WHO Won?!?

An Irreverent Look at the Oscars
Volume 1: 1927-1943

2nd Edition

by

Robert James, Ph.D.

An Imagination Archives Publication

This is a work of historical scholarship and analytical editorial criticism. No endorsement by the Academy of Motion Picture Arts and Science for this work or its conclusions is suggested or implied. Trademarked terms Oscar ®, Oscars ®, Academy Award ®, and Academy Awards® are used in historical and editorial context. This work only offers speculative analysis and in no way suggests original winners of any awards, or nominees for said awards, are, or can be, altered.

WHO Won?!? An Irreverent Look at the Oscars, Volume 1: 1927-1943

First Edition © 2012 & Revised Second Edition © 2014, Robert James

All rights reserved.

No part of this book may be reproduced, scanned or distributed in any printed or electronic form without permission.

ISBN-13: 978- 0692317211
ISBN-10: 069231721X

Cover Art by Emmy Gray (missemmygray@gmail.com)

All images used are in the public domain, and are acquired from Wikimedia Commons.

WHO Won?!?

An Irreverent Look at the Oscars

Volume 1: 1927-1943

2nd Edition

To the memory of

my mother and father,

who never forgot the popcorn

&

To my Catherine:

"Some Kind of Wonderful"

Table of Contents

Introduction i

PART ONE: 1927-1933 PREVIEW 1

CHAPTER ONE: 1927-28 5

CHAPTER TWO: 1928-29 29

CHAPTER THREE: 1929-1930 49

CHAPTER FOUR: 1930-31..................................... 65

CHAPTER FIVE: 1931-32 83

CHAPTER SIX: 1932-33.. 107

Intermission:

PART TWO: 1934-1943 PREVIEW 139

CHAPTER SEVEN: 1934 141

CHAPTER EIGHT: 1935... 165

CHAPTER NINE: 1936... 193

CHAPTER TEN: 1937 223

CHAPTER ELEVEN: 1938 255

CHAPTER TWELVE: 1939 299

CHAPTER THIRTEEN: 1940 357

CHAPTER FOURTEEN: 1941 423

CHAPTER FIFTEEN: 1942 479

CHAPTER SIXTEEN: 1943 527

Afterword 573
Roll the Credits! 575
Index 579

Endnotes 613

INTRODUCTION

Something is terribly wrong with the Oscars. Has been, for over eighty years.

More often than not, they go to the wrong people, and to the wrong movies.

I'm here to fix that annual tragedy. I know you're relieved. I know I was, when I was done writing this book. You should enjoy yourself. I certainly did, as I kicked out idiotic films that should have never been made, much less handed Oscars. I've seen almost every single film nominated in the past eight decades, and quite a few that weren't, and I've come to one conclusion.

The Academy of Motion Picture Arts and Sciences doesn't have a clue what it's doing, more often than not.

Fortunately, I do. Believe me: you can trust me.

Why, you say? Who the hell is this guy to think he can rewrite Oscar history?

It's a valid question, since I am about to give the finger to generations of Oscar voters, deprive winners of their Oscars, and decide what should have happened, rather than what did happen.[1] You may get upset, particularly if I'm taking away your very own Oscar. To which I say, if you are that dense and shallow that a fictional "let's pretend" drives you to anger and tears, then you have no business being in Hollywood.

Or maybe you do. After all, the Oscar tends to go to the weepers and the histrionics...

---

[1] Allow me this legal disclaimer: In no way, shape or form am I actually taking away anybody's Oscar or nominations, or handing an Oscar or nomination to anybody. This is an intellectual exercise, purely for entertainment purposes, and is not intended to deny the existence or fact of the historical Academy Awards, nor to subvert in any legal way said ownership of these intellectual trademarks and copyrights.

Who I am involves many things. As Walt Whitman said of all Americans, "I am large, I contain multitudes." I suppose one could say I am a bit of an arrogant, pompous ass, given my penchant for quoting dead poets and suggesting I know better than Hollywood. I won't say it, of course, but others have. But given the raging egotism of Hollywood, I think I am in the minor leagues when it comes to arrogance, pomposity, and thinking I know better than anyone else as to what should happen. Opinions are like assholes; everybody's got one. But I would suggest that while these are my opinions, they are educated opinions, driven by decades of watching films, reading film history, and being fascinated by the electoral whims of Hollywood and America in general.

By profession and training, I am two things, neither of which is either particularly respected or highly paid in America. I am a teacher, and a literary critic. If teaching was respected, it would be a lucrative profession, instead of the comparative widow's mite it earns against other advanced degrees. As to literary criticism, the less said the better. Writing articles a handful of people might read in my lifetime is not my idea of a useful career. That it was at one point seems, to me at least, to be a sign I've grown up...somewhat. I earned my Ph.D. from UCLA in 1995, and then promptly disembarked from academia and began teaching in an inner-city high school. I have now taught teenagers for the better part of two decades, and if that doesn't qualify me for recognizing bad decisions and immature thinking in Hollywood, I don't know what will.

But my profession aside, I do love the movies. Much of my life has been spent in the dark, watching the lights play on the screen. As a boy, my family piled into the station wagon and went to the drive-in, for a double feature and Mom's cold popcorn. My friends and I fought over the TV Guide so we could search for a 3 am Friday night showing of the Godzilla film we hadn't seen yet. My best friend's father was a night owl who would wake us up in the middle of the night so we could indulge ourselves in seeing Tokyo destroyed once more (he fought in the Pacific in WWII; I suspect that he saw it as just retribution). As a teenager, the Balboa Theater in Newport Beach switched from endlessly showing *Deep Throat* and turned itself into a first class revival house, playing a new double feature every few days. I took to sitting in the balcony, in this old, musty, curtain-ripped and cockroach-infested movie house, and all I cared about were the films I had never seen. The VHS tape led to haunting video stores. When I was a student at UCLA, I often went to their film department after classes, and sat in their state of the art theater and watched original prints of many of the films in this book. When the DVD emerged, and it became apparent that Hollywood intended to squeeze every last drop of profits from its film libraries, I bought and bought. And on cable, TCM has become my favorite channel, and the DVR my favorite technological possession.

As a child growing up in the Sixties and Seventies, I was exposed to practically every film Hollywood made in the sound era. I may not have watched them all, but the opportunity was there. Prior to the advent of the VHS tape, local television stations aired three basic kinds of programming: local news several times a day, reruns of old television series during the daytime, and then, gloriously showing Hollywood all night long, every night, and almost every weekend hour as well. I believe that my generation will be the last to be fully immersed into the history of Hollywood, because the VHS tape and its successors on DVD (in various formats) have had an ironic effect: practically every film has been made available, while simultaneously eroding the awareness of those films for the general public. Once local stations used old movies as a way of filling the hours, but VHS tapes caused their ratings to plummet. They then turned to syndicated programming and infomercials to pack their evening and night hours. And so, Laurel and Hardy, Abbott and Costello, the Three Stooges – all have disappeared from Sunday mornings and UHF afternoons. *Creature Features* no longer fills the eyes of young boys and girls settling in for a Sunday afternoon of classic frights, and so, waves of moviegoers have no idea who Karloff or Lugosi are. *The Wizard of Oz* isn't a yearly event any longer. *Casablanca* isn't run. *The Million Dollar Movie* is no more. Anybody can rent these films, or find them on cable, or even own them. But few people do, unless they already know about them. Classic Hollywood is relegated, as a cultural phenomenon, to people growing older, and black and white film is seen by young people as stupid and boring.

I do my best to change all that. My children absolutely adore the Marx Brothers, Frankenstein, and Stan & Ollie. I show my students *The Music Box* at least once in their four years in my school, and their laughter shows me that Laurel and Hardy haven't lost their magic. I own many of the movies I talk about in this book, and I do my best to make them available to friends and family and students. My classroom is covered in old movie posters so teenagers will ask about them, and I can point them to all the books I've read that will tell them more, and to the movies they need to see.

So if all that doesn't provide me with some street cred when it comes to trusting the worth of my alternative prescriptions for Oscar gold, then you're out of luck. You've bought the book, so you might as well read it now.[2]

So sit back, make some popcorn, and maybe even grab a pen and some paper. You might just make a list of films you want to see, or see again.

Just find someone who hasn't seen them yet, preferably some child who hasn't decided that old movies are boring, and black and white is some ancient ritual torture. Just don't start with *Sunset Blvd.* or even *Bambi*; they'll never recover...

If they're a little older, and squirming, try this out on them: "It isn't an old movie if you've never seen it before!"

What I think I can promise you is that I haven't given an award to a single stinker – which is far more than the Academy can say.

Trust me on this one.

And pass the popcorn.

---

[2] Thanks for the royalties, by the way; buy some more copies as presents – I have kids who need to go to college.

PART ONE: 1927-1933

PREVIEW

Before I begin on my merry little trail of destruction, revenge, and justice, let's get the rules straight.

First, I kept to the categories that the Academy themselves created. I may occasionally slip in a snide comment about their value, or linger for a minute about losing one, but I played in their ballpark. On the other hand, I did ignore the five nominee rule, for a number of reasons. The Academy let the number fluctuate for decades. The number five has always been arbitrary, allowing in too many candidates some years and denying too many in others. What is more important, I hope this book draws attention to as many wonderful movies as possible, and an arbitrary limit would prevent that publicity. So if some of you think I'm playing tennis without a net at times, all I can say is more movies need love.

Second, I tried my best to see every movie that had anything to recommend it for Oscar worthiness. My local library, video stores, my own collection, TCM, YouTube, Netflix, and UCLA helped assure as close a degree of completion as was feasible. If the film was simply unavailable, I made a note as to its unviewed status (this was much less of a problem after the early Thirties). Tragically, some films have been lost, such as Lon Chaney, Sr.'s turn as a vampire in 1927's *London after Midnight*.[3] Hopefully, some sleuth will track them down.

---

[3] I am aware that Lon Chaney never used the Sr., and that his son Creighton was forced to use Lon Chaney, Jr. Unfortunately, I found many young readers confused by the

Third, I stuck primarily to American films, although recognized foreign masterpieces often make their way into these pages, like exchange students invited to stay awhile. I did look at the release date in the United States to determine their year of eligibility, just as the Academy did. It wouldn't be fair to challenge what the Academy chose if they didn't get a chance to see it. For most foreign films, that means the year in which they are considered will be different from the year in which they were made. If I've missed anything great, let me know. But just encompassing the huge numbers of American films which deserved consideration was exhausting enough – for now.

Fourth, I stayed away from the technical categories, simply because I am truly unqualified to venture any opinions in those areas.

Fifth, I invited friends and family and internet participants into the conversation whenever and wherever possible, to check my own impressions and suggest other takes.

Finally, my criteria for suggesting when an Oscar should have gone to someone other than the person who historically received it are as follows. While it is inherently unfair to judge the past by the standards of today[4], the point of movies is to watch them. The difference between a classic and something which was just made long ago is the capacity of audiences to return, enjoy the film afresh, and then to return again to see something in the film they had not seen before. Why is it that I have watched Stan and Ollie push that piano up the stairs over a hundred times, and still laugh every bit as much as I did the first time, but that a film like *The 40-Year-Old Virgin*, which caused my sides to hurt the first time, merely evokes a half-hearted grin on repeated viewings? Life is short; Art is long. Only when we dig through the garbage the cultural engines of each generation heap upon us do we discover the diamonds buried within, and try to pass them along.

One suggestion. Many of the movies discussed in the first four chapters are extremely difficult to find, and most people have never seen these obscurities (for some of them, I wish that was still true for me). If you find your eyes glazing over, you may want to move to Chapter Five, which finds Hollywood in full golden glory. Go ahead; I won't mind. But you'll be missing out on the first righteous act of setting those fools straight – and some really good movies!

---

difference without this designation, and I hope those who care will recognize that this helps keep the uninitiated a little less confused.

[4] Especially in such matters as special effects, which doom so many classic fantasy and science fiction films to the status of historical artifacts, or kitsch, or both, but also in issues such as musical and acting styles, mobility of the camera, and so forth.

One last note: I use footnotes to make asides, humorous and otherwise; endnotes with Roman numerals are for the bibliographically obsessed. Please read the footnotes, or you'll miss good stuff!

I hope you enjoy reading this as much as I did writing it.

CHAPTER ONE: 1929 AWARDS
1ˢᵗ Show

Movies released between August 1ˢᵗ, 1927 and July 31ˢᵗ, 1928[5]

THE SCENE OF THE CRIME:

On May 16, 1929, the first Academy Awards banquet was held in the Blossom Room at the Hollywood Roosevelt Hotel, where the Academy's offices were located. The first hosts were Douglas Fairbanks, Sr., perhaps the greatest swashbuckler the screen has ever known (whose career was about to be destroyed by the switch to sound) and William C. de Mille, the older brother of Cecil B. DeMille, and father to famed choreographer Agnes de Mille.[6] The awards were handed out after the food and dancing, in just a few minutes. The winners (and everybody else)

---

[5] Fasten your seatbelts; this is going to be a bumpy footnote. For the first five years, films from different calendar years competed against each other, since the eligibility period ran from August 1ˢᵗ of the first year to July 31ˢᵗ of the next. The first Academy Awards, given in 1929, were for films made between August 1, 1927 through July 31, 1928. In 1930, for the first and only time, they held two Academy Award ceremonies. The first covered films made from August 1, 1928 to July 31, 1929; the second honored films made in the back end of 1929 and the front end of 1930. The fourth show, held on November 31, 1931, covered films made from August 1, 1930 through July 31, 1931. The fifth event, held on November 18, 1932, granted awards to films made between August 1 1931 and July 31 1932. There was no award show in 1933. Maybe this all confused them as much as it confused me. The sixth Academy Awards, covering films made in the latter half of 1932, and all of 1933, was held on March 16, 1934, and things cleared up from that point on, as all future shows covered the previous calendar year.

[6] They spelled their last names differently.

knew who was going to win before anybody showed up that first year. The second year, they got wise to the dramatic potential and didn't tell anybody before the show.

Sadly, a number of speeches then ensued, from William C. de Mille to Louis B. Mayer, all breaking their arms patting themselves on their own backs. Then Al Jolson sang, after complaining he wasn't given an Oscar (he joked that he needed a good paperweight). He made fun of Jack Warner, the head of the studio who produced Jolson's groundbreaking *The Jazz Singer*, which ushered in the age of sound (Warner Brothers had received a special Oscar for that innovation that evening): "For the life of me, I can't see what Jack Warner can do with one of them. It can't say yes." Jolson sang; everybody went home.

Nothing was broadcast or filmed.

The categories that year were odd, enough so that they dropped many of them the next year. Smart people. As Henry David Thoreau said, "Simplify. Simplify." Too bad they ignored him later on.

Best Picture was then called Outstanding Production.[7] Somewhat redundantly, they also had a category called Unique and Artistic Picture, a kind of second Best Picture award. Apparently, the gods of commerce would get the first; the gods of art would get the next. Hollywood never tried to separate the two ever again (guess which one usually wins?). The movies operated in two main categories, as did the theater that spawned them, as Gerald Mast and Bruce Kawin have pointed out: "The two dominant theatre genres were melodrama and farce; they were to become the two dominant film genres as well… Melodrama was a world of pathos, not of tragedy, of fears and tears, not of ideas. No action was irreversible; no matter what mistake the good-hearted character made, it would eventually be erased by his or her essential goodness."[i] Hollywood hasn't changed all that much in a century, has it?

The Academy divided the Best Director[8] awards into two categories: Best Direction (Dramatic Picture) and Best Direction (Comedic Picture). They dropped this split for the next year, never to happen again. Comedy, as a result, has largely been ignored, almost as much as the horror, western, and musical genres. Hollywood takes itself way too seriously at the Academy Awards and rarely lightens up in its award selection. Make us laugh, thanks, but no thanks. Make us cry, and you get a naked man with a sword. Weird people.

---

[7] I'm just going to call it Best Picture to avoid confusion.
[8] The Academy lists this as Best Directing, but practically everybody calls this Best Director, so we will do so as well.

For the first, last, and only time, they gave an Oscar for Best Writing (Title Cards) to Joseph Farnham. I refuse to say anything about this. My wife thinks I read too much as it is. We'll let Farnham keep it for whatever movies they had in mind; the Academy never bothered mentioning.

They also handed out an Engineering Effects Oscar, never to be presented again. The ancestor of today's technical awards, Hollywood took years before it recognized the craft of screen technology. Not glamorous enough, I suppose. I'm as guilty as the Academy is, but then the technical awards tend to be completely justified, given as they are by the technicians themselves. They don't need justice.

Numbers of nominations per category fluctuated, unlike the five that have been used for most of my lifetime; the awards were often based on an entire year of work, rather than specific films, an idea that has merit in years where nominees sometimes undercut themselves by turning in more than one film of great work.[9]

WHAT THEY GOT RIGHT:

Best Cinematography: Charles Rosher and Karl Struss won for *Sunrise: A Song of Two Humans*, over George Barnes, for *The Devil Dancer, Magic Flame,* and *Sadie Thompson*

I feel bad for George Barnes, who got nominated for three films (*The Devil Dancer, Magic Flame, Sadie Thompson*), but history has proven the Academy utterly correct in selecting Charles Rosher and Karl Struss for F.W. Murnau's silent masterpiece, *Sunrise: A Song of Two Humans*.

Sunrise tells of a man conspiring with his lover to kill his wife, and failing, and the redemption that follows. The wife is played by Janet Gaynor, the winner of the Best Actress Oscar for this year's work, which includes this film, *Street Angel,* and *Seventh Heaven.* Renowned to this day for the utter beauty and inventiveness of the cinematography, *Sunrise* remains viewable primarily for the camera work. A box-office dud, at least compared to its enormous costs, *Sunrise* won the Oscar for Unique and Artistic Picture. An early prestige film, Fox rarely allowed

---

[9] All details about the annual Oscar ceremonies come from the indispensable and highly readable *Inside Oscar: 10th Anniversary Edition*, by Mason Wiley and Damien Bona, Ballantine Books, 1996.

any director the kind of freedom (and budget) that Murnau enjoyed on this film.

Few silent pictures – for that matter, few sound pictures – have ever equaled the fervent dreamlike quality of the scene in the swamp, and the use of fades within scenes, such as the opening railroad imagery, or the totally unexpected (and somewhat astonishing, given the technology of the time) walk of the redeemed couple through traffic, and into the field of flowers. The last scenes on the lake, from the moonlight honeymoon, to the nightmarish search, are nicely mirrored. *Sunrise* influenced practically everyone in Hollywood, not the least of whom was John Ford, and made Hollywood "dolly happy."[ii]

Best Art Direction: William Cameron Menzies won for *Tempest* and *The Dove*, over Harry Oliver, *Seventh Heaven*, and Rochus Gliese, *Sunrise*

Menzies would go on to many other films, most famously *Gone with the Wind*, wherein control freak David O. Selznick actually said that "Menzies is the final word" when it came to the look of the film. Menzies also directed the burning of Atlanta scenes. In addition, he directed the cult classics *Things to Come* and *Invaders from Mars*. *Tempest* stars John Barrymore in a Russian Revolution picture; *The Dove* featured Norma Talmadge, Gilbert Roland and Noah Beery, and was set in Mexico originally. Two very different kinds of sets, and Menzies does a fine job in both. So, a well-deserved Oscar.

One note here: Fritz Lang's future parable *Metropolis*, with art direction by Otto Hunte, Erich Kettlehut, and Karl Vollbrecht, should have been nominated for their future city. I came very close to arguing they should have won the award, but so many of the sets look ludicrous today. For that matter, Karl Freund, Gunther Rittau, and Walther Ruttman's cinematography deserved mention as well. If there had been a special effects Oscar, *Metropolis* should have won. Given that the technical Oscar this year went to Roy Pomeroy's pioneering work on *Wings*, I find it hard to choose; since I am not even remotely close to being qualified to judge technical issues, I have thus remained out of the conversation on this one. Sorry, *Metropolis*.

WHAT THEY GOT WRONG:

The great travesty of the awards came when the governing board removed Charlie Chaplin from the running from the directing, writing, and acting categories by handing him a "special first award" for *The Circus*. Chaplin was an independent who controlled his own studio, and was a partner in United Artists. The studios had to recognize his genius, but they didn't want the competition for their own films. Never again would any nominee be removed from the race and handed a consolation prize.

At the time, the film community made a great uproar over Charles Farrell being left out completely. Farrell was the co-star of the smash hit *Seventh Heaven*, which had been nominated for Outstanding Picture and was cited in star Janet Gaynor's Best Actress Oscar. Farrell and Gaynor made over a dozen films together, based on the success of *Seventh Heaven*. His career would last through the sound era and end up on television in *My Little Margie*. He also served as Palm Spring's mayor for much of the Fifties. (Farrell's performance is discussed below, in the Best Picture section).

Here are the "winners" the Academy chose (feel free to do your best Dr. Evil impersonation here):

> **Outstanding Production (Best Picture):** *Wings*
> **Unique and Artistic Picture:** *Sunrise*
> **Best Actor:** Emil Jannings, *The Way of All Flesh* and *The Last Command*
> **Best Actress:** Janet Gaynor, *Seventh Heaven*, *Sunrise*, and *Street Angel*
> **Best Direction (Dramatic Picture):** Frank Borzage, *Seventh Heaven*
> **Best Direction (Comedic Picture):** Lewis Milestone, *Two Arabian Knights*
> **Best Writing (Adaptation):** Benjamin Glazer, *Seventh Heaven*
> **Best Writing (Original Story):** Ben Hecht, *Underworld*

Outstanding Production (Best Picture): *Wings* won, over *The Racket* and *Seventh Heaven*

Wings survives as a movie we can readily watch (although for some bizarre reason, the movie wasn't released on any home format until the 2012 DVD). Directed by the WWI ace William "Wild Bill" Wellman, *Wings* stars the future Mr. Mary Pickford, Charles "Buddy" Rogers, and the "It Girl" herself, Clara Bow. This WWI tale of star-crossed lovers, tragic misunderstandings and the most realistic fight scenes in Hollywood up to that point was a huge critical and commercial success. *Wings* has moments that still thrill, and sentimental scenes that make a modern audience cringe (this is true of many silent films). But once they're in the air, you can see where most of the dogfight scenes in Hollywood history start their contrails. The overly contrived love stories don't sit well today. In the death scene, overtones would seem to imply that the two male leads were more than just friends, a sign of how differently we view male physical contact today. Sadly, Clara Bow playing a saintly good girl just doesn't work (see the Best Actress category below for why). The end of the film is painfully artificial, and in many ways, undercuts the reality of the war. *Wings* has not aged well as a result of the human elements, but its battle scenes became the template for such things. Later on, the Academy retroactively decided this would be the film to carry the honor of being the first Best Picture, thus dismissing *Sunrise* from its status as co-first. But *Wings* doesn't deserve its Best Picture status – and neither do the other two films nominated in this category, *The Racket* and *Seventh Heaven*.

Long thought lost, Howard Hughes' *The Racket* was found in a Hughes repository at the University of Nevada and beautifully restored in 2004. The back story to the movie is intriguing, as it is based heavily on Al Capone, whose nickname Scarface is turned into Nick Scarsi. The corrupt government of Chicago actually banned the play and then the film because the story cut too close to the bone. The original theater cast included Edward G. Robinson playing the Capone character; he was wooed away by Warner Brothers on the basis of the play's success. Supposedly, the gangsters portrayed in the movie threatened producer Hughes and cast members out of rage at having their lives and corruptive influence too clearly shown to the public. *The Racket* tells the story of a good cop and his war with the evil gangster. The subplot concerns the gangster's little brother and a floozy out to ruin him. Today, Louis Wolheim as Scarsi proves to be the most attractive part of the experience, with his smashed nose and resilient attitude (he was also in director Lewis Milestone's *Two Arabian Knights* this year, and would later be in *All Quiet on the Western Front*). The street set is almost as elaborate as the one in *Sunrise*. The camera shots are often interesting, and the action keeps flowing, so long as Wolheim is on the scene. When the story shifts to the clean cop's exile, and the reporters begin providing "humor," the movie falls apart. Some of the narrative drive returns when the good cop arrests the little brother, and starts to build a case; the gangster tries to rescue his kid brother, and things come to a close. *The Racket* helped to establish the gangster genre, but for the most part, the movie wallows in dead ends and failed attempts to interest audiences, instead of staying focused on Wolheim – and thus does not deserve its nomination for Best Picture.

Seventh Heaven remains a curious little piece of melodramatic fluff, set in the dregs of society, where the hero has a golden heart and an arm of iron, and his greatest dream is to get promoted from sewer worker to street sweeper. Seriously. No ironic overtones. That's it: street sweeper. Charles Farrell is a big strapping lunk, and he does have some screen presence. Janet Gaynor plays the younger sister of a pair of down-on-their-luck prostitutes (the prostitution isn't shown, but signaled fairly strongly). They have a rich aunt and uncle. After being whipped repeatedly by her sister (with a real whip), Gaynor stands up and tells her uncle the truth that they haven't been good. The older sister then lashes her down the street until Farrell stops the beating and stands up for Gaynor lying senseless on the ground. When the sister rats out Gaynor to the cops for being a prostitute like her, Farrell claims she's his wife, and the cop says that Farrell will be investigated, which shall surely cost him his promotion. Gaynor then offers to pose as his wife and goes home with Farrell. The love story plays out rather predictably from there, as both Gaynor and Farrell become much better people, through severe suffering, and the whole things wraps up in a scene right out of a Catholic postcard. More of a bad made-for-TV movie than anything, *Seventh Heaven* is a sign of the overweening sentimentality of the period that this film would dominate so much of the year. It didn't even deserve a nomination – as the Academy decided about *The Jazz Singer*.

In terms of sheer impact on the film industry, *The Jazz Singer* may just be the most important movie in history, because it changed the entire course of the cinema by making sound mandatory. The Board declared the film to be ineligible for any award in the belief it would be unfair to have a sound film compete with silent pictures (hence the special award to Warner Brothers for developing sound). Actually watching *The Jazz Singer* today reveals neither jazz nor singing. Jolson shamelessly mugs and cries his way through the role of a young Jewish singer trapped between the worlds of his cantor father and show business. The scenes in blackface are excruciating to watch (to be fair, Jolson did exert a great deal of effort to support black civil rights in the theater). Why the first half of the century thought he was the greatest entertainer in the world is next to impossible to understand, particularly when Louis Armstrong and Bing Crosby are around before WWII. Armstrong and Crosby would so utterly change the nature of singing as to make Jolson impossible to take seriously. Jolson's greatness required you to be in the same room with him to feel anything other than mystification (not unlike much of Laurence Olivier's acting). This film and performance are the very essence of schmaltz (one contemporary reviewer called it a "pleasantly sentimental orgy").[iii] Were it not for being the moment sound took over, nobody would care about this dreck – especially when there are works of genius we need to consider, which the Academy should have included.

Buster Keaton's Civil War comedy *The General* remains the artistic high mark of his career, and a film that continues to astonish viewers today. I had the great joy of watching many Keaton films at LA's Silent Movie Theatre with an audience and an organist in his eighties; *The General* rocked the house. Two actual trains were used in the filming, including a massive destruction scene, and while other Keaton films make me laugh more, no other Keaton film has this strong a narrative and visual explosiveness (literally, in the train wreck). When you add in what are often considered his two other best films, *Steamboat Bill, Jr.*, which has his finest moment, where the front of the house falls on him, perfectly framing him with the upstairs window, and 1928's *The Cameraman* with its Tong war, the Academy was criminally negligent in never even nominating Keaton. They performed penance for this when they gave Buster Keaton an honorary Oscar in 1959. *The General* deserved consideration as Best Picture, in the spirit of recognizing a body of work. Unfortunately, it was released too early in 1927; despite this, some Academy voters tried to write it in, and failed. I go on at length for an ineligible film, because if you haven't seen *The General*, you really should.

For Best Picture, were it not for the early release date, *The General* should have won the Oscar. *Steamboat Bill, Jr.* was eligible, and while not the masterpiece *The General* is, is well worth a nomination. The movie has a number of classic gags, beyond that of the falling house. The bit with the hats got the biggest laugh of the film when it played at the Silent Movie Theatre. Buster's fight against the wind remains masterly comedy.

One last choice presents itself, although it could just as easily go into the other Unique and Artistic Picture category. Given the rules of the time, foreign films released in America were eligible, if they were released within the appropriate dates: as such, I offer Fritz Lang's *Metropolis*.[10] This seminal science fiction film became the template for practically every vision of the future ever made, even unto today, and of all the films made this year, it remains the one most often seen. The image of the robot turning into a woman remains indelible – and one which the makers of the Karloff *Frankenstein* and *Bride of Franken-*

---

[10] *Metropolis* was almost completely restored in 2010. Honestly, if you haven't seen this version, you've missed the movie entirely; it certainly never made much sense to me before.

stein must have seen. The opening of the film immediately creates a very different kind of city, with its mighty machinery, followed by workers who are little more than part of the machines they serve; like prisoners, they await behind bars for work to begin and end. I would bet writer Thea von Harbou had read H.G. Wells *The Time Machine*, as she lays out a working class deep beneath the city, and a cultured leisure class above, like Wells' Morlocks and Eloi before their civilization fell. The sons of the leisure class have everything catered to them, including a garden with futuristically attired girls (nude and nearly nude) who are intended as playmates for the young rich men. One of those sons, Freder, meets a young woman, Maria, who interrupts their play in paradise with the children of the working class; she insists that rich and poor are brothers. Love blooms at first sight, although complications ensue (don't they always?). The choreographed workers at their machines still repulse the free mind.[11] The stalking of the young Maria through the catacombs, first with candlelight, and then with a flashlight, is a remarkable achievement, given how hard it could be to film in darkness. The acting styles range from naturalistic to highly stylized; the modern response (well, mine anyways) is to fight back laughter at how silly they look clutching their hearts. Oddly, for a science fiction film set in the future, the Biblical imagery (the names, the Tower of Babel, the machine as Moloch, the Flood, and so forth) render it as a morality tale. The story itself has been accused of supporting the idea of the Wise Master, which would make the moral and artistic tangle of this film resemble nothing so much as the same difficulties a modern viewer encounters in watching *Birth of a Nation*. Hitler loved this movie; von Harbou became a Nazi supporter. But Fritz Lang came to America. Reportedly, he turned down the offer of control of the German film industry from Joseph Goebbels himself – although the only source of that story is Lang himself; but he left while Harbou stayed, which seems ample evidence of his dislike of the Nazis. *Metropolis* reads more like a conflict between capitalism and the individual than it does a beneficent praising of any kind of Fuehrer. In fact, the robot Maria is clearly ridiculing the power of the demagogue, by showing how easy it is to pervert that power for selfish reasons (as Adolf Hitler did a few short years after this film was made).

So, a complicated decision for this Oscar. Ultimately, I would argue the Oscar should have gone to *Metropolis,* because it remains the most inventive and striking. That the Academy ignored it is perhaps under-

---

[11] Frederick Taylor, the founder of scientific management, would have loved the efficient motion.

standable, because they were celebrating American films first and foremost, and also because *Metropolis* didn't screen here in its full form. But hindsight should be 20/20, and *Metropolis* is clearly the biggest – and best – production of the year. *Metropolis* should have won the Oscar for Best Picture.

Unique and Artistic Picture: *Sunrise* won, over the documentary *Chang: A Drama of the Wilderness,* and *The Crowd*

Unique and Artistic Picture was a one-time oddity. The Academy seemed to want to point to a set of films which were not commercially motivated so much as they were serious attempts to be new and different (which Hollywood has never done well, being much more comfortable with "do it again, only more so.")

Sunrise rightfully won for Best Cinematography, which seems to have taken up the artistic intent behind this award in future years (the award tends to go to the deliberately beautiful films). But the tale itself, of a man who cheats on his wife and plots to kill her, quickly devolves into a standard and forced story of redemption and forgiveness. The wife, played by Janet Gaynor, is a pathetic wretch. The husband seems to be lurking about in a simian pose for much of the picture. Once the couple reconcile, *Sunrise* turns into a comic tale of the country hicks in the big city (there's even a drunken pig, followed by a pig chase). *Sunrise* has charming moments, until you remember he almost murdered her that morning. *Sunrise* is a film relying on tricks to make its impressions, rather than on an honest story. Not that there's anything wrong with tricks – most movies turn to at least some, particularly with modern special effects – but the film itself seems to gloss over the real pain involved in the rush to get to the redemption. The story has aged badly, even as the imagery is quite inventively fresh; but style, without substance, only goes so far – and for a Best Picture Oscar, not far enough. *Sunrise* should not have won the Oscar, although the nomination is deserved.

Chang, most recently made available in the aftermath of Peter Jackson's remake of *King Kong*, is not a documentary, but filmmakers Ernest B. Schoedsack and Merian C. Cooper filmed on location in Siam (today's Thailand), using real people and wildlife, finishing with a rented elephant herd they made stampede for the film's climax. While the story is somewhat fictionalized – the home was rebuilt to accommodate the camera, the pet monkey was trained, the finale was staged – *Chang* is a kind of early National Geographic special, and a forerunner to Disney's True Life Adventure series of the late Forties and Fifties. *Chang* is definitely not a politically correct film; the centerpiece is a hunt for predators, including not one, but two slain tigers, one of whom is shot on camera. That it was nominated along with *Sunrise* and *The Crowd* is a sign of how highly respected Cooper and Schoedsack were. The nomination should stay, if only because *Chang* led them to RKO and their masterpiece *King Kong*.

Most film historians feel King Vidor's *The Crowd* should have won. Surprisingly, Louis B. Mayer himself prevented the Board from choosing his own studio's picture (MGM had released *The Crowd*). As *The New York Times* related in 1972, Mayer didn't want the award, "because it wasn't a big money-maker for MGM...it was unglamorous, against the studio's image."[iv] Mayer also believed that if it won, or MGM won too many awards, people would think he had jiggered things in MGM's favor (apparently, everybody thought rigging things was a grand idea the next year – see Chapter Two). He kept the Board sitting for hours past midnight until they gave the award to *Sunrise* instead. According to Anthony Holden in *Behind the Oscar*, Mayer did the same thing to other MGM winners as well that year. He only allowed the Oscar for Title Writing to go to an MGM picture. Paramount, Fox and United Artists took home the other Oscars. Denying *The Crowd* violates the very idea of honest awards, because the film is one of the masterpieces of the silent cinema. The film opens on Independence Day, 1900 with the birth of John Sims, the light of pride in his father's eyes. The father teaches John that he is special, and could someday be president. The film then begins to undercut that promise, in a way that must have infuriated Mayer and those who wanted to sell the American dream unalloyed by realistic expectations: Vidor kills off the father on his son's twelfth birthday. The shot of the boy coming up the stairs is quite stark in its beauty, but what follows is even more remarkable. Vidor takes us into the concrete jungle of New York; his camera goes up the side of a skyscraper, into one of the multitude of windows, and we get the most famous image of the film: an enormous room, filled with the same exact desks, all being manned by the same exact workers. *The Crowd* is about modern conformity and the cookie cutter necessity of employment, as opposed by the traditional American expectation of exceptionalism. On their first date, John and Mary fall in love (or at least lust), prompted by the Tunnel of Love. On the way home, John proposes marriage, inspired by an ad for buying a home. Love itself has become commercialized in the modern city. At times, I felt like I was watching the inspiration for Arthur Miller's tragedy *Death of a Salesman*. Miller seems to have taken the main character in this film and split him into two for further dramatic conflict: the big dreams of Willy Loman, forcing his son to think greatness will be his, and the dark realizations of Biff, who knows there is no place for greatness in the modern urban world for all but a few. The camera wizardry intoxicates at times, perhaps none so giddily as the camera going down the slides at Luna Park ahead of the dating quartet. This film also has the most honest appraisal of pre-wedding night jitters I've ever seen. In the end, John comes to an accommodation of his expectations and the harsh reality of modern urban life: he learns to laugh at it all, and accept his place. Not the answer Louis B. Mayer wanted either, but one that is at least possible. Pragmatism reigns.

In the end, while I felt all three films deserved the nomination, I found myself drawn to giving the finger to Louis B. Mayer for denying King Vidor and *The Crowd*. Of the three, *The Crowd* has most retained its effectiveness as a film. *Sunrise* is beautiful to watch, but the story is very, very hard to take seriously (see below in the Best Actress category for more on why). Therefore, the Oscar for Unique and Artistic Picture should have gone to *The Crowd*.

Best Actor: Emil Jannings won for *The Way of All Flesh* (now a lost film) and *The Last Command*, over Richard Barthelmess for *The Noose* and *The Patent Leather Kid*

Emil Jannings is perhaps best known today for the professor who falls in love with Marlene Dietrich in *The Blue Angel*, but he ended up as a committed Nazi who wholeheartedly supported Hitler. Anybody who loved Hitler doesn't deserve an award. What else he deserves, I leave to those of you with inventive imaginations and sadistic streaks.

Richard Barthelmess became famous in the films of D.W. Griffith, most notably as the Chinese lover in *Broken Blossoms*. After his career slowed over the Thirties, he quit acting to enlist in the naval reserve in WWII, never to return to the profession. His performances in his two nominated films are serviceable as a boxer going to war in *The Patent Leather Kid*, and reportedly quite strong in the very short gangster film *The Noose*, of which the only copy seems to be in the Museum of Modern Art in New York.[12] Regardless of the unavailability of the movie, Barthelmess was on the original committee to create the awards. Does the phrase "insider trading" mean anything to you? Barthelmess loses his nomination.

The nominees for this year originally included Charlie Chaplin, who was removed by the Governing Board from the competition. Chaplin should have retained his nomination in this category, as well as the oth-

---

[12] Feel free to offer me a trip to New York to see it sometime.

ers in which he was removed. His performance in *The Circus* was excellent, but not the glory that was to come in *City Lights*. Chaplin plays the Tramp to perfection in *The Circus*, and he certainly deserved a nomination.

But what about other possibilities?

John Barrymore never received an Academy Award. Despite being widely regarded as the greatest actor in the world, the Hollywood moguls personally disliked him. He wrecked himself through alcohol and womanizing; like Lord Byron, he was "mad, bad and dangerous to know." In *Tempest*, he plays a Russian peasant officer who ruins his career through falling in love with a princess. Set during WWI and leading to the Russian Revolution, the film is at times uncomfortable in its depiction of an ugly, scheming Communist – the Communists were quite despicable enough without this caricature – but Barrymore's performance is strong. Two scenes in particular remain fresh in their capacity to express emotion without any words: when he sees the Princess for the first time and falls in love, and when he is stripped of his status as an officer because he has been caught in the bedroom of the Princess. Barrymore mars his performance by touches of overacting, and the mannerisms he relied on instead of thinking through the role, but compared to other male performances this year, Barrymore should have been nominated.

Lionel Barrymore's performance in *Sadie Thompson* remains one of his best, as the reformer who discovers his sensual desires are more powerful than his religious beliefs. The performance is excellent, particularly in Barrymore's frenzied eyes, and should have been worth a nomination (see Best Actress and Writing for more on *Sadie Thompson*).

The silent-film actor whose dramatic reputation remains the greatest after all these decades has to be Lon Chaney, Sr. He was one of the biggest stars in the world while he was alive, and was successfully transitioning to sound pictures when he was felled by throat cancer. The Man of a Thousand Faces was becoming the Man of a Thousand Voices as he took on speaking parts. More than likely, he would have been cast as the Frankenstein Monster and as Dracula, thus depriving both Boris Karloff and Bela Lugosi of their stardom. In 1927 and 1928, Chaney appeared in a wide range of films and roles: the now-lost vampire picture *London after Midnight* (stills show a very toothy grin); *Mockery*; *The Unknown* (with a nicely turned performance by a young Joan Crawford); *The Big City*; *Laugh, Clown, Laugh* (with a very young Loretta Young); and *West of Zanzibar* (eligible in next year's awards). While not the film roles he is best known for today – the Phantom of the

Opera and the Hunchback of Notre Dame – those movies contain an astonishing variety brought to life with different makeup, body language, and verve. Burt Lancaster once told Chaney biographer Michael Blake that the moment in *The Unknown* when Chaney realizes the woman he loves, loves another, was "the most emotionally compelling scene he'd ever seen an actor do."[v] Three of Chaney's films – *The Unknown*; *Laugh, Clown, Laugh;* and *West of Zanzibar* – were in the top-ten grossing films of 1927 and 1928. Lon Chaney was never once nominated for an Oscar, despite his box-office power and his extraordinary acting ability. In a year in which a body of work was the nominating factor, rather than a single movie, Lon Chaney should have been immediately nominated, without question.

Of all the serious dramatic actors we still watch from the silent era – and there aren't many who survived the wholesale shift in acting styles and tastes – Chaney remains the most fascinating. The reason that he wasn't even nominated may be because the grotesque and the gothic have never been valued by the Academy Awards (and it didn't help that Chaney didn't participate in Hollywood social circles). Horror movies have won fewer awards than any other genre, despite the heights they reached as an art form before they descended into the gore fests of the Seventies to the present. But Chaney's films were not always in the horror genre, as with *Tell It to the Marines*. As Orson Welles said, Chaney was "a great deal more than a makeup artist. He was an actor of great power and enormous eloquence. Certainly I've never heard a tribute to Chaney of anything like the dimensions he deserves."[vi] Lon Chaney, Sr. was a consummate artist, living his roles, tortuously and indelibly, and we need to honor his memory as the most versatile actor of his generation. Chaney should have won the Oscar for Best Actor.

Best Actress: Janet Gaynor won for *Seventh Heaven, Sunrise,* and *Street Angel,* over Gloria Swanson, *Sadie Thompson*; and Louise Dresser, *A Ship Comes In*

As for Janet Gaynor, her turn in *Seventh Heaven* finds her doing her best Lillian Gish imitation. The actress has always struck me as more than a little annoying, but playing a prostitute with a heart of gold, she clearly went over well back then. Julia Roberts did this sort of thing more amusingly in *Pretty Woman*.

Sunrise shows Gaynor in a somewhat better light, although as in *Seventh Heaven*, she relies upon almost comatose responses to trauma to get across to the audience (and in *Sunrise*, there's a moment where she's channeling Lillian Gish...again). Once more, she is playing a character who becomes almost unbelievably good, to the point of cloying stickiness. Gaynor was, like many stars, creating a screen persona – and the experience either works for you or it doesn't. I just couldn't bear to be in her presence for very long. Put yourself in her shoes: your husband has been cheating on you, he's just barely kept himself from killing you, you run away while he follows you...and then, he buys you some bread, some flowers, and goes into a church with you where a wedding is taking place...and you forgive him. The man just came within an inch of drowning you...and you forgive him. Some women do this, but we usually call them victims. *Sunrise*, and Gaynor, want the audience to see her as sympathetically heroic, the ideal wife and mother. In the twenty-first century, that kind of behavior just doesn't appeal to most of us (or shouldn't). The last film for which she was cited doesn't make things much better.

Street Angel marked her third nominated performance. Once again, she is teamed with Charles Farrell from *Seventh Heaven*. And yes, once again, she is playing a good girl forced to flirt with prostitution, this time due to a sick mother needing medicine they can't afford. Gaynor is more natural and lively in this film than in her previous Frank Borzage film, *Seventh Heaven*. Borzage clearly had paid attention to F.W. Murnau's *Sunrise* before he made this film (down to several plot elements, as well as cinematography choices). But what is it with killing your woman and Janet Gaynor?!? Once more in *Street Angel*, she is playing a woman who is almost murdered by her man, this time her fiancée. Yet again, we get this overwhelmingly corny salvation, with the same heavy-handed reliance on redemption and Godly lessons learned. Ultimately, whenever I see Janet Gaynor, the words simpering and whining come to mind, and whatever charm she has drains away, particularly since I don't find love and violence to be complementary. The not so subtle sadomasochism of Gaynor's three films is disturbing, not as sadomasochism, but that it is counterbalanced by these sappy happy endings. Actors can make this stuff work, and apparently, Gaynor did for her generation – but I just find myself wincing, then looking for an insulin shot. She should have never won an Oscar, nor been nominated, for any of these performances.

Gloria Swanson in *Sadie Thompson* plays a bad girl who wants to change her ways, first through the love of a soldier who is willing to marry her; then when denied that love by Lionel Barrymore's rigid puritan beliefs, through the redemption of God at Barrymore's hands. But when it turns out that the man – a minister in the original, but just a prude in the film version, in a concession to the Hays Office) – is sexually attracted to her, she denies him and returns to the love of her soldier again. The final reel of the film is missing; a photo montage reconstruction exists. Reportedly, Barrymore commits suicide out of shame at his own lust, thus freeing Swanson. Swanson garnished excellent reviews for this performance, and for good reason. She's rash, brash, confident, sexy, playful, sassy, and anti-authoritarian – the very embodiment of the Twenties generation. Her sensuality, resentment, hostility, spirituality, and sheer longing for a life of her own, on her own terms, remain true, even to modern audiences. She definitely earned this nomination.

Louise Dresser, from *A Ship Comes In*, ended her career in a string of films with Will Rogers in the early Thirties. The public recognition of this nomination was in many ways the high point of her career, but she had a fascinating life: she was discovered by Theodore Dreiser's songwriter brother, Paul Dresser, who gave her his last name and said she was his little sister; she starred with Lon Chaney, Sr., Buster Keaton (a lifelong friend), and Rudolph Valentino, among others. But the film itself, about an immigrant husband accused of planting a bomb who then asserts his patriotism in his defense, was completely unavailable for viewing. Dresser's husband is persecuted for a crime he did not commit, his son dies fighting for his country, and when he is finally exonerated, happily goes back to being a janitor. It all sounds more than a little contrived and awkward, but there is no way of knowing, so we will have to set any discussion of her nomination aside.

As to other performers who deserved selection, few stars have ever equaled Clara Bow for sheer sex appeal. Bow became known as the "It Girl" after making *It* in 1927. As Elinor Glyn famously wrote, "IT" was "that quality possessed by some which draws all others with its magnetic force. With 'IT' you win all men if you are a woman – all women if you are a man."[vii] That same year, Clara Bow also made *Children of Divorce*, which follows naturally after "It," apparently, and then *Hula* (after the divorce, doesn't everybody dance?). Gary Cooper, by the way, made some of his first appearances with Clara Bow, with whom Cooper had an infamous affair (he plays the reporter in *It*). Believe it or not, Bow was also the female lead in *Wings* as well, which makes her lack of a nomination more than a little puzzling, until you view the different performances – and when you realize that upper crust Hollywood didn't like Clara Bow socially. In *Wings*, she has to be a goody two-shoes, and she's not very good at it; playing the bad girl in *It* she's marvelous. Her bad girl shows she isn't really bad, she's just drawn that way. Clara Bow acts like a vamp, but when a man on a first date tries to get fresh, she slaps him to put him in his place – and the next day, goes into his office and lays her body all over his desk?! Conflicted is the word that comes to mind. In *Wings*, once she's in France, and has her eyes opened, the role becomes more suited to what worked well for her on the screen, and the performance improves. So she should have been given a nomination for Best Actress, because she was in many ways the most exciting female star of the Twenties, and still quite watchable today.

Having recognized her performances for the eligible year, however, doesn't bring her the statue. I would like to suggest one more performance that should have been nominated, that of seventeen-year-old Brigitte Helm as Maria and her robot double in *Metropolis*. While her Maria is stiff and somewhat unconvincing – playing a saint-like figure is never easy – it does grow more interesting when Rotwang stalks her. Her turn as the robot, both in the costume and as the evil Maria, is compelling and unique, and one of the great performances of the silent era.

But not as great as that of Gloria Swanson. Her performance shines in comparison to Bow, Gaynor, and the rest, particularly given how well Swanson still plays today in *Sadie Thompson*. Even though she publicly rooted for Gaynor, Gloria Swanson should have received the Oscar for Best Actress.

Best Direction (Dramatic Picture): Frank Borzage won for *Seventh Heaven*, over King Vidor, *The Crowd*, and Herbert Brenon, *Sorrell and Son*

In these days of the director being seen as little short of God, one has to stop and really examine what the role of the director is: he decides when to start and stop the scene, he decides where the camera goes, and he tries to influence the choices the actors are making. He may also write, he may also star, he may have a hand in the editing, he may even produce. Okay, so maybe he is God, at least on the set, if the star's not so big. Billy Wilder once said "A director must be a policeman, a midwife, a psychoanalyst, a sycophant, and a bastard."[13] But I have wondered why the Best Picture Oscar and the Best Director Oscar aren't one and the same, and the only answer I can come up with is that producers run the studios, and they want an Oscar too. So, I tend to gravitate towards having the Best Picture and the Best Director go hand-in-hand, except when I don't, of course. As the great Ralph Waldo Emerson said, "A foolish consistency is the hobgoblin of little minds." Don't be small. To quote the great Oliver Norville Hardy, "Be big!"

Frank Borzage's direction on *Seventh Heaven* has some interesting moments. He starts underground, and it's a strange place to begin a

---

[13] Qtd. in Ed Sikov, *On Sunset Boulevard*, p. 176.

movie, in the sewers. He uses an early tracking shot following the whipping of Janet Gaynor through the streets by her alcoholic prostitute of a sister. I'm also impressed with the wonderful shot of the camera rising and rising and rising while Gaynor and her co-star Charles Farrell climb six flights of stairs (hence the title, *Seventh Heaven*). The movement of the camera up or down the stairs was used in later films, including Alfred Hitchcock's *Blackmail* and G.W. Pabst's *Pandora's Box*. But the direction, like the story, takes some heavy-handed turns. That the Oscar went to him does not bode well for the Academy's tastes, as he deserved no award – but Borzage should be left with a nomination.

Herbert Brenon should have been nominated for *Laugh, Clown, Laugh* rather than *Sorrell and Son*, which no longer exists in a complete print; at least that way, we could have watched it. An odd film, *Sorrell and Son* shows a WWI veteran who returns home to raise his son after his wife abandons them; in his old age, and suffering from cancer, his son (now a doctor) euthanizes him. Brenon gives us the first example of the Academy patting itself on the back for nominating daring films, but then rarely giving them the actual award.

Of the directors working in 1927 and 1928, many have been forgotten, some are remembered for single films, and some continued their careers into the sound era and became even bigger legends (John Ford, for example, who deservedly won more Best Director Oscars than anybody else). William "Wild Bill" Wellman, the director of *Wings*, belongs in that last category, if for nothing else than the fact he later directed *The Public Enemy, Nothing Sacred, The Ox-Bow Incident,* and *Battleground*. But what was the Academy thinking when they handed the Best Picture to *Wings*, and then didn't even nominate Wellman? But then, they didn't nominate F.W. Murnau either, and his *Sunrise* won the other Best Picture Oscar!

It's not like the field was crowded, with only three nominees for dramatic direction. Plenty of room for Wellman, so he should have been nominated for directing *Wings*. Wellman put flight into movies in a way nobody had before. Not only that, but he visually experiments in interesting ways on the ground as well, including placing a camera on a swing with two lovers, which can be quite dizzying at first. I cannot recall seeing one peculiar camera move anywhere else before this movie – the camera is rolling towards the character, and zooming in at the same time, while the character keeps backing away. Most unusual. The montages of the war also remain striking. In fact, the parts of the film that stay fresh, having to do with the war, were what Wellman wanted the picture to be; Clara Bow and the love story were forced on him by the studio, and it shows.

Like Wellman, F.W. Murnau should have been nominated for Best Director. Murnau, perhaps most famous today for directing the horror classic *Nosferatu*, was brought here from Germany to make an Expressionist film. *Sunrise* was the result.

Tod Browning was not nominated in this year, despite having directed *London After Midnight* and *The Unknown*. Like most of Browning's films – most famously *Freaks* – these two explore the grotesque. *London After Midnight*, also known as *The Hypnotist*, is one of the most famous lost films (the last known print was burned in the Sixties). TCM did put out a photo reconstruction of the film, which is worth looking at, as *London After Midnight* was the most commercially successful of all the Browning-Chaney, Sr. collaborations. *The Unknown* is the tale of an extra-thumbed murderer who hides his distinguishing digits by pretending to be an armless wonder in a carnival sideshow. His secret is discovered by the father of the woman he loves, so Chaney murders him. He then has his arms amputated for real when he finds that his love object can't stand the touch of a man's hand – only to return to find she has fallen in love with another. Death ensues. Almost operatic in its intensity, *The Unknown* was one of the year's biggest hits (as was *London After Midnight*), but not the kind of thing the Academy has ever liked. Browning's direction was functional, but hardly inventive. His camera was static, and he often encouraged actors to go over the top, which was a stylistic quirk being outmoded in the better silent films of the late Twenties. He has a love for quick cutting between actors for their reactions, particularly in scenes where characters are watching each other, secretly or otherwise. As always, Chaney's face is the most interesting thing in Browning's films, as would Bela Lugosi's eyes in Browning's *Dracula*. Browning's great strength as a director was in choosing stories which would titillate and obsess his audiences, and when combined with a great actor like Chaney, the results were (and are) fascinating. Browning should have been nominated.

Now that we've pointed out the omissions, let's return to the final official nominee.

King Vidor maintained an active career in Hollywood for over half a century, and for good reason. The director of *The Big Parade, Duel in the Sun,* and *War and Peace,* among many other well-known films, Vidor also solved the infamous William Desmond Taylor murder at the end of his life, as detailed in Sydney Kirkpatrick's compelling book, *A Cast of Killers*. In *The Crowd*, he crafted his finest film. Vidor's innovative use of new camera movements, incorporating models, dissolves, and overhead tracking shots was remarkable. The famous scene that slides up the skyscraper, heads in through the window, and floats over this amazingly depressing scene of 200 men working at 200 desks is unforgettable. The movie itself is one unrelenting disaster after another, as a couple meet, fall in love, marry, and constantly have to cope with the grind of everyday life, as well as major tragedy. Ending on a hopeful note, *The Crowd* was clearly a serious film, trying to cope with the problems of modern conformity and the false promises of the corporate world. And so, the Oscar for Best Direction (Dramatic Picture), should have gone to King Vidor. Given that he was robbed of the Best Picture (Artistic) by his own boss, this is sweet justice. The Academy made up for this oversight with an honorary Oscar in 1979.

Best Direction (Comedic Picture): Lewis Milestone won for *Two Arabian Knights*, over Ted Wilde, *Speedy*

Speedy is a typical Harold Lloyd comedy, amusing as always, but hardly a brilliant film. Babe Ruth makes a nice cameo appearance, and some wonderful shots of Luna Park at Coney Island charm, but the movie is mostly an excuse to string one gag after another, none of them really building towards anything – so no nomination should have been given.

Lewis Milestone would later direct *All Quiet on the Western Front* and *Of Mice and Men*, as well as *Ocean's Eleven* and the Marlon Brando *Mutiny on the Bounty*. *Two Arabian Knights* features Louis Wolheim and William Boyd as two WWI soldiers who hate each other, but eventually escape their POW camp by way of the Middle East and a harem. The unveiling scene in *Two Arabian Knights* is as sexy and romantic an encounter as any in the silent cinema (and far better than all the love scenes in *Seventh Heaven*, for example); one of the chase scenes would have done Keaton proud. Milestone should keep his nomination, but the Best Director of comedy is somebody we all know and love today.

Chaplin is Chaplin, but *The Circus* isn't the ambitious *The Gold Rush* nor is it the incandescent *City Lights*. What it is, is funny. And in a year where the category was comedic direction, what better director, and what better film? Chaplin should have won, hands down, for Best Direction (Comedic Picture).

Best Writing (Adaptation): Benjamin Glazer won for *Seventh Heaven*, over Anthony Coldeway, *Glorious Betsy*, and Alfred Cohn, *The Jazz Singer*

Hollywood is notorious for destroying books they adapt by completely ignoring what made the book wonderful in the first place. On the other hand, a slavish adaptation doesn't work either, because film is different from print, and watching is different from reading. The ability to cut prudently, to recast the written word, and to maintain the elements of the original story which make that story work is a great art, and not one that is generally appreciated outside of this award.

The problem I have with all three of these nominations is that the films are abominable dreck: banal, sentimental hogwash of the lowest order, and based on sources even more deservedly obscure than the films that were adapted from them. They therefore should all lose their nominations.

I have nothing against sentimentality in a film – the great John Ford's films have touches throughout – but only when in service to the picture as a whole, and not as the entire purpose of the picture. Melodrama can be worth watching, and still forms the vast output of most film and television, but these things are like junk food: fattening, bad for your health, deadening to the palate, and interchangeable.

Awards should be given to those films which rise above the rest, in their quality and originality. Writing awards should be given for freshness of treatment, and not for simply forming the basis of a hit film, as these three nominations so obviously were. Other adaptations this year were far more interesting, and hits as well, if commercial success is to be used as a yardstick – and there's no reason it shouldn't be, as one factor among others. When lots of people like something, this does not necessarily equate to a lack of art.

Among those others, Thea von Harbou adapted *Metropolis* from her own novel. But as she became a fervent Nazi, I have no desire to award her anything.

One of the classics of the silent era, *King of Kings*, came out very early in 1927, and was left out of consideration for that reason. Otherwise the film, the direction of Cecil B. DeMille, the portrayal by H.B. Warner of Jesus, and the adaptation of the Biblical source would all be under consideration. All of Jesus' dialogue consists of Biblical quotes, and Warner projects a marvelous sense of the divine, even if it is a bit like watching a painting act...or maybe that is what makes it work so well. The opening scene and the resurrection scene, shot in two-strip Technicolor, are sinfully opulent – I love the jaguar and swans! The trick shots with the Seven Deadly Sins trying to keep Mary Magdalene from repenting are very well done. The first appearance of Jesus is when he heals the blind, and we are made to see at the same time. *King of Kings* is still a very reverent film, made more interesting by the use of lighting and shadows that are quite masterful at times. Not eligible, but well worth your time now that you know about it.

But another obvious choice went ignored (obvious, once you dig a bit into the source material): *Sadie Thompson* was based on a play by the same name, which was itself based on W. Somerset Maugham's classic short story, "Rain." Gloria Swanson "wanted to make my *Gold Rush*" and set out to do so with this film, writing the screenplay with director Raoul Walsh. *Sadie Thompson* would be the last film in which he would ever act, since he lost an eye in an accident shortly thereafter. Swanson had to navigate a hailstorm of protest from various sources, despite having the Hays Office's verbal agreement to allow the story to be filmed. The profanity of the original source was toned down, although many viewers claim to be able to lip read a number of foul words. As one contemporary reviewer recognized, in the May 1928 *Motion Picture Magazine*, "despite the fact that Reverend Davidson...is reduced from the cloth to a plain blue-nose reformer, and that Sadie's words of denunciation are subtly deprived of their sulphur, the screen version is remarkable for its fidelity to the stage original."[viii] Ultimately, the film was a great success at the box office, and remains fascinating today.

Therefore, both a nomination and an Oscar for Best Writing (Adaptation) should have gone to Gloria Swanson and Raoul Walsh for *Sadie Thompson*.

Best Writing (Original Story): Ben Hecht won for *Underworld*, over Charlie Chaplin's rescinded nomination for *The Circus*, and Lajos Biro, *The Last Command*

Let's start by restoring Chaplin's nomination, and then dropping Biro from the discussion entirely. *The Last Command* has a great central conceit: what if a Russian general ended up in Hollywood as an actor playing a Russian general? But Biro then surrounds that great idea with several deal breakers: one, we are asked to believe that a committed female revolutionary would fall in love with a fat old general just because he loves Russia; two, that a train he has just escaped from just happens to go across a bridge that conveniently collapses to cover up his escape; and three, that the revolutionary turned director would get all mushy and sentimental over him. Stupid isn't good writing. Biro is just outclassed by Hecht and Chaplin.

Ben Hecht was one of the best screenwriters in history. With his co-writer Charles MacArthur, he wrote plays, including *The Front Page* (best known in the incarnation with Cary Grant and Rosalind Russell, *His Girl Friday*) and *Twentieth Century*. He worked for great directors, including Alfred Hitchcock (*Foreign Correspondent, Lifeboat, Rope, Notorious*), John Ford (*The Hurricane*), and William Wyler (*Roman Holiday*). *Underworld* was a film Hecht actually disowned before its release, asking that his name be taken off the credits. Directed by Josef von Sternberg, *Underworld* is the tale of a gangster who rescues a down-and-out lawyer who then both fall in love with the same woman. Eventually, after a shootout, the gangster does the right thing and gives up the girl. Hoke. Gritty and visually impressive, but the story is pure hoke. Hecht would get far better in the future. Given the general lack of originality in Hollywood – then as now – this film does have some striking moments, particularly in the acting of Clive Brook and the signs of director Joseph von Sternberg's coming of age as a director. An odd little bit with a kitten, before and during the final shootout, seems to me to be the strangest touch in the film (even if they do reach for the sentimental lever – threaten a kitten, and watch the tears start). But Hecht's central conceit – that a violent oaf of a gangster would willingly give up freedom for no reason other than that he wants to do the right thing – is just utterly unbelievable. *Underworld* is generally considered the movie that launched the gangster genre (which would make James Cagney and Edward G. Robinson stars shortly), but it would be surpassed by later iterations of the world of the criminal. Hecht was right to want his name off this, and he should be stripped of his Oscar and his nomination.

Chaplin's *The Circus*, like almost all of his films, is endlessly inventive in terms of gags, but also in setting up the emotional payoff of the film. Shamelessly sentimental, which is why audiences at silent film showings tend to laugh more at Keaton than Chaplin in this, our more cynical age. Chaplin was an intense taskmaster, insisting on take after take in the drive to perfection. During the filming of *City Lights*, he even sent the entire crew home – with pay – for several weeks while he figured out how to resolve a plot problem (if that's not writing, what is?). The ideas in *The Circus* are as good as any of Chaplin's films, and one in particular is indelible: the scene with the monkeys clambering over Chaplin while he desperately tries to stay on the high wire. How Chaplin ever got the monkey to put his tail into Chaplin's mouth is beyond me.

Chaplin had greater moments as an actor (*City Lights*, for example; more on this later) and a director (*The Gold Rush*). But *The Circus* is as good as anything he ever wrote, and considerably better than what came after *City Lights*, and all the more amazing that he made the film while going through a vicious divorce from Lita Grey. His seventeen-year-old wife was pregnant, and spilling their private lives onto the front page; Chaplin's desire for his wife to perform fellatio was called "abnormal, unnatural, perverted, degenerate, and indecent."[ix] With press like that, one may start to feel some sympathy towards the Academy for wanting to avoid an Oscar being won by Chaplin. William Randolph Hearst's mistress Marion Davies was named as one of Chaplin's lovers, causing further social uproar. Finally, Chaplin paid his wife a million dollars to gain a divorce. Then the government sued him for a million dollars in back taxes...and the movie sets burned down and had to be rebuilt. Hard year for the Little Tramp, yet *The Circus* shines beautifully. I actually prefer it to *The Gold Rush*, simply because Chaplin isn't trying so hard for greatness. The film doesn't have the directorial ambition of *The Gold Rush*, but the gags remain fresh, visually bright, and reminiscent of the slapstick on which Chaplin had built his career. Chaplin should have won the Oscar for Best Writing (Original Story).

CHAPTER TWO: 1930 AWARDS
2nd Show

Movies released between August 1st, 1928 to July 31st, 1929

THE SCENE OF THE CRIME:

This year, the ceremony moved to the Cocoanut Grove at the Ambassador Hotel. The location has not been preserved, as the hotel has been turned into a high school in Los Angeles, but in the Twenties and for many decades, it was a favorite nightspot for Hollywood royalty. William C. de Mille again hosted the show, which was broadcast on the radio. In order to make my life easier, they reduced the number of categories from twelve to seven.

This year, they didn't announce the winners ahead of time. Thus began the time-honored tradition of guessing who would win, and the creation of numerous ulcers, panic attacks, and nervous breakdowns for those nominated.

Except for the fact that for the first (and last time), there were no nominees announced. This may have made the evening more of a surprise for the attendees, but my life certainly got harder. Unofficial lists of nominees have been constructed by scholars examining the notes of the judges, but the names are all educated guesswork. As we have nothing better, we will run with the guesses.

More than anything else, this was the year the judges rigged the elections so their own studios benefited from the awards. Crooked and unbelievably self-serving, these Academy Awards might best be dropped entirely. Perhaps no other year more deserves a complete do-over.

The radio broadcast lasted an hour, so the bloating had apparently begun from the previous year's fifteen minutes.

WHAT THEY GOT RIGHT:

Nothing. Absolutely nothing. A travesty of a ceremony, if ever there was one. As a sign of that corruption, this is the only year in the ENTIRE history of the Academy Awards where no film won more than one Oscar. The outrage was such that the voting rules were completely changed to a one person, one vote policy, away from a handful of judges choosing the winners. We're not at Price, Waterhouse yet, but the path there was laid out of the anger over this year's awards.

WHAT THEY GOT WRONG:

Everything. Absolutely everything. Are you not paying attention?

There were seven categories. Here they are, along with their "winners":

Best Picture: *The Broadway Melody*
Best Actor: Warner Baxter, *In Old Arizona*
Best Actress: Mary Pickford, *Coquette*
Best Director: Frank Lloyd, *The Divine Lady*
Best Writing: Hans Kraly, *The Patriot*
Best Cinematography: Cedric Gibbons, *The Bridge of San Luis Rey*
Best Art Direction: Clyde de Vinna, *White Shadows in the South Seas*

Every single one of those awards was an act of double-dealing and gross manipulation. Even if they deserved the award, they shouldn't have received them. One of the points of this book is justice, and justice will be served. I will consider films that were apparently nominated, simply because they lost to self-serving judges. They slighted almost every silent film made that year, in the reverse of their self-serving argument against the talkie *The Jazz Singer* the previous year. In 1930, silent films were ignored in favor of the tripe Hollywood made with sound. The only silent that won an award was *The Patriot*, for writing.

Best Picture: *The Broadway Melody* "won" over *Alibi*, *Hollywood Revue*, *In Old Arizona*, and *The Patriot*

Part of the problem in making any selection this year lies in the poor quality of films in general, as the studios stumbled their way through the switch to sound.[14] This would be the last year that a silent film was up for Best Picture. *The Patriot* is now a lost film, the creation of the great director Ernst Lubitsch, who never received an Oscar other than an honorary one (and was again snubbed by the AFI when they put out their 100 greatest films list a few years ago).

Sadly, Lubitsch's film can't be considered. All that remains of it are a few scraps in the UCLA archive, and a trailer. What I've seen of it reveals Emil Jannings to be a massive, overacting ham, and the rest of the cast to not be much better, if the tiny snippets are any indication. The sets do impress in this story of Czarist Russia and court intrigue.

Widely seen as the first movie musical, *The Broadway Melody* just isn't very good. Like *The Jazz Singer*, important doesn't necessarily mean quality. Case in point: the novel *Uncle Tom's Cabin* started the Civil War (or so Abraham Lincoln joked), but you would have to pay me large amounts of money to ever read it again. *The Broadway Melody* belongs in the same category of important but not worth your time more than once. The backstage musical has a few decent songs, written by future MGM producer Arthur Freed and his partner Nacio Herb Brown, although they play "Broadway Melody" waaaaaay too many times in a row. That they are delivered by a ham doing his best Al Jolson impression and a mediocre sister act just makes us long for Bing Crosby, Fred Astaire, Gene Kelly – anybody but these people. Like most MGM pictures, the look is crisp and elegant, and the lead women are dressed to the height of fashion of the period. The sister act's uncle stutters and stammers, and the girls laugh at him, supposedly in good humor. Mixed in with laughing at his disability is a lot of skin and bathing for the girls (the Hays Office was never as energetic in its censorship as the later Joseph Breen regime was). *Broadway Melody* takes every op-

---

[14] As the dean of American film critics, Andrew Sarris, once said, "...most film historians have considered 1929 the worst year artistically in the history of the American cinema." *"You Ain't Heard Nothin' Yet"* p. 11.

portunity to have the girls strip down to silk underwear. One bizarre note: there is a scene in which the dancer stays en pointe, tap-dancing on her toes. Truly unusual, but one freaky dance should not a Best Picture Oscar make, so no nomination is warranted. Just because something is first does not make it best.

Remember that as a truth of other genres besides the musical.

Alibi is one of the earliest gangster films, a genre that would dominate much of the early sound era, along with musicals; guns and tap shoes make dandy sound effects. *Alibi* was directed by Roland West, best known today for his suspected complicity in the death of his mistress, actress Thelma Todd. The film starts off with some interesting images accompanied by their sounds, put into a rhythmic pattern: a prison guard swinging his billy club like a western trick shot artist, a prison bell, the prisoners emerging from their cells to the beat of the tapping billy club, and then, Chester Morris being released from prison.[15] The sets were designed by William Cameron Menzies, and show his sense of space and art deco style. The fluidity of the camera surprises, given the endless complaints about early sound pictures having no camera movement; watch as the camera tracks in and around the nightclub scene. Sadly, the sound tricks and camerawork end up the best things about the film; the acting is stagy, the dialogue stiff, and the few signs of life in the film have nothing to do with the plot or the characters. *Alibi* is definitely not worth a nomination for Best Picture.

Hollywood Revue has no story. Instead, we get a grab-bag of almost every star MGM had access to as an excuse to let the stars each have sound. Laurel and Hardy, for example, make their first sound appearances, in a half-baked magician sketch that never really lets them develop their humor. Buster Keaton does a dance in drag (one that Fatty Arbuckle had already done in a silent picture he made with Keaton), showing yet another example of MGM ruining Keaton's career, something that began after Keaton's last great film, *The Cameraman*. *Hollywood Revue* did introduce the song "Singin' in the Rain," in two versions: one with Cliff Edwards (known as Ukulele Ike, and later, the voice of Jiminy Cricket), and an everything-but-the-kitchen-sink finale shot in two-strip Technicolor, under a giant Noah's Ark. Jack Benny shows up periodically. We get a Romeo and Juliet sketch, which supposedly ruined the silent film star John Gilbert's career. Lon Chaney, Sr. refused to appear, so they sing "Lon Chaney's Gonna Get You If You

---

[15] West also directed Morris in *The Bat Whispers*, one of the influences on Bob Kane when he designed Batman.

Don't Watch Out." All in all, a mediocre film, and not one deserving any kind of Best Picture nomination.

The western *In Old Arizona* has two distinguishing marks, as the first sound picture to be filmed on location, and as the project where actor-director Raoul Walsh lost his eye in an accident (a jackrabbit jumped through the windshield while they were returning). Some nice framing shots open the picture – ones I suspect Walsh himself directed – but the action scenes are staged unbelievably poorly (the director who replaced Walsh likely did these). The entire film is plagued by wooden acting (as are many films of the early sound era). The surprise ending is telegraphed so far ahead there isn't any surprise in it at all. In no way does *In Old Arizona* deserve a nomination, and should have been removed from consideration on its own merits...or lack of them.

Other films would have been far finer nominations.

First off, they should have celebrated Laurel and Hardy's classic comedy *Big Business*. The tale of the boys trying to sell Christmas trees, and discovering the irascible James Finlayson resisting them every step of the way, is priceless. The tit-for-tat destruction that follows remains funny eighty years later. Although a short, it deserved the Oscar nod.

William Wellman directed Louise Brooks in her best American film, *Beggars of Life*. A gritty story of an abused girl who kills her abusive stepfather then goes on the road as a hobo, *Beggars of Life* is very good, and a film that points directly at Louise Brooks' greatest role in next year's *Pandora's Box*. I found the depiction of the threat of sexual abuse, rape, and the general sense that women are property to be unexpected but brutally honest. That sense of harsh reality is matched, awkwardly, by poorly written attempts at humor and sentimentality. An unbalanced film, but one worth a nomination.

The Docks of New York was made a year after Josef von Sternberg's huge success with his early gangster film, *Underworld*. George Bancroft stars in both. *The Docks of New York* begins in the bowels of a ship, with Bancroft playing a coal stoker with only one night of leave. The chalk graffiti shows explicitly their goal: naked women and booze. An incredibly charismatic film for the eye (see Cinematography), *The Docks of New York* is one of the masterpieces of the silent screen for that alone. Director von Sternberg was never better than in this film, which deserves a nomination.

So does Erich von Stroheim for his nineteenth century Viennese tale of seduction, *The Wedding March*. Von Stroheim was obsessed with detail and shot films so long they couldn't possibly be released. Ultimately, he self-destructed against the increasing restrictions of the studio system – who, to be fair, need to make a profit to stay in business.

Any director who consistently goes vastly over budget and doesn't make back that expense is going to be left out. Von Stroheim began as an actor under D.W. Griffith, and became known as "The Man You Love to Hate." He once starred in a WWI propaganda film wherein his character was trying to rape a mother, ripping off her clothes with his teeth; when her crying baby distracted him, he threw the baby out the window. *The Wedding March* is a marred film, hacked into pieces before release, but it's still better than anything the Academy nominated.

Damnably, the Academy completely ignored Lillian Gish's pet project, *The Wind*. Lillian Gish's performance is a tour-de-force, playing a woman on the frontier forced to marry against her will because of economics, fear, and male desire. The direction, by Victor Sjöström (usually rendered as Seastrom in English), is brilliant, juxtaposing the driving furies of human emotion with the physical winds and cyclones of the prairies, perfect visualizations of how human beings cope with overwhelming forces: nature, human passions, and the cruelties of those who have power over those who do not. Watching this film, seeing the constantly blowing dust and wind, must be taken as a symbolic experience, because there's no way any environment that has this much dust and wind could ever support farm life for long (the Dust Bowl hadn't happened yet, but *The Wind* seems a grim foreboding of that ecological disaster). Surprisingly, this was an MGM film, one Louis B. Mayer could easily have promoted for Oscars. Irving Thalberg immediately approved Gish's proposal for this project, so perhaps Mayer's jealousy over Thalberg's genius had already begun at this point. One suspects that Mayer disliked it for the same reasons he disowned *The Crowd* the previous year: both are deliberately somber, downbeat films that tackle serious issues. Despite being a silent, *The Wind* deserved a nomination, and what is more, overwhelmingly outclasses every single film they apparently nominated for Best Picture. Two bad musicals, a poor excuse for a western, and a crime melodrama can't compete with *The Wind*.

But one film can.

The critical darling of this year remains *The Passion of Joan of Arc*, directed by Carl Theodor Dreyer and recounting the trial of St. Joan. A French film, and one released in the United States within the eligibility period, Dreyer's film remains astonishingly different. Once thought lost, and rediscovered in, of all places, a janitor's closet in an insane asylum in Sweden (no comments, please), *The Passion of Joan of Arc* must be seen to be believed. Faces like these had never been in movies before, and rarely since; no makeup was used. Joan of Arc is played by Renee Maria Falconetti, her eyes are beyond compare. Shot in a series of close-ups, very few shots encompass more than a few faces. Quick cutting keeps the pace moving along, as the interrogation of Joan by her English captors rolls out. Based on the original transcripts of the trial, *The Passion of Joan of Arc* attempts to recreate history, but with none of the tedium many historical films indulge in the name of verisimilitude. Within a few moments, we are completely immersed in the trial itself, in a time machine of cinema. Falconetti's performance – the only one she ever had on film – is, perhaps, a bit too weepy, a touch too monotonous in its constant crying. But those eyes! The only eyes in all of silent cinema to challenge them are those of Maria in *Metropolis*. Dreyer's film is truly unique, and should have won the Academy Award for Best Picture.

Best Actor: Warner Baxter "won" for *In Old Arizona*, over Chester Morris, *Alibi*; Lewis Stone, *The Patriot*; George Bancroft, *Thunderbolt*; and Paul Muni, *The Valiant*

Warner Baxter should not have won for *In Old Arizona*, not just because any award from fixed voting is wrong, but also because his performance in this western is, to put it plainly, cheesy. If that isn't the worst Spanish accent in the history of filmmaking, I don't know what is – except for the other Spanish accents in the movie. And if those reasons weren't enough, he wasn't even initially cast; only Raoul Walsh's car accident brought him the part. Walsh filmed this as a two-reeler, and the dailies were so good the studio asked for it to be extended into a full-length film. One wonders what Walsh would have been like, but the jackrabbit had his own say in the matter (rabbits committing suicide and mutilation of movie stars definitely make an impact...). Baxter has a few comic touches with the roguish part, but not enough to warrant an Oscar. He has a habit of launching into romantic purple prose, then undercutting it with a self-effacing comment. It's a bit like Valentino turning into Groucho Marx, but without the charm of either.

Chester Morris had a long career in Hollywood, up into the television era. Best known today for a whole series of films as Boston Blackie, a former thief turned crime solver, Morris is charismatic, and Boston Blackie is a fun character. The gangster pic *Alibi* is neither charismatic nor fun. At this point in his career, his emotional range went from a smirk to a stiff upper lip, with little in between. He does have one good scene where he cowers in fear, but definitely not worth a nomination for Best Actor.

Lewis Stone is out of the discussion, simply because *The Patriot* is lost.

George Bancroft and Josef von Sternberg reunited in *Thunderbolt*, which also co-starred Fay Wray before *King Kong* stereotyped her as the screamer. Essentially a remake of the archetypal gangster film *Underworld*, the movie doesn't have much of the interest of other von Sternberg work. As in *Underworld*, there is another cat, this time a squeeze toy. But it isn't *Thunderbolt* that Bancroft should have been nominated for, but von Sternberg's *The Docks of New York*. Bancroft's acting has significantly improved since *Underworld*; watch his face for the subtle reactions after he saves the prostitute from drowning. But *Thunderbolt* is a talking picture, with all the requisite drawbacks of early sound film; *Docks* isn't. Bancroft should have received his nomination for *The Docks of New York*.

Paul Muni would come to dominate the acting world of the early Thirties, as he proved himself a chameleon. In *The Valiant*, he plays a murderer who does the noble thing. The movie is more atmospheric than one would expect, with a surprisingly mobile camera. Ultimately, however, *The Valiant* is just a filmed stage play, particularly in the second half. Muni's performance has moments of intensity, particularly when he's not talking. Compared to the other nominated performances, Muni is good – but not good enough for a nomination.

As for those the academy ignored completely, once again Lon Chaney, Sr. deserves a nomination, this time for *West of Zanzibar*, where he plays a father who unknowingly ruins his own daughter in a misguided act of revenge.[16] Chaney runs an emotional gamut few actors have ever displayed in any era: from hatred of another, to horror, to self-loathing, to pity, in under a few minutes, with just the looks on his face. *West of Zanzibar* is not a great movie, but it holds by far the most interesting performance of the year. Chaney should have won again for Best Actor, for the first back-to-back Oscars in this alternate history. No other silent film dramatic actor persistently remains so watchable, fascinating, compelling.

Best Actress: Mary Pickford "won" for *Coquette*, over Betty Compson, *The Barker*; Bessie Love, *The Broadway Melody*; Corinne Griffith, *The Divine Lady*; Jeanne Eagels,[17] *The Letter*; and Ruth Chatterton, *Madame X*

This category has the greatest travesty of Oscar history: Mary Pickford, a major silent film star known as "America's Sweetheart," campaigned intensely to win this award for *Coquette*, a film that practically begs for a silver nitrate fire to incinerate the film stock. If any one award forced the Academy to change its voting practices, this one did.

---

[16] See Chapter One, under Best Actor, for a discussion of this performance
[17] The first posthumous nomination, as she died of a heroin overdose.

As Wiley and Bona put it in their invaluable book *Inside Oscar*, the controversy swirled around "how the Academy could possibly have given Best Actress to Mary Pickford in a movie nobody liked."[x] Pickford had invited the judges to tea at her mansion, Pickfair; this award resulted. It didn't keep her career from tanking. After three more flops, she stopped making pictures. *Coquette* was an attempt to stop playing the kinds of girlish roles she was famous for; she cut her famous hair, bobbing it, and set about ruining men's lives. This would be akin to Shirley Temple playing Lolita. Even her biographer calls this "inferior work."[xi] Her performance defines the term "wooden." Not only did Pickford not deserve the Oscar, she didn't deserve the nomination, or as history has proved, even a career after *Coquette*.

Ruth Chatterton in *Madame X*, Corinne Griffith in *The Divine Lady*, and Bessie Love in *The Broadway Melody* aren't worth an Oscar, thus removing them from consideration here. Having to sit through all three of their movies would make a good punishment for any detention hall in high school. Most of them are awkward, stiff, and worst of all, boring, especially when compared to the actresses the Academy didn't even bother mentioning. Ruth Chatterton would have some other movies that aren't so painful to watch, but the fallen woman melodrama *Madame X* isn't one of them. Posturing, emoting, and faked sobbing on cue isn't good acting (or good directing). Lucille Ball does a much better drunk on Vitameatavegamin commercials. I wish the Academy didn't have this weakness for handing actresses the Oscar for endless crying and emotional wailing, but they do. Griffith plays Lady Hamilton, the love of Lord Nelson in England during the Napoleonic Wars (Laurence Olivier and Vivien Leigh would later cover the same story in *That Hamilton Woman*). Griffith is overacting much of the time, which is not uncommon in the pre-talkie era. Griffith's performance isn't as awful as others, but in a film about a great romance where the naval battles outshine the romance, Griffith has clearly not done her job (Marie Dressler is much more fun in the movie as her mother). Bessie Love has some sparkle at times in *Broadway Melody,* but not enough to overcome the rest of the boredom she inflicts.

The Letter was later enthusiastically remade with Bette Davis in the Jeanne Eagels part of an adulterous wife who kills her lover and then faces a blackmailer. At the time I wrote the first edition, only a single print of *The Letter* remained, and I had not had a chance to see it. Warner Archives in the interim made the movie available on DVD, and film fan Robert Alan Bryan was kind enough to send me a copy. Eagels' performance certainly isn't going to replace Davis' more accomplished turn, but compared to the other actresses nominated this year, Eagels seems full of nuance and detail. Compared to Davis, she just looks like a consumptive trying to avoid death's arrival (heroin isn't a good idea, kids...). Eagels' least amateurish moment comes when she testifies on the stand, lying her way through a version of events designed to turn her into a victim of a drunken lout. Her reliance on mannerisms elsewhere is discomforting, but fairly typical. She is far enough ahead of Pickford and the others that I would suggest leaving the nomination.

Betty Compson's part in *The Barker* is an endless series of pouting and whining. She would be much better in *The Docks of New York*, playing the prostitute who is rescued from suicide by sailor George Bancroft. She has a grittier role, and indubitably helped by the genius of von Sternberg for filming fallen women. Compson should be granted a nomination for *The Docks of New York* instead.

And as is usually the case in the early years of the Academy, the true artists were ignored.

Renee Maria Falconetti's eyes should have a nomination for *The Passion of Joan of Arc* (see above in Best Picture).

Lillian Gish's performance in Victor Sjöström's *The Wind* is delicate, nuanced, and compelling. Gish is completely riveting and honest as the wind drives her insane. Few performances can match it in the silent era – and neither can any of these sound nominations, which are sound only because you can hear them. Artificial, creaky, and downright trivial, most of the other performances nominated in this category are textbook examples of how not to act. The looks in Gish's eyes, the sense of growing horror, the rape she endures, and the murdering justice she metes out – all are done in the silent manner she had not only mastered, but practically invented as well. She should most definitely have been nominated for Best Actress.

Victor Sjöström directed another great silent film actress, Greta Garbo, in *The Divine Woman*. Only one reel exists of this film, and shows Garbo shifting from domestic goddess to angered slut to devoted lover in under a minute. I suspect that she deserved an Oscar nomination, especially compared to the ridiculously bad actresses that the Academy shoved forward this year, and even on such slim evidence, I would happily name her as Oscar material. When we add that to her performance as a woman denied her true love in Clarence Brown's *A Woman of Affairs*, it seems very clear the Academy was snubbing her, which would not be the case when the voting became based on the entire membership in the next year of eligibility. Garbo's biographer Karen Swenson calls *A Woman of Affairs* "the first of Garbo's films to withstand the test of time."[xii] I would agree. Watch the scene in the hospital with the roses; you will probably agree Garbo deserved a nod.

Fay Wray got her major break in Erich von Stroheim's *The Wedding March*, and the fact that the performance wasn't recognized with a nomination can only be taken as a sign of how the awards this year were rewards for loyal employees, and the withholding of them as punishment for not being good little boys and girls. Her performance is natural, believable, and touching, even when what she is asked to do – sacrifice herself to perhaps the most churlish lout in the history of American cinema – is in service to the egotistical mania of Erich von Stroheim, who places himself at the center of this film, and assumes that everyone will, of course, want him as much as he thinks he should be wanted. Any actress who had to do a love scene with von Stroheim and his ego deserves at least a nomination.

Of all these performances, none remains as masterful and persistently intriguing as Lillian Gish, whose career dominated the silent era as the best actress of her generation. *The Wind* is the capstone of her silent pictures. It's not a performance style that would ever work in the sound era, and Gish's career never returned to these heights, but *The Wind* proves she knew what she was doing. As Gish's biographer Charles Affron said, "*The Wind* contains the summa of Lillian's artistry in the mimetic registers of speechless acting."[xiii] In other words, she is a damn good artist. Gish should have received the Oscar for Best Actress.

Best Director: Frank Lloyd "won" for *The Divine Lady*, and was also up for *Drag* and *Weary River*, over Harry Beaumont, *Broadway Melody*; Irving Cummings, *In Old Arizona*; Lionel Barrymore, *Madame X*; and Ernst Lubitsch, *The Patriot*

The recipient of the Best Director award, Frank Lloyd, is the only winner to not have his film nominated for Best Picture; also, he was one of the judges...do the math. At the time, *Variety* called the film "spasmodic, episodic, and anemic."[xiv] As I've said before, no award should have gone to someone who helped jigger the rules to get the statue – but especially for a director this mundane. He is remembered today for the Clark Gable/Charles Laughton *Mutiny on the Bounty*, for which he was nominated, but did not win. *The Divine Lady* is a kind of precursor to *Mutiny*, since it has naval scenes and a romance. *Drag* and *Weary River* both star Richard Barthelmess. *Drag* is still another predictable melodrama, with a young playwright who marries one woman while he's in love with another. *Weary River* is a moralistic play about a gangster going straight by playing music in the prison band. None of these movies has any particular appeal today, other than to those interested in the transition from silent to sound pictures, and Lloyd shouldn't have been nominated for any of them.

Harry Beaumont produced a musical monstrosity in *Broadway Melody*. Regardless of its importance historically, he made a very bad film. He should be stripped of his nomination.

Irving Cummings loses his as well. Raoul Walsh's work on the early parts of *In Old Arizona* is evident, because as soon as the film was recast without him, the movie loses all visual interest – and any claim on the nomination.

Lionel Barrymore is best known as an actor today, particularly for the evil Mr. Potter in *It's a Wonderful Life*, but he had a brief career as a director. The composition of a number of the scenes in *Madame X* reflect a real sense of life surrounding these actors; sadly, the actors sound like bad audio-animatronics at Disneyland. The voicing is unbelievably awkward. Barrymore, like most of Hollywood, had not learned how to do sound; the training was all in imagery. As a silent film, this would have been far more brilliant. In short, a flawed nomination, and not one he really deserved. As Scott Eyman has observed in *The Speed of Sound*, as a director, Barrymore "quickly proved himself one of the worst in the business...*Madame X* is a landlocked, paralytic antique whose grotesque style only emphasizes source material that was passé even then."[xv] I agree – no nomination.

As a lost film, *The Patriot* cannot be judged, but on Lubitsch's reputation alone, his nomination is a good one.

As for those who were not recognized, many easily surpass the crap the Academy picked.

William Wellman deserves a nomination for *Beggars of Life*, which is proof he was capable of directing more than action scenes, as he did so well in *Wings*. Some of his more interesting choices as a director include the imposition of the flashback of the threat of sexual abuse over the face of Louise Brooks, as she recounts the murder of the would-be rapist (her adoptive father), as well as a moment of touching intimacy within a haystack between the runaway hoboes. While the emotional content of the film is unduly leavened by poor attempts at humor and a happy ending that relies on us thinking a brutal hobo actually has a heart, Wellman should have been nominated for the darker corners of this film.

As I've suggested above, Josef von Sternberg hit an artistic peak in *The Docks of New York*. Every single shot is striking, and serves to move the story ahead, with little or no wasted effort, in a considerably more believable and compelling romance than Frank Borzage's *Seventh Heaven*. He should have a nomination.

Carl Theodor Dreyer's *The Passion of Joan of Arc* is a directorial tour de force (discussed above). Nothing like it had been seen before, or since. And as such, nothing like it can compare, because there is nothing like it, which is true of many of Dreyer's films, such as *Vampyr*. Dreyer should have been nominated.

Erich von Stroheim's direction of *The Wedding March* certainly merits consideration. Like his butchered masterpiece *Greed*, *The Wedding March* was shot long and edited short; thus, we have only guesswork as to what it would have been like to see the entire thing. The second half (more or less) was released as *The Honeymoon*, the last copy of which was lost in a fire a few days after Stroheim died in 1957. Stroheim's direction has one major flaw, in that he never learned William Faulkner's lesson: "In writing, you must kill all your darlings." As Ernest Hemingway taught, it's not what you leave in, it's what you leave out. Irving Thalberg said Stroheim had a "footage fetish."[xvi] A nomination, certainly, but as a total film experience, less than what it could have been in the hands of someone willing to be selective. Stroheim should have been a novelist; he could have written as long as he wanted. Film is a medium that requires pacing and brevity to make its greatest statements. I'm not saying they shouldn't make long films, but each moment has to keep the story moving ahead. Stroheim never seems to have understood that – or that everyone would not be as fascinated with his character as he so obviously is.

Finally, Victor Sjöström had two films to be considered: the almost completely lost Garbo film, *The Divine Woman*, and his masterpiece, *The Wind*. I think I have made it perfectly clear that *The Wind* is a masterpiece that needs to be seen by any film lover. Victor Sjöström deserves the nomination, and were it any other year, he should have won the Oscar.

Having said that, the most unique picture of the year has to be *The Passion of Joan of Arc*. Nothing else equals its originality, even if the film itself remains static in its emotional development, playing a single note of sorrow with little of the more verbal defiance one expects from Joan of Arc. The genius of Carl Theodor Dreyer's direction demands the recognition of the Academy Award for Best Director.

Best Writing: Hans Kraly "won" for *The Patriot* and also got a nod for *The Last of Mrs. Cheyney*, over Elliott Clawson for *The Cop, The Leatherneck, Sal of Singapore*, and *Skyscraper*; Tom Barry for both *In Old Arizona* and *The Valiant*; Josephine Lovett, *Our Dancing Daughters*; and Bess Meredyth for both *A Woman of Affairs* and *Wonder of Women*.

Hans Kraly should lose his Oscar, because of the corruption of the Academy; also, *The Patriot* is a lost film. Sorry, Hans. *The Last of Mrs.*

Cheyney stars Mrs. Irving Thalberg, Norma Shearer, as well as Basil Rathbone. Set among the rich socialite set, Shearer plays a thief posing as a rich widow, who is uncovered; blackmail and a tidy resolution ensue. The film was remade twice. Not a great script, actually. Murky, at best. Sorry again, Hans. No nomination is merited.

Elliott Clawson wrote the screenplays for both *The Phantom of the Opera* and *West of Zanzibar*. The four films for which he was being considered have a common fault: they don't star Lon Chaney, Sr., but they do star Alan Hale, who would be more famous as Errol Flynn's sidekick in many films, as well as the father of the Skipper on *Gilligan's Island*. *The Cop* only exists in a nitrate print in the Library of Congress, so I was unable to view it. From reports of those who have, it's a fairly well written cop drama, with a ridiculously dumb ending. Stupid endings do not equal good writing. *The Leatherneck* is a buddy film, told from the point of view of a court-martial for desertion. Minor at best. *Sal of Singapore* exists in UCLA's archive, but it is unavailable, as it is awaiting restoration. Finally, *Skyscraper* has some nice shots of workers building a skyscraper, and is another buddy movie, as one friend tries to get his injured friend to buck up and live again. None of these are at the caliber of Clawson's better work – and why wasn't he nominated for *West of Zanzibar*? A strange film, yes, and racist in the imperialist way most of the western world was then, but a nicely twisted dark plot that lets Lon Chaney get in one of his finest acting moments. Clawson should have a nomination for *West of Zanzibar*.

Tom Barry was nominated for both *In Old Arizona* and *The Valiant*. *In Old Arizona* is based on the O. Henry story, "The Caballero's Way," but the released version is padded, and all too often, the dialogue is as awful as the acting. *The Valiant* tells the story of a murderer, who then proceeds to hide his identity to protect his family. The script is reasonable in its construction, but then, that was due to the original play *The Valiant* adapts. The dialogue is stiff, and unconvincing – and not deserving of a nomination any more than *In Old Arizona* does.

On the plus side, women were finally being recognized for a field they tended to dominate in the silent era: writing. Many of the most highly paid and respected writers in pre-talkie Hollywood were women. Josephine Lovett's *Our Dancing Daughters* was a major hit for Joan Crawford, and which made her a star (she reportedly went around the town, taking pictures of all the marquees with her name on it). The film's opening scenes, shot into a three-part mirror of Crawford's dancing feet, which then shows her slip being put on over them, is one of the most risqué and suggestive moments of the silent cinema (was she dancing nearly naked?). The film plays with the inversion of expectations so common in Twenties' images of women – the bad girl usually turns out to be the good girl. Clara Bow's stardom lived on different versions of that; one contemporary reviewer in *The New York Mirror* called Crawford's part a "typical Clara Bow role." *Our Dancing Daughters* has a reverse image as well, and shows the supposed good girl is, in fact, the bad girl. Opening the film with shots of mirrors only reinforces this twinning and twisting, and for that, one would like to credit the writer. Indeed, Crawford herself claimed that she snuck into the story department one night and stole the script so she could angle for the part more effectively. Josephine Lovett clearly deserves the nomination.

The other woman nominated, Bess Meredyth, had a very successful career, which included the Tyrone Power *The Mark of Zorro*, and the Claude Rains film noir, *The Unsuspected*. While *Wonder of Women* is now a lost film, *A Woman of Affairs* stars Greta Garbo and John Gilbert, and was adapted from a bestselling novel by Michael Arlen, *The Green Hat*. The second film to try and capitalize on the success of the torrid *Flesh and the Devil*, *A Woman of Affairs* is famous for its love scene and the hospital scene at the end, when Garbo receives roses from John Gilbert (see Best Actress above for more). Well worth a nomination for Meredyth.

As for those who were not nominated, let's begin with *The Wind*. Frances Marion's adaptation of the novel of the same name by Dorothy Scarborough should have been nominated. The ending of *The Wind* is a tacked-on happy one that doesn't fit well with the rest of the film (and cheapens it); in the novel, the Lillian Gish character wanders off to die in the desert. But this is hardly the writer's fault, as the original ending was filmed, then was changed at the studio's insistence (or so one version of the story goes; another says it was never filmed). Frances Marion and *The Wind* should have been nominated.

Laurel and Hardy's writing crew deserved a nom for the endlessly inventive *Big Business*. Riffing off of each other is far harder than writing drama, where the outcomes are often to be found repeated and repeated. Nobody ever did destruction with more panache than Laurel and Hardy. H.M. Walker received the credit for the titles, but the Oscar nomination should go to the uncredited Leo McCarey and Stan Laurel, and their gag men. Hardy was usually off playing golf while they figured these things out. Perhaps even funnier than *Big Business* is the lesser known *Wrong Again*. There is a horse, a piano, and a nude statue. The greatest double takes in the history of comedy come in this film. See these for those days when you are absolutely convinced that life sucks. So, in this year of double nominations, Stan Laurel & Co. should get nominations for both *Big Business* and *Wrong Again*.

Finally, we could not do better than to select Buster Keaton's last great film: *The Cameraman*. After this, his genius would be constrained and deflated by the studio system at MGM. Keaton maintained a career into the Sixties, with minor performances and behind-the-scene gag writing. Keaton's ability as a performer and director has often been recognized. But his capacity to construct brilliant gags and a narrative to contain them has often been ignored. *The Cameraman* deserves a nomination, and what is more, I think it to be the most compelling story of the year, especially in its capacity to reward more than one viewing. Buster Keaton and his gag men thus should have won the award for Best Writing for *The Cameraman*.

Best Cinematography: Clyde de Vinna "won" for *White Shadows in the South Seas*, over John Seitz, *The Divine Lady*; Ernest Palmer for both *Four Devils* and *Street Angel*; Arthur Edeson, *In Old Arizona*; and George Barnes, *Our Dancing Daughters*

Clyde de Vinna should not have his Oscar, as with all the winners this year. *White Shadows in the South Seas* is, however, unique, in that the film was shot entirely in Tahiti. Pretty as a postcard when the scenery is shown, it becomes mundane when the story intrudes. As a matter of principle, he should not have the Oscar, but he should retain his nomination.

John Seitz's camerawork on *The Divine Lady* deserves some consideration. Seitz's career spans decades, from 1909 to after WWII; he is perhaps best known for his association with director and writer Billy Wilder on *Double Indemnity, The Lost Weekend,* and *Sunset Blvd.* While the story limps along, the production values reflect the money spent upon it. The battle scenes are what drew the nomination. Seitz should stay.

Ernest Palmer can only be judged on *Street Angel*, because F.W. Murnau's *Four Devils* is a lost film. *Street Angel*, for which Janet Gaynor was given the Oscar the previous year, isn't eligible, so Mr. Palmer should be out of the running.

Arthur Edeson's work on *In Old Arizona* is location shooting for the most part, and functional, but hardly worth an Oscar. Some nice opening shots, but most of the film is trivially shot, with little to recommend it. No nomination is deserved.

George Barnes' camerawork on *Our Dancing Daughters* is compelling and creative, particularly in the suggestiveness it makes possible. He should keep his nomination.

As for those who went without a nomination, I offer three.

Roy H. Klaffki is listed as the cinematographer of *The Wedding March*, although there were others uncredited, and Erich von Stroheim claimed credit as well. The film has a wonderful sheen, but the cinematography does not draw attention, nor does it seem to particularly serve the story.[18] Still, *The Wedding March* is head and shoulders above the original nominees for this year, even in its butchered state, and deserves a nomination.

The Wind has a gritty, filthy look to it, beyond what I have already said about it. John Arnold should have been nominated – especially when you consider he also was the cinematographer on two of the movies they nominated for Best Picture, and so had the commercial success (*The Broadway Melody* and *Hollywood Revue* are both his work). From *The Wind*, the shots of the horses in the storm and the men heading to round them up remain as striking as those of Gish looking through the window near the end of the film as the corpse is uncovered by the wind. For *The Wind*, Arnold should have the nomination he so richly deserved, and for a far better film than his musicals.

Finally, Josef von Sternberg and Harold Rosson should have been nominated for *The Docks of New York*. The lighting alone is astonishing, varying itself depending on the scene. Although Rosson was given credit for the cinematography, and would later help make Jean Harlow a star (and his wife), von Sternberg is well known to have been in charge of the look of his lighting and camerawork. *Docks* is an absolutely fascinating film to watch, even when ignoring the plot (not unlike *Sunrise*). Sternberg had improved his craft tremendously in the year since *Underworld* (and made two other films, including *The Last Command*). Take one look at the scene where Bancroft is getting off the ship for the first time. Notice the lighting above on deck, and in the middle, and on the dock – it's a painting, and far from the only one in the film. He and Rosson deserved a nomination, and what is more, they should have received the Oscar for Best Cinematography, for the finest sense of composition of the year.

P.S. In 2012, the *Sight and Sound* poll of movie critics and directors placed the Soviet filmmaker Dziga Vertov's *Chelovek s kino-apparatom* (*Man with a Movie Camera*) on their top ten list. I'm having a very hard time accepting a piece of Communist drivel like *Man with a Movie*

---

[18] I find that a mobile camera is often more interesting as not, but not because of some desire for movement. John Ford and Howard Hawks rarely move the camera, but both of those men were geniuses at picking the exactly correct framing of the scene. Most people aren't, and a moving camera can add some energy to an otherwise static film. I also have no hostility to displaying style, as long as there is substance to match. As Andrew Sarris said, "Critics who argue that technique should not call attention to itself are usually critics who do not wish to call attention to technique." *"You Ain't Heard Nothin' Yet"* p. 266.

Camera as one of the greatest films ever made. In terms of technique and style, perhaps, but this is like bronzing the best poop you've ever had. It may be pretty, but that doesn't make it a good idea. What's next, Leni Riefenstahl's *Triumph of the Will*? D.W. Griffith's *Birth of a Nation*? This kind of ranking is what happens when critics forget that propaganda isn't something to be dismissed in favor of presentation. The values – or lack of them – being served have to be considered in the judgment of a film. *Man with a Movie Camera* basically argues that the Soviet Union was a nifty idea and everybody is just plum happy to be living in a dictatorship that just may have been a few shades closer to hell on earth than Nazi Germany. So, no nomination, despite the cineastes who are probably preparing to burn me in effigy even as I speak. See what watching Soviet claptrap leads to?

Best Art Direction: Cedric Gibbons "won" for *The Bridge of San Luis Rey*, over William Cameron Menzies for both *Alibi* and *The Awakening*, Mitchell Leisen, *Dynamite*; Hans Dreier, *The Patriot*; and Harry Oliver, *Street Angel*

Cedric Gibbons would go on to hold the record for the most nominations (39) and the most wins in this category (11), but on general principle, he should not have this one for the adaptation of Thornton Wilder's novel of a collapsed bridge and the meaning of death, *The Bridge of San Luis Rey*. Hans Dreier's work *The Patriot* has an interesting look, in what remains of the film, but not enough to merit its nomination. Harry Oliver and *Street Angel* should also be out; by the Academy's own rules, the movie wasn't eligible.

William Cameron Menzies, who won the first Oscar in this category the year before, was nominated for two films, *Alibi* and *The Awakening*. *Alibi* in particular has some beautiful set pieces, in the opening, and in the club scenes. He should keep his nomination.

Mitchell Leisen's work on Cecil B. DeMille's *Dynamite* might be worth considering, except for the fact that it wasn't released in the eligibility period.[19] Leisen went on to a successful career as a director, including the Fredric March *Death Takes a Holiday*, scripts from both Billy Wilder and Preston Sturges (both of whom he pissed off so much they became directors themselves), and several *Twilight Zone* episodes. But he should not have been nominated for this story of a woman who marries a condemned man for his fortune, only to see him get an unexpected reprieve.

---

[19] Remember: the nominations were cobbled together after the fact from the notes of the judges, and are thus not official nominations, checked for eligibility.

Oddly, the Academy ignored one of the most influential films of the year by passing over Joan Crawford's breakthrough *Our Dancing Daughters*, which built on her turn as the love interest in Lon Chaney, Sr.'s *The Unknown* the previous year. Cecil Beaton's Art Deco sets are something to behold, as are the costumes, and Joan Crawford's dancing. F. Scott Fitzgerald said of her, "Joan Crawford is doubtless the best example of the flapper...young things with a talent for living."[xvii] Why this film was not nominated is a mystery, but *Our Dancing Daughters* should have been.

Of all the films I saw from this year, no set was more detailed than *The Wedding March*. Erich von Stroheim destroyed his career in the monomaniacal pursuit of detail, and every single shot in this film shows it, to the point of wrecking any narrative drive or a sense of balanced character (the lout who accompanies Fay Wray to the scene outside of the church is so broadly crass that one can only cringe). We get an apple orchard in the film, in full bloom – and each of the thousands of blossoms had to be hand-tied to the branches. Designed by Richard Day and von Stroheim, *The Wedding March* is the very definition of excellent art direction. It deserved a nomination, and had von Stroheim not driven his studio masters mad with budget overruns in the service of that art direction, he and Day would have been nominated. What is more to the point, they deserve the Oscar. *The Wind* reproduces the claustrophobic feel of being trapped within the storm, both without and within; *The Wedding March* goes *The Wind* a number of steps better in its glorious decadence, wallowing in this fairyland Vienna. *The Wedding March* should have the Oscar for Best Art Direction

CHAPTER THREE: 1930 AWARDS
2nd Show of the Year, 3rd Show Overall

Movies released between August 1st, 1929 and July 31st, 1930

THE SCENE OF THE CRIME:

    For the only time in Academy Award history, two shows were held in the same calendar year. On November 5, 1930, they gathered in the Fiesta Room at the Ambassador Hotel. The host this time was Conrad Nagel, actor and Academy president. The evening got off on a bad foot (after the food and dancing) with a fifty-minute harangue from Will Hays on how wonderful the film industry was now that he had cleaned it up (self-congratulation is never fun…unless, of course, I'm the one doing it). For the first time, different presenters handed out each award, a tradition that continues to this day. Once again, the winners knew ahead of time – or at least two of them did, as Norma Shearer and George Arliss took pictures with their awards two days earlier. Rumors persist that MGM employees were pressured to vote for Norma Shearer, who was married to MGM bigwig Irving Thalberg. Joan Crawford quipped that Shearer was treated so well because "She sleeps with the boss."

    One of the highlights of the evening was a talking film with special Lifetime Achievement honoree Thomas Edison. Somewhat ironic, as most of the movie moguls in the room had fled the East Coast to start Hollywood because Edison had been suing them for copyright infringements in the early days of the industry. Edison's film ran at the end of the night, which seemed a fitting tribute to an art form he had played such a large role in making possible.

They kept all the award categories from the previous year, and added a new one: Best Sound Recording.

WHAT THEY GOT RIGHT:

Once again, not much. The stink of corruption still floats over some of these awards, particularly those of Norma Shearer, for Best Actress, and her brother Douglas, for the new Oscar for Sound Recording. Eventually, you would think they would see clearly.

But if they did, I wouldn't be writing this book, you wouldn't be reading it, and we would have never met. That would be sad, no?

Surprisingly, Universal made a good showing this year with the anti-war picture *All Quiet on the Western Front*. Universal was never respected by the other film studios, particularly MGM. This film began the tendency of the Academy to go for big, bloated pictures with a message. It makes them feel Important. I'm not saying there won't be moments the Big Issue Picture is quite good; I'm just not going to agree with them very often. What they may have seen as a Big Issue often isn't. This is not to say *All Quiet on the Western Front* isn't worth watching – it is. But it is most definitely a message picture, and weakest when pontificating, rather than showing us what the war was like.

For the first time, each branch of the Academy voted for the nominations with all members of that branch; then, the entire Academy voted on the final awards. Still doesn't mean they were right, though…

But there are two categories in which I am inclined to agree: Best Cinematography and Best Art Direction.

Best Cinematography: Joseph T. Rucker and Willard Van Der Veer won for *With Byrd at the South Pole*, over Arthur Edeson, *All Quiet on the Western Front*; William Daniels, *Anna Christie*; Gaetano Gaudio and Harry Perry, *Hell's Angels*; and Victor Milner, *The Love Parade*.

A visual record of Admiral Byrd's aerial conquest of the South Pole, *With Byrd at the South Pole* is a unique film, unmatched for a long time as a film in the tradition of *Grass* and *Chang*, and in the direct line to the myriad nature films of Walt Disney and National Geographic. Impressive footage, but is this art? Yes, it is, and often of a high order. Beginning awkwardly with Admiral Byrd reading from cue cards in a painfully obvious way, *With Byrd* quickly becomes a lyrical and indispensible historical record. In two years, after this and *Tabu* (shot in Bora Bora), the cinematographers changed the rules so that only films made in America could qualify, which strikes me as rigging things again, but I can feel the frustration of those trapped in the studio. Who can compare studio limitations with this kind of live footage, at least at this stage of early sound? *All Quiet on the Western Front* has moments of good camerawork, but nothing stands out as particularly artistic. *Anna Christie* is a very muddy film, with little to recommend it except some work at night and in the fog, but the bulk of the film bores in terms of its cinematography. *Hell's Angels* got the nomination because of the flying scenes, but Howard Hughes did little that Wellman and his cameramen hadn't already mastered in *Wings*. *The Love Parade* doesn't have much in terms of how the eye sees it either. Rucker and Van Der Veer deserve their award for *With Byrd*.

Best Art Direction: Herman Rosse won for *King of Jazz*, over William Cameron Menzies, *Bulldog Drummond*; Hans Dreier, *The Love Parade*; Jack Okey, *Sally*; and Hans Dreier, *The Vagabond King*

Sadly, Bix Beiderbecke was ill before filming his piece for the musical collection *King of Jazz*. Star Bing Crosby got involved in a car accident in which he was driving drunk, and had to be brought to and from the set from jail each day. I enjoyed seeing Joe Venuti and Eddie Lang playing (perhaps the finest jazz violinist and guitarist of the Twenties). Rosse designed some interesting sets – a giant book, a bandstand, various flashy backgrounds, and a giant piano for the band to play in. Fun stuff, if way over the top with the most unique sets of the year (with the possible exception of Laurel and Hardy's *Brats*, which you should see as soon as possible). The other nominees don't even come close.

WHAT THEY GOT WRONG:

Once again, almost all the major categories. Here they are, along with their "winners":

Best Picture: All *Quiet on the Western Front*

Best Actor: George Arliss, *Disraeli*
Best Actress: Norma Shearer, *The Divorcee*
Best Director: Lewis Milestone, *All Quiet on the Western Front*
Best Writing: Frances Marion, *The Big House*
Best Sound Recording: Douglas Shearer and the MGM Sound Dept., *The Big House*

Best Picture: *All Quiet on the Western Front* won, over *The Big House, Disraeli, The Divorcee,* and *The Love Parade*

All Quiet on the Western Front won, but when we compare the film to the other pictures they nominated, it's not hard to see why, given that few people (outside of film historians) have since bothered watching *The Big House, Disraeli, The Divorcee,* or *The Love Parade*. *Disraeli* is a dinosaur from the nineteenth century theater with sly one-liners, some melodramatic spy-fluff, and lots of "Rule, Britannia" feel (see Best Actor for more). *The Divorcee* is a dated attempt to display the hypocrisy of the double standard regarding infidelity, even it did launch the pre-Code era of more open sexuality (see Best Actress for more). Neither of those should have been nominated. *The Love Parade* is, on the other hand, classic Ernst Lubitsch, full of the naughty innuendo and comic touches one expects from this director (see the Director and Actor categories for more), and should be seen far more often, as it belongs on the list of Best Picture nominees.

All Quiet on the Western Front is definitely a worthy nomination. The film remains one of the great indictments of war. In the pacifist, isolationist spirit of 1930 America, *All Quiet on the Western Front* must have wrung a chord of reassurance for strongly held principles in large areas of America. A very brave film, *All Quiet on the Western Front* exhibits the brutality of war, the fear of the soldiers, and the rapid abandonment of civilized expectations in favor of survival. At times, *All Quiet on the Western Front* is every bit as unsettling as the opening of *Saving Private Ryan*, including one shot with a pair of hands left grabbing the barb wire, after the rest of the soldier is blown apart. Grittiness and reality surround the plot, from a soldier soiling himself under his first attack to a soldier telling a pompous officer to kiss his butt. The film is even honest about sex, in a classy, restrained way. *All Quiet on the Western Front* retains much of its power and conviction more than eighty years after its making. But a greater picture remains to be seen.

The prison story *The Big House* is also still worth watching; it feels like a Warner Brothers movie that escaped onto the MGM lot. The opening scenes may be the most accurate ever done on what it is like to enter into prison, and Robert Montgomery makes a sympathetic figure for the viewer; we are drawn into the slammer as he is. Wallace Beery plays a big goon who has a penchant for lying and then denying that he lied; Chester Morris plays his smarter cellmate. Montgomery is the novice, in jail for killing someone when driving drunk. *The Big House* earns its Oscar nomination.

The Academy ignored several great movies, including the best one of the year.

Rouben Mamoulian's *Applause* was a financial disaster, coming as it did in the days after the stock market crash, and telling a tragic tale, which explains why the Academy ignored it. Torch singer Helen Morgan plays a burlesque queen, in a part originally intended for Mae West. Had West starred in it, the film would be much better known today. Morgan reportedly put on some weight and wore a cheesy blond wig to play the role, in an early bid for living the part (think De Niro in *Raging Bull* for a later version of this gambit). She's got a great voice, but she's not the best actress, even in this era. Mamoulian spares no punches in exposing the seamy side of life, especially in the sequences showing close-ups of the burlesque dancers. I am put in mind of nothing so much as the Brobdingnagian section of Jonathan Swift's *Gulliver's Travels*; distance is sometimes the source of aesthetics. *Applause* can be a very ugly experience, and it's easy to see why it didn't gain a wider audience – but the Academy should have nominated it.

As they should have for Alfred Hitchcock's *Blackmail*, the very first British sound feature film; Hitchcock made a silent version concurrently. Already staking out his territory as the master of the thriller, Hitchcock presents an insider's tale of Scotland Yard, with betrayal, voyeurism, sexual assault, murder, a man caught between murder and love, and yes, a little blackmail. On almost every level, *Blackmail* is a far better film than most of what was released this year, as one would expect from Hitchcock. But an even greater game was afoot.

The German *Pandora's Box* adapts Frank Wedekind's plays *Erdgeist* (1895) and *Die Büchse der Pandora* (1904); Alban Berg based his opera *Lulu* on the same materials. Lulu, a kept woman, is played by Louise Brooks, who just shimmers with life and the glow of the beautiful and the young. One can see quite clearly why Hollywood might have had more than a little discomfort at approving this film; Lulu is a young woman trading upon sex and the flesh to achieve material success. The film is strikingly well-made, with almost no wasted action. The scene in the theater prop closet between Lulu and her older lover – ranging from argument to manhandling to temper tantrum to hysterical laughter to making out – has more emotional honesty than the majority of American films to that date...put together. Not healthy, this seduction of the older man (who is engaged to another) by the amoral Lulu, but very real. The hanging wolf skin is a marvelous touch for a scene that all too often would be portrayed as one sided; clearly, both the older man and the younger sex kitten are chasing each other, depending on the turn in the relationship.[20] On their wedding day, her status as the object of lust and love from a number of different sources (including her new stepson) brings on violence, and the husband's death from a gun in her hands (I leave unsaid how that occurs, since it is one of the turning points of the film, and fascinating to watch). A trial follows, as do other complications. That the film also contains what may be the first open portrayal of a lesbian only added to its unsuitability to the Academy. The honesty in this film comes not from the concern with unhealthy passion and sexual behaviors outside of the norm; rather, *Pandora's Box* remains a landmark film because it admits more than the kind of rosy, sunny sexuality American cinema had almost exclusively concerned itself with, when it did admit such things existed as more than titillation. *Pandora's Box* feels like a film about fifty years before its time, from its cinematography to its acting to its direction. *Cabaret* lies in this film's direct lineage. Beyond a doubt, worthy of a nomination, for the film, the director G.W. Pabst, and the star, Louise Brooks. When you consider that Pabst and Brooks also made *Diary of a Lost Girl* in the same year of eligibility, it is clear that cinema was at its best in their collaboration this year. *Pandora's Box* should have won the Oscar for Best Picture.

Best Actor: George Arliss won the Oscar for *Disraeli*, with another nomination for *The Green Goddess*, over Wallace Beery, *The Big House*; Maurice Chevalier for both *The Big Pond* and *The Love Parade*; Ronald Colman for both *Bulldog Drummond* and *Condemned*; and Lawrence Tibbett, *The Rogue Song*

George Arliss won for *Disraeli*, a role he had done on stage and the silent screen. Throughout the decade, and past it, playing historical figures often led to Oscar gold. Arliss was also nominated for a second role s a villainous rajah in the Indian colonial potboiler *The Green Goddess*, but named only for *Disraeli* (the same narrowing is true of Norma Shearer). For the next awards, the rules would be rewritten to allow only one performance to be nominated per acting category per year.

---

[20] Later on, there is a stuffed crocodile when someone blackmails Brooks; I'm still trying to figure out what that means, but it feels like it should mean something.

Arliss belongs to the nineteenth century, as he plays the Victorian prime minister, Disraeli. His hair is ridiculous, looking as if he had a giant upside down question mark on his forehead; portraits of Disraeli show that Arliss has gone way beyond the original idiotic hairstyle. Arliss can be fun to watch, but his performance doesn't convince us we are watching the real thing in the slightest. Arliss is obviously having a ball, and at times, so are we, but he really isn't giving a deep performance. No Oscar is really necessary, but Arliss should keep the nomination. Just keep the hair away from me.

Wallace Beery was one of the biggest stars in Hollywood, and one who made the transition very successfully into sound. The character of Butch was written for Lon Chaney, Sr., whose death gave more than one actor their break (Karloff and Lugosi, to name two). His performance as an inmate in *The Big House* still works, if a bit repetitively. He dominates the film, having both the best lines, and delivering them with relish. Playing Butch catapulted Beery to being the best paid actor in the world, for a time. He earned his nomination.

Ronald Colman's performance as a detective in *Bulldog Drummond* secured his transition to a talking picture star. His rich, noble tone would maintain his career well for the next two decades, and remain one of the great voices of the cinema. This movie would also spawn many sequels, including a late performance by John Barrymore. Colman is mannered, happy, and full of savoir faire. Not a serious role, but an exuberant one. Colman's film was a smash success, and deservedly so. *Bulldog Drummond* feels like a Hitchcock film, actually. The dialogue is crisp, the editing fast, and the sets are wonderful. Granted, most of the actors around Colman still haven't figured out how to act and talk at the same time, but Colman's performance points in the right direction, especially verbally. As for *Condemned*, Colman plays a thief sentenced to Devil's Island, where he falls in love with the warden's wife, who returns the favor. The warden, understandably, is not amused. Colman should keep the nomination for his voice alone.

In the naughty court musical *The Love Parade*, we get Maurice Chevalier, who always played Maurice Chevalier – tongue firmly in cheek, happy, excited, and ready to burst into song. Most careers in Hollywood are based on producing a screen persona, then milking it: Clark Gable, for example, always played Clark Gable, and was usually enjoyable on screen. Chevalier clearly was a breath of fresh air as he brought his French accent to town, but eighty years later, he's hard to take seriously as an actor. He's fun, yes, but one doesn't give acting awards for smirking – usually. (I will shortly make an exception or three.) Chevalier was also nominated for *The Big Pond*, a poor man meets rich girl movie that cries out for Lubitsch, and does Chevalier little credit. He should keep the nomination for *The Love Parade*.

The Czarist tragedy *The Rogue Song* brought us Lawrence Tibbett. This opera singer is quite famous, but the film exists only in fragments, so there's no real way of knowing (sad, because Laurel and Hardy were the comic relief). But acting is not why Tibbett was cast, so no nomination should have been given to him.

None of these actors deserved the actual Academy Award. So allow me these choices from left field: let's nominate Groucho, Harpo, and Chico Marx for *The Cocoanuts*. Yes, it's a horrible film. Most of the Marx Brothers movies were really, really bad, and the prime reason to have invented the fast forward button on your remote – except when the brothers are doing their best to wreck the film around them by being funny. *The Cocoanuts* was the first time most of America had seen these professional smartasses calmly, cooly, and maniacally overthrow every sacred cow in existence; in the dictionary under irreverent, there you will find the Marx Brothers enshrined as the word's definition. And of the three in this film, *The Cocoanuts* is clearly Groucho's show, as it so often was. I'm not sure if you would call it acting, but any one of the Marx Brothers is more fun to watch than what passed for acting this year – or most other years. Groucho should have gotten the Oscar for Best Actor.

Best Actress: Norma Shearer won for *The Divorcee*, and was also nominated for *Their Own Desire*, over Greta Garbo, for both *Anna Christie* and *Romance*; Nancy Carroll, *The Devil's Holiday*; Ruth Chatterton, *Sarah and Son*; and Gloria Swanson, *The Trespasser*

Norma Shearer's performance in the marriage melodrama *The Divorcee* is stilted and artificial – and I could swear in her first scene, she keeps looking over Chester Morris' shoulders to read from cue cards. She probably wasn't, as she was known for obsessive rehearsals, but it looks like she is, which means in a love scene, she chose to keep avoiding eye contact with her lover. Not a good idea. I was shocked to see her chewing food with her mouth open, especially since she was a woman marketed as the essence of class. Did nobody have manners back then? Shearer provides a prime example of why the Academy Awards weren't to be trusted in these days, because of the block voting the studios demanded from their employees. But she's also an example of how time withers the false and feeds the true (*Their Own Desire* isn't any better, and please don't ask me to explain the plot; life is too short for that). Shearer could improve; her performance in next year's *A Free Soul* is considerably more interesting, but only as good as whoever was in the scene with her. Watch her with Clark Gable, and she becomes smoother, more believable, sexier. With Leslie Howard, she becomes as stiff and artificial as he almost always was. And with Lionel Barrymore, the ham emerges. But she did not deserve the Oscar for *The Divorcee*, surrounded as she is by second-rate actors and bad dialogue (which still plagued her in *A Free Soul* when she was forced to say things like "And suddenly the moonbeams turned to worms...and crawled away.")

Greta Garbo's first talking appearance in *Anna Christie* screams its own significance – dirty, lowdown, Eugene O'Neill importance. *Anna Christie* is the last kind of film one expects from glossy MGM (shockingly out of place is a credit for "Gowns by Adrian"). The characters are all drunkards, poorly dressed, and in need of baths. The O'Neill play is a classic of the American theater; this movie...is not. Garbo's performance is largely remembered for her first line: "Giff me a viskey, ginger ale on the side. And don't be stingy, baby." Anna Christie was raped, and the event is obliquely referenced, as is her time then spent as a prostitute ("Men again. Men all the time. Oh, how I hate them."). This is definitely pre-Code Hollywood. The film is very, very talky – and dull. Perhaps Garbo should have kept her mouth shut. Except for the brilliant performances in *Ninotchka, Queen Christina*, and *Camille*, I don't find much joy in her sound performances, but her voice is an attractive one. She still hasn't learned how to stop acting as if she was in a silent film – she puts her hand to her head and through her hair waaaaaay too much. She tends to over-emphasize emotion, using her entire body. Compared to other performances, one can see justification for the nomination, but I felt none of the wonder a few of her films engender. I tend to agree with Richard Schickel, who called this a "static and ludicrous film."[xviii] However, the German version of the film has a more interesting, less mannered performance (the early sound films were often filmed in one or more foreign languages; you haven't lived until you've seen Laurel and Hardy in multiple languages). Garbo's comfort level with German was obviously higher than her English; she gives a better performance in every way. As for *Romance*, Garbo plays (once again) a woman with a shadowy past and too many lovers. Unlike *Anna Christie*, she's taking no chances playing her usual glamorous self, and needs no nomination. Garbo should keep her nomination, but for the German version of *Anna Christie*.

The less said about Nancy Carroll and Ruth Chatterton the better. In *The Devil's Holiday*, Nancy Carroll is playing yet another bad-girl-who-realizes-she-wants-to-be-good-and-so-reforms-at-the-end role. Chatterton was nominated for Best Actress two years in a row, this time for

Sarah and Son; I can't explain why without resorting to conspiracy theories, since *Sarah and Son* is more or less the same basic tearjerker mother worshipping her son-who-doesn't-know-her role as her previous outing in *Madame X* (with a little opera and an accent thrown in for class[21]). No nominations for either Carroll or Chatterton.

Gloria Swanson again was nominated, this time for her first talkie, *The Trespasser*. This is the film she made when *Queen Kelly* tanked, and it was reasonably successful – then. She is forced to sing; we are forced to listen. It's not a bad voice, a bit like Jeanette MacDonald, but Swanson's career went into a nose dive for a reason. This may be it. No nomination.

As for those who were passed over, think of Mary Duncan in F. W. Murnau's *City Girl*, playing the title role. Duncan made very few films, because she married well and left the business (later becoming known for her charity work, as well as being friends with Rose Kennedy). Duncan is wonderful in this lesser-known Murnau film, showing spunk and fire as a waitress who marries a country boy and comes into conflict with his dictatorial father. The joy of the run through the wheat fields is felt in every frame. Too bad Duncan didn't make many films, as she had it in her to be one of the great ones. And honestly, I found *City Girl* to be a far more satisfying, believable story than *Sunrise*. While not the cinematographic masterpiece *Sunrise* is, *City Girl* is on a simpler, more elegant plane of art. Less is often more. Duncan should have been nominated.

We might also consider the African-American actress Nina Mae McKinney, all of sixteen and full of life, who deserved a nomination for her role as the devilish Chick in King Vidor's *Hallelujah* (see the Director category for more). It's an overdone performance, but not any more so than Greta Garbo's English performance in *Anna Christie*. Not for nothing was McKinney known as the "dusky Clara Bow." McKinney is by turns spunky, over-the-top, conniving, and downright wrong – even when she converts, it seems done as a calculation to get the preacher to be her man. So why wasn't she selected? Racism is the most likely reason. It would be decades until we reached Dorothy Dandridge, but McKinney blazed that trail.

But as I've said above, Louise Brooks more than deserved a nomination for *Pandora's Box* (as well as for *Diary of a Lost Girl*). She should have won the Oscar. Watch five minutes of her playing Lulu and you will see why.

---

[21] She sounds, strangely enough, exactly like Latka's girlfriend Simka from *Taxi*.

1931-1932

Best Director: Lewis Milestone won for *All Quiet on the Western Front*, over Clarence Brown, for both *Anna Christie* and *Romance*; Robert Leonard, *The Divorcee*; King Vidor, *Hallelujah*; and Ernst Lubitsch, *The Love Parade*

Lewis Milestone was a versatile director, having won for the comedy award two years previously.[22] *All Quiet on the Western Front* is a big, difficult film, and well worth a nomination. The direction is sure and inventive. Milestone uses sound brilliantly, especially in the scenes in the classroom where the noise of the crowd and the parade, the blind support for the war, empowers the vile recruitment of the innocent. The teacher who convinces his whole class to enlist en masse may be the most dangerous fool ever portrayed in film or literature. The sense of reality is highly detailed, and often shot through the frame of a door or a window (John Ford had a penchant for this framing device, most famously at the end of *The Searchers*). Milestone should have edged a few overacted scenes back to more believability, but overall, it's an excellent job of direction. He should keep his nomination.

Clarence Brown's version of *Anna Christie* is far less interesting than the German one, shot on the same sets by Jacques Feyder. Brown shouldn't have been nominated (the also-ran *Romance* isn't any better). Odd, how the famous versions of early talkies pale in some respects to the foreign language versions; watch the Spanish version of *Dracula*, and other than the massive loss of Bela Lugosi and Dwight Frye, la pelicula is far more interesting to watch.

Robert Leonard doesn't deserve a nomination for *The Divorcee*, which is an awkwardly paced, poorly directed film. It has its moments, but those are largely from sticking a finger in society's eye.

King Vidor's decision to make an all-black musical largely filmed in the South was an odd one. Viewing *Hallelujah* today is a mix of pleasures and embarrassments. The documentary feel of some of the location shooting is excellent, as is the sense that Vidor is doing his best to portray black life as realistically as possible. But the stereotypes creep in, of sensuality and violence being somehow inherently black. *Hallelujah* is another step in the constantly shifting Vidor canon; that versatility may be part of the reason why he isn't better known to the general public today. Directors who specialize tend to gain a public image – think Hitchcock and thrillers, Scorsese and gangster pictures, Lucas and pulp adventure. Vidor has made a brave film here, even if it is somewhat dated. He should keep his nomination.

---

[22] Only by denying Chaplin, of course; I felt the award unjustified. His film *Two Arabian Knights* was a comedy, but set in WWI, which explains why he was chosen to direct this movie.

Ernst Lubitsch definitely earned a nomination for this first musical to actually tell a story through song. The "Lubitsch touch" is in ample evidence, as the sexual innuendoes fly fast and furious. *The Love Parade* is a stunningly beautiful movie, with a number of comic moments. My two favorites are when the camera pulls away so Maurice Chevalier can tell a dirty story in silence, and the ambassador's reaction to the marriage between queen and consort. But the songs are beyond awful, with the exception of the roustabout comedy number, "Let's Be Common." Still, *The Love Parade* is a far better film than any of the musicals nominated before (and some since), even if the end is more than a bit sexist, as the man asserts his "natural" dominance (a fairly typical attitude of the period).

Other directors should have gotten a nod from the Academy.

Rouben Mamoulian was a rising star, on his way to making *Dr. Jekyll and Mr. Hyde*. *Applause* was acclaimed in its day by the critics, and Mamoulian was highly praised, particularly for his camerawork. Mamoulian deserved a nomination for *Applause* (see Best Picture above).

Hitchcock should have been nominated for *Blackmail*. The play of light and shadow, the sense of motion, the glimpse of the small detail leading to the next action, the director cameo, the comic moments – the endless stream of small touches reveal a man already in control of his craft and heading into art.

As I've argued previously, *Pandora's Box* should have led to a Best Director nomination for G.W. Pabst. Of all the eligible films this year, *Pandora's Box* remains the most striking and unusual, the least touched by age. Pabst should have won for Best Director.

Best Writing: Frances Marion won for *The Big House*, over George Abbott, Maxwell Anderson, and Del Andrews, *All Quiet on the Western Front*; Julian Josephson, *Disraeli*; John Meehan, *The Divorcee*; and Howard Estabrook, *Street of Chance*

The Big House was written by one of the best of the silent screenwriters, Frances Marion. That she survived into the sound era is a testament to her ability, since most women fell by the wayside in favor of smart-cracking men. *The Big House*, however, can't quite decide what kind of movie it wants to be: scathing indictment of the prison system? Comedy? Romance? The dialogue wanders from inspired to dull and back again. Any writer that thinks a first declaration of love should include the phrase "I get sort of a chokey feeling" isn't on top of her game.²³ *The Big House* has its moments, but it lacks a consistency throughout – a problem with many films, admittedly, but one I am willing to excuse depending on how good the good bits are. The best parts of the film are based on first-hand research Marion did in prison visits, and for that realism alone, she can keep the nomination – but she didn't deserve the Oscar.

The gang on *All Quiet on the Western Front* definitely earned the nomination. While not a perfect adaptation, it is a remarkably effective one, preserving the spirit of Erich Maria Remarque's classic. The mob can have their nod.

Disraeli is more or less the version of the stage play that George Arliss had been in for decades. Not particularly original, and not deserving of an Oscar nod.

The Divorcee is an attempt to show the double standards of male and female infidelity, and as such, is a brave move – but the dialogue is strictly mechanical and awkward. It's not an interesting picture to listen to at all. The nomination should stay, for pricking at hypocrisy.

Howard Estabrook was one of the most respected screenwriters of this period, winning the next year for *Cimarron* (actually a very poorly written movie). He was also very prolific, writing the screenplays for both the 1929 and 1946 versions of *The Virginian*, Howard Hughes' *Hell's Angels*, and the Selznick adaptation of *David Copperfield* in 1935. He was nominated this year for *Street of Chance*, starring William Powell and Jean Arthur – a well-plotted crime melodrama, and well enough done for this sort of thing. He can keep the nomination.

As to other scripts, a few merit consideration.

Bulldog Drummond has some choice moments of verve and wit, but then, almost anything in Ronald Colman's voice is fun to hear. It deserved a nomination.

Of the two G.W. Pabst films, it is not *Pandora's Box* that features unique and original writing. In some ways, *Pandora's Box* is a good example of a film rising above its screenplay, but *Diary of a Lost Girl* is a far more telling script, although not executed as compellingly as *Pandora's Box*. Part of the problem lies in the actors surrounding Louise Brooks being less effective, particularly the seducer. *Diary of a Lost Girl* starts with a father who regularly beds his housekeepers, and then confronts the father with an employee who has done the same thing to

---

²³ After deciding this for myself, I found biographer James Curtis in full agreement: "Frances Marion had a genius for doping out the broad parameters of a screenplay...But her dialogue was hopelessly hackneyed, leading Thalberg in the Thirties to treat her as a 'ditch digger.' He had her scripts rewritten by dialogue specialists like Anita Loos and Donald Ogden Stewart..." *James Whale: A New World of Gods and Monsters*, p. 337.

his daughter. Not as luminescent as she was in *Pandora's Box*, Brooks still shines as the daughter who has to deal with the consequences of her seduction, which seems to have happened while she was unconscious. But the movie then takes her through the standard social condemnation to a coming of age tale, first with yet another unconscious seduction, and then quite a different take on things. The ending is still unexpected, and not in the way the Jack the Ripper ending is in *Pandora's Box*. The moral ascendancy of Brooks' character is quite unusual. This movie feels like what Charles Dickens would have written if he had let himself admit sex existed in his books. Rudolf Leonhardt adapted the Margaret Böhme novel, and he merited a nomination.

But the best writing of the year, even if it includes a remarkably stupid plot and a large number of boring characters, is that of Morrie Ryskind, adapting George S. Kaufman's play for the Marx Brothers, *The Cocoanuts*. "Do you want to be wage slaves? Well, what makes wage slaves? Wages!" "Right now, I'd do anything for money. I'd kill somebody for money. I'd kill YOU for money...Ah no, you're my friend. I'd kill you for nothing." "One false move and I'm yours!" "Why-a duck? Why-a no chicken?" Actually, there's really no telling who to give the Oscar to here – the Marx Brothers were notorious for ad-libbing. The Oscar should have gone to Ryskind, Kaufman, and the Marx Brothers. Yes, I know Harpo never speaks. He's still got better dialogue than the rest of the movies made this year.

Best Sound Recording: The first Oscar in this category went to Douglas Shearer and MGM for *The Big House*, over John Trilby and RKO, *The Case of Sergeant Grischa* (a lost film); Franklin Hansen, *The Love Parade*; Oscar Lagerstrom and United Artists, *Raffles*; and George Groves and First National, *Song of the Flame* (also a lost film)

The entire sound departments for each studio were nominated, but a single individual was named to receive the award in their stead. Just on general principle, Shearer should have not won this award. MGM was one of the last to jump on the sound wagon fully, and it seems unfair to allow the award to stand. Who else should have won? Of all the musicals made this year, *The Love Parade* sounds far better; Lubitsch used sound to great effect, and the recording engineer served him well. Normally, I will not talk about this category, but corruption and nepotism must be stopped. Franklin Hansen should have won.

By the way, if you've never seen Ronald Colman in *Raffles*, it's a fun Samuel Goldwyn production. Not a great film, but a fun bit of high-class thievery of the British sort (made in America, of course). The sound announces itself from the dark: British bobbies slurping up their tea, followed by a fade-in on the visuals of same.

CHAPTER FOUR: 1931 AWARDS
4th Show

Movies released between August 1st, 1930 and July 31st, 1931

THE SCENE OF THE CRIME:

On November 10, 1931, the attendees gathered at the Biltmore Hotel, in the Sala D'Oro. Nobody bothered to let the guests know where they were sitting ahead of time, so everything was an hour late. The emcee this year was Lawrence Grant, an actor known for a range of supporting roles in everything from *Bulldog Drummond* to *Son of Frankenstein* and *Dr. Jekyll and Mr. Hyde*. They observed a moment of silence in memory of Thomas Edison, who had just died. Political commentary was featured for the first time, as the head of the American Newspaper Publishers Association joked that in Arkansas, they did have a few Republicans and "other varmints." This, with Republican Vice President Charles Curtis in the room, and due up to speak next. Quite a few people followed a comedian out into the lobby out of boredom, but they were herded back in. Child actor and nominee Jackie

Cooper slept through most of the awards on Marie Dressler's shoulder (or lap, depending on which account you read). Cooper's uncle, Norman Taurog, won for Cooper's movie, *Skippy*, but the victory was largely based on Taurog surviving a car accident in Oscar's first sympathy win.

The writers went back to the original split categories of Original Story and Adaptation. After this ceremony, cinematographers, tired of losing to pretty pictures shot overseas, had the rules rewritten to insist that their Oscar only went to work filmed in America.

Another change resulted from this year, when Norma Shearer announced the winner for Best Actress, and might have named herself. It wouldn't be the last time a candidate could have given herself the Oscar; it happened at least once. You'd think the Academy would have figured this out...

Everybody complained how long and boring the ceremony was. If they only knew what was to come...

WHAT THEY GOT RIGHT:

Best Actress: Marie Dressler won for *Min and Bill*, over Irene Dunne, *Cimarron*; Norma Shearer, *A Free Soul*; Ann Harding, *Holiday*; and Marlene Dietrich, *Morocco*

Marie Dressler saw her career revive itself with the previous year's *Anna Christie*, walking away with the picture, despite "Garbo Talks!" She became a major star, in the unlikeliest second act of any actor in American cinema. You've never seen anything like Dressler before or since. She is a true original. *Min and Bill* is a crude oceanfront love story between Dressler and Wallace Beery. Dresser plays Min, a scrappy broken-down tavern keeper with a crusty outside and an inside as soft and warm as a fresh-baked biscuit, Marie Dressler won the hearts of a Depression-torn America. *Min and Bill* isn't a perfect movie; it can't decide what it wants to be at times, inserting a slapstick boat chase shortly after establishing itself as a comic character study with serious undertones. Compared with the other performances this year, there really was no contest. Seeing her wale the tar out of Wallace Beery is enough to earn her the award; Beery was a horrible human being, nowhere near as charming as the louts he tended to play; an alcoholic, he beat his first wife Gloria Swanson. Dressler deserved this Oscar.

Irene Dunne has a thankless character to play in the Western *Cimarron* as a bigot who is required to be a good wife, with little or no complaint, as her husband abandons her repeatedly, and she goes on loving him. She does turn into a strong female character, as she runs the newspaper without him, and eventually becomes a congresswoman, but it just isn't a role I could bring myself to watch again. I barely managed the first time. No nomination should have been given.

See last year's Best Actress for more on Norma Shearer's performance in *A Free Soul*, for which she should not have a nomination due to her hammy delivery of bad dialogue.

Ann Harding is nearly forgotten today, despite her considerable beauty and trademark long blonde hair. She never quite got into a major classic film, although she had a long career on Broadway and in Hollywood. Her turn in *Holiday* as the unhappy rich daughter looking for a place in the sun is overshadowed by the 1938 remake with Katharine Hepburn and Cary Grant. Unfortunately, the only copy of the Harding version is in the Library of Congress.[24]

Marlene Dietrich made her American debut in *Morocco*, directed, as she had been in the German *The Blue Angel*, by Josef von Sternberg. Sternberg crafted her image, making her into a star over the first years of the Thirties. Pairing her with Gary Cooper and Adolphe Menjou put her in the best of company. Dietrich was more beautiful in this film than in *The Blue Angel* (although not the stunner Sternberg made her in next year's *Shanghai Express*). The character makes more sense as well: a world-weary entertainer, coming to the end of her line. As in *The Blue Angel*, Dietrich plays a nightclub entertainer. She immediately begins challenging the sexual boundaries by dressing as a man for her opening night. She also kisses a woman on the lips in the audience, driving the men crazy...and then tossing the flower she took from the woman to Gary Cooper. I have to admit, I'm not quite certain this is singing. Dietrich has a very odd voice. She sounds flat to my ear at times. But then, I may have just seen Madeline Kahn's brilliant parody of Dietrich, Lili von Shtupp, one too many times in *Blazing Saddles* to ever take the original seriously. Dietrich comes out in a bathing suit and feather boa for her next number, offering apples like Eve to Adam. Volumes have been written about the sexual twisting of Dietrich's life and roles. In the end, Dietrich's role in *Morocco* offers her more to do than she has in next year's *Shanghai Express*, where she's pretty much part of the scenery; here, her capacity to portray wounds and hurts born in the past convinces. She deserved the nomination.

---

[24] Feel free to invite me on a trip to Washington D.C. I'd love to have a chance to see the movie. And hey – if you've never seen the Smithsonian in all its glory, you'll never know why D.C. is actually worth keeping as our capital! We'll need at least a week, and I'd like to bring the wife and kids too – your treat, of course.

Best Sound Recording: How the hell do I know? Let's let Paramount Studio keep this one. At least it's not Douglas Shearer again...

WHAT THEY GOT WRONG:

Quite a lot. Again. This is becoming a broken record. Get used to it.

Best Picture: *Cimarron*
Best Actor: Lionel Barrymore, *A Free Soul*
Best Director: Norman Taurog, *Skippy*
Best Writing (Adaptation): Howard Estabrook, *Cimarron*
Best Writing (Original Story): John Monk Saunders, *The Dawn Patrol*
Best Cinematography: Floyd Crosby, *Tabu*
Best Art Direction: Max Rée, *Cimarron*

Best Picture: *Cimarron* won, over *East Lynne*, *The Front Page*, *Skippy*, and *Trader Horn*.

Cimarron was the only Western to win Best Picture, for over half a century. Too bad it didn't deserve the Oscar. But then, neither did *East Lynne*, *Skippy* or *Trader Horn*. You could drop all four of those movies into the trash can, and very few people would complain, least of all me. *Cimarron* is racist, empty spectacle (bad acting abounds; see below in Writing for more on the film); *East Lynne* is sheer Victorian melodrama, and what is worse, BAD Victorian melodrama; *Skippy* can be remembered primarily for the peanut butter named after it (basically, *Skippy* is a Little Rascals episode on steroids, and nowhere near as amusing as Spanky and Alfalfa); *Trader Horn* is only remembered for its live footage of Africa (which MGM would endlessly reuse in their Tarzan films); the film indulges the fascination Hollywood occasionally had for white hunter films, with all the racist implications. We even get a white goddess, ala H. Rider Haggard's *She* (and played with B-picture camp by Edwina Booth, who picked up malaria and ruined her career). In what may be the most ridiculous thing in the entire movie, the romantic lead carries around a guitar... for most of the picture. No case. No strap (until late in the film). He's climbing a mountainside, and the guitar is in one hand. He's hacking through jungle, and the guitar is in one hand. Dumb. Thankfully, we seem to be past the moment in our cultural evolution in which watching two rhinos being shot and killed is seen as entertainment. And if Harry Carey says "lad" one more time, I am going to slap him. Most racist moment? "Don't you understand? White people must help each other." No nominations for any of them in this category.

The sole remaining official nomination for Best Picture was for *The Front Page*, based on a play by Ben Hecht and Charles MacArthur, which would later reach its greatest version in *His Girl Friday* (a minority prefers the Billy Wilder take). Black humor emerges, right from the opening shot of a flour bag being used to test a gallows: "Sunshine Flour Ensures Domestic Happiness," we read on the bag, right before it drops. Adolphe Menjou and Pat O'Brien turn in credible performances, and the direction by Lewis Milestone is effective in trying to make it more than a filmed version of the play. The sound and camerawork aren't perfect, but both are trying to move past the restrictions of early sound films. Hecht and MacArthur get in some wonderful little comic digs, here and there – at one point, they mention the hanging of George "Kid" Cukor (Cukor had just started his career as a first-rate director). We even get a joke about using an official press release as toilet paper, and – I kid you not – the first flipping of the bird in American cinema. Definitely pre-Code Hollywood, and lots of fun – a good nomination.

Now try these on for size: *The Public Enemy. Little Caesar. The Blue Angel. Animal Crackers. Dracula.* And in the name of all that is holy and wonderful, *City Lights*. How could they have left those out?! Yes, I know most of *Dracula* is plain awful, a stage play being filmed. But it retains its power, in all its wooden glory. *The Blue Angel* has that accursed Nazi, Emil Jannings, and a Marlene Dietrich who is a bit chunky and sings like the illegitimate love child of Minnie Mouse and Goofy. The whole film is, underneath it all, an act of revenge by Josef von Sternberg on the teacher from his childhood who terrorized him. *The Public Enemy* has the poster child shot of domestic violence (grapefruit, anyone?). *Little Caesar*? Yes, this is the death of Rico. *Animal Crackers* is, like most of the Marx Brothers movies, marred by the plot and secondary characters (but still funny, funny, funny – use that fast forward button!). But the hands down, no questions need be asked, how-could-they-have-been-that-monumentally-stupid-move-of-all-time award goes to the Academy for not only not giving *City Lights* the Best Picture Award, but not even NOMINATING it?!?

City Lights is Chaplin's finest moment, and the most emotionally satisfying, hysterically funny film he ever made. I have watched it dozens of times, and still find myself tearing up at the end out of genuine sorrow and joy. *City Lights* is a masterpiece, and should have won the Oscar for Best Picture.

P.S. I would consider Luis Buñuel's surrealist film *L'Âge d'Or*, but it wasn't shown in the United States until 1933, and then only very briefly in New York. It would be 1979 before it saw release here. You should see it; there's really nothing like it – but *City Lights* is still far better.

P.P.S. While it's not a movie I would nominate for Best Picture, I might suggest John Ford's *Up the River*, a prison caper flick that is the only movie to star both Spencer Tracy and Humphrey Bogart. Tracy plays a very charismatic con, while Bogart, believe it or not, plays a rich kid who made a mistake. Fun stuff, until it is marred by a blackface routine. The existing print jumps and skips, but functions.

P.P.P.S. And while you're at it, Alfred Hitchcock's *Murder!*, while not one of his best films, is still quite enjoyable, with a highly mobile camera and halfway decent sound. Many of his plot obsessions show up here in early forms. Herbert Marshall stars, playing a bit riper than he should. The camera work is more interesting than the story, a whodunit, which Hitchcock didn't care for much.

Best Actor: Lionel Barrymore won for *A Free Soul*, over Richard Dix, *Cimarron*; Adolphe Menjou, *The Front Page*; Fredric March, *The Royal Family of Broadway*; and Jackie Cooper, *Skippy*

How could they not have nominated Chaplin?!? The final scene of *City Lights* is the single greatest acting moment in the history of cinema up to that point, and still remains in my top ten of all time.

Instead, they gave the award to Lionel Barrymore for *A Free Soul*, a story of a daughter torn between her drunken lawyer father (Barrymore) and a gangster lover (Clark Gable). Sorry, Lionel. Sheer ham – head shaking and hair hanging do not a Best Actor Oscar make. *A Free Soul* is occasionally interesting, but only when Gable is on the screen. I usually enjoy watching Lionel Barrymore, but this isn't one of those times. He still hasn't learned how to rein the performance back in for talkies. He will...mostly. Barrymore deserved neither Oscar nor nomination (his brother John was having considerably more fun playing Svengali this year).

Adolphe Menjou's turn as Walter Johnson in *The Front Page* is as wicked as you could ask for, and well worth a nomination.

And as for the rest – Jackie Cooper in *Skippy*, Richard Dix in *Cimarron*, and Fredric March in *The Royal Family of Broadway* – they not only shouldn't get the award or a nomination, but they should have been replaced by James Cagney in *The Public Enemy*, Dwight Frye and

Bela Lugosi in *Dracula,* and Edward G. Robinson in *Little Caesar.* Fredric March is the best thing in *The Royal Family,* but that isn't saying much in this rip-off of the Barrymores' celebrity (it has its moments of fun, mostly when the actors go off the deep end). The film March should have gotten a nomination for is *Laughter,* a story of a gold digger who realizes her mistake and chooses the funny, artistic March instead (see below in Writing). Even though his Barrymore pastiche has its moments, *Laughter* shows March's comedic talents off to much better effect in one of the best performances of his all too often staid career, and helped build his stardom.

James Cagney became a star because of the gangster classic *The Public Enemy*. Martin Scorsese has called this role the "birth of modern acting."[xix] Were it not for *City Lights* and that final shattering scene, I would agree. Cagney plays an amoral monster, capable of anything, and he doesn't just act this role – he lives it as a charming monster, like Humbert Humbert and Hannibal Lecter. As with Karloff in *Frankenstein* (another monster), complete immersion and absolute authenticity become the bywords. They are not actors anymore; they are icons. Both *Frankenstein* and *The Public Enemy* are marred by weak supporting actors who haven't learned how to act for sound pictures – the spouse and best friend in *Frankenstein*, the brothers in *The Public Enemy*. But Karloff and Cagney – now there's an alliterative pairing worth inventing a time machine for! – only emerge as greater actors for the contrast. Tom Powers made Cagney's career, and for damn good reason.

That other gangster classic *Little Caesar* did the same thing for Edward G. Robinson. Warner Brothers, unlike much of Hollywood in this period, championed the common man, the outsider, the immigrant, which is why the gritty realism and ironic humor of the Warner Brothers movies tend to play better today than the glossy artificiality and upper class obsessions of MGM and other studios. Both Tom Powers in *The Public Enemy* and Rico in *Little Caesar* pay for their crimes – and this in pre-Code Hollywood – but their risings remain fascinating, because the basic American values of individualism, hard work, risk-taking, and rule-breaking are displayed with such force and cunning. Americans are somewhat schizophrenic when it comes to the rule of law; we definitely are a nation of people who follow the rules (we have less graft and corruption than most, if not all, of the world), but we also love our outlaws. After all, the quintessential play of that most American game baseball is the steal. But we also expect the umpire to enforce the rules fairly and impartially. Edward G. Robinson brings panache, power and fervor to the role – but even when he's dressed to the nines, nobody would call Rico elegant. He's a thug, through and through. Cecil

B. DeMille had noticed a curious thing: he could show sex and sin, as long as it was couched in Biblical terms, and the sinners were punished. That paradox is paralleled in the gangster flick, wherein violence and lawbreaking can be reveled in by the audience, so long as the villain gets his due at the end. Tragedy, according to Aristotle, should evoke pity and terror in the audience, who then have their unhealthy emotions purged through the catharsis of the fall of the hero. Gangster films survive to this day on this orgy of violence, followed by a purging. The bad guys have to pay, so we can get on with our lives. Michael Corleone in *The Godfather II* may be alive and in charge at the end, but his humanity is gone, and that is the price he paid, and worse than being shot up like Rico. Edward G. Robinson was the first great gangster star, followed shortly by Cagney; both of them would return to the genre throughout their careers. I think Cagney's performance has aged better, because it is a more nuanced one, but Robinson definitely deserved a nomination.

Like *The Public Enemy* and *Little Caesar*, *Dracula* had to be carried by the power of its star. *Dracula* is cursed with stagy direction by Tod Browning, overly restrained camera work (Karl Freund, in other places masterful), and a wooden supporting cast. But Bela Lugosi's performance was enough to carry the film; when you add in the maniacal performance by Dwight Frye, you've got movie magic. Edward van Sloan as Dr. Van Helsing is also considerable, although pretty much the same again in *Frankenstein*. We forget today what a romantic, dangerous performance Bela Lugosi gave, and the degree to which his vision of the vampire has remained the one all the future vampires would be challenging – and failing. Along with his rich, textured voice and deep hungering eyes, Lugosi crafted his performance with the most expressive hands in film history. Watch the film again, and see if you don't agree: like Karloff as the Frankenstein monster, Lugosi would be forever typecast because of the immense power of his performance as Count Dracula. Finally, Dwight Frye should also have been nominated; he goes from showing us a reasonable, well-mannered real estate agent to give the best performance as a lunatic of all time. The image of him looking up the stairs is priceless – and just as other stars have been parodied, so too has Frye's Renfield remained a star turn. Both Lugosi and Frye should have been nominated.

But Chaplin should have received the Academy Award for Best Actor.

Best Director: Norman Taurog won for *Skippy*, over Wesley Ruggles, *Cimarron*; Clarence Brown, *A Free Soul*; Lewis Milestone, *The Front Page*; and Josef von Sternberg, *Morocco*

Chaplin, *City Lights*, 'nuff said. None of the rest who were actually nominated and won even come close. Good night, Brown, Milestone, Ruggles, Taurog, and even Josef Von Sternberg (who could just as easily been nominated for *The Blue Angel*). Milestone and von Sternberg do some interesting things in their films, but they offer no contest with Chaplin and *City Lights*. Besides, Norman Taurog, who won, was a real bastard: to make his nephew Jackie Cooper cry for one scene, he threatened to shoot the boy's dog if he didn't weep. Taurog should be covered in Skippy peanut butter and tossed in the local dog pound.

Just to be fair, William Wellman should have been nominated for directing *The Public Enemy*. In the words of Martin Scorsese, the direction of this very violent film is "elegant."[xx] So many grace notes abound: the shots out of the dark; the policeman's hand outstretched into the light[Cagney's face and hands and motion; and the baby carriage full of booze. *The Public Enemy* continues to grab audiences by the throat and shake them, despite the awkwardness of almost the entire cast outside of Cagney. He's real; they are patently cardboard (Joan Blondell and Jean Harlow being notable exceptions). In many ways, this is Wellman's best film, and as influential as *Wings* proved to be. But since *City Lights* is Chaplin's best film, welcome to one of those years in which excellence gets beaten out by genius.

Best Writing (Adaptation): Howard Estabrook won for *Cimarron*, over Seton Miller and Fred Niblo, Jr., *The Criminal Code*; Horace Jackson, *Holiday*; Francis Faragoh and Robert N. Lee, *Little Caesar*; and Joseph L. Mankiewicz and Sam Mintz, *Skippy*

Cimarron was based on a novel by Edna Ferber (she also wrote *Show Boat* and *Giant*). They don't write 'em like this any more. Pick your reasons: boredom, maturity, tolerance. For the love of all the writing gods, who would name their main male character Yancey Cravat?!? And his son is named Cimarron Cravat. There's also a guy named Grat Gotch, which I nominate as the worst name in film history. Ridiculous. I picked up a copy of *Cimarron* from my school library to read, and nobody had checked it out since 1965...who knew my students had such good taste? The script does a reasonable job translating this to the big screen, but that's not saying much. The tale of the Oklahoma land rush is just begging for cinematic expression, because chases and greed often make tempting stories.²⁵ But let's be real here: the land that was being chased down was stolen from the Indians who had been promised it, and paid for it in the blood of the Trail of Tears. The film also has one of the worst racist depictions of blacks in the boy servant Isaiah, who gets excited over a wagonload of watermelons, and acts like slavery still exists, and was a good thing. To be fair, Yancey does defend the rights of Indians in his newspaper editorials, and he understands and uses Indian culture, and he may be part Indian. What is left unexamined is his wholehearted support of stealing Oklahoma from the Indians, while he condemns whites for stealing from the Indians. I'm not kidding. The script is that conflicted and confused. He says how awful it is the government only paid a $1.40 an acre to the Cherokee, then he can't keep himself from going out to grab some more land. He does end up preventing government graft at their expense. The same kind of contradiction – between stereotypes the film is promoting and countervailing evidence – comes when Isaiah bravely goes to rescue Yancey's son in the middle of a gunfight. The film wants to be enlightened, while remaining prejudiced. What also sticks out is Yancey's defense of the Jewish notion salesman Sol Levy (who ends up spread eagled like Jesus on the cross at one point…and they draw it out long enough for it to be obvious).²⁶ *Cimarron* may have once appealed to whites proud of their grandpappies, but we have no reason to continue passing this film on as the best picture of its year. It isn't – but it shouldn't have been then either. Over-acting and stereotypes can't be fixed by one exciting land rush and some gunfighting. One last complaint: Yancey takes off for five years, never sends a single postcard or letter, shows back up out of the blue after abandoning his wife and kids to fend for themselves…and the wife takes him back, with only a bare whisper of a complaint, until

---

²⁵ Ron Howard did his take on it in the dull *Far and Away*.
²⁶ And yes, I understand the arguments about the historicity of cultural artifacts; we aren't supposed to judge the beliefs of yesterday by the standards of today. I'm never going to accept any bowdlerization, nor would I suggest not watching these films or reading problematic books. I use *Birth of a Nation* to teach students the ways in which racism was rampant in early twentieth century America, as well as how to recognize propaganda. But such films need to be put in context; if I just show them Griffith's seminal work without preparation and commentary, doesn't that suggest I agree with what's being said? At some point, don't we have to consider that these beliefs are in fact flaws, and may lessen the artistic worth of a piece? Don't we believe that the greatest art must find new audiences with each generation? I'm not in favor of being politically correct just to be politically correct. A substantial gap exists between setting out to demonstrate black inferiority, and using terms that were common to the period. *Huckleberry Finn* shows racism and slavery to be wrong. The language and ideas Twain uses aren't acceptable today, but their use reflects the reality of the day. But having a black boy beg a white man as his "massah" and seeing watermelons as a reason to run away from his mother, as happens in *Cimarron*, is far closer to *Birth of a Nation* than *Huckleberry Finn*.

he chooses to defend a whore in court. Even after that, she is happy with him...until he proposes making the Indians citizens. You can pick your jaw up off the floor now. No award, and no nomination, were merited.

We've got two gangster pictures which got nominations, *The Criminal Code* and *Little Caesar*. *The Criminal Code* plays on the prison grounds established by the previous year's hit *The Big House*. Setting up a conflict between the code of silence, and the right thing, *The Criminal Code* is well-written, and well-acted. Walter Huston and Boris Karloff give excellent performances. *Little Caesar* is taken from the novel of the same name by W.R. Burnett, based on the life of Al Capone, but it plays with the same kind of good guy/bad guy friendships that so many gangster films did. Douglas Fairbanks, Jr. does the best he can with a gangster who would rather be a dancer, but the role is a dopey one to begin with, even if it does let Edward G. Robinson reply to Fairbanks' desire to dance with cracks about making other people dance (the Fairbanks character is based on George Raft, who later moved from dancing to acting).[xxi] The dialogue is often snappy, and it sounds clichéd today because this film started the clichés. Like Cagney, Robinson's voice and delivery were often parodied, but the lines from *Little Caesar* are more interesting in and of themselves, and both movies deserve the nominations they received in this writing category.

Holiday is an adaptation, and a very good one by most accounts, of the Philip Barry play (better known in the remake with Katharine Hepburn and Cary Grant). As I've said above in Best Actress, the film is not available.

Skippy is a flaccid little morality tale. We get a dog, and following the unwritten rule of all dog stories, the dog must die. Why anybody thought this deserved Oscars is beyond me.

Other movies need more attention than they were given.

I wish somebody would explain how *The Front Page* didn't get nominated in all this, for more than Best Picture. My guess is that Howard Hughes, who produced this, didn't have much respect around Hollywood, nor did he control the studio votes needed to push a nomination through for anybody who wasn't liked. They'd already given him enough in the one nod. Ben Hecht and Charles MacArthur wrote the original play, which was adapted by Bartlett Cormack and Charles Lederer, who did such a good job they should have been nominated.

One bizarre experience I would like to recommend to those of you who have seen the Humphrey Bogart *The Maltese Falcon* as many times as I have (not likely, but let's say you've seen it at least twice so you don't feel so bad). The original adaptation, starring Ricardo Cortez (real name, Jacob Krantz), feels like major déjà vu. The novel is faithfully presented (more or less), and the direction is competent from Roy del Ruth. The actors aren't as memorable as Bogart, Peter Lorre, and Sydney Greenstreet, but Cortez fills the role with the sex appeal Sam Spade carries in the novel better than Bogart does, and Dwight Frye is just as threatening as the hood Wilmer. Greenstreet and Lorre outshine this version's Cairo and Gutman. Mary Astor isn't particularly attractive (she's always been the weakest link in the Bogart), but while Bebe Daniels is sexier, she isn't as convincing an actress. One nice touch: Sam Spade has a picture of Lulu (Louise Brooks) on his wall, as if she's an old flame. Maude Fulton and Brown Holmes wrote the screenplay, with uncredited assistance from Lucien Hubbard. The Cortez *Maltese Falcon* isn't going to replace the Bogart version, but the writers did such a good job they deserve a nomination (even with their tacked on fake ending). And finally, as an adaptation, the 1936 version with Warren Williams and Bette Davis is wretched, but as a goofy detective flick, *Satan Met a Lady* is worth watching...once.

Again, we come to the Marx Brothers, this time with *Animal Crackers*. Morrie Ryskind adapted his play, co-written with George S. Kaufman, Bert Kalmar, and Harry Ruby. Big dumb boring plot, interrupted by manic genius and the best one-liners and routines of the year: "How much would you charge to run into an open manhole?... Just the cover charge."; "He thinks I look alike."; "One morning I shot an elephant in my pajamas. How he got in my pajamas, I don't know." Harpo, Chico, and the flash. Groucho and the introductions. Best of all, Groucho and Chico discussing the cost of the orchestra. Brilliant, brilliant, brilliant! Can you say Oscar? I knew that you could! Now, can you say Hungadunga and spell semicolon? Ryskind could, which should have won him the Oscar for Best Writing (Adaptation).

Best Writing (Original Story): John Monk Saunders won for *The Dawn Patrol*, over Rowland Brown, *Doorway to Hell*; Harry D'Abbadie D'Arrast, Douglas Doty and Donald Ogden Stewart, *Laughter*; John Bright and Kubec Glasmon, *The Public Enemy*; and Lucien Hubbard & Joseph Jackson, *Smart Money*

The Dawn Patrol is better known for the Errol Flynn version from 1938, but this Howard Hawks version stars Richard Barthelmess and Douglas Fairbanks, Jr. Neil Hamilton[27] has the Basil Rathbone role as the commander; a horrible actor, the film improves when he's not

---

[27] Hamilton later played TV's Commissioner Gordon from the Adam West *Batman*. More than thirty years later, his acting style hadn't changed much; camp it was, and camp it stayed, by being so deadly serious.

there. Someone should have thought about not mixing American and British accents in a British unit, as they jar. Bad acting dooms parts of this tense screenplay; in 1938, things became remarkably better as the acting improved, but they also cleaned up the dialogue and presentation. John Monk Saunders gets credit for a tough take on the war, but many stiff lines remain. The nomination was a good idea, but not the award. He got to be married to Fay Wray, so he shouldn't feel too bad.

Doorway to Hell stars Lew Ayres, but the reasons to watch this film are two: Dwight Frye, and James Cagney, in his second movie. While Lew Ayres is badly miscast as a gang lord who wants to get out of crime, the story isn't bad. It's just not Oscar quality, and Rowland Brown shouldn't have received a nomination.

Laughter stars Nancy Carroll and Fredric March, and was written by Donald Ogden Stewart, who would go on to shine in *The Prisoner of Zenda* and *The Philadelphia Story*. *Laughter* only really works when Fredric March is on screen; quite literally, he's the spark that makes this engine run. Before he shows up, a suicidal ex-lover of the former showgirl turned millionaire's wife has the best line: "I can call you from hell and reverse the charges." March plays another former paramour, a musician who gleefully ignores social niceties. Frank Morgan, later the Wizard of Oz, portrays the millionaire husband. The film literally doesn't play well, with a soundtrack that needs serious help, as does the entire cast before March comes in. Just watch how bad Nancy Carroll is when March isn't on screen, and how she sparkles when he is, to see how good March is. The subplot about the suicide drags and doesn't mesh well with the rest of the film. *Laughter* is thus one part melodramatic mess, and one part proto-screwball comedy. Stewart would learn much better in the future. No nomination.

If you have to pick one of these nominated films by longevity and influence alone, *The Public Enemy* would far and away be the most likely choice. The script takes an unusual view of crime, placing the tale of the older good brother and two younger bad boys in the historical context of childhood and the attractions of the criminal life in a boy's love of mischief. The movie starts in 1909, then moves forward by leaps and bounds, ending up in Prohibition. Everything escalates to the final brutal ending, which remains as shocking today as it was then. John Bright and Kubec Glasmon wrote the screenplay. Bright helped to found the Screen Writers Guild; *The Public Enemy* was the height of his career. Glasmon never did better than this film either.

Lucien Hubbard and Joseph Jackson wrote *Smart Money*, the only film to have both James Cagney and Edward G. Robinson together. Cagney's star turn in *The Public Enemy* hadn't happened yet, so Cagney gets a decidedly second-banana role. Boris Karloff shows up very briefly as a pimp (that's the implication of the role). The story tries to recreate *Little Caesar* while making Robinson's barber-turned-gambler more sympathetic. It works, but it's definitely not up to the level of *The Public Enemy*, much less *Little Caesar*.

If you haven't figured it out already, the Oscar for Best Writing (Original Story) should have gone to Charlie Chaplin for writing *City Lights*. As Andrew Sarris said, *City Lights* is "precariously balanced between the domains of comedy and tragedy. Charlie is his own Don Quixote and his own Sancho Panza, a knight and a knave, a fool both damned and divine."[xxii] Perfection demands respect – and Oscar gold.

Best Cinematography: Floyd Crosby won for *Tabu*, over Edward Cronjager, *Cimarron*; Lee Garmes, *Morocco*; Charles Lang, *The Right to Love*; and Barney "Chick" McGill, *Svengali*

Tabu won the Oscar, but we return again to the question of photographing nature, or manipulating light and shadow into art. One rarely operates at either end of that spectrum, but generally, leaning towards art produces more interesting results. *Tabu* is by F.W. Murnau, the director of *Nosferatu* and *Sunrise*. Filmed in Tahiti and Bora Bora using a native cast and crew, the film juxtaposes the paradise before Europeans arrived with colonialism. I suspect the film was financed to be able to show nudity. Murnau's final outing *Tabu* revels in its simplicity and understanding of Polynesian culture. But I am not convinced that its cinematography is anything other than serviceable. The camera is just an eye here; there is no sleight of hand, no magic in its imagery. Murnau made the film with Robert Flaherty, most famous for the Eskimo documentary, *Nanook of the North*. Flaherty co-wrote the film, but he was expecting to co-direct. Floyd Crosby was the cameraman (his son is David Crosby, the musician). The rest of the crew were natives. The film likely won on the basis of Murnau's reputation, and the location shooting. The occasional naked breast probably didn't hurt any, but the Oscar statue already has enough gratuitous nudity, don't you think?

Cimarron does take in big views, but since when do big views alone make for fine cinematography? (I do think there are times David Lean substitutes pretty pictures for substance, especially after *Lawrence of Arabia*). You have never seen falser riding scenes in close up. The horses aren't even moving (not that this is the cinematographer's fault, but I need somewhere to complain about it). The movie just looks pedestrian most of the time, and should not have received a nomination.

The Right to Love now exists only in one reel, in UCLA's archive, and is not available for viewing.

Svengali stars John Barrymore (in my vote for worst makeup of the decade). *Svengali* has one really surprising shot – the camera begins in a close-up of Barrymore's face, as he exerts his hypnotic power, then the camera tracks back, moving – somehow – out of a window and into the rooftops, in an effective bit of trickery. The camerawork on Svengali's eyes reminds one of what they did with Lugosi's eyes in *Dracula*. A good nomination.

Of all these films, the one with the most enduring and influential cinematography remains that of von Sternberg looking at Marlene Dietrich, through the eyes of Lee Garmes. *Morocco* has an astonishing visual grace. The film looks like they studied Rembrandt, mixing light and shadow, both in its backgrounds, and in Dietrich's face. Lee Garmes was rightly nominated for this movie, which also co-starred Gary Cooper. The Academy would make up for their failure to award Garmes this by giving him the Oscar for making a very similar film later in *Shanghai Express* (Dietrich, von Sternberg, foreign locales, danger and dangerous love). Garmes had a career that proves him more than a stand-in for von Sternberg, including *Scarface* and *Gone with the Wind*. In this same year of eligibility, he shot *City Streets*, starring Gary Cooper, for director Rouben Mamoulian; the scenes where they interrogate Sylvia Sidney are beautifully atmospheric, and would have fit right into a von Sternberg film. *Morocco* looks real, but real in the way in which a dream should look real. Garmes (and standing behind him, von Sternberg) should have received the Oscar (see next year's cinematography for more).

Best Art Direction: Max Rée won for *Cimarron*, over Stephen Goosson and Ralph Hammeras, *Just Imagine*; Hans Dreier, *Morocco*; Anton Grot, *Svengali*; and Richard Day, *Whoopee!*

Can anybody explain the irony of an Oscar for a western winning for a category originally called interior decoration?! If one talks simply about the look of the film, perhaps. *Cimarron* is spectacular in its scale, and the film does move at times. The nomination should stay, but not the award.

Just Imagine is a truly bizarre film, part science fiction, part musical, part romance, part just plain weird (finally released on DVD in 2009). Starring El Brendel and Maureen O'Sullivan, *Just Imagine* occupies a world all its own, drawing on *Metropolis* and its own crazed sense of the ridiculous. Movies like this made science fiction look bad (there wouldn't be another major American studio science fiction film until the Fifties). If this had been released in the Sixties, with the right hallucinogenic, it might have become quite a cult hit. As it is, you just watch with your mouth open at the glorious goofiness. Welcome to the wondrous world of...1980! Names have been replaced by numbers, and the government selects your mate...and everybody flies their own hovering plane through the sky...and bursts into song (the songs invariably destroy the charm of the film). The lab looks like *Metropolis* had an affair with an Art Deco lounge. One surprising slap-in-the-face joke: all the future plane manufacturers are Jewish; El Brendel suggests someone finally got even with Henry Ford, who was a notorious anti-Semite; even today, some Jewish-Americans refuse to buy Fords. The rocket ship and some of the props were reused in the Buster Crabbe *Flash Gordon* and *Buck Rogers* serials. The nomination should stay.

Morocco has all the look of a lived-in world, a Morocco that probably makes tourists disappointed in the real thing for its beauty and grime (light and shadow again, in the cinematography and the sets). A well-deserved nomination for Hans Dreier, who had a first-rate career as the head of Paramount's design department for decades, with scads of nominations and three Oscars, including one for *Sunset Blvd*.

Svengali has sets that begin in a claustrophobic tone, and an inn nobody could possibly run affordably. Anton Grot had a wonderful career for the next 20 years, including *Little Caesar, Footlight Parade, Captain Blood, A Midsummer Night's Dream,* and many more. The nomination should remain.

Whoopee! is an Eddie Cantor vehicle, remaking the Florenz Ziegfeld stage hit. Samuel Goldwyn produced this in two-strip Technicolor, making Eddie Cantor a movie star. Were there an Oscar category for Best Song this year, "Makin' Whoopee" would likely be the winner. Although Cantor made the song a hit – and vice versa – the rolling eyes must have worked better on stage than on camera; Cantor wears out his welcome quickly. Gus Kahn was one of the great lyricists, and "Makin' Whoopee" one of the high points of his career. The movie betrays the common racism of the period (*Whoopee!* is of a piece with *The Jazz Singer* in some ways; the blackface performance is even more offensive than Jolson's). But the issue is the interior decorations, which are functional, but not all that interesting. My only guess is that it was Busby Berkeley staging the dances that attracted them. No nomination.

All of these movies pale next to an epic tale of invention and discovery. *Die Frau im Monde* (*Woman in the Moon*), directed by Fritz Lang from a novel by his wife Thea von Harbou, was the first serious attempt to show a flight to the moon. A very inventive sequence shows the power of images to recount plot early on; it's a kind of visual memory we rarely have in sound film. Surrounded by some twaddle about gold on the moon and spies trying to get the plans, the movie really comes alive when the rocket appears. From that moment on, the film has all the drama it needs in the glory of exploration and spaceflight. Lang gets so much right, because Hermann Oberth was the scientific adviser – Oberth was one of the leading rocketry experts in the world. Coming to this film after the Apollo moon landings undercuts the excitement a bit, but I was astounded at how much they got right, not the least of which is the hysteria and public fascination that would accompany the early Apollos, as well as the discovery that the point of space travel is to know the Earth better. Much is seriously wrong too, like breathable air on the moon, but the intense plausibility of the enterprise made this movie special, and the sets and model work made it possible. Easy decision then: the Oscar for Art Direction should have gone to *Die Frau im Monde*.

CHAPTER FIVE: 1932 AWARDS
5th Show

Movies released between August 1, 1931 and July 31st 1932

THE SCENE OF THE CRIME:

On November 16, 1932, Hollywood gathered at the Fiesta Room of the Ambassador Hotel. An original piece of music composed for the banquet was played, and the show was broadcast on national radio for the first time. Conrad Nagel hosted. Conrad who, right? Nagel was a founding member of the Academy, and a silent film star who survived into early talkies on the strength of his voice. Believe it or not, they were tabulating the votes at the actual ceremony. Seriously. The Academy also didn't announce the winners; they flashed their images on the wall. Apparently, somebody wanted silent pictures again...

The Academy announced there was to be no "speechifying." Nagel then launched into a long speech. The gathering observed a moment of silence for three recently dead dignitaries: F.W. Murnau (killed in a car accident), Thomas Edison (honored two years in a row), and George

Eastman. Walt Disney was granted a Special Award for creating Mickey Mouse. Disney reciprocated by providing a color cartoon caricaturing the acting nominees, *Mickey's Parade of Nominees*. Chaplin was supposed to be there to hand the award to Disney. After the massive snub he received the previous year for *City Lights*, no wonder he refused to come.

The Academy let the number of nominations in each category float even more than before: eight for Best Picture; four for Writing (original story); two for Cinematography, three for the rest. Only Paramount was nominated for Sound Recording – they won. The Academy added three new Short Subject awards, and they let the experts pick those – Walt Disney, Laurel and Hardy, Mack Sennett, and a few others. The insiders then proceeded to nominate themselves, which normally would enrage me, but this time, for damn good reason, it doesn't (see below).

Fredric March won the Best Actor Oscar for *Dr. Jekyll and Mr. Hyde*. While the awards continued, someone counting the votes noticed Beery was only one vote behind March, which under the rules at the time, constituted a tie, and Beery was brought up at the last minute for his performance in *The Champ*. Later on that evening, March got off one of the great Oscar quips. He and Beery had recently adopted children: "It seems a little off that Wally and I were given awards for best male performance of the year."

WHAT THEY GOT RIGHT:

Best Short Subject (Comedy): I don't care if Laurel and Hardy helped choose themselves for their Oscar. *The Music Box* is the funniest half hour in the history of...well, history. I've seen it over one hundred times. It never fails to cause my sides to hurt. The boys received a huge round of applause. For once, the Academy was prescient and correct in all respects.

Best Short Subject (Cartoon): I also don't care that Walt Disney helped select his own *Flowers and Trees*, since it was the first cartoon to use Technicolor. Disney was constantly innovating, and we should reward one of the few people in Hollywood history who hated doing the same thing twice. Disney holds the record for the most Oscars and the most Oscar nominations for one reason, and one reason only: quality. The Silly Symphonies were his way to experiment with new animation methods, while Mickey Mouse paid the bills. After *Flowers and Trees*, the Silly Symphonies' use of color out-earned even Mickey for a time.

Nothing else came close to matching it this year (except his other color Silly Symphonies). Bravo, Walt!

Best Short Subject (Novelty): Mack Sennett should keep his Oscar for Novelty Short Subject for *Wrestling Swordfish*. The old man deserved it, if for nothing else than discovering Chaplin.

Best Cinematography: Lee Garmes won for *Shanghai Express*, over Ray June, *Arrowsmith*, and Karl Struss, *Dr. Jekyll and Mr. Hyde*

The Academy got this one right for every single nomination in the category, even if they did leave some worthy cinematographers out.

Lee Garmes won for *Shanghai Express*, and one can see why. Finally, Dietrich looks beautiful, at times stunningly so, as Shanghai Lil, the woman with a shady past on this train running through Chinese intrigue. Excellent work for Garmes, and well deserving of the award. As I've noted above, it's hard to distinguish Garmes' contributions from those of von Sternberg, but Garmes is officially credited with this stylish intensity and beauty. Dietrich claimed in her autobiography it was mostly von Sternberg (see below in Best Director for more). *Shanghai Express* is a gorgeous film; like *Morocco*, it brings a foreign world to life, in detail, in the very breath of a fantasy made real. If you watch Dietrich from *The Blue Angel* through Garmes' work on *Morocco* and *Shanghai Express*, you can see her steadily growing more attractive as von Sternberg and Garmes craft an increasingly richer understanding of their canvas. An excellent award by the Academy.

June's cinematography in *Arrowsmith* is serviceable, but never really comes alive until we get to the jungle at the end. The nomination was well-deserved for this alone.

Karl Struss' work on *Dr. Jekyll and Mr. Hyde,* with its revolutionary transformations, was duly recognized. Working with Perc Westmore on makeup, Struss used a series of colored filters of his own invention to reveal or conceal makeup in successive layers, thus letting Fredric March transform from Jekyll to Hyde in front of our eyes, in the camera and with camera shifts to his hands then back to accommodate more changes, all to astonishing effect. Some transformations were more conventional, with the camera stopping and March holding still while they added makeup, then rolled the camera again. The filter secret remained hidden for decades until director Rouben Mamoulian revealed it. But even before the transformations, Struss and Mamoulian were playing camera games, starting with an organ being played from the point of view of Jekyll, the shadow of whose head can be seen on the organ, but not the shadow of the camera. The camera then continues to act as Jekyll's eyes, dollying out into the hallway, until it pans into a mirror, where all of a sudden Jekyll is there, and we don't see the camera's reflection. We are ourselves Jekyll and Hyde throughout the film, as a result of these camera innovations, and must examine our own inner selves, as he does. When Dr. Jekyll first encounters the prostitute Ivy, and she tempts him, the image of her gartered leg swings over the image of Jekyll asserting his innocence. Struss' cinematography is just as impressive throughout. Struss was the cameraman on *Sunrise*, and was well known for his innovative work. Were it any other year than that of *Shanghai Express*, I would argue the Oscar should have gone to him.

Two other films should have been nominated for cinematography.

Carl Theodor Dreyer, the director of *The Passion of Joan of Arc*, next made *Vampyr*. Both were financial disasters and artistic triumphs, although *Vampyr* would take decades to be recognized fully. Cinematographer Rudolph Maté worked closely with Dreyer to create the film's unique look, a kind of dream world filled with fogs and shadows and haze. They discovered that a light reflected into the lens would produce this effect. Maté went on to a career in Hollywood, including *To Be or Not to Be, Foreign Correspondent, Gilda,* and *The Pride of the Yankees*. *Vampyr* remains an ambiguous, unsettling film which thrives in a world of its own, not unlike *The Passion of Joan of Arc*.

Finally, James Wong Howe's work on *Transatlantic*, his first sound picture, rescued his career, as he had been thought to have been a relic of the silent era. *Transatlantic* used deep focus extensively, an extremely difficult technique which keeps the foreground and the background all in focus (Gregg Toland made deep focus famous ten years later in *Citizen Kane*). Surprisingly, this film has never been released on DVD or VHS, and is very rarely seen. Howe not only uses deep focus, but he has a very mobile camera few were capable of in 1931 – one shot had to have been done on a crane, as the camera flies through the air and into the set of the port's entry building. Howe restored his reputation with *Transatlantic*, and the film deserves to be better known.

WHAT THEY GOT WRONG:

I don't know what's wrong with these people. I guess they all decided this book needed to be written before I was born. Why else would they keep on making such bad choices?

Best Picture: *Grand Hotel*
Best Actor: Fredric March, *Dr. Jekyll and Mr. Hyde;* Wallace Beery, *The Champ*
Best Actress: Helen Hayes, *The Sin of Madelon Claudet*
Best Director: Frank Borzage, *Bad Girl*
Best Writing (Adaptation): Edwin Burke, *Bad Girl*
Best Writing (Original Story): Frances Marion, *The Champ*
Best Art Direction: Gordon Wiles, *Transatlantic*

Best Picture: *Grand Hotel* won, over *Arrowsmith, Bad Girl, The Champ, Five Star Final, One Hour with You, Shanghai Express,* and *The Smiling Lieutenant*

Ok, people, let's try these movies on for size: *Frankenstein* and *Scarface*. Well, hell, even add *Tarzan the Ape Man* and *Freaks* for two major cult films, and *Platinum Blonde* as the one Capra film everybody ought to know better. What do we get in their place? In no particular order, nothing, next-to-nothing, creaky star-studded pictures, weepies, second-rate John Ford, Dietrich-obsessed von Sternberg, and Chevalier-obsessed Lubitsch (with not one, but two best picture nominees).

Grand Hotel won for Best Picture...somehow. *Grand Hotel* is not very grand, but it is in a hotel. *Grand Hotel* is the only movie to ever win Best Picture and be nominated for nothing else (there's that whiff of corruption again). The first film to have an all-star cast, *Grand Hotel* was MGM's biggest moneymaker of the year, setting the precedent for bloated, big-budget, poorly scripted, all-star extravaganzas. *Grand Hotel* has not aged well. Ensemble casts need to have a single story to bind them all together; all this one has is the idea that it happens in one hotel. Set in Germany, the only actor to have a German accent was Wallace Beery, despite most of the characters being German. Garbo has her Swedish accent of course, which I suppose could pass as German to an uneducated ear. Beery is sorely miscast as the German industrialist Preysing; seeing this big lummox as a businessman (even one about to go under) works just about as poorly as his solitary German gutturals. Nobody seems to have considered how silly he would sound. Beery does play the lecher aspects fairly well. Barrymore is once more shamelessly mugging (you pick which one, Lionel or John...either one works), but Barrymore also has moments of great emotional honesty (you pick one, Lionel or John...either one works). Joan Crawford is clearly having fun, but what an unfortunate name for her character (it rhymes with phlegm...did nobody think about such things back then?). Garbo is tortured, and honestly, somewhat unpleasant to watch.[28] "I vant to be alone" is her famous line, but like many famous lines, misquoted, as it is actually "I just want to be left alone." *Grand Hotel* has moments worth watching, and some interesting choices in how the story is told. The opening, using the telephone bank and shifting from character to character, is a serviceable idea, given how many characters need to be introduced, but movies (like good fiction) should be about showing, not telling, and much of this seems forced. Essentially, the flaws in the film come from the need to continually move to the next character, thus undercutting the narrative momentum over and over again. Granted, the theme of each character's tale is that they have all come to the end of their rope, but that commonality doesn't really support the constant switching. Not the best picture of the year; as one contemporary critic said, "dull to the point of complete enervation."[xxiii] Bloat should not equal Oscar gold. Neither nomination nor Best Picture Oscar should have been given.

Arrowsmith is based on a novel by America's first Nobel Laureate for Literature, Sinclair Lewis (an author largely ignored by academia, but well worth reading). Lewis was awarded the Pulitzer Prize for *Arrowsmith*, but declined it on principle. A cycle of Sinclair Lewis films resulted from this adaptation of the story of a man of science and his dedication to research. John Ford directed for producer Samuel Goldwyn (see below for more on Ford), and it was a critical and commercial success. Watching the movie today, we can see why. *Arrowsmith* is fast-paced, idealistic, and a bit dunderheaded about science, but all in all, a well-meant film worth a nomination.

Bad Girl is yet another romance from Frank Borzage. This one has a naughty tinge to it from the title to the opening scene, wherein a woman who appears to be the bride confesses fear, and the maid says, "After you've done it eight or nine times, you won't give it a thought." Turns out they're not talking about sex...but they got ya! Too bad it goes downhill from that. It's just another warmed-over version of *Seventh Heaven*. Girl meets guy, guy wants a better job, guy has to protect her by offering marriage...it wasn't that good a plot to begin with, and this verges on plain awful. No nomination should have been given.

The Champ is a big, fat male weepie. Wallace Beery plays a big fat male; Jackie Cooper does the weeping. Written by Frances Marion, from the original story by Sidney Howard, *The Champ* is an enjoyable

---

[28] Which may be the point with the diva she is playing, but I am not so sure it isn't Garbo playing a part she didn't really want. The idea that someone that tall and lanky could be a prima ballerina is more than a little ridiculous. As Donald Spoto remarked, "Garbo...very nearly destroyed the picture" (from *Possessed*, p. 93).

movie about a washed up fighter raising his boy, directed by King Vidor. Good thing there's not a dog, since they'd probably shoot it so we'd cry more. The nomination should stay.

Mervyn LeRoy directed Edward G. Robinson in *Five Star Final*, building upon Robinson's star-making turn in the previous year's *Little Caesar*. Boris Karloff has a role as Isopod, a deceitful reporter; the film was released two months after his breakthrough as the monster in *Frankenstein*. Robinson plays a newspaper editor, whose publisher resurrects a forgotten murder case. Social complications result from digging up old dirt. Pre-Code women abound, including a floozy who comes for a job after certain...favors were granted; her breasts are an actual subject of conversation. Karloff gets to be sleazy, sanctimonious, drunk, remarkably pleased with himself, and terrified. Marian Marsh, on the rise after being menaced by John Barrymore in *Svengali*, is fresh as the daughter of the murderess. Frances Starr as the mother is so bad an actress, at times it's almost camp. H.B. Warner has a very difficult scene where he is required to pretend utter happiness while also conveying absolute horror, and carries it off touchingly. The film isn't quite sure what it wants to be: hard hitting expose of the newspaper world, or soap opera weepie? Robinson is still looking for a part as good as Rico in *Little Caesar* and is reduced to obsessive hand washing as his dominant character trait. Second-rate Robinson at best, and the most interesting thing is Karloff. The nomination was still a good idea for the better parts.

The Smiling Lieutenant starts and ends with sex. Well, this is pre-Code Hollywood, and Ernst Lubitsch. It's all off camera, but it does quickly establish Maurice Chevalier's character: the girl leaves his front door with a smile, even though we never see him. He's also a rogue, since a bill collector came to the door right before she did – guess which visitor got what she wanted? Throughout the film, there is a glowing sheen to these people, as if they were somehow animated. Lubitsch produces a beautiful look in his pictures, as always. The songs aren't more than rhyming ditties, however. *The Smiling Lieutenant* is a lusty little piece of strudel. Not very filling, mind you; just dessert, and a frothy one at that. A good nomination, nonetheless.

One Hour with You is yet another Ernst Lubitsch musical with Maurice Chevalier (George Cukor began directing this one, but Lubitsch took over). Sex, sex, and more sex. Except for when there's sex. We meet Chevalier with a beautiful blonde on his lap, and a cop telling him to stop making love in the park: Cop: "You can't make love in public!" Chevalier: "I can make love anywhere." Cop: "No, you can't!" Blonde: "Oh, but officer, he can! He can make love anywhere!" Chevalier, incredibly pleased: "Darling!" This is the Lubitsch touch, and here it is again: the blonde is Jeanette MacDonald, and they are, as Chevalier soon assures us with a look into the camera, actually married. So what we think is naughty and not allowed, is naughty and matrimonial: "I am married, and I like it. I'm sorry to disappoint you." *One Hour with You* begins as a paean to wedded sexual bliss; temptation soon comes in the form of the wife's amoral best friend (well, if temptation didn't come, we wouldn't have much of a movie). As Oscar Wilde said, "I can resist anything...but temptation!" Will Chevalier? The nomination should stay.

And on another note, will Marlene Dietrich? *Shanghai Express* continues Josef von Sternberg's seven film obsession with Dietrich, begun in *The Blue Angel* and *Morocco*. *Shanghai Express* may just be von Sternberg's best film with Dietrich. From the opening shots, the sense of life's complications, a foreign land, and the depth of each and every character are presented with the minimum of brush strokes. Each little daub implies an entire history behind it. For example, when the porter tries to get on board to deal with a customer complaint, Warner Oland's imperious refusal to move and his insistent shove back on the porter is done in under five seconds – but we know this character is much more than what he seems to be, and that he has a purpose in boarding the train. We are shown, not told, over and over again – except for, oddly enough, Marlene Dietrich's Shanghai Lily. We have to have it explained to us that she is a "coaster," a woman who lives by her wits up and down the Chinese coast. Mysteries board this train, and take us with them. Unfortunately, they don't tend to work themselves out in satisfying ways; in the end, *Shanghai Express* and Dietrich are just eye candy. Sexy to look at, but not much more. The nomination should stay – barely.

And now for those movies the Academy was myopic enough to ignore.

Platinum Blonde is a substantial Capra film, and one with much to recommend it: great acting, a compelling story, a purpose. More and more, I return to this early Capra as an indication of the stellar career he would have from *It Happened One Night* onward. See more under Best Actor, Best Actress, and Best Director. Better still, just see *Platinum Blonde*. You won't be disappointed. I sure wasn't – the film should have been nominated for Best Picture.

The same goes, even more so, for *Frankenstein* and *Scarface*. Both of them have Boris Karloff (guess which one has him, of all things, bowling?). Both were major commercial hits (*Frankenstein* was the #1 movie of the year). Both of them have great directors – James Whale and Howard Hawks. Both films have more life, more real pulsing excitement and thrills and depth to them than anything the Academy nominated this year. Yes, *Frankenstein* has some bad actors – the fiancée and the best friend are so stiff Dr. Frankenstein should have used them for parts instead of the corpses he and Igor dig up. The fiancée is played by Mae Clarke, who is somewhat better as a prostitute in Whales' previous film, *Waterloo Bridge*, and as the target of Cagney's grapefruit in *The Public Enemy*. Colin Clive is more than awful, except during the graveyard and creation scenes, when his mania emerges most fully. Having to watch Clive in love scenes is like being forced to eat overripe tomatoes. On the other hand, *Scarface* has its own weak acting – the so-called comic relief simply doesn't work, if it ever did. Why someone as Machiavellian and determined as Scarface would ever put this fool in as his secretary is never explained – if Muni is so concerned about his public image, why does he have an illiterate boob for a front man? Yes, *Scarface* does revel in violence (for the most part, Brian de Palma's version is only a matter of difference of degree, not kind[29]). I also wonder why Muni has an accent, and his mother has an accent...but his younger sister has no accent at all, which tears the willing suspension of disbelief. George Raft starts his coin-flipping gimmick here. Of all the films made this year, these two have been watched for generations by viewers, very few of whom have gone on to film school.[30] *Frankenstein* remains the seminal horror film; *Scarface*, the seminal gangster film. Horror movies existed before *Frankenstein*, as some gangster flicks came before *Scarface*. Hawks actually made *Scarface* in 1931, before *Little Caesar* and *The Public Enemy*, but arguments with the censors delayed its opening until 1932. After *Frankenstein* and *Scarface*, no film in either genre could fail to reference them. More than their sheer importance, both movies are so damn much fun to watch. Having to pick between the two of them is next to impossible, and really comes down to these factors: those weak actors in *Frankenstein* versus the bad comic relief in *Scarface*; the added morality lessons the censors forced onto *Scarface*; tellingly, the fact that *Frankenstein* has lost a considerable amount of its power to horrify, whereas Tony Camonte's brutality is still with us; and just as tellingly, the ending where Tony turns coward, rather than continuing the character arc he has followed from the beginning. But *Frankenstein* has

---

[29] As Andrew Sarris says of the original, "Before Tony is dispatched, a new record is set for murders on the screen." Truly, nothing is new under the sun...or the gravestone. *"You Ain't Seen Nothin' Yet"* p. 268.
[30] *Tarzan the Ape Man* was also a favorite for decades, but it seems to have fallen by the wayside, not least because of its racism, which is why I'm not promoting it. *Freaks* gets no love either, as it is an exceptionally disturbing and completely ridiculous film.

several scenes which live in our popular memory still, and the mythic qualities of the creation scene mean *Scarface* should lose out to *Frankenstein* for the Best Picture Oscar – by a neck bolt.

Best Actor: Fredric March in *Dr. Jekyll and Mr. Hyde* and Wallace Beery in *The Champ* tied, leaving behind Alfred Lunt from *The Guardsman*

I feel bad for famed theatrical star Alfred Lunt; most years, those who don't win the statue can at least commiserate with others who don't win. Alfred Lunt was the only loser that night. Sadly, *The Guardsman* isn't good enough to overtake the original winners for Best Picture, Wallace Beery or Fredric March – or those I am about to suggest should have been nominated. Let's be clear; Lunt and Fontanne (see Best Actress) were great stage stars, but what works on the boards rarely works on the screen. *The Guardsman* shows us theatrical acting at its contemporary best, but not quite great movie acting. The story is inventive, but not performed well for the screen: a jealous actor pretends to be his wife's Russian lover to forestall the real thing. Nomination da, award nyet.

Fredric March's performance as Dr. Jekyll and Mr. Hyde is by far the best that dual personality have ever received (Spencer Tracy hated playing them). March is a bit hammy in both roles, as he almost always was, but the parts seem to demand exaggeration, as the good and the bad in human nature are separated and distilled. Whenever an actor dons makeup, the temptation is to credit the makeup and not the actor, but this is almost always a mistake. March well deserved a nomination, and the only reason I am denying the appropriateness of his Oscar is because another actor in makeup playing a classic monster outclasses him – as we will see.

Wallace Beery's turn as the boxer on his last legs is still effective. But he tended to play one type from one movie to the next – unreliable, joshing, drinking, loveable as a fat old dog. I have a hard time believing him as a boxer, because he is so out of shape, and moves so awkwardly. But audiences bought him, and so did the Academy. But since I'm the only one who matters here (well, and you, of course, dear reader, but you've been awfully quiet while I made all these choices – you should speak up more!), I don't think he deserved his Oscar. I've seen Beery play this same character in *Min and Bill* and *The Big House*, although his love for the boy Dink is new, as is his half-hearted attempt to be noble. Reportedly, Beery kept making life difficult for Jackie Cooper on the set, out of what Cooper believed was jealousy. And, as a boxer, he looks like a little kid fighting – not exactly playing the former heavyweight champion of the world convincingly. *The Champ* was the high point of Beery's career; it was all downhill after this. He should keep the nomination, but greater performances went unrecognized this year.

As for those the Academy overlooked, Robert Williams in *Platinum Blonde* plays one of the great American smartasses. Sadly, Williams died of peritonitis shortly after filming his best performance; I suspect he might have had an excellent career in the Thirties, ending up as a great character actor as he aged. His ability with snappy patter and knowing glances points the way to the Cary Grant of *His Girl Friday* and the James Stewart of *The Philadelphia Story* (*Platinum Blonde* seems to lay the groundwork for the reporter-rich girl subplot there). I could do without the gum chewing, and I could really do without the simultaneous gum chewing and smoking, but one can't have everything. Williams deserved a nomination.

And so did Paul Muni. *Scarface* begins one of the most celebrated careers of the Thirties. Like Lon Chaney, Sr. (and Meryl Streep), Muni would be famous for immersing himself within the role. Muni's greatest acclaim would come from playing famous historical figures, starting here with his impression of Al Capone – or what the media had made of Capone. As Scarface, Muni announces his presence on the screen by hiding behind a warm towel in a barber shop (a scene referenced in Muni's *I Am a Fugitive from a Chain Gang*). When the cop comes to bring him to headquarters for questioning, Muni becomes the very definition of disdain for authority, a position that played well in the early Thirties world of the Depression – as the Marx Brothers knew so well. If Muni doesn't quite muster the physical menace of a gangster, then neither did the diminutive Cagney in *The Public Enemy* or the rotund Robinson in *Little Caesar*. Like them, he has something far more important: attitude. Cagney had amorality, Robinson had ambition, but nobody looked like they were enjoying themselves more than Muni, who seems to have invented the smirk. If Muni has a shortcoming, his style is still too theatrical, as Martin Scorsese has pointed out in his interview with Roger Ebert.[xxiv] Ultimately, this theatricality leads me to deny that the Oscar should have gone to Muni.

One of the great injustices of the Academy lies in their hostility to Boris Karloff as an actor. To a certain degree, this idiocy was part and parcel of the Academy's hostility and neglect of the horror genre – but it still cannot be forgiven. Karloff's acting is always compelling, nuanced and highly individual, and almost always overcame the roles he was given. Like Louis Armstrong and Bing Crosby, the material simply didn't matter; one note, and we're hooked, even on the worst songs ever written. One sight of Karloff, one hearing of his magnificent voice, and who cares what else happens in the movie? Trapped in B pictures and stereotyped, Karloff, even in the most awful dreck, is captivating. From the thousand movies I watched for this volume, no actor was more likely to get a family member to stop what they were doing and watch; over and over again, Karloff brought them in and kept them there. In his breakout role in *Frankenstein*, Karloff is absolutely stunning, with no performance before or since like it (except his own return to the role in *Bride of Frankenstein*). His portrayal of the monster outdoes every actor who has ever tried it (including Robert De Niro), and most actors who haven't tried it. He mesmerizes, turning what could have been a one-note performance trapped in makeup into a compelling, nuanced, driving display of the essence of acting. Nobody lived that role the way Karloff did, bringing out the innocence of a newborn, the pity and longing for acceptance in his eyes, the terrifying grief and anger of rejection, and the murderous longing for revenge. That the Academy didn't recognize him was unbelievably short-sighted, myopic, and downright blind – pick your own adjective for a lack of simply looking. They had eyes, but they could not see.

So let's take care of that right now: Boris Karloff should have won for Best Actor, for a timeless performance that remains the greatest in the history of the horror genre, and the best of the year.

Best Actress: Helen Hayes won for *The Sins of Madelon Claudet*, over Marie Dressler, *Emma*, and Lynne Fontanne, *The Guardsman*

Want to know what Irving Thalberg, the head of production at MGM, thought about this victory? "Let's face it. We win Academy Awards with crap like *Madelon Claudet*."[xxv] If Thalberg could recognize how bad that film is, who am I to disagree? Of course, Thalberg also thought his wife Norma Shearer was a great actress, and as of this year, little evidence has been shown to prove that. While Helen Hayes wasn't anything special in this trash, she does shine in at least a few scenes, particularly when she is shown her baby for the first time, even though she didn't want him. But Hayes is trapped in this soapy weepie, and the more noble she is supposed to be, the stagier and less believable her performance becomes. She sacrifices her life by becoming a rich man's mistress, then a streetwalker, to be able to raise her illegitimate son from afar. At times, I want to institute a rule that no actress can cry more than once in a film if she wants a career. No Oscar should have been given, especially for any performance in a film that tries to convince us a bad paint-by-number is art – or that the purpose of a woman's life is self-sacrifice for a male.

As for Marie Dressler, *Emma* is a fun movie, full of slapstick and Dressler eating up the scenery and her fellow actors. She should keep her nomination.

Lynne Fontanne was the most famous stage actress of her day; as I've said above in Best Actor in regards to her husband, this doesn't translate all that well. Still, *The Guardsman* is at times fun, and an important artifact. Nomination da, award nyet.

We've got a serious problem. Despite this being an era in which female stars dominated, few seem to have found roles they could dig into this year. No wonder Hayes won – she had so little competition!

So let's stretch things a bit here. We could nominate Dietrich for *Shanghai Express*, but other than one touching scene, what she's doing is pretending to be a canvas for Josef von Sternberg and Lee Garmes to paint upon in light and shadow. Posing isn't acting. As director Clarence Brown pointed out in discussing Garbo and Dietrich, "Anybody who knows them both would not mention Dietrich in the same breath as Garbo. Garbo gets her effects from herself. All the director has to do is lead her gently along, and she will do the rest. But Dietrich is all director. Her works convey the impressions of a man with a gun – standing over her, forcing her through every action, all the time."[xxvi] No Dietrich need apply.

Frank Capra directed Jean Harlow in *Platinum Blonde* (she would hit her commercial peak in next year's *Red Dust* with Clark Gable). The Capra film opens in a newsroom, redolent of *The Front Page*. A reporter, played by Robert Williams, is assigned to investigate the rich family paying off a show girl, called "the human cash register." In earlier Harlow films, she would have been cast as the show girl; here, she gets to play a society ingénue who eventually marries the reporter. Harlow actually manages to pull off a reasonable upper class society accent, and a good amount of the attitude (Katharine Hepburn would do it much better in *The Philadelphia Story*, but that's no shame – Hepburn did pretty much everything better). Harlow's great moments in this film come when she gets the chance to use the expectation that she will behave in a loose, immoral fashion, then surprises us when she does the exact opposite. The look on her face when she thinks the reporter is blackmailing her for sex, only to find out he wants lunch, is as good as acting without words gets in this period. When we find out that she intends to use the reporter as men in other films used her, the reversal hits us again, and our original anticipations are returned in deeper satisfaction. Harlow becomes a more and more unattractive character as the film goes on, which again runs against her typecasting. Capra was not the first major director to cast Harlow – William Wellman used her in

The Public Enemy – but he gives her the chance for a great performance. Capra's disdain for the hypocrisies and mores of the rich comes through here as a major topic of his films. Harlow is quite good in the film, which should have been enough for a nomination for Best Actress.

But the other female lead in *Platinum Blonde*, Loretta Young, is better as the reporter's pal who secretly loves him. Young turns in an attractive performance, and one that hasn't yet taken on the burden of stardom that would so often weigh down her later pictures (with the notable exception of her best film, *The Bishop's Wife*). Here's how good Loretta Young is: we would rather be with her than Jean Harlow. Yes, the role plays off of the silent, suffering lover, and yes, the film seems to take as a matter of course that women should serve their men, and not the other way around. But those common expectations of the early Thirties are wrapped in a larger theme: that every human being should be who they're supposed to be, and not who other people want them to be. As Shakespeare said, "Let me not to the marriage of true minds / Admit impediments. Love is not love / Which alters when it alteration finds, / Or bends with the remover to remove." Young carries that message in the subtle banked fires of her eyes, and in her desire for the man she loves to be the playwright he is meant to be, and not the plaything Harlow thought she married. Her look of absolute joy as her beloved breaks out of his gilded cage is priceless. Loretta Young deserved a nomination.

As did Miriam Hopkins for her turn as the prostitute Ivy in *Dr. Jekyll and Mr. Hyde*. Hopkins was better known for her comedic abilities, but here, she must move from a sexual temptress who haunts Dr. Jekyll's Victorian mores so much that he unleashes Mr. Hyde, to an abused woman who must feign love for Mr. Hyde at the peril of body and soul, while conveying her absolute disgust at his every touch. Hopkins turns in a rounded, unexpected performance, and one that the Academy should have recognized with a nomination.

We might also consider Greta Garbo for the potboiler *Mata Hari*. She's far more nuanced and sure of herself in this than in *Anna Christie*; she's become a much better actress, in almost every way (and considerably better than in *Grand Hotel*). The plot is fairly conventional spy stuff, with some sexy dancing and intrigue thrown into the mix. Ramon Navarro talks, and he's not bad. Garbo takes this muck and makes it worth watching. A nomination seems to be in order, given the generally poor quality of acting this year.

Another choice would be Barbara Stanwyck in *The Miracle Woman*, the Frank Capra film loosely based on evangelist Aimee Semple McPherson. Exposing the fakery of faith cons, *The Miracle Woman* plays like a female version of *Elmer Gantry*. Rarely before or since has such raw emotional power been combined with such believability, such touching sweetness (this, despite the presence of a blind love interest and a ventriloquist dummy). As she goes from anger to deception to redemption, Stanwyck comes into her full powers in this film, building on her breakthrough role in Capra's 1930 *Ladies of Leisure*. She and Capra attack religious and social hypocrisy in America, even if it is telegraphed more than explored. The Academy shied away from this assault, ignoring it completely. Americans in 1931 weren't ready for this film; they aren't ready for it now. Stanwyck should have won the Oscar for Best Actress this year.

Best Director: Frank Borzage won for *Bad Girl*, over King Vidor, *The Champ*; and Josef von Sternberg, *Shanghai Express*

Bad Girl? Not really (see Best Picture). Frank Borzage's direction of the actors moves towards an attempt at showing an awareness of the Depression, and I rather suspect Borzage had watched *The Crowd* a few too many times before he made this. I know that Borzage has his admirers (Martin Scorsese among them), but his films just have no flair and little humor; the outcomes are often unbelievable. I literally have no idea why they gave Borzage the award, except that A) they really liked him, and B) they had terrible taste. He definitely didn't deserve this Oscar – or even a nomination.

King Vidor was a chameleon. Here's a slice from his filmography: he went from the comic (Marion Davies in *The Patsy*) to the bitterly realistic (*The Crowd*) to a Southern, all-black musical (*Hallelujah*) to a western (*Billy the Kid*), then back to comedy (another Marion Davies, *Not So Dumb*) to realism (*Street Scene*) to tearjerker (*The Champ*). Part of the reason this critically respected director isn't known better today is because we don't know how to pigeon-hole him. *The Champ* plays off of the celebrity of Wallace Beery and Jackie Cooper, in a film highly reminiscent of the sentimentality of Charlie Chaplin's *The Kid*. Cooper famously cries his heart out at the end of the film; one wonders if Vidor had to threaten to shoot his dog the way Cooper's uncle Norman Taurog had on *Skippy*. Overall, it's a competent film, with little of the special qualities Vidor brought to *The Crowd* and *Hallelujah!* The nomination should stay, but I for one wish Vidor had been allowed to pursue his pet projects more, rather than these melodramas.

Josef von Sternberg was busily transforming Marlene Dietrich into a sex goddess, beginning with *The Blue Angel* and moving right into *Morocco* and *Shanghai Express*, which may be the height of their collaboration. Von Sternberg's mastery of lighting was never better used than in turning Dietrich into a creation of light and shadow and sex. While the story is not particularly interesting, the way it is told remains riveting. *Shanghai Express* has been described as *Grand Hotel* in a train, and there is that ensemble feel, but *Shanghai Express* is far more focused and controlled, as are the characters, than in that bloated, misbegotten excuse for a Best Picture. The entire film is drenched in restraint, and those struggling against that restraint; the Chinese civil war rages about them as an exterior reflection of the emotional struggles within. The two former lovers, played by Dietrich and Clive Brook, try to work through the layers of repression and pride they have put on as armor; in the end, however, Dietrich seems to be much better posing than she is acting (and moving your eyes around a lot isn't acting, Ms. Dietrich!). With von Sternberg (and a few other directors), the line of duty between direction and cinematography is not just blurred, it's violated. The look of the film is due as much to von Sternberg as it is to Lee Garmes. A prime example of this presents itself when Dietrich is told to pray, and through a cross of shadows, all we see are Dietrich's hands in supplication. Von Sternberg reached one of his peaks with this film, at least visually, if not in terms of narrative. Look at the dolly shot in the train passageway as it follows Dietrich and see if you don't agree as to the artistry. Audiences certainly did; *Shanghai Express* was the top moneymaker of the year.[31] The nomination should stay, and the Academy should be applauded for making it.

But how could they have left out John Ford? Soon, he would regularly appear in this category. Ford was on his way to becoming, in my opinion (and many others), our greatest American director. As Orson Welles said when asked from whom he had learned to direct, he said, "I prefer the Old Masters, by which I mean John Ford, John Ford, and John Ford." Ford would win an unprecedented and unmatched four Oscars for Best Director, balancing art and commerce brilliantly. *Arrowsmith* opens quickly, as it does in the novel, cutting from pioneer grandmother to curious boy to over-anxious med student to doctor – which is when we see Ronald Colman's face for the first time. Many shots are framed by doorways (a favorite of Ford's) and already display Ford's penchant for "cutting in the can" to prevent producers (in this case, Samuel Goldwyn[32]) from changing the picture very much. Move-

---

[31] I know, I've already labeled *Frankenstein* the #1 movie of the year – and it was, for 1931; *Shanghai Express* ruled 1932. Remember that the dates for eligibility are not yet the same as the calendar year.
[32] Ford was not the only director who distrusted Goldwyn. Billy Wilder was extremely dismissive of Goldwyn: "He was a titan with an empty skull – not confused by anything he read, which he didn't." Qtd. in Ed Sikov, *On Sunset Boulevard*, p. 161.

ment, narrative drive, painterly images, sentiment without mawkishness, awareness, honest characters, humorous touches – all these and more are evident here. Ford had directed stars before (notably Harry Carey), and he was capable of making stars (Victor McLaglen and John Wayne especially) and choosing future stars (Spencer Tracy and Humphrey Bogart), but here, for the first time, he has a major star capable of depth and charisma in Ronald Colman. Ford makes the most of it. A few awkward touches mar *Arrowsmith*, especially the way Colman proposes on the first date, which isn't believable because we haven't seen their attraction conveyed in any significant way. Not a perfect movie, and not a film I would want to see more than once, but *Arrowsmith* does form the model for a series of films about medical research, most famously in *The Story of Louis Pasteur* (1936) and *Dr. Ehrlich's Magic Bullet* (1940). Ford deserved a nomination.

As did Rouben Mamoulian, for *Dr. Jekyll and Mr. Hyde*. The cast acts beautifully; the movements of the camera are brilliant (see Cinematography above).

James Whale had a wicked sense of humor, which would fully emerge from the hints in *Frankenstein* when he made *The Invisible Man* and *Bride of Frankenstein*. Whale was finding his way in *Frankenstein*, as can be seen from his failure to evoke real acting from all of his performers, but when he could convince Colin Clive to let loose, as in the creation scene, and with Boris Karloff perfect in his portrayal of the Monster, he clearly knew how to direct. The humor remains true to this day; who else would reveal the living Monster by having him walk into the room...backwards? The pity and terror in Karloff's performance was set free by Whale. He should have received a nomination – as should Howard Hawks.

Scarface begins with the claim to being a true story – and then attacks the government for not doing anything to stop the gangs. The title cards then turn the finger towards the audience: "The government is your government. What are YOU going to do about it?" In a perhaps not-so-subtle joke (probably aimed at the censors who insisted on the moral platitudes), the film then begins with a shot of the streetlight in the darkness, then swings to a janitor cleaning up after a stag party (get it? We need to clean up the gangs!). From the earliest frames, Howard Hawks is crafting his first great film (Richard Rosson directed some additional scenes, which usually stick out like sore thumbs). The dollying camera, the shift in sound the closer we get to the talking, the use of shadows to build suspense, the whistling of the killer as he gets closer to his target, the casualness of the killing, the passage of time by superimposing the blazing Tommy gun over the flying pages of the calendar...I could go on and on, but wouldn't you rather go watch this instead? Look for the "x" at every death. *Scarface* should have been Howard Hawks' first nomination as Best Director.

Finally, Frank Capra had an amazing year attacking American hypocrisy and exposing our national double standards by making us laugh at them, with both *The Miracle Woman* and *Platinum Blonde*. *Platinum Blonde* has what I think is Jean Harlow's best acting before *Dinner at Eight*, as a result of Capra's direction and inversion of audience expectations about her. We see one wonderful shot of Harlow kissing the reporter through a sheet of falling water, and all told, this may be the sexiest kiss and makeout shown on the screen up to this point (Capra liked it so much he did it again in *Lady for a Day*). When you consider that Jean Harlow had her best performance so far here, and Loretta Young one of her best, the art of the director in bringing out the best of his actors is clear. *Platinum Blonde* and *The Miracle Woman* show Capra reaching for films that matter, after a career spent largely making entertaining fluff. Frank Capra should have had a nomination for Best Director.

Like Best Picture, this category basically comes down to the choice between *Frankenstein* and *Scarface*. Rather than repeat the argument there, let us consider the role of the director. He (or she) guides the actors through their performances, deciding when a take is good enough; he decides where to place the camera, and when to begin and end the shot. In the era when studio producers had far more control over casting and the script, the director's job was more limited than it became later. We have to therefore look at the acting, and what the director chose as satisfactory. What that comes down to, for me, is the Best Director Oscar should have gone to Howard Hawks, rather than James Whale. I just can't forgive Whale for how bad the acting of the fiancée and best friend are. While I think *Frankenstein* is marginally the better picture, Hawks would prove himself to be the better, more enduring director over Whales, whose career can be summed up in three films: *Frankenstein, The Invisible Man,* and *Bride of Frankenstein*[33]. Hawks' films include *His Girl Friday, Bringing up Baby, The Big Sleep, Sergeant York, Ball of Fire, To Have and Have Not, Red River,* and (probably) *The Thing*. All of those were made before Whale committed suicide, so opportunity was not the issue. Hawks began his rise to greatness with *Scarface*, and he deserved the Oscar (which he never won in reality).

---

[33] Some would add *Show Boat*, which I can tell is the best film version – but also leaves me cold.

Best Writing (Adaptation): Edwin Burke won for *Bad Girl*, over Sidney Howard, *Arrowsmith*; and Percy Heath & Samuel Hoffenstein, *Dr. Jekyll and Mr. Hyde*

Bad Girl...isn't. Corny dialogue to boot, despite a seemingly suggestive opening. The film starts off with a bang then fizzles into weepie. And not even good weepie (although there is a convincing crying scene towards the end...from the husband, no less). The plot sets up the two not to trust each other, but everything turns out all right in the end. Strictly soap. No award and no nomination should have been given.

Sidney Howard turned *Arrowsmith* into a movie, but an honest adaptation of the novel still awaits us. Read the novel, and you will see why the movie fails to be faithful to the source material from the opening announcement: "The story of a man who dedicated his life to service and his heart to the love of one woman." This is not quite what the book is about, but it is what audiences of the period wanted from their heroes (and, mostly, still do). Having read the book, I think the flaws in the movie are largely those of not staying true to the spirit of the novel. Lewis sets out to show the ways in which science works (which the movie hardly does), but also to criticize and satirize society, in order to purge it of its sicknesses. Remarkably little of this purpose remains in the film, but when Howard's script lets it peek through, the film picks up more power. All traces of criticism of small-town life have been erased, and now government and small-minded bureaucracy has become the target. Not surprising, given this was the Depression. Howard may not have been responsible for this winnowing and lessening, but in an era when the script was almost sacrosanct after being approved by the producer, he must have had a major hand in it. *Arrowsmith* is still a good script, but not the best adaptation of the source material; the lab chat is beyond vague. No scientist would ever talk that way. The nomination should stay for what works.

Robert Louis Stevenson was served better by Heath and Hoffenstein (and don't they sound like a vaudeville act?). Percy Heath died in 1933, shortly after receiving his nomination; Samuel Hoffenstein would go on to other remarkable work, including Astaire and Roger's *The Gay Divorcee*, uncredited work on *The Wizard of Oz*, and *Laura*. *Dr. Jekyll and Mr. Hyde* comes across fairly well, although their screenplay seems to be based more on the Victorian stage version than the novella. Worth a nomination.

We might consider *Tarzan the Ape Man*. I would, but Cyril Hume and Ivor Novello absolutely destroyed the character by reducing him to an idiot who can't speak English. You might try reading the original by Edgar Rice Burroughs, although I warn you: Burroughs was racist, although no more so than the majority of whites in his time. Hume would go on to a long career, perhaps reaching his peak in *Forbidden Planet*; Novello was an actor (he did some work for Hitchcock), songwriter (best known for the WWI classic, "Keep the Home Fires Burning") and writer. No nomination.

The greatest omission came in not nominating *Frankenstein* (for any awards). The original Mary Shelley novel has little or no action for much of its length; it's a philosophical treatise, and not a particularly interesting one much of the time, except to literary scholars (I should know; I am one, and I have the Ph.D. to prove it). *Dracula* is a far more interesting novel to most modern readers. This adaptation has kept *Frankenstein* in print, as generations of readers have sought it out after seeing Karloff. I wish the soap opera moments were excised, but the graveyard scene, creation scene, and the great hunt at the end, have rarely been equaled. "It's alive! It's alive!" The writer, John L. Balderston, also adapted *Dracula* and wrote *Bride of Frankenstein*. He should have been nominated.

Scarface has a screenplay by Ben Hecht, based on a novel by Armitage Trail (a pen name for Maurice Coons, which isn't much better). Hecht largely ignored the novel. He and Hawks "patterned its Capone-ish characters after the Borgias."[xxvii] In terms of the narrative arc, the movie plays out much like *Little Caesar*. A small-time gangster moves up the ranks, seeing those above him as weak and easy to take out, leading to the big time, then an ultimate downfall. Part of this is due to the nature of the beast – how many stories can you tell about organized crime? – and part of it is due to using the same source material of Al Capone. Overall, the script is less important than the direction and acting, which make of a story we've already seen something very special. The point here is style, not substance. We've seen this story before; we've just never seen it told quite this well before. Hecht should have a nomination.

Jo Swerling adapted the story for *Platinum Blonde*, from the original by Harry E. Chandlee and Douglas W. Churchill. Swerling had a great career, often working with Frank Capra; he wrote *The Pride of the Yankees* and *It's a Wonderful Life*. *Platinum Blonde* is as good, at times, as any Capra film. We are dealing with a love triangle, and unrequited love, and many other standard elements of romance films, but they're done sharply and with verve. The overarching theme of social criticism of the rich and their shortcomings works well to drive the love story. Robert Riskin provided additional dialogue, so the nomination is shared by the two of them. They deserved a nomination.

In the end, the Oscar in this category should go to the movie that best recasts the original source material without losing the heart of the original. *Frankenstein* doesn't do that, because the original material is so utterly different from the film. *Scarface* also ignores the original novel. *Dr. Jekyll* pulls on the Victorian play as much as it does Stevenson, but it does so with the intent of getting to the root of that twisted tree. The Oscar should have gone to Heath and Hoffenstein for *Dr. Jekyll and Mr. Hyde*.

Best Writing (Original Story): Frances Marion won for *The Champ*, over Grover Jones and William Slavens McNutt, *Lady and Gent*; Lucien Hubbard, *Star Witness*; and Adela Rogers St. John, *What Price Hollywood?*

Let's dispose of those last three immediately. *Lady and Gent* is a paean to boxing clichés and tripe; *Star Witness* is an extremely unlikely story of a grandfather insisting on truth over the safety of his grandchildren; *What Price Hollywood?* is just an early version of *A Star Is Born*, which really has three versions too many already.[34] None of them should have received any nomination.

Frances Marion understood her audience with *The Champ*. Anybody who can make us want to see Wallace Beery again, and Jackie Cooper cry some more, must know what they're doing. On the other hand, even then, it was clear that Beery's champ is an awful father, full of lies and alcohol and betrayal. Seen through today's eyes, the child Dink is the enabler in this unhealthy relationship. Love is there, yes, but how can Dink ever trust his own father? Beery gets to be noble for a change. One of the most effective moments in the film comes with the dialogue, when Jackie Cooper finally calls his father Daddy when he's sure the man he's called "The Champ" for the whole film is about to lose the big fight. The ending is sheer cornball – and I don't mean the death scene. I mean what Marion has Cooper do after his father dies, going through every character saying "I want the Champ" and then seeing his mother, with whom he has spent a total of less than one day since he was a baby, and then having her pick him up as if he was an infant. We fade out to the strains of a childhood lullaby. Assuming of course it is Frances Marion coming up with this ending, Marion doesn't deserve the Oscar because this undercuts everything the Champ tried to teach his son: don't give up; don't cry; keep your chin up. Instead of growing up, Dink is reduced to a little baby in the arms of American Motherhood – a mother, I remind you, who abandoned her child as a baby for a rich husband.

---

[34] To be fair, Constance Bennett makes it worth watching once.

The Champ is a mess of unexamined parenting styles and values; all the script is really interested in is getting the audience, particularly the male audience, to cry. I didn't. No Oscar should have been given.

Again, we come to the Marx Brothers. Are you sensing a pattern here? You ought to by now, or you're not paying enough attention! Maybe you need a nap. Or a snack. Go on. Sleep! Eat! I'll wait for you. Feel better now? Good! Because I'm about to applaud S.J. Perelman, Arthur Sheekman, Groucho, and the host of gag writers who worked on *Monkey Business*. The story begins as the Marx Brothers are stowaways on a luxury liner. Unlike their previous two films, *Monkey Business* was written specifically for the screen. The film is anarchy at its best – in fact, some countries banned it because they were afraid it would cause their citizens to move towards anarchy. Seriously! Try these moments on for size. The Marx Brothers, pretending to be Maurice Chevalier to get off the boat. Groucho: "Is it true you're getting a divorce as soon as your husband recovers his eyesight? Is it true you wash your hair in clam broth? Is it true you used to dance in a flea circus?" Madame Pucchi: "This is outrageous! I don't like this innuendo." Groucho: "That's what I always say. Love flies out the door when money comes innuendo." "Oh, I know it's a penny here and a penny there, but look at me. I worked myself up from nothing to a state of extreme poverty." Well worth a nomination.

Looking abroad, French filmmaker René Clair wrote and directed *À Nous la Liberté* (translation: *Freedom for Us*). Clair's comedy is a truly original film, but a comedy with social daggers hiding in its smiles, through its comparison of prison with the factory – visually, they're nearly exact duplicates. The only major difference? The factory is more efficient at removing freedom. Long before the Nazis plastered "Arbeit macht frei!" all over Germany, Clair was making fun of the idea in this film. Famously, the film's producers sued Charlie Chaplin for supposedly copying scenes a few years later for *Modern Times*; the film's director, René Clair, was not a part of the suit, and believed Chaplin could have anything he wanted (and rightfully so – the movie is a Chaplin homage from start to finish, and could easily have starred him). Chaplin and his crew denied ever having seen the film; they settled out of court. Born in Paris, Clair emigrated to Hollywood before WWII, where he made the classics *I Married a Witch* and *And Then There Were None*, among other lesser films. *À Nous la Liberté* remains his most famous French film, and for good reason. While his artistic director was nominated for an Oscar, he himself was not – and given the weak competition they nominated for this category this year, and despite the

Marx Brothers, Clair's inventive script deserved both a nomination and the Oscar for Best Writing (Original Story).

Best Art Direction: Gordon Wiles won for *Transatlantic*, over Lazare Meerson, *À Nous la Liberté*; and Richard Day, *Arrowsmith*

Transatlantic is set upon an ocean liner; James Cameron would have been proud to use the sets for *Titanic*. Think of it as *Grand Hotel* at sea (everybody seems to call it that – you might as well too). Gordon Wiles won the Oscar for his very first film as art director. He would go on to his death in 1950 working in Hollywood – and not a single one of his films is a classic. But he got things right in this movie: the recreation of the ship and the art deco look are definitely worth a nomination, but I am suggesting the award should go to wonders even greater.

À Nous la Liberté was a shock, since no foreign films had been nominated for an Award, and few ever would be until they created the Foreign Film category. One can see why the art directors in the Academy nominated the film. The prison sets are truly oppressive, but what drew the attention of voters was the striking visual mirroring in the factory scenes, including the conveyor belts moving both their work, and their food, past the workers. If Chaplin did see this film – and there's a good chance he did – he took those ideas and went hyperbolic with them, to much greater comic effect, in *Modern Times*. The nomination should stay.

Arrowsmith is really not worth a nomination in this category. Basic small town, fake labs, and tropical huts that look much like they do in every film that uses any of those settings. So, no nomination should have been given.

The Academy ignored better choices, as it so often did.

Surprisingly, *Grand Hotel* was not nominated for its spectacular art deco hotel sets. It did deserve a nomination.

Finally, how could they have left out *Frankenstein*?!? Granted, some of its village scenes were on the same sets as *All Quiet on the Western Front*, but the laboratory and the dungeon, with their German Expressionist influences, and the wonderful gadgetry, are all absolutely original and unforgettable. By far, this is the most memorable looking film of the year, and the most influential. Charles D. Hall worked primarily for Universal, including *Dracula, All Quiet on the Western Front*, and *Bride of Frankenstein*. Later, he did *My Man Godfrey* and several Hal Roach productions, including some Laurel and Hardy, and *One Million B.C.* While he was nominated for two of his more obscure films, he never won – until now. Bless you, Charles D. Hall – and thank you for so many great sets! You should have received the Oscar for Art Direction![35]

---

[35] Hall's crew included Frank Grove, Kenneth Strickfaden, and Raymond Lindsay, who created the lab equipment. Cited in Tino Balio, *Grand Design*, p. 301.

CHAPTER SIX: 1934 AWARDS
6th Show

Movies released between August 1st, 1932, and December 31st, 1933

THE SCENE OF THE CRIME:

Finally, they decided to make the terms of eligibility equivalent to the calendar year. This makes a larger number of films eligible this year, because for the only time, a year and a half of movies fill the pool. So, I have to work harder, but then, the films are getting consistently better, so it balances out nicely. Thus, 1933 is the only year not to have an Oscar night.

The awards took place on March 16, 1934, again in the Fiesta Room at the Ambassador Hotel.

They tried their best to avoid the mistakes of the previous year. The seating arrangements were handled by the studios ahead of time. There would be no late announced ties again. Best of all, they brought in Duke Ellington as the dance band!

If you don't know Duke Ellington's music, you are seriously deprived – and less perceptive and intelligent a reader than I had hoped you would be. Please fix this flaw in your character immediately.

Just as wise as choosing Ellington, they picked Will Rogers to host the evening, thus inaugurating a long and often fruitful tradition of comedians hosting the show.

This Academy Awards also saw Walt Disney cement the nickname Oscar, when he referred to the statues as such.

The greatest embarrassment of the evening came when Will Rogers called up "Frank" to get the Best Director award...and Frank Capra tried to come up to get Frank Lloyd's award. Capra never forgot the shame.

At the end of the evening, they even read off the voting results for each category, thus further embarrassing the losers.

More importantly, at least the acting awards seemed to be based on genuine acting ability, rather than studio manipulation. Doesn't necessarily mean I'm going to agree with their judgment...

The two absent winners, Charles Laughton and Katharine Hepburn, were neither one of them very popular in Hollywood.

Also all over the place were the number of nominations – up to ten for Best Picture, three for most of the others, but four for sound recording...and EIGHTEEN nominations in a new category, Best Assistant Director, which then got to hand out SIX Oscars...in the same category! Silly people. I'm not even going to try and judge that one, either this year, or any other (eventually, they dropped the award).

WHAT THEY GOT RIGHT:

Best Actress: Katharine Hepburn won for *Morning Glory*, over Diana Wynyard, *Cavalcade*, and May Robson, *Lady for a Day*

Winner Katharine Hepburn made her debut opposite John Barrymore in *A Bill of Divorcement*, a story about love and insanity (not necessarily the same thing, but getting closer all the time for celebrities). When the filming was done, Hepburn turned to Barrymore and announced, "I will never have to play another scene with you." Barrymore hit back, "But my dear, you never have." Another version of this sounds more like Hepburn. Barrymore kept pinching her fanny. Hepburn snapped, "If you keep doing that, I'm going to stop acting." Barrymore then said, "I wasn't aware that you'd started, my dear." With those (possibly) apocryphal stories, Hepburn began her combative love-hate relationship with Hollywood. This quintessential nonconformist was an actress dedicated to her art even after she became a wildly successful star. *Morning Glory*, for which she won her first of a still unmatched four Best Actress Oscars, has her playing a young ingénue with the stage name of Ava Lovelace, dedicated to the theater, before she has ever made it into her first Broadway play. She's a chatterbox in *Morning Glory* (and another one in *Little Women*). Having been on the stage in New York, she handled dialogue very well, but she's already learning to perform naturally, in the screen manner. Hepburn puts across the young actress taking on airs in an attempt to appear sophisticated, but her earnestness keeps stumbling through, especially as she is compared to established actresses in the casting office, both of whom are fake as fake can be, to illustrate the differences. As she pays her dues, the facade crumbles as the real character emerges. Hepburn does a wonderful drunken Hamlet and Juliet (I honestly got chills down my spine the first time I saw this.) The Academy seems to have surprised itself when it gave her this Oscar; like Laughton, she didn't bother appearing at the Awards ceremony. She rarely did. No matter; she reigned as the greatest actress in Hollywood for much of the next half century. She deserved the Best Actress Oscar for *Morning Glory*.

Diana Wynyard in *Cavalcade* shows everything that is wrong with stage-trained actors of the period being brought into movies. She's constantly playing to an audience that isn't there, rather than living the role. She puts a quaver into her voice, then looks away from Clive Brook, then back, then away for a longer time. I don't for a minute buy her performance, and it bodes poorly for the Academy that they gave her a third place. She resembles Norma Shearer more than a little, and both of them seem to have gone to the same bad acting school. No nomination should have been given.

May Robson was seventy-five when she filmed *Lady for a Day* for Frank Capra, playing Apple Annie, a poor woman who has lied to her daughter from afar for her entire life about being rich. Given Marie Dressler's unexpected celebrity over at MGM, starring a senior citizen seemed to be good business. Robson remains charming in the role, as does Warren Williams as Dave the Dude, a gambler who makes Apple Annie's subterfuge work, when her daughter appears unexpectedly and must be fooled into thinking her mother is in fact a rich socialite. Robson well deserved her nomination, and it launched her on a series of excellent supporting roles in *Alice in Wonderland, Bringing up Baby*, and *The Adventures of Tom Sawyer*, among others. She's as good as Marie Dressler, and often better used by her directors.

So who else should have been nominated?

Henrietta Crosman in John Ford's *Pilgrimage* deserved a nod. Watch her when the mayor reads the telegram from the war department; few actresses from this decade can match her ability to convey a range of emotions. Her transformation from cold-hearted, selfish crotchety old lady to fully human is heart-wrenchingly satisfying. When we compare her performance in this Ford film with her usual upper-class snootiness she was typically typecast in – *The Royal Family of Broadway, Up the River* – we can see how truly deep this actress reached into herself when given an opportunity to carry an entire film.

After playing the evangelist to the hilt in *The Miracle Woman*, as well as a series of other roles, Barbara Stanwyck turned to *Baby Face*. Starting as low as one could go – waitress and scenery in her father's blue-collar, tenement speakeasy – Stanwyck uses her sex appeal and her body to sleep her way to the top. Unabashed, driven, cold, and cynical, here is the forerunner to her femme fatale in *Double Indemnity*. Stanwyck had been playing characters on the edge of society: women with married lovers, mail-order brides, gun molls. Now she just didn't dance on the edge of acceptable behavior – she dove right in to the depths of cynicism and manipulation. We wouldn't see another character like this as the heroine until the rise of film noir in the Forties. Stanwyck deserved a nomination.

As did Greta Garbo in *Queen Christina*. Playing a bisexual, cross-dressing queen – the kind with a crown, not restrictive underwear – Garbo outdid herself in this pre-Code historical extravaganza (see Best Picture below for more).

Writing (Adaptation): *Little Women* won for Victor Heerman and Sarah Y. Mason, over Robert Riskin, *Lady for a Day*; and Paul Green & Sonya Levien, *State Fair*

Before I go to the nominees, let me kick *Cavalcade*, the supposed Best Picture of the year. Why give a film the best picture and the best director Oscars, but NOT nominate the film for the writing?!? Especially when the source material is a Noel Coward play? Answer: because the nominations by the writers picked decent work, and the general Academy voted for the ones they liked. The writers knew the adaptation of *Cavalcade* was awful; they left it out. What does this teach us? Pay more attention to writers! If you don't, you'll get crap like *Cavalcade*.

The three films nominated for this Oscar have their fans still. The first two tell solid stories well, and earned their nominations. This version of **Little Women**, starring Katharine Hepburn, remains my favorite and the closest in spirit to the book. *Lady for a Day* is a touching, heartwarming story full of characters right out of Damon Runyan, which makes sense, since that's who Capra favorite Robert Riskin was adapting. Every note of dialogue fits the characters perfectly. My particular favorite is Guy Kibbee's Judge Blake, a pool hall hustler who speaks as if he'd swallowed a dictionary, a thesaurus, and Emily Post, yet still has the rogue in his mouth. Both *Little Women* and *Lady for a Day* definitely deserved their nominations as inspired, faithful adaptations.

On the other hand, *State Fair* is not my idea of a good story. A few years later, this would be Ma and Pa Kettle's pig pen. I have no objection to stories about rural settings and farm folk – the novel and original film version of *Charlotte's Web* were childhood favorites I still cherish – but without Will Rogers, would anybody care about this? No nomination was deserved (see Best Picture for more on all three of the original nominees).

As for what was left out, does it surprise anyone that the writers didn't nominate the adaptation of *A Farewell to Arms*? The writers knew what butchery had been committed (see Best Picture for more).

My problem lies in what they failed to nominate – what a surprise, right?

Joseph L. Mankiewicz and William Cameron Menzies should have been recognized for doing the best adaptation Hollywood has ever made of a book that is basically unadaptable: Lewis Carroll's immortal *Alice in Wonderland*. Sorry, Mr. Disney, your version comes in second, closely followed by the 1949 Louis Bunin puppet version. And as for Tim Burton's empty eye-candy travesty, the less said the better. This *Alice* was created by people who had breathed the book in with every step of their childhood (see Best Art Direction for more).

Based on a play by Caroline Francke and Mack Crane, *Bombshell* parodies Hollywood even better than *Sullivan's Travels* and *Singin' in the Rain*. John Lee Mahin and Jules Furthman crafted a witty, self-reflexive jab at the moviemaking business and the publicity machines that still stings today. Perhaps the greatest surprise in it is a black maid who isn't subservient, but sassy – she responds to criticism with a snappy warning that she knows where the bodies are buried. *Bombshell* is Jean Harlow in her funniest starring role (see Best Actress for more). Mahin and Furthman should have a nomination.

Howard J. Green and Brown Holmes wrote the screenplay for *I Am a Fugitive from a Chain Gang*, based on Robert E. Burns' book, *I Am a Fugitive from a Georgia Chain Gang*. Burns was an actual fugitive, escaping from a chain gang more than once, and on the lam after publishing his book; after the movie, he was still on the run, until New Jersey granted him asylum. For their terrific story, adapted with punch and style, Green and Holmes should have been nominated (see Best Picture for more).

R.C. Sherriff adapted H.G. Wells' *The Invisible Man* for James Whale. Sherriff's screenplay shines with fervor and dark humor, although much of that may be due to Whale himself. Although it spawned a host of sequels and imitators, nobody has ever done better in drawing out the novel's essence onto the screen than Sherriff. Sherriff would go on to write *Goodbye, Mr. Chips* and *Mrs. Miniver* among other things. This version of *The Invisible Man* brings the book to life as no other Wells adaptation ever has, while still remaining true to the source (some minor changes were made, particularly in creating the fiancée and her father, and having Griffin murder Kemp; the movie is also updated to the 1930s). Wells himself objected to one aspect, because he felt his scientist was turned into a madman, but Wells generally objected to anything anybody else did besides himself (see Best Picture for more); he ended up approving the screenplay.[xxviii]

Waldemar Young and Philip Wylie adapted H.G. Wells" classic novel, *The Island of Lost Souls*, brilliantly, if somewhat disrespectfully. The glamour of this film, and Charles Laughton's performance, has led to two remakes, both of them less than the original, with Burt Lancaster and Marlon Brando both trying to outchew Laughton's performance. They failed. Waldemar Young was the Mormon leader Brigham Young's grandson; he wrote *London after Midnight*, *The Sign of the Cross*, *Cleopatra*, and *The Lives of a Bengal Lancer*. Philip Wylie used to be a very famous writer, best remembered now for his science fiction novels *Gladiator* and *When Worlds Collide*. But in his day, he was known as a fierce social critic, particularly in blaming American mothers for most of our social problems in *A Generation of Vipers*. They did a bang-up job on *The Island of Lost Souls* (Wylie also helped with *The Invisible Man*, although he went uncredited). Wells hated this adaptation, as Dr. Moreau was turned into a villain; Britain banned it for 25 years. I think it deserves a nomination, for taking Wells' ideas and carrying them even further than Wells did – which is saying something – and crafting an undeniable classic (although usually I resent altering the book, in this case, the adaptation is so much better than the source material – see Best Picture for more).

Trouble in Paradise remains an extremely witty script. Samson Raphaelson wrote the screenplay, based on an adaptation by Grover Jones of a play by Aladar Laszlo. Raphaelson was a very successful writer in Hollywood, from *The Jazz Singer* to Hitchcock's *Suspicion*; he also wrote many times for Lubitsch, including *The Merry Widow* and

The Shop Around the Corner. Raphaelson deserved a nomination (see Best Picture and Best Director for more).

When we watch a film, the writing shines through primarily in the plot and the dialogue. After we find out what happens, and we watch again, we are drawn not to what happens, but to the flavors of how it happens, to the magic of the acting, the imagery, and to the words we long to speak ourselves. Great writing can handle repetitive readings – or viewings, in movie terms. Of all these films, which ones bear us through them again and again, and make us feel that we are reading the book itself (or seeing the play)? Using those criteria, *Little Women* rightly earned the Oscar this year (although *The Invisible Man* comes very, very close to winning). Louisa May Alcott herself would have been proud of this film. The Academy got this one right.[36]

Best Short Subject (Cartoon): Disney's *Three Little Pigs* won, over their own *Building a Building*, and Walter Lantz, *The Merry Old Soul*

Disney deservedly won. As no less an expert than Chuck Jones noted, *The Three Little Pigs* was the shifting point of animation into a true art form: "The biggest thing Disney contributed was that he established the idea of individual personality…he and a fellow named Ub Iwerks…created the idea that you could make an animated cartoon character who had a personality and wasn't just running and leaping in the air like tiny toons. The breakthrough really was *Three Little Pigs*…that's where personality was developed."[xxix] Little comic touches abound, even in the background; the first pig has female piggy pinups; the brick house pig has a picture labeled "Father" on the wall – and the picture shows sausages. This cartoon and the song "Who's Afraid of the Big Bad Wolf?" genuinely helped Americans work their way through the darkest days of the Great Depression. FDR's election seemed to go hand in hand: "The only thing we have to fear is fear itself." Heady days, when some ink and celluloid and a tune could change the mood of a nation. A well-earned Oscar.

As for the other nominations, *Building a Building* featured Mickey and Minnie Mouse, in glorious black and white. Set on a construction site, Mickey defends Minnie's honor against the villainous Peg Leg Pete,

---

[36] Tino Ballio makes the observation that *Little Women* began an extended attempt by Hollywood to gain legitimacy by adapting the classics, as in the adaptations of Shakespeare, Dickens and Tolstoy which would soon follow this movie's success. The movie companies made sure that teacher lesson plans were distributed for many of these films, to encourage acceptance – and attendance – in the hinterlands. *Grand Design*, p. 63.

with a bunch of comic gags thrown in. Average Mickey fare, but fun, and worth a nomination.

Walter Lantz, who would later be more famous for inventing Woody Woodpecker, did his best with *The Merry Old Soul*, which featured the character stolen from Walt Disney, Oswald the Lucky Rabbit. As a teacher, I'm opposed to plagiarism; as a moral human being, I'm opposed to theft. Oh, wait – that's the same thing, and still wrong. Oswald was brazenly taken from Disney through a crooked contract, which providentially forced him to invent Mickey. No nomination should have been given to Lantz, even if this cartoon does have decent caricatures of Chaplin, Garbo, Keaton, Joe E. Brown, Laurel and Hardy, Will Rogers and others (which explains the nomination more than anything else).

Still, the Fleischer Studio should have received a nod for their seminal Betty Boop cartoon, *Snow White*. Roland C. Crandall singlehandedly animated this milestone, much of it to the music of Cab Calloway. Betty Boop plays Snow White, of course. But the reason people remember this is the middle section, when Ko-Ko starts singing "St. James Infirmary Blues" and the animation becomes surreal. This *Snow White* is the complete opposite of the Disney Snow White, and one that has become a cult classic.

Best Short Subject (Novelty): I'm beginning the trend of ignoring short subjects, this time for Novelty. *Krakatoa* won. I'm not going to argue with a volcano – are you?

WHAT THEY GOT WRONG:

The Academy is improving...somewhat. They persist in nominating glossy melodramatic fecal matter, but then, that still goes on today. Any year where they recognize Charles Laughton, Katharine Hepburn, and Walt Disney increases their batting average substantially. But then, given that they've been batting less than .100, that isn't very hard to do. Their worst decision this year? Handing three Oscars to one of the most putrid movies ever made, *Cavalcade*.

Best Picture: *Cavalcade*
Best Actor: Charles Laughton, *The Private Life of Henry VIII*
Best Director: Frank Lloyd, *Cavalcade*
Best Writing (Original Story): Robert Lord, *One Way Passage*
Best Cinematography: Charles Bryant Long, Jr., *A Farewell to Arms*
Best Art Direction: William S. Darling, *Cavalcade*

Best Sound Recording: Paramount, *A Farewell to Arms*
Best Short Subject (Comedy): RKO, *So This Is Harris*

Best Picture: *Cavalcade* won, over *A Farewell to Arms, 42nd Street, I Am a Fugitive from a Chain Gang, Lady for a Day, Little Women, The Private Life of Henry VIII, She Done Him Wrong, Smilin' Through,* and *State Fair*

Once again, they nominated a pile of films, and gave the Oscar to the worst of their choices. I will trade you *Cavalcade, A Farewell to Arms, She Done Him Wrong, Smilin' Through* and *State Fair* for *Duck Soup, The Invisible Man, King Kong, M,* and *The Mummy*. The Academy's prejudices against comedy and horror again prevented them from seeing genius. Let's give the Academy credit however: they did nominate one of the best musicals (*42nd Street*), a groundbreaking film of social realism and injustice (*Chain Gang*), Frank Capra (*Lady for a Day*), George Cukor and Katherine Hepburn (*Little Women*), and Charles Laughton (*The Private Life of Henry VIII*). But as we shall see, they left out so many great films, in favor of garbage.

And speaking of garbage, as Scott Eyman has written, *Cavalcade* received "undeserved success."xxx *Cavalcade* is based on a Noel Coward play, which should mean some measure of sophisticated wit. The movie tells the story of an English family, beginning in the dark days of the Boer War in 1899, on the verge of the twentieth century. We learn all this in the introductory titles. That's the best part of the film; it all goes downhill from there. The acting is veddy, veddy, veddy British. But if the British ever actually talked like that and acted like that, I will eat blood pudding. Everybody is insufferably posing, emoting, and pronunciating throughout the movie. The upper classes are good looking; the lower classes are not. The servants are happy to be servants (and unhappy when not serving); everybody wants to fight for the empire; a couple in love has nothing but love; everybody is dressed beautifully, and dirt doesn't exist (you'd think this was an MGM picture rather than Fox). The youngest son can't stop being all upper class and bouncy; I'm shocked he doesn't bound into a scene and yell, "Tennis, anyone?" Bad things do happen, but only to make a point, or to show how veddy, veddy serious this all is supposed to be. Get drunk and break your daughter's doll? You get run over by a fire wagon and die. Muse about the nature of love and suggest it isn't permanent, and an iceberg takes you down when you honeymoon on the Titanic. This is what passes for irony in this movie. Want to show how awfully wrong war is? You get killed on the last day of the war. Is it irony if it's this obvious? Historically, Anglophilia is an occupational hazard in Hollywood, and often for good reason. *Cavalcade* isn't one of them, and should have received no Oscar and no nomination. There's a damn good reason the film is hardly ever seen today. I could have gone the rest of my life without it.

Ernest Hemingway had an opinion on Hollywood's take on *A Farewell to Arms*: he told the producers to place it in their anal cavity. He was furious about the alternate ending in which Catherine survives, among other artistic obscenities. But even in the main version where she dies, director Frank Borzage has taken the tragic love story and removed the tragic. *A Farewell to Arms* is about loss: the loss of World War I, the loss of life, the loss of innocence, the loss of love, loss, loss, loss. Hemingway was one of the great writers of the twentieth century, combining that deeply tragic sense of the world with the cleanest, simplest style in the history of the English language.[37] Because his novels and stories are deceptively easy to read, Hollywood has raided them many times, and only rarely captured what Hemingway was actually saying. While the cast of this film was fine – Gary Cooper and Adolphe Menjou in particular – the master of romantic melodrama Borzage failed to perceive the story he had on his hands, and cheapened this classic tale. Yes, touches exist to suggest bad things are happening: the dead soldier who opens the film; the references to dying soldiers; the chain of ambulances (which look like toys, because they are); the disgrace of out-of-wedlock pregnancy; and on a surprising note, the apparently forced seduction of the virginal nurse (a scene that departs from the novel substantially). All too often, as someone once said of Kurt Vonnegut, these touches bittercoat the sugar pill. Sheer window dressing. Little is wrong with Cooper in the role of Frederic Henry, or Menjou as the Italian doctor. Cooper became one of Hemingway's best friends, and even served as the inspiration for the character of Robert Jordan in *For Whom the Bell Tolls,* which Cooper then went on to play in the screen version. I can even stand Helen Hayes as Catherine (even though I can't see why Gary Cooper should find her so beautiful). But the film only presents the romantic side of the story, or uglies things up for fake effect, and keeps almost none of the tragic qualities that make the novel so deeply rich. Want an example? The film stages a bombing raid, for the sole purpose of having Cooper and Hayes do the "cute meet" so beloved in romances. About halfway through, they depart from the novel almost entirely and turn it into dreck (although the great retreat is handled well, even though the reason is never explained,

---

[37] For those of you who think he was a misogynist, sexist, macho faker, I suggest you shut up and go read "Up in Michigan," the single finest portrayal in American literature of the anguish a young girl can experience at the hands of a man.

which was one of Hemingway's main objections). The ending is an incredibly well-acted betrayal of Hemingway (screenwriter Oliver H.P. Garrett prostituted Faulkner's *Sanctuary* similarly in 1933's *The Story of Temple Drake*, completely reversing the ending of the classic novel). No nomination should have been given.

Moving along, *42nd Street* has a number of things going for it: a great choreographer in Busby Berkeley, a great title song, another standard in "You're Getting to Be a Habit with Me," and some snappy dialogue. My favorite line: "It must have been hard on your mother not having any children." Other than that, and given we have to put up with Warner Baxter, George Brent and Dick Powell, what have we got? Competent but hardly inspired direction from Lloyd Bacon, Bebe Daniels failing to impress again after the awful *Broadway Melody*, Ruby Keeler's uninspired singing and enthusiastic but limited dancing, a very young Ginger Rogers playing a loose girl named "Anytime Annie," a functional but hardly interesting plot of a producer broke and likely to have another nervous breakdown, and the usual cornball romances. So why do we still watch *42nd Street*? Busby Berkeley, Busby Berkeley, and Busby Berkeley. A giant train set. Multiple inlaid circular, rotating stages. A city skyscape made out of dancers. Once you get to the actual show, and Berkeley does things nobody has ever done before in the history of entertainment with synchronization and overhead camera shots and unbelievable set decoration, you will see why *42nd Street* works and why backstage musicals have copied it ever since. Moreover, this is the film that resurrected the movie musical and made it a regular offering in the theaters for the next three decades. As it is pre-Code, sexual references and innuendo abound, which gives it a realism that musicals would omit until the genre stopped being made (with rare exception).

All told, three great musicals emerged this year: *42nd Street*, *Gold Diggers of 1933*, and *Footlight Parade*. What do all three of them have in common? Warner Brothers and Busby Berkeley. *Gold Diggers* was directed by Mervyn LeRoy, who was set to helm *42nd Street* until his health sidetracked him. *Gold Diggers* has another great song, "We're in the Money"; Ruby Keeler and Ginger Rogers are back, as are several of the supporting cast. Warner Brothers got smart; this time, they started with a Berkeley number, with Rogers singing and a whole chorus line dressed up in coins (Rogers was dating Mervyn LeRoy at the time; this film got her noticed by RKO, which cast her with Fred Astaire in *Flying Down to Rio*). In many ways, *Gold Diggers* is a more interesting film than *42nd Street*, because it doesn't take itself as seriously, which is odd for a film about the Depression – but the ending is one of the most serious responses to the Depression ever put on film. *Gold Diggers* casts off most of the things that bored us. Much of this is due to Mervyn LeRoy, and learning from *42nd Street*. Joan Blondell helps. We see little person Billy Barty as a baby who escapes from his stroller. Dick Powell is substantially better than in *42nd Street*. Warren Williams and Guy Kibbee are perfect supporting cast. Granted, *Gold Diggers* is basically *42nd Street* done over again, but who cares? After "We're in the Money" with a Pig Latin chorus at the end, Berkeley outdoes himself with "The Shadow Waltz" – neon violins, anyone? – and "Remember My Forgotten Man," which may be the most famous musical number to point straight at the Depression.

Finally, we get Jimmy Cagney hoofing it in *Footlight Parade*. Cagney began as a song and dance man. His first theatrical job, believe it or not, was in drag! His style remains unique and vivid. Once again, Warner Brothers put Busby Berkeley in charge of the choreography; this time, unfortunately, we get Lloyd Bacon back directing. No classic songs appear either. That doesn't matter as much as it might, with James Cagney and Joan Blondell leading us. Ruby Keeler and Dick Powell are back, with comic relief from Guy Kibbee and Cagney pal Frank McHugh. Yes, *Footlight Parade*, like *Gold Diggers*, is more or less another remake of the backstage musical. But when you've got Cagney, especially in his prime, you've got verve and excitement. Berkeley does three main numbers, steadily increasing in complexity and originality, but none of them quite matching *Gold Diggers*. Cagney is the reason to watch, but in terms of overall quality, *42nd Street* should have been replaced with *Gold Diggers of 1933* for the nomination: better songs, better numbers, better overall plot. Now, if Warners had only cast Cagney in all three musicals!

I Am a Fugitive from a Chain Gang is Warner Brothers at their realistic, social consciousness best, driven by Darryl F. Zanuck before he left the studio. Directed by Mervyn LeRoy, the film and the book on which it was based led to the breakup of chain gangs, thus making it one of the handful of films which actually changed American history. The movie crusades against the persecution of the innocent and the brutality with which society punishes its criminals; Warner Brothers often hit that theme, including another 1933 picture, *The Mayor of Hell*, starring Jimmy Cagney as a political appointee turned reformer of a juvenile penitentiary. Such protests played well in the inner city theater chains Warners owned. *Chain Gang* plays the injustice for all its worth, and earned its Oscar nomination.

Lady for a Day remains a sentimental winner, with Damon Runyan's street sense and Capra's growing mastery driving this story of a gangster helping a poor alcoholic woman pretend to be rich for a single day. Definitely worth watching, and the nomination makes perfect sense even today. Originally, Capra wanted Marie Dressler for Apple Annie, James Cagney or William Powell for Dave the Dude, and W.C. Fields for Apple Annie's pretend husband. What he got instead were three actors turning in the greatest performances of their careers, in a picture that showed Capra at the top of his game. One can well understand Capra thinking he was the Frank that Will Rogers was summoning up – after all, *Cavalcade* was a lousy movie to beat his heartwarming piece of Americana. Until WWII, Capra could do almost no wrong as a director. After WWII, except for *It's a Wonderful Life*, he could do no right. The hitting streak accelerates with *Lady for a Day*, a solid nomination by the Academy.

The 1933 *Little Women* persists as the best adaptation of this often-filmed Louisa May Alcott novel for two reasons: George Cukor and Katharine Hepburn. From the opening titles looking like a nineteenth century Christmas card to the final scenes, this adaptation is literate and brimming with the spirit of antebellum New England. Edna May Oliver is a delightful old coot as Aunt March. Hepburn brings a kind of no-nonsense, gruff edge to her character, which was new to feminine sensibilities, and can still surprise viewers expecting a more gentle approach. All of the actresses do a fine job bringing these little women to life. *Little Women* enchants us still, and deserves its nomination.

Without a doubt, *The Private Life of Henry VIII* belongs on the list for Best Picture. The entire film is lavishly decorated and costumed, the supporting performances are as good as they got in this era, and Charles Laughton remains unmatched in his portrayal of Henry VIII. Alexander Korda produced and directed. The camerawork is inventive, the sound excellent, the dialogue both witty and bawdy, and the narrative flow serviceable. My only complaint lies in them leaving out the historical impact of his epic horniness, the cataclysm of which drove England out of the Catholic fold, laid the roots of the Spanish Armada, and set England on the path to world domination. But then, that would have made a very different film; what *Private Life* wants to do is let Laughton play around, be naughty, and storm about in kingly ways. As such, it's a lark, with some tremendous acting.

She Done Him Wrong is of a lesser variety of naughty spree. I'm not sure how the film ever got nominated for Best Picture. Mae West is fun, but only for brief moments. I realize some readers may be throwing this book across the room right now, especially after I forgave the Marx Brothers for how bad huge bleeding chunks of their movies are. Allow for this fundamental difference: the Marx Brothers don't care about how poor their supporting cast and story are, because they're just there to have fun and be subversive. In a Mae West movie, she behaves as if all the bad acting and poor excuse for a plot actually matter. Yes, she is still tossing off that marvelous attitude and those drawled innuendos that must have shocked and titillated, and I do find her very sexy (more so than Jean Harlow, quite often – but then, I've always found smart women sexier). Most famous line? "Why don't you come up some time and see me?" But Cary Grant hasn't really learned to be Cary Grant yet (he and Mae West are both more interesting and better directed in their next film, *I'm No Angel*). I suspect Paramount threw their support behind this and *A Farewell to Arms*; Mae West was keeping Paramount afloat financially. How else did they leave off Ernst Lubitsch, for either *Design for Living* or *Trouble in Paradise*? *She Done Him Wrong* tries one too many plot lines, one too many love interests, an attempted suicide, and a stereotypical black maid who serves as the punching bag for Mae West's wit once too often (once is too often). Example: she calls her maid "eightball." The Jewish stereotype isn't much better. *She Done Him Wrong* should not have received a nomination.

The same goes for *Smilin' Through*. The only good thing I can say about *Smilin' Through* is that it isn't *Cavalcade* – but that's like saying being crapped on by a seal is better than being crapped on by a walrus. I can't even begin to describe how ridiculous the plot is, but I suspect the writers at MGM had discovered reefer madness, and not in a good way (not that there is any good way; too many great artists have been rendered powerless by that stuff...but then, let's not bring up Paul McCartney right now). While I've got the opportunity, here's one of the puzzling mysteries of the Thirties: how did Leslie Howard ever get to be a star? Perhaps I've seen *Gone with the Wind* one too many times, but the man's the walking definition of a wimp. I can appreciate intelligence, class and sensitivity in a man – after all, I see myself in the mirror every day – but Leslie Howard isn't doing much more than a bad imitation of any of that in most of his movies. I am grateful to him, because he more or less gave Humphrey Bogart his career by insisting that he be cast in *The Petrified Forest*, but how he ever became a leading man is as much a mystery as how the bellicose Teddy Roosevelt ever got the Nobel Peace Prize. Here, we are asked to believe in the kind of quack spiritualism that was rife in the Twenties. From the opening shots of *Smilin' Through*, I refused to buy into the plot, because it's done with so little grace and so much earnestness. Have these people never heard of irony or self-deprecation? Failing that, how about a good swift kick in the rear? The cinematography is done well, thanks to Lee Garmes, and Fredric March is effective at times (and again, as she did in *A Free Soul,* Norma Shearer gets better in a strong male's company, but only when the tone is comic or sexual). However, that's not enough to save this turkey. The movie should not have been nominated, even if the kid is cute, but Norma Shearer...isn't. Her worst line? "I've been an awful prune." Clearly, this was MGM once again jiggering with the voting to get one of their films on the ballot.

Miracle of miracles, Janet Gaynor actually made a movie where she didn't annoy me...as much. She still sounds like Minnie Mouse, although not quite as charming. Gaynor does a decent turn as Will Roger's daughter in *State Fair*, until she gets all serious and noble – and boring. Of course, Will Rogers prefers his prize hog Blue Boy, but then, so does the man who wants to marry Gaynor. Rogers even went so far as to refuse the gift of the hog after the film was done: "I just wouldn't feel right eatin' a fellow actor."[xxxi] *State Fair* is bucolic humor at its...best. Some nice camerawork on the rides at the state fair, but otherwise, a basic film, with romances (for both brother and sister...and the pigs – guess which love affair is the most interesting?). They should not have given a nomination for this hog slop.

Perhaps because of the year-and-a-half period of eligibility, but also because the studios were so desperate to make money in this deepest year of the Depression that they were willing to take risks, more great films need to be considered in this chapter than in any year before 1939: *Duck Soup, The Invisible Man, King Kong, M* (1933 US premiere), *The Mummy; White Zombie, Sons of the Desert, Dinner at Eight, Boudu Saved from Drowning, Queen Christina, Pilgrimage, Trouble in Paradise, Design for Living, Alice in Wonderland, Bombshell, Baby Face, The Island of Lost Souls, The Bitter Tea of General Yen, American Madness,* and *Flying Down to Rio* (ok, that isn't a great film, but it does have the first pairing of Fred Astaire and Ginger Rogers!).

So, I'm going to offer up appropriate movies that should have been nominated to convince you of their cinematic melt-in-your-eyes goodness, in no particular order (I don't want to be predictable, after all...).

Dinner at Eight is worth watching for one classic scene: Marie Dressler and Jean Harlow walking down the hall together, talking; I have rarely laughed as hard as I have at Dressler stumbling and then telling Harlow, with a pat on the arm, "My dear, that's something you need never worry about it." There – now you have a damn good reason to go watch the movie. Directed by George Cukor, produced by David O. Selznick, and adapted by Frances Marion and Herman J. Mankiewicz from a play by George S. Kaufman and Edna Ferber, *Dinner at Eight* is an obvious attempt to replicate the success of *Grand Hotel* and cash in on the all-star cast. Cukor was on a roll, working with some of the biggest stars MGM had over the previous two years. Cukor would hit his commercial stride with this film, and go on to *Little Women*; both films were in the top ten moneymakers of the year. Selznick, who was married to Louis B. Mayer's daughter Irene, needed that hit to counter the jokes around town that "the son-in-law also rises." *Dinner at Eight* is considerably better than its model, *Grand Hotel*, since it refuses to take itself as seriously, despite the Depression context. The casting considerably improves, with Jean Harlow and Wallace Beery playing nouveau riche westerners, Lionel Barrymore and Billie Burke as their social betters in financial trouble, and Marie Dressler as a bankrupt retired stage star. Overall, well worth a nomination, even with the rough spots (the ingénue Madge Evans among them).

White Zombie may be Lugosi's best film, as a whole film. Lugosi plays Murder Legendre, a zombie master in Haiti. A young woman about to be married becomes another man's obsession, who pays Lugosi to use black magic to draw her to him. Things don't end well. Produced and directed by the independent Halperin brothers, and shot on the cheap in Hollywood, apparently Lugosi took a major hand in rewriting and even directing parts of the movie. *White Zombie* was the first film to use zombies as its subject; its style points the way to Val Lewton's classic, atmospheric horror films of the Forties (most famously, *Cat People*). In some ways very old-fashioned, even to awkwardness, *White Zombie* remains an unusual experience (see Cinematography for more).

Morning Glory should have been nominated. Not a perfect ending, but few movies are more of an insider's version of acting and the theater, with strong performances from C. Aubrey Smith and Adolphe Menjou, and that Oscar-winning performance from Hepburn.

Boudu Saved from Drowning remains a witty, subversive film, directed by Jean Renoir, contrasting the freedom of the classless tramp Boudu, with the social mores and hypocrisies of the bourgeoisie. Boudu is played by Michel Simon, who has a marvelous physicality, including a stunt where he sits suspended in a doorway (Chaplin would have loved this gag). Renoir, the son of the Impressionist painter, would go on to his masterpiece *Grand Illusion* in 1937.

Over in Britain, they imported the director of *Pandora's Box*, G.W. Pabst, to make *The Adventures of Don Quixote*, starring the Russian opera superstar, Feodor Chaliapin, in English, French, and German versions at the same time. The look of Quixote and Sancho Panza is perfect, even if the songs in the English version are not what you would hope for in a Chaliapin film. Well worth a look.

Baby Face may be the ultimate pre-Code film, featuring Barbara Stanwyck as a woman sleeping her way to the top. More than one person has suggested that *Baby Face* is the best introduction to pre-Code movies. I would agree, if for nothing else than the chance to see John Wayne in a rare non-Western film in his period of exile from the A-list after his debut as a star, *The Big Trail*, bombed. Believe it or not, a German shoemaker sets Stanwyck off on her seductive path upward by trying to get her to read Nietzsche. Superwoman, anybody? Her father sells her body; he fails at last, because she decides to take control. As she says to her father, "I'm a tramp, and who's to blame? My father...nothing but men! Dirty rotten men. And you're lower than any of them!" The movie doesn't go in for subtlety; a minute after she lambastes her father, he is killed by his beer still blowing up. Stanwyck watches him burn with satisfaction. The movie gets even more daring from there. The influence of *The Crowd* is clear, as the camera moves up the skyscraper, jumping up levels as Lily works her way up the bedroom ladder. Great jazz and blues soundtrack too – using "St. Louis Woman" as a motif works very well, since the song is about a prostitute. The ending is about as fake as fake could be, but probably mandated by the expectations of the audience. Despite that falsehood, for sheer chutzpah, *Baby Face* should grab a nomination...and shake it in your face.

As should Greta Garbo in *Queen Christina*, directed by Rouben Mamoulian. Garbo forced MGM to cast her former lover John Gilbert in the part of her lover in the movie, over their strident objections (Gilbert was an alcoholic on his last legs, and had proven to be box-office death). Gilbert is effective and charming; if only he had been in this kind of movie when sound began, he might have made the transition. C. Aubrey Smith gives one of his best performances as Christina's simple, gruff manservant. Like most MGM productions, the sets and costumes are elaborate. Considerable gender-bending takes place; in 1934, this movie could not have been made. The final scenes have a power and grace Garbo never reached before.

Let's turn to four horror films the Academy was snobbish enough to ignore completely. James Whale made his first nearly perfect film with *The Invisible Man*, allowing his black comic genius to emerge. Yes, *Frankenstein* is amazing, but I cringe at the bad acting Whale let slip there. Claude Rains became a hit in a film where he wasn't even seen until he was dead. Rains' voice made him a star. John P. Fulton's special effects made him invisible. Una O'Connor is her usual hysteric self. The opening images of Rains coming through the snow, and into the inn, are indelible, as are many other scenes, especially the unveiling scene: "He's all eaten away!" Whale's humor revels in the naughty idea of a naked man running around (even with pants on, singing "Here we go gathering nuts in May."). Throughout, *The Invisible Man* is a delight.

H.G. Wells was adapted twice this year, with Charles Laughton in *The Island of Lost Souls*. Laughton gives the greatest performance in cold calculation and cruelty as a mad scientist – and I include Colin Clive's insane turn as Dr. Frankenstein. Supported by Bela Lugosi in a bit role as the Sayer of the Law, with – believe it or not – Alan Ladd and Randolph Scott made up as two of the creatures, Laughton is malevolently good.

Karl Freund, a master cinematographer, made his directorial debut with *The Mummy*. Boris Karloff created his second screen legend with Imhotep, the Mummy, enduring hours of agonizing makeup for one brief scene as the mummy, then more to age him for his modern incarnation, Ardath Bey. I think William K. Everson said it best in *Classics of the Horror Film*: *The Mummy* is "the closest that Hollywood ever came to creating a poem out of horror."[xxxii] Endless remakes would attempt to recapture the magic; all of them fail. Karloff the Uncanny – as he was uniquely billed – remains unmatched in the role. Freund was not an actor's director; much of the surrounding cast is as wooden and unbelievable as they were in *Dracula*, which he had shot for director Tod Browning.

If *M* doesn't scare the fecal matter out of you, you're probably as evil as Peter Lorre's character, a child murderer. Granted the film was made in 1931, but it didn't premiere here in the U.S. until 1933, which makes it eligible (see below in Best Actor and Best Director, for more). *M* remains a masterpiece.

Going from terror to laughter, we turn to Stan and Ollie. Laurel and Hardy never made a better full length picture than *Sons of the Desert*, with the possible exception of *Way Out West*. For once, they found an idea that could sustain an entire picture: the boys want to go to a convention; their wives don't. Everything proceeds from there. The gags roll out fresh, from the "exhausted ruler" to a happy Stan at the end. If it wasn't for *Duck Soup*, I'd say *Sons of the Desert* was the funniest film of the year.

Like Laurel and Hardy, Frank Capra was on a roll. *American Madness* and *The Bitter Tea of General Yen* preceded *Lady for a Day* – and his next film would be *It Happened One Night*. *American Madness* shows us the banking system at its worst and its best. Walter Huston does a good turn as the head of a bank in serious trouble. The opening of *American Madness* shows the interior workings of a bank better than anybody else ever has; the power and security of the safe is undercut by the frailty and weaknesses of the men who work in it. Money seems to be so much paper, except to those with power, like gangsters and crooked bankers. Huston's character does his best to make banking into a human affair, which personalizes the Great Depression. He's the mirror image of Mr. Potter from *It's a Wonderful Life.* Indeed, many of the elements from *American Madness* were reworked into that later film, including the bank run and the good will of the community towards the compassionate banker. Capra also worked on a new way to speed up the film: "I speeded up the pace of the scenes to about one-third of a normal scene. If a scene played normally in sixty seconds, I increased the actors' pace until it played in forty seconds. When *American Madness* opened, there was a sense of urgency, a new interest, at work. The audience loved it."[xxxiii]

From Americana, we go East. *The Bitter Tea of General Yen* is a truly unusual film, in which a forbidden love between an Asian general and a white missionary woman was explored. Not surprisingly, it bombed at the box office, given the typical anti-Asian prejudices of the American public at the time (take a look at the Jeanne Eagels version of *The Letter* for a particularly ugly example). Swedish actor Nils Asther played General Yen. Capra was already pushing Hollywood's limits; to actually cast a Chinese actor to play Yen would have broken them; Yen's suicide at the end seems to have been the only acceptable way to tell this story for Capra. Barbara Stanwyck played the missionary. After being captured by the General and held in hopes of a seduction, in a dream Stanwyck sees a barbaric and stereotyped Asther breaking into her bedroom to rape her; a European clothed and masked Asther then breaks in to save her, revealing himself to her, and then we see the screen's first Asian-Caucasian kiss. Capra is deliberately playing with images to try and get the audience to consider their own stereotypes: a traditional Chinese man isn't acceptable, but an assimilated one...is? *Bitter Tea* is a very complex film, at times unaware of how it is promoting the very images it is questioning; *Bitter Tea* needs to be seen by anyone trying to understand the ways that stereotypes and unspoken assumptions craft our sense of The Other in American culture.

Pilgrimage is such a good film, and not one which John Ford fans tend to remember – including myself. Watching *Pilgrimage* for the first time, after a lifetime of my father encouraging me to love John Wayne and Henry Fonda in Ford films, remains one of the highlights of writing this book (see Best Actress above and Best Director below for more). That this film wasn't nominated for any awards whatsoever is one of the many sins of the year for the Academy.

After nominating two films the previous year directed by Ernst Lubitsch, the Academy proceeded to ignore perhaps his best film, *Trouble* in *Paradise*, and his most subversive, *Design for Living*. Maybe they missed Maurice Chevalier, who wasn't in either. Lubitsch's first non-musical comedy of the sound era, and considered by many to be his best film, *Trouble in Paradise* begins, continues, and ends in irony. For a movie that promises sexual paradise (the titles are set over a bed), we open with a short, fat unattractive man dumping garbage into a gondola...and then beginning to sing "O Sole Mio" the way gondoliers do for lovers in Venice. A crime has been committed, and all we see are the shadows of the thief as he removes his disguise. We then cut to Herbert Marshall, playing a well-dressed "Baron" being offered a menu; he announces, to the waiter, what must have been Lubitsch's inside joke about movie-making: "Beginnings are always difficult."[38] Lubitsch then signals to us, subtly, that the Baron is not nobility, but the thief, by showing a small leaf stuck to his clothes. His love interest, played by Miriam Hopkins, is also masquerading as nobility; she is a pickpocket. Almost everybody in *Trouble in Paradise* is pretending to be someone else. Edward Everett Horton, like Karloff, is always worth watching, even in bad films; here he plays Marshall's victim.[39] Irony, irony, irony. We expect a kiss; we get a shakedown. Deep in the film, Lubitsch sets up this wonderful shot of two mirrors and a bed that implies so much more than is being said. As Scott Eyman put it so well, the film is a "dazzling Mobius strip of erotic collusion, genial irony, and...visual lyricism and elegance"[xxxiv] Lubitsch was rarely better than *Trouble in Paradise*.

And rarely more controversial than he was in *Design for Living*. Based on a Noel Coward play (as was the awful *Cavalcade*), *Design for Living* stars Fredric March, Gary Cooper, and Miriam Hopkins (who was also in *Trouble in Paradise*). Ben Hecht wrote the screenplay. Favorite line? "A bicycle seat is a little hard on Lady Godiva's... historical background." To watch the three leads go round and round in friendship, love, rivalry and passion is to see Lubitsch thumbing his nose at all the censors in America. And yet, he gets away with it – and America loved it, putting *Design for Living* in the top ten earning films of the year. I honestly don't think this movie could be made today, with a major cast and director, and still come up with the same sexual answer this film does. While not a perfect movie, *Design for Living* remains worth watching.

---

[38] Marshall was missing a leg from WWI, but doesn't look like he has a wooden leg in his elegance.
[39] Those of us who grew up watching *Rocky and Bullwinkle* know Horton best as the narrator of *Fractured Fairy Tales*.

So, *Trouble in Paradise* should have gotten Lubitsch a nomination. He reached an artistic and commercial high this year. A few years ago, the American Film Institute put out their best 100 film list; notoriously, Lubitsch was nowhere to be found. I suspect that these pre-Code works were not a part of the viewing childhood of those critics; I know I had never seen these movies before writing this book, because they were never on mainstream television, then or now. They deserve far wider recognition.

In addition, one of the most unusual pictures ever made is the anthology picture, *If I Had a Million*. Eight directors, including Ernst Lubitsch who guided the project, worked with almost thirty writers to produce these tales of total strangers being given a million dollars each. In this year of the Depression, the idea of a million dollars being dropped out of the sky was very exciting. The stars included Gary Cooper, Charles Laughton, and W.C. Fields. The Fields bit about roadhogs is priceless. Not a picture I would nominate for this highest award, but one you really should see at least once.

And now, I've got just two words for you: *King Kong*. Okay, more than two words: Fay Wray, screaming. Dinosaurs. The Empire State Building. Biplanes. What has to be a candidate for the greatest last line of any film: "'Twas Beauty killed the Beast." I've watched it well over a hundred times since I was a child, and *King Kong* still fascinates. You have no idea how desperately I want to make this the Best Picture of the year. But if I did that, I would have to betray the Marx Brothers and their finest achievement.

Duck Soup nearly ended the Marx Brothers' careers. Were it not for Chico Marx playing cards with Irving Thalberg, we might never have had *A Night at the Opera*. Chico was an infamous gambler; he and Thalberg often played together, and one night, they got to talking about the end of the brothers' Paramount contract because of *Duck Soup* failing at the box office. Thalberg offered them a chance at MGM and the hit of *A Night at the Opera*. *Duck Soup* is the quintessential Marx Brothers movie, finally stripped of all the idiocies one has to use the fast-forward button to get past. Leo McCarey, the great comedy director who had first worked with Laurel and Hardy, matched the Marx Brothers (most of their directors were second-rate hacks). The boys went after war itself in this picture, ridiculing national posturing and aggression by showing its roots in egotistical maniacs and petty jealousies. Benito Mussolini banned the picture, because he thought it was aimed at him; the Marx Brothers were "ecstatic."[xxxv] Arguably, this is the greatest comedy ever made. Despite the astonishing competition, *Duck Soup* should have won the Oscar for Best Picture of the year.

Best Actor: Charles Laughton won for *The Private Life of Henry VIII*, over Leslie Howard, *Berkeley Square*; and Paul Muni, *I Am a Fugitive from a Chain Gang*

Before discussing Laughton's performance, let's examine the two actors who lost.

As for Leslie Howard, perhaps the less said the better (see *Smilin' Through* in Best Picture for why). In the once-lost *Berkeley Square*, Howard plays a man transported back in time to London shortly after the period of the American Revolution, to meet his ancestors. Apparently, H.P. Lovecraft, the great horror story writer, loved this film (he would, with his rampant Anglophilia and dislike of the modern).[xxxvi] As for me, TCM made it possible to see *Berkeley Square* shortly before going to press. I may never forgive TCM or read Lovecraft again. Lovecraft had clearly lost his sanity to Cthulhu by the time this movie came out. The movie is little but talk, talk, talk. Howard is more robust than usual, although still trapped in a dream state as an actor. Regardless, he's the only one in the movie with even a semblance of charisma to him, but that's not saying much. Howard should not have been nominated.

Paul Muni's performance in *I Am a Fugitive from a Chain Gang* remains brilliant. In most of these early years, he would have won, particularly given his growing reputation as a very versatile actor. His performing style has moved away from the staginess that plagued his acting in *Scarface*, and that's all to the better; Muni plays an everyman who is looking for a place in life after the horrors of WWI. A quieter, more natural approach served that purpose well, even if he slipped into the old habits occasionally. He earned the nomination.

Let's put off Laughton again, and let me recommend three more actors, all of whom should have been nominated: Fredric March, Claude Rains, and John Barrymore.

Fredric March starred with Cary Grant and Carole Lombard in the WWI flying film, *The Eagle and the Hawk*. Grant starts off awkwardly in the harsher role, but improves as the character becomes more human; March begins as a joyful fellow, then turns steadily more dejected and depressed as the war grinds him down. Many of the fight scenes are lifted from *Wings* and *The Dawn Patrol*, but this film makes an antiwar statement as powerful as that of *All Quiet on the Western Front*. March's performance is the best of his career up to this point, as good if not better than *Dr. Jekyll*. The only explanation I have for his omission here is his win in the previous year. By itself, the look on his face when he sees the first casualty of war should have earned him a nomination.

In *The Invisible Man*, Claude Rains had to act with none of his face showing – and in some scenes, with none of his body either. Everything had to be done through body language and voice. Watch a scene or two in the movie twice: first, with the sound turned off, and see if you don't agree that you know what is going on anyways, with just gestures from Rains; then turn the sound back on, and look away, and see if the voice doesn't do the same thing. Rains gives us one of the subtle, enduring performances in horror history, which I would rank only behind Karloff as Frankenstein. Rains deserved a nomination.

John Barrymore's performance in *Dinner at Eight* may be the most honest thing he ever did. Essentially, he played himself, exposing his age, alcoholism, and ruined life that rooted the heart of this biting comedy to the life of the performer who has run his course. Barrymore deserved a nomination for finally dropping the mannerisms and the fakery for a wrenching farewell to the acting profession. After this film, he would rarely find material worthy of him (a notable exception being next year's *Twentieth Century*, directed by Howard Hawks). If you ever want proof of how good a director George Cukor was, watch *Dinner at Eight*. Barrymore should have been nominated.

And now, back to the original winner for Best Actor, Charles Laughton in *The Private Life of Henry VIII*. Laughton's win marked the first time a performer won the Oscar for a performance filmed outside of the United States. Laughton's take on the earthy King Henry VIII remains a tour-de-force of this magnificently diverse actor, who seldom made a film that was not eminently watchable. Korda begins the story on the day Anne Boleyn is executed, thus omitting both Catharine of Aragon and the departure of England from the Catholic Church. That material is covered brilliantly in other films, most finely in *A Man for All Seasons*, but not here. Laughton gets the chance to play the lusty king from the height of his power to a doddering remnant, with each stage done to perfection. His appearance, after minutes of setup, suitably impresses with the royal stature of a monarch. People were genuinely surprised when Laughton won, but when you watch his performance as Nero in *The Sign of the Cross*, released very soon after *Private Life*, it makes more sense. Laughton went from the most openly heterosexual performance ever done in film to the most openly homosexual performance in under three months at the movie houses. Seeing these two parts is like seeing two entirely different actors. Add in the performance those two sandwich, in *The Island of Lost Souls*, and you've got a remarkable actor on a roll. Therefore, it pains me to argue he should not have received this Oscar, because I so love his performance.

But another non-American deserved it even more, for the searing highlight of his entire career: Peter Lorre, in *M*. Directed by Fritz Lang in what may be the best film for either of them, Peter Lorre evokes more sheer evil than almost any other performance in movie history. Much as I love Lon Chaney, Sr. and Boris Karloff, Lorre's child murderer terrifies me far more; aware as we are today of the presence of these monsters in our lives, the reality of the character's depravity haunts our dreams after seeing this movie. Lorre's face is infinitely malleable, revealing a wide range of emotions with just a look. I enjoy watching Laughton, but having seen Lorre, I know the face of evil. Peter Lorre should have won the Oscar for Best Actor.

Best Director: Frank Lloyd won for *Cavalcade*, over Frank Capra, *Lady for a Day*; and George Cukor, *Little Women*

Frank Lloyd won. I have no idea why. *Cavalcade* is staid, still, and uninspired, like watching bad dinner theater, without the rubbery chicken. Frank Lloyd was a serviceable director, but not more than that. He does handle crowd scenes decently, and he milks the soap opera. But craftsmanship should lead to art, and *Cavalcade* is anything but art. Glossy and mildly diverting, yes, but best? Not even close, so Lloyd should have received no Oscar and no nomination.

As for Frank Capra, who was on his way to becoming the dominant director of the Thirties, *Lady for a Day* is an inventive picture, and well-directed. One can understand his belief that he had been chosen, and his grief that the competent hack Frank Lloyd was the one who beat him. Capra would return to triumph when he swept the next year's awards with *It Happened One Night*. He definitely deserved this, his first nomination.

As did George Cukor, for **Little Women** (and he could just as easily been nominated for **Dinner at Eight**). Cukor would be known for his ability to direct great pictures starring women, and this version of Louisa May Alcott's classic really is one of his major triumphs. While Hepburn would go on to greater roles (including more than one for Cukor), none of the other actresses in this movie ever gave a more touching, robust performance. Between this and **Dinner at Eight**, Cukor proved he could play among the best directors Hollywood had. Cukor should keep his nomination.

Because the Academy was only listing the top three vote-getters, we really don't know who else was up. James Whale should have been for *The Invisible Man*; Alexander Korda should have been for *The Private*

Life of Henry VIII (see Best Actor and Best Picture above for both films). Even more, John Ford should have been included.

From the opening moments of *Pilgrimage,* we are in the presence of a man who is entering into a personal world of artistry after more than a decade of learning his craft and gaining enough commercial clout to wring permission, now and again, for a film to please himself. John Ford remains the greatest director America produced during the studio era, and arguably, in the history of film. Not every film is a masterpiece, but he has a higher percentage than practically anybody else. *Arrowsmith* has nothing on *Pilgrimage*. We begin in rural Arkansas, on a farm set that is reminiscent of F.W. Murnau's for its beauty and reality. These characters are real. Nothing is forced; nothing is artificial; only slight traces here and there show that the film is coming out of early Thirties' acting styles. The simple elegance of his camera setups is striking, but he can also indulge in surprising effects, as when the young man tosses a stone into a dark pool, and the camera watches the surface smooth itself out again into the reflection of the young girl he loves. The emotional honesty and intensity of this film first peaks when the mother receives word that her son has been killed. I rarely cry during movies, but this scene blurred my vision, much as the end of *City Lights* does.

At the opposite end of the emotional spectrum lies Fritz Lang's *M*. From the opening shots of a child singing a song about a murderer then picking out the next "victim" in their game, the clash between childhood innocence and the evil that awaits them in the world is depicted brilliantly. Peter Lorre appears initially in shadows, kindly talking to a child who may be his next target. The first time we see Lorre, he is looking in a mirror as we reflect upon the nature of the murderer, almost as if we ourselves were a suspect. First, we wonder who the killer will be; once we know that, the narrative drive comes from watching the police trying to figure it out. Ultimately, and in a brilliant reversal of the normal expectation that the police will solve the crime, the criminal world hunts down M and puts him on trial. Even today, the one unforgiveable crime in prison is to hurt a child; most child molesters and child murderers have to be kept in solitary confinement or the other inmates will kill them. Lang's evocation of this story continues to make viewers uncomfortable. Lorre's performance, as I've said above, remains riveting and unforgettable. Images drive the tale, which is as it should be: the empty staircase, the empty plate, the empty chair, the ball rolling away, the floating balloon – all pointing at the missing child; the juxtaposition of the leading criminals and the leading policemen brainstorming in smoke-filled rooms; the reflections of the children with kitchen utensils and Lorre's face as he struggles with his compulsion to kill (and eat his victims?); the chalk M the beggars place upon Lorre's shoulder. Lang should have been nominated for Best Director, because he was never better than in this film.

But then, neither was Ernst Lubitsch. As I've pointed out above (in Best Picture), Lubitsch hit all his marks this year in *Trouble in Paradise*. He should have been nominated for Best Director. And in this, perhaps his greatest film, he should have won. Lubitsch perfected the comedy of manners, of attraction, of sex and love and innuendo. *Trouble in Paradise* and *Design for Living* remain hallmarks of comic invention, and social defiance. *M* instills in me a far deeper despair for humanity, but Lubitsch makes me to want to be human all the more. Ernst Lubitsch should have won the Oscar for Best Director.

Best Writing (Original Story): Robert Lord won for *One Way Passage*, over Frances Marion, *The Prizefighter and the Lady*; and Charles MacArthur, *Rasputin and the Empress*

One Way Passage isn't much more than romantic melodrama. William Powell, still too serious for the good of his career, plays a convicted murderer; Kay Francis, near the height of her stardom, plays a woman dying. They fall in love aboard the ship back to San Francisco. Neither one of them know the other is going to die (until they know, but they don't let the other one know they know, but we know they know, so the fact that they don't know that the other one knows...ok, I'll stop now that you know). The comic relief to all this comes from the second pair, Frank McHugh (always good for a laugh) and Aline MacMahon, as a thief and a con artist. The end is so corny you start looking for the butter. *One Way Passage* is the kind of contrived plot Hollywood loves to put across, without a trace of irony. Definitely not the film that deserved the Oscar, and not a movie I'd recommend seeing more than once, unless tragic melodrama is your cup of tea. Given what else they could have given the award to, to hand it to this serviceable, emotionally manipulative, forced, minor film is just incomprehensible. I did enjoy the opening, which lets William Powell be playful, as he would be for most of the rest of his career. It's all downhill after that.

Frances Marion was continuing her string of hits at MGM as the most successful female screenwriter of the Thirties. *The Prizefighter and the Lady* is a truly bizarre film, starring Myrna Loy, and featuring Jack Dempsey, Primo Carnera, and Max Baer. The romance between Loy and Max Baer's character is just an excuse to get to the climax of the film, the fight for the heavyweight championship between Baer and Carnera (which actually happened not too long after this film was released). For boxing fans, worth a look – but not an Oscar nomination. Three other reasons to avoid this film: Max. Baer. Sings.

Rasputin and the Empress is god-awful stuff, with more scene-chewing from the Barrymore brothers, joined by their sister Ethel (this is the only film with all three Barrymores). Nobody believed it then; nobody believes it now. Lionel seems to be channeling his brother's performance as Svengali; jokingly, his beard was called the fourth Barrymore. While there are moments that point towards a decent film, *Rasputin* so badly twisted the truth that the royal wife of one of Rasputin's assassins sued and won. Now if we could just get everyone who is the subject of a Hollywood biopic to sue, we might start actually getting some truth out there. I've gotten to the point where I assume any film that advertises itself as based on a true story is invariably going to prove to be a massive lie. In other words, in Hollywood, the truer a story is supposed to be, the more fictional it is. *Rasputin* is a curiosity piece, and nothing more. No nomination should have been given.

Now we come to the two amazing, original, fabulous stories and screenplays the Academy decided weren't worth their time: *King Kong* and *Duck Soup*. For sheer audacity, neither one of them can be beaten. *Kong* has the plot and the better ending; *Duck Soup* has far better dialogue. I've watched both films more times than I can count. Both deserved nominations: for *Kong*, James A. Creelman and Ruth Rose; for *Duck Soup*, Bert Kalmar and Harry Ruby wrote the story and songs, Arthur Sheekman and Nat Perrin wrote the additional dialogue; the Marx Brothers ad-libbed as well. Both movies were ignored by the Academy. Of the two, I would choose *Duck Soup* for the writing. The Marx Brothers never had a finer script or story. This time, they had an entire country to run – and ruin: Freedonia. Guess who's president? Groucho Marx as Rufus T. Firefly! For once, the plot actually makes sense, although not as much as the jokes: political intrigue, corruption, and war. I have never once fast-forwarded *Duck Soup*. I have used the rewind button a few times. Some things need to be seen more than once to fully savor. Margaret Dumont: "I welcome you with open arms!" Groucho: "Is that so? How late do you stay open?" It goes on for a good five minutes unabated. "You know, you haven't stopped talking since I came here? You must have been vaccinated with a phonograph needle." Harpo and the sidecar. Chicolini and Pinky (Chico and Harpo) as the spies. The lemonade stand. "I've got a good mind to join a club and beat you over the head with it." "I wonder what ever became of me." Groucho wooing Margaret Dumont ("But I can't see the stove.") All the Grouchos. "Well, who you gonna believe, me or your own eyes?" The mirror scene. Chico's trial. And at long last, no harp or piano playing!

That alone should have been worth the Oscar for Best Writing (Original Story)!

Best Cinematography: Charles Bryant Lang, Jr., won for *A Farewell to Arms*, over George Folsey, *Reunion in Vienna*, and Karl Struss, *The Sign of the Cross*

A Farewell to Arms (in its restored version) shows the kind of visual grace Lubitsch had trained Paramount cameramen to shoot in *Trouble in Paradise*. As Scott Eyman points out, Victor Milner's cinematography in *Trouble in Paradise* had a "rich, opulent, luminous surface that became the Paramount house style."[xxxvii] According to the American Society of Cinematographer's obituary of Charles Lang, "the major studios all had a distinctive "look," and the much-emulated Lang style of lighting became heavily identified with Paramount throughout the Thirties and Forties."[40] The ASC may not have been aware that *Trouble in Paradise* preceded *Farewell* by several months on the Paramount lot. The seduction scene owes a great deal to Erich von Stroheim and the apple blossoms in *The Wedding March*. Charles Lang should keep his nomination, but Milner deserved one as well for *Trouble in Paradise*.

George Folsey shot the Marx Brothers' first two movies, as well as a number of musicals and my favorite Hepburn-Tracy comedy, *Adam's Rib*. But for *Reunion in Vienna* for MGM, he only produced the typical MGM gloss. Nothing special here which deserves any nomination.

Karl Struss' work on *The Sign of the Cross* is phenomenal. Scott Eyman points out the craft in his biography of Cecil B. DeMille: "Cameraman Karl Struss revived a trick from the silent days and shot the entire film through a bright red gauze, which gave the images the lambent glow 'of a world remembered,' in Struss' words. In talkies, gauze was used for close-ups, especially for leading ladies, but Struss' gambit gave the film a luminous quality that makes the movie one of DeMille's most exquisite visual experiences."[xxxviii] If Eyman says it, I'm prepared to agree. Watching *The Sign of the Cross* today remains enjoyable largely due to Struss, and the excesses of Laughton and Claudette Colbert as the Emperor Nero and Poppaea; the main love story is unconvincing. The nomination was worthy.

---

[40] To further elucidate: "A studio's specialty genres obviously dictated a certain look. Warners, for example, developed a somber house style for its social-problem pictures. To fit with the realism of these pictures, the style consisted of austere, flat lighting and highly contrasted images. To complement MGM's opulent and sophisticated house style, [art director Cedric] Gibbons imposed on MGM's pictures a consistency of style and mood; settings were bathed in brilliant high-key lighting that created a soft gray-white glossy look." Tino Ballio, *Grand Design*, p. 96.

But other films produced striking achievements in cinematography, and went completely ignored – Victor Milner in *Trouble in Paradise* being a prime case.

White Zombie was shot by Arthur Martinelli, a silent film cameraman whose career lasted thirty years in Hollywood. Done on an extremely low budget, the film has continued to draw fans through its atmosphere and imagery, and the creative choices that had to be made to get the job done. Watch, and pay particular attention to the carriage ride in the night that opens the movie, the scenes in the sugar mills, the use of shadows throughout – and, of course, Lugosi's eyes. Martinelli should have been nominated.

King Kong remains as much a matter of the wizardry of the camera as it is the result of Willis O'Brien's crafting of Kong and his dinosaur opponents, which were carved by Marcel Delgado. The extensive use of glass paintings, rear projection, miniatures, and inserts of live action had never been brought to this level of artistry, and all within the camerawork of Edward Linden, J.O. Taylor, Vernon L. Walker, and Kenneth Peach. Put together with Willis O'Brien's painstaking stop-motion animation, they created a feast for the eyes and imagination. They should have won the Oscar for Best Cinematography.

Best Art Direction: William S. Darling won for *Cavalcade*, over Hans Dreier and Roland Anderson, *A Farewell to Arms*, and Cedric Gibbons, *When Ladies Meet*

Let's dispose of the three the Academy thought merited mention; no nominations were deserved for any of them.

To give the Oscar to William S. Darling for *Cavalcade* is like giving the award to a wax museum that only has figures of your great-grandparents. None of these costumes or sets produces a sense of anything other than being stuck on a bad sound stage without a sandwich. He deserves no award and no nomination.

As for *A Farewell to Arms*, I don't think so. While the look by Hans Dreier and Roland Anderson is reasonable, it isn't as realistic a depiction as the earlier *All Quiet on the Western Front* managed to be. They should not have been nominated.

When Ladies Meet is just more Cedric Gibbons doing his MGM pretty stuff. He often deserved the nominations he got, but not this time. The film is more famous in the Joan Crawford / Robert Taylor version from 1941. A lady writer has a novel with a fictionalized affair; she becomes friends with the wife of the man with whom she had the affair. Pretty nonsense at best, and not deserving of a nomination.

What I really cannot fathom is how the Academy could have ignored the three prime candidates for stunning art direction: *King Kong*, *Alice in Wonderland* and *The Sign of the Cross*. Actually, if we remember studio block voting, I can understand it pretty well: RKO was a minor studio; Paramount threw its support behind *A Farewell to Arms*.

Alice in Wonderland was a big production, with lots of money and invention going into the costuming and set design, trying to bring to life the Tenniel illustrations of the Lewis Carroll classic. They succeeded, through the efforts of William Cameron Menzies (who went uncredited), costumer Newt Jons, and makeup legend Wally Westmore. Since there were no Oscars for costuming and makeup, all three should have a nomination here. Every set is full of surprises. Watching Alice fly down the staircase and out the door still has me scratching my head as to how they did it. Think of the following: Cary Grant as the Mock Turtle; Edna May Oliver as the Red Queen; W.C. Fields as Humpty Dumpty; Gary Cooper as the White Knight; Edward Everett Horton as the Mad Hatter. Wonderful costumes and makeup, verging on the creepy and the fantastic at times, make this movie visually stimulating.

Mitchell Leisen went uncredited for his art direction on *The Sign of the Cross*, Cecil B. DeMille's epic of the persecution of Christians after Nero's burning of Rome. Leisen got credit for the costumes, and although DeMille always had a major hand in the design of his set, Leisen did excellent work. Take one look at Claudette Colbert bathing in a huge tub of ass's milk to see why. The streets of Rome look as if they'd been lived in for centuries; Nero's palace is decadence itself. Leisen deserved a nomination (with DeMille's hand on his shoulder).

We come then to a film that transcends the usual categories and emerges as a myth-making, once-in-a-lifetime experience. *King Kong*, with all its bad acting (Bruce Cabot), hammy acting (Robert Armstrong), and implicit racism, remains the one film from this year that must be seen to be believed. Far better than its more technically advanced homage by Peter Jackson, *King Kong* comes to life, and remains alive, eighty years after its making. Special effects genius Willis O'Brien is the force behind Kong's magic, and even though others have the on-screen credit for this category, all the histories about *Kong* name O'Brien as the man to honor. And so I do as well: Willis O'Brien and his crew should have won the Oscar for Art Direction, for making Kong the stuff of dreams.

Best Sound Recording: Paramount and Franklin Hansen won for *A Farewell to Arms*, over Warner Bros and Nathan Levinson for *42nd Street, Gold Diggers of 1933*, and *I Am a Fugitive from a Chain Gang*

Warner Brothers invents sound...then they never win this award?! Yes, they gave them a special Oscar for inventing the process, but why didn't they ever earn one in these early years? Here they are with three nominees, and the other studio's film wins. Nathan Levinson and Warner Brothers deserve kudos for all three of these movies, not the least of which is the last. The final spoken words of *Chain Gang* are famous, coming out of the darkness: "I steal."

But not the Oscar. Yes, *A Farewell to Arms* has impressive sound, particularly in the small sounds that often are missed in other films of the period. You can hear the difference, if you listen carefully.

But since I'm not going to discuss this category again, it's time for some justice: Warner Brothers should have the Oscar.

Short Subject (Comedy): RKO won, for *So This is Harris*, over RKO; *Preferred List*; and Universal, *Mister Mugg*

I simply can't explain what is wrong with the Academy. After showing their absolute genius the year before in this category with Laurel and Hardy's *The Music Box*, they proceed to name three shorts nobody has ever heard about since – all of which should have been discarded as unworthy.

In this same period, Laurel and Hardy made *Scram!; Their First Mistake; Towed in a Hole; Twice Two; Me and My Pal; Midnight Patrol; Busy Bodies;* and *Dirty Work*. Talk about an embarrassment of riches – especially when you consider they made the full-length *Pack up Your Troubles, Fra Diavolo,* and *Sons of the Desert* that year too. Some of their greatest moments came in these shorts. In *Scram!*, they play vagrants who have an hour to get out of town; trouble ensues with a rich drunk, rain, a piece of gum, a key, an umbrella, a storm drain, and a policeman – and that's just in the second scene. *Their First Mistake* was in bringing home an adopted baby without checking with Oliver's wife first. As Stan says, "You know, I'm not as dumb as you look." The boys also play with confusing some sexual stereotypes (something they did again in *Twice Two*). *Towed in a Hole* has the boys selling fresh fish; Stan suggests they catch the fish too, and cut out the middleman. They buy a boat...and it doesn't go well, except for our laughter. Stan plays tic-tac-toe with himself. *Twice Two* is cross-dressing, gender-bending at its funniest. Stan marries Ollie's sister, and Ollie marries Stan's sister. Guess who plays the sisters? *Me and My Pal* is all about the wedding and the jigsaw puzzle, and that damned last missing piece. *Midnight Patrol* has Stan and Ollie playing cops on the night beat; for once, they get to be the authority figures (and screw up even worse than usual). *Busy Bodies* takes place in a sawmill. Whatever doesn't get destroyed gets cut in half – literally! *Dirty Work* has Stan, Ollie, and a mad scientist. I need say no more than this: Chimney sweep Ollie gets turned into a chimp.

Of all these great shorts, perhaps the finest is *Me and My Pal*. Like *The Music Box, Me and My Pal* is organized around one great idea: a jigsaw puzzle distracts and detains everyone. The Oscar should have gone to this hilarious half hour comedy classic.

Intermission...

PART TWO: 1934-1943

PREVIEW

Prior to the outbreak of WWII, and well into that war's early years, Hollywood was in its greatest glory, creating consistently high levels of commercial art. Oddly enough, it occurred under the harsh restrictions of Joseph Breen and the Production Code, which severely constrained what could and could not be shown on the screen. Beginning on July 1, 1934, every Hollywood film had to pass the stern eye of Breen and his staff, backed up by the power of the newly formed Catholic Legion of Decency. Without Breen's approval, a film literally could not be released without a firestorm of controversy and protests (Howard Hughes used that to his advantage when distributing the non-approved *The Outlaw*, his tribute to Jane Russell's attributes). Working under the censorship of the Breen Office restricted the kinds of stories the studios could produce. In my opinion, having to follow the rules forces people to get more creative. As Robert Frost said, writing poetry without rhyme is like playing tennis without a net. If "anything goes" in an artistic medium, quality tends to go down. What could be daring becomes offensive; what could be risqué becomes blatant. With censorship, a certain artificiality does enter into the worldview, but the root of the word is art, after all. When strict rules are established, the game of learning how to bend without breaking becomes a subversive delight. Little is more fun in art than slipping one past the censors. In the early twenty-first century, we are witnessing the return to traditional forms in music, poetry, and art. Once we're three revolutions past the revolution, all we can really do is put the tennis net back up, because nothing is left to rebel against.

Hollywood's golden age was golden for a reason. The studios could be oppressive; the censors could force a willful denial of reality. But even the B-pictures can be worth watching, and while many of the A-pictures have lost their interest for us, what has remained is higher in both quantity and quality than any similar period. Which, infuriatingly, renders some of the choices the Academy made in their glory years even more bizarre and incomprehensible, until we realize that the studios kept playing games with the voting, and people could still be shortsighted in the face of excellence.

Finally, the calendar year determines the eligibility year, which makes everything a little less confusing. Hollywood is less confused too: the transition to sound has been completed, and actors are finally figuring out how to act and talk at the same time. Now if they can just master the patting-the-head-and-chewing-gum-at-the-same-time routine.

CHAPTER SEVEN: 1935 AWARDS
7th Show

Movies released in 1934

THE SCENE OF THE CRIME:

On February 27, 1935, the glitterati gathered at the Biltmore Bowl in the Biltmore Hotel, hosted by now-forgotten author, actor, and humorist Irvin S. Cobb. Shirley Temple received a special child-sized Oscar, after being called "the loveliest Christmas present that was ever given to the world." No, I have no idea why Cobb said that in February either, but Temple had made nine films in 1934, all of them wildly successful. Walt Disney scored his third Oscar in a row for Best Cartoon, this time *The Tortoise and the Hare*. The Oscars went musical, with the first Best Score and Best Song awards (notorious for how wrong they usually are), as well as a new award for Best Film Editing. I'm going to ignore this new category, as I already have enough to do in this book. I'm going to do the same for Sound Recording. Judging editing requires far more patience and insight then I have the time to acquire; learning to understand style in literature also requires the most effort, and still remains an ongoing project after thirty years of practice. I just can't do editing justice; it literally would require an entirely separate book, to say nothing of an entirely separate professional career (since the first edition, I have made a reasonable stab at it in the Special Features on my accompanying blog "Who Should Have Won the Oscars?" at rjameswhowon.wordpress.com).

For the first time, one film swept the five major Oscars. It would be over forty years before it happened again.

WHAT THEY GOT RIGHT:

Finally, finally, finally the Academy got it right, with four short words: *It Happened One Night*. Why is the movie so great? We get Frank Capra, in full mastery of his American material; crisp, funny, dramatic dialogue from Robert Riskin; and Clark Gable and Claudette Colbert at their absolute best. As Pauline Kael put it, they "became Americans' idealized view of themselves – breezy, likable, sexy, gallant, and maybe just a little harebrained."[xxxix] Capra was given the Best Director award with the same line that had led to his public humiliation the previous year: "C'mon up and get it, Frank!" His same table guests returned to witness this triumph. Frank Capra ruled the night. The audience shouted out the movie's title in unison when it won Best Picture.

Claudette Colbert had to be retrieved from the train station to come and get her Oscar, since she had decided to go on vacation instead; Shirley Temple gave Colbert her award. Prior to the ceremony, in regards to the Best Actress category, furor was unleashed when Bette Davis (*Of Human Bondage*) and Myrna Loy (*The Thin Man*) weren't nominated. A write-in campaign ensued, but to no avail. Bette Davis later claimed her own studio boss Jack Warner had stolen the award from her by ordering all Warners employees to vote for anybody but Davis (whose performance in *Of Human Bondage* was done at RKO, so one can see why Warner wouldn't push for Davis, especially given how argumentative she had been). As one Oscar historian puts it, "There was no way around it. Bette Davis had been passed over on purpose."[xl]

Best Picture: *It Happened One Night* won, and rightly so, over *The Barretts of Wimpole Street, Cleopatra, Flirtation Walk, The Gay Divorcee, Here Comes the Navy, The House of Rothschild, Imitation of Life, One Night of Love, The Thin Man, Viva Villa!,* and *The White Parade*

Again, I offer you a trade: I will give up – forever – *Flirtation Walk, The House of Rothschild, One Night of Love, Viva Villa!* and *The White Parade* in exchange for John Ford's *The Lost Patrol*, Alfred Hitchcock's *The Man Who Knew Too Much*, Ernst Lubitsch's *The Merry Widow*, W.C. Fields' *It's A Gift*, and Howard Hawks' *Twentieth Century*. Any takers? I didn't think so.

It Happened One Night shattered the mold in many ways. The film proved Columbia Pictures and studio head Harry Cohn were no longer on Poverty Row; they had joined the ranks of the major studios. Frank Capra was now the most celebrated director in Hollywood, and would remain so for much of the next decade. A new genre had developed under his guidance and sensibilities, as Donald Spoto points out: "Frank Capra's *It Happened One Night*, released early in 1934, had established screwball comedy as the most successful form of escapist entertainment at the height of the Great Depression. Audiences loved to see the rich satirized and the poor elevated, and they loved romantic endings."[xli] Certainly, others contributed to the development of the genre: Ernst Lubitsch was its grandfather, with films like *Trouble in Paradise*. But the form required the imposition of censorship to bring it forth, and 1934 saw *Twentieth Century*, *The Thin Man*, and *It Happened One Night* create the category in full (reaching its height in 1938's *Bringing up Baby*).[41] The story for *It Happened One Night*: spoiled rich girl (Claudette Colbert) goes on the run; reporter breaking away from his life (Clark Gable) runs into her on a bus, realizes she is the story of the year. They come together, in hostility, deception, and comic frustration, and learn from each other. Love happens, but not easily. Both Gable and Colbert were trapped; both become free. Few perfect movies exist; *It Happened One Night* is one of them.

On a lesser plane, *The Barretts of Wimpole Street* tells the romance of Robert Browning and Elizabeth Barrett Browning, the Victorian poets (she was the more famous in her day). Barrett was an invalid until Browning whisked her out of her repressive father's home, giving her a life and a son in wedded bliss in Italy. The father is brilliantly played by Charles Laughton; Browning, alas, is not. Fredric March turned in one of his worst performances, as he himself recognized: "I think [director]

---

[41] Film scholar Ed Sikov has even more pointed commentary on the nature and structure of the genre: "With screwball comedies, audiences laughed at the nagging hatred that develops between two people in love. Indeed, in screwball comedies, fighting *was* loving– a way for two equals to express mutual respect and commonality of purpose. To set these ridiculous sparring matches in motion, screenwriters were in constant need of 'meet-cutes' – funny setup scenes that bring two unlikely people into such close proximity that, following genre convention, they can do nothing but start some sort of emotional or physical brawl." *On Sunset Boulevard: The Life and Times of Billy Wilder*, p. 121.

Sidney Franklin paid more attention to Norma and maybe he let me get out of hand...[the character] brought out the worst ham elements in me, and I feel I failed in the role."[xlii] Norma Shearer was nominated for Best Actress playing Browning; and for once, I'm not disagreeing. She truly brings out the invalid in Elizabeth, and the abused child – but the main reason to watch this film is to see Laughton as a cold-hearted, controlling, and possibly incestuous father. For Laughton's sake, I support the nomination for Best Picture.

Cecil B. DeMille's *Cleopatra* was even more sexually provocative than last year's *The Sign of the Cross*; he opens the film with a beautiful female who, if she is not naked, is wearing a diaphanous cloth which reveals her nipples. As usual, the sets and costumes are immaculate, and often historically based. Claudette Colbert's Cleopatra is suitably imperious. Oddly, they cast the usually wisecracking Warren Williams as Julius Caesar, which works better than one would expect. Henry Wilcoxson has the best role of his life as Marc Antony. Nobody ever did crowd scenes better than DeMille; every person in them seems alive, a real person. If they had had a category for costumes this year, Travis Banton would have won; they're unbelievable. The script rewrites history for dramatic effect; Shakespeare pulled it off better in his history plays. The nomination stays for a good spectacle, which in most ways is better than the color remake with Elizabeth Taylor.

Flirtation Walk is yet another Frank Borzage romance, this one with Dick Powell, Ruby Keeler, and Pat O'Brien. Delmer Daves wrote the screenplay (Daves would be better known for *Dark Passage* and *An Affair to Remember*). Powell and Keeler get a chance to try a romance with a minimum of singing; marching in formation at West Point substitutes for the Busby Berkeley dance numbers of their earlier films. Powell is a cadet; she is the daughter of the commandant. *Flirtation Walk* isn't a bad film, but it certainly isn't Oscar quality – so no nomination.

Fred Astaire and Ginger Rogers made their first excellent film together in *The Gay Divorcee*. The American musical would never be the same. Astaire remains the finest dancer the screen has ever known; Rogers, as they say, had to do everything he did, "only backwards, and in high heels." A goofy looking man with a charming wit, when he began to move, Astaire was elegance personified. *The Gay Divorcee* had been a Cole Porter musical, *The Gay Divorce*; the imposition of the Production Code in 1934 mandated a change from a happy divorce (a no-no, obviously) to the acceptable happily divorcing woman (no, the demand doesn't make sense to me either). Astaire pursues Rogers, who thinks he's a gigolo sent to help her establish grounds for a divorce. As so often in musicals, the plot is just an excuse for dancing and singing. Fortunately, the numbers include "The Continental" and "Night and Day" (see Best Song below for more). Unfortunately, other numbers intrude, too few of which have Fred and Ginger dancing together. For some reason, they dropped most of the Cole Porter songs from the play. As a plus, Edward Everett Horton plays his usual loveable dunderhead. An important film, although not a perfect one; the nomination is a good choice.

Here Comes the Navy stars Jimmy Cagney and Pat O'Brien in the first of a series of military films the two made (and remade). Combative from the start, Cagney and O'Brien put on a fun show. Whether it qualifies for the Best Picture is questionable. Fun, yes – but anything other than an excuse for male rivalry and fisticuffs, no. As an historical artifact, *Here Comes the Navy* does provide us with footage on the *USS Arizona*, lost at Pearl Harbor, as well as extensive footage of one of the Navy's dirigibles. But those don't qualify it for a nomination, which *Here Comes the Navy* should not have received.

The House of Rothschild is yet another historical drama with George Arliss, which also has Boris Karloff in the second starring role (and billed ahead of both Loretta Young and Robert Young – no relation). Nunnally Johnson wrote the screenplay. Arliss deliberately chose this project as a way to attack anti-Semitism, which was on the rise in Germany. The movie begins in Prussia in 1780, in a time of Jewish persecution. Darryl F. Zanuck went along, which is ironic, since he was the only non-Jewish producer running a studio in Hollywood. The film is problematic, since it makes a virtue out of the very things for which Jews were being attacked: financial manipulations, deceptiveness, greediness, and the accumulation of money to gain power. German propaganda minister Joseph Goebbels, who was in charge of the German film industry, didn't ban the movie; he had it edited to emphasize this stereotype. Yet, the film also accurately depicts the horrible disadvantages that Jews had to cope with in Europe, thus driving them to the very behaviors for which they were then attacked. Arliss plays a dual role, as the founder of the Rothschild banking empire as it spread across Europe, and then as the younger Nathan. Arliss' acting is still as stagey and artificial as ever, and more damagingly, the film gets no dramatic thrust as it moves forward episodically. Karloff is very much the best part of the film, as the villainous Baron LeDrantz. Nothing else really brings us back to this film, even with the final reel being an experiment in three-strip Technicolor. *The House of Rothschild* should have not been nominated (the film was selected, in my opinion, because it was Fox's biggest moneymaker of the year).

Imitation of Life stars Claudette Colbert, Warren Williams, and Louise Beavers (later a star of her own television show, *Beulah*). Colbert and her black housemaid Beavers open up a pancake and syrup concession, using the maple syrup Colbert's dead husband used to sell, and Beaver's secret pancake recipe (a very enlightened view, showing women running their own business). Beavers has a light-skinned daughter, named Peola, who is capable of passing for white; Colbert has a daughter as well (who will eventually fall in love with the same man as Colbert). The movie attempts to be daring, in that it explores issues of skin color and race, as Peola decides to pass for white as an adult, and reject her mother. Stereotypes still creep in, despite the attempt to be enlightened (critic Jeff Stafford draws particular attention to these issues and their contemporary reception).[xliii] One could argue Colbert takes advantage of Beavers, and the store's sign does what Aunt Jemima's maple syrup has done for decades now (and other black images used to do, as in the now-extinct Sambo's restaurant chain). I'm not sure what to make of the exchange about how smart Peola is; her mother says "We all starts out that way. We don't get dumb till later on." Racism? Commentary on how blacks had to behave to survive racism? The film gives no clue, and I suspect the screenwriter was just using the stereotype for attempted humor. But then, when Peola comes home crying, and insists she won't ever be black, her mother counsels "You gotta learn to take it. You might just as well begin now." No other film made it so clear what blacks had to suffer in America. *Imitation of Life* is at heart a melodrama, but one that explores serious issues of motherhood, race, and the role of women in the professional world (it was remade with Lana Turner in the Fifties, and didn't work as well). The nomination was a good one.

One Night of Love is a freak, a film about opera that became a hit. Real-life opera singer Grace Moore plays Mary Barrett, who wants to study under Guilo Monteverdi, famous opera teacher. Romantic complications ensue. Who cares? The point of this film is the music – or should be. Moore has a lovely voice, having started out in musical theater (she introduced Irving Berlin's "What'll I Do"), then taking vocal training and spending sixteen seasons at the Met until she was killed in a plane crash in 1948. So far as her songs go, Moore is a good singer, but not a great one – and even less as an actress. She is mediocre, at best – just like this movie. The nomination shouldn't have been given to *One Night of Love*.

The Thin Man proved to be critical in the careers of both William Powell and Myrna Loy. Both of them had their public personas changed forever by this film and the series that followed, as well as their other on-screen partnerships. Powell had been a heavy on the silent screen, and was finding his way into melodramas before *The Thin Man* cast him into the comedic romances which have proved to be his enduring legacy (*My Man Godfrey* being a major achievement). Loy had been cast as foreign vamps, most infamously in the MGM big-budget *The Mask of Fu Manchu*, starring Boris Karloff; Loy's scenes of sadism have seldom been matched. *The Thin Man* moved her into comedic roles, often as wives; as she herself said, *The Thin Man* "finally made me..." after more than 80 films."[xliv] While the alcoholic hijinks have lost some of their froth and some of the supporting cast overacts, *The Thin Man* remains a wonderful romance, with a decent murder mystery (as it should, since it is based on the Dashiell Hammett novel). More importantly, *The Thin Man* remains one of the few films to ever show a married couple who are still in love, and happily so. The joy Loy and Powell bring makes *The Thin Man* still sparkle like few movies before or since. The two would go on to make more movies together than any other male and female couple: fourteen films, many of them classics. America became certain they were married; no amount of publicity could convince otherwise. *The Thin Man* deserves this nomination.

Viva Villa! stars Wallace Beery as the hero from the Mexican Revolution; David O. Selznick produced. Jack Conway directed, but Howard Hawks was the original director. Problems abounded on the location shootings in Mexico; Lee Tracy (who played the reporter, based on John Reed) was a major drinker, and at one point, urinated on the heads of Mexican cadets from a balcony.[xlv] Hawks was fired after hitting MGM head Louis B. Mayer in an argument over retaining Tracy. *Viva Villa!* doesn't seem like the kind of film MGM would ever make, since the upper classes are the villains, but the movie was the year's top moneymaker (the early Thirties saw a huge shift in our relations with Latin American countries, as FDR launched into the Good Neighbor Policy). Watching the film today, one is struck by the brutality of the landowners, and the cruel injustices the peasants face. But the film's casting unconsciously produces a racist dimension, as the peasants who have no speaking parts are all played by Mexicans, but the ones who talk are played by Anglo-Americans. Beery's performance as Villa proves durable, even through his bad Mexican accent. Mostly, the movie is an excuse for Beery to wallow humorously in violence and sex. All in all, no nomination was deserved (if only Hawks could have finished the film, I might be saying something very different).

The only reason to watch *The White Parade* is if you're a rabid Loretta Young fan (that, and you really like UCLA, which has what seems to be the only remaining copy). Had they stuck to nurse training, and not gone for the stale romance, it might have worked, but as it is, *The White Parade* is nothing but a weepy melodrama, and not a particularly good one at that. Where's a bedpan when you need one? No nomination would have been a better choice.

Even though I agree with the Academy in honoring *It Happened One Night*, they still nominated movies malodorous and maladjusted – and not in a good way. Let me point you to the choices they should have made, as I've suggested above.

W.C. Fields' first great sound comedy appeared in 1934 (what Fields movies come before have got some funny bits, but not in sustained length): *It's a Gift,* directed by Norman McLeod from a screenplay by Jack Cunningham, is based on a play Fields had been in, which was itself based on a story by Charles Bogle (none other than W.C. Fields himself.) Many of Fields' classic routines are here: shaving in the bathroom nearly turns into murder; the child about to be hit ("He's not going to tell me I don't love him!"); Mr. Muckle, the blind man in the grocery store; "kumquats!"; the constantly interrupted nap on the porch ("Wake up and go and sleep!"); Carl L-a-F-o-n-g; and the folding chair. All for an orange grove – and a fifth of gin. While certainly not the equal of last year's *Duck Soup*, or this year's masterpiece *It Happened One Night*, *It's a Gift* is a contender for the funniest movie of the year, and should have been nominated.

The Lost Patrol is one of John Ford's best entertainments, but with a somber, angry core, set in WWI in Mesopotamia (the same visual and narrative territory *Lawrence of Arabia* would inhabit three decades later). Ford crafts a tale of a patrol being taken down, man by man, by an almost unseen enemy. Victor McLaglen plays the unnamed sergeant; Boris Karloff gets to go crazy as a religious fanatic named Sanders (for some, Karloff's performance goes overboard). Their officer is killed; the sergeant takes over, with no idea what their orders are. McLaglen leads them to an oasis, wherein things go badly wrong. Grace under pressure, the importance of duty, the bonding of men, the dangers of fanaticism – Ford's themes of his mature works begin taking root here, in ways his earlier works had barely touched. Ford always claimed it as one of his favorite movies. The Academy should have nominated it.

Ernst Lubitsch's *The Merry Widow* stars Jeanette MacDonald and Maurice Chevalier. While we've seen this territory before from Lubitsch, this may just be his best musical. And more importantly, it's Jeanette MacDonald's last great movie before getting trapped in musical schlock with Nelson Eddy.⁴² Lubitsch has to cope with the imposition of the Production Code, and yet finds ways to be naughty: the maids all knowing exactly where Chevalier lives; the inkwell draining as MacDonald writes about Chevalier; "I know what to do, but am too old to do it."; the king's sword belt; "Have you ever had diplomatic relations with a woman?" The can-can was never can-cannier. But the movie is more than just titillation for a change: "For the first time in a Lubitsch musical, music is not a metaphor for sex, but for love."[xlvi] Unlike *The Smiling Lieutenant*, it is the husband, and not the wife, who must learn to behave and submit. Lubitsch was never better, or funnier, in one of his musicals; *The Merry Widow* should have been nominated.

Alfred Hitchcock had little following in the United States, except for a small group of devotees. His films rarely did big business here, showing mostly in New York to the art house crowd. *The Man Who Knew Too Much* changed all that, becoming "the first Hitchcock film to score with critics – and audiences – in the United States."[xlvii] Hitchcock loved the story so much he remade it with Jimmy Stewart and Doris Day in the Fifties; most fans still prefer this original.[xlviii] That popularity comes mostly from the presence of Peter Lorre as the villain, providing sinister focus, and pointing directly at the rising menace of Adolf Hitler. Lorre was brilliant, and Hitchcock provides him with his first great role in a film outside of Germany. The director even points slyly at Lorre's role as a child murderer in *M*, when the girl about to be kidnapped tells Lorre she isn't interested in his pretty watch, since she's not a child. But the playful family at its heart, a family more interesting by far than that of Stewart and Day in the remake, also provides an attraction, as does Hitchcock's directorial glee in telling this story. Hitchcock's fluid camera moves, economic editing, and mastery of suspense all seduce the audience into his story. The Academy ignored this film entirely, having already done obeisance to Britain the year before in handing its Oscar to Charles Laughton. *The Man Who Knew Too Much* deserved a nomination for Best Picture, Lorre for Best Actor, and Hitchcock for Best Director.

Howard Hawks' *Twentieth Century* starred John Barrymore and Carole Lombard for Columbia Pictures (who threw all their support behind the Capra film rather than diluting their chances to finally win some Oscars). Ben Hecht and Charles MacArthur wrote the script,

---

[42] I am apparently far from alone in bemoaning her teaming with Eddy instead of Chevalier. Andrew Sarris agrees: "Maurice Chevalier, the increasingly wary and resigned man of the world, is to be supplanted by Nelson Eddy, a callow, wooden, and single-minded suitor to the increasingly coy and saccharine Jeanette MacDonald. As with the Marx Brothers, the vinegar of Paramount is sweetened with the sugar of Metro." *"You Ain't Heard Nothin' Yet"* p. 41.

based on the play *Napoleon of Broadway*; Preston Sturges did some work on the screenplay as well, although uncredited. Few stories have ever done better to lay out the ways in which theatre people dramatize themselves constantly, privately as well as publicly (if you've never hung out with actors, or even worse, theatre majors, you don't know how bad it can get). *Bombshell* and *Morning Glory* are but fertilizer to the crop of hothouse orchids in *Twentieth Century*. If only Columbia hadn't made that other picture this year, *Twentieth Century* might have had a chance – at a well deserved nomination.

P.S. One of the best French films of the Thirties was released this year, but not in the United States. *L'Atalante* would not be seen on American screens until 1947, and is thus ineligible. I highly recommend the film; as Roger Ebert says, "This is the kind of movie you return to like a favorite song, remembering where you were and how it made you feel, and how its feet smelled."[xlix]

Best Actor: Clark Gable won for *It Happened One Night*, over Frank Morgan, *The Affairs of Cellini*; and William Powell, *The Thin Man*

Clark Gable reached his first great role in *It Happened One Night*. Tough, manly, funny, and more American than any star had ever been before this, Gable's turn as Peter Warne made him a superstar, a position he would hold until his death a quarter-century later. Gable was sent to make this film at Columbia Pictures as a punishment by Louis B. Mayer at MGM: "I'd like to spank him," Mayer supposedly said, for being a "bad boy."[l] Gable showed up on his first day drunk.[li] Gable never had a better comic role; other than playing Rhett Butler in *Gone with the Wind*, *It Happened One Night* was his greatest acting achievement. The Oscar should remain on his mantelpiece.[43]

Frank Morgan (the future Wizard of Oz) got a nod for *The Affairs of Cellini*, an historical melodrama starring Fredric March as the sculptor Cellini, directed by Gregory La Cava (most famous for *My Man Godfrey*). As J.R. Jones so aptly described *The Affairs of Cellini*, this "inspired wisp of Hollywood candy floss" shows Morgan off well as the Duke who pursues Cellini's model and former lover, while Cellini pursues the Duke's wife.[lii] Morgan does his patented fluster and bluster throughout the movie, bringing out the comic angles of power and adultery as effectively as anybody did in the Thirties. Morgan was generally

---

[43] Gable fought being cast in all three of his greatest roles, *It Happened One Night*, *Mutiny on the Bounty*, and *Gone with the Wind*. This is why certain actors should be kept on a leash and smacked on the nose with a rolled-up screenplay when they don't know any better. Sometimes, even Louis B. Mayer was right.

a welcome presence in whatever movie he was in, and *The Affairs of Cellini* is no exception. Want some proof? Nobody besides Morgan could have made this seduction line anything more than ridiculously stupid: "Don't call me milord. I'd prefer that you call me Bumpy." A worthy nomination for a silly tickler of a performance.

As I've said above, as a result of *The Thin Man,* William Powell moved from the pompous detective Philo Vance and a few romantic roles into the joking, witty parts he is best remembered for today. His occasional foray back into serious drama (*Manhattan Melodrama,* for example) makes us long for the comic sparkle in his eye. Nick Charles is Powell's defining moment. As Roger Ebert has said, "William Powell is to dialogue as Fred Astaire is to dance. His delivery is so droll and insinuating, so knowing and innocent at the same time, that it hardly matters what he's saying."[liii] Powell deserved this nomination as Nick.

The Academy went three for three here, but they still missed worthy choices to nominate.

Had it been any other year than this, John Barrymore would have finally won his Academy Award. His role as the theatrical producer Oscar Jaffe was the funniest thing he ever did. Howard Hawks once told about going after Barrymore for the role: "He said, 'Mr. Hawks, just why do you think I would be any good in this picture?' I said, 'It's the story of the greatest ham in the world, and God knows you fit that.' And he said, 'I'll do the picture.' He never even read it."[liv] Hawks and Barrymore were a perfect match, and *Twentieth Century* remains Barrymore's last great performance. Barrymore should have been nominated. Barrymore had an explanation for why he wasn't: "This town is filled with hypocritical old biddies who are afraid that if I win, I'll show up drunk to accept it. And I just might."[lv]

Who else should have been nominated? Peter Lorre, as the villainous mastermind in Hitchcock's *The Man Who Knew Too Much,* and Charles Laughton, as the most abusive father in pre-WWII films in *The Barretts of Wimpole Street* (see Best Picture above for more on both).

Best Actress: Claudette Colbert won for *It Happened One Night*, over Norma Shearer, *The Barretts of Wimpole Street*; and Grace Moore, *One Night of Love*

Claudette Colbert had one helluva year. Not only did she luck into *It Happened One Night,* but she also made *Cleopatra* for Cecil B. DeMille and *Imitation of Life* for John M. Stahl. Three very different roles: one romantic screwball comedy, one historical epic, one socially conscious melodrama. Colbert didn't want to make *It Happened One Night*; Capra had almost ruined her career with her first film, which he directed.

She had to be paid $50,000, double her normal rate, and they had to be done in only one month. When shooting ended, she reportedly told friends she had just finished "the worst picture in the world."[lvi] She couldn't have been more wrong. Colbert deserved her Oscar for *It Happened One Night*, playing Ellie Andrews. She had been sexy before; she had been funny before; never before and rarely since was she both. She explored the ways in which women were trapped by American males, and could escape those bonds through humor, sexiness, and standing up for oneself. Colbert was never better, and proved herself the rightful recipient of Best Actress Oscar.

Norma Shearer was once again nominated for Best Actress, but this time, she deserved it for *The Barretts of Wimpole Street*. One can feel the life in her being shut down, destroyed by her father. The reverse doesn't work quite as well with Fredric March as Robert Browning, but since the movie focuses heavily on her relation with her father, March doesn't detract as much as he might. As always, Shearer is only as good as her male star; give her Gable, she's fabulous; give her March, not so much. But give her Charles Laughton, and you get the best Elizabeth Barrett Browning one could ask for in 1934.

In *One Night of Love*, Grace Moore isn't anybody's idea of a great actress – or shouldn't be. She doesn't deserve this nomination (see Best Picture above for why).

Hollywood was annoyed when two actresses seemed to be frozen out by studio block voting: Myrna Loy in *The Thin Man* and Bette Davis in *Of Human Bondage*. I would agree, as you've seen. Grace Moore and Norma Shearer are weak substitutes compared to Loy and Davis.

As I've said above, Myrna Loy's role as Nora Charles was a game changer for her. Smart, coy, active, and funny, Loy was everything one could ask for in an actress in a comedy. More importantly, she was, in every way, the equal of the male. Marriage never looked so good (even through the alcoholic haze, which no longer seems as funny as it once did). The next Thin Man movie should have had Grace Moore as the murder victim, for stealing Loy's nomination for Best Actress.

Bette Davis' turn as a Cockney tart was also a major career boost for Davis, who had been battling with Jack Warner for better roles. When she made *Of Human Bondage*, she assumed this would show Warner she was right; instead, Warner refused to allow her to be loaned out for *It Happened One Night*, and cast her in a dumpy role as a housewife instead. Norma Shearer herself campaigned for Davis to win for Best actress, and a write-in vote ensued (the Academy was also answering charges that the nominations were all "propaganda"; the Screen Actors Guild actually required actors to resign from the Academy due to their power struggle with the studios).^lvii The Academy then lied about her taking third place; the uproar forced the Academy to change its nomination rules the next year.

Watching *Of Human Bondage* today, one wonders why anybody was all that excited. Davis goes over the top with this performance, and it hasn't aged well. Then again, neither has the movie or Leslie Howard's performance. Is it just me, or did he specialize in pathetic? Bette Davis herself agreed, saying his "whimpering adoration in the face of...brutal diffidence was difficult for me to believe."^lviii I suspect people were amazed back then because Davis was willing to go unglamorous in the role, that she appeared to be as sick as the character, and that she had a Cockney accent. Davis plays a disdainful, manipulative, lying, cheating shrew of a character. What, precisely, did Howard's character find attractive? As an exercise in self-abuse, *Of Human Bondage* works. Davis deserved a nomination, compared to the rest of the year, but Colbert's Oscar was well won: ask yourself who seems more human, more fully rounded? Davis' character is more of a caricature of a human being than anything else, and her famous scene rebuking Howard is mostly histrionics. Davis was so anxious to prove herself a serious actress she left out the human touch.[44]

Others charged racism for the first time at the Oscars. *Imitation of Life* featured Claudette Colbert, but it also starred Louise Beavers. As one columnist pointed out, "I also lament the fact that the motion picture industry has not set aside racial prejudice in naming actresses. I don't see how it is possible to overlook the magnificent portrayal of the Negro actress, Louise Beavers, who played the mother in *Imitation of Life*. If the industry chooses to ignore Miss Beavers' performance, please let this reporter, born and bred in the South, tender a special award of praise to Louise Beavers for the finest performance of 1934."^lix It would not be until Hattie McDaniel and *Gone with the Wind* that the Academy began addressing this, if only tentatively. Watch the scene where her light-skinned daughter Peola comes home crying, and pay attention to Beavers' face when her daughter blames her for being black, and you'll agree: Beavers should have been nominated for *Imita-*

---

[44] To be fair, few were more important in developing the potential of the screen actor: "She broke the old mould for female stars: she didn't want to get up on that screen and be decorative, to be glamorous like Garbo, to be sympathetic like Janet Gaynor, to pose as an actress like Norma Shearer: she wanted to *act*, to illuminate for audiences all the women she found within her – waitresses, dowagers, spinsters, harridans, drunks. She fought to play them all. All subsequent screen stars owe her a debt, in that she proved that an actress could be an excellent judge of material, and her dedication destroyed a lingering belief that stage acting was 'superior' to film acting." David Shipman, *The Great Movie Stars*, p. 149.

tion of Life, "the first time in American cinema history that a black woman's problems were given major emotional weight in a major Hollywood motion picture."[lx]

Carole Lombard should also have been nominated for Best Actress for her comedic breakthrough in *Twentieth Century*. Just watch as Lombard goes from portraying a terrible actress to a great one to a spoiled diva, all in a few minutes. Brilliant! To be able to stand up to Barrymore at his finest, match him blow for humorous blow, and come off his equal – now that's acting!

Best Director: Frank Capra won for *It Happened One Night*, over Victor Schertzinger, *One Night of Love*; and W.S. Van Dyke, *The Thin Man*

Frank Capra was the quintessential director of the Thirties, both artistically and commercially. Working in the lowest of the major studios (or the highest of the Poverty Row studios), he was given unprecedented artistic freedom to pursue his visions of America. Although all too often thought of as a populist liberal, he was in fact a conservative Republican. But his pictures define the American dream in its sunniest possibilities in the Thirties. The rich are often skewered (and why shouldn't they be?); the poor are often celebrated. But the money is not the issue, in either case. Character is. Concern for following one's better self is. Following the Golden Rule is. Capra had great successes. *It Happened One Night, Mr. Deeds Goes to Town, Mr. Smith Goes to Washington,* and *It's a Wonderful Life* rank among the best films ever made, and taken together, provide us the best picture of what it means to be an American at the top of our game. He made interesting failures: *Lost Horizon* and *Meet John Doe* foremost among them. He made eccentric films, particularly *You Can't Take It with You,* and the goofy *Arsenic and Old Lace*. His career went into complete collapse in the Fifties, as few other great directors have. I cannot say enough of a man unjustly accused as a purveyor of "Capracorn." America means more after seeing his films, and all without being deceived. We really can be the people Capra thought we could be, on our best days.

On the other hand, the less said about Schertzinger and *One Night of Love*, the better. The nomination is one of those occasional ones where the Academy tries to get all high-toned, for no good reason other than to make themselves feel classy. Look at us! We like opera! Before you go thinking bad things about me, I own recordings of over a hundred operas. *One Night of Love* just isn't a good movie, and shouldn't have been selected.

Woody Van Dyke was known as "One-Take Woody." He actually shot all of *The Thin Man* in sixteen days, with a few retakes the following month. The film's mystery is a bit confusing at times, and some of the secondary roles don't play as well as they should. But Van Dyke was the one who insisted on Powell and Loy for these roles, and knew they could be both hysterically funny and romantic; for their casting alone, he deserved this nomination. Insight and speed were Van Dyke's gifts as a director, even if his films rarely went beyond skimming the surfaces.

Which, oddly enough, is often what a certain British import was often accused of. Nothing could be further from the truth. Alfred Hitchcock should have been nominated for Best Director for *The Man Who Knew Too Much* (see Best Picture above).

Finally, if you don't think Howard Hawks deserved a Best Director nomination for *Twentieth Century*, then consider this: he got John Barrymore to give his last great performance, and Carole Lombard to give her first. If that's not directing, what is? Hawks should have been nominated.

Best Writing (Adaptation): Robert Riskin won for *It Happened One Night*, over Frances Goodrich and Albert Hackett, *The Thin Man*; and Ben Hecht, *Viva Villa!*

Robert Riskin deserved his Oscar. *It Happened One Night* remains justly famous for everything about it, not the least of which is the dialogue. Remember these scenes? The hitch-hiking and donut-dunking explanations of Gable. The "Walls of Jericho" going up: "Don't be a sucker. A good night's rest'll do you a lot of good. Besides, you got nothing to worry about: the walls of Jericho will protect you from the big bad wolf." The Walls of Jericho coming down. I'll let Claudette Colbert's leg speak for itself. But as for the rest of her, I'll let Gable speak Riskin's words: "Why didn't you take off *all* your clothes? You could have stopped *forty* cars." Colbert's comeback: "I'll remember that when we need *forty* cars." Riskin is a major reason so many of Capra's films are as great as they are – and the Academy should be congratulated for giving the writer this Oscar.

Even so, Frances Goodrich and Albert Hackett give Riskin a run for his money in their worthily nominated screenplay for *The Thin Man*. Dashiell Hammett's novel is wonderful, but the relationship of Nick and Nora Charles, even with the alcohol, remains the happiest, most joyful marriage in Thirties cinema. Much of that is due to the dialogue, as well as the sheer joy Loy and Powell bring to their work. "Waiter, will you serve the nuts? I mean, will you serve the guests the nuts?" Nick, to

Nora, after sending her on a long taxi ride: "How'd you like Grant's tomb?"; Nora: "It's lovely. I'm having a copy made for you." Nick, in a bar, demonstrating proper technique: "The important thing is the rhythm. Always have rhythm in your shaking. Now a Manhattan you shake to fox-trot time, a Bronx to two-step time, a dry Martini you always shake to waltz time." Nora, to Nick: "I read where you were shot five times in the tabloids." Nick, responding: "It's not true. He didn't come anywhere near my tabloids." Classic! Goodrich and Hackett merited this nomination.

Ben Hecht wrote *Viva Villa!* Much of Villa's life was heavily fictionalized; the original screenplay had to be rewritten due to objections by the Mexican government and Villa's widow.[lxi] Chances are, this did not serve the truth. Perhaps it doesn't matter, since the movie starts off by announcing it was not even trying to be the truth, but was rather "inspired by a love of the half-legendary Pancho Villa and the glamorous country he served." Hecht tried to provide Villa with a specific motivation, by inventing the scene where Villa's father is whipped to death because he dared to protest the illegal seizure of his land; Villa stabs the overseer in the back in an alley, then takes off into the countryside: "Injustice was his nurse, oppression his tutor." In the end, it's a wallow in the mud with Beery. No nomination should have been given.

Other movies deserved more consideration from the Academy.

Death Takes a Holiday should have been nominated for Best Writing (Adaptation). The great Maxwell Anderson, and Gladys Lehman, adapted the play by Alberto Casella; Fredric March stars as Death; Mitchell Leisen directed. Better known today in its Brad Pitt remake, *Meet Joe Black*, the original version remains charming, and the special effects quite impressive for 1934. I'm not about to have it replace Riskin's triumph, or even Goodrich and Hackett's work on *The Thin Man*, but I would choose it over Hecht's *Viva Villa!* any day.

I would say the same thing about MGM's adaptation of Robert Louis Stevenson's classic adventure tale, *Treasure Island*. Reuniting the stars of *The Champ*, Jackie Cooper and Wallace Beery, *Treasure Island* also has Lionel Barrymore, with Victor Fleming directing. John Lee Mahin wrote the screenplay, and a fine job he did too. Louis B. Mayer ruined the classic ending by insisting that Cooper had to have a crying scene, and a happy ending; the studio mogul had never even read the book.[lxii] By far, this *Treasure Island* has my favorite Wallace Beery performance, as scoundrels were his forte, and Long John Silver scoundrels with the best of them (I shall forego talking like a pirate. You're welcome). An excellent adaptation, even with Mayer's piddling in the pot.

WHAT THEY GOT WRONG:

Not much, for a change. But enough to keep me busy.

The awards for Best Score went to the head of the studio music department from 1934-1937; I'm going to ignore them, and list the folks who actually composed the music.

Here are the ones the Academy was dopey enough to give awards:

Best Writing (Original Story): Arthur Caesar, *Manhattan Melodrama*
Best Cinematography: Victor Milner, *Cleopatra*
Best Score: Victor Schertzinger and Gus Kahn, *One Night of Love*
Best Song: Con Conrad and Herb Magidson, "The Continental," *The Gay Divorcee*
Best Art Direction: Cedric Gibbons and Fredric Hope, *The Merry Widow*
Best Short Subject (Cartoon): Walt Disney, *The Tortoise and the Hare*
Best Short Subject (Comedy): RKO Radio, *La Cucaracha*

Best Writing (Original Story): Arthur Caesar won for *Manhattan Melodrama*, over Mauri Grashin, *Hide-Out*; and Norman Krasna, *The Richest Girl in the World*

What can you do when a film decides to blatantly announce its tear-jerker status, and settles in for a good cry? All you can do is hope it's better than *Manhattan Melodrama*, my nominee for the worst title of the year (and most others). Not content with starting the film off by bumping off the parents of the two boys who grow up to be Clark Gable and William Powell, five minutes later their adoptive father is dead. Does the word overkill mean anything to you? Powell and Gable (and love interest Myrna Loy) do the best they can with this manipulative nonsense, enough so that it's a somewhat enjoyable movie, but they overcome the writing rather than being lifted up by it (as they would be in a good screwball comedy, or one of the better Thin Man entries). *Manhattan Melodrama* is as good as writer Arthur Caesar ever got, but it shouldn't have been good enough for Oscar – or John Dillinger, who got what he deserved when the FBI shot him down when he went to see this film. *Manhattan Melodrama* deserved neither nomination nor award.

A young Mickey Rooney appears in *Manhattan Melodrama*, and then in *Hide-Out*, the latter of which stars Robert Montgomery as a wounded gangster who hides out on a farm; Maureen O'Sullivan plays the farm girl. Love happens – doesn't it always with a farm girl in the movies? Decent story, with Montgomery having to learn what it means to be human rather than on the make all the time. *Hide-Out* got the gloss from MGM in the city scenes, and the farm life is happy, as it rarely is in reality.[45] Fine if you like this sort of thing, but this is the kind of picture that *Variety* once famously titled "Sticks Nix Hick Pix." Not Oscar quality from Mauri Grashin (who started out as a gag writer for Laurel and Hardy, hit this high point, and went downhill afterwards). No nomination should have been given.

The Richest Girl in the World starred Miriam Hopkins, Joel McCrea and Fay Wray in Norman Krasna's script. Krasna would go on to write *White Christmas* and *Indiscreet*. *Richest Girl* shows us one of the corniest plots of all: the richest girl in the world, played by Hopkins, wants to be loved for herself instead of her money. Fay Wray plays her friend who is helping her out by swapping identities with her. McCrea meets Hopkins, who is pretending to be Wray; they are attracted to each other, but Hopkins needs to be sure. The screenplay works, because of the performances, and the minor but believable twists that follow. An enjoyable little film that so wants to be directed by Ernst Lubitsch it hurts. The nomination should stay.

I'm going to stretch the term "original" to include *The Black Cat*, "suggested by the immortal Edgar Allen Poe classic," "The Black Cat." The movie and the book have nothing to do with each other except for the title. Literally everything else is different (a black cat does show up repeatedly). Peter Ruric[46] wrote the screenplay, and it's a doozy.[lxiii] Starring Boris Karloff and Bela Lugosi together for the first time, *The Black Cat* explores some very dark events. Karloff plays Hjalmar Poelzig; Lugosi is Dr. Vitus Werdegast; Lugosi was never more elegant. Lugosi is returning from prison camp to confront his great enemy, Karloff, who betrayed his country in the war, sent Lugosi to prison, and stole Lugosi's wife and daughter. Karloff's character is loosely based on Satanist Aleister Crowley. Karloff has a gallery of women, frozen in life by his embalmer's art (and suggesting not just Satanism and sadism, but also necrophilia, as Bret Wood has pointed out).[lxiv] The film very much belongs in the German Expressionist tradition (best known in *The Cabinet of Dr. Caligari*). For those who disdain all the supernatural dressing that usually goes with horror films, *The Black Cat* explores the true

---

[45] I ought to know; I used to have to rake up horse pens; I helped slaughter a pig. By the way, cows are the dumbest animals on the planet – we're doing them a favor eating them. I had two, named Hamburger and Steak. Delicious. My editor, by the way, insists sheep are dumber. I don't know – sheep have at least figured out how to get shorn rather than skinned...

[46] A pen name for George Carol Sims, who published in the pulps as Paul Cain.

human horror of betrayal, sadism, and the cruelty to which humans are all too often prey. *The Bride of Frankenstein* rips off the final moment of the film. Peter Ruric should have won the Oscar for this outrageous tale.

Best Cinematography: Victor Milner won for *Cleopatra*, over Charles Rosher, *The Affairs of Cellini*, and George Folsey, *Operator 13*

Victor Milner's work on *Cleopatra* won, and other than showing off the sets and costumes, I can't see why. The photography is no better than a typical Abbott & Costello movie. The battle scenes show some style, but that's about it (and some of the footage was lifted from DeMille's 1923 *The Ten Commandments*), in terms of camerawork. No Oscar and no nomination was deserved.

Charles Rosher's work on *The Affairs of Cellini* makes everybody seem to be lit by auras of light. We get no pretense of filming reality in sixteenth century Florence. *The Affairs of Cellini* is a frothy romp, not a historical picture. Rosher helps everybody – even bumbling Frank Morgan – to look as if they were stepping out of an ad for the local Renaissance Fair. Even the torture chamber looks like fun. Rosher was a cinematography pioneer, having shot *Sunrise* for F.W. Murnau. He would go on to a career filming mostly mediocrities, but *The Affairs of Cellini* shows the kind of silky, attractive work he was capable of achieving – and earns him this nomination.

Operator 13 is a Civil War movie starring Marion Davies and Gary Cooper; Davies left MGM after making this movie. Folsey was nominated for the Oscar thirteen times for cinematography; he never won. He isn't winning this time either; basic MGM gloss is all we get.

Several other movies would have been much better choices in this category.

For Universal's *The Black Cat*, John J. Mescall shot the film as if the German expressionists were cut loose in America. *The Black Cat* looks like no other movie ever made in the Thirties, with a bright lighting like that of a hospital, contrasting with the deepest possible shadows. The last five minutes of the movie are a cinematic tour de force of cutting and camera angles. Mescall deserved a nomination.

The Lost Patrol is a stark, minimalist vision of men against an unseen enemy in the desert. Photographed by Harold Wenstrom, Ford's poetics of the West begin to emerge in this tale of grace under pressure in the desert. As Mike Lorefice puts it, "Harold Wenstrom's standout claustrophobic cinematography shows the soldiers have everywhere and nowhere to escape."[lxv] Wenstrom never made a better movie; he deserved a nomination for cinematography.

They passed over Joseph Walker, unaccountably, for *It Happened One Night*. Walker went on to shoot *Mr. Smith Goes to Washington*, *His Girl Friday*, and *It's a Wonderful Life* (along with many other classics). Watch the scene in the haystack, the beautiful ways in which the moonlight plays, the shimmering beauty of the night – and tell me if Walker doesn't deserve a nomination, and the Oscar for Best Cinematography. That's right – *It Happened One Night* should have won yet another.

Best Score: Victor Schertzinger and Gus Kahn for *One Night of Love*, over Kenneth Webb and Samuel Hoffenstein, *The Gay Divorcee*, and Max Steiner, *The Lost Patrol*

With this first Best Score Oscar, the Academy rolled over and gave it to the opera wannabe, *One Night of Love*. Sadly, they named the wrong people; Gus Kahn wrote the lyrics for one song, not the score; Schertzinger does seem to have contributed to the score. The Academy was confused, but then, they were trying something new. Rex Bassett and Lou Silvers did the arranging.[lxvi] I love opera, but this score isn't quite it, and should have received neither Oscar nor nomination.

I suspect the Academy nominated *The Gay Divorcee* for the songs, rather than the surrounding score, but on the other hand, the songs do need to be orchestrated. Bit of confusion there, and for many other nominations down the road (eventually the Academy would try to separate original scores from adaptations more than once). The nomination should stay for the fine way Kenneth Webb and Samuel Hoffenstein bring out the beauty of Cole Porter's music – and Porter should have been added to the nominees.

The last candidate, Max Steiner, should have won an Oscar the year before for his brilliant, groundbreaking score on *King Kong*, but they didn't have the category yet. As the historian of movie scores Gary Marmorstein has said: *King Kong* was "the first complete original soundtrack...the first underscore that...greatly enhanced its film."[lxvii] For that revolutionary work, and for his ebullient, martial, sentimental, and yes, a bit overbearing score for John Ford's *The Lost Patrol*, Max Steiner should have been recognized. But this year, greater mastery was at work elsewhere, and as usual, the Academy failed to nominate it.

Never before, and rarely since, have a score and a director worked so intimately together. Franz Lehar's music for his operetta *The Merry Widow* met its match in Ernst Lubitsch. As the director's biographer has recognized, "The score is a masterpiece, and Lubitsch is its equal, adapting his cutting strategies to the rhythm of the music…The sense of freedom, of film perfectly timed to the mathematics of the music, is exhilarating."[lxviii] Lorenz Hart added some lyrics to the songs, but truly, the songs are almost beside the point; the story and the score are partners in this dance. A passel of people worked on the adaptation and orchestration; the Oscar should have gone to all of them: Herbert Stothart, Charles Maxwell, Paul Marquardt, Leonid Raab, and Franz Lehar himself for good measure. *The Merry Widow* is what the Best Score Oscar should be all about: the tune and the tale, waltzing along.

Best Song: Con Conrad and Herb Magidson won for "The Continental," from *The Gay Divorcee*, over Vincent Youmans, Edward Eliscu, and Gus Kahn's "Carioca" from *Flying Down to Rio*; and Ralph Rainger and Leo Robin's "Love in Bloom" from *She Loves Me Not*

I will now proceed to prove to you, beyond a shadow of a doubt, how boneheaded the Academy voters were then. The song that should have won is "Night and Day" by Cole Porter, from *The Gay Divorcee*. If you don't know that song, what the hell is wrong with you?!? I suggest the Frank Sinatra rendition from *A Swingin' Affair*. Sheesh – do I have to teach you EVERYTHING?!?

"The Continental," "Carioca," and "Love in Bloom" are so minor in comparison, we might as well consider it emotional abuse to force them to compete against such mastery.

Some other songs they didn't bother nominating include "I Only Have Eyes for You"; "I'm in the Mood for Love"; and "On the Good Ship Lollipop" – hey, that Temple kid was cute! All three of those would have been better than the ones they nominated. Why does the Academy have no ear for music?!

Don't bother telling me that "Night and Day" wasn't written for the movie. Over the years, the Academy has handed nominations and Oscars for Best Song to tunes that clearly weren't written for the movies. If they can break their own rules, so can I, just this once – at least for Cole Porter and this song.

The Oscar should have gone to Cole Porter for "Night and Day," a classic work of elegant passion.

Best Art Direction: Cedric Gibbons and Frederic Hope won for *The Merry Widow*, over Richard Day, *The Affairs of Cellini*; and Van Nest Polglase & Carroll Clark, *The Gay Divorcee*

Cedric Gibbons and Frederic Hope helped Ernst Lubitsch reach his musical peak in *The Merry Widow*. We are launched into yet another imaginary kingdom in Eastern Europe; romance suffuses every set. The nomination was deserved, but really, for nothing we haven't seen before. The Oscar should have been saved for something truly original.

Don't look for the real Renaissance in Richard Day's sets on *The Affairs of Cellini*. Rather, we are occupying a fantasy reality which only serves to set the stage for the attempted sexual and political hijinks of a plot to be found recycled on television sitcoms like *Three's Company*. The only difference is the costumes and the sets, and superior acting in this sexual farce. Day started off his career serving the monomaniacal Erich von Stroheim, went on to collaborate with John Ford on *Young Mr. Lincoln*, and ended with the historical accuracies of *Tora! Tora! Tora!* In between, Day worked on over two hundred and sixty other films. His sets for *The Affairs of Cellini* are quite supportive of this sexual romp, particularly the Duke's court. Sometimes they even look lived in and dirty, and not in the naughty way. Day deserved this nomination.

Polglase and Clark did serviceable work on *The Gay Divorcee*. Recreating a beautiful seaside resort hotel for most of the scenes creates the proper mood. The nomination should stay.

Three other films should have been brought up for Oscar consideration.

Universal let Charles D. Hall, the genius of the sets on *Frankenstein*, go wild on *The Black Cat*, under the direction of Edward Ulmer, who had worked in Germany with Max Reinhardt, Fritz Lang and F.W. Murnau. Ulmer is generally given kudos for the sets, but the credits list Hall; chances are, they worked together. Karloff's castle is a masterpiece of Art Deco design, stripped of all warmth and charm; the horrors it hides are brought to life in a Gothic spirit brought into the twentieth century. *The Black Cat* is a unique visual experience, in terms of both cinematography and sets, and deserved a nomination for art direction.

Babes in Toyland (aka *The March of the Wooden Soldiers*) has haunted the Christmas dreams of children for generations. Laurel and Hardy didn't want to make the movie; Hal Roach made them, after spending a substantial amount for the rights to Victor Herbert's operetta. The sets reproduce a fairy tale world of Mother Goose, Santa Claus, and an underworld of nightmares: Mother Hubbard's shoe, the toy workshop (and the giant wooden soldiers), and the scariest caves ever. I'm also surprised Disney didn't sue, since a live action Mickey Mouse clone appears, along with the Three Little Pigs and a snippet of "Who's Afraid of the Big Bad Wolf?" Unfortunately, I can't give credit where credit is due, as the movie does not list the art direction, and the Internet Movie Database only lists a property master who is unlikely to be the correct person (the local Laurel & Hardy fan clubs can't locate the information either).

The Scarlet Empress has to be seen to be believed. The film that Sternberg called a "relentless excursion into style" is a feast of costuming and set direction, like a Cecil B. DeMille production taken over by opium eaters. Andrew Sarris describes it as "a tapestry of tyranny so intricately woven and so luminously lit that audiences and critics of the time were stupefied."[lxix] The movie is violent, with a surprising amount of frontal nudity for a film made right when the Production Code was being imposed forcefully by Joseph Breen and the Legion of Decency. *The Scarlet Empress* has sets full of gargoyles, pierced saints, and skeletons, as well as naked women acting as offering plates at dinner, and a clock that flashes a fur coat to reveal a naked woman. Some of the doors are so heavy and elaborate nobody could possibly open them alone. Dietrich still isn't acting in her role as Catherine the Great; as Roger Ebert has pointed out, for Sternberg, "Whether she could act was beside the point for him; it would have been a distraction."[lxx] Sam Jaffe plays the idiot heir, a gargoyle himself. Sternberg even goes so far to have the final shot of Dietrich next to a horse – a sly reference to the apocryphal legend that Catherine died while having sex with a horse (the harness supporting the horse above her supposedly broke). *The Scarlet Empress* has art direction by an uncredited Hans Dreier; Sternberg's influence must also be given the credit. Dreier and Sternberg should have received the Oscar for Art Direction.

Best Short Subject (Cartoon): Disney won for *The Tortoise and the Hare*, over *Holiday Land* from Columbia and Charles Mintz; and *Jolly Little Elves* from Universal and Walter Lantz

Yes, Disney deserved to win, but not for the lackluster *The Tortoise and the Hare*. This year, the truly innovative work was being done in the black and white Mickey Mouses, as Disney's animators began to hit the peaks on their learning curves. *Playful Pluto* entertains far more than *The Tortoise and the Hare*, despite one similar running gag. Disney's animators were making steady advances in the depiction of character, especially Norm Ferguson, whose work in *Playful Pluto* has been called "the big one" in "the milestones in our learning process" at Disney because "it was an outstanding example in its time of how to picture to the audience what the character was thinking, how it felt about that happening, and the motivation of its action."[lxxi] Pluto, Mickey, some yard work, a hose, flies, and some fly paper – and the drawings come alive as they never have before. *Playful Pluto* deserves the Oscar.

As for the competition, *Holiday Land* and *Jolly Little Elves* share a common shortcoming: they're not even in the same ballpark as Disney. No nominations were deserved for either.

Best Short Subject (Comedy): Once again, the Academy gave the award to second-raters – who are not even worth mentioning – while one of the greatest of all Laurel and Hardy shorts, *Them Thar Hills*, went unnoticed. *Them Thar Hills* places Laurel and Hardy (Hardy in a cast from gout) into a trailer, runs them to a place where the well has been filled with moonshine, then brings in a married couple out of gas. The wife stays with Laurel & Hardy, and the good mountain "water." One of the classic tit-for-tat routines climaxes the movie. Laurel & Hardy should have taken home the gold.

CHAPTER EIGHT: 1936 AWARDS
8th Show

Movies released in 1935

THE SCENE OF THE CRIME:

On March 5, 1936, the Academy gathered at the Biltmore Bowl in the Biltmore Hotel. Academy President Frank Capra was the host, but he almost gave a party to which nobody came. The various guilds (writers, directors, actors) decided on a boycott in an attempt to break the Academy's power as a studio tool. The studio bosses were abandoning their own creation, for its failure to control the unions. Only a few stalwarts maintained their loyalty: David O. Selznick, Darryl F. Zanuck, Cecil B. DeMille, Frank Capra, and Clark Gable, among others.[lxxii] Capra allowed write-in votes, to counter charges that the nominations had been jiggered (only forty members remained from the boycott). Price Waterhouse was brought in to tally the votes. Finally, to make sure people would show up, Capra decided to give an honorary Oscar to D.W. Griffith, to celebrate the man more responsible for American movies being an art form than anybody else. That night, Griffith received the first standing ovation in Academy history.

Capra's efforts worked – barely. Tickets were handed out to studio employees who normally never had a chance to attend. Some stars came, but not many. Bette Davis didn't come in a formal dress, shocking many. The actual awards didn't get handed out until midnight.

Harry Cohn joked that since Columbia had won so many awards the year before, he had made sure his studio put out no good movies this year (they were only nominated for sound recording – and lost).

A first: Dudley Nichols refused to accept the Oscar he had won for writing *The Informer*, due to his support for the Writers Guild.

Another first: the Academy began a brief period of awarding a choreography category, which they called Best Dance Direction.

The Academy reworked the Writing categories, splitting it into Original Story and Screenplay. The tweaking would continue for decades.

WHAT THEY GOT RIGHT:

I feel so bad for the Academy. They got so much right last year, and now they go right back to making such bad decisions. One step forward, two steps back...but here's what they did get right.

Best Cinematography: Hal Mohr won for *A Midsummer Night's Dream*, over Ray June, *Barbary Coast*; Victor Milner, *The Crusades*; and Gregg Toland, *Les Misérables*.

For the first, last, and only time in Academy history, a write-in candidate won the Oscar. Hal Mohr's work on *A Midsummer Night's Dream* raised an uproar when it wasn't even nominated. Capra had to allow write-in votes to counter the charges of corruption. Mohr produced a singular look for German director Max Reinhardt's only Hollywood film, an adaptation of Shakespeare's *A Midsummer Night's Dream*. Mohr replaced Ernest Haller when he couldn't give Reinhardt what he wanted; Mohr produced the bright, enchanted shimmer of the finished film. Nothing like it had ever been seen before. The beautiful if slightly over-long montage of faeries awakening to the moon in the forest has to have been largely due to Mohr. A bravely won Oscar, built from outrage at excellence denied.

Ray June's camerawork on *Barbary Coast* served a script by Ben Hecht and Charles MacArthur; Howard Hawks directed Miriam Hopkins, Edward G. Robinson and Joel McCrea in this tale of the Gold Rush in California. The film opens in fog and night, lit by lanterns.

Looking at Miriam Hopkins, one can see they've been studying how Sternberg lit Dietrich. After that, the film looks quite run of the mill. Walter Brennan begins his long string of playing old coots with an eccentric nicknamed "Old Atrocity." Somebody really should have told Edward G. Robinson not to wear what looks like lipstick and eye shadow. The earring was not a good idea either. The film earned no other nominations, understandably so. The nomination should stay, for the opening, Hopkins, and the scenes in the moonlight.

Victor Milner shot *The Crusades* for Cecil B. DeMille. Milner also did Lubitsch's *Trouble in Paradise*, and he would go on to *The Lady Eve* and *The Palm Beach Story* for Preston Sturges. *The Crusades* stars Loretta Young and Henry Wilcoxson (Marc Antony from DeMille's *Cleopatra*) as the Princess of Navarre and King Richard the Lionheart. Young is somewhat miscast, as I never quite believe the supposed religious fervor. Wilcoxson plays yet another Antony, only more so. C. Aubrey Smith gives us a great religious fanatic lighting the flames for the Crusade. Fiction rules history, and Milner captures it all for DeMille in a "glorious schlock pageant."[lxxiii] The nomination should stay.

Gregg Toland continued to build his reputation as one of our great cinematographers, as he headed towards his masterpiece, *Citizen Kane*. *Les Misérables*, beautifully restored to the best possible condition in 2007, proves him in full command of his abilities. Toland's framing of faces to reveal the nuances of their expressions creates a sense of reality beyond most other cinematographers. As always, the cinematographer's art in black and white is the interplay of light and shadow, of the deepest blacks and the starkest whites, and all the shades of gray in between. Given that the director of *Les Misérables*, Richard Boleslawski, was far better known for his ability in directing acting rather than his imagery, one has to credit Toland with the sheer visual power of much of this film. The Academy made a good choice here.

What also remains incomprehensible is that *The Informer* was not nominated at all for the cinematography, since it is what the film is most famous for these days. From the opening credits, as shadows move through a dark, barely lit landscape, Joseph H. August's cinematography is stark and compelling. August deserved a nomination as well.

Best Short Subject (Cartoon): Disney won for *Three Orphan Kittens*, over Disney's *Who Killed Cock Robin?* and MGM's *The Calico Dragon*, from Harman-Ising

Disney had pulled so far ahead of the other studios' animation departments by this point that competition largely didn't exist. The nomination of MGM's *The Calico Dragon* can only have been due to MGM's studio block voting (the title card even imitates Disney slavishly); the whole cartoon could have come out from Disney a couple of years before. *Who Killed Cock Robin?* is remembered for its parodies of Mae West, Bing Crosby, and Harpo Marx, but the parody hasn't aged well. Disney and his animators were hitting their full stride in 1935, and plans were being laid for *Snow White and the Seven Dwarfs*. Disney should have been nominated for *The Band Concert* too, one of the most inventive of all the Mickey Mouse cartoons. Mickey's band twirls into the sky on a cyclone, refusing to stop playing the overture to *William Tell*. For me, *The Band Concert* is the ultimate in the kind of animation that had begun with *Steamboat Willie*, and nothing can match its manic qualities from the Disney studio. But the studio was heading towards a new kind of animation, one focused on realism and a deeper sense of character, and in that vein, the Oscar went to the Silly Symphony *Three Orphan Kittens*, a visual delight, from the snow effects, to the lighting in the basement, to the reflections of the kittens in the kitchen floor. The camera moves fluidly across the screen; shifts in perspective also strike new touches, as they move away from the proscenium view to pan in and out. The animators make us care for these little abandoned house-breakers (I strongly suspect this short inspired *The Aristocats* decades later). The cartoon is marred by a stereotypically happy black maid and a black doll calling for Mammy. Still, for artistic advances and experimentation, *Three Orphan Kittens* deserved its Oscar.

WHAT THEY GOT WRONG:

Man, did they get things wrong again! Either shake your head sadly here, or if you like being dramatic, do the face-palm. Until we get to the audio version of this book, you're just going to have to supply your own special effects...

Best Picture: *Mutiny on the Bounty*
Best Actor: Victor McLaglen, *The Informer*
Best Actress: Bette Davis, *Dangerous*
Best Director: John Ford, *The Informer*
Best Writing (Original Story): Ben Hecht and Charles MacArthur, *The Scoundrel*
Best Writing (Screenplay): Dudley Nichols, *The Informer*
Best Score: Max Steiner, *The Informer*

Best Song: Harry Warren and Al Dubin, "Lullaby of Broadway," *Gold Diggers of 1935*
Best Dance Direction: David Gould, "I've Got a Feelin' You're Foolin'," *Broadway Melody of 1936*
Best Art Direction: Richard Day, *The Dark Angel*
Best Short Subject (Comedy): MGM, *How to Sleep*

Best Picture: *Mutiny on the Bounty* won, over *Alice Adams, Broadway Melody of 1936, Captain Blood, David Copperfield, The Informer, Les Misérables, The Lives of a Bengal Lancer, A Midsummer Night's Dream, Naughty Marietta, Ruggles of Red Gap,* and *Top Hat*

I'm not saying the Clark Gable/Charles Laughton *Mutiny on the Bounty* isn't a great movie; it is, despite some minor flaws and mundane pacing in the middle. The early scenes of getting ready to sail and the building tension on the ship are excellent. The film becomes too episodic after the first half hour, and really loses its narrative drive and any sense of complexity once they reach Tahiti; the film picks back up with the mutiny. The ending suggests a happy outcome for the mutineers; as a teenager, I was shocked when I discovered that Fletcher Christian and all but one man were soon murdered on Pitcairn. But of the five times this book has been filmed, this remains the very best by a wide margin. Charles Laughton gives a masterful performance; Clark Gable and Franchot Tone turn in excellent work as well, although not on Laughton's level (but then, few actors did – see Best Actor below). The sense of historical reality is serviceable, although not the peak of sailing naval pictures (*Master and Commander* comes first in my mind). MGM and Irving Thalberg lavished money on their production, reconstructing two British sailing ships, then towing them to Tahiti for location shooting (and being forced to use Catalina off the coast of Los Angeles for the majority of the film). The result was a good action picture, and one that I've watched every few years with pleasure. The nomination should stay, but not the Oscar.

Alice Adams stars Katharine Hepburn and Fred MacMurray, and was based on a Booth Tarkington Pulitzer Prize novel, and directed by George Stevens (his first important film). Hepburn was nominated for Best Actress (see below). *Alice Adams* relentlessly depicts the social consequences of money and class in America (a subject we rarely admit exists these days). In the hands of Capra, Hepburn's character would have stuck her tongue out at the rich. Here, her brother is the one who doesn't approve of social climbing; in this, he's like his father. The cruelties of women enforcing their ranks surround the frailties of Hepburn as she tries to break into their circle. Her hunger to be accepted and desired pains us, especially when we realize how vain and petty the in-crowd is. The dinner party towards the end couldn't be more awkward and uncomfortable. Hattie McDaniel's maid is meant to be amusing; she might have been, once. Tarkington's original downbeat outcome was sacrificed on the altar of happy endings, turning the film to the trivial, and should have never been nominated.

Broadway Melody of 1936 stars Jack Benny, Eleanor Powell and Robert Taylor. Benny plays a gossip columnist on the radio (imitating Walter Winchell). Taylor is a producer, putting together *Broadway Rhythm*. Eleanor Powell is Taylor's childhood sweetheart, who wants in the show. He won't let her, so she masquerades as a French entertainer Benny has invented. Buddy Ebsen and Frances Langford show up. MGM was clearly flexing its studio votes getting this on the ballot. Taylor is atrocious, especially when he does something he thinks is singing. Powell is pretty darn bueno, especially when she does a drop-dead impression of Kate Hepburn in *Morning Glory*. Nevertheless, none of this comes close to what a Best Picture should be, so no nomination should have been given.

Captain Blood was Errol Flynn's breakout role. Directed by Michael Curtiz, Flynn is marvelous as the swashbuckling doctor wrongfully imprisoned and enslaved. I've always loved Flynn's movies since I was a kid, and time has not changed that opinion. Sometimes, I even agree with myself. *Captain Blood* and Flynn still buckle a swash as nobody has before or since. Basil Rathbone is marvelous as the pirate Levasseur, and the duel scene is the best in cinema history up to that point, largely due to the fight choreographers Ralph Faulkner and Fred Cavens, Rathbone's mastery of the sword, and Flynn's natural grace and savoir faire. Olivia de Havilland, like Flynn, became a star because of this film. Lionel Atwill extended his record as one of the best screen villains as Colonel Bishop, the cruel plantation owner and father of Arabella (de Havilland). Also starring: the wonderful fighting ships, which were miniatures – eighteen foot miniatures! Never before had naval combat looked so real, so exciting, even if some combat from a silent picture was spliced in. *Captain Blood* isn't the perfect swashbuckler, but it's in the top ten (several of which star Flynn and de Havilland). A few moments strike as overwrought, and Flynn should never be called upon to do much acting. As Peter O'Toole says as the Flynn character in

My Favorite Year, "I'm not an actor! I'm a movie star!" The nomination should stay.[47]

David O. Selznick forced his father-in-law Louis B. Mayer to make *David Copperfield*. Thankfully, Selznick won out, and with the help of director George Cukor, put together a dream cast that remains unmatched to this day. Freddie Bartholomew was found for David Copperfield after eight months of searching, then more time wasted over parental squabbles. Basil Rathbone began to build his reputation as a superlative villain this year as Mr. Murdstone (David's stepfather), cemented it with Pontius Pilate in *The Last Days of Pompeii* and the pirate Levasseur in *Captain Blood*, and finished off the year as the cruel Marquis St. Evremonde in *A Tale of Two Cities*. The other actors include Jessie Ralph as Peggotty, Edna May Oliver as Aunt Betsy, and in the most perfect casting in the entire year, W.C. Fields, who replaced an unhappy Charles Laughton in the role of Field's lifetime as Mr. Micawber. Watching the first rushes with Laughton, one of Selznick's assistants said, "Laughton looks as if he's going to molest the child."[lxxiv] Una O'Connor and Lionel Barrymore eat up the scenery in small roles. Written by Howard Estabrook and rewritten by British novelist Hugh Walpole, *David Copperfield* remains the best adaptation of any Dickens novel Hollywood has ever done (the British have had a few to equal it, notably the David Lean *Great Expectations*). What is more, I think it may be Selznick's best film, with the possible exception of *Gone with the Wind*. As Selznick's biographer David Thomson argues, *David Copperfield* "is the first film that identifies the terrible beauty of a child's apprehensions and the way they burn unceasingly through duller adulthood. David never did anything better."[lxxv] The nomination most definitely should stay.

The Informer tells the story of Gypo Nolan, who rats out one of his best friends to get a reward. Victor McLaglen stars as Gypo. The opening title cards lay out that we are in a Judas tale in 1922 Dublin, torn by rebellion and British oppression. The critics of the period fell over themselves praising it: "...they...compared *The Informer* favorably to Sternberg's *The Docks of New York* and Hawks' *Scarface*." Watching it today can be a jarring experience since we expect one of Ford's greatest films, but as Scott Eyman has so ably observed, "one generation's shattering masterpiece is another's threadbare warhorse."[lxxvi] The film is too earnest, too absorbed with its own seriousness. The drunken scenes some see as played for comic effect are merely pathetic, as Gypo blows

---

[47] The 12-year-old in me is very happy right now. Now, if I could only punch that school bully in the face, and get rid of those zits, life would be perfect...

his thirty pieces of silver on drink and showing off. We've seen so many later films, many of them directed by Ford himself, which know how to tell a tragedy better. The nomination should stay, as the film is still worth watching for the better parts, but we are just partway to the mature genius Ford would become by the end of the Thirties.

Les Misérables retains a special place in my memory, as the very first film based on a classic novel any of my teachers showed me. The magic of words becoming images remains intoxicating – and often infuriating, as Hollywood destroys the heart of the thing they're trying to bring to life visually. A very sad graveyard could be made of the books Hollywood has murdered. *Les Misérables* is not one of them, for once. From its opening scenes, wherein Jean Valjean (Fredric March) is sentenced to ten years in the galleys for stealing a single loaf of bread to feed his starving nephews and nieces, the heart is torn in sympathy for those wretched poor who have exhausted all of their options. March is good, but Charles Laughton as Inspector Javert is brilliant in one of the peaks of this actor's nearly unmatched career. Had Laughton not been nominated in *Mutiny on the Bounty*, he surely would have been for this film. Javert is a tortured soul, the child of criminals, who spends his life in manic pursuit of the law in compensation for his unfortunate choice in parents. Laughton's face – which he described as looking like "the behind of an elephant" – fascinates in its endless subtleties.[lxxvii] *Les Misérables* was Darryl F. Zanuck's response to David O. Selznick's Dickens adaptations over at MGM; this film's concern with the poor and social justice points directly at Zanuck's production of *The Grapes of Wrath* in a few years. Director Richard Boleslawski was an actor's director; March was never better in a dramatic role, and Laughton rarely matched himself here. The nomination should stay.

The Lives of a Bengal Lancer stars Gary Cooper and Franchot Tone; the inimitable C. Aubrey Smith appears as well. Set in British colonial India, *The Lives of a Bengal Lancer* ostensibly tells a war story between the British army and a local rebel (by definition, in Hollywood, rebelling against imperial control makes you a villain...unless your name is Luke Skywalker). The first real story is that of a young man on his first assignment, under the command of his martinet father; the second, and better story, is the competition between Gary Cooper's veteran and Franchot Tone's mocking newcomer, as they work through their dislike, and try to help the young son cope with his father's devotion to duty. Cooper plays a flawed character (something he would rarely do as he became a bigger star); Tone has the smirk and the jabbing wit down perfectly. *The Lives of a Bengal Lancer* is that rare beast: an adventure tale driven by character conflict, and a well-earned nomination.

A Midsummer Night's Dream remains the best Shakespeare film to emerge from Hollywood in the Thirties. Based on a wildly successful production at the Hollywood Bowl, German director Max Reinhardt was signed up for a film version even before opening night. Apparently, fleeing from the Nazis is good for your career; just ask Fritz Lang. Everybody who was anybody in Hollywood came out for the performances under the stars. Warner Brothers then went to work making this version of Shakespeare's comic masterpiece, to the immortal music by Felix Mendelssohn – arranged by another refugee, Erich Wolfgang Korngold. This *Midsummer* charms and pops, even as it occasionally has to drag some dead weight. (Dick Powell, anybody? I thought not.) Fortunately, Mickey Rooney's turn as Puck is wild, if a bit annoying. Rooney played much of his role in a cast after breaking his leg tobogganing. James Cagney as Bottom continues to surprise with his excellence; indeed, the mechanicals have never been funnier than with Cagney and Joe E. Brown. Had there been a Best Supporting Actor category this year, both should have been nominated, as they give brilliant comic turns. Olivia de Havilland announced her incipient stardom at age 19 as Hermia. Bette Davis was going to be cast, but she was fighting with Jack Warner – again. Reinhardt didn't direct the film so much as he did the actors. William Dieterle actually shot the movie, with Hal Mohr on the camera (see Best Cinematography above). A box-office failure, Reinhardt's *Midsummer* has proven to be the most interesting film version thus far. The nomination is well deserved.

Based on the Victor Herbert operetta, *Naughty Marietta* was the first film to team Jeanette MacDonald with Nelson Eddy. Neither of them would ever do much apart again. Macdonald plays a princess avoiding an arranged marriage by fleeing to America disguised as her maid, when she is captured by pirates. Nelson Eddy rescues her. She avoids being forced to marry a colonist by implying she was a prostitute (hence the "naughty" part). This folderol is but an excuse for the two of them to sing. One could call it singing; on the other hand, Al Capp once described what they do as "depraved sincerity."[lxxviii] They do have impressive voices, but great singing doesn't necessarily involve a beautiful voice (just think Bob Dylan, Janis Joplin, or Louis Armstrong). Why this groaning creaker of a film ever got nominated for a Best Picture Oscar can only be chalked up to the respect Hollywood had for profits – and MGM studio block voting. "Sweet Mystery of Life," indeed. As Michael Phillips has noted, "One of the film's biggest problems is Nelson Eddy, who seems incapable of expression. Critics called him 'the singing capon' (a capon being a castrated chicken), and the name fits. He seems unable to feel; he sits or stands stock-still, shoulders squared, with his beautiful baritone booming out, as if from a broken marionette."[lxxix] We should feel sorry for MacDonald, whose successful career was yoked to Eddy until he killed it. No nomination should have been given.

Ruggles of Red Gap is basically a version of James Barrie's *The Admirable Crichton* sent west (but then, turned sideways, so is *My Man Godfrey*). Directed by Leo McCarey, *Ruggles* examines American attitudes towards class, individualism, and self-reliance, all through the prism of a British servant who learns to discard his class-based views in favor of a more American independence. Charles Laughton turns in yet another top-notch performance as the butler Ruggles, who seeks to live his own life; this year, Laughton could do no wrong (see Best Actor). Laughton's rendition of the Gettysburg Address sends chills up my spine each and every time – reportedly, it brought the speech back to American prominence, having largely been forgotten.[lxxx] *Ruggles* is an excellent nomination.

Top Hat is, arguably, the finest musical Fred Astaire and Ginger Rogers ever made – which means, by definition, *Top Hat* may be the finest musical ever made, period. That the Academy nominated it reflects eternal credit upon them. We can explain numerous reasons for *Top Hat* not winning: the Academy rarely honors musicals; even though the story and songs are different, Astaire and Rogers had made films like this one before, including some of the same cast members (hello, Edward Everett Horton!) and the same director, Mark Sandrich. The difference here lies in the mastery of several extraordinarily difficult art forms: music and lyrics, brought to perfection by Irving Berlin (see Best Song below); choreography, by Astaire and Hermes Pan (see Best Dance Direction below); and three other necessities: acting, singing, and dancing. Fred Astaire could act, as could Ginger Rogers, well enough to carry a movie. But in motion, Fred Astaire and Ginger Rogers are the very personification of grace and elegance and style. Both of them realized that they had to continue to act when the singing and dancing began (which is why most musicals fall flat on their faces, because they stop acting at the moment their characters are about to be fully realized). What is more, even though Astaire had a less than robust voice, what he had more than anybody outside of Bing Crosby and Louis Armstrong was rhythm. The man sang like he danced. Irving Berlin and Cole Porter preferred him above all others to introduce their songs on stage and screen, and for damn good reason: nobody else could bring a song's poetry to life on its own merits better than Astaire. Add in Rogers, and you've got magic; as Katharine Hepburn said, "Fred gives Ginger class, and Ginger gives Fred sex." Both are more as a team than they would ever be apart.^{lxxxi} *Top Hat* brought it all together: story, humor, romance, singing, and dancing, in one of the true American art forms, the musical. Not a single misstep mars *Top Hat*. *Top Hat* should have won the Oscar for Best Picture.

Allow me three codas.

The Academy shamelessly omitted nominations for three other outstanding films: Alfred Hitchcock's *The 39 Steps*; James Whale's *Bride of Frankenstein*; and the Marx Brothers' *A Night at the Opera*. All three approach perfection, and along with many of the Academy's choices, rendered this year one of the most difficult to reconsider. Hitchcock's *The 39 Steps* is one of his great suspense masterpieces (see Best Director for more). *Bride of Frankenstein* is one of those rare things: a sequel that betters the original. The imagery of Frankenstein on the cross opens up all kinds of thoughts about the role of the outsider, the exile, and the castoffs of society, at the hands of a persecuting majority. Funnier, better acted all around (even Karloff matches and exceeds his original performance), with a deeper story and better supporting cast (Ernest Thesiger is priceless), *Bride of Frankenstein* is my favorite horror film.[48] I came within a hair's breadth of choosing it as the Best Picture, but if it is one of the handful of horror films to approach art, then *Top Hat* beats it by being the very definition of musical art.

As for *A Night at the Opera*, the Marx Brothers produce a classic comedy, but one somewhat drained of their insanity, as Thalberg put them in service to a romance, which tames them to a degree. *Top Hat* beats them all, which is saying something. Makes me almost want to believe in Santa Claus. But as Chico says, "You no canna foola me. There is no sanity clause."

Best Actor: Victor McLaglen won for *The Informer*, over Clark Gable, Charles Laughton, and Franchot Tone, *Mutiny on the Bounty*

Victor McLaglen received the Oscar for Best Actor, largely because the three *Mutiny* nominees split the MGM studio vote. John Ford reportedly got McLaglen drunk and hung over for several scenes, but McLaglen's son and Ford himself denied this. McLaglen never reached these heights again, quickly becoming a first-rate character actor, usually in John Ford films, often with comic overtones. McLaglen definitely remains one of the best parts of the film, which is his finest moment as a star. Gypo's love interest is turning to prostitution because they're

---

[48] Karloff should have been nominated again for Best Actor, so let's consider him so. We can just keep it our little secret, and make fun of people who never read the footnotes...

starving; if only they had the twenty pounds to get to America. Dangling in front of him is the reward for turning in his friend, which is precisely the money they need to escape from Dublin and destitution. What is worse, he's refused to kill someone, so the IRA has kicked him out; the British think he's still with the rebels, so he has no one to turn to. What will Gypo do? And having done it, how will he live with himself? The outcome is almost certain from the beginning, investing the tale with something of Greek tragedy. McLaglen definitely deserved a nomination, but only the three-way split of votes on *Mutiny on the Bounty* ever got him the Oscar for Best Actor, which should have gone elsewhere.

Mutiny on the Bounty secured three Best Actor nominations, an unmatched feat to this day. Charles Laughton's Captain Bligh is a right bastard, a cruel disciplinarian for whom power and authority are all. Clark Gable's Fletcher Christian comes across with verve, humor and compassion, easily outdoing the performances of Marlon Brando and Mel Gibson in the same role. Franchot Tone's young enthusiastic midshipman Byam acts as our viewpoint character, as we learn the ways of the British navy (which sailors called a "floating hell"). All three performances deserved nominations, Laughton most of all. Laughton creates the ravaging insecurity at the heart of Captain Bligh, a "self-made man" who is still on the make and needs to assert absolute control over all others in order to maintain his sense of superiority. Without this heart of pain, Bligh would be nothing but a cardboard villain. Laughton's Inspector Javert from *Les Misérables* is even more undermined by his sense of social insecurity; when you match these two masterful turns with the charming performance as Ruggles the butler in *Ruggles of Red Gap*, particularly in the recitation of the Gettysburg Address, you can see this was Laughton's year. Watch all three performances, and not only will you see the voice and face used differently for every character, but the entire body language from stance to walk is unique, and utterly indicative of the inner life of each. Laughton deserved the Oscar for Captain Bligh, a role with which he would be forever identified. But before we celebrate, allow me to pass out one necessary gesture of respect.

As *David Copperfield's* Mr. Micawber, actor and part became one: W.C. Fields lived this role as few actors ever have. I would argue he had inhabited a Dickensian world for much of his life. Charles Dickens was his favorite author, and Fields had committed much of his work to memory. *David Copperfield* is a fabulous movie, and Fields' Micawber is reason #1. Allow me to prove how good an actor Fields is: he actually convinces you he likes a child. Fields would never again be given this kind of opportunity, primarily because he could so easily overwhelm a film. In *David Copperfield*, he fit himself perfectly into the tight collar of the role. He deserved a nomination (had there been a Best Supporting Actor category this year, he would have sewn it up easily).

Even so, Laughton should have won.

Best Actress: Bette Davis won for *Dangerous*, over Katharine Hepburn, *Alice Adams*; Miriam Hopkins, *Becky Sharp*; Merle Oberon, *The Dark Angel*; Elisabeth Bergner, *Escape Me Never*; and Claudette Colbert, *Private Worlds* (they nominated six due to a tie vote)

Bette Davis got the Oscar, as she herself said, as a "consolation prize" for not winning the previous year for *Of Human Bondage*.[lxxxii] *Dangerous* co-starred Franchot Tone in this tale of a lover trying to help the formerly famous actress played by Davis overcome alcoholism. Watching *Dangerous* today, one wonders what all the fuss was about; but then again, so did Davis, who thought Katharine Hepburn deserved to win for *Alice Adams*. *Dangerous* is sheer melodrama, so soapy you need to hose it down to see it clearly. As an actress, Davis is still learning her craft (see *Jezebel* below for that turning point), and I think the reason why her contemporary actors were so taken with her, as in *Of Human Bondage*, was that she was willing to play ugly in this age of glamour. Davis would never have gained any attention at MGM; only a gritty studio like Warners would have done it for her, and even then she had to fight, which is another reason why Davis was so respected by other actors trapped in the studio system. Davis does have her moments in the film: her drunken soliloquy of Juliet's death scene; a few snatches of seductiveness here and there; her conniving vulnerability and hostility as she attempts to get a divorce. Today, Davis' performance is the only reason to watch *Dangerous*; nothing else about the film – plot, direction, cinematography, the cast – is worth your time. But while I do think Davis earned the nomination, she did not deserve the Oscar, as she herself admitted.

Katharine Hepburn's nomination in *Alice Adams* is for a dutiful daughter who wants more than her father can provide, but she can't bring herself to tell him that. She loves her father; her mother is a nag, but both women feel the difficulties of finding a socially advantageous marriage without the funds necessary to provide the niceties of social contact. Hepburn rarely played a role this insecure and namby-pamby as she grew into her maturity; it's jarring, knowing what was to come, but Hepburn makes it work somehow. The scenes with her father, and her confrontation with her father's employer, are the best part of it. The nomination should stay, even if I don't like Alice very much.

Miriam Hopkins stars as *Becky Sharp*, the first feature length Technicolor film. Directed by Rouben Mamoulian, this adaptation of the William Makepeace Thackeray classic *Vanity Fair* does a credible job bringing to life the most infamous social climber of literature. Mamoulian took over for another director, and reportedly reshot everything from scratch. I suspect not, for about a third of the way into the film, the camera starts moving, and Mamoulian was famous for his mobile camerawork. Before the scenes in Belgium, *Becky Sharp* is a static, theatrical presentation of the novel, with little life outside of Hopkins and a handful of the supporting players. Hopkins was perfectly cast, bringing her blend of sexy charm and deviousness to a boil. Hopkins deserved her nomination, because she is the best part of the film. Like Hepburn in *Alice Adams*, Hopkins makes the movie worth watching, even if neither performance is their best work. She should keep her nomination.

Merle Oberon received a nod for *The Dark Angel*. Lillian Hellman co-wrote the screenplay – her first Hollywood assignment – adapting the weepie play about a girl and two boys who grow up together. Oberon plays the woman who loves one of the men, both of them love her, and WWI gets in the way. Fair warning: blindness and noble self-sacrifice are involved, perhaps a bit too much so, but tolerably. Oberon made her first American film appearance. Her performance is restrained and unconvincing for the most part; at times, she goes overboard in a display of bad acting. Fredric March isn't much better, as the ham comes out. Merle Oberon survived on her beauty alone. She cries more falsely than almost any other actress. Part of the problem is the ridiculously overwrought melodrama in which she's trapped. But the job of an actor is to master the material he or she is given; that she really never succeeds is why she should not have her nomination for this piece of tripe.

Elisabeth Bergner played Gemma Jones in the British *Escape Me Never*, a role she had on stage in London and on Broadway. To quote *The New York Times* reviewer of the day, "Deep down under the exterior glitter of Bergner and a splendid British cast, Margaret Kennedy's odyssey of an unearthly sprite and a mad genius is still in the approximate neighborhood of claptrap."[lxxxiii] I couldn't agree more. Bergner's performance here in *Escape Me Never* as a wild child seems overly mannered. The next year, Bergner would co-star with Laurence Olivier in *As You Like It*. She also seems to have been the model for Margo Channing, the Bette Davis character, in *All About Eve*. As for the movie as a whole, the live footage of Venice in the Thirties is enchanting, but that's about the best thing I can say. The plot is indeed claptrap; the performances have little spark or snap to them, including Bergner's. As for the nomination, I suspect this is a case of Hollywood being overly impressed with a foreign and theatrical reputation. Bergner simply doesn't play well on the screen – so no nomination should have been given.

   Claudette Colbert teamed with director Gregory La Cava in *Private Worlds*, a melodrama set in an insane asylum. Colbert plays a psychiatrist who comes into conflict with Charles Boyer as a dictatorial new director; Joel McCrea plays a psychiatrist who teams with Colbert. Colbert couldn't be a more kind, understanding, and saintly caretaker. One of the pleasures of her performance lies in her obvious authority and power in the role, as so many women's roles were supposed to be in the popular conception of Thirties movies, and so few have proven to be as I've watched these movies. Moreover, one of the attractions of *Private Worlds* is the platonic friendship between McCrea and Colbert, which is quite unusual for the period – and by far the best aspect of the film, which ends up running into melodramatic clichés and the obligatory romantic ending between opponents. Colbert's nomination is a good one; I can't think of a healthier or saner human being in Thirties film.

   For the un-nominated, Olivia de Havilland made two fine appearances: as Hermia, in *A Midsummer Night's Dream*, and as Arabella, in *Captain Blood*. Of the two, Arabella is far better. In this swashbuckler, de Havilland supplies the romance: she is lively, perky, stubborn, lovely, compassionate and sparkling. De Havilland would go on to play Errol Flynn's love interest repeatedly, but never better than here. How any man could fail to fall in love with the actress after seeing this movie is just as much a puzzle as to how any woman could resist the same attraction for Flynn. De Havilland should have been nominated, and after watching the ladies this year, she gives the freshest, most convincing performance by far. The Oscar should have gone to Olivia de Havilland for *Captain Blood*.

Best Director: John Ford won for *The Informer*, over Henry Hathaway, *The Lives of a Bengal Lancer*, and Frank Lloyd, *Mutiny on the Bounty*

   Ford won for *The Informer*. No other movie this year was so obviously aiming for art; who else but Ford could have gotten the performance he did from Victor McLaglen? Ford's special touch can be seen from the opening scenes. As McLaglen is pursued by the wanted poster for his friend, we hear a sentimental song recalling old times and friendships coming from a street singer. The film is drenched in darkness and fog, at least in part due to necessity; the sets were so cheaply made, Ford had to resort to this felicitous atmosphere to preserve the willing suspension of disbelief. Reveling in the night, and in McLaglen's first-rate performance, Ford changed his standing permanently with *The Informer*, gaining "a critical reputation he would never entirely lose and bestowed upon him a leader's role within the industry."[lxxxiv] Looking ahead, Ford would become much better. *The Informer* was an indispensable step toward the fusion of entertainer and artist that was to come – but should not have won the Oscar.

Henry Hathaway's work on *The Lives of a Bengal Lancer* works quite well, in a functional, minimalist way. Little effort is wasted on anything but telling the story clearly and cleanly, and what's wrong with that? Storytelling is a dying art form these days in Hollywood; most everybody seems to have forgotten how. Hathaway does a far better job directing than Frank Lloyd did on *Mutiny on the Bounty*.

Lloyd's direction on *Mutiny on the Bounty* is the weakest part of the film, as it is largely static, with little inventiveness, and ignorant of the necessary pacing to make almost the entire middle section of the film work properly. Lloyd remained the studio drone he was on *Cavalcade*. What fascinates about *Mutiny on the Bounty* would more than likely have happened regardless of who directed, since it was Thalberg who pumped the money into the movie and cast it. Laughton was great regardless of directors; Gable was always Gable (but look at *It Happened One Night* to see what Gable was capable of with a first rate director like Frank Capra). Lloyd seems more in love with the ship then he does with the story, and the shots of the *Bounty* sailing remain the ones most cinematically compelling. The nomination should stay, but I suspect the quality of the film is there despite Lloyd, not because of him.

So what of those the Academy ignored?

One might point to another John Ford film made the same year as *The Informer*: Will Rogers' last movie, *Steamboat Round the Bend*. Written by Dudley Nichols, who also wrote *The Informer*, *Steamboat* tells the story of a patent medicine salesman who comes to race a steamboat. Personally, I have a hard time watching the Ford/Rogers collaborations, because of Stepin Fetchit playing the most racist characters in American film prior to Jar Jar Binks (who is, if you watch, clearly pointing at Stepin Fetchit as inspiration). Scott Eyman suggests two categories for Ford: "*Steamboat Round the Bend* features Ford the entertainer, rather than Ford the artist."[lxxxv] I suggest *Steamboat* as a counterpoint to *The Informer*, so one can see both of Ford's major categories of movies (which he would learn to merge by the later Thirties, with *Stagecoach* and *The Grapes of Wrath*). The steamboat race is wonderful. *Steamboat Round the Bend* makes a nice companion piece to *The Informer*, even if we have to put up with Jar Jar...er, Stepin Fetchit.

Like Ford, Alfred Hitchcock was rapidly improving, producing one of his masterpieces in *The 39 Steps*. One of the best British films he would ever make, *The 39 Steps* starred Robert Donat and Madeleine Carroll. Two words are all you need to remember this one: Mr. Memory. From the opening shots, Hitchcock lets us see we aren't in the hands of a mundane moviemaker. We get shots of feet entering a theatre, the seats, the back of Donat's head, and then the music hall orchestra opens up, and Mr. Memory is on stage. We are in an act of voyeurism, watching Donat watch the show. Shots ring out, panic follows, and Donat picks up a strange woman. The game, as Sherlock Holmes occasionally said, is afoot. Hitchcock's odd humor continues to emerge. When the cleaning woman finds a dead body, her scream becomes the scream of Donat's train. The final scenes thrill both in visual and narrative terms. Hitchcock's American reputation would take time to build, but *The 39 Steps* moved him much closer.

And yet, even more than Ford and Hitchcock on their way to artistic perfection, we need to pay homage to a director who hit his artistic height, a feat he would never reach again. If *Top Hat* is the perfect musical, and that largely due to Fred Astaire and Hermes Pan, then *Bride of Frankenstein* is largely due to James Whale, and horror films just don't get any better than this, if what you want from a horror film is black humor, a mirror to society, and a call to social justice. That, and a hellishly good time. Watching *Bride* today unfolds as a far richer experience than I had remembered as a child, when all I cared about were the thrills.[49] Like reading *Huck Finn* and watching *Rocky and Bullwinkle*, *Bride of Frankenstein* operates as both a child's adventure and as an adult's invitation to reconsider some very basic assumptions. I am put in mind of Chaplin's Tramp, who often lived on the margins, and who was rejected by those who were "normal." Consider three scenes: the capture and crucifixion of the monster; the scene with the hermit (so brilliantly parodied in *Young Frankenstein*), and the creation scene of the Bride. In each, Whale's humor points out the harsh demands for conformity that society makes, and the frustrated failures and persecution of those individuals whom society refuses to accept. Like science fiction, horror often gets away with things a mainstream film can't, because the assumption this is all pointless kid's stuff provides major cover. I don't think any other genre could have made it past the censorship

---

[49] Try the vantage point of having seen *Gods and Monsters*, a fine film in and of itself about the making of *Bride* and the life of James Whale.

office with so many pointed references to the persecution of Christ. Small touches throughout the film surprise and startle: the owl watching the monster's first kills, Una O'Connor's ironic "He's alive!" for both the monster and Dr. Frankenstein; the monster and his reflection; the monster's discovery of music, and language, and wine; the longing for connection and friendship. James Whale should have been nominated for *Bride of Frankenstein*, and he should have won the Oscar for Best Director. It might have made the difference between continued achievement, and the decline that actually occurred in just a few years.

Best Writing (Original Story): Ben Hecht and Charles MacArthur won for *The Scoundrel*, over Moss Hart, *Broadway Melody of 1936*; and Don Hartman & Stephen Avery, *The Gay Deception*

Ben Hecht and Charles MacArthur won for *The Scoundrel*, which they also directed. Noel Coward stars in this supernatural tale of personal redemption. Coward plays a publisher who is morally bankrupt (leave it to two writers to "invent" a publisher who is certain to be damned...). He dies, but is given a chance to return to life to find one single person who cares about him enough to mourn his passing. Hecht and MacArthur are playing with a plot that has been used in a variety of other modes, such as Beauty and the Beast, or the Flying Dutchman. The dialogue is brutal, venomous, and quite the best part of the movie – but the category here is story, not screenplay. The outcome is the predictable one, which is why the Oscar should have gone elsewhere.

Moss Hart's original story for *Broadway Melody of 1936* isn't all that original (the movie is a sequel, after all). Hart wrote two classics for the stage, *You Can't Take It with You* and *The Man Who Came to Dinner*, and later directed the initial stage production of *My Fair Lady*. *Broadway Melody of 1936* should have no nomination, mostly because the story is more than a little ridiculous and repetitious.

Stephen Avery and Don Hartman received a nomination for *The Gay Deception*, which is not some Thirties version of *The Crying Game*. Frances Dee plays a lottery winner who decides to spend it all on high living; she meets a bellhop who is actually a prince in real life (Francis Lederer, who was the son in *Pandora's Box*). William Wyler directed. The story amuses, as it works through the Cinderella story, combined with something of *The Prince and the Pauper*. I found *The Gay Deception* to be one of the best unknown films of the Thirties, sweet, funny, and romantic, perfect for the next time you want to share a movie with somebody you'd like to fondle. The nomination stays.

And what about the films the Academy ignored?

One of the most original story ideas for the year is the very first movie about lycanthropy, *Werewolf of London*, starring Henry Hull and Warner Oland. Written by John Colton, and based on an original story by Robert Harris, *Werewolf of London* began a long chain of werewolf films, the best of which were this and Lon Chaney, Jr.'s *The Wolf Man*. Stylishly filmed, although clearly on a budget, *Werewolf of London* retains a strange charm, and plays up the tragic angle, and should have earned a nomination.

Ladies and Gentlemen, I offer you, in the center ring, the gentleman who should have won the Oscar for Best Writing (Original Story) of the year 1935: Mr. Charles Bogle, ably assisted by Mr. Sam Hardy. Mr. Bogle will be attempting to deceive you as to his true identity, but do not be bamboozled; keep your eye on *The Man on the Flying Trapeze*, Mr. William Claude Fields! Ah, Yes! Charles Bogle is none other than one of the many pen names of W.C. Fields, the world's greatest juggler, and one of the funniest men who ever lived. He plays Ambrose Wolfinger, a henpecked husband and lush (now there's a surprise) who finds himself trapped in a whopper of a lie. For years, to make one of my best friends lose it completely in public, no matter where we were, all I had to do is lean over and say "Hurry, Ambrose, hurry!" You'll need to see the movie to see why. But if three little words can cause repeated crackups, the idea has to be worth an Oscar. Just don't look for any trapezes. Godfrey Daniel!

Best Writing (Screenplay): Dudley Nichols won for *The Informer*, over a whole cartload of writers for *The Lives of a Bengal Lancer*; and Talbot Jennings, Jules Furthman, and Carey Wilson for *Mutiny on the Bounty*

Dudley Nichols won for *The Informer*. He refused to accept the award, out of loyalty to the Screen Writers Guild, which was protesting the Academy's interference in labor relations. Nichols was the usual scribe on John Ford's more artistic efforts. Nichols reproduces the heart of the original novel, bringing strife-torn Dublin to life as few other movies ever have. Written with Ford on his ship the *Araner*, Nichols' script is a work of quality, even if the ending is more than a little ridiculous (why would anybody's mother forgive an informer who caused her son's death?!). The nomination should stay, but not the award.

The Lives of a Bengal Lancer seems to have been written by a cast of thousands: Waldemar Young, John L. Balderston, Achmed Abdullah, Grover Jones, and William Slavens McNutt. Beware hordes of wandering writers! They're hungry, and have no compunction against long pig (pass the BBQ sauce...). Based on a novel by Francis Yeats-Brown, *The

Lives of a Bengal Lancer is set in India, when it was under British imperial control (as so many adventure movies were, most famously *Gunga Din*). Allow me to set aside the colonial issues. I am very aware of the implications this movie makes about the rightness of the Empire; Hitler loved the movie so much he made the S.S. watch it, for its implications of white superiority.[lxxxvi] But *The Lives of a Bengal Lancer* is full of witty dialogue and solid character conflict, the very stuff of excellent story telling. How anybody managed to herd this many writers is a miracle. A well-deserved nomination, even with the implied rightness of colonial control.

Charles Nordhoff and James Norman Hall wrote three books about the *Bounty* mutiny: one about the mutiny itself, one about the return to England by Captain Bligh, and one about the survivors on Pitcairn Island. Classics of seafaring literature, they are as readable today as they were when first published in the early Thirties. Talbot Jennings, Jules Furthman, and Carey Wilson and other uncredited writers turned out a serviceable script. Some of the writing could have been smoothed out into a more flowing script, rather than the episodic and somewhat static picture we get in the middle. More care should have been taken to enliven the Tahitian scenes, and to deepen the reasons for romance; the love scenes are entirely too limp. The nomination should stay, but tighter scripting would have brought them the Oscar.

Other writers needed recognition this year as well.

W.P Lipscomb adapted Victor Hugo's gargantuan novel *Les Misérables* for Darryl F. Zanuck (he also worked on *A Tale of Two Cities* over at MGM). Nothing less than a massive miniseries would ever do to encompass the entirety of the novel. Lipscomb and Zanuck (a writer himself) extracted the heart of the story, and made it sing. The opening of the film compares the persecution of Jean Valjean for a crime he had to commit (stealing bread for his starving nieces and nephews) with the persecution of Javert for a crime he could not help committing (having criminals for parents). Absolutely perfect structuring of a story aims the two men – and their moral answers to their quandaries – at each other. Valjean will steal again, only to be helped by a kindly and forgiving bishop, and so learn to forgive and give to others ("I learned life is to give, not to take," taught the bishop); Javert learns never to forgive, to be harsh to all, including himself, in enforcing the law. Lipscomb deserved a nomination, even if huge bleeding chunks of the novel lie on the floor beside the typewriter, including a very unsatisfying reversal of the book's ending, which hammers home the theme of the need for human forgiveness rather than the false ending of the movie.

On the same grounds, Howard Estabrook and Hugh Walpole should have been nominated for adapting *David Copperfield*. Dickens' novel is enormous; Estabrook and Walpole got it all into one movie, saving every scene of consequence (see Best Picture above for more).

Bride of Frankenstein is a beautifully written and filmed movie (see Best Picture and Best Director). More than any other film this year, I am drawn to the situations and scenes devised by the script, and by James Whale's interpretation. William Hurlbut and John Balderston took the Mary Shelley novel and the 1931 film, and devised an absolutely brilliant and fresh look at the situation. They begin with one creation scene – Mary Shelley, Byron, and Percy Shelley on a stormy night as Mary invents the tale – and end with another creation, that of the Bride. Whale plays up that circular structure by casting Elsa Lanchester (the wife of Charles Laughton) as both Mary Shelley and the Bride. In addition to the scenes discussed above in Best Director, let me point to other felicities: the character of Dr. Praetorius, played by Ernest Thesiger, his bottle creations (brought to brilliant life by special effects wizard John P. Fulton), and the first meeting of Praetorius with the monster in the graveyard scene, itself a black mockery of a Catholic mass (and the mirror image of the good hermit's sharing of bread and wine and prayer). A nomination should have gone to William Hurlbut and John Balderston – and the win should have, except for a little matter of a comedy at the opera house.

Irving Thalberg saved the Marx Brothers' career, by giving them a new contract, and then providing them with a structure and a creative process that allowed them to become commercially successful again. He had the writers produce a script, then sent them with the Marx Brothers on the road to work out the material, test it, expand it through improvisation and further writing, then test it some more. By the time they were ready to film, the Marx Brothers had their new routines mastered. *A Night at the Opera* and *A Day at the Races* were the result. While in some way the boys were tamed by having to serve a romance, *A Night at the Opera* still finds them in classic form. The writing was the engine that drove that success. George S. Kaufman and Morrie Ryskind deserve a nomination – and yes, once again for a Marx Brothers movie, they should have received the Oscar for Best Writing (Screenplay). What's the point of this book if we can't recognize genius? Think of the wondrous set-pieces and one-liners: Mrs. Claypool: "I've been sitting right here since seven o'clock"; Otis B. Driftwood: "Yes, with your back to me. When I invite a woman to dinner I expect her to look at my face. That's the price she has to pay." "Hey you. I told you to slow that nag down. On account of you I almost heard the opera." "And now, on with the opera. Let joy be unconfined. Let there be dancing in the streets, drinking in the saloons, and necking in the parlor." The contract scene. The stuffing of the stateroom ("And two hard-boiled eggs.") The disguised aviator speech. "Of course you know this means war!" And that little night at the opera. Writing doesn't get much better than this – which is why *Night at the Opera* should take home the Oscar here.

Best Score: Max Steiner won for *The Informer*, over Herbert Stothart, *Mutiny on the Bounty*; and Ernst Toch, *Peter Ibbetson*

Let's start with the losers this time.

Mutiny on the Bounty features a score by Herbert Stothart, functional and appropriately uplifting, but hardly anything you particularly find yourself humming or wanting to hear again. Stothart was a studio work horse, often brought in because he could be relied upon to be serviceable and timely. He won the Oscar for Best Score for *The Wizard of Oz*. The nomination should stay for *Mutiny on the Bounty*.

Peter Ibbetson stars Gary Cooper and Ann Harding, with a nominated score by Ernst Toch. Toch, like Arnold Schoenberg, had fled to Hollywood to escape Nazi persecution. Toch did piecework for the studios: "Owing to the 'eeriness' of his modernist idiom, Toch was quickly typecast as a specialist of horror and chase scenes, and he was to have a hand in most of the mysteries coming out of the Paramount studio for the next several years" – like Bob Hope's *Ghost Breakers* and *The Cat and the Canary*. *Peter Ibbetson* was the rare exception. That movie, and his later Oscar nominated *Ladies in Retirement,* were both "oddly dark-toned entertainment[s]."[lxxxvii] The film itself, a romantic fantasy, has its moments, served especially well by the score and the cinematography of Charles Lang (which was not nominated); Cooper is badly miscast, but he does the best he can with a role Leslie Howard probably wanted. The nomination is well earned.

Max Steiner's score on *The Informer* won, announcing itself from the opening credits as a story of importance, weaving in Irish tunes, and generally keeping the movie rolling along as well as he had with *King Kong*. In many ways the prototype to Ford's later scores incorporating American folk tunes, Steiner's work on *The Informer* definitely deserved an Oscar nomination, but another man deserved the statue more.

What seems more than a little ridiculous in hindsight was ignoring Franz Waxman's score for *Bride of Frankenstein*. Menacing, suspenseful, and thoroughly original, this music has become more and more recognized as the classic it is. As James Curtis has summarized, Waxman "produced what is probably still to this day the greatest score ever written for a horror movie. Three distinctive themes, representing the Monster, the Bride, and Thesiger's Pretorius, weave leitmotifs throughout...The score is alternately romantic, exciting, and horrifying as it builds to a clamorous creation scene..."[lxxxviii] Waxman should have been nominated.

What seems even more ridiculous was the omission of Erich Wolfgang Korngold's rousing score for *Captain Blood*. One of the few pieces of Thirties film music still played in concerts today, Korngold's score powers the adventure, as a score should: "...few film scores are more rousing: trumpets go off like roman candles, drums roll across the sea."[lxxxix] Korngold should have been nominated for this, his "first original, symphonic composition for the screen...written in the grand manner...the blueprint for all of Korngold's subsequent work for the screen: richly melodic, sumptuously orchestrated, and replete with superbly heraldic passages...Film music more or less came of age with Korngold, who in this one film showed what could really be achieved with a symphonic score."[xc] Korngold might just as easily have been nominated for *A Midsummer Night's Dream*, even though he didn't write the music; his arrangement, according to his biographer, introduced the idea of leitmotifs into film scoring: "The idea of giving characters a musical calling card was highly influential. Other composers quickly grew out of the 'one tune' score and began to identify their characters much more strongly in musical terms."[xci]

What seems beyond ridiculous was the omission of the score for *Top Hat*. Irving Berlin wrote the music, which was arranged by Max Steiner (he and the RKO music department also contributed original pieces). *Top Hat*'s score is romantic, lyrical, comic, and transcendent, and the one score of the year to outdo Korngold's two achievements. Irving Berlin and Max Steiner should have been nominated, and what is more, the Oscar for Best Score should have gone to them for *Top Hat*.

Best Song: Harry Warren and Al Dubin's "Lullaby of Broadway" won from *Gold Diggers of 1935*, over Jerome Kern, Dorothy Fields, and Jimmy McHugh's "Lovely to Look At" from *Roberta*, and Irving Berlin's "Cheek to Cheek" from *Top Hat*

The winner, "Lullaby of Broadway" is a very good song – but compared to "Cheek to Cheek," "Isn't This a Lovely Day?" and "Top Hat, White Tie and Tails" from *Top Hat*, it's distinctly second class. With music by Harry Warren and lyrics by Al Dubin, "Lullaby of Broadway" became a standard. Sung by Winifred Shaw and Dick Powell, I suspect the number won more for the unique Busby Berkeley number than for its own merits. The Oscar definitely wasn't the best choice, but a nomination seems a good idea.

"Lovely to Look At" from *Roberta* is but one of the great songs in this Astaire and Rogers musical. But then, we are talking music by Jerome Kern, one of the giants of American songwriting. This time out, with lyrics by Otto Harbach, Dorothy Fields, and Jimmy McHugh, we get "I'll Be Hard to Handle," "Smoke Gets in Your Eyes" and "I Won't Dance" as well. Irene Dunne and Randolph Scott also star, but things never quite gel in this lesser entry in the RKO musicals. Still, the four songs I've mentioned here should have received nominations – but the Oscar for Best Song should have only gone to Irving Berlin for "Cheek to Cheek."

Irving Berlin's songs for *Top Hat*, including "Cheek to Cheek," represent one of the highest peaks of American songwriting. I simply cannot do justice. Go watch the movie again. Better yet, may I suggest Ella Fitzgerald's *The Irving Berlin Songbook*? Your ears will thank me.

Best Dance Direction: David Gould won for "I've Got a Feelin' You're Foolin'" from *Broadway Melody of 1936* and "Straw Hat" from *Folies Bergere*, over Leroy Prinz for "Elephant Number – It's the Animal in Me" from *The Big Broadcast of 1936* and "Viennese Waltz" from *All the King's Horses*; Bobby Connolly for "Playboy from Paree" from *Broadway Hostess* and "Latin from Manhattan" from *Go into Your Dance*; Busby Berkeley for "Lullaby of Broadway" and "The Words Are in My Heart" from *Gold Diggers of 1935*; Sammy Lee for "Lovely Lady" and "Too Good to Be True" from *King of Burlesque*; B. Zemach for "Hall of Kings" from *She*; and Hermes Pan for "Piccolino" and "Top Hat" from *Top Hat*

Let me start with the hellish stinkers and work my way up to heavenly.

"Hall of Kings" from *She* is just a big fat goofy wallow in crazy temple worship. *She* was intended by Merian C. Cooper to be his follow-up to *King Kong*. Pauline Kael called *She* "hilarious, terrible, essential... Camp like this is a rarity."[xcii] This adaptation of H. Rider Haggard's classic adventure novel failed at the box office. The novel itself doesn't read well anymore; we don't celebrate being white, colonial, and imperial the way great-grandfather Lord High Muckety-Muck did. No nomination should have been given for this nonsense.

Winifred Shaw, best known for her famous number in *Gold Diggers of 1935* (see below), starred in *Broadway Hostess*, from which Bobby Connolly was nominated for "Playboy from Paree." A forgettable song and number, and the movie is even worse. Here's *The New York Times* reviewer from 1935: "Sitting through the new film at the Strand is like having to be polite to the boss while he tells an old story badly. With a thoroughness that is nothing short of sinister, the manufacturers of 'Broadway Hostess' have succeeded in rounding up all the clichés of the Broadway comedy-with-music cycle and herding them into one photoplay."[xciii] Sadly, Connolly's other nomination "Latin from Manhattan" from *Go into Your Dance* isn't much better, with Ruby Keeler and Al Jolson on their downward career paths. Jolson sings, with corn; Keeler gets trapped in a Busby Berkeley rip off, whose only moment of creativity is a giant Earth rotating with dancers up and down the stairs on it. No nomination should have been needed here either.

King of Burlesque has one reason to watch it: Fats Waller! The great piano player and composer was featured in the Alice Faye musical. Sammy Lee was nominated for "Lovely Lady" and "Too Good to Be True." Other than that, basic Alice Faye, whose movies were never Oscar caliber even on her best days. No nomination should be here, despite Waller.

The Big Broadcast of 1936 stars Bing Crosby, Burns and Allen, Ethel Merman, Bill "Bojangles" Robinson and the very young Nicholas Brothers (sadly, we also have to put up with Amos n' Andy in blackface). Leroy Prinz was nominated for the "Elephant Number" from this film; he was also nominated for "Viennese Waltz" from *All the King's Horses* (oh look, a waltz! Snore...). The "Elephant Number (It's the Animal in Me)" features Ethel Merman and elephants dancing. You'd think the Merm and elephants would be awesome. Not so much. No nomination should have applied.

The dances in *Broadway Melody* use a lot of camera tricks, as well as a Rogers and Astaire clone. They're serviceable, but mostly recycle gimmicks others invented first, or perfected later. Eleanor Powell's tap-dancing in "Broadway Rhythm" is the best number in the movie (they didn't nominate it; instead, the award went to "I've Got a Feelin' You're Foolin'"). The ballet wasn't done by David Gould; Albertina Rasch was such a cruel taskmaster that the ballet dancer's slippers filled up with blood, and Powell lost four nails on her right foot.[xciv] Buddy Ebsen does a novelty number with his sister Vilma. Gould was also nominated for "Straw Hat" from *Folies Bergere*, which is second-rate Chevalier. The Oscar went to the wrong dances – and the wrong dance director.

Gold Diggers of 1935 marked the first time Busby Berkeley was allowed to direct an entire film himself. "Berkeley makes the narrative world more like the musical world by stylizing it...by setting everyday activities to rhythm."[xcv] The opening action in the film is done to music, in rhythm; all of life becomes a dance. Starring Dick Powell, Adolphe Menjou and Gloria Stuart (most famous today as the old woman from

Titanic), *Gold Diggers* is one more great musical from Warner Brothers. Berkeley was nominated for the "Lullaby of Broadway" and "The Words Are in My Heart" numbers. "Lullaby" begins in a vast blackness, with a spotlight showing one woman's face as she begins to sing. We are then launched into a wild world of a dream, which ends in the woman's apparent murder by a veritable army of synchronized tap dancers. She then wakes up. "The Words" features an entire range of pianos, transported into the swaying and circling movements of dancers (Berkeley has dancers inside the pianos themselves, hidden for the most part, creating his geometrical patterns). As always, Berkeley's world is unique unto itself – and a well-deserved nomination.

Hermes Pan was given credit for the choreography on *Top Hat*, specifically naming two numbers: "Piccolino," which is the most like Busby Berkeley that Pan got in the film, and "Top Hat, White Tie and Tails," which isn't like Berkeley at all. What is the difference? Fred Astaire. According to Richard Jewell, author of *The RKO Story*, Pan and Astaire collaborated together on Astaire's dances.[xcvi] Astaire should have been nominated as well. More importantly, "Piccolino" should not have been, as it has dated the most of all the numbers. Instead, "No Strings (I'm Fancy Free)," "Isn't This a Lovely Day?" and most importantly, "Cheek to Cheek" should have been chosen. "Fancy Free" sets into motion the love interest and complications from the film, serving a narrative purpose by expressing a firm and joyful resistance to romantic entanglements, modulating into the soft caresses of desire after Astaire meets Rogers. Strenuous tap becomes sand and soft shoe after love enters; the dance becomes the story, and vice versa. "Isn't This a Lovely Day?" moves us towards involvement, showing how attraction can grow, all without touching. Joy and excitement lead to that first touch, and thrilling synchronicity. "Top Hat" comes when the romance is troubled with mistaken identities; Astaire is at his most violent, "killing" dancers. "Cheek to Cheek" may be the greatest five minutes and twenty seven seconds in the history of American dance. Fred may have hated Ginger's dress, but nothing could be more beautiful. All told, Astaire and Pan moved the dance numbers away from what Berkeley was doing, with his intricate maneuvers by large numbers of dancers and props, to focusing on the entire dancer, even to the point of insisting that the camera use only full shots of Astaire dancing. As Jewell points out, the camera returned to a "much more simple, pure, classical...way of shooting." As often as possible, Astaire used single takes, which allowed no fakery. Astaire simply had to be perfect. As a result, while Berkeley wows and shocks, Astaire woos us to love dance. One is the passion of a one night stand, which stales with repetition; the other is a lifelong love affair. Which would you prefer? Astaire and Pan should have won the Oscar for Best Dance Direction for the several brilliances of *Top Hat*.

Best Art Direction: Richard Day won for *The Dark Angel*, over Hans Dreier and Roland Anderson, *The Lives of a Bengal Lancer*, and Carroll Clark & Roland Anderson, *Top Hat*

The Dark Angel gives us the wealthy mansions of the gentry and aristocracy, before WWI, as well as a country inn, and various war scenes. Richard Day would go on to *The Grapes of Wrath, A Streetcar Named Desire,* and *On the Waterfront.* With *The Dark Angel*, Day does well, although not so well as the one who should have won. No Oscar should be his, but not a bad nod otherwise.

Hans Dreier and Roland Anderson were nominated for *The Lives of a Bengal Lancer.* One can see why, as the feeling of a British army camp in India is created from whole cloth. Some location shots were incorporated into the film, but for the most part, *The Lives of a Bengal Lancer* was made in Southern California. Dreier and Anderson did an excellent job, although I still laugh at the award category, which names a flick mostly shot outside for "interior" decoration. The nomination should stay.

Carroll Clark worked under Van Nest Polglase at RKO, but in *Top Hat*, Clark and Roland Anderson completely outdid themselves with their sets. The Venice-inspired canals are their most stunning creation, all done up on art deco steroids, as we enter the setting for the knitting up of the tangled love story, and the glory of the final dances. A great nomination, without question.

As is usual in these early years, the Academy ignored other excellent choices.

As there is, of yet, no Special Effects category, I would like to suggest a British film from Gaumont: *The Transatlantic Tunnel*. This science fiction tale about constructing a tunnel beneath the Atlantic Ocean was a major production, starring American Richard Dix (*Cimarron*) and British Leslie Banks (*The Man Who Knew Too Much*); George Arliss and Walter Huston play the prime minister and the president. But the real star remains the special effects: the tunnel, the tremendous drilling machines, the oppressive sense of the difficulties involved. A nomination should have been in order.

In another of Universal's Poe-inspired horror films, *The Raven*, Karloff is Edmond Bateman, and Lugosi is Richard Vollin, a brilliant but deranged surgeon. We meet Lugosi reciting a verse from Poe's poem, "The Raven." Lugosi's hobby is building the torture devices from various Poe stories, including the razor-sharp pendulum. Lugosi saves the life of the daughter of a judge; Lugosi falls in love with her; the judge does not agree. Karloff is a criminal who wants his face changed. Horror follows. The use of shadows is extensive; the camerawork increases the claustrophobic foreboding. Poe's poem "The Raven" fills many of the spaces of the movie, as well as the obsession with death that permeates so much of his work. The movie goes for little of the deeper level of last year's *The Black Cat*, but the terrifying aspects of the film are more intense and based largely on the set designs, which should have earned Charles D. Hall a nomination for Best Art Direction.

Another strange omission for this category is *The Crusades*. Like most of DeMille's movies in this period, the sets are exhaustively researched, and look lived in and real (they ought to – many of them had already been used in *The Lives of a Bengal Lancer*). The costumes breathe history. The armor looks like real armor (well, more often than not). Perhaps it is all a bit too pretty at times, but far less so than almost any historical film before the late Sixties. Roland Anderson worked under DeMille, uncredited as his art directors so often were. He and DeMille deserved a nomination.

As did *Bride of Frankenstein*. The sets look like German expressionists were cut loose for one more romp in Hollywood (ironically, *The Informer* displays this influence as well). Charles D. Hall put together sets that both replicated and extended the look of the original. The castle, the woods (looking like WWI has visited them), the idyllic hermit's glen, the dungeon, the cemetery, and the creation scenes all display a power unmatched in any other film this year. Given that there was no makeup category, I would like to give a nod to Jack Pierce, the greatest makeup genius of the Thirties and Forties. Altering his original makeup for the monster to reflect the burning at the end of the first movie, Pierce produced an even more startling and battered look for Karloff. Charles D. Hall should have been nominated – and he should have won the Oscar for *The Bride of Frankenstein*.

Best Short Subject (Comedy): Ignore the flotsam they did nominate; the Oscar in this category should have only gone to the funniest sequel in the history of the movies, Laurel and Hardy's *Tit for Tat*. The boys open up an electronics store, only to discover the grocery store next door is owned by the husband and wife they ran into in the mountains in *Them Thar Hills*. The husband becomes convinced Oliver is making the moves on his wife; wholesale comic destruction builds from the small upwards. What are you waiting for?!? Go watch it! And tell the boys they should have another Oscar!

CHAPTER NINE: 1937 AWARDS
9th Show

Movies released in 1936

THE SCENE OF THE CRIME:

On March 4, 1937, the Academy returned to the Biltmore Bowl at the Biltmore Hotel in downtown Los Angeles. Another comedian took over the hosting duties, George Jessel (star of the original theatrical production of *The Jazz Singer*). Even though very few actors still remained officially in the Academy due to disputes with the Screen Actors Guild, more of them showed up this year. Jessel made a plea for short speeches; he was ignored (as is usually the case). Walt Disney gave an Oscar to himself when he announced the winner of the Best Short Subject (Cartoon) category. Bette Davis became infuriated when Jessel forgot to call her up to make the Best Actress presentation.

Suspense was destroyed, because the press were told the winners ahead of time, and nominees could just go down to the press room and end the anticipation.

For the first time, the Academy recognized Best Supporting Actors and Actresses, even if they only got plaques instead of statuettes. Also for the first time, the Irving G. Thalberg Award was announced to be given in the next year, for the producer who had the "most distinguished body of work in a single year." Norma Shearer, Thalberg's widow, was making her first public appearance since Thalberg's death, on the arm of Louis B. Mayer. She cried when the audience applauded.

The eligibility restrictions on films made outside of the United States were dropped for both Cinematography and Art Direction.

Other than cartoons, I will be dropping Short Subjects entirely.

WHAT THEY GOT RIGHT:

Not very much. But the one thing they got right, the Academy really got right.

Best Director: Frank Capra won for *Mr. Deeds Goes to Town*, over William Wyler, *Dodsworth*; Robert Z. Leonard, *The Great Ziegfeld*; Gregory La Cava, *My Man Godfrey*; and W.S. Van Dyke, *San Francisco*.

Frank Capra won his second Best Director award for *Mr. Deeds Goes to Town*; I could not agree more. The movie begins in disaster, as a rich man dies in an automobile accident. The flip side of the coin is that someone will inherit twenty million. *Mr. Deeds* pivots back and forth between the incipient disaster and the beneficial boon. Nothing is ever left unflipped; both sides are explored. Capra's economical style focuses on the building of character, and the humor and tragedy inherent in every move humans can make. Gary Cooper plays Longfellow Deeds, a small town poet and tuba player who inherits a fortune. Jean Arthur plays Babe Bennett, a reporter trapped by her duplicity. Capra was on top of his game again in *Mr. Deeds*. For evidence, look at the Best Picture, Best Actor, Best Actress, and Best Writing (Screenplay) categories. Not a single false note exists in the movie. Frank Capra is the reason.

William Wyler tackled Sinclair Lewis' novel *Dodsworth* with the help of Walter Huston. *Dodsworth* tells the story of a mighty industrialist – a mighty unhappy industrialist – who has just sold off the factory he spent his life building. Now, he and his wife are heading off to a life of their own, traveling to Europe. Wyler was best known for providing a solid realism, along with a depth of character and feeling in an economical, no-nonsense style. Wyler received more nominations for Best Director than anybody else in history, and they were almost all well-earned. Wyler tells stories exceptionally well, and *Dodsworth* is no exception. As Sinclair Lewis himself said, "I do not see how a better motion picture could have been made from...the novel."[xcvii] The nomination should stay.

As for Robert Z. Leonard, I suppose one might receive credit for managing the monster that is *The Great Ziegfeld*, but a shorter film, with crisper writing and a few less songs, would have made for a better movie. Leonard never moved much beyond competent carpentry as a reliable studio director, with little or no vision beyond doing what he was told. No nomination should have been given.

Gregory La Cava turned in a masterful film in *My Man Godfrey*. If it weren't for Frank Capra operating on an even higher level of achievement, the Oscar should have gone to La Cava. From the opening credits (which are quite inventive for the period) to the closing marriage, La Cava crafts a wonderful comedy of manners that responds to the Depression in similar ways to that of *Mr. Deeds*. Godfrey, played by William Powell, is a Forgotten Man, brought into the circle of Carole Lombard's rich but quite loony and disconnected family; Godfrey turns their lives into something far more real and human. La Cava would never be better, but even so, Capra gets closer to perfection. I'm just glad we have both this and *Mr. Deeds*; I've watched them over and over again, with increasing pleasure.

W.S. Van Dyke was a consummate craftsman, working on budget, if not under budget, and often bringing in commercially successful films time after time due to his diligence. The *Thin Man* movies proved his gifts of comedy; *San Francisco* proves he should have stayed with the laughs, as things never really sparkle. The film does open with one of the most riotous New Year's Eve street parties ever, reproducing San Francisco shortly before World War I, and filling the streets with drunken, happy people. I suspect you would have to be drunk to be happy about this movie getting a Best Picture nomination, as much of it is hackwork. But the earthquake shatters, and Spencer Tracy becomes a star. Van Dyke gets the credit for bringing those two together. The nomination should stay – barely.

Left out of the mix was a German immigrant who should have been recognized. Fritz Lang took a number of years to finally put together his first American film, after some false starts. *Fury* is not a perfect film; I am not even sure it is a great film. The second half of the film plays falsely, particularly in the courtroom scenes and the ending. What is it then? Serious, well-intentioned, and Germanic in its tone and outlook. If *M* is about the righteous persecution and justified vigilante killing of an utterly evil child murderer, then *Fury* is about the dangers of righteousness and vigilantism. Spencer Tracy turns in a furious performance as the unjustly targeted innocent who engineers revenge against the mob who tried to burn him to death (see Best Actor below). Oddly, MGM released this film, which feels very Warner Brothers. Lang's sense of Americana is growing, and he is learning the differences between his homeland and a democracy, but at its heart, *Fury* is about the Nazis and the ways in which they manipulated the truth to instill the terror of the crowd, to ride the mob mentality to power. *Fury* is Lang's warning that we must not fall prey to gossip, to the blind fear that drives us en masse to make bad decisions. Told in a simple, documentary style, *Fury* works as that strong warning. Lang should have received a nomination for Best Director for this brave film.

Finally, Alfred Hitchcock was again ignored for one of his best Thirties British films, *Sabotage*. Hitchcock adapted Joseph Conrad's seminal spy novel *The Secret Agent*. The showpiece of the film is the montage of the boy unknowingly carrying the bomb into Piccadilly Square. Hitchcock shows himself to be a most accomplished director of physical motion and suspense in this, his first true mastery of the camera for an extended sequence. The whole film doesn't operate on this level, but you can see with sureness his future achievements around the corner. The Academy should have nominated Hitchcock for this film.

WHAT THEY GOT WRONG:

More and more, every year. I just simply do not know what was wrong with those people. I suspect they continued to manipulate the results to suit their commercial needs. Reportedly, Louis B. Mayer cut a deal with Darryl F. Zanuck to swap block voting: if Zanuck's people voted for *The Great Ziegfeld* for Best Picture, Mayer's lackeys would vote for Paul Muni for Best Actor. And people wonder why I get mad...

Best Picture: *The Great Ziegfeld*
Best Actor: Paul Muni, *The Story of Louis Pasteur*
Best Actress: Luise Rainer, *The Great Ziegfeld*
Best Supporting Actor: Walter Brennan, *Come and Get It*
Best Supporting Actress: Gale Sondergaard, *Anthony Adverse*
Best Writing (Original Story): Pierre Collings and Sheridan Gribney, *The Story of Louis Pasteur*
Best Writing (Screenplay): Pierre Collings and Sheridan Gribney, *The Story of Louis Pasteur*

Best Cinematography: Gaetano Gaudio, *Anthony Adverse*
Best Score: Erich Wolfgang Korngold, *Anthony Adverse*
Best Song: Jerome Kern and Dorothy Fields, "The Way You Look Tonight," *Swing Time*
Best Dance Direction: Seymour Felix, "A Pretty Girl Is Like a Melody," *The Great Ziegfeld*
Best Art Direction: Richard Day, *Dodsworth*
Best Short Subject (Cartoon): Walt Disney, *Country Cousin*

Best Picture: *The Great Ziegfeld* won, over *Anthony Adverse*, *Libeled Lady*, *Mr. Deeds Goes to Town*, *Romeo and Juliet*, *San Francisco*, *The Story of Louis Pasteur*, *A Tale of Two Cities*, and *Three Smart Girls*

The Great Ziegfeld is one of the worst choices for Best Picture in the history of the Academy Awards. I love William Powell and Myrna Loy (even as Flo Ziegfeld and Billie Burke), and moments in this movie charm, but as one critic said at the time, *The Great Ziegfeld* was "an atrocious production...a picture false in biography, a glittering avalanche of legs and tinsel, a truer demonstration of the stupidity and rank barbarism of these times had never been more ably given."[xcviii] Lavish budgets and overblown dance scenes do not a Best Picture make. The film is too long at almost three hours with 23 songs. Too much of a not always good thing, and in a biopic, too much glossing over of the truth; the word "sanitized" comes to mind. The fun drains out of the picture as the hustler becomes the Great Man. Ray Bolger's dance is the best of the movie; Fanny Brice has the best comic moments. We have to put up with blackface again. *The Great Ziegfeld* deserved neither Oscar nor nomination.

Anthony Adverse stars Fredric March, Olivia de Havilland and Claude Rains in the screen version of one of the biggest bestsellers of the Thirties. Set in the late eighteenth century, March plays Adverse, a bastard child raised in an orphanage, and then, unknown to Adverse, by his grandfather Bonnyfeather, played by Edmund Gwenn. De Havilland plays the daughter of his father's cook, and a future opera singer and lover of Adverse...and Napoleon. Where's James Michener when you need him? Time has not been kind to either the movie or the novel, as both have lost their fame and luster. But even then, feelings ran hot against this film among those who had read the novel in the height of its fame. As *The New York Times* critic of the day said, *Anthony Adverse* is "a bulky, rambling and indecisive photoplay which has not merely taken liberties with the letter of the original but with its spirit... For all its sprawling length, [the novel] was cohesive and well rounded.

Most of its picaresque quality has been lost in the screen version; its philosophy is vague, its characterization blurred and its story so loosely knit and episodic that its telling seems interminable."[xcix] Far too much happens in far too short a space; Selznick would face a similar problem soon in adapting the huge *Gone with the Wind*, and end up with a movie almost twice as long as *Anthony Adverse* in order to do *Gone with the Wind* justice. Part of the reason for the decline of this film has to do with how March has to spend much of the film as a slave trader, and the film asks us to accept this as a legitimate way to wealth (after some hand-wringing over it). March's African mistress is a bit hard to swallow as well. What works today are the sets, the score, and the supporting cast, most of whom got nods from the Academy. Other than that, not so much. You'll notice that none of the leads got nominations, then or in these pages, and for good reason. No nomination should have been given.

Libeled Lady gives us a screwball comedy with an all-star cast: William Powell, Myrna Loy, Spencer Tracy, and Jean Harlow. Real-life lovers Harlow and Powell weren't paired; Tracy went with Harlow, and Powell went with Loy, the woman most of America assumed he was married to in real life. Tracy plays a newspaper editor who has to get married to his girlfriend Gladys or lose her. Harlow's appearance in a bridal gown, full of fury at being stood up once more, remains one of the great entrances. Tracy's paper has published a false story about socialite Myrna Loy (hence the title). Tracy then decides to sic a notorious lady killer on Loy. The lady killer comes in the form of William Powell; if he can bring the whiff of scandal into her life, the lawsuit will fail. Romance and hijinks follow. An outstanding nomination (see Best Writing (Screenplay) below for more).

Frank Capra produced another one of his masterpieces in *Mr. Deeds Goes to Town*; apparently, the Academy was getting used to it, since they chose the mediocre *Ziegfeld* over this classic vision of American virtues. Every single character in this movie is an eccentric in word and deed, even when they are pretending not to be. Americans love to be considered individuals; conformity is the danger to one side, and community is the benefit to the other. Where we place ourselves in that continuum remains the essential American choice. In a classed society, choices are few and far between. Here, it can be a daily decision. *Mr. Deeds* plays with this, as few films have before or since. The trial scene at the end brings all these threads together in a sad, funny, enlightening romp through Americana. Definitely a worthy nomination.

Romeo and Juliet was Irving Thalberg's gift to his wife, Norma Shearer. Thalberg lavished two million dollars on this adaptation of

Shakespeare's tale of star-crossed lovers, over double the initial budget. Only Warner Brothers' plans to make *A Midsummer Night's Dream* convinced Louis B. Mayer to let Thalberg have his way. Unfortunately, the film was grossly miscast. Romeo and Juliet are teenagers, but Shearer was thirty six and Leslie Howard forty four. John Barrymore (Mercutio) was in his fifties. Thalberg then chose an excellent director in George Cukor, but Cukor had no experience with Shakespeare. Irving Thalberg died on the night of the premiere; the film followed him shortly to the same place. *Romeo and Juliet* has its highlights, among them Edna May Oliver as the Nurse and Basil Rathbone as Tybalt (see Best Supporting Actor below). But when Romeo is old enough to be a grandfather, and Juliet's old enough to be a cougar, something is terribly wrong – and the acting doesn't change our minds in the slightest. Cukor also stages the worst fight scenes of any major director in film history. Simply awful, even with Basil Rathbone's genius with the blade. No nomination would have been the right choice.

San Francisco wasn't the first time Hollywood destroyed a city. *Deluge* drowned New York; *The Last Days of Pompeii* did in the Romans. Hollywood has often gone for the disaster picture; destruction, like sex and love, usually sells – and if you put the three together, you've got yourself a blockbuster...or a financial disaster. *San Francisco* definitely belonged to the former. Clark Gable and Jeanette MacDonald received top billing as Blackie Norton and Mary Blake, but the movie belongs to Spencer Tracy's Father Mullin (and the special effects). MacDonald is getting painfully upright, moving past her Lubitsch days of naughtiness; on the other hand, her opera singing is quite good. Gable is playing Gable, with little of the humor we saw in *It Happened One Night*. The earthquake can't happen soon enough. The nomination should stay, for Tracy and the Richter scale.

The Story of Louis Pasteur is yet another one of the biographies that George Arliss made Hollywood love (well, what they loved were the profits, but Hollywood often confuses love and money). Paul Muni starred, along with his beard (see Best Actor below). If you love milk – or dogs, or mothers, or sheep (hopefully not at the same time) – you should really see this movie at least once. I had to watch it twice, which is really once too many. The nomination should stay, as *The Story of Louis Pasteur* became the paradigm for Hollywood biographies (see Best Actor and the Writing categories below for more).

A Tale of Two Cities was David O. Selznick's follow-up to his masterpiece *David Copperfield*. Ronald Colman even shaved off his famous mustache to play the role of Sydney Carton. Edna May Oliver and Basil Rathbone were back; Freddie Bartholomew and W.C. Fields were not (and more's the pity). W.P. Lipscomb, who had done a bang-up job on *Les Misérables* over at Fox the year before, adapted the screenplay, with the help of comic writer S.N. Behrman; Selznick would have done much better to get British novelist Hugh Walpole back again. Selznick would have done even better to have kept George Cukor as director, instead of studio hack Jack Conway. Future horror greats Val Lewton and Jacques Tourneur arranged the excellent "revolutionary sequences" (Lewton and Tourneur later created *Cat People* and *I Walked with a Zombie*). Sadly, Selznick was not emotionally invested in *Two Cities* – his father had learned English from *David Copperfield*, and had read the book aloud to David as a boy. Selznick was on the way out the door of MGM as well, to create his own production company. *A Tale of Two Cities* comes a distant second to *David Copperfield*, but still well worth watching, despite its overwhelming earnestness. The most memorable performance is that of Blanche Yurka, playing Madame De Farge, she of the clacking knitting needles. Basil Rathbone is a right bastard as the Marquis St. Evrémonde, running over a child, then chastising the parents for endangering his horses. Edna May Oliver snaps off some great sarcastic comments. Colman brings a world-weary humor to life, and has that wonderful final speech: "It's a far, far better thing I do than I have ever done before. It's a far, far greater rest I go to than I have ever known." The problem lies in the romantic leads, who are about as interesting as cold instant mashed potatoes; we can never quite understand why Colman is love-sick for the woman. The nomination should remain, but the main course of the lovers should really be sent back to the cook, who should have known better.

Three Smart Girls wins this year's "What were they thinking?!?" award – or would have, if they hadn't selected *The Great Ziegfeld* as the winner. I've got nothing against Deanna Durbin; she has a marvelous, operatically trained voice, and was one of the best juveniles of the Thirties. But Best Picture?!? For this piece of mundane fluff?!? No. Never. You want a measure of how minor it is? *Three Smart Girls* is a musical...with no nods in any of the musical categories. Mischa Auer plays a no-good Count, in one of the few charming moments; Ray Milland isn't bad either. See Best Writing (Original Story) below for more on why there should be no nomination.

Many great films were completely ignored in this category.

Dodsworth deserved a nomination (see Best Director above, and Best Actor below, for why). A very young David Niven appears early in his career.

I can't understand why the Academy didn't pick *Swing Time*, directed by George Stevens, with Fred Astaire and Ginger Rogers, one of their absolute peaks as screen partners. See Best Song and Best Dance Direction below for more on why *Swing Time* should have been nominated for Best Picture.

Unbelievably, the Academy couldn't be bothered to nominate one of the greatest comedies of the Thirties: *My Man Godfrey* – but at least they gave it SOME nominations, unlike one of the other highly regarded comedies, *Modern Times*. Each should have been nominated for a Best Picture Award. Both *My Man Godfrey* and *Modern Times* have this in common with *Mr. Deeds*: they are all comic responses to the Great Depression. *Mr. Deeds* requires an unexpected inheritance; *Godfrey* requires a financial genius living as a homeless person; all *Modern Times* requires is the genius of Chaplin.

The Academy completely snubbed Charlie Chaplin in what many consider to be his greatest film (I'm not one of them; my vote goes to the sublime perfection that is *City Lights*). *Modern Times* was one of the top ten most profitable movies that year, coming only behind *San Francisco* and *The Great Ziegfeld*, so they haven't got the excuse of ignoring a flop. The rejection of Chaplin can be chalked up to a number of reasons: Chaplin was making his last silent picture; he had gone through a number of scandals; he ran his own studio and was beholden to none; he had snubbed the Academy. But I prefer to think of it as sheer jealousy. Chaplin wrote, produced, directed, composed, and starred in *Modern Times*. While I think his performance and creativity in *Modern Times* come as signs of significant (but not substantial) decline from his earlier work, *Modern Times* should have been nominated for Best Picture. I wouldn't suggest Best Actor, because none of the emotional depth is here which we saw in *City Lights*; likewise, Chaplin's directing and cinematography have become pedestrian compared to others. But the picture as a whole works as well as any did this year. The scenes in the factory, with the feeding machine and Charlie's incorporation into the machine itself, remain as funny and biting as any satire ever filmed. The cocaine mistake in the jail and the nonsense song amuse as well. But *Modern Times* has little of the narrative structure of *City Lights*, as it strings one comic scene after another, with occasional moralizing; it's not the best thing Chaplin ever wrote, even if it is better than much that was to come. Here's an example of what's wrong with the thematic issues of the picture being a defense of the common man and the worker. After having become a part of the machinery himself, the Tramp later ignores the plight of another worker caught in another machine to have lunch. Does anybody else see a contradiction there? Chaplin's politics were always more than a little confused, as several of his biographers have pointed out; it wouldn't matter, but much of what people tend to celebrate about this film is its political stance, which is murky at best. I think it should be nominated for being funny – and that ought to be enough to put it into contention for the Best Picture.

But not enough to win, against a movie that was both funny, and seriously engaged in the difficulties of the Great Depression, and the nature of wealth, civic responsibility, and plain everyday humanity. *Mr. Deeds Goes to Town* should have won for Best Picture, primarily because I find myself wondering what Chaplin was thinking, and not in a good way; as for *My Man Godfrey*, I just find *Mr. Deeds* diving deeper into the human need for individuality and freedom.

Best Actor: Paul Muni won for *The Story of Louis Pasteur*, over Walter Huston, *Dodsworth*, Gary Cooper, *Mr. Deeds Goes to Town*; William Powell, *My Man Godfrey*, and Spencer Tracy, *San Francisco*

Paul Muni finally won his Oscar for *The Story of Louis Pasteur*. Too bad he didn't deserve it. Allow me to defer to W.C. Fields, who was not happy about Muni winning: "Any actor knows that comedy is more difficult, requires more artistry. It is pretty easy to fool an audience with a little crepe hair and a dialect. It seems to me that a comedian who really makes people laugh should be as eligible for an award as a tragedian who makes people cry. This isn't a case of sour grapes with me because I didn't grow any grapes last year. I didn't even sow a wild oat."[c] I couldn't agree more. *The Story of Louis Pasteur* doesn't have what I would consider great acting. Milk, yes. Rabies, yes. Sheep, yes. Mothers and dying babies, yes. An occasional smirk on Muni's bearded face, yes. But overall, I think the Oscar was given because Muni had been passed over before (and from Darryl F. Zanuck's swapping of votes with Louis B. Mayer).[ci] Muni turns in an enjoyable performance as his career was hitting its peak; it would go into decline as acting styles changed. Muni would soon be a victim of his own success, trapped into the George Arliss niche of recreating historical figures, with essentially the same performance over and over again. That performance begins here in *The Story of Louis Pasteur*. No Oscar should have been given, but he should keep the nomination.

Thankfully, the Academy nominated William Powell for *My Man Godfrey* instead of *The Great Ziegfeld*. Powell was meant for comedy, and even when his movies aren't perfect, he almost always is. *My Man Godfrey* was one of his career peaks, and still pleases every bit as much today. Watching Powell putting Carole Lombard in the shower makes me crack up every time I see it. Seeing Powell put everything that is out of order back into order feels very Shakespearean; at the end of each of the Bard's plays, all that was wrong is now right. *Godfrey* has that feel of one of Shakespeare's comedies, a sense of completion and rightness that remains deeply satisfying. Throughout, Powell's performance is restrained, with every facial gesture and vocal inflection perfectly placed. The nomination is beyond deserved; it's righteously correct. Take that, *Ziegfeld*!

Spencer Tracy is one of my favorite actors of classic Hollywood. *San Francisco* was his first nomination, playing Father Mullin (Tracy would win his second Best Actor Oscar playing Father Flanagan in *Boys Town* two years later). Tracy first shows up onscreen in boxing togs, and he knocks down Clark Gable in the sparring ring. From that point on, he brings life to the stale story (as does the earthquake). If every priest were like Tracy's Father Mullin, we'd all be Catholic. Problem is, Tracy isn't playing a leading role; he really should have been nominated for Best Supporting Actor. So he should be moved there for *San Francisco*. In this category, he should have been nominated for a different performance, that of the persecuted innocent turned vengeful 'ghost' in Fritz Lang's *Fury*. Tracy had an enormous range as an actor, even while he rarely (if ever) overacted. Tracy in *San Francisco* is holiness, goodness, humanity, and toughness all at once; Tracy in *Fury* is revenge and rage personified. Now, add in his comic performance in *Libeled Lady*, and you begin to see the true capacity of this actor's actor.

Walter Huston brings out the unhappy core of the business class in *Dodsworth*, the dissatisfaction at the heart of earning money and power for the sake of earning money and power, when there is not some greater purpose to it all. His wife wants a life, after Dodsworth has sold off his factory to give her what she most wants. Huston is hard, craggy, and about as Midwestern American as one could ask – which also includes a certain kind of rough charm and humor and enthusiasm. Quite rapidly, what Dodsworth and his wife discover is that they have very little in common. Mrs. Dodsworth meets David Niven; Dodsworth meets Mary Astor. Difficulties result. Mrs. Dodsworth meets a Frenchman; Mr. Dodsworth meets French historical monuments. Difficulties result. Throughout, Huston provides a pragmatic, very American response to the world of Europe and his wife's new...interests. He returns to America; she stays behind in Europe. He confronts her; they reconcile; then she strays again in Vienna. Watching Huston work through the sadness, betrayal, and acceptance, followed by a new birth of self and freedom, is riveting. The nomination was surely worthy – but still outclassed this year by a character named Longfellow.

Gary Cooper turned in his first classic comic performance in *Mr. Deeds Goes to Town*. Like all the greatest comedies, as Howard Hawks pointed out, this story could have been shot as a tragedy as well. As Longfellow Deeds, Cooper brings his aw-shucks cowboy style to this deeply serious film, and one which causes us to laugh throughout. Deeds is a true American eccentric, writing poetry on greeting cards, playing his tuba with joy, and refusing to be forced into anything other than being himself...until love, evident betrayal and ultimate redemption bring him through the crucible of temptation. Cooper had done comedies before, particularly *Design for Living*; in *Mr. Deeds*, he found his first indelible performance, comic or otherwise. Watch him in the courtroom scene at the end, and see how great an actor Cooper was: dejection, hope, strength, and humor come through in tuba-sized proportions. The nomination would be the first of many for this American icon, and one he really should have won, even as fine as Powell, Huston and Tracy were this year. The Oscar should have gone to Gary Cooper for *Mr. Deeds*.

P.S. I would recommend watching Charles Laughton in *Rembrandt* from this year as well. While the overall film is somewhat brittle and slow, Laughton's performance is a quiet revelation; the scene where Laughton's Rembrandt remembers his dead wife is the single finest elegy in British film history. I am not one for open displays of grieving, but Laughton opens the grave every time.

P.P.S. I would also recommend watching Humphrey Bogart in *The Petrified Forest* in his breakthrough role as Duke Mantee. While the film itself is sometimes klutzy and excessively stagy, and Leslie Howard's performance is his usual fey boredom, Bogart made people wake up and realize how good he could be playing bad guys. Compared to later Bogart, it's minor and overly mannered, but how wonderful to watch actors claim new territory.

Best Actress: Luise Rainer won for *The Great Ziegfeld*, over Irene Dunne, *Theodora Goes Wild*; Gladys George, *Valiant Is the Word for Carrie*; Carole Lombard, *My Man Godfrey*; and Norma Shearer, *Romeo and Juliet*

Preposterous, that Luise Rainer won for what is essentially a supporting role, playing Anna Held, Ziegfeld's first female star, a little French bon-bon of a diva. Not very filling, even with her famous crying on the phone bit – which plays a little scary, so when my then thirteen-year-old daughter watched it with me, she said "her big bug eyes are creeping me out." Luise Rainer proves a match for Powell, but others turned in more enduring work, not least the wonderful comic performances of Irene Dunne and Carole Lombard, and the forgotten but reportedly good dramatic performance of Gladys George, all of which went by the wayside in the voting (the less said about Shearer's abominable Juliet the better). Therefore, no Oscar should have been awarded, but Rainer should keep the nomination for what she does give.

Irene Dunne's turn in the classic screwball comedy *Theodora Goes Wild* continues to please. Co-starring Melvyn Douglas, and based on a story by Mary McCarthy, *Theodora* tells the story of a small-town girl who secretly writes a steamy romance novel. She fights hard to protect that anonymity, until the big city and Douglas loosen her up. Dunne delights as Theodora, beginning as a prim young woman, then putting on one of the most charming drunks of the decade. Both main characters are trapped; each helps the other become free – and few stories are better suited for comedy, romance, or serious drama. Let freedom ring! Irene Dunne should keep her nomination.

Valiant Is the Word for Carrie features Gladys George as a woman with a shady past, an outcast who befriends a young boy, then later brings him and a young girl to the big city. George goes straight and raises them both. As adults, bad stuff happens to them, and George gets even more valiant. George is most famous for playing the club owner in love with James Cagney in *The Roaring Twenties*, and as Miles Archer's widow in *The Maltese Falcon*. *Valiant Is the Word for Carrie* is the third film for which she should be remembered, which I finally saw in 2014 for this 2nd edition. Before, I did manage to see the Three Stooges in *Violent Is the Word for Curly*, which seemed to make people happier about me not seeing the rarer full-length soaper. I am very happy now to have seen both George and Curly, to the point of wishing they'd worked together. George lifts *Valiant Is the Word for Carrie* on her capable back. When trapped in a melodrama this blatantly manipulative, actors can do one of two things. They can either force the material into something more realistic, as Bette Davis would soon learn to do, or they can take it drop-dead serious, and play it for all its worth – which is what George does. She gives herself completely over to the sentiment, scrubs up every soapy moment, and wrings every tear out of us. When she gets indignant, few actresses of the period could match her. Despite the sappy material, George makes us believe it all matters, and for that, she earned her place here.

Carole Lombard proved herself the best comedienne on the Thirties screen (outside of Margaret Dumont). *My Man Godfrey* matches her with William Powell, and the pairing couldn't be better. One of the best scatterbrained performances in film history, Lombard's role as Irene Bullock comes across as champagne being uncorked without a glass waiting for it – until Godfrey appears. Lombard was never better, especially when she finds her sense of self-worth and asserts herself at the end – she deserved this nomination.

Norma Shearer was nominated for *Romeo and Juliet*. Respect for her husband Irving Thalberg and the power of the MGM studio voting bloc explain this terrible choice. As the biographer of director George Cukor so rightly recognized, "Cukor managed to get Shearer's readings clear, but because she was not much of a dramatic actress, her performance never rose above adequacy."[cii] Oscar nominations should not have been given for "adequate" – and I would choose a much harsher word.

Can somebody please explain why they left out Jean Arthur, from *Mr. Deeds Goes to Town*? Granted, Arthur had an odd voice, and a less than classic beauty, but under Frank Capra's direction, she turned in two of the finest performances in American film history in *Mr. Deeds* and *Mr. Smith Goes to Washington*. In *Mr. Deeds*, she plays Babe Bennett, a cynical newspaper reporter who sets out to turn Longfellow Deeds into a month of paid vacation by pretending to be a "lady in distress" and suckering Deeds. Eventually, love intercedes, and the "crucifying" gives way to human compassion and the need for the truth. Her heartfelt testimony in the court still rips me apart every single time. Arthur deserved a nomination – and the Oscar for Best Actress.

Best Supporting Actor: Walter Brennan won for *Come and Get It*, over Mischa Auer, *My Man Godfrey*; Stuart Erwin, *Pigskin Parade*; Basil Rathbone, *Romeo and Juliet*; and Akim Tamiroff, *The General Died at Dawn*

I love Walter Brennan, but even I don't think he deserved the Oscar for this role. Blame the extras, who loved him even more than I do and voted for him every time they could. Brennan himself admitted this was why he won three times (eventually, the extras would lose their votes over this kind of crowd behavior – the more powerful members of the Academy apparently wanted to keep dumb choices for themselves...). Brennan gave Oscar-worthy performances, but this isn't one of them. Too much overblown Swede. *Come and Get It* is an oddity. Directed by both Howard Hawks and William Wyler, produced by Samuel Goldwyn, and based on a novel by Edna Ferber (the author of *Cimarron* and *Giant*), *Come and Get It* is a logging romance, where the two romantic leads are Walter Brennan and Edward Arnold. I'll give you a minute to recover from that. The main reason to watch this film is to try and figure out which director did which scenes. Other than that, unless you really, really love cutting down trees, and Frances Farmer as the love interest, or want to see Joel McCrea smacked around by his father,

Come and Get It isn't much of an invitation. No Oscar should have been given – not even a nomination.

Mischa Auer put together a career in the mid-Thirties playing down-and-out eccentrics who relied on others for their financial support. He had a unique face, one that could broadcast both bemusement and dismay simultaneously. I would love to have him as the Dauphin in a version of *Huckleberry Finn*. In *My Man Godfrey*, he plays Carlo, the kept pet of the rich wife: her protégé. Auer had the face of a basset hound. He does the best gorilla impression ever. He deserves his nomination.

Stuart Erwin plays a hick rube named Amos with an unexpected gift for football in *Pigskin Parade*. Erwin's role in this seminal Twentieth Century-Fox musical would be the high point of his career; he would go on to make *The Bride Came COD* and *Son of Flubber* – not exactly shining moments in any filmography. Today the film is better known for the first major appearance of Judy Garland. MGM loaned her to Fox to give her a chance to see what she could do. She stole the picture – even though Betty Grable and Jack Haley were there as well. Stuart Erwin got top billing, and this Oscar nomination – which in the words of one musical historian was a "miracle."[ciii] I can only credit Fox's block voting for the nomination, which is far from deserved for this minor character actor. No nomination should have ever been given.

Basil Rathbone was cited for his role as Tybalt in *Romeo and Juliet*. Man, could he use a sword! His voice was nearly unparalleled in Hollywood, and this role increased his stature as a screen villain substantially. Although Rathbone has very little screen time, when he is on, the entire movie comes alive – a godsend in this mortuary of a film. Rathbone was rightly named here, but he could just as easily been nominated for his evil, cruel fop Marquis St. Evremonde in *A Tale of Two Cities*.

Akim Tamiroff was nominated for Lewis Milestone's *The General Died at Dawn*. Based on a screenplay by Clifford Odets and starring Gary Cooper, *The General Died at Dawn* is yet another of the movies set in China which Hollywood seemed to dabble in regularly during the Thirties (*The Bitter Tea of General Yen* and *The Good Earth* being two others). Tamiroff plays General Yang with Asiatic makeup, his thick accent, and the supposed stoicism of the Orient. I suspect this nomination was for the makeup. Tamiroff should not have been named for this wooden performance.

Spencer Tracy should have been nominated in this category for his role as Father Mullin in *San Francisco* (see Best Actor). At the time, Tracy was seen as a leading man, and this category was meant for the character actors, not the stars. Silly idea. Tracy should get the nomination here.

And what about the rest of the boys? The ones they left out in the cold?

Thomas Mitchell exults in fighting against conformity and social expectations as the newspaper editor in *Theodora Goes Wild*. Watch the scene when he finds out Theodora's secret – I defy you not to split your face smiling. He should have been nominated for Best Supporting Actor.

Paul Robeson's recreation of the role that made him famous is the best part of the second film version of *Show Boat*. Universal poured big bucks into this production, and it shows, from the opening credits, with those unique paper cutout titles through the intense level of detail in almost every scene. James Whale directed; Irene Dunne starred. *Show Boat* was a landmark in the history of the American Broadway musical, exploring issues of miscegenation and race, but a few moments of racist stereotypes creep through, in the "happy slave" mode particularly. Robeson overcomes those sour spots, and steals the movie with his rendition of "Ol' Man River." He should have been nominated for the power of his voice and the pain in his eyes.

And now, let's consider John Carradine. *The Prisoner of Shark Island* tells the true story of Dr. Mudd, a physician who treated John Wilkes Booth's broken leg the night as Booth fled his pursuers after Lincoln was shot. Mudd was arrested, tried, and found guilty by association, then sent to prison for years, until his actions during an epidemic gained him early release. Mudd is played by Warner Baxter, in the best role of his career, while his sadistic jailer is played by John Carradine – a role Carradine would tune to such perfection that Ford would have him portray much the same part the next year in *The Hurricane*. Watch and listen to Carradine when he first realizes Mudd will be under his control. Vitriol has a face; vindictiveness has a voice. The sheer glee Carradine feels at being able to punish Mudd is frightening. Carradine deserved a nomination.

Eugene Pallette's bullfrog voice and demeanor should have earned him a nomination as the patriarch of the nuttiest family of the year in *My Man Godfrey*. Watch the scene when he first meets Godfrey, emerging from Irene's bedroom and picking up his hat, coat and suitcase. Godfrey has just delivered breakfast on his first day butling; the father assumes Godfrey has just slept with his daughter. Look at Pallette's eyes, and the quick assessment of the situation, as he begins to unbutton his coat to deliver the fatherly thrashing. His facial expressions endlessly amuse. The Thirties and Forties had the greatest character actors of all time, and Pallette was one of the best (watch him in *The Adventures of Robin Hood* as Friar Tuck for another great scene-stealer). Pallette deserved a nomination – and the Oscar for Best Supporting Actor.

Best Supporting Actress: Gale Sondergaard won for *Anthony Adverse*, over Maria Ouspenskaya, *Dodsworth*; Beulah Bondi, *The Gorgeous Hussy*; Alice Brady, *My Man Godfrey*; and Bonita Granville, *These Three*.

Gale Sondergaard made her screen debut in *Anthony Adverse*, and won for her first role. Sondergaard remains far better known for her vain appearance in *The Mark of Zorro*. In *Anthony Adverse* she plays a conniving maid with the ridiculous name of Faith Paleologus, who steals Anthony's birthright. Sondergaard was so successful in the role she was typecast into playing evil women for the rest of her career. Watching her today, she isn't that impressive. Still, she deserves a nomination, if for nothing else than having to act through that name. But giving her the Oscar is like adding bananas to a peanut butter sandwich, then frying the whole mess. It made Elvis fat, which should be enough warning for everybody else not to go there.

Maria Ouspenskaya is better known these days for her famous gypsy in *The Wolf Man*, intoning the myth of the werewolf: "Even a man who is pure in heart and says his prayers at night, may become a wolf when the wolfbane blooms, and the autumn moon is bright." In *Dodsworth*, she plays the Baroness, the mother of the boy Mrs. Dodsworth wants to marry. Imperial, cold, and dominating, Ouspenskaya is marvelous in this tiny role. The nomination should stay.

The Gorgeous Hussy stars Joan Crawford as Peggy Eaton, the subject of America's first presidential sex scandal; Lionel Barrymore plays Andrew Jackson, who defended Eaton's somewhat questionable name (he had nothing to do with the questionable part). James Stewart is stuck in here, with sideburns, no less. Beulah Bondi was nominated for playing Rachel Jackson, who in real life died before Jackson was inaugurated. Crotchety, loving, and decidedly looking like she could breathe fire out of her pipe, Beulah Bondi brings Rachel to life even better than Barrymore does the General. She actually uses the words "weasel juice" effectively. If that's not acting, what is? Her capacity to portray old love, one deepened with time and persecution, as well as her dying words, remain the best part of the film, along with Barrymore's substantially accurate Jackson. Still, *The Gorgeous Hussy* would have been far better in the pre-Code era, when they could have shown more clearly the reasons Eaton was disdained, and Crawford could have cut loose a bit more. Too much gorgeous, not enough hussy. As it is, some good performances can't save the picture, especially given its gross inaccuracies and reworkings, I could at least tolerate those if they made the story work, but they don't. I'm surprised this hasn't been remade, and done openly and honestly. Beulah Bondi deserved her nomination.

William Wyler directed *These Three* from a script by Lillian Hellman, adapting her own play, *The Children's Hour*. Merle Oberon, Miriam Hopkins and Joel McCrea star. Bonita Granville is the young teenager who tells a lie about her two schoolteachers. In the original Broadway play, the lie accused the two female leads of lesbianism; in this sanitized version, Granville says one of them spent the night with the other's fiancé. Granville's performance brings meaning to the words "spoiled rotten lying little brat" and "drama queen," forming a perfect argument for corporal punishment. A good nomination for a young actress who would go on to play the definitive Nancy Drew, as well as appearing in *Now, Voyager* with Bette Davis.

Alice Brady put in a brilliant performance as the mother in *My Man Godfrey*. If you look up the word airhead in the dictionary, you will find a picture of Brady as Mrs. Bullock. She seems to live in a special world of her own; you want to ask her what color the sky is where she is, because it certainly isn't blue. Pink with polka dots, perhaps. She hears and sees pixies in the morning. She spouts the most preposterous baby talk to her dog. She keeps Mischa Auer as her pet protégé Carlo. If any performance made the rich look like the fatuous, vapid lot most of them are, this is the one. Absolutely worth a nomination – and the Oscar for Best Supporting Actress. Nobody was better than Alice Brady this year.

Best Writing (Original Story): Pierre Collings and Sheridan Gribney won for *The Story of Louis Pasteur*, over Norman Krasna, *Fury*; William Anthony McGuire, *The Great Ziegfeld*; Robert Hopkins, *San Francisco*; and Adele Comandini, *Three Smart Girls*.

How can you win an Oscar for an original story for a biography of a real person? Well, we are talking Hollywood; most of their biographies are sheer fiction. Some degree of creativity would have to be used, in the manner of presentation. I would also expect that an official source not be named in the credits, as that would tilt things over to the adapted category. The problem with *The Story of Louis Pasteur* is that the narrative is mundane, and deals with much of the story in a perfunctory, superficial way. So, goodbye, Pierre Collings and Sheridan Gribney! Goodbye, *Louis Pasteur*. Go drink your milk – Pasteurized, of course. They should not have received the Oscar or a nomination.

To even suggest William Anthony McGuire for *The Great Ziegfeld* is to ignore the very concept of story. Stringing together empty dance and song numbers from second-rate singers and dancers isn't writing. The picture drags on and on, with little relief or consistent interest. The dialogue has little snap or zest. Plus, once again, this is a biography of a real person, with no originality in subject matter or presentation. No nomination should have been given.

Robert Hopkins' story for *San Francisco* isn't new either. We've seen it before, between Clark Gable and William Powell in *Manhattan Melodrama*; we will see it again in film after film, twice more with Tracy and Gable: the male love story, with a woman tossed in for grins and giggles. Usually, one of them dies, dramatically. The difference here is putting it in the Great San Francisco earthquake. Anita Loos wrote the screenplay, and while much of it is forced and trite, the power of the quake cannot be denied, because it is focused on the human costs. Gable is forced to play a religious conversion with little basis other than that the woman he loves isn't dead, which could just as easily be explained in his sense of the world as a piece of luck. What is great about the movie is not the story, nor is it the dialogue, which comes across as graceless and merely functional. No nomination was warranted.

Adele Comandini's nomination for *Three Smart Girls* befuddles. I like the title; smart women are so much more fun than dumb ones. Three daughters want to get their parents back together, and keep their rich idiot of a father from marrying a gold digger. Disney did this (somewhat) better later on in *The Parent Trap*. Largely an illogical sentimental pile of folderol, which I can demonstrate quickly: their father hasn't seen them in ten years, and not a trace of resentment do the girls display. Ten. Long. Years. No phone calls. No post cards. Nothing. But they love Daddy, and isn't he a dear? No nomination should have been made, for that alone.

Finally, we are left with Norman Krasna's nomination for Fritz Lang's first American film, *Fury*. I believe this to be the most original story of the year, and Krasna should have received the Oscar for Best Writing (Original Story). See Best Director above for why, although if you've been good little boys and girls and are reading every word as you should, you'd already know this. Off to bed with no supper for you!

Best Writing (Screenplay): Pierre Collings and Sheridan Gribney won for *The Story of Louis Pasteur*, over Frances Goodrich and Albert Hackett, *After the Thin Man*; Sidney Howard, *Dodsworth*; Robert Riskin, *Mr. Deeds Goes to Town*; and Eric Hatch & Morris Ryskind, *My Man Godfrey*

Talk about having your cake and eating it too! Two Oscars for the same movie, for the same writers. Too bad they didn't deserve either. The screenplay patently plays loose with the facts. Why does Hollywood do this with true stories? Why not just make up a different story, rather than turning a fascinating true life into an ABC Afterschool Special all the time? However, the nomination should stay, for two reasons: Paul Muni does turn in an enjoyable performance with their dialogue, and they do present science much more accurately than previous Hollywood depictions. But there should be no Oscar. Besides, their mouth is too full of cake to make an acceptance speech.

Frances Goodrich and Albert Hackett adapted Dashiell Hammett's specially commissioned treatment for a follow-up in *After the Thin Man*. Were it not for the Academy rule against sequels for Best Writing (Original Story), I'd argue the Oscar should have gone to Hammett. *After the Thin Man* is a worthy successor to the original, with even more fun from William Powell and Myrna Loy as Nick and Nora Charles, our drunken detectives. Jimmy Stewart has an early, atypical appearance. Asta the dog is back – with Mrs. Asta. The whole series is well worth your time.

Sidney Howard did a credible job turning Sinclair Lewis' classic novel *Dodsworth* into a fine screenplay. Indeed, I think this may be the best adaptation of Sinclair Lewis ever filmed, mostly due to Howard's faithful but streamlined adaptation. Best line: "Love has got to stop someplace short of suicide." A good nomination here.

Before I turn to the two best screenplays of the year that they did nominate, let me point out one they didn't: *Libeled Lady*, by Maurine Watkins, Howard Emmett Rogers and George Oppenheimer, based on a story by Wallace Sullivan. One line after another brings laughs: When Spencer Tracy sees the woman he loves married to another man, in order to carry out his plot, he cries "She may be his wife, but she's engaged to me!" William Powell: "I thought that was rather clever of me"; Myrna Loy: "Yes, I thought you thought so." Wonderful nonsense. The trout-fishing scenes alone are worth the price of entry. Why they failed to nominate it, I can't explain.

But they did recognize Eric Hatch and Morris Ryskind's script for *My Man Godfrey*, which is a thing of beauty. A classic comedy of manners, in which almost everybody is pretending to be something they're not, and by the end, they have become more than they were. Some first-rate zingers add the sparkle: "All you need to start an asylum is an empty room and the right kind of people." "If you're going to be rude to my daughter, you might as well at least take your hat off!" "The only difference between a derelict and a man is a job." Great stuff, for a great nomination.

Robert Riskin wrote another classic script for Frank Capra in *Mr. Deeds Goes to Town*, giddily funny, yet rooted in very serious issues. Comedy gains depth when it deals with serious issues: wealth, small town virtues, community, eccentricity, conformity, and love percolate through the humor, leading us to reconsider our entire worldview. Situation after situation resolves itself comically, and the dialogue rolls off as easily as Longfellow Deeds' tuba oom-pah-pah. Capra and Riskin weren't above stealing from themselves; they replay the echo in the mansion bit from *Platinum Blonde* to great effect (hey, if Handel and Bach can plagiarize themselves, why not Riskin and Capra?). The film added two regional words to the common American tongue: doodle and pixilated. Perhaps no expression of common human decency has been clearer since the Bible gave us the Golden Rule: "From what I can see, no matter what system of government we have, there will always be leaders and always be followers. It's like the road out in front of my house. It's on a steep hill. Every day I watch the cars climbing up. Some go lickety-split up that hill on high, some have to shift into second, and some sputter and shake and slip back to the bottom again. Same cars, same gasoline, yet some make it and some don't. And I say the fellas who can make the hill on high should stop once in a while and help those who can't. That's all I'm trying to do with this money. Help the fellas who can't make the hill on high." The elegance of simplicity cannot be overstated. The Oscar for Best Writing (Screenplay) should have found a perfect home with Riskin and *Mr. Deeds*.

Best Cinematography: Tony Gaudio won for *Anthony Adverse*, over Victor Milner, *The General Died at Dawn*, and George Folsey, *The Gorgeous Hussy*

Tony Gaudio's camerawork on *Anthony Adverse* remains effective, producing a wide variety of times of day and night, and setting the mood for the tale of a bastard finding his way through life. The shots done during candlelight particularly impress, as does the fight scene between Claude Rains and his wife's lover, deepened with the kind of shadows Michael Curtiz would perfect. Gaudio earned his nomination, but better shooting happened elsewhere, so no Oscar should have been given.

Victor Milner's work on *The General Died at Dawn* is masterful. The camera moves when it needs to move, concentrates when it needs to concentrate. The light shifts and moves as well, deepening the shadows and brightening the eyes of the actors with great fluidity and grace.

Milner was proving himself one of the best cameramen in the business with his work on this film.

MGM again used their studio block voting to get the nomination for George Folsey on *The Gorgeous Hussy*. While the photography is quite up to the normal high level of MGM's films, for the most part, it isn't distinguishable from any other MGM film of the period. A few highlights impress: Joan Crawford expressing her love in the moonlight streaming in at the window, and the mourning in the church, with the sunlight streaming in from the stained glass window. Apparently, Folsey was quite good with streaming. The nomination should stay.

Other cameramen ought to have been recognized by the Academy.

Ted Tetzlaff should have been nominated for *My Man Godfrey*. From the beginning of the film in the trash heaps, with the fogs of the bay and the lights from the street casting all into shadow, we are in the hands of a master cinematographer. Tetzlaff's camerawork is smooth, elegant, and economical (as it would be on Hitchcock's *Notorious*). As David Thomson describes it, Tetzlaff produced "...the glossy satanic black and white of *My Man Godfrey*."[civ] I couldn't agree more.

Finally, we come to a film that, despite its flaws, presents a glimmering Shakespearean tale, with the courts of the city, and the Forest of Arden: *As You Like It*. Two cinematographers worked on this adaptation: Jack Cardiff, who later won an Oscar in 1947 for *Black Narcissus*, and Harold Rosson, ex-husband of Jean Harlow and the man who shot *The Wizard of Oz* and many other worthy pictures. The cinematography and the score (see below) are by far the best parts of the film, although several of the supporting cast bring their roles successfully to life. Leon Quartermaine as Jacques gives a wonderful "All the world's a stage." The two actors playing the Dukes couldn't be more aristocratic. Olivier hasn't learned how to act for the camera yet. But the clean, crisp quality Rosson and Cardiff bring to the sets, faces, and costumes remains impressive, as does the translucent, dream-like quality of the scenes in Arden. Cardiff and Rosson should have won the Oscar for Best Cinematography this year.

Best Score: Warner Brothers and Leo Forbstein (and not composer Erich Wolfgang Korngold) won for *Anthony Adverse*, over Warner and Max Steiner, *The Charge of the Light Brigade*, Selznick and Max Steiner, *The Garden of Allah*; Paramount and Werner Janssen, *The General Died at Dawn*; and RKO & Nathaniel Shilkret, *Winterset*

The Academy used to nominate the studio and music department for the score, rather than the composer. The official Academy database now lists the composer as well, thus rectifying their previous error, so I will follow them in their chastened path.

Erich Wolfgang Korngold composed the score for *Anthony Adverse*, but the Oscar went to the head of the music department, Leo Forbstein. Korngold was furious, and refused to accept the Academy Award when Forbstein offered it, waiting until after Forbstein's death. *Anthony Adverse* now seems one of his minor works (although his Violin Concerto can be found here). Korngold would learn with time to score fight scenes beautifully; one can hear the roots of *The Adventures of Robin Hood* and *The Sea Hawk*. But overall, I would not consider it to be worthy of the Oscar itself, as it isn't Korngold's best work, and the entire film is over-long and over-done. No nomination should have been given

Max Steiner's score for the Errol Flynn *The Charge of the Light Brigade* is stately, martial and thrilling, particularly in the famous cavalry charge. The movie itself easily drives any history teacher up the wall with its lack of historical awareness (I should know; I teach history, and it drove me batty). Regardless of the utterly fictional nature of the movie, *The Charge of the Light Brigade* excites, in large part due to the score, and the excellent action scenes. Curtiz's trademark shadows play throughout effectively. A very good nomination indeed.

Max Steiner received another nomination for *The Garden of Allah*, produced by David O. Selznick and starring Marlene Dietrich and Charles Boyer. A horrendously difficult shoot resulted in a film best known for its color cinematography and little else. *The Garden of Allah* has an oriental score by Steiner that effectively conveys romance and mystery. Too bad the film is so remarkably stupid. Only Dietrich fanatics, those who want to see early color photography, and people who adore Max Steiner could possibly find this mess worth watching. Perhaps because the score has been imitated and used in so many other pictures set in the Middle East, the music sounds clichéd at times, but the nomination should stay for what persists in the ear.

The General Died at Dawn has music by Werner Janssen; Janssen would be nominated for a number of Oscars for his scores in the Thirties and Forties, almost all for forgettable movies. When you say a man's most famous film is the Marx Brothers' lackluster *A Night in Casablanca*, you've pretty much summed up his career as a second-rate composer. Janssen's score for *The General Died at Dawn* is bombastic and overbearing, although it does have a few nice moments when quiet suspense is needed. Overall, though, it's clichéd. No nomination should have been made.

Winterset, starring Burgess Meredith in his screen debut, is based on a Maxwell Anderson play about a son who tries to clear his executed father's name. The score by Nathaniel Shilkret has an interesting jazzy note here and there, and a constantly shifting array of tones. Overall, the music is effective, perhaps more so than the movie itself, which is eminently forgettable, and badly acted, except for John Carradine as the father and Meredith as the son. The nomination should stay.

What shocks music lovers today is the horrendous omission of Sir William Walton's score for the first Laurence Olivier Shakespeare film, *As You Like It*. James Barrie (*Peter Pan*) worked on the screenplay, but far more importantly, Walton's music for the movie is an absolute winner. Light, airy, touching, and highly effective – especially in a film marred by no chemistry whatsoever between Oliver and his Rosalind, an annoying Germanic-toned Elisabeth Bergner – Walton's music remains as wonderful to hear today as it should have then. The Oscar should have gone to Sir William Walton for *As You Like It*.

Best Song: Jerome Kern and Dorothy Fields' "The Way You Look Tonight" won from *Swing Time*, over Cole Porter's "I've Got You Under My Skin" from *Born to Dance*; Arthur Johnston and Johnny Burke's "Pennies from Heaven" from *Pennies from Heaven*; Richard A. Whiting and Walter Bullock's "When Did You Leave Heaven" from *Sing Baby Sing*; Walter Donaldson and Harold Adamson's "Did I Remember" from *Suzy*; and Louis Alter and Sidney Mitchell's "A Melody from the Sky" from *Trail of the Lonesome Pine*

I can live with "The Way You Look Tonight" winning from the Astaire-Rogers *Swing Time*, by Jerome Kern and Dorothy Fields. The problem is, I can't live without Cole Porter's "I've Got You Under My Skin" from the Eleanor Powell *Born to Dance*. If we are choosing on the basis of the original performance, then the Fred Astaire rendition would outdo the lesser-known, less rhythmic Virginia Bruce "Skin" from *Born to Dance*. But I prefer to consider the song in terms of the numbers of ways it has been rendered over the years, and of the two, "Skin" has proven the greater song (even if this is choosing between the greater of two great goods). Much as it pains me to decline a Jerome Kern/Dorothy Fields number, I can't deny Cole Porter – this time. May I recommend the Sinatra version from *Songs for Swingin' Lovers*? You're welcome. Cole Porter should have the Oscar for Best Song for "I've Got You Under My Skin."

As for the other songs they nominated, a few are worth pointing out, even if it's just for the novelty. We can be happy that they did nominate "Pennies from Heaven," from the movie of the same name, with music by Arthur Johnston, and lyrics by the talented Johnny Burke. But then, they had Bing Crosby and Louis Armstrong singing it. Hard to go wrong with two men who could swing what was written on a cheap bar's bathroom wall.

The Academy went from great to bad with "When Did You Leave Heaven," from *Sing, Baby, Sing*, music by Richard A. Whiting, and lyrics by Walter Bullock, which sounds like a bad pickup line. No nomination should have ever been given.

"Did I Remember," from *Suzy*, has music by Walter Donaldson, and lyrics by Harold Adamson...and it's sung by Jean Harlow (likely a dubbed voice) and Cary Grant. Not a great song, and they must have known it, since for most of the song they're talking over it. The song deserved no nomination.

"A Melody from the Sky" is from *The Trail of the Lonesome Pine*, with music by Louis Alter and lyrics by Sidney Mitchell, and sung by Cliff Edwards (better known as the voice of Jiminy Cricket). A minor song, with no basis for nomination.

The Academy also chose to neglect some classics: two more from *Swing Time* and Jerome Kern and Dorothy Fields: "A Fine Romance" and "Pick Yourself Up"; Johnny Mercer's "I'm an Old Cowhand" from *Rhythm on the Range*; and Irving Berlin's "Let's Face the Music and Dance" from *Follow the Fleet*. American music was in its golden age; we live in an age of iron (and not in a good way, metalheads...). Fortunately, we have recordings to remind us of the greatness we once enjoyed in abundance.

Best Dance Direction: Seymour Felix won for "A Pretty Girl Is Like a Melody" from *The Great Ziegfeld*, over Dave Gould for "Swingin' the Jinx" from *Born to Dance*; Bobby Connolly for "1000 Love Songs" from *Cain and Mabel*; Russell Lewis for "The Finale" from *Dancing Pirate*; Busby Berkeley, "Love and War" from *Gold Diggers of 1937*; Jack Haskell for "Skating Ensemble" from *One in a Million*; and Hermes Pan for "Bojangles" number from *Swing Time*

The dances in *The Great Ziegfeld* are showy, but not the best of the year. Many of them are downright boring, even the celebrated "A Pretty Girl Is Like a Melody," which cost a quarter of a million dollars, back when that kind of money meant something. The staircase turning into a cake, filling the screen, pleases on first sight, but ultimately, it's a pretty stunt with little life to it. No Oscar or nomination should have been handed to Seymour Felix.

Born to Dance has Jimmy Stewart as a sailor on leave, helping Eleanor Powell achieve her Broadway dreams. Dave Gould put together the "Swingin' the Jinx" number, which has Powell tap-dancing on a giant battleship set. Too much battleship, but not enough Powell, who was an outstanding dancer. The nomination should stay for her.

Bobby Connolly was nominated for "I'll Sing You a Thousand Love Songs" from *Cain and Mabel*, a mostly forgettable romance between showgirl Marion Davies and prizefighter Clark Gable. Connolly can't save this mess. Thankfully, Gable doesn't sing. Unfortunately, Davies does, and it more or less killed her career. No nomination should have been given.

Russell Lewis choreographed "The Finale" for the Frank Morgan vehicle *Dancing Pirate*, a mediocre film shot in Technicolor and whose only reason for viewing is to see a brief appearance by a very young Rita Hayworth with her family, The Dancing Cansinos. "The Finale" doesn't go much beyond minor Spanish flamenco formations. This dance should not have been nominated.

Busby Berkeley put together "Love and War" from *Gold Diggers of 1937*. Dick Powell, Joan Blondell, and a cast of hundreds follow Berkeley's commands to the last toe tap and plotted move. What do we get this time? Synchronized oversized rocking chairs; one rocking chair gets so big a tap dancer can go to town on it; a bomb blows it up, and it reassembles into a cannon; war, kissing, and marching follow. Too bad the song sucks. The nomination should stay.

Jack Haskell choreographed "Skating Ensemble" from *One in a Million*, starring the great skater Sonja Henie. Henie skates, although nowhere near as acrobatically as today's best. The nomination should stay for a pleasant time.

Hermes Pan was named for the "Bojangles" number from *Swing Time*, but seen today, and setting aside the historical context, what an embarrassment. Fred Astaire in blackface was not a good idea. Actually, anybody in blackface is not a good idea, but at least Astaire doesn't go for the white mouth and eyes. My assumption is he felt he was being respectful, and that in keeping the blackface to a minimum, he was avoiding the racist aspect. But the opening shot has a caricature of a black man as well, which adds to the discomfort of viewers today. Besides the blackface, "Bojangles" is mostly just tricking the audience through some visual effects, rather than focusing on choreography; it's faking it up, instead of showing something truly and simply. What could the Academy have chosen instead? "Pick Yourself Up" is just such joyous abandon and flinging happiness; Ginger Rogers was never better, with her "most glorious two minutes." "Waltz in Spring Time" has been called the "best dance number they ever did, because it is so complex."[cv]

But the greatest of them all, in terms of telling the story and utterly devastating the audience emotionally is "Never Gonna Dance." The entire point of choreography is symbolized by this absolutely perfect number. Hermes Pan and Fred Astaire should have won the Oscar for Best Dance Direction for "Never Gonna Dance" from *Swing Time*.

Best Art Direction: Richard Day won for *Dodsworth*, over Anton Grot, *Anthony Adverse*; Cedric Gibbons, Eddie Imazu, and Edwin B. Willis, *The Great Ziegfeld*; William S. Darling, *Lloyds of London*; Albert S. D'Agostino and Jack Otterson, *The Magnificent Brute*; Cedric Gibbons, Frederic Hope, and Edwin B. Willis, *Romeo and Juliet*; and Perry Ferguson, *Winterset*

Richard Day's work on *Dodsworth* is nicely done, and considerably difficult not to accept as the winner. From the giant factory to the more intimate moments, the world of *Dodsworth* is made real on the screen. Day had to reproduce a shipboard, Paris, Switzerland, an upper class American home, Vienna, Italy, and others. Quite effective work, and well deserving of a nomination, but the Academy ignored something even more impressive. The nomination should stay, but not the Oscar.

Anton Grot got a mention for *Anthony Adverse*, a big sprawling historical epic one would have expected from MGM rather than Warner Brothers. Grot's work in reproducing eighteenth century Europe proves to be exceptionally effective. We feel the differences from our present day in each scene, even if a certain quality of the soundstage remains (but back then, when didn't it?). Grot did an excellent job, and the nomination should remain.

I can see why they nominated *The Great Ziegfeld*; reproducing Ziegfeld's sets and going beyond the great showman does require some talent. The film dazzles in its opening scenes, with the recreation of the carnival sideshow, as we see the dancer Little Egypt competing with Sandow, the strongman. Everything from the costumes to the backgrounds shows the money they poured into the film, but money and glitz aren't everything. Style, curiously, is largely absent from the film. Astaire and Rogers did far better on their lower budgets at RKO. No nomination for wasting money.

Lloyds of London is most famous today for making Tyrone Power a star. So how do you make a film about insurance interesting? Turn it into a love story, of course – wherein Power falls for the wife of his hated rival. Oh, and while you're at it, toss in a sea battle...with some insurance on those vessels! *Lloyds of London* feels like a George Arliss or Paul Muni film to a degree, but the only real historical accuracy resides with the sets, which recreate the look of England during the Napoleonic wars about as well as any film did in the Thirties. I particularly enjoyed the seaport and Lloyd's coffeehouse, which had a feel of being well-lived in, unlike the kind of gloss this film would have had at MGM. William S. Darling would later win in this category for *Anna and the King of Siam*; he does well enough here to deserve his nomination.

The Magnificent Brute stars Victor McLaglen in an odd stew of a film, involving steel mill workers, a floozy, some missing money, and romance – with a kid tossed in to remind people of *The Champ*. The nomination for Albert S. D'Agostino and Jack Otterson rests on the robust recreations of the steel mill's working, portrayed effectively enough to keep the nomination.

Romeo and Juliet won a nomination for Cedric Gibbons and crew. The film is a veritable hodgepodge of antiques and styles, and never forms a clear sense of place and scene: "On one side were costume designer Adrian and resident art director Cedric Gibbons, and on the other were Cukor and Oliver Messel, who did the sets. The result was an incoherent look, pleasing neither side."[cvi] Or me. I've seen sets that clashed less in dinner theater (although the balcony scene is set in a huge garden terrace that pleases the eye). No nomination should be given for wasting even more money than they did on *The Great Ziegfeld*.

Perry Ferguson's work on *Winterset* seems a little out of place for an Oscar. To a modern eye, normal sets, nothing special – though speaking as a Bruin, I enjoyed the shot of UCLA's Royce Hall standing in for an eastern law school. A nice miniature shot of a prison seems more theatrical than cinematic. The main set, a poor, dark alley, looks even more like a theater set. No nomination should have gone for this B-picture masquerading as something important (playwright Maxwell Anderson's reputation has been in steep decline for decades, and for good reason).

And even with that long list, they missed their target completely.

The British *Things to Come* is largely unwatchable these days, save as a record of the past's vision for the future. Despite the cast including Ralph Richardson, Raymond Massey, and Sir Cedric Hardwicke, the film as a whole has aged badly.[50] H.G. Wells' writing grew increasingly pedantic and strident as he became more famous; as science fiction writer Ted Sturgeon punned, he sold his birthright for a pot of message. What remains compelling are the designs, from William Cameron Menzies, the director, and Vincent Korda. If you can disengage your logic, you might enjoy it. You ought to have plenty of practice; Hollywood

---

[50] The science of the space gun is ridiculously stupid, as it was when Jules Verne proposed it; as Larry Niven and others have pointed out, any humans would be a thin red paste on the floor if we launched to outer space that way.

requires you to be as dumb as possible to watch most of its output these days. The costumes are a hoot; apparently, everybody in the future has no problem walking through doors with their giant shoulders (among others, the Marchioness of Queensbury worked on the designs). The future is full of light, curves, and lots of transparent tubing for elevators and pneumatic cars. I wonder if Vegas knows about this? The futures of barbarism and rebirth remain visually impressive, even after these decades now of CGI and huge budgets for science fiction and fantasy films. Menzies and Korda deserved a nomination, and what is more, they should have received the Oscar for Best Art Direction.

Best Short Subject (Cartoon): Disney won for *The Country Cousin*, over MGM, *The Old Mill Pond*, and the Fleischer Studio, *Popeye the Sailor Meets Sindbad the Sailor*

Disney continued their dominance of this category with *The Country Cousin*, a Silly Symphony that presents a modern version of the Aesop's fable about the country mouse and the town mouse. *The Country Cousin* shows the kind of lush animation Disney was developing, as well as focusing on more elaborate ways to present character other than broad humor, as it did in the Mickey Mouse and Donald Duck cartoons that paid the bills for the experimentation of the Silly Symphonies. The score is perfectly synchronized to reinforce the actions and humor of the plot. Timothy Mouse from *Dumbo* can be traced back to this country mouse getting drunk on champagne. Disney should also have been nominated for *Thru the Mirror*, wherein Mickey does the Alice routine and steps into the mirror world, which is wild, and wildly animated. But the Oscar should have gone to an even more impressive cartoon.

MGM was nominated for *The Old Mill Pond*, which presents cartoon versions of famous black entertainers as frogs, including Louis Armstrong, Ethel Waters, Fats Waller, Cab Calloway, Bojangles Robinson, and Stepin Fetchit. We're back at the issues of historical context and the persistence of acceptability of presentations that can only be seen as racist now. MGM was doing its best through the Harman-Ising team to catch up to Walt Disney. In terms of its animation, *The Old Mill Pond* is competent enough, if uninspired. As parody, it fails completely, and not because it's racist (which it arguably is). *The Old Mill Pond* commits the cardinal sin of boredom, which should never receive any nominations.

Finally, the Max Fleischer Studio, the creators of Betty Boop and Popeye, as well as the animators for the first Superman cartoons, got a nod for *Popeye the Sailor Meets Sindbad the Sailor*. Like MGM, the Fleischers were doing the best they could to keep up with Disney. They pulled out all the stops for this long adventure cartoon. As a technical achievement, the cartoon is not up to Disney's rising standards, yet they do use a rolling camera effect that was very expensive to produce, as it involved shooting three-dimensional circular sets, one frame at a time. Wht the Fleischers did manage to do was produce human figures more capably than Disney did at the time, even if they are caricatures. Bluto plays Sindbad. Wimpy shows up with his hamburgers, as does Olive Oyl, the most unattractive sex symbol in movie history. The Fleischers, like Disney, had developed a stable of fully realized characters; it would take time for Warner Brothers and MGM to do the same. While *The Country Cousin* remains years ahead of what the Fleischers were capable of, Popeye simply never had a better cartoon (except perhaps the meetings with Ali Baba and Aladdin). The Oscar should have gone to *Popeye the Sailor Meets Sindbad the Sailor*.

CHAPTER TEN: 1938 AWARDS
10th Show

Movies released in 1937

THE SCENE OF THE CRIME:

On March 10, 1938, once again, the Academy returned to the Biltmore Bowl of the Biltmore Hotel. This year, the Academy charged fifteen bucks a ticket, mostly to keep out the extras, who had managed to annoy all the stars the year before when they so packed the dance floor that few of the celebrities could dance. This year, the Academy had made nice with the various guilds, and each guild's president attended. Dudley Nichols accepted the Oscar he had refused previously for *The Informer*. Given the fiasco of the previous year's leaks in the press room, for the first time, all of the winners were kept secret, as the press promised to not release the results before the Awards were given. Bob "Bazooka" Burns hosted.[51]

---

[51] Burns was a radio and movie comedian who made a specialty out of the country bumpkin, and a unique instrument made out of stove pipes and a whiskey funnel, which he named a "bazooka."

For some silly reason, they gave a wooden Oscar with a moveable mouth to Charlie McCarthy, Edgar Bergen's dummy.

The Academy chose to honor screen comedy pioneer, Mack Sennett, with a special Oscar; W.C. Fields made the award.

Some imposter showed up and claimed he represented Alice Brady, the Best Supporting Actress. To this day, nobody knows who he was, or where Brady's Oscar is.

The very first Irving G. Thalberg Award was given to Darryl F. Zanuck.

WHAT THEY GOT RIGHT:

Best Director: Leo McCarey won for *The Awful Truth*, over William Dieterle, *The Life of Emile Zola*; Sidney Franklin, *The Good Earth*; Gregory La Cava, *Stage Door*; and William Wellman, *A Star Is Born*.

Leo McCarey was one of the great comic directors of all time, and never better than he was with *The Awful Truth*. Ironically, then, when McCarey won, he was annoyed they hadn't given it to him for *Make Way for Tomorrow*; "Thanks, but you gave it to me for the wrong picture."[cvii] McCarey, like many known for comedy, wanted to be taken seriously. Doom usually results, but *Make Way for Tomorrow* is worth watching. Orson Welles later said, "That's the saddest movie ever made. It would make a stone cry."[cviii] The great French director Jean Renoir lauded McCarey as "one of the few directors who understand human beings."[cix] *The Awful Truth,* starring Irene Dunne and Cary Grant, brings the screwball comedy closer to the perfection it would reach in *Bringing up Baby*. What is remarkable is that McCarey, who cut his teeth with Laurel and Hardy, improvised most of the script on the set, which makes the writing nomination it received more than a little suspect for the wrong attribution. The method drove Grant and Dunne to distraction, until they realized they were in the hands of an improvisational master. What we get with *The Awful Truth* is a dissertation on modern love, complete with adultery (on both sides, possibly). And divorce. And reconciliation. All that, and a dog. Named Mr. Smith (and yes, that's Asta). I told you it was fun, didn't I? McCarey's direction (and dialogue) is witty, suggestive, and endlessly entertaining. He deserved the Oscar for this, and not for the well-meaning *Make Way for Tomorrow*. Make 'em laugh. As the nineteenth century thespian Edmund Kean said on his deathbed, "Dying is easy; comedy is difficult." Take your statue, Leo. Be grateful. We certainly are!

William Dieterle was nominated for *The Life of Emile Zola*. The film doesn't take many chances, telling the story quickly, with a few flairs here and there. We mostly watch the movie because it won Oscars, and for Muni's performance. Dieterle's direction is competent, but hardly inspired. He would get much better in *The Hunchback of Notre Dame* and *The Devil and Daniel Webster*. The nomination should stay, if only because most bio-pics tend to bore, and this one usually doesn't.

Sidney Franklin stretched beyond the typical MGM glossy, don't upset the applecart style in *The Good Earth*. Not much of a stretch, mind you, but a bit outside the normal run of the richest studio. But Franklin tells the story cleanly; he gets the best he can out of his two leads, neither of whom should have ever been cast (see Best Picture and Best Actress for more). Unfortunately, MGM wasn't the studio to be making this, as they could not help but glamour up the story, rendering it false through such touches, as well as casting stars instead of actors capable of completely submerging themselves in the role. In the second half, when the second wife appears, she is so repellent I cannot imagine why she has every male wrapped around her little...finger. Only Franklin can be held responsible for not evoking a more attractive performance out of her. Franklin does do his best to bring this ungainly beast of a film to rein, and for the effort, the nomination should stay.

Gregory La Cava went from the zany genius of *My Man Godfrey* to the more dramatic and less enjoyable *Stage Door*. La Cava manages to produce a variety of emotional moods, and move from the comic to the tragic, if in a somewhat off-putting way. La Cava has to negotiate a large cast, and provide them with unique moments to differentiate them all. He does so effectively, making the nomination worthy. See Best Picture below for more.

William Wellman, better known as the hard-hitting action director of *Wings*, turned in a melodramatic tale with *A Star Is Born*. Wellman and cameraman W. Howard Greene haven't quite figured out how to light color film; they should have shot this in black and white, because their attempts at atmospheric lighting just don't work. Oddly, the Academy gave Greene a special Oscar for the cinematography; clearly, they didn't know any better. Wellman's characters all seem two-dimensional stereotypes, with a few exceptions. The comic bits with Edgar Kennedy and Andy Devine aren't bad, just a little forced. All the color shots of mid-Thirties Hollywood at the beginning fascinate. For a movie that ends in a famous suicide scene, *A Star Is Born* strives for comedy for much of its first half (screenwriter Dorothy Parker's influence comes through here). Gaynor and March had a good comic sense; they're far better when they're being funny. Things go downhill from there; the ending is contrived and forced. Go back to your action pics, Wild Bill, or go make a full-on comedy (he listened to me! See *Nothing Sacred* below). No nomination should have been given.

Best Dance Direction: Hermes Pan won for the "Fun House" number in *A Damsel in Distress*, over Sammy Lee for "Swing Is Here to Stay" from *Ali Baba Goes to Town*; Dave Gould for "All God's Children Got Rhythm" from *A Day at the Races*; Bobby Connolly, for "Too Marvelous for Words" from *Ready, Willing and Able*; Harry Losee for the "Prince Igor Suite" from *Thin Ice*; Busby Berkeley for "The Finale" from *Varsity Show*; and Leroy Prinz for the "Luau" from *Waikiki Wedding*

Well, the Academy got it right, with one proviso: Fred Astaire should have been included in the nomination. Hermes Pan and Astaire were an unbeatable pair in the Thirties, producing classics, dance after dance. This time, Ginger Rogers wasn't around. *Shall We Dance* came out this year, but compared to earlier Astaire-Rogers films, the dances were lackluster, except for the roller-skating tap dance of "Let's Call the Whole Thing Off." *A Damsel in Distress* paired Astaire with Joan Fontaine, George Burns and Gracie Allen. Major problem: Fontaine could neither dance nor sing. Despite music by the Gershwins, a script co-written by P.G. Wodehouse from one of his own novels, and some inspired Astaire dancing, the film bombed. The Oscar was given for a number without Fontaine, set in a fun house: "Stiff Upper Lip." Inventive and unique, even if devoid of emotional impact, when compared with everything else being danced this year, "Stiff Upper Lip" deserved to win. Astaire, Burns and Allen all do a wonderful job negotiating their way through the obstacles of the best fun house ever: slides, moving floors, rotating floors and tunnels, and crazed mirrors. Pan and Astaire deserved the Oscar for Best Dance Direction.

Sammy Lee choreographed *Ali Baba Goes to Town*, which starred Eddie Cantor in a dream vision, wherein he is a sultan. Perhaps I should stop there. Then again, he didn't. Cantor speaks to an African tribe by talking like Cab Calloway and putting on blackface. This is what used to pass for humor, and the dead silence should have taken the nomination away.

Dave Gould was nominated for *A Day at the Races* with the Marx Brothers. One doesn't usually think of the Marx Brothers as dancers, other than Groucho's crazy kicking, but *A Day* has "All God's Children Got Rhythm." Seen today, the piece is more than a little racist, but put into historical perspective, it's impressive. Ivie Anderson, who sang most of the Thirties with Duke Ellington, has a great part in it. The nomination should stay, for her sake. As for the movie itself, *A Day at the Races* has its moments, but of the major Marx Brothers' films, *Day* has the fewest laughs – except for the tutsi-frutsi ice-a cream! Oh, and Harpo's examination by Groucho. Um, and Harpo's charades. Er, and Groucho, the floozy and the midnight rendezvous. Ok, I confess: *A Day at the Races* is still better than most comedy movies – and I especially like seeing Ivie Anderson.

Bobby Connolly choreographed *Ready, Willing and Able*, which was Ruby Keeler's last movie for Warner Brothers. Yet another backstage musical, *Ready, Willing and Able* is largely forgettable Ruby Keeler fare, with uninventive choreography for the most part. But then we get that giant typewriter, with Ruby tapping from key to key with Lee Dixon, as women's black stocking-clad legs strike the paper. Connolly deserved the nomination for this dance alone, even if either Berkeley or Pan would have done much more with it.

Harry Losee was nominated for the "Prince Igor Suite" in Sonja Henie's *Thin Ice*. One assumes it's skate dancing; I have no way of knowing. The movie wasn't available. But I like Sonja Henie; she should keep the nomination on ice for now...yes, I'm ducking. Please put down the crowbar...

Busby Berkeley continued his own way with *Varsity Show*. One of the best things about the movie is the black dance team Buck and Bubbles, who are effervescent. But Berkeley choreographed the finale, for which he received the nomination. Berkeley got a huge bleacher full of dancers, and began to play as he always did. Fun stuff, for which Berkeley should keep the nomination.

The less said about Leroy Prinz and *Waikiki Wedding*, the better. Martha Raye and Bing Crosby are fun, but this isn't Oscar-level choreography, not by a long shot.

Best Short Subject (Cartoon): Disney won for *The Old Mill*, over the Fleischer Studio, *Educated Fish*, and Charles Mintz, *The Little Match Girl*

The Old Mill, like so many other Disney cartoons, was a groundbreaking event, this time showcasing the studio's profoundly important invention of the multi-plane camera, and moving the studio ever closer to the kind of reproductions of reality that would be hallmarks of their feature length animated films. The multi-plane camera allowed the reproduction of depth and movement, lifting animation to new heights of art. *The Old Mill* doesn't have much of a story: animals live in an old mill, and a storm comes. What it does have are eye-popping animated effects. Watch the opening scene, as we go from the shimmering spider web to the camera entering into the animation itself, with multiple layers achieved through the innovations of the multi-plane camera. I doubt any other studio could have produced the water effects. Astonishing to this day, *The Old Mill* would deserve an Oscar even if it were to be released anew.

As for its competition, *Educated Fish* and *The Little Match Girl*, the other studios should have been embarrassed to even try. *Educated Fish* is yet another attempt by the Fleischer Studio to catch up to Disney; they don't even come close this time with a school of fish. Hah. Hah. I did find the Mae West worm amusing. *The Little Match Girl* finds Columbia going so cute it's creepy, as they try to find some story to match Disney. The screen is very, very busy; they haven't learned yet that less is usually more. Some nice animation effects are achieved, but the story never really moves beyond rank sentimentality, especially in its version of heaven. No nomination was warranted for either.

As usual, the only real competition was from Disney itself, in another classic Mickey Mouse cartoon, *The Clock Cleaners*. Mickey had begun to turn away from the trickster into the respectable, boring middle class mouse he became. Donald Duck and Goofy are equal partners. The animators have clearly learned from the Silly Symphonies, and few Mickey Mouse cartoons ever milked an idea as this one does. As Mickey, Goofy and Donald clean the town clock, every amusing permutation comes out (Goofy's main riff is a clear takeoff on Harold Lloyd's *Safety Last*). The Academy should have nominated this instead of the other two they did – and perhaps the same trio with the haunted house in *Lonesome Ghosts*, which is also well worth your time, particularly in the payoff at the end.

WHAT THEY GOT WRONG:

Wrong? Who said the Academy ever gets anything wrong?!? Oh, yeah, that was me.

Best Picture: *The Life of Emile Zola*
Best Actor: Spencer Tracy, *Captains Courageous*
Best Actress: Luise Rainer, *The Good Earth*
Best Supporting Actor: Joseph Schildkraut, *The Life of Emile Zola*
Best Supporting Actress: Alice Brady, *In Old Chicago*
Best Writing (Original Story): William Wellman and Robert

Carson, *A Star Is Born*
Best Writing (Screenplay): Heinz Herald, Geza Herczeg and Norman Reilly Raine, *The Life of Emile Zola*
Best Cinematography: Karl Freund, *The Good Earth*
Best Score: Universal Music Department, *One Hundred Men and a Girl*
Best Song: Harry Owens, "Sweet Leilani," *Waikiki Wedding*
Art Direction: Stephen Goosson, *Lost Horizon*

Best Picture: *The Life of Emile Zola* won, over *The Awful Truth, Captains Courageous, Dead End, The Good Earth, In Old Chicago, Lost Horizon, One Hundred Men and a Girl, Stage Door,* and *A Star Is Born*

The Life of Emile Zola is yet another Paul Muni bio-pic. This time, the French writer of *Nana* and other socialist novels comes into Muni's hands. The Warner Brothers seem to have intended the film as a sly attack on Hitler's actions and attitudes towards the Jews by focusing on the Dreyfus Affair, which showed the French government to be anti-Semitic to the core at the turn of the century. But they tell the story without really letting the audience know why Dreyfus was being persecuted, which undercuts the entire point of attacking anti-Semitism; a finger points at his record, showing his religion to be Jewish, while the French military leaders ask how somebody like that could have made it onto the general staff. An inherently weakened picture, *The Life of Emile Zola* was far from the best made this year. The first half is mediocre at best, but the second half makes up for it, as the trial takes over to provide narrative drive. The nomination should stay, but not the Oscar.

The Awful Truth couldn't be better. See Best Director above, and a whole bunch of other stuff below. Damn funny movie, and a great nomination.

Victor Fleming's *Captains Courageous* adapted Rudyard Kipling's famous novel. Starring Spencer Tracy, Freddie Bartholomew, and Lionel Barrymore, *Captains Courageous* tells the story of a rich, spoiled boy fished out of the sea by Spencer Tracy, and taught the realities of life with Tracy and the other fishermen, captained by crusty Barrymore. Bartholomew plays a real stinker of a kid: a conniving, insensitive, heartless creature who makes an excellent argument for legislating retroactive birth control. Tracy plays an uncharacteristic role, using curled hair and an awkward accent, as he guides Bartholomew to a more human maturity (see Best Actor below for more on Tracy). Fleming does a good job keeping the story moving, and making Bartholomew's transformation believable. Of course, one of the stages in that transformation is for Barrymore to haul off and wallop Bartholomew across the head so hard he lands in a pile of fish. The phrase "child abuse" was coined considerably later, but at this point, everybody in the audience is so sick of Bartholomew that the smack must have been a relief. Wrong, but a relief nonetheless. The movie's false note comes in Tracy's death scene, which is entirely too uplifting and noble. Despite this, the nomination should stay.

Dead End proved to be another step in Humphrey Bogart's path to stardom, as well as granting the Dead End Kids a career for a decade and more. Based on the play by Sidney Kingsley, with a screenplay by Lillian Hellman and direction by William Wyler, *Dead End* names Sylvia Sidney and Joel McCrea as the stars, but it was Bogart and the Dead End Kids who emerged as the center of attention, along with Best Supporting Actress nominee Claire Trevor (also see Best Supporting Actor). *Dead End* may be the most emblematic of Depression Era films, daring to show poverty in the midst of plenty, and calling for social action without ever saying a word, by simply juxtaposing the sufferings of the poor with the blessings of the rich. More than that, *Dead End* shows how poverty is a breeding ground for crime, and how difficult it can be to stay to the straight and narrow when there seem so few rewards for moral behavior to counter those of the wages of sin. An excellent nomination.

The Good Earth, based on Nobel Laureate Pearl S. Buck's bestselling novel, was one of the last major projects Irving Thalberg was working on when he died (the film is dedicated to him as "his last great achievement"). Pearl S. Buck wanted only Chinese actors cast, and looking back, she was at least half right. Paul Muni has no business being in this film; he looks absolutely ridiculous in makeup. Luise Rainer is more problematic, as she does project a certain dignified quality, a stoicism that was associated in the West with the "oriental" character back then. Such a stereotype was more a product of western imperialism and false perceptions than it was a reality, which means Rainer is creating a false impression of the essence of Chinese culture (see Best Actress below for more). Like *San Francisco*, the movie largely exists as an excuse for a special effects disaster, this time locusts, which are rendered effectively for the time. Moreover, Buck's novel was the bestselling book in America in the early Thirties, in much the same way that *Gone with the Wind* would dominate the middle Thirties in the bookstores. If this movie was such a great adaptation, why wasn't it nominated for the writing category? Overall, the film has dated badly, but then, so has Pearl S. Buck. Who reads *The Good Earth* these days, unless some high school teacher forces them? I had never seen this film before writing this book; I have no intention of ever seeing it again. No nomination should have been given.

In Old Chicago is Darryl F. Zanuck's attempt to replicate the success of the disaster flick from MGM, *San Francisco*. They had an earthquake; he has a fire. They had Clark Gable, Spencer Tracy, and Jeanette MacDonald; he has Tyrone Power, Don Ameche, and Alice Faye, who go to show why MGM was rightfully able to claim they had more stars than heaven. *In Old Chicago* is but one in a long, terribly frustrating line of examples where Hollywood shouts "me too!" and proceeds to make the same film others did, only more so. The movie has not aged well. We start with a foolish Irishman who gets himself killed racing in a covered wagon with a locomotive. He leaves behind Alice Brady to raise their sons, Tyrone Power and Don Ameche, in boomtown Chicago. Alice Faye shows up to destroy the narrative thrust every time she sings. One good brother, one bad brother, one woman between them – but the point of the movie, like *San Francisco*, is to show off the special effects and destroy a city. By the way, you've never seen an uglier cow than the one who knocks over the lantern. You'd swear she needs plastic surgery to be in a Hollywood film. On top of all that, Tyrone Power basically stalks and sexually assaults Alice Faye...and she likes it. The cow should have refused the nomination.

Frank Capra made the mistake of most Hollywood powerhouses: he took his commercial success – often quite artistic – and set out to make Art with a capital A. He made up for it later with *Mr. Smith Goes to Washington* and *It's a Wonderful Life*, but we still have to swallow hard before subjecting ourselves to sitting through *Lost Horizon*. Parts of the film are very good, yet others are so awkward as to make me want to go to a séance and ask Capra just what the hell he was thinking (or perhaps Columbia head Harry Cohn, who took the editing away from Capra out of frustration, whereas Capra might have succeeded if left alone). Ronald Colman stars in this adaptation of James Hilton's novel by Robert Riskin. Hilton's popularity has largely vanished today, known only for the film adaptations (this, and *Goodbye, Mr. Chips*). *Lost Horizon* is a fantasy, a longing for a utopia of timeless perfection. The problem with all utopias is this: they're boring. When all problems have been solved, we don't have paradise: we have the land of the lotus eaters. Human beings need challenges, not perfection. Ronald Colman apparently never learned that, as he seeks Shangri-La. The film takes a small group of disconnected refugees from a war, puts them in an airplane, and crashes them into Hilton's perfect place: adventurer Colman and his brother, along with business man and swindler Thomas Mitchell, paleontologist Edward Everett Horton, and a prostitute. They reach the

Valley of the Blue Moon, where we find Sam Jaffe, playing the High Lama (Jaffe got the part after two other actors passed away, each time right after they were cast. Talk about bravery!). H.B. Warner plays Chang, the High Lama's right hand man. *Lost Horizon* does its best to provide some dramatic tension, with the mystery of how the refugees were brought to Shangri-La. As in most utopias, everything is talk, talk, talk as they explain how paradise works. The dialogue needs to crackle, and it doesn't here, which surprises, because Riskin and Capra were quite good at that. We are left with the voices, particularly that of Ronald Colman, to try and carry the story forward, as well as Edward Everett Horton attempting comic relief. The camerawork remains rather static as well, although the snow work is starkly beautiful. All told, an interesting failure, but a failure nonetheless. The nomination should stay for making the attempt.

One Hundred Men and a Girl is yet another Deanna Durbin lightweight movie getting nominated for Best Picture. I don't mind Deanna Durbin, but her vehicles aren't what I think of when I think "Best Picture." True, this one has Leopold Stokowski, Eugene Pallette, and Mischa Auer, but just because we've got some interesting side dishes doesn't mean the meal's a good one. Today, Deanna Durbin would have a Disney Channel series at best; she and Hannah Montana could guest star on each other's shows. Of course, they'd have to call it something besides *One Hundred Men and a Girl*; too many people would think it was pornography. On that note, let me just say "no nomination needed" and get out of the way before people start throwing things at me.

Stage Door stars Katharine Hepburn and Ginger Rogers in yet another backstage story. Adolphe Menjou shows up; Lucille Ball, Eve Arden and Ann Miller get very early appearances. Rogers and Hepburn are unwilling roommates in the boarding house called the Footlights Club, along with over a dozen other wannabe theatrical divas. Rogers is street smart and tough; Hepburn is haughty and high-toned. Both have dialogue that zings (see Best Writing (Screenplay) below). When Hepburn arrives, and tosses her furs on the bed, Rogers picks them up and sniffs, "Fresh kill?" Hepburn snaps back, "Yes, I trapped them myself." In some ways, this is another version of *Morning Glory*, although Hepburn is a far more mature and capable actress by 1937. Adolphe Menjou is Adolphe Menjou again, playing the impresario. Rogers plays more or less the same role as in the musicals with Fred Astaire, but without much dancing. Hepburn has to play a bad actress, and does so by cold readings and no emotional affect whatsoever; Hepburn would be parodied for years to come for "The calla lilies are in bloom again." The ending turns unfortunately melodramatic, but this does give me a good reason to deny they should have the Oscar. All those wisecracks almost got to me.

A Star Is Born stars Fredric March and Janet Gaynor, and if you've been with me since the first year of this harangue, maybe you know enough to stop right there. Gaynor was annoying enough in silents; add sound and color, and you've got one long whine to go with the pastels. I swear, every time she takes in breath, she sounds like one of my dog's squeaky toys. I can never figure out why Fredric March falls in love with her character, or why they give her a contract; we never see her supposedly great screen test, or more than a few seconds of her films. We're told she's fabulous, but we never see it. Much potential was wasted here, through miscasting Gaynor as the young ingénue, and for the film not preparing the groundwork for March's decline adequately. Like great literature, they should show, not tell. This movie tells all the time. "No nomination" should have been what they were told.

Once again, the Academy neglected some truly great films.

Nothing Sacred, produced by David O. Selznick and directed by William Wellman, stars Fredric March and Carole Lombard. Ben Hecht wrote the screenplay, but when Selznick insisted on a happy ending, Hecht walked out; Dorothy Parker and Ring Lardner, Jr. (and others) came in for rewrites. This screwball comedy may be the funniest thing Fredric March ever did, and Carole Lombard reaches her peak. An opening note does feature a stereotypically slow black man, and his large family; we also get an Indian "joke"; these kinds of idiocies often passed for humor back then. On the other hand, when a group of children show up to serenade Lombard, every single ethnic group seems represented, which appears to be an argument on Wellman's part for integration far ahead on the PC curve. As the tale continues, Lombard's desire to have fun meets up with March's desire for a great story; cynicism is the driving force here. Wellman has a real touch for comedy, although he's better known for action. Just keep him away from the melodrama (like *A Star Is Born*). At the dance, we get a marvelous comic image of a very short bald man dancing with a very tall woman, and spying on Lombard under her armpit every so often. The classic fight scene at the end remains the best part of the film. *Nothing Sacred* should have been nominated for Best Picture.

As should Selznick's other great film of the year, the best version of Anthony Hope's novel *The Prisoner of Zenda*, starring Ronald Colman, with Douglas Fairbanks, Jr. and David Niven. Not only does the film contain some very fine acting, thrilling swordplay, and tender romance, but it has some of the finest special effects prior to CGI. How Ronald Colman shakes hands with himself is a mystery; they must have had to do a high number of takes to get the timing perfect. But attention to that kind of detail is a hallmark of Selznick pictures of the mid-Thirties; later, as Selznick's addiction to methamphetamines grew, he would spiral out of control and ruin at least two Hitchcock pictures, if not more. Here in *The Prisoner of Zenda,* as in *David Copperfield,* the result is a sparkling adaptation (while the Dickens is a widely read classic still, the Hope novel would be forgotten without the films). Selznick being an independent, and releasing through an ailing United Artists, must have cost him some nominations (which is also true for the next picture I'm advocating as well); that, and he seems to have thrown his support behind *A Star Is Born* instead. Selznick was always a busy little beaver; methamphetamines will do that to you. *The Prisoner of Zenda* deserved a Best Picture nod instead of *A Star Is Born.*

Laurel and Hardy made *Way Out West,* and like *Sons of the Desert,* this long film is every bit as good as one of their classic shorts. Proudly affixed to the credits, at long last recognizing the truth of the matter, is the title card proclaiming *Way Out West* to be "A Stan Laurel Production." Laurel and Hardy's long films are beloved by fans; I oughtta know; I've been one since I was a kid. But all too often, the boys were far better served by the short form. *Way Out West* is one of the excellent exceptions. From the moment they appear, with Stan pulling Ollie behind a mule, the comedic inventiveness never flags. First Ollie goes into the pond. Then Stan walks right through the pond; Ollie follows, only to find the hole Stan missed. Stan then drags Ollie behind the mule, with his clothes drying on a rack overhead. Stan tries to hitchhike, but can't find his thumb. Then Stan does the Claudette Colbert leg bit from *It Happened One Night,* and it works just as well for him. Their greatest musical moment arrives here as well, as they sing and "commence the dancin'." Astaire and Rogers have serious competition...at least in the entertainment category. A gold mine is involved, as is a chiseling James Finlayson. As always, Ollie gets exasperated; Stan gets confused; the audience is laughing. What more could you want? Oh, right. A damn Academy Award nomination for Best Picture! Right, Ollie? Right, Stanley!

Finally, the Academy found a way to weasel out of having failed to nominate another great film by handing its creator a special Oscar. Walt Disney's *Snow White and the Seven Dwarfs* remains groundbreaking. The Academy tried to cover up ignoring *Snow White* by having Shirley Temple give Walt an Oscar with one large Oscar and seven small ones in a row – the next year. Personally, I don't like cop-outs, and animation remains one of the most disrespected art forms of America (baseball, jazz, pizza, and comic books are a few of the others).

Much later on, the Academy would create a separate category to keep long animation out of consideration completely for Best Picture. While I don't personally find *Snow White and the Seven Dwarfs* to be Disney's best – that honor would go to *Pinocchio* for the height of artistry, *Bambi* for the depth and honesty of storytelling, and *Fantasia* for sheer gumption – I find it incomprehensible that the Academy was so cowardly. Or maybe I don't; Hollywood hates taking chances. *Snow White* deserved a nomination as Best Picture. Watch the scene where Snow White escapes into the forest; I challenge you to find a more terrifying two minutes in the history of American cinema. Watching the film remains as fresh today as it was when it opened, and every single feature length animated picture comes directly from here.

In the end, I think the Best Picture should go to a film that bears repeated viewings, and still brings joy and insight every time. At that, the choice winnows to *The Awful Truth, Nothing Sacred, The Prisoner of Zenda, Snow White and the Seven Dwarfs*, and *Way Out West*. When I polled friends and family, the choices narrowed further to *Snow White, Way Out West,* and *The Awful Truth*. Any of them would be excellent selections. What it comes down to me is thinking over my past forty years, and which of those films I've returned to the most, and which gave the most rewards for that time spent. On that basis, *The Awful Truth* should take the Oscar for Best Picture. Three careers came to perfection in that film: Cary Grant became Cary Grant, and Irene Dunne and Leo McCarey would never be better. What more could you want? Get the Oscar, Mr. Smith! Good boy.

Best Actor: Spencer Tracy won for *Captains Courageous*, over Charles Boyer, *Conquest*; Paul Muni, *The Life of Emile Zola*; Robert Montgomery, *Night Must Fall*; and Fredric March, *A Star Is Born*

Much as I love Spencer Tracy, Harpo Marx hair and a goofy accent do not an Oscar equal. The role of Manuel the Portuguese fisherman in *Captains Courageous* was one Tracy never wanted and fought against; that he turned it into Oscar gold is a sign of the respect the community had for Tracy, and, I think, a desire to reward him for the great work he had been turning in before this movie. Tracy does the best he can, given what the role demands. He deserves a nomination for the effort, but not the Oscar, given what the Academy ignored (be patient; we're getting there!), and the false notes that erupt in the death scene, wherein it is played solely for sentimentality, and not for true emotion and realism. Tracy would rarely allow such blunders in his films as his star power grew.

Charles Boyer was chosen for his role as Napoleon in Greta Garbo's *Conquest*. At least they didn't cast Maurice Chevalier, although that might have made a more interesting film. *Conquest* is about a sexual tryst in a time in Hollywood when such things just weren't allowed. Boyer is decent in the role, looking very Napoleonic, but the makeup may have been too much, since Boyer also looks uncomfortable. Worse, he simply doesn't have any chemistry with Garbo. Occasionally, Boyer gets a wild look in his eyes when talking about his empire, and you can feel the world conqueror emerging, if only momentarily. But it all seems forced and unnatural. No nomination.

Paul Muni received another Oscar nomination for his title role in *The Life of Emile Zola*. Muni digs into the role with theatrical gusto, as he usually did. Muni lived his roles, researching them and driving himself to perfection, at least in his own terms. Muni is quite good as Zola, but not markedly different from his role as Louis Pasteur. Muni never really overcame his stage training, although he learned to tone it down as time went on. Muni clearly enjoys himself here as Zola the crusader, a character that Warner Brothers loved to have as their heroes, fighting against social injustice. Muni does deserve a nomination here, for what I think is his last good performance. Still, not the epitome of great screen acting that the Oscar should represent.

Robert Montgomery had been stereotyped as a light romantic lead, occasionally with a caddish side. With *Night Must Fall*, he broke out and turned in a bravura performance as a psychopathic killer. Montgomery was so sure of himself, he even invested his own money to help finance the production (thus breaking one of the cardinal rules of Hollywood: ALWAYS use somebody else's money). Montgomery seems a bit off at first, but then that may be me just coming to him from watching his earlier frothy films. He quickly becomes the part, lying fluidly to charm the old woman, played by Dame May Whitty, whose money he is already eying. Her niece, Rosalind Russell, is suspicious and attracted at the same time. Murder follows. At the end, Montgomery grows a bit too stagy for the role, which may be due to the play dominating his memory, as he'd seen it himself on Broadway. But Montgomery walks the path begun by Peter Lorre in *M* as we move towards *Psycho* and *Cape Fear*, and all the human monsters that have come in our films since, so his nomination should stay, if only as a warning of the horrors awaiting us.

Looking back, no actor was more widely respected or honored in the Thirties and Forties than Fredric March – which makes his relative obscurity today even more of a surprise. The man was either in every important picture of those two decades, or up for consideration for the leading role. Watching him now, a certain porcine quality does touch his acting every now and then, as it does with Muni. He was also a cad on the set, regularly trying to sleep with his leading ladies. Shelley Winters once said she had never known anybody else who could act out a heart-wrenching scene and pinch her butt at the same time.[cx] *Nothing Sacred* finds March having fun in the role. His performance in *A Star Is Born* has him reaching the other direction, after the initial comic scenes. March is a good screen drunk. Perhaps his finest moment in the movie is when he is saying goodbye to his wife; the look of resignation and determination to end it all comes across heart-breakingly. The nomination should remain.

One of the many things I can't understand about the Academy is their general neglect of some of their greatest stars. Cary Grant never won an Oscar; he was only nominated twice, for two of his weakest performances. *The Awful Truth* finds Archibald Leach in complete possession of that miracle of masculine charm, grace, and goofiness in full flower as "Cary Grant." By 1937, he had developed an array of subtle expressions, vocal inflections, and physical movements that still make him the most eminently watchable star of the twentieth century. Observe his face as he tries to figure out what to make of his wife's male companion at the beginning of the movie. Catch his classic pratfall with the chair at the recital. Grant's look of glee when Dunne is embarrassed at the nightclub is worth the price of admission alone. *The Awful Truth* cemented Grant's stardom, propelling him to the status of one of Hollywood's best actors and greatest leading men. Why he didn't receive a nomination is a mystery even the Sphinx can't solve. Cary Grant should have won the Oscar for Best Actor for *The Awful Truth*.

Best Actress: Luise Rainer won for *The Good Earth*, over Irene Dunne, *The Awful Truth*; Greta Garbo, *Camille*; Janet Gaynor, *A Star Is Born*; and Barbara Stanwyck, *Stella Dallas*.

Luise Rainer won back-to-back Oscars, then self-destructed her career. *The Good Earth* would prove to be her grand finale. When Alfred Hitchcock became frantic over his chances to win an Oscar in the early Forties, his wife Alma finally snapped, "for Chrissakes don't take it so seriously. Just remember, this is the group that gave an Oscar to Luise Rainer. Twice!"[cxi] I know what Mrs. Hitchcock meant, yet I prefer Rainer's performance here as the good wife O-Lan to her weepy, creepy turn in the previous year's *The Great Ziegfeld*. I'm still going to argue she should not have won her Oscar, however. Watching *The Good Earth* today, one can only wish that Thalberg had gone through with his original idea of casting Anna May Wong in the role. Shot as a silent film, Rainer might have gotten away with it; her face and body language can be quite expressive. But once she opens her mouth, and the German accent stumbles out, all suspension of disbelief goes willingly away. Bad casting. And what is more, what is a dirt-poor farmer's wife doing wearing makeup in China?! No Oscar, but she should keep her nomination for what she does get right about the role: the stubborn streak, the work ethic, the charm of her half-smile.

Irene Dunne's turn in *The Awful Truth* proved to be the high point of her career. She would never be funnier, more beautiful, or more self-assured. What more can I say? Just this: she makes Cary Grant look even better with her than he does by himself. Now that takes talent. The nomination should stay.

When Rainer won, the audience was shocked; they fully expected Garbo to win for *Camille*. Garbo turned in what is widely regarded today as her greatest serious performance of her career (I would point to *Ninotchka* as her best, but I find laughing more enduring than weeping). Irving Thalberg worked hard to craft this update to the nineteenth century warhorse, dying before filming was complete; as he said privately, "The problem of a girl's past ruining her marriage doesn't exist anymore. Whores can make good wives. That has been proven."[cxii] The story was the basis of Verdi's *La Traviata*, and more recently, *Moulin Rouge*. Co-starring Robert Taylor, who shows he has finally learned how to act, *Camille* still succeeds in wrenching tears, largely due to Garbo's performance, and George Cukor's deft direction. Garbo acts more understated, nuanced, and alive than she ever has been before. A well-deserved nomination.

Janet Gaynor? No, no, no. A thousand times no. Whiny, whiny, whiny. I will say this: she's more fun drunk than sober. And I'm not talking about myself, despite needing more alcohol to put up with her (hic). She has a nice drunk scene with Andy Devine wherein, shock of all shocks, she's actually amusing for a minute. She also has some funny moments imitating Greta Garbo, Katharine Hepburn, and Mae West. Enough so that I think she would have been far better off in comic parts, preferably in a supporting role; she could have easily become the Judy Holliday of the Thirties. Oddly, Fredric March was more effective in this movie when he was drunk too. Gaynor should have played the whole movie that way. God knows there's no other way I could bring myself to watch this one again. No nomination should have been given for *A Star Is Born*.

Barbara Stanwyck starred in the tearjerker *Stella Dallas*. King Vidor directed this paean to motherly sacrifice. Stanwyck came to the role after a couple of years of not particularly memorable roles. The imposition of the Production Code stole her thunder as an actress who loved pushing the boundaries. *Stella Dallas* was a reinvention of her screen personality, just as *Ball of Fire* and *Double Indemnity* would be later. Stanwyck deliberately starts out playing the role as a bit of a tart, setting her cap for the boss, as she had in pre-Code films. But by the end, she has transformed herself into the poster child for loving mothers (to the point of the audience needing insulin at times). Hallmark Cards should erect a statue in her honor. The nomination stays, just as long as a free box of Kleenex comes with it.

Of all these performances, none was more accomplished, subtle, comic or touching than that of Irene Dunne in *The Awful Truth*. Watch the scene at Cary Grant's rich fiancée's house, as she puts on a trollop act to end all trollop acts – while also ending Grant's engagement. Incredibly funny stuff – and worthy of the Oscar for Best Actress, which Irene Dunne should have won for *The Awful Truth*.

Best Supporting Actor: Joseph Schildkraut won for *The Life of Emile Zola*, over Ralph Bellamy, *The Awful Truth*; Thomas Mitchell, *The Hurricane*; H.B. Warner, *Lost Horizon*; and Roland Young, *Topper*.

Joseph Schildkraut won for portraying Captain Alfred Dreyfus, the centerpiece of the infamous Dreyfus Affair in *The Life of Emile Zola*. Schildkraut had a long career in Hollywood, often playing slimy, unattractive characters. Here, he plays against type, as a good soldier and family man who is unjustly accused, persecuted and imprisoned for the espionage he did not commit. Schildkraut fills the role with intense emotional pressure, but perhaps a touch too much melodrama, as does Muni; they are both too stagy for the screen. But he does rend the heart as we watch him punished for a crime he did not commit. He should keep the nomination, but the Oscar should have gone to a performance far more lasting.

Ralph Bellamy seems to have made a career out of playing the second banana, most famously in *The Awful Truth* and *His Girl Friday*. Here, he is after Irene Dunne. As an oil man and rancher from Oklahoma, he gets caught in the meat grinder between Grant and Dunne as they work through their divorce back to each other. It should be a thankless role, but Bellamy makes more of it than anybody else could have. His dance scene with Dunne is one of the funniest things in the movie. The nomination is an excellent one.

Thomas Mitchell earned a nomination for his role as the drunken doctor who acts as the voice of reason (a role he would replicate and improve in *Stagecoach* later). *The Hurricane* was John Ford's contribution to the disaster film genre, along with Dorothy Lamour and her sarong. Jon Hall (a star of the later Invisible Man series) and Mary Astor also star with Raymond Massey and John Carradine. Based on a novel by *Mutiny on the Bounty* authors Charles Nordhoff and James Norman Hall, *The Hurricane* featured cutting edge special effects with the hurricane, put together by James Basevi, the wizard behind *San Francisco*'s earthquake. The location footage is quite lovely, and the studio shots just as effective. Mitchell's performance stands out in *The Hurricane*, and although I think he's far better in *Stagecoach* playing almost the same role, he does deserve a nomination here.

H.B. Warner, most famous as Jesus in the silent *The King of Kings* and part of the wax museum in *Sunset Blvd.*, plays Chang in *Lost Horizon*, the man who guides the war refugees to Shangri-La. Warner is calm, inscrutable, and endlessly willing to explain everything. I suppose this kind of quiet serenity isn't easy to project without inducing sleep; Warner is very successful in that. The nomination should stay.

Roland Young had to go up against Cary Grant and Constance Bennett in *Topper*, and he steals the show. One of the regular ugly questions about the Supporting categories is how often leading roles get stuck into this to prevent competition, or ensure nominations and wins, and vice versa. Roland Young wasn't a star, but given that the movie is named after his character, and he spends much of the time onscreen with disembodied voices, it may be a stretch to not have him in the starring category. But let it be. Watch Roland Young play an old fuddy-duddy who finds a way to live again, and you will know how much he deserved this nomination. The drunken walk through the hotel lobby alone is worth nominating him.

Finally, we reach a man moving towards stardom, but still making the best he could with supporting roles. Humphrey Bogart went from the terror of his role as a gangster in *The Petrified Forest* to a more nuanced, believable performance as a gangster on the run back to his slum roots in *Dead End*. Bogart shows up early in the picture, and quickly dominates the proceedings as Baby Face Martin. Bogart has finally found his strengths in this role, projecting menace without resorting to the mannerisms he used in *The Petrified Forest*. Now, a look in his eyes, a quick body motion, a restraint of his passions projects his incipient greatness as an actor. What is more, watch his hurt and disappointment when his mother rejects him. Even more, watch the erotic nostalgia which suffuses his face when he holds Claire Trevor for the first time in years, and the horror in his face when he realizes what she has become. Bogart should have been nominated – and what is more, no supporting actor stole a film this year as Bogart did in *Dead End*. Joel McCrea never knew what hit him. The Oscar for Best Supporting Actor should have gone to Bogart.

Best Supporting Actress: Alice Brady won for *In Old Chicago*, over Claire Trevor, *Dead End*; Dame May Whitty, *Night Must Fall*; Andrea Leeds, *Stage Door*; and Anne Shirley, *Stella Dallas*

I suspect Alice Brady won for *In Old Chicago* because they failed to give her the Oscar previously for her top-notch performance in *My Man Godfrey*. The Academy has a nasty habit of missing their first, best opportunity, then making it up later for a secondary, undeserving performance. Here, she plays Mrs. O'Leary, the hard-working laundress whose butt-ugly cow starts the Chicago fire. Brady isn't bad as Mrs. O'Leary; she just isn't as good as she was in *My Man Godfrey*. The script gives her so much less to do, and *In Old Chicago* just isn't up to that classic comedy either. No award or nomination should have been given for what is essentially a thankless role.

Dame May Whitty made her talking picture debut recreating her Broadway role as the old woman who lets the murderous Robert Montgomery into her home in *Night Must Fall*. The seventy-two-year-old plays a curmudgeon who becomes enamored of the young Montgomery; that he is, unknown to her, a liar and a killer only increases the tension in the tale. Whitty is good in the role, and deserved a nomination.

Andrea Leeds plays an actress who may have already had her only moment of glory in *Stage Door*. Against the wisecracking Katharine Hepburn and Ginger Rogers, Leeds has to carry the emotional burden of the film, a job she does poorly for much of the film, playing it too broadly, and without convincing emotion. She is supposed to be the best actress in the boarding house, but little evidence is offered to us to prove that assertion. She does have one true moment when she tries to teach Katharine Hepburn how to read a scene; the aftermath is why she deserves the nomination.

Anne Shirley's performance in *Stella Dallas* has not aged well, as the ungrateful daughter for whom Barbara Stanwyck sacrifices everything. Widely praised in 1937, seen today, she comes across as namby-pamby and one-dimensional. As one critic has put it, "she is such a simpering twit that her mother, rather than devoting her life to her, should have strangled her at birth."[cxiii] Hey, he said it, not me. But it's still true. Part of the problem is the writing; no way in this little nursery could a mother as tacky and coarse as Stella Dallas ever produce this little piece of genetic treacle. No nomination was deserved.

Claire Trevor is only on the screen for a few minutes as Humphrey Bogart's childhood sweetheart turned prostitute in *Dead End*. Let's just put it this way: she was so good, she played another prostitute for John Ford in *Stagecoach* two years later, that time with a heart of gold. Perhaps no other moment in *Dead End* instructs the crowd as to the cost of poverty on a good person's life than that of Trevor telling Bogart to take a good look at her. Trevor is the only actor in the film operating at Bogart's level; she not only deserved the nomination, she should have won the Oscar for Best Supporting Actress.

Best Writing (Original Story): William Wellman and Robert Carson won for *A Star Is Born*, over Robert Lord, *Black Legion*; Niven Busch, *In Old Chicago*; Heinz Herald and Geza Herczeg, *The Life of Emile Zola*; and Hans Kraly, *One Hundred Men and a Girl*

When William Wellman and Robert Carson were named for *A Star Is Born*, Wellman tried to hand it to Selznick: "Here, David, you take it; you wrote more of it than I did."[cxiv] Wellman was being modest, and getting a little payback for Selznick's endless interference during filming. The story was so popular they filmed it twice more under this title, and more than a few times in various plagiarisms. But then, *A Star Is Born* rips off *What Price Hollywood?* by simply making the love interest and the drunk the same character, so one good theft deserves another. The tale of two careers heading in opposite directions remains potent. The nomination should stay.

Robert Lord's story for *Black Legion* offered Humphrey Bogart another opportunity to stretch his acting. Bogart's character joins a white supremacist group, which in 1937, was a brave thing for a studio film to portray, what with the KKK still lingering from its heights of power in the Twenties, and the American Bund rising. Bogart plays a machinist who gets passed over for a promotion in favor of an intellectual with a Polish last name. My concern with the nomination is again the fact that this is largely not an original story; it is one taken from the headlines, and based on a real person. The Black Legion existed, and was in the headlines; Bogart was playing out a real-life story, which had been reported in a series of newspaper articles. But *Black Legion* hits hard, and lets Bogart shows his capacity to play more than a heavy, which is what he'd become stereotyped as, after previously being stereotyped as the young society boy with a tennis racket on Broadway. What Lord does with the real-life material is original, and thus deserves a nomination in this category.

I'm still having trouble understanding how they can give a Best Writing (Original Story) nomination to historical retellings and biographies based on published works. So, as a matter of principle, I'm arguing *The Life of Emile Zola* should not be nominated, because the credits even name the source material!

I came close to dropping *In Old Chicago* for the same reason, but the movie has an actual original plot line. Well, I use the word "original" loosely – actually, we get yet another version of the two men competing for the same woman we have seen again and again. *San Francisco* at least had an original twist, in that Spencer Tracy's priest wanted to save Jeanette MacDonald, not marry her. *In Old Chicago* ultimately becomes a bore, and largely unbelievable in its family dynamics. No nomination should have been given for the lack of plausibility.

One Hundred Men and a Girl stars Deanna Durbin as A Girl. With A Voice, of course. Her father is the unemployed trombone player Adolphe Menjou, who wants a job with Leopold Stokowski. A lost purse, stolen money, a ton of complications later, and you've got Stokowski conducting an orchestra of 100 unemployed men and That Girl. Hans Kraly had the idea for this piece of well-toned fluff, the kind of thing Disney would do to death later on – and still does on the Disney Channel in a variety of guises. Given how few original ideas Hollywood seems to have had this year, we'll let the nomination stand, if only because I'd rather hear Durbin sing the opera her voice was meant for, instead of bad pop – which they inflict on us in this movie too, unfortunately.

As for other original ideas, you try it. Hollywood doesn't do original very often; when they find one, they beat it to death, which is why originality is on the endangered species list.

But let me make one suggestion: Laurel and Hardy, *Way Out West*. Jack Jevne and Charles Rogers were credited with the original story; one wonders, don't one, if Stan Laurel was being generous in keeping his name off the list. Jevne also did the screenplays for *Topper* and Danny Kaye's *Wonder Man*. Rogers contributed to numerous Laurel and Hardy productions. Putting Stan and Ollie into the Old West was sheer genius, as is much of this film. Just watch Stan light his thumb and you might agree. And if you don't agree, write me an angry email. I get the feeling you won't be alone. In any case, Stan Laurel and his boys, Jack and Chuck should have been handed a nomination and the Oscar for Best Writing (Original Story).

Best Writing (Screenplay): Heinz Herald, Geza Herczeg, and Norman Reilly Raine won for *The Life of Emile Zola*, over Viña Delmar, *The Awful Truth*; John Lee

Mahin, Marc Connolly and Dale Van Every, *Captains Courageous*; Morrie Ryskind and Anthony Veiller, *Stage Door*; and Alan Campbell, Robert Carson, and Dorothy Parker, *A Star Is Born*

The Life of Emile Zola was yet another Paul Muni biopic. Staid, earnest, and lacking in any dialogue I've ever heard real people speak, the picture also provides little understanding of Zola, other than in the most superficial way. Basically, they made most of it up, and they even admit that in the opening credits. What we get is another version of the story that made Muni famous: the man wronged and rejected by society, crusading to correct social ills. Muni did it for chain gangs; he did it for germs; now he's doing it for anti-Semitism (although that aspect is played down). Warner Brothers loved these kinds of social crusaders, and so do I, but after awhile, they get repetitive. As I've said before, Hollywood loves more of the same, only more so. Had they been more accurate in their history, they might have gotten somewhere – but they weren't, and they didn't. No Oscar or nomination should have been given.

Marc Connolly and Dale Van Every did a competent job updating Rudyard Kipling's *Captains Courageous*. The heart of the story persists, which is all we can ask from an adaptation. The nomination should stay.

Morrie Ryskind and Anthony Veiller adapted *Stage Door* from the play by Edna Ferber and George S. Kaufman. Ryskind brings his wisecracking genius from his multiple outings with the Marx Brothers. "We started off on the wrong foot. Let's stay that way." "When I get back to my room, you're the only thing I want to find missing." "A pleasant little foursome. I predict a hatchet murder before the night's over." Great stuff. The nomination most assuredly should stay.

A Star Is Born has a great first half, bringing together the star and the wannabe. Comedy dominates. But when it's time to go to the dark side, we're unprepared for it; the argument that Norman Maine is box office poison never really makes any sense, other than that the writers want a suicide at the end of a film. Great idea for a movie, but weak execution. Hey – maybe they'll make it again someday! No nomination should have been given.

One picture that should have been nominated was *Easy Living*, with a screenplay by Preston Sturges. *Easy Living* stars Jean Arthur, Edward Arnold, and Ray Milland, and was directed by Mitchell Leisen. Sturges would go on to prove himself one of the greatest writer-directors in Hollywood history (*The Lady Eve, Sullivan's Travels, The Miracle of Morgan's Creek, Hail the Conquering Hero*). *Easy Living* gives us a great screwball comedy, with Arthur as a working class girl who tries to return a very expensive fur coat that falls out of the sky one day. She tries, and she ends up with a hat, a lost job, a lavish suite at a hotel, and Ray Milland. Assumptions romp their way through the slapstick. Few writers have ever done funny satire as well as Sturges. While he isn't at his peak yet, he's heading there.

But better still is a willingness to look at marriage, love and adultery, and make us laugh about these things in such a way as to get us to reconsider the nature of them all. The script for *The Awful Truth* was based on a play by Arthur Richman. Viña Delmar would go on to write little else of consequence, but there's a reason for that: all the books that touch on this movie emphasize McCarey improvising most of the action and dialogue on the set. As Ralph Bellamy remembered, he was "informed he was to show up on the set the following Monday for filming. Bellamy had no script, no dialogue, or even a hint about his upcoming scene so he went to see the director, but received no help at all from the perpetually upbeat McCarey. 'He just joshed and said not to worry, we'd have lots of fun but there wasn't any script'."[cxv] Delmar will have to share the nomination with McCarey, therefore, and a most worthy one it is. *The Awful Truth* couldn't be better written. Let's try two lines for evidence: Irene Dunne: "You've come back and caught me in the truth, and there's nothing less logical than the truth." Cary Grant: "In the spring, a young man's fancy lightly turns to what he's been thinking about all winter." Much more awaits you. Viña Delmar and Leo McCarey should have won the Oscar for Best Writing (Screenplay).

Best Cinematography: Karl Freund won for *The Good Earth*, over Gregg Toland, *Dead End*, and Joseph Valentine, *Wings over Honolulu*

Karl Freund has a special place in my boyhood heart for directing Boris Karloff in *The Mummy*. Long before *The Good Earth*, he had returned to a job he was far better at: cinematographer. Most Americans are more familiar with him for his long work shooting *I Love Lucy*. Freund won the Oscar for Best Cinematography, and from the opening shots, we can see why: in a very painterly way, a village in China is lovingly depicted in a rural beauty and grace anybody who has ever lived on a farm will know is a crock of duckshit. Still, Freund's mastery of light and shadow, and his ability to frame poetically, is substantial. Watch the scene on the wedding night as the door closes off the light cast outward onto the mound of dirt wherein the peach pit has been buried. Likewise, the scene shot up from the water as Luise Rainer washes the clothes. Camerawork must be relied on to reflect those subjects they couldn't show in the Thirties, such as childbirth; the juxtaposition of the storm with the birth may be going over the top a bit, but Freund does his best to bring this to life visually. No Oscar was deserved, but the nomination should stay.

Gregg Toland continued to increase his mastery of the camera with *Dead End*, as he headed toward the career highs of *The Grapes of Wrath*, *The Long Voyage Home* and *Citizen Kane*. Throughout *Dead End*, the dull, harsh lights of the New York heat inform the audience of the difficulties of poverty, but the showcase scene for Toland's art comes when Bogart hides in a junk room, and Joel McCrea follows him in: the dust, the streaming light, the flash of the gun fire all lead us towards film noir. Toland deserved this nomination.

Joseph Valentine was nominated for *Wings over Honolulu*, a Ray Milland military romance potboiler that is so completely forgotten even Turner Classic Movies doesn't show it. Universal should have been ashamed to allow it in this category. I was so ashamed for them, I didn't even watch it. Oh wait, I couldn't! It isn't on video; it never gets shown on cable. The only reviews I could find on it lambasted its lack of military knowledge, and its rampant sexist attitudes. The nomination was apparently for the aerial photography, of which there is less than five minutes. No nomination should remain for a film this obscure – and apparently, deservedly so.

The un-nominated James Wong Howe should have been chosen for *The Prisoner of Zenda*, which has some of the most beautiful shadows you've ever seen. C. Aubrey Smith's magnificent nose has never looked more aristocratic. The entire look of the film is fantasy, with shimmering tones and candle light. Wonderful camera angles abound. Howe was one of the great cinematographers, with a career that ran from the silents through *The Rose Tattoo* and *Hud*. In *The Prisoner of Zenda*, the final duel between Rudolf and Rupert of Hentzau looks like the inspiration for the greatest sword fight of all time, that between Errol Flynn and Basil Rathbone in *The Adventures of Robin Hood*. Howe was there first, shadow fighting on the wall. Howe not only deserved a nomination for Best Cinematography; he deserved the Oscar.

Best Score: Charles Previn and Universal won for *One Hundred Men and a Girl*, over Alfred Newman, *The Hurricane* and *The Prisoner of Zenda*; Louis Silver, *In Old Chicago*; Max Steiner, *The Life of Emile Zola*; Dimitri Tiomkin and Morris Stoloff, *Lost Horizon*; Oscar Straus, *Make a Wish*; Herbert Stothart and a host of others, *Maytime*; Alberto Colombo, *Portia on Trial*; Roy Webb, *Quality Street*; Frank Churchill, Leigh Harline, and Paul Smith, *Snow White and the Seven Dwarfs*; Victor

Schertzinger, *Something to Sing About*; W. Frank Harling, Milan Roder and John Leipold, *Souls at Sea*; and Marvin Hatley, *Way Out West*

No category would be more in flux for the first decade or more of its existence then Best Score. From 1934 to 1937, the head of the music department would receive the nomination, rather than the composer or composers. From 1937 to 1945, any studio got a nomination automatically, simply by submitting a movie for consideration. They would eventually try a variety of categories (original and adapted, musical and dramatic, and so forth) before simplifying the matter. I have chosen to restore, to the best of our knowledge, the names of the original composer (the Academy Awards official database does the same); I have also been forced to skip more than I would prefer, simply because so many of these were nominated by the one film one studio rule, rather than on the basis of quality; many of these have vanished into archives, or are gone completely.

Let's be clear: Deanna Durbin and Leopold Stokowski won this one, not the score for *One Hundred Men and a Girl*; nobody is credited with the score, for good reason: there isn't one, outside of what Stokie brought to the studio. *One Hundred Men and a Girl* uses a kind of classical warhorse approach to the score, giving us Stokowski conducting everything from Tchaikovsky's 5th symphony to Liszt's Hungarian Rhapsody to Verdi's *La Traviata*. The Academy fell all over itself to prove they were classy. I'm just not sure how you can give an Oscar for a score when there is no score. Neither award nor nomination should have been given.

The Hurricane brings us Alfred Newman, and a rousing sound it is, as Newman underscores the injustice of European colonization, the romance of the lovers, and the terrors of the hurricane. Good stuff. The nomination should stay.

Newman composed an absolutely first-rate score for *The Prisoner of Zenda*. The menace of Raymond Massey is increased, subtly; the glories of Flavia's beauty and the love Rupert finds in her are suggestively embroidered; the thrill of combat and victory have never sounded better (outside of Korngold's *The Adventures of Robin Hood* score, that is). The theme of the film, with its soaring romantic reassurances, cannot be forgotten (except by old absent-minded professors like me, so don't ask me to hum it...) What a great nomination!

The score for *In Old Chicago*, by Louis Silver and a passel of uncredited composers, brings back a whole string of Victorian tunes and throws them together in the sound track. John Ford's composers would do this sort of thing far better. The music works for the story – which isn't very good, so that's not saying much – but isn't much more than serviceable. No nomination was deserved.

Max Steiner's work on *The Life of Emile Zola* is yet another competent entry in this excellent composer's filmography, but hardly his most inspired work. Mostly, it's predictable – when there's trouble, the score is disturbed; when Zola decides to fight, the score swells. Granted, that's what it's supposed to do, but one expects some surprises with one's expectations. What is more, very little of the film actually has music. The nomination should stay, if only for sheer competence.

The score for *Lost Horizon* is by Dimitri Tiomkin and Morris Stoloff. Not one of the better scores, as it is overly intrusive and obvious. I think film music can be so much more than this. Much of the film has no music at all, and what we do get just doesn't add anything significant. No nomination should have been given.

Make a Wish tells the story of ennui-ridden composer Basil Rathbone, who finds inspiration in a singing boy, played by Bobby Breen, whose production company made this treacle. Jay Silverheels, the future Tonto of Lone Ranger fame, made his feature film debut here. The score is by Oscar Straus, who would reach his career height with Max Ophüls' *La Ronde* in 1950. One word for the score for *Make a Wish*: schmaltz. I'd use other words, but there are children in the room. We've heard this kind of thing done over and over again, and we don't need to hear it again. Thankfully, most of the film has no score at all, but what is there should only earn one thing: no nomination.

Maytime stars Nelson Eddy and Jeanette MacDonald in yet another of their repetitive movies, although it is generally regarded by people who care as their best film, and MacDonald named it her favorite role.[cxvi] I managed not to fall asleep while I watched it; I account that an astonishing act of will. Herbert Stothart wrote the score, but he lifted sections of Tchaikovsky's Symphony #5, as well as numerous other sources.[52] Film score composers "borrow" from classical music all the time; I am inclined to remove any nomination in which the majority of the score isn't the property of the person who is being nominated, or clearly attributed as an adaptation. Herbert Stothart doesn't deserve this nomination.

Portia on Trial came out of Republic Pictures, one of the better of the Poverty Row studios. They remain best known today for their movie

---

[52] As one very perceptive commentator has remarked, "Various passages from this symphony were used in the 1937 motion picture *Maytime*, starring Jeanette MacDonald and Nelson Eddy. The music appears not only in some of the background score, but also in the form of a sung pastiche invented by Herbert Stothart as a fictitious French opera entitled *Czaritsa*, "composed" by the character Trentini for the lead soprano (MacDonald)." [http://www.youtube.com/watch?v=cG6oNJYOr28]

serials, and for being John Wayne's studio in the late Forties and early Fifties, including the release of *Rio Grande* and *The Quiet Man*. Alberto Colombo labored in relative obscurity as a composer for movie serials and B-pictures, such as *Zorro Rides Again*. The film itself only exists at UCLA, and was unavailable for viewing. No nomination should have been allowed, if the other Republic nominations over the next several years are any reliable guide to quality.

Quality Street stars Katharine Hepburn as a spinster pretending to be her own niece. Based on a James Barrie play few people remember, *Quality Street* was one of the reasons Hepburn was seen as box office poison. The score is by Roy Webb, and is very romantic, with plenty of flute, harp, and violins. Pleasant enough, but like the movie, not anything that gathers much interest outside of Hepburn or Barrie fans. No nomination should have been made.

Something to Sing About is Jimmy Cagney's third-best musical, after *Yankee Doodle Dandy* and *Footlight Parade*. Independently produced by Cagney after walking away from Warner Brothers, *Something to Sing About* relates the story of a New York bandleader going Hollywood. The film was made on the cheap – and it shows – but the music by Victor Schertzinger is serviceable swing. Watch this movie for Cagney's dancing, particularly when he gets a chance to hoof it with two old vaudeville friends, Johnny Boyle and Harland Dixon. Dwight Frye plays a foppish makeup man, which was unexpected, as was the Japanese manservant who pretended to be unable to speak fluent English (the film is homophobic, but deliberately undercuts racism; go figure...). The score deserved a nomination, if only to encourage independent production.

W. Frank Harling (*Stagecoach*), Milan Roder (Korngold's orchestrator) and John Leipold (*Union Pacific*) were nominated for *Souls at Sea*. The score has moments of charm, especially in its trumpet and brass flourishes, and the romantic music for George Raft when he looks at a new girl, but most of the music is perfunctory and clichéd. The nomination can stay, for the moments when it breathes some originality.

Way Out West takes the typical Laurel and Hardy tune and extends it further than we've heard before. We also get a number of musical numbers, not the least of which is the sublime "Trail of the Lonesome Pine." But it's unlikely this would have been nominated had it not been for the one studio, one nomination rule operating. The nomination can stay for Marvin Hatley, who composed the Laurel and Hardy theme, "Ku-Ku," also known as "The Cuckoo Song." Few other tunes have been heard so many thousands of times, and still retain the power to bring a smile.

Finally, *Snow White and the Seven Dwarfs* built off the experience gained from the Silly Symphonies, wherein color, story, animation techniques and music were constantly pushed to the limits to find what the animation medium could do in the hands of true artists. Frank Churchill, Leigh Harline, and Paul Smith produced a score as good as anything Hollywood had made for their own musical romances, and far more memorable than any other score of the year. The first few bars of *Snow White* resound in the memory from the first hearing: harp, strings, brass, and human voices mix into that ineffably romantic, fairy tale feel. The tunes of the songs work their way into the score, reinforcing their dramatic impact when they are sung by the characters. The magic mirror mystifies in the tremulous woodwinds and strings behind his speech. The queen's menace is intensified by deep brass and strings. The flight through the forest mixes percussion, brass and strings into one truly terrifying accompaniment. Snow White's relations with the animals are backed up by all the brighter colors of the orchestra: flutes, harps, the higher ranges of strings. The orchestration is rich with these kinds of color shifts, to reinforce at every moment the action on the screen in a textbook example of what a score is supposed to do, throughout the entire film. What is more important, *Snow White* set a standard for future musicals, as Disney was hoping: "Really, we should set a new pattern – a new way to use music – weave it into the story so somebody doesn't just burst into song."[cxvii] *Snow White and the Seven Dwarfs* should have won the Oscar for Best Score.

Best Song: Harry Owens' "Sweet Leilani," won from *Waikiki Wedding*, over Frederick Hollander and Leo Robin's "Whispers in the Dark" from *Artists and Models*; Harry Warren and Al Dubin's "Remember Me" from *Mr. Dodd Takes the Air*; the Gershwins' "They Can't Take That Away From Me," from *Shall We Dance*; and Sammy Fain and Lew Brown's "That Old Feeling," from *Walter Wanger's Vogues of 1938*

God help us all..."Sweet Leilani"?!?!? Blame the extras; they were allowed to vote, and apparently, the Gershwins were too sophisticated for the unwashed masses. Let's make this clear. Anybody who prefers "Sweet Leilani" over "They Can't Take That Away From Me" by George and Ira Gershwin from *Shall We Dance* needs a serious transplant of taste, rhythm, and ears. At least the Academy nominated the Gershwins for this song, even if they also forgot "They All Laughed" from the same film, and "A Foggy Day" and "Nice Work If You Can Get It" from *A Damsel in Distress*. For that matter they also forgot Irving Berlin's "I've Got My Love to Keep Me Warm" from *On the Avenue*, Cole Porter's "In the Still of the Night" from *Rosalie*, and Richard Whiting and Johnny Mercer's "Too Marvelous for Words" from *Ready, Willing and Able*. All six of those omitted songs definitely deserved a nomination. I suspect the extras just preferred Bing Crosby to Fred Astaire; I can understand that, to a degree. Still, "Sweet Leilani" seems to confirm that the masses are indeed unwashed.

For that matter, so was the Academy, for nominating "Remember Me" and "Whispers in the Dark." They cleaned up a bit for "That Old Feeling," by Sammy Fain and Lew Brown.

But then they went and forgot *Snow White*. Seriously, while they're not the adult art the Gershwins, Berlin and Porter produced, few movie songs have lasted as long in the popular consciousness as those by Frank Churchill and Larry Morey for *Snow White*: "Whistle While You Work" and "Someday My Prince Will Come."

And how could they have missed their own theme song, "Hooray for Hollywood" by Richard Whiting and Johnny Mercer from *Hollywood Hotel*?

Still and all, the Oscar should have gone to the Gershwins for "They Can't Take That Away From Me," a song that encompasses longing and love, and the permanent memory and regret that losing that love can bring. Trust me; I just took a shower.

Best Art Direction: Stephen Goosson won for *Lost Horizon*, over Cedric Gibbons and William Horning, *Conquest*; Carroll Clark, *A Damsel in Distress*; Richard Day, *Dead End*; Wiard Ihnen, *Every Day's a Holiday*; Anton Grot, *The Life of Emile Zola*; John Victor Mackay, *Manhattan Merry-Go-Round*; Lyle Wheeler, *The Prisoner of Zenda*; Hans Dreier and Roland Anderson, *Souls at Sea*; Alexander Toluboff, *Walter Wanger's Vogues of 1938*; William S. Darling and David S. Hall, *Wee Willie Winkie*; and Jack Otterson, *You're a Sweetheart*

Stephen Goosson put together the paradise of Shangri-La for Frank Capra's *Lost Horizon*; apparently, the Academy approved. He and Frank Capra practically reproduced a mythical Tibet for the film, and the depth of research shows. The enormous sets built for Shangri-La also reflect a kind of utopian dream-works – although to me, they rather look like some clean college campus (which, for a teacher, is a kind of utopia, provided tenure is involved). The scenery is beautiful, and one can accept the existence of this paradise. However, I am not sure this wasn't simply a consolation prize to Frank Capra through Stephen Goosson, since Capra won neither Best Director or Best Picture. (Goosson also did the honors on Leo McCarey's *The Awful Truth* this year). The nomination should stay, but not the Oscar.

Carroll Clark was nominated for the Fred Astaire musical *A Damsel in Distress*, which has one intricate set that makes the nomination entirely worthwhile (see Best Dance Direction above for why).

Richard Day's work on *Dead End* attempts to provide a tenement slum, but he failed, because everything outside still looks far too much like a stage set. But the interiors create a dark sense of poverty successfully. The smell of desperation is in the walls. The nomination should stay for that visual stench.

Wiard Ihnen got a nomination for showing Mae West that *Every Day's a Holiday*. Welcome to the late Victorian era. Nice costumes. I would be willing to bet the Academy would nominate almost any film in this category if it was set in the Victorian period. They loved bustles, apparently. No nomination should ever be given for Grandma's underwear.

Cedric Gibbons and William Horning reproduced early nineteenth century Poland in *Conquest*. Beautifully elaborate, as most MGM productions were, *Conquest* deserved its nomination for its palace scenes. At the other end of the century, Anton Grot reproduced France in *The Life of Emile Zola*. Very effective sets, even if obviously on a sound stage or a back lot all too often (but then, that applies to most of Hollywood's movies in the Thirties and Forties). The nomination should stay, even if Devil's Island doesn't look very devilish.

Nelson Eddy and Eleanor Powell are badly mismatched in *Manhattan Merry-Go-Round*. Cab Calloway somehow manages to be boring. Joe Dimaggio shows up, and is forced to sing. John Victor Mackay gave them a recording studio for the gangsters to take over. Weird movie, and not in a good way. No nomination should have been made.

Souls at Sea stars Gary Cooper and George Raft as they struggle to sail through intrigue in the mid-nineteenth century. The movie is a surprising indictment of slavery, showing the horrors of a slave trader's ship (and obliquely, commenting on racism in 1937). Hans Dreier and Roland Anderson give us ships, docks, a court, several inns and taverns, staterooms, a shipwreck and a lifeboat. The nomination should stay.

Walter Wanger's Vogues of 1938 is an excuse for Joan Bennett to dress up and Warner Baxter to watch. The nomination for Alexander Toluboff seem to be more for the dresses than the sets; the costume category was not yet invented. No nomination should ever be given for pretty flufferies.

Wee Willie Winkie stars Shirley Temple in John Ford's version of Rudyard Kipling's classic tale of India (don't expect much resemblance to the original story, however). As always in a John Ford film, the setting is as authentic as the budget will allow. This time, the feel of nineteenth century India, and a British army camp, is so real you want to wipe the sweat off the screen. David S. Hall, best known for this film and *The Greatest Story Ever Told*, and William S. Darling, who worked repeatedly with Ford, prove themselves equal to the task of satisfying the great director, and are well deserving of a nomination.

Alice Faye burdens us again in *You're a Sweetheart*, a backstage musical comedy romance. Yeah, designing a stage is hard work. No nomination should ever be given for the obvious, Jack Otterson.

Finally, and out of alphabetical order, Lyle Wheeler's work on *The Prisoner of Zenda* is marvelous, creating this imagined European postage stamp of a country brilliantly. Beginning with the hunting lodge, the total reality of this fantasy realm is established. One of the curious problems of inventing an imaginary kingdom is that it must seem more real than real places, and Wheeler succeeded admirably. The pomp and majesty of the coronation scene has rarely been equaled (producer David O. Selznick was one of the world's greatest admirers of royalty). Ditto for the ball. Wonderful stuff, and well worth the Oscar Lyle Wheeler should have received for Best Art Direction.

CHAPTER ELEVEN: 1939 AWARDS
11th Show

Movies released in 1938

THE SCENE OF THE CRIME:

On February 23, 1939, the Academy once again took over the Biltmore Bowl at the Biltmore Hotel, hosted by Academy President Frank Capra. A radio black-out was broken when a local radio station reporter was caught illicitly broadcasting from a locked booth; fire axes convinced him to stop. Bob Hope came to give out the Best Short Subject Oscars; he joked that the table full of awards looked "like Bette Davis' garage." Teen movie stars Deanna Durbin and Mickey Rooney got small Oscars. Walt Disney picked up a special Oscar for *Snow White and the Seven Dwarfs*, with one normal size Oscar and seven little ones, even though the film had been nominated only for Best Score the previous year. Shirley Temple gave it to him with some laughs for their repartee. Hal Wallis of Warner Brothers got the Thalberg Award. Spencer Tracy and Bette Davis both picked up their second Oscars for Acting. Disney extended his streak to six. Tracy was later forced to donate his Oscar to the real Boys Town, but he insisted on getting a duplicate one for his home (the first one had already annoyed him, since it was inscribed to "Dick Tracy").

To prevent another "Sweet Leilani" fiasco, the Academy stripped the Best Song voting away from the extras. Thank you. Thank you. Thank you.

The Academy allowed the music departments to completely screw up any sense of logic, reason or clarity by creating two categories out of an old one: Best Score, and Best Original Score. Now, I don't particularly have any problem with that, if you want to recognize a truly original score that the composer crafted from all new material, then recognize the possibilities of arranging already composed material (Bach and Handel did this in traditional musical structures, as have many other composers since then). But the Academy then proceeded to allow the same movie score to be nominated in BOTH categories! Very, very confusing, and it makes me want to try and straighten them out here too (they really ought to be paying me for all this, don't you think?). The problem is, it isn't always clear what is original, and what is recycled. You'll just have to bear with me – at least I'm trying to do the right thing here! Which is more, I'm afraid, than the Academy usually did.

WHAT THEY GOT RIGHT:

Musically, they didn't do too badly, successfully picking the two best scores of the year. But then they went and blew it with the Best Song...will these people never learn?

Best Original Score: Erich Wolfgang Korngold scored a righteous win for *The Adventures of Robin Hood*, over Victor Young, for both *Army Girl* and *Breaking the Ice*; Werner Janssen, *Blockade*; Marvin Hatley, *Block-Heads*; Alfred Newman, *The Cowboy and the Lady*; Richard Hageman, *If I Were King*; Herbert Stothart, *Marie Antoinette*; Russell Bennett, *Pacific Liner*; Louis Silvers, *Suez*; and Franz Waxman, *The Young in Heart*

The Adventures of Robin Hood remains the quintessential adventure movie score: uplifting, ecstatic, dramatic, thrilling, and achingly romantic. Erich Wolfgang Korngold does it all, in a seamless score that has set the bar for every single adventure film to follow (and quite a few other genres as well). As Rudy Behlmer so aptly describes, "His style for the Flynn swashbucklers resembled that of the creators of late nineteenth century and early twentieth century German symphonic tone poems. It incorporated chromatic harmonies, lush instrumental effects, passionate climaxes, all performed in a generally romantic manner. Korngold's original and distinctive style was influenced by the Wagnerian leitmotif, the orchestral virtuosity of Richard Strauss, the delicacy and broad melodic sweep of Puccini, and the long-line development of Gustav Mahler."[cxviii] What he said! Honestly, I should go back in time and buy the entire Academy a leg of mutton and a cask of ale for this award. Huzzah!

Army Girl tells the story of the resistance in the US Army to shifting from cavalry to tanks. A totally forgotten picture from poverty row Republic Studios, for which Victor Young composed a perfunctory military score for the military scenes, and some violins for the love scenes. James Gleason is the most enjoyable part of the movie, as a gruff but comic defender of the tank. Several actors and actresses in this film may be the worst I've ever seen (and I've seen *Plan Nine from Outer Space*...sober). Young's score only shows up occasionally, and never to great effect. Once again, the one nomination per studio rule applied here. No tanks.

Breaking the Ice was yet another Bobby Breen musical, this one also scored by Victor Young. Breen was a male version of the young Deanna Durbin, with a voice quite accomplished for his age. The score is run of the mill Hollywood musical, with nothing memorable to recommend its nomination – which should therefore be gone.

Werner Janssen's score for the mediocre antiwar film *Blockade* really doesn't deserve a nomination (see Best Writing (Original Story) for more). Janssen never composed for a first-rate film; his work, like the films he was chosen to score, remains second-rate. *Blockade* is no exception, and would never have been nominated without the special rules governing this category.

As was also certainly true for Marvin Hatley's work on Laurel and Hardy's *Block-Heads* (see *Way Out West* above for more). *Block-Heads* is the one where Stan stayed in the trenches for twenty years after WWI was over, because nobody ever relieved him of duty. *Block-Heads* does have a more extensive score than previous Laurel and Hardy outings, but even so, it's not particularly inspired or memorable. We get some rousing martial music for the war scenes, some relaxed strolling music for the reunion scene (which is then beaten to death though repetition), and not much else. Briefly considering it in comical terms, *Block-Heads* unfortunately indulges in too many fat jokes at Ollie's expense, but there are some funny moments: the giant pile of cans, the shadow window shade, Stan's punching, Stan smoking his hand. The final plot twist steals from earlier Laurel and Hardy shamelessly. No nomination should have been given to Hatley this time around.

Alfred Newman scored *The Cowboy and the Lady*, starring Gary Cooper and Merle Oberon. Cooper plays a rodeo cowboy who falls in love with the daughter of a presidential hopeful – played by Oberon, who doesn't fit this very American role well. Fun little romantic comedy, but Cooper is at his most stereotyped aw-shucks. The music does have that riveting western sound of fiddle, accordion and bouncy rhythm, as it begins in the city with a touch of hot swing. Like many films of the period, the score only shows up sporadically. What we do get is quite good, as Newman often could be (he really was one of the great ones). I love the way he uses a trombone as a kind of moaning lonely voice against the violins. A well-deserved nomination.

Richard Hageman's music for *If I Were King* is only heard from time to time, but is competent and touching. While still not the equal of Korngold, Hageman does a fine job romancing us with his strings. The nomination should stay (see Best Supporting Actor below for more).

Herbert Stothart's work on *Marie Antoinette* is eminently forgettable, as so many of his scores were. Stothart would have done far better to have used music from the late eighteenth century as the score; after all, this is the great era of Mozart and Haydn. No nomination should be given for a lack of taste.

Russell Bennett produced a rugged, athletic score for *Pacific Liner*, a tale of an epidemic loose on board a transport ship. Were it not for Erich Korngold's magnificent work on *The Adventures of Robin Hood*, I would argue the Oscar should have gone to Bennett. His use of brass is quite different from the typical string-laden Hollywood score, although he loves the violins as well. *Pacific Liner* is a little-known film with a B-film budget and cast, who all do their best to rise above the material. My only complaint is that the score is rarely heard. Bennett keeps his nomination; he would go on to work most famously on the film versions of numerous Rodgers and Hammerstein adaptations.

Suez is another Tyrone Power pseudo-historical epic in the mold of *Lloyds of London*. Loretta Young shows up for the romantic part; the Suez Canal shows up for the rest. Don't expect historical accuracy in the slightest; the descendents of the canal builder, Ferdinand de Lesseps, sued for libel.[cxix] But since music and historical accuracy rarely have anything to do with each other in movies, Louis Silvers' score should be heard on its own merits. Silvers had a career that stretched from *The Jazz Singer* through *Young Mr. Lincoln* and more. Here, Silvers pulls together an entire music department, including David Raksin and Ernst Toch, to deliver a decent if hardly inspired score: lots of romantic violins, some Egyptian style music, a bit of martial marching, a little mystery music when needed. Nowhere do we hear the kind of controlling themes that might help pull this episodic dullard together as a film (*Lloyds of London* is more compelling). Really, nothing anybody would ever remember, for either the score or the movie. No nomination.

Franz Waxman's score for *The Young in Heart* is sprightly and lively. *The Young in Heart* is a caper movie from David O. Selznick, starring Douglas Fairbanks, Jr., Janet Gaynor, Paulette Goddard, Roland Young and Billie Burke. Think con artists meet Miss Moneybags; they discover their humanity. Apparently, after seeing Gaynor do her comic bits, Selznick decided to put her into the humorous mode entirely; Gaynor is (wait for it)...enjoyable. There, I said it. She's good in this movie – although less so when she has to get all sad and weepy. Roland Young and Billie Burke build on their partnership from *Topper* and come across beautifully as sentimental old reprobates. Waxman's score does them all good service, and shows a sense of humor all its own. When the grifter father has to get a job as a car salesman (for the "Flying Wombat"), Waxman brings in a fat tuba rendition of Wagner's "Ride of the Valkyries" for just a moment: death approaches in the shape of a job. An excellent nomination.

I've moved the nomination for Max Steiner's score for *Jezebel* from Best Score to Best Original Score here (see Best Score below for why).

Best Score: Alfred Newman won for *Alexander's Ragtime Band* (he was also nominated for *The Goldwyn Follies*), over Victor Baravalle, *Carefree*; Morris Stoloff and Gregory Stone, *Girls' School*; Max Steiner, *Jezebel*; Charles Previn and Frank Skinner, *Mad About Music*; Cy Feuer, *Storm over Bengal*; Herbert Stothart, *Sweethearts*; Marvin Hatley, *There Goes My Heart*; Boris Morros, *Tropic Holiday*; and Franz Waxman, *The Young in Heart*

Alfred Newman took Irving Berlin's music and crafted a competent, worthwhile accompaniment of the master's songs. But I am of the opinion that Best Score should really go to the composer of the music, as well as the orchestrator, especially when the vast majority of the music is songs, and not score. We watch *Alexander's Ragtime Band* for the songs, not for the filler that Newman made of the songs. So Newman should keep his Oscar – but Irving Berlin should have been added to the name on the award.

Newman also scored *The Goldwyn Follies*, which is a mess (see Best Song and Art Direction for more). We find Newman doing his best to bring a swinging quality to movie music here, as he did with Berlin's music in *Alexander's Ragtime Band*. Once again, he is providing filler between a great composer's songs, this time George Gershwin, as well as orchestrating the songs. Newman's music is pleasant enough, and versatile, but all we really remember are the Gershwin songs, which Newman orchestrates well enough. Let's add George Gershwin, and let Newman share the nomination.

Carefree received a nomination for Victor Baravalle, but as we've just seen, how can anybody get the nomination when Berlin wrote the music for this one too? I suspect that the nomination was rigged. Yes, I know there is a score tying the songs together, and the songs have to be orchestrated; it still doesn't make sense to me, since that would be somewhat akin to handing the Nobel Prize for Literature to the editor instead of the writer. Once again, Berlin should have been nominated as well; having done so, the nomination should stay (for more on this Fred Astaire-Ginger Rogers picture, see Best Song and Art Direction below).

A low budget film from Columbia, *Girls' School* has a lot of adolescent love and nonsense at a – you guessed it – girls' school. The only star of note is Ralph Bellamy, with supporting cast Noah Beery and Marjorie Main. Few have bothered seeing *Girls' School* since 1938. Morris Stoloff got the nomination, but the IMDB says Gregory Stone provided the score; Stone never rose above B-pictures like *Jungle Jim in Pygmy Island*. Largely a forgettable score from a forgettable movie, which should not have been worth a nomination.

For *Jezebel*, Max Steiner put together a competent score which opens with strings and harps, but nothing compared to the glories of his *Gone with the Wind* score next year. For the most part, we don't even notice Steiner's work, which isn't, in my mind, the mark of a great score. Not that I want it to drown out the action or the actors, but we ought to be able to remember the music if it truly makes an impact. The final scenes are the memorable part of the film, as a human chorus wordlessly joins the beating drum, brass and strings to assure the audience of the nobility that Bette Davis has finally reached, that she is a Jezebel no more. My problem with nominating him in this category has to do with this question: what, precisely, is Steiner adapting? Much of this seems original. So the nomination should be moved there.

Charles Previn (father of André) and Frank Skinner compiled the score for *Mad About Music*, starring Deanna Durbin. The score is brisk, supports the songs, and keeps things moving along effectively in the long stretches between songs. A reasonable, if uninspired, nomination.

Storm over Bengal is a typical Indian adventure story, and a Republic low budget clone of other pictures: two brothers in love with the same woman; British imperial control is threatened by Indian upstart, the British have to stop it – and do. Scorer Cy Feuer worked almost entirely on B-Pictures, including quite a few with John Wayne. The high point of his career was scoring *Angel and the Badman* – and being nominated for *Storm over Bengal*. I've always had a fondness for B pictures; they're one of life's great guilty pleasures. Unfortunately, I could not locate a copy of the film; UCLA's copies are non-circulating, so I have no idea of the quality of the score. My bet is no nomination.

Here come Jeanette MacDonald and Nelson Eddy again, singing as woodenly as a lumber yard in yet another teaming, this time named *Sweethearts*, lifted from a Victor Herbert operetta. Herbert Stothart again received credit for his horde of arrangers and composers working for him; again, I find it incomprehensible that anybody ever thought the vast majority of his work was worthy of an Oscar, nomination or otherwise. He shouldn't be getting one here either.

There Goes My Heart is another Hal Roach full length comedy, ripping off *It Happened One Night* and starring Fredric March as a reporter and Virginia Bruce as a rich heir taking a job in a salesgirl in a department store in order to have a normal life; Eugene Pallette shows up as March's newspaper editor. Marvin Hatley (of Laurel and Hardy tune fame) provides the usual forgettable score. No nomination should have been given.

Dorothy Lamour, Ray Milland, and Martha Raye take a musical *Tropic Holiday* from Paramount. Mexico is the setting, and yes, there are bullfights. The score is by Boris Morros, according to the Academy, but the Internet Movie Database also credits Gordon Jenkins, later famous as one of Frank Sinatra's best arrangers. I have no way to judge the score, as the film was available nowhere. The one review I found was not kind, however. We shall have to reserve judgment.

Franz Waxman was nominated in two categories for *The Young in Heart*; he really belongs above in the Best Original Score category. No nomination should be here then.

Best Art Direction: Carl J. Weyl won for *The Adventures of Robin Hood*, over Lyle Wheeler, *The Adventures of Tom Sawyer*; Bernard Herzbrun and Boris Leven, *Alexander's Ragtime Band*; Alexander Toluboff, *Algiers*; Van Nest Polglase, *Carefree*; Richard Day, *The Goldwyn Follies*; Stephen Goosson and Lionel Banks, *Holiday*; Hans Dreier and John B. Goodman, *If I Were King*; Jack Otterson, *Mad About Music*; Cedric Gibbons, *Marie Antoinette*; and Charles D. Hall, *Merrily We Live*

The Adventures of Robin Hood is the first Technicolor masterpiece – and the sets and costumes were designed for that in mind. *Robin Hood* has absolutely beautiful costumes, particularly for Maid Marian and Prince John. Watching the great entry of Robin Hood into the feast, we can see the reasons why the Academy chose this film to honor. Granted, we're not looking at realism here. What we do see is a setting for adventure and romance. The tables, the candles, the chairs, the food, the costumes, the enormous torches, the heraldry, and so much more – all done with an eye to drench us in Technicolor. Carl J. Weyl would go on to more fabulous work on *Casablanca, The Big Sleep*, and *Yankee Doodle Dandy*. An utterly justified Oscar – perhaps the taste of the Academy may be hoped for after all. At the least, this Oscar gives me pause from condemning them...momentarily.

Other films also justified their selections. David O. Selznick turned his hand from Charles Dickens to that most famous of American authors, Mark Twain, for *The Adventures of Tom Sawyer*. Twain's paean to boyhood joys and adventures received the full Technicolor treatment, along with a search for a Tom Sawyer equivalent to Selznick's famous search for a David Copperfield that resulted in Freddie Bartholomew becoming a star. Selznick would do the same thing more famously in looking for his Scarlett; many have noted that this movie prefigures *Gone with the Wind*, with much of the same crew ending up on that 1939 film. Norman Taurog directed, but both George Cukor and William Wellman came in for retakes and additional scenes. The end result is oddly unsatisfying, despite the profusion of excellent bits. The whitewashing scene, the funeral, and the graveyard are particularly good, but the film makes too much treacle out of Becky and Tom's "relationship" (unlike the novel), forcing the child actors into fakery. Jim is a child used for racist comic relief. Sid, the good cousin, also gets turned into more of a priss then he was in the novel. Looking at the award, what makes it difficult to single out Lyle Wheeler here is the presence of production designer William Cameron Menzies, who was given credit for the most memorable part of the film, the cave sets. Much of the film looks like a fairy tale America, rather than the kind of lived in town, but clearly, this was deliberate. William Cameron Menzies should have been given a nomination along with Wheeler.

Bernard Herzbrun and Boris Leven used the big budget well on *Alexander's Ragtime Band*. Recreating San Francisco in the early twentieth century, from the upper crust of the Fairmont Hotel, to the down and dirty Barbary Coast, to various nightclubs, *Alexander's Ragtime Band* is beautifully crafted. While the film itself is overrated, the sets show studio Hollywood at its most efficient. The nomination should stay.

Alexander Toluboff (*Stagecoach*) was nominated for *Algiers*, but I have the same problem with this nomination as I have for James Wong Howe's cinematography: the outdoor scenes in the Casbah, which are quite impressive, are from the French original. But when the American cast is in the scene, the issue goes away (to a degree). Toluboff does do some impressive work in reproducing the Casbah, giving a claustrophobic feel of a very old maze, inhabited by human rats. Despite my misgivings over the usage of another film's work, the nomination should stay.

Van Nest Polglase was selected for still another Fred Astaire-Ginger Rogers musical, this time for *Carefree* (after *Top Hat* and *The Gay Divorcee*; he would go on to other nominations for *Citizen Kane* and *My Favorite Wife*). Polglase does a nice job putting together sets for a medical building and office, as well as a country club. But what brought the nomination are the dream sets, produced after Ginger Rogers consumes shrimp with whipped cream, welsh rarebit with extra cheese, lobster with gobs of mayonnaise, cucumbers in buttermilk, and strawberry shortcake. I'm not all that impressed, but then I've seen *Murder, My Sweet* and its drug-induced visions, as well as Dali's dream sets on *Spellbound* (see Best Song for more). Polglase should keep his nomination.

Richard Day was picked for *The Goldwyn Follies*, a musical that casts Adolphe Menjou as a movie producer searching for what Americans want to hear; the movie uses that as an excuse to toss at us every music act Sam Goldwyn could sign up. That Ben Hecht was responsible for the script just scares me – what some people won't do for money! Goldwyn wanted to create a musical franchise that would keep generating sequels; he failed miserably (he would eventually find his man in Danny Kaye). The sets for this film are predominantly offices, homes, and soundstages, and nothing particularly striking, and usually too stagy. Much of the film was made on real studio lots, so I'm unclear precisely what this nomination was for, except perhaps the fact that it was filmed in color. No nomination should have been given (see Best Song and Best Adapted Score for more).

Holiday is an adaptation of a Philip Barry play, starring Cary Grant and Katharine Hepburn (the three would later come together again for the superior *The Philadelphia Story*). The mansion set is spectacular, yet cold and intimidating as it reinforces the imposing power of the family who owns it, and the oppression it places upon the children who are expected to live up to that social standing. One room within, the play room, reflects the warmer human values the mansion all but forbids. This set alone earned Stephen Goosson and Lionel Banks their nomination. Goosson ran Columbia's art direction for a quarter-century, including many of Frank Capra's films; Lionel Banks did *Mr.*

Smith Goes to Washington and *His Girl Friday*. *Holiday* has excellent art direction, and earned its nomination.

Hans Dreier and John B. Goodman got to go medieval for Ronald Colman and Basil Rathbone in *If I Were King*. As elaborately designed as *Marie Antoinette*, *If I Were King* reproduces the France of Francois Villon and Louis XI as well as anybody could have in the studio system. The sets look well-aged, and the costumes suitable. Dreier was a perennial Oscar nominee in this category; Goodman worked on everything from *Shadow of a Doubt* to Clint Eastwood's television series *Rawhide*. They should keep their nomination.

Jack Otterson's work on the Deanna Durbin *Mad About Music* seems effective for a typical Durbin vehicle. Hotel rooms, a Swiss town, a rural school, a church, a hotel lobby and more work quite well. Fair nomination, if largely clichéd (as Otterson's work so often was, stuck as he was on the B-movie groove at Universal – but he did do *The Wolf Man*).

MGM's powerful art director Cedric Gibbons was nominated for *Marie Antoinette*, having gone mad with over 11,000 photographs of Versailles.[cxx] The sets and costumes, by far, are the best part of the film, along with John Barrymore and Robert Morley's supporting performances. Only MGM could have put together this kind of over-the-top spectacle, and then forget to fill it with any substance. Magnificent sets, but the actors tend to be lost in it all, as Norma Shearer simply isn't up to carrying this kind of picture (not that she's capable of carrying a small picture either). Good nomination, but only if you like stunning excess.

Merrily We Live was a Hal Roach feature length film trying to build on the success of *Topper* the previous year, and so brought back Constance Bennett and Billie Burke (see Best Supporting Actress). The sets give us a wealthy, well-appointed home. As such, the look is well done by Charles D. Hall, better known for *Frankenstein* and *Bride of Frankenstein*. The cars in particular are stunning, beautiful and gleaming, and earn the nomination.

WHAT THEY GOT WRONG:

Hoooo, boy. 1938 is a big, big, boo-boo year, the rotten little brats. Hollywood should be taken out and spanked regularly for this one. Just wait until you see the absolutely perfect film they overlooked completely; you'll be lining up outside by the woodpile for your chance to go at them. Bring your own belt.

Best Picture: *You Can't Take It with You*
Best Actor: Spencer Tracy, *Boys Town*
Best Actress: Bette Davis, *Jezebel*
Best Supporting Actor: Walter Brennan, *Kentucky*
Best Supporting Actress: Fay Bainter, *Jezebel*
Best Director: Frank Capra, *You Can't Take It with You*
Best Writing (Original Story): Eleanore Griffin and Dore Schary, *Boys Town*
Best Writing (Screenplay): George Bernard Shaw, Ian Dalrymple, Cecil Lewis, and W.P. Lipscomb, *Pygmalion*
Best Cinematography: Joseph Ruttenberg, *The Great Waltz*
Best Song: Ralph Rainger and Leo Robin, "Thanks for the Memory," *The Big Broadcast of 1938*
Best Short Subject (Cartoon): Walt Disney, *Ferdinand the Bull*

Best Picture: *You Can't Take It with You* won, over *The Adventures of Robin Hood, Alexander's Ragtime Band, Boys Town, The Citadel, Four Daughters, Grand Illusion, Jezebel, Pygmalion,* and *Test Pilot*

You Can't Take It with You is one of Frank Capra's most celebrated films, and for sheer eccentricity and hostility to the overweening arrogance of the rich, you can't do much better. Lionel Barrymore, Edward Arnold, Jean Arthur and Jimmy Stewart all turn in marvelous performances; Robert Riskin's screenplay of the Moss Hart and George S. Kaufman Broadway hit is first-rate. The supporting players, including Mischa Auer and Spring Byington, are all delightful. No film has ever celebrated the great American tradition of non-conformity more than this one. I love this movie. So why strip it of its Oscar for Best Picture? Because three movies go this wonderful film one better by reaching the peak of each of their genres. What shocks is that the Academy completely, totally, and idiotically snubbed one of them. So sad; I had begun to feel they were at least nominating the best, even if they weren't always giving them the Oscar.

The first of the three films I prefer to *You Can't Take It with You*, *The Adventures of Robin Hood*, simply couldn't be any better. A perfect cast: Errol Flynn as the greatest swashbuckler of all, Olivia de Havilland as his love Maid Marian, Basil Rathbone as the furious and violent Sir Guy, Claude Rains as the villainous, conniving Prince John, Eugene

Pallette as Friar Tuck, and Alan Hale as Little John. Not a single note is out of place – not least with the magnificent score by Erich Wolfgang Korngold. The pacing is perfect, launching us into the story immediately, and never letting up on the emotional thrills, leavened with perfect humor. The movie gives us three epitomes of film history: the greatest entrance of all time when Flynn swaggers into the castle, a deer thrown across his back; the greatest escape of all time, when he fights his way out; and the greatest sword fight of all time, between Flynn, Rathbone, and all those shadows. For the first time, Technicolor actually works the way it should have; the restoration in particular brings out the form's glories. Director Michael Curtiz's run of film masterpieces begins this year with this movie and *Angels with Dirty Faces*. That run would peak in *Casablanca,* one of the few consistent contenders for the greatest film of all time (and with good reason). Much as I love Frank Capra's *You Can't Take It with You, The Adventures of Robin Hood* must be accounted the greatest adventure film in Hollywood history. I could name a few other possibilities, but having seen the film almost two hundred times, I am still excited by *The Adventures of Robin Hood. Robin Hood* could easily have won the Best Picture Oscar of 1938 instead of Capra's comedy – but even *Robin Hood* falls to another in the end.

But first, let's go over who else they did nominate.

Alexander's Ragtime Band was intended to be Irving Berlin's life story, but he was uncomfortable with the idea: "...Berlin's Russian-Jewish, Lower East Side roots made him squirm – he didn't hide them so much as de-emphasize them – and he objected to Darryl F. Zanuck about being the sole focus of a screen biography...Gradually an amalgam of music men, including the recently deceased George Gershwin (1937) was worked out."[cxxi] Fox put their biggest stars, Alice Faye and Tyrone Power, together with a bigger budget, and went to town with Berlin's songs. The result is enjoyable; Faye is better here than *In Old Chicago*. Even so, Ethel Merman belts out more impressive songs than Faye, especially with "Heat Wave." The problem is Tyrone Power. How do you have a major musical when the lead male neither sings nor dances? I do love Power in *The Mark of Zorro*, but many of his other films have faded fast (*Nightmare Alley* has its fans as the most bizarre film ever made by a major movie star). What is more, *Alexander* is just another version of *In Old Chicago*, with the same cast. Overall, the movie just doesn't meet the standard of the Astaire-Rogers musicals over at RKO. No nomination should have been given.

Boys Town was MGM's biggest moneymaker for the year, bringing Spencer Tracy his second Oscar for Best Actor and making Mickey

Rooney into an even bigger star. Based on a real place that still exists today, *Boys Town* tells the heartwarming story of Father Flanagan's crusade to create a place to rescue homeless boys and reform them. Mickey Rooney becomes the poster child for hardened criminals as Tracy does his best to bring him around. The movie works well for what it is; the scene where little Pee-Wee gets hurt would rip the heart out of anybody. The ending is idiotic – see Best Writing (Original Story) below for more. The nomination should stay, for what does work.

In *The Citadel*, Robert Donat plays a doctor in a coal town, crusading to better the situation of the workers. Rosalind Russell plays his love interest, Ralph Richardson his best friend. Donat takes up a posh practice until the death of his friend restores his virtues. Bitterly earnest, *The Citadel* was King Vidor's attempt to show how the medical profession cares more about money than it does about ideals. The film and Donat's performance have not aged well. As online critic Chris Dashiell has so perceptively noted, "This was a prestige picture for Metro, and it was nominated for several Oscars. It seems that prestige often requires a certain level of mediocrity."[cxxii] Sadly, this has proven to be true of many A-films of MGM as well as those of other studios of the period. Watching it today, I find myself wondering if people didn't already know that many doctors cared more about money than helping. The first half is better than the second, so long as there is some hope and a touch of humor. But as the seriousness grows, so does the feeling we are being strapped to a pew for the sermon. No nomination should ever be given for force-feeding us morality.

Four Daughters is a pleasant enough little movie that made John Garfield a star. I really have no explanation for that; I don't find him all that interesting in most of his movies, but then, I've seen Jack Nicholson, who does the dark side much better. Starring Claude Rains as a music teacher and widow with (you guessed it) four daughters, the movie wrings some unlikely romances and marriages out of the ladies and their suitors. An enjoyable melodrama, which I find is actually marred by John Garfield's depressed and neurotic rebel figure. He just doesn't belong, and his suicide is based on his realization that he doesn't belong. The satisfaction comes when he is dead and Priscilla Lane can marry the right guy, after having married the wrong guy to make her sister happy. I don't know about you, but that level of self-sacrifice stretches the bounds of my sense of reality. *Four Daughters* spawned several sequels, all of which are worth watching, particularly if you like Claude Rains and Priscilla Lane. The nomination should stay, but you have to just bury your logic, which is something melodrama seems to require more of than any other genre.

The very first foreign film nominated for Best Picture, and a true classic of world cinema, *Grand Illusion* was directed by the great Jean Renoir, and stars Jean Gabin and Erich von Stroheim. Released in the United States in 1938, *Grand Illusion* must have made an enormous impression for studio Hollywood to have nominated it. *Grand Illusion* remains a unique experience – and one of the greatest pleasures I got out of writing this book, since I had never seen it. Set in WWI, *Grand Illusion* tells the story of French soldiers escaping a German POW camp. More than that, the film exposes the class issues that continue to dominate European culture, examines the nature of war, and suggests that nationalism blurs the human bonds we should share with each other. *Grand Illusion* is the second of the three films I prefer to *You Can't Take It with You*, and I came close to choosing it for what should have been Best Picture of the Year. As I consider *The Adventures of Robin Hood* the greatest adventure film of all time, I would place *Grand Illusion* as the very best prisoner of war film; even so, it is more than that. Like a great epic novel, *Grand Illusion* explores an entire society in microcosm, inviting us to repeated viewings to savor the ironies and observations Renoir and his cast worked into their collaboration. Renoir gave Stroheim the first opportunity he had had for many years to indulge his obsession for detail; other than *Sunset Blvd.*, Stroheim never had a better performance. Renoir fully restored *Grand Illusion* after WWII from a surviving print the Americans saved from the Nazis, who hated the film and destroyed every print they could. The film as it exists today is complete. The nomination of *Grand Illusion* shows how classy the Academy could (and can) be.

Jezebel always strikes me as Bette Davis getting revenge on David O. Selznick for making *Gone with the Wind* without her. Her role is more or less Scarlett O'Hara (see Best Actress below). As a whole picture, *Jezebel* has its moments, but flaws persist in keeping it from being the film it could have been. First and foremost, Henry Fonda has no business being in this movie (the bad hair should have been the first clue); as Wyler's biographer has so aptly noted, "Fonda was basically miscast in the role..."[cxxiii] Second, the film exists as a reason to punish Bette Davis' Julie Marsden as a Jezebel; when she defies the social expectations and norms of her restrictive society, she has to be crushed in the course of the plot (*Jane Eyre* does the same thing with Mr. Rochester). Jezebel's spirit has to be broken to male domination, and she must be reined in to satisfy the audience. Well, I am one audience member who wasn't satisfied. One of the many reasons to prefer *Gone with the Wind* to this pre-emptive strike of a movie is the fact that Scarlett never breaks (and yes, she does pay the price for that indomitability). Third,

Jezebel is also a film that should have been made in glorious Technicolor, given that the plot hinges on Davis' insistence on wearing a bright red gown to the Olympus Ball, where no unmarried woman was allowed to wear anything but white. Yes, I have an imagination, but the point should have been carried visually. Technicolor was available; after all, this is the year of *The Adventures of Robin Hood*. Despite this, Wyler makes it work, when all dancers clear the entire dance floor rather than be seen as accepting Davis and the red dress.[53] Fourth, the picture's depiction of happy slaves is part and parcel of the moonlight and magnolias take on the antebellum South which Hollywood (and the South) constantly promoted (among the slaves are Eddie "Rochester" Anderson and Matthew "Stymie" Beard). Fifth and finally, the picture essentially repeats the now worn-out Thirties formula of a troubled love story merging into a disaster pic: instead of the earthquake of *San Francisco* or the fire of *In Old Chicago*, we get malaria. I'm tired of seeing this plot twist over and over again. As a whole, *Jezebel* is best seen as Bette Davis' first truly great performance, and for that, it deserves a nomination for Best Picture.

The next film the Academy selected is far better known to most moviegoers in its later incarnation as *My Fair Lady*. *Pygmalion* has one thing going for it the musical did not: a screenplay by the original playwright, George Bernard Shaw. Shaw, who also won a Nobel Prize in Literature, was not amused by getting the Academy Award for Writing (Screenplay): "It's an insult for them to offer me any honor, as if they had never heard of me – and it's very likely they never have. They might as well send an honor to George for being King of England."[cxxiv] Much of that was his public pose as a curmudgeon; he actually displayed the Oscar in his home. Shaw was responsible for casting the wonderful Wendy Hiller as Eliza (see Best Actress); would that he had only been listened to when he requested Charles Laughton as Professor Henry Higgins. Instead, we get Leslie Howard, who managed to snag a "co-directed by" credit with Anthony Asquith. Surprisingly, as a second choice, Howard proves to be quite good, turning in what I would argue is the best performance of his all-too-overrated career (see Best Actor below). Hidden in the titles: David Lean, future director of *Great Expectations* and *Lawrence of Arabia*, edited the film. Not only should this film keep its nomination for Best Picture, but I would argue this may be the best filmed version of any Shaw play.

---

[53] The scene was based on a Hollywood white ball where Norma Shearer violated the same rule. One outraged guest said, "Who does Norma think she is – the house madam?" http://www.imdb.com/title/tt0030287/trivia

Test Pilot stars Clark Gable, Myrna Loy, and Spencer Tracy, and was directed by Victor Fleming, *Test Pilot* replays the kind of male love story we have had in *Manhattan Melodrama* and *San Francisco*. Been there, done that – only this time, we get planes, and the good guy dies. The planes are the best part of the movie – beautiful things, as planes were in the late Thirties, all shine and silver. Gable is at his rakish, devil-may-care best; Tracy plays grumpy and loyal; Loy is just enjoying everything with her *Thin Man* charm. A fun movie, even if the story is somewhat repetitive and indulgent of the kind of misogynist sadomasochism the period's films often engage in; Myrna Loy says "Tell him I want to be slapped." Howard Hawks, one of Victor Fleming's best friends, borrowed one of the scenes for his 1939 *Only Angels Have Wings*, wherein fliers refuse to recognize the name of a dead aviator. Tracy has a great death scene that steals the picture from Gable. Myrna Loy always said this was her favorite role. Worth your time – once. The nomination should stay.

The Academy ignored better choices.

Among the films they should have nominated, I would first point out *Angels with Dirty Faces*. A great gangster picture that also addresses the social problem of juvenile delinquents and the source of crime (more realistically than *Boys Town*), *Angels with Dirty Faces* also has three vital performances from James Cagney, Pat O'Brien, and Humphrey Bogart, and the first-rate direction of Michael Curtiz (see Best Director, Best Actor, and Best Writing (Screenplay) below for more). An unforgettable film that rewards multiple viewings, *Angels with Dirty Faces* could have easily replaced *Alexander's Ragtime Band*, *Boys Town*, *Four Daughters*, or *Test Pilot* on the original balloting. I have to assume that Warners threw its support behind *The Adventures of Robin Hood* instead. *Angels with Dirty Faces* tells the story of Rocky (Cagney) and Jerry (O'Brien). Both are petty criminals as children; Cagney gets caught, but O'Brien runs faster and escapes. Cagney gets put into reform school, and learns how to be a better criminal; O'Brien becomes a priest. The stage is set for their clash as adults, over the fate of the Dead End Kids, who aren't as well integrated into this film as they are in *Dead End*, even though they are the motivation for the famous ending. Bogart plays a lawyer who rips off Cagney, and then pays the price for that betrayal – but Cagney pays too, setting up for the famous final scene (see Best Actor below for more). As film critic Dana Polan points out, *Angels* is about seduction – the ways in which the images we have of others seduces us into imitating other behavior: the seduction of movies, of newspaper stories, of gangsters.[cxxv] The movie has a sly sense of humor; when Cagney is expecting police to interrogate him, he is sitting on his bed reading the magazine *Detective*. Even more, consider it in Machiavellian terms: good triumphs through lies, evil attracts through truth, and power is gained by whatever means necessary. Is there another studio film that so cynically pushes for idealism, exposing the way in which our impressions of reality form that reality? A brilliant film, *Angels with Dirty Faces* should have been nominated for Best Picture.

As should *The Lady Vanishes*, starring Margaret Lockwood, Michael Redgrave, Paul Lukas, and Dame May Whitty in this quintessential example of a Hitchcock film: comic, romantic, suspenseful, thrilling (the New York Film Critics chose it as the best picture of the year). Hitchcock used the success of this movie to launch his career in America, snagging a favorable contract with David O. Selznick.[54] *The Lady Vanishes* concerns the disappearance of Dame May Whitty on a train; everything follows from that mystery. One of the many memorable moments concerns a pacifist attempting to deal rationally with the fascist forces attacking them; he is killed for this attempt. Hitchcock clearly was making a statement about Hitler, and the approaching war many now saw coming in Europe. A wonderful film – the Academy should be slapped for not nominating it (see Best Director for more).

But a greater travesty was the Academy completely snubbing the third picture to outdo *You Can't Take It with You*, along with *The Adventures of Robin Hood* and *Grand Illusion*: *Bringing up Baby*. Howard Hawks never made a better movie – ever. If *Scarface* begins the gangster genre, then *Bringing up Baby* brings the screwball comedy to its absolute perfection. As Pauline Kael would have it, "it may be the movies' closest equivalent to Restoration comedy."[cxxvi] What the great and grand mystery remains is how the Academy – and the American public – could have completely ignored this astonishing achievement. Did they have no eyes? No ears? No sense of humor? How could this film have bombed at the box office?!? *Bringing up Baby* tells the story of Cary Grant, a paleontologist trying to find funding for his museum, and the final bone for a dinosaur he's been reconstructing for years. Grant has a fiancée, who may be the single coldest, least emotional woman ever put into an American film. He comes into contact with a slightly crazed, ditzy heiress, Katharine Hepburn, who proceeds to turn his life upside down with a dog, a lost bone, a leopard, a rich aunt, a big game hunter, a drunken groundskeeper, an angry small town constable, and love. Throughout, each incident leads logically to the next, played

---

[54] A relationship which would prove to be both productive and troubling, in many ways; for more, see the first-rate Hitchcock biography, *Alfred Hitchcock: A Life in Darkness and Light* by Patrick McGilligan.

as seriously as any drama would have, but with a level of laughter one finds in the best of comedies. At the end, when everything (literally) is in ruins, the illogicality of love is matched by the inevitability of love, and the characters resign themselves to being happy – as does the audience. *Bringing up Baby* proves itself to be an enduring classic, the pinnacle of the screwball comedy, and a film that should not just have been nominated for Best Picture, but should have won the Academy Award for Best Picture of 1938.

Best Actor: Spencer Tracy won for *Boys Town*, over Charles Boyer, *Algiers*; James Cagney, *Angels with Dirty Faces*; Robert Donat, *The Citadel*; and Leslie Howard, *Pygmalion*

 This really hurts; Spencer Tracy did not really deserve the Best Actor Oscar – again. I didn't want to admit that, but neither his role in *Captains Courageous* or *Boys Town* really should have won. MGM's studio block voting once again delivered an Oscar to somebody other than the finest performance of the year. Not that Tracy isn't as good as an actor could get in this particular role as a good priest, but it's the role itself that limits Tracy. Father Flanagan has nothing but goodness in him, and Tracy does that beautifully; but I suspect the real Father Flanagan was not quite this saintly all the time (even if there is a movement to canonize him). Tracy shows barely a sign of frustration or fluster once he gets going on his project. That limitation, and the fact Tracy has already played this exact type before in *San Francisco*, lead me reluctantly to argue against his Oscar. Tracy does quiet nobility better than anybody else ever has – with the possible exception of Pat O'Brien in *Angels with Dirty Faces* – but it still isn't enough for who should have won this year. He still deserves a nomination.

 Charles Boyer uttered his most famous line of all in *Algiers*: "Come with me to the Casbah." Except, as with so many other famous lines, he never actually said it. As the immortal Yogi Berra put it, "I never said most of the things I said." Boyer didn't want to make this American version of *Pepe le Moko* (which was not seen in the US until 1941). I wish they'd listened to his hesitancy, or allowed him more freedom. Boyer was forced to imitate the original actor Jean Gabin scene for scene, even down to hand gestures. He does project an air of that now vanished staple of detective fiction, the gentlemanly thief (like Raffles), and a more light-hearted charm than Gabin, but with little of Gabin's intensity, sense of serious threat, or ennui. Saddled as he was with the beautiful but wooden Hedy Lamarr, Boyer did the best he could, but in almost every way, he and this remake pale next to the original French version. On the other hand, Chuck Jones created the immortal Pepe le Pew in honor of this performance, and for that alone, the nomination should stay.

I consider James Cagney's performance in *Angels with Dirty Faces* to be the finest of his career. He moves beyond the malevolence of Tom Powers in *The Public Enemy* to a fuller, more nuanced turn as Rocky, the boy who couldn't run fast enough to avoid a life of crime. Trapped, he rises to the top. Throughout, Cagney is unbelievably good, working into his portrayal the real quirks of a rounded human being – the shoulders rolling and straightening, the vocal habits, the smirk in the eyes and mouth. When Cagney is finally captured by the police, the look of glee and satisfaction at having made such a great show of defiance and violence is stunning. The ending of *Angels* must be seen, because for the first time in American film history, a performance is so rich and intense that ambiguity of motivation fills it. Cagney deliberately left it open: did his character turn coward, or did he fake it? Watch the last shot of Cagney's face; grim determination fills the entire screen. From that point on, it's Curtiz's direction, and Cagney's voice, hands, and shadows that rip us to pieces. A great nomination.

Too bad that is so rarely true. Witness Robert Donat, whose problem in *The Citadel* is that he is earnest, serious, and deadly boring. He seems to walk through the role like a zombie. Watching the electric Ralph Richardson next to the stale Donat is to know the difference between beautiful wallpaper – and wallpaper paste. Donat has an atrocious Scottish accent, from which his usual British tones keep escaping. He does have some nice moments, as when he brings the newborn baby back to life, gets tipsy, and blows up the typhoid-ridden sewer to save the town. But once he gets married to Rosalind Russell (who is largely wasted), and grows pompous, I felt like I'd been sold a ticket to a sermon instead of a movie. No nomination was merited.

Leslie Howard's turn in *Pygmalion* is nigh short of miraculous, for he doesn't make me want to turn off one of his movies for the very first time. He finally shows some backbone and gruffness in one of his roles, leading me to suspect that the annoying feyness of most of his work was deliberate, which makes it all the worse. Seeing him lurk about the streets in the opening scenes, as he listens in on various dialects, invokes immediate comparison with Rex Harrison, and not unfavorably. As he talks to Wendy Hiller's incomparable Eliza, he actually evokes the kind of class prejudice and intolerance Shaw intended for him to have – all due to the language barrier her dialect imposes on her. What is more, Howard had a talent for physical touches he rarely explored; watch him walking up the stairs when Eliza has given him back the jewelry. All in all, a well-deserved nomination for an actor trapped in roles that have aged remarkably badly.

And now, on to those the Academy snubbed.

Errol Flynn should have been nominated for *The Adventures of Robin Hood*. As Roger Ebert so pointedly puts it: "Because Errol Flynn in later life became a caricature of himself and a rather nasty man, it's exhilarating to see him here at the dawn of his career. He was improbably handsome, but that wasn't really the point: What made him a star was his lighthearted exuberance, the good cheer with which he embodies a role like Robin Hood. When George C. Scott was asked what he looked for in an actor, he mentioned "joy of performance," and Flynn embodies that with a careless rapture. Watch his swagger as he enters John's banquet hall and throws a deer down before the prince, full knowing that the punishment for poaching a deer is death. Surrounded by his enemies, he fearlessly accuses John of treason against his brother Richard the Lionhearted, and then fights his way out of the castle again. Another actor might have wanted to project a sense of uncertainty, or resolve, or danger; Flynn shows us a Robin Hood so supremely alive that the whole adventure is a lark. Yes, his eyes shift to note that the exit is being barred and guards are readying their swords, but he observes not in fear but in anticipation."[cxxvii] What Mr. Ebert said! In Like Flynn!

And for my last candidate, I should like to point once more at Cary Grant, this time for *Bringing up Baby*. Grant took everything he had crafted as a star, and completely inverted it to play Dr. David Huxley, the paleontologist in search of the missing intercostal clavicle. "Cary Grant" was handsome, suave, urbane, charming, graceful and smooth-talking; Dr. Huxley became myopic, bumbling, clueless, awkward, clumsy, and mush-mouthed. He went from pursuing the woman to being pursued. The two things he kept were his absolutely perfect sense of humor and his immense capacity to carry a story forward. His improvisations on the set, honed by his time with Leo McCarey, remain some of the finest moments in the movie – and none more so than when he is wearing the frilly negligee and leaps into the air, crying "I just went *gay* all of a sudden." Perhaps he made the audiences of 1938 uncomfortable, but the joke would probably have sailed over the heads of most of them, as the word meant "happy" to all but those few aware of the connotations.[55] The rumors of Grant's homosexuality or bisexuality have been denied repeatedly by those who knew him best, as well as those who

---

[55] "Gay meaning 'homosexual' became established in the 1960s as the term preferred by homosexual men." http://oxforddictionaries.com/definition/english/gay

have scrupulously investigated the evidence.⁵⁶ All throughout the film, Grant is the innocent trying to cope with the crazy things that are happening, and doing so in the most amusing way possible. An absolute classic performance, which should have gained him a nomination for Best Actor.

But not, by a hair, the Oscar. While Grant was as good in this as he ever had been, one man went even further, by being better than he ever would be again – as well as almost anybody else for years to come. James Cagney in *Angels with Dirty Faces* transcends his entire considerable career by literally remaking himself as an actor, taking every gangster he had ever played, including his breakthrough role in *The Public Enemy*, and fusing those characters into the summation of what it means to be an actor. Up to that point in film history, no other actor had turned himself inside out on screen, in the manner they would be using in Method acting in the next two decades. Cagney performs a miracle, creating a truly ambivalent performance that can be interpreted, with real satisfaction either way, as either the act of the greatest coward or the bravest man ever seen on film. James Cagney should have won the Oscar for Best Actor for this fearless performance.

Best Actress: Bette Davis won for *Jezebel*, over Norma Shearer, *Marie Antoinette*; Wendy Hiller, *Pygmalion*; Fay Bainter, *White Banners*; and Margaret Sullavan, *Three Comrades*

Jezebel is the movie in which Bette Davis finally learned how to channel her enormous energy and love of risk-taking into real acting. As Jan Herman has so capably proven, William Wyler is the reason Davis moved past being a showy actress whose performances surprised, to become a real actress whose performances convinced: "As filming continued, Wyler convinced Davis that every moment need not be played with equal fervor. During rehearsals he had realized that was her greatest weakness...Davis learned how to modulate her performance and tone down her mannerisms." Davis herself recognized this fundamental change: "He made my performance. It was all Wyler. I had known all the horrors of no direction and bad direction. I now knew what a great director was and what he could mean to an actress...Willy really is responsible for the fact that I became a box-office star."[cxxviii] Watching

---

[56] The same is true for the allegations made against Spencer Tracy and Laurence Olivier, and I suspect a number of other celebrity targets. I am not arguing that many homosexual and bisexual men have not hidden their sexuality, often marrying as protection or for other reasons; I am simply stating that all too often, these charges are made to sell books, without any credible evidence.

Jezebel after *Of Human Bondage* and *Dangerous*, I can finally see why she was accounted by her peers as their best actress. Her performance is breathtaking in its audacity, assuredness, and control. Watching her sweep into her engagement party shockingly dressed in her riding clothes still makes audiences gasp – even those who don't care about the niceties of antebellum mores one bit. I find myself within a hair's breadth of agreeing with the Academy that she deserved the Best Actress Oscar – but one performance outdoes even this magnificence.

Norma Shearer's nod for *Marie Antoinette* seems more out of respect for the dead than for her performance. Her husband Irving Thalberg had been planning *Marie Antoinette* for her before he died; he intended it to be one of her last roles before she retired. She hadn't been in a movie for two years before this, and honestly, she shouldn't have been in this one either. MGM reportedly forced her to take the role, given how much they had already spent, and the profits her return to the screen could mean for the studio. Watching Shearer having to pretend to be a young excited girl is even worse in this movie than it was in *Romeo and Juliet*. Shearer is lost in the spectacle, unlike John Barrymore, who seems to dominate even all that scenery as Louis XVI, and Robert Morley, who is bogglingly stupid as his heir and her husband. Shearer just tries to cope with goggle eyes and breathlessness, then puts on slutty for awhile. To be fair, when she is about to be sent back to Austria, and she realizes her friends are merely ones of advantage, Shearer does have a nice scene of having to accept her imminent failure (Joseph Schildkraut looks ridiculous as the lover who abandons her when she is being sent back home). As always, when she has a strong male lead, she responds with some degree of life; Tyrone Power tries, but if he couldn't pull off this kind of stiff romance, I'm not sure anybody could. The film would have been far better off to cut him out entirely, and focus on the court politics (but even then, the writers chose to come up with this nutty jewel caper instead of something real). For that matter, the entire film is based on the ridiculous conceit that the French revolution was the result of courtly intrigue, rather than the genuine revolution against monarchy that it was (minor piffle is mouthed from the monarchs about how they want to help the people, but they're beyond unconvincing). The movie just drags and drags, and most of the boredom is due to Shearer. I don't drink coffee, but I could have used a cappuccino intravenous drip to stay awake. Was it wrong of me to cheer the guillotine going up at the end? Do I need to say it? Apparently, I do: no nomination should have been given to Shearer for a film Pauline Kael called a "resplendent bore."[cxxix]

Wendy Hiller got her film break in *Pygmalion*, and here's how superb she is: I completely forgot Audrey Hepburn's performance in *My Fair Lady* while watching her. She is "deliciously low" as the flower girl; by the end, she is more regal than the Queen herself. Hiller is simply the best Eliza the screen has known. Audrey who?

Margaret Sullavan received a nomination for *Three Comrades*. Sullavan is best known today for *The Shop Around the Corner* and *Back Street*; *Three Comrades* was her only Oscar nomination for Best Actress. She plays a young woman in postwar Germany, wrapped up with Robert Taylor and the other two comrades, Robert Young and Franchot Tone. Sullavan brings a quiet reality to the world of acting, and given the overacting and histrionics that tended to mark the common run of performance in the Thirties, she must have seemed a breath of fresh air. Unlike Katharine Hepburn and a few others, she has not retained that freshness; she reminds me of a slightly less wholesome June Allyson, another actress whose performances have lost much of their luster. *The New York Times* raved: "The word admirable is sheer understatement. Her performance is almost unendurably lovely."[cxxx] *Three Comrades* is the only film to give F. Scott Fitzgerald a screenwriting credit, even though the majority of the film does not use his script at all, as producer Joseph L. Mankiewicz rewrote most of it.[cxxxi] Based on a novel by Erich Maria Remarque (most famous for *All Quiet on the Western Front*), *Three Comrades* was turned from the serious politically-charged novel Remarque wrote into yet another Frank Borzage melodrama. One exception to this: watch the completely unexpected scene wherein Franchot Tone hunts down Robert Young's murderer, and you'll wish Borzage had taken more chances as a director. The editing is brilliant, cutting back and forth between Tone and his prey, as some of the glorious strains from the Handel *Messiah* emerge from the church where Tone exacts vengeance. In the end, and compared to the other performances in this category, Sullavan's nomination should stay, as she does tend to dominate the film effectively, if quietly.

In *White Banners*, Fay Bainter plays a homeless woman named Hannah, who has come to town in search of the son she gave up for adoption, to see how he has turned out. The boy is played by Jackie Cooper; Claude Rains also stars. Bainter and Rains do their best to keep the film from getting too syrupy, even though Bainter has a kind of Stella Dallas self-sacrificial role to play in this hosanna to true motherhood. Rains has never displayed more glee than in his role as a teacher inventing the refrigerator in his spare time; the banter he displays with everyone is first-rate stuff. Bainter should keep the nomination

Once more, however, the Academy ignored the best choice.

Like Cary Grant for *Bringing up Baby*, Katharine Hepburn took everything she had built personally, and turned it inside out as heiress Susan Vance. She had played very insecure characters before (notably in *Alice Adams*), but for the most part, her roles were brash, confident, smart, sure of themselves – much as she was. Certainly, her typical stubbornness and persistence came through, but she also became an airhead, incapable of sustaining any thought beyond what she wanted at the moment – and what she wanted was Cary Grant. Hepburn had never been the sexual aggressor in her films; here, she pursues Grant with abandon, damning the consequences. The result has remained with me as long as any role she ever played, and never fails to charm, despite her inability to perceive any reality other than her emotional longings. Hepburn should have been nominated for *Bringing up Baby* – and she should have won.

Best Director: Frank Capra won for *You Can't Take It with You*, over Michael Curtiz for both *Angels with Dirty Faces* and *Four Daughters*; Norman Taurog, *Boys Town*; and King Vidor, *The Citadel*

Frank Capra won the Best Director Oscar (again) for one of his classics. In any other year, I would be applauding, as you might have guessed from my discussion of *You Can't Take It with You* above in Best Picture. Capra doesn't make one misstep, although I do find the ending slightly unbelievable, which often were Capra's one fault; *Meet John Doe* is the most infamous of these occasionally unsatisfying endings. Frank Capra should definitely keep his nomination, but the Oscar should have gone to a director who made an even greater film. Stick around and maybe I'll tell you!

Michael Curtiz was nominated for *Angels with Dirty Faces* and *Four Daughters*, but why not for *The Adventures of Robin Hood*? Certainly, he had a co-director, William Keighley, who began *Robin Hood*, which may have undercut the voting. Roger Ebert splits their roles thus: "Keighley did most of the outdoor scenes, Curtiz did most of the studio shooting."[cxxxii] Think of these three films by Curtiz, all in one year: *Four Daughters*, one of those weepy, overcooked melodramas; *Angels with Dirty Faces*, one of the hallmark gangster films, with Cagney's greatest performance; and *Robin Hood,* the greatest buckler of swashes of them all. As Dr. Drew Casper of USC has pointed out: "Other than Hitchcock, no director can claim as many brilliant films as this man can."[cxxxiii] While I would add John Ford and Howard Hawks to that short list, Casper has the right of it. Curtiz is woefully underrated as a director, and that reputation should have been cemented this year. Just look at

Angels with Dirty Faces, and compare the way in which the young version of Cagney's character is captured by the police and dragged away while his hands clutch at the fence, with the scene at the end where Cagney is violently attempting to avoid the electric chair, and watch his hands clutching in the same way. Few directors have this level of imagery and circular structure. The death scene is visually stunning, in Curtiz's use of the shadows on the bars, the tracking shot of Cagney, and then the cut away from Cagney's face to use only shadows, sounds, and close-ups on Cagney's hands, before focusing entirely on Pat O'Brien's face, which conveys an intense emotion and believable sorrow, grace, and gladness all at once, punctuated by the single tear.

The Adventures of Robin Hood is another visual stunner from Curtiz, and nowhere more so than in the final sword fight between Rathbone and Flynn, with its thrilling use of shadow fighting, close-ups, and framing to bring the audience to the edge of their seats. Curtiz is terribly underrated as an artistic director who was also very commercial – like Hitchcock, Ford, and Hawks. Curtiz deserved the nomination for *Angels with Dirty Faces* and *Robin Hood* (instead of the minor *Four Daughters*).

Norman Taurog is back again to make young boys cry in *Boys Town*. I still haven't forgiven the bastard for threatening to shoot his nephew Jackie Cooper's dog. No nomination should have gone to a movie that essentially could have filmed itself, given the by-the-numbers sentimentality it projects (see Best Picture and Best Actor above for more).

In *The Citadel*, King Vidor is once again playing with the conflicts between idealism and reality, in the same way that he was in such classics as *The Big Parade* and *The Crowd*. Some directors gain subtlety and humor as they get older; others calcify. Unfortunately, Vidor seems to have belonged to the second group, if this film is any indication. The film has little of the adventurousness and experimentation of Vidor's earlier work. No nomination was deserved.

Moving on to the directors the Academy ignored, we find two major omissions.

Trying to explain Alfred Hitchcock's greatness as a director can be difficult. He chose stories which in the hands of other directors would be the sheerest pulp, then he turned this dross into gold (Louis Armstrong did much the same with hack songs). *The Lady Vanishes* seems to me to be the moment Hitchcock brought together all of the elements he had been toying with for years, to produce the kind of film that would mark him as one of best of all directors. In his deft mixing of genres, his unmatched pace, his capable plotting, his use of dramatic, unusual angles to make a point (as when he films up through the two drugged drinks), and in his generally satisfying endings, Hitchcock had found his métier. *The Lady Vanishes* should have brought Hitchcock a nomination.

But more flummoxing than leaving out Hitchcock, I simply cannot understand how the Academy could have overlooked Hawks' work on *Bringing up Baby*. The screwball comedy requires the most delicate handling of the subject matter – sex – in an era when that could never be openly discussed without the nuance of innuendo, and plays that subtlety off against the broadest strokes of physical comedy. Hawks made several screwball comedies, both before and after *Bringing up Baby* – the best of them being *Twentieth Century* and *His Girl Friday*. As a master of the form, he brought to this film a wonderful sense of the absurd and the inevitable. Watch the opening, wherein Cary Grant's dilemma is laid out brilliantly: he is a scientist dedicated to his profession, but he has no life outside of his intercostal clavicle. He's about to marry an icicle, and doesn't know how to get out of it. When he meets Katharine Hepburn, a woman who does nothing but cause him trouble, his life begins to unravel. The shot of Grant riding on the sideboard of the car, moving him away from the man Grant's trying to convince to help give the museum money, shows him literally getting carried away; perversely, the camera shows him from the waist up as he speeds off. Throughout the film, Hawks chooses the most economical, perfect frames for the action and comic responses. Hawks is the closest thing classic cinema has to Ernest Hemingway; both of them believed in cutting the fat, expressing things without folderol and filigree, and maintaining grace under pressure. Hawks should have been nominated for Best Director, and he should have won this year, despite the phenomenal achievements of Michael Curtiz.

Best Supporting Actor: Walter Brennan won for *Kentucky*, over Gene Lockhart, *Algiers*; John Garfield, *Four Daughters*; Basil Rathbone, *If I Were King*, and Robert Morley, *Marie Antoinette*

Walter Brennan won for *Kentucky*, as he had before on the strength of his popularity with the extras, who selected him regardless of the quality of his performances. Brennan plays one of his typical old coots in this tale of feuding families in horse-breeding Kentucky. Loretta Young and Richard Green play the young lovers in a Romeo-and-Juliet plot for which we all know the ending the second we see them. Brennan does a good job as old Uncle Peter, spouting and sputtering, and he gets to die, but Brennan isn't doing much more than phoning in this copy of the other times he's done this shtick. He should keep his nomination because he's always worth watching, but he didn't deserve the Oscar (and he knew that).

Gene Lockhart had a very good year in 1938, between his nominated performance as Regis, the informer in *Algiers*, and a memorable performance as Bob Cratchit in MGM's *A Christmas Carol*. Lockhart is at his two-faced best in this part, whereas he is in absolute earnestness as Cratchit. Lockhart plays an honest toad: "I'm an informer, not a hypocrite." But so much of the performance is a mimicking of the original (even more so than Boyer's twinning of Jean Gabin), that I can't in all honesty suggest Lockhart should keep the nomination. Now, if only Chuck Jones had invented a character based on Lockhart, that would be a different story…

John Garfield became a star playing the doomed musician in *Four Daughters*. I find his performance a weak forerunner of the kind of thing Marlon Brando and Montgomery Clift would do in the Fifties, and about as appropriate in this film as a wedding guest showing up in jeans and a t-shirt when everybody else was in formal wear. He just doesn't fit the story very well, or maybe the story doesn't fit him. Suicide is the only way to make this mess work out, but I never buy Garfield taking that route. No nomination should have been given.

Basil Rathbone was up for *If I Were King*, starring Ronald Colman and directed by Frank "Mutiny on the Bounty" Lloyd; Preston Sturges wrote the screenplay for this medieval version of *The Prisoner of Zenda*. Ronald Colman plays poet Francois Villon, who gets to be king for a day. Rathbone plays Louis XI, a king constantly manipulating things to his liking. Rathbone, unfortunately, looks to me like Sherlock Holmes in one of his disguises, rather than inhabiting the role truthfully. He constantly seems to be playing a part as the king, rather than being the king. What is more, he throws his deep resonant voice, one of his great gifts, into an annoying upper register. He's like the caricature of a king, rather than a king. No nomination was deserved…for *this* performance.

Robert Morley's turn as the doomed King Louis XVI proved that boneheaded dorks existed in the eighteenth century. Louis XVI probably remains the greatest argument against monarchy who ever lived. Morley does that argument justice. An utter fool for the first half of the film, he does find a backbone when he wants to keep his wife from being sent back to Austria, only to collapse back into blubber when he doesn't get his way. Very little of this movie is worth watching more than once, but Morley remains effective, and a good choice.

And now for the performances the Academy should have selected.

One of them was the compellingly quirky Edward Everett Horton in *Holiday*. For the first time, Horton is playing an eccentric who feels like a real person. I don't think I've ever seen a character actor with more glee at living life to the fullest. As Professor Potter, Horton does everything he can to keep Cary Grant on the path to nonconformity (*Holiday* is the film wherein Grant does most of his acrobatic flips). Horton had a long career adding zest to every film in which he appeared; he was never more central to the tone of a film than he was for *Holiday*. Horton should have been nominated.

Astonishingly, neither Basil Rathbone nor Claude Rains were nominated for *The Adventures of Robin Hood*. Rathbone has rarely been equaled for his ability to project menace and handle a sword as Sir Guy, but Claude Rains produces a far subtler threat in Prince John. His is the movement behind the scenes, the conspiratorial dangers we still face today in the halls of power: a terrible, unending selfishness, the drive to power for power's sake, the need to aggrandize oneself regardless of the consequences. Both Rathbone and Rains should have been nominated, but for the silky corruption of his performance, Rains should have won the Oscar for Best Supporting Performance for his Prince John (particularly when considering his other excellent roles this year in *White Banners* and the father in *Four Daughters*).

Best Supporting Actress: Fay Bainter won for *Jezebel*, over Miliza Korjus, *The Great Waltz*; Billie Burke, *Merrily We Live*; Beulah Bondi, *Of Human Hearts*; and Spring Byington, *You Can't Take It with You*.

In *Jezebel*, Fay Bainter plays Aunt Bell, who is constantly troubled by her niece's unconventional ways – and Bette Davis does indeed discomfort Bainter. I think Bainter won because she stands in for the audience's desire to see Davis reined in, and can express their frustration when Davis fails to follow the expectations of both the world of 1852 New Orleans, and the audience of 1938 America, who wanted to be titillated by a strong woman defying the rules, but could not accept that defiance without some kind of comeuppance (as when Scarlett loses Rhett, or as in *Woman of the Year*, when preview audiences demanded Katharine Hepburn's character be humiliated). Bainter's performance has aged badly, to the point of not believing she could possibly be real. Neither Oscar nor nomination was a good idea.

Miliza Korjus plays Carla Donner, an opera star and the other woman in the movie biography of the Waltz King Johann Strauss, *The Great Waltz*. A lavish biopic from MGM starring Luise Rainer, *The Great Waltz* was directed by a French import, Julien Duvivier, but both Victor

Fleming and Josef von Sternberg came in for uncredited reshoots.[cxxxiv] Korjus was a Polish soprano; this was her only American film. Overall, *The Great Waltz* is a ridiculously bad movie, and not even remotely connected with the truth, as even the film admits up front: "We have dramatized the spirit rather than the facts of his life, because it is his spirit that has lived – in his music." In other words, we're going to string together a bunch of his waltzes, have Luise Rainer play his true love and long suffering wife, then have Strauss get tempted by an artistic slut until even the trollop realizes that it would be wrong to break up a marriage. In reality, the opposition to Strauss came from his father; once his father died, his career took off. Strauss never married the woman the movie claims he did, nor did he have an affair with Carla Donner, the singer played by Korjus. Korjus is not particularly pretty, and she seems to force the cute at times. Her smile is one of the biggest fakes in film history. She does have a lovely voice, and when she sings, the fakery gets toned down (mostly). Reviewers thought she stole the movie; that wasn't hard, given how bad the rest of the actors are. No nomination was merited.

Merrily We Live is most often thought of as a rip off of *My Man Godfrey*; instead of a butler, we get a chauffeur – after a whole chain of lost men being saved by Burke being a "philanthropist." The family is even screwier than that of *My Man Godfrey*: a richer and grumpier father, a playboy brother, and not one but TWO scatterbrained sisters. Lest we forget, we also get Billie Burke at her ditziest. As a whole, the movie is trying too hard to be funny, and Burke has done this routine before – and so did Alice Brady, far better, in *My Man Godfrey*. No nomination should be given for being a copycat.

Of Human Hearts stars Jimmy Stewart, with Beulah Bondi as his mother (a common pairing of these two actors, most famously in *It's a Wonderful Life*). Stewart plays a Civil War doctor who gets chastised by Abraham Lincoln (played by John Carradine) for ignoring his mother, after she had sold everything she owned to support him through medical school. Another of Hollywood's hallelujahs to motherhood, *Of Human Hearts* gives Bondi a chance to shine as the kind of eternally self-sacrificing mother we have seen in *Stella Dallas* and elsewhere (although without the prostitution). Bondi is her usual crusty but loveable self, but she's good enough at it to deserve a nomination.

In *You Can't Take It with You*, Spring Byington is the woman who writes the plays because somebody delivered a piano to their house by mistake. She has a marvelous little comic role; I especially love the bit with the kitten acting as a paperweight on the manuscript, and her completely innocent way of being fascinated with everything, and asking the most ridiculous questions straight-faced. A small but enjoyable role, and one that deserved a nomination.

The one unforgettable performance in this category was the one the Academy utterly ignored: that of May Robson as Mrs. Carlton Random in *Bringing up Baby*. Never has an actress turned in a performance so imperiously befuddled. From her first reaction to Cary Grant in his borrowed negligee to the increasing exasperation she displays towards the antics of Katharine Hepburn and Grant, Robson turns in the last great performance of her career. She should have received a nomination, and she should have won the Oscar for Best Supporting Actress.

Best Writing (Original Story): Eleanore Griffin and Dore Schary won for *Boys Town*, over Irving Berlin, *Alexander's Ragtime Band*; Rowland Brown, *Angels with Dirty Faces*; John Howard Lawson, *Blockade*; Marcella Burke and Frederick Kohner, *Mad About Music*; and Frank Wead, *Test Pilot*.

Boys Town exists; Father Flanagan was real; Mickey Rooney's character is an amalgam of real boys who were helped. The narrative is basic, with no unique qualities, a bare-bones approach, and a ridiculous ending. How is this original? Answer: *Boys Town* isn't, and shouldn't have been nominated. The writers were Eleanore Griffin and Dore Schary, who would go on to work on many other MGM films. Griffin came up with the story for *The Harvey Girls*, starring Judy Garland; Schary would eventually take over MGM from Louis B. Mayer, after becoming a producer for such groundbreaking films as *Battleground*. *Boys Town* was just a minor stepping stone, and not worth an Oscar or a nomination.

Irving Berlin received a nomination for the story behind *Alexander's Ragtime Band*, largely because the movie had begun as an attempt to film his life story by Darryl F. Zanuck. Berlin talked him out of it, but Berlin's songs formed the framework of this movie, which is largely why we still watch the movie. The plot, such as it is, remains a mundane love triangle. The songs are anything but mundane; they are the backbone of the Great American Songbook. But they shouldn't have been enough to gain a nomination for story. Let's go listen to Ella Fitzgerald's *Irving Berlin Songbook* instead. Come along! Come along!

We have an absolutely first rate story from Rowland Brown in *Angels with Dirty Faces* – one so good that dozens of other films and TV shows and pulp novels would rip it off shamelessly. Two young boys, best friends from the poorest slums, and one goes good, the other goes bad – and they confront each other as adults. The dialogue in this film is taut and to the point; the story never lags. A far better story in terms of its realism and emotional honesty, *Angels with Dirty Faces* deserved its nomination. Brown would go on to film noir, including *Kansas City Confidential*, but *Angels with Dirty Faces* was his career high.

Blockade was Hollywood's attempt to wax noble about the Spanish Civil War. Henry Fonda is badly miscast as a Spanish peasant; Madeleine Carroll plays a spy. Writer John Howard Lawson later became one of the Hollywood Ten, persecuted by the House Committee on Un-American Activities after WWII. *Blockade* is one of those movies the Academy nominates when it wants to pat itself on the back for being good human beings standing against violence and bloodshed. Like many well-meaning diatribes, it hasn't aged well, not just because of its intense earnestness, but more because of the clumsy ways in which it expresses that earnestness. When Fonda turns to the audience in an anti-war appeal, breaking the fourth wall also tears what little willing suspension of disbelief the film held for me in the first place. Chaplin's *The Great Dictator* would make much the same mistake with his speech at the end, although Chaplin pulls it off somewhat better than Fonda. Lawson's script was also hamstrung by the restrictions the Breen Office placed on the references to the Spanish Civil War. No nomination should have been made for this failed antiwar story.

Marcella Burke and Frederick Kohner came up with *Mad About Music*, based on an interesting idea, although I don't know whether I'd call it very original. Deanna Durbin plays a young girl in Switzerland who pretends to have a famous father; she then has to convince an Englishman, played by suave Herbert Marshall, to pretend to be her father. We've seen this kind of plot more than once; it's a very effective way to produce hijinks, especially when you add a neglectful famous mother and her conniving agent. Durbin does a lovely "Ave Maria." Fun vehicle, done with about as much class as this plot can handle. Marcella Burke began her career with this credit – and only had one other, in 1956! Way to stay optimistic, Ms. Burke! Kohner did a little better, staying in the business until he ended with the Gidget franchise. The nomination for *Mad About Music* should stay.

Frank Wead was nominated for *Test Pilot*. Wead turned to screenwriting after an accident invalided him out of the military.[57] *Test Pilot* is one of his more famous scripts. We've seen this picture before, but not with planes. The sense of what it means to fly, and the emotional burdens of test pilots' friends and families, comes across sincerely and ef-

---

[57] Wead would later be the subject of the John Ford film, *On Wings of Angels*, starring John Wayne as Wead.

fectively. Wead should keep his nomination (see Best Picture above for more).

And now for the true most original story of the year, despite the fact that the Academy ignored the film completely: Hagar Wilde and *Bringing up Baby*. Put a frustrated paleontologist, a rare dinosaur bone, a ditzy heiress, a dog, and a leopard who pines for the song "I Can't Give You Anything But Love" and what should you have? Oscar gold, Baby!

Best Writing (Screenplay): George Bernard Shaw, Ian Dalrymple, Cecil Lewis and W. P. Lipscomb won for *Pygmalion*, over John Meehan and Dore Schary, *Boys Town*; Ian Dalrymple, Elizabeth Hill, and Frank Wead, *The Citadel*; Lenore Coffee and Julius J. Epstein, *Four Daughters*; and Robert Riskin, *You Can't Take It with You*

George Bernard Shaw and company did an outstanding job producing a cinematic version of Shaw's play *Pygmalion*: deleting the longer speeches, adding scenes Shaw himself had wanted in the original but couldn't afford, and bringing out the essential quality of the play – without feeling like a theatre production at all. In adapting a play, asking the playwright isn't necessarily the best choice, as the author often can't rethink the story in film terms. Here, Shaw and the other writers do a magnificent job. An excellent nomination, and the Oscar could easily remain on Shaw's shelf – except for the one screenplay adaptation the Academy chose to ignore completely, which leads me to move away from Shaw.

But first, the other nominations:

John Meehan and Dore Schary took a sentimental look at one of the great charitable organizations of the last century, Boys Town, and created MGM's biggest hit of 1938. As I've pointed out already, *Boys Town* will warm the cockles of your heart and make you cry. But it spins on a ridiculous coincidence, devolving into artificial melodrama rather than continuing to build on the true human relationships they had been following. We're expected to believe a bank robbery happens just at the right time for Mickey Rooney to reform by ratting out his brother, and that the boys all arrest the bad guys. This might work in a Little Rascals short, but not in a serious movie. The nomination should stay for the emotional qualities, but the false turn at the end lessens their craft.

The Citadel adapts the novel by A.J. Cronin. A decent story, told with as much righteousness as the emotionally restrained director and cast can muster. The novel itself was influential in changing the ethical standards of the medical profession in Britain. Numerous adaptations have been made accordingly, of which this version is far from the most faithful. The radically altered ending in particular violates Cronin's ideas. Ian Dalrymple, Elizabeth Hill, and Frank Wead didn't deserve this nomination.

Four Daughters was based on a novel by Fannie Hurst, who also wrote the original *Imitation of Life*. Nobody reads Fannie Hurst any more. The script has its amusing moments, but the melodrama is heavily overplayed, which is not helped by John Garfield's anti-hero angst. No nomination should have come to Lenore Coffee (who wrote mostly second-rate melodramas for thirty years) and Julius J. Epstein (*Casablanca*).

Robert Riskin's adaptation of *You Can't Take It with You* has its detractors; many feel the delicate balance and nuances of the play were hammered and bludgeoned into a more two-dimensional attack on the rich. The movie's portrayal of the tycoon who finds his heart again is overdone, and his conversion does play falsely at times. Edward Arnold does the best he can with the role, but he's asked to be Ebenezer Scrooge without laying the groundwork for that salvation as Charles Dickens did. Even then, let's remember that Dickens is writing a fantasy in *A Christmas Carol*, one I want to believe in, as I do all fairy tales, but wishing doesn't make it so. Riskin and Capra would ponder the same issues again in *Mr. Smith Goes to Washington*, *Meet John Doe*, and *It's a Wonderful Life* with varying degrees of success.[58] Riskin should keep the nomination, although I have friends who are angry about the changes to the play.

A number of other screenplays were unjustly ignored.

First, *The Adventures of Robin Hood* went through a long gestational process.[59] The two credited writers are Norman Reilly Raine (*Tugboat Annie*; *The Private Lives of Elizabeth and Essex*) and Seton I. Miller (*Scarface*; *G-Men*; *The Black Swan*). They, along with the writers who worked on it before them, found the strongest skeleton from the original ballads and legends, lifted the best parts from previous film versions, and crafted a supple, fast, action-driven tale of Robin Hood that remains the finest version of all time. They should have been nominated.

Billy Wilder and Charles Brackett's screenplay for Ernst Lubitsch's *Bluebeard's Eighth Wife* should have been recognized. One of the funniest moments comes with a shop window sign that says "English Spoken" – and the next line says "American Understood." Gary Cooper

---

[58] The one false note in *Mr. Smith* is Claude Rains' senatorial suicide attempt; when they got to *Meet John Doe*, they realized it was more interesting and convincing to let the good guy have a dark side and change (even if they couldn't figure out how).
[59] For just how long, find the seminal research on this and other classic films by the genial and well-informed Rudy Behlmer, in *America's Favorite Movies: Behind the Scenes*.

plays a millionaire who has had seven wives – and he wants Claudette Colbert as the eighth. Very sneaky, Lubitsch; the film starts off with Cooper just wanting to buy the tops of pajamas. While the argument goes past the censors, thousands of women are considering Gary Cooper nude from the waist down. The dialogue is excellent: "Have you ever had a waiter look at you with untipped eyes?" "Please let me apologize from the bottom of your bathtub." Ultimately, it's a slick little film that manages to be about sex when they couldn't talk about sex, by making it about true love and marriage. While it's not top of the line Lubitsch, or Wilder and Brackett, *Bluebeard's Eighth Wife* is worth a look.

In the final summation, the same snubbed movie deserves the Best Writing (Screenplay) Oscar: *Bringing up Baby* launches one surprise after another, never allowing the pace or the humor to slacken. Of course, much of that is due to the editing and direction and acting, but in the beginning was the Word, and these words are pretty darn bueno: "When a man is wrestling a leopard in the middle of a pond, he's in no position to run." Katharine Hepburn: "Your golf ball, your running board, your car? Is there anything in the world that doesn't belong to you?" to which Cary Grant replies, "Yes, thank heavens, you!" "You know why you're following me? You're a fixation." Good stuff, but even better in the movie. The structure of *Bringing up Baby* is also circular, in that we end where we began in the lab, but with a difference: instead of being with a woman who is obsessed with Grant's career, he ends with a woman who is obsessed with him as a person – as he is with her. Very few scripts ever approach this perfection; that the screenplay could also support improvisation makes it the equivalent of a classic American song. When Peter Bogdanovich "borrowed" the story to remake it as *What's up, Doc?* in 1972, we had more evidence for a new generation that the story was infinitely flexible and capable of reinterpretation. Dudley Nichols and Hagar Wilde should have been nominated for this category, and they should have won the Oscar for Best Writing (Screenplay).

Best Cinematography: Joseph Ruttenberg won for *The Great Waltz*, 1-2-3-ing over James Wong Howe, *Algiers*; Ernest Miller and Harry Wild, *Army Girl*; Victor Milner, *The Buccaneer*; Ernest Haller, *Jezebel*; Joseph Valentine, *Mad About Music*; Norbert Brodine, *Merrily We Live*; Peverell Marley, *Suez*; Robert de Grasse, *Vivacious Lady*; Joseph Walker, *You Can't Take It with You*; and Leon Shamroy, *The Young in Heart*. Long waltz; wasn't it?

Joseph Ruttenberg had a fabulous career as a cinematographer, with a filmography widely varied and respected, shooting everything from *The Philadelphia Story* and *Gaslight* to *Brigadoon* and *Gigi*. He won the Oscar for *The Great Waltz*, one of his decidedly lesser collaborations. Nothing is wrong with the cinematography, other than what he's being asked to film: a huge, crashing bore of a story, tied to some famous waltzes. MGM films were almost always the most polished films around; they have also turned out, by and large, to be empty wastes of time and money.[60] *The Great Waltz* is no exception. Other than the music – admittedly the only excuse for filming this – only Ruttenberg brings any life to this corpse at all. He constantly shifts the perspective of the camera, especially during the performances. For the dances, in particular, Ruttenberg tries his best to keep the eye entertained as well as the ear. The best known scene, that of the creation of "Tales from the Vienna Woods," proves Ruttenberg's best work here: pastoral, dreamlike, and romantic, as Strauss and the slut ride in a carriage (rear projection ruins much of the effect, unfortunately). We also get some of the most extreme close-ups ever done to this date. I can see why they gave Ruttenberg the Oscar; without him, everybody would have walked out of the movie, or fallen asleep. He should keep the nomination for trying so damn hard to provide life support, but the Oscar should have gone to another cinematographer.

James Wong Howe's work on *Algiers* is problematic, as some of the film was lifted entirely from the French original, and other scenes are mere copies. One wonders if Howe was nominated for his own excellent work, or for those outdoor scenes of the Casbah from the French version. After watching *Algiers* first, I then ran *Pepe le Moko* side by side, starting and stopping when necessary. Let's compare the first few minutes of each. The films both open in police headquarters, looking at a map and dollying out slowly (the American map is more elaborate; also, the American version begins after a written explanation of the Casbah and Pepe Le Moko). As the cameras dolly out to the left, we see the police in a very similar office, although posed somewhat differently – but the camera moves are nearly identical. But then the next few

---

[60] Right before going to press, I read Andrew Sarris' *"You Ain't Heard Nothin' Yet": The American Talking Film, History & Memory, 1927-1949*. A very readable summation of his cinematic judgments at the end of his life, the book also served to confirm many of my own independently drawn conclusions. Among them, that MGM wasn't all it was cracked up to be: "Metro was clearly the most popular (box-office grosses) and most prestigious (Oscars) of all the studios, and yet its standing among film scholars, historians, and cultists is quite shaky indeed." Sarris goes on to defend MGM somewhat, but the consensus is clear: MGM may have had the all the stars in heaven, but they could have used a few touches of hell now and then to liven them up. P. 22-23.

shots differ substantially: Howe's work is fuzzier, while the original is sharp; then again, the French film has been restored for the Criterion Collection, as opposed to a standard print for *Algiers*. The original cuts back and forth, framing the actors' faces in more compelling ways, while the American remake tends to be more mundane with characters we aren't going to see much – but when it comes to Inspector Slimane, who is hunting Pepe with careful intelligence, Howe's camera lingers on him, signaling to the audience his importance. I rather think this is due to the direction, rather than the cinematographer, but at this remove, who can tell? Knowing how accomplished Howe was, I'm inclined to give him the benefit of the doubt over the occasional imitations. At the fence's office, Howe's version is darker, more atmospheric, and more romantic than the original. In the final summation, the two versions each have their different visual attractions, even as the American remake lifts what it wants from the original. Howe's nomination was earned.

Ernest Miller and Harry Wild were nominated for *Army Girl* (see Best Score above for more on this picture). Ernest Miller photographed dozens of westerns for Republic; Harry Wild would begin his career that way, but end up shooting *Gentlemen Prefer Blondes* and *Son of Paleface*. Their work on *Army Girl* shows the expertise they built shooting on the cheap, finding ways with the camera to make the most of the low budgets Republic gave them. The obstacle course between the tank and the horses is particularly well done, given the action emphasis Republic Pictures always had. Miller and Wild do a decent imitation of Frank Capra's way of filming love scenes as well. They should keep their nomination.

Cecil B. DeMille once again used Victor Milner to shoot one of his historical epics, this time a tale of pirates and American history during the War of 1812, in *The Buccaneer*, starring Fredric March as Jean Lafitte.[61] Milner does his usual excellent job, bringing DeMille's version of the past alive, albeit in a kind of glowing romanticism few would see as realistic today. To a degree, this kind of luminosity is overdone, particularly when filming some very ugly pirates (including a charismatic, comic Akim Tamiroff). Milner's camera roams in interesting ways as well, as when he has it circling about the room when March tries to convince his pirates to support America against the British. Milner shoots his battle scenes as well as anybody did in the Thirties (other than John Ford's cinematographers). The sword fight in the jail isn't

---

[61] DeMille's son-in-law Anthony Quinn would remake the film in the late Fifties; he has a bit part as one of the pirates in this first version.

anywhere near the thrills of *The Adventures of Robin Hood*, but it still satisfies the eye – or rather, how Milner films the prisoners' reactions while March fights as if he's stuck in molasses. The night scenes in the swamp have a curious dark bluish tinge I can't recall seeing other than in silent films. Milner deserves the nomination.

As does Ernest Haller for *Jezebel*. Haller brings a wonderful use of tracking shots to this southern tale, instilling in the story some much-needed vitality, particularly when Bette Davis isn't front and center. Indeed, Haller has one of the most mobile cameras I've seen up to this point (although much of that motion may be Wyler's artistic vision as well). What is more, Haller does something quite remarkable, and akin to what Lee Garmes and Josef von Sternberg did for Marlene Dietrich: he takes a very odd looking woman and brings out her beauty to the point of astonishment. Bette Davis has never looked more real, and yet she is here a vision of beauty. Haller should be given much of the credit – and a nomination (Haller would go on to *Gone with the Wind*, *Rebel Without a Cause*, and many other classics).

Joseph Valentine's work on the Deanna Durbin vehicle *Mad About Music* is an odd one to pick. Durbin's movies were fairly low-budget and focused on watching her sing, with little reason to splurge on camerawork. *Mad About Music* is no exception. Average, at best. No nomination should be given to a man who would do far better working with Alfred Hitchcock later.

Merrily We Live has an extremely bright palette of glowing whites. Norbert Brodine would go on to shoot *Of Mice and Men* and *Kiss of Death*. Here, so much is harshly lit I felt like I needed sunglasses. No nomination for hurting my eyes.

J. Peverell Marley shot a huge variety of films over his career, from the Basil Rathbone *The Hound of the Baskervilles* to Vincent Price's *The House of Wax*. In *Suez*, he performs solid work, with a camera that moves and rolls more than most did in this period. Nothing striking emerges, no single image to burn into the eye. We simply get competence with an advance of technical know-how, with little to inspire. Marley should keep his nomination, as a sign of that mastery of technique, but the statue should only go to the artist who moves beyond mere efficiency.

Vivacious Lady stars Ginger Rogers as a nightclub entertainer who falls in love with Professor Jimmy Stewart, whose family and former fiancée then make trouble for the pair. George Stevens directed this screwball comedy, which showcases Stewart approaching his true screen presence, and Rogers moving away from being second banana to Fred Astaire. A fun movie, overall, although parts drag; the most famous scene of the film is the catfight between Rogers and Stewart's former intended. As for the camerawork by Robert de Grasse, it's competent, although hardly inspired (he only had one great film, *The Body Snatcher*, before heading into series television). What may have impressed back in 1938 is the occasional fluidity of de Grasse's rolling close-ups; we tend to forget how hard such things were to accomplish back then. When Rogers is leaving Stewart, de Grasse's use of shadows appropriately reflects the darkening emotional palette. The nomination should stay for those touches, even if the film as a whole doesn't look much better than a typical TV-movie today.

You Can't Take It with You is the least distinctive of all of Capra's great black and white films. Cinematographer Joseph Walker was capable of so much more visually, instead of what looks and feels like a filmed play. Competent, yes; Oscar-worthy, no.

Leon Shamroy's camerawork on *The Young in Heart* is eminently serviceable. He would only really blossom as a cinematographer in color, including *Leave Her to Heaven, The King and I,* and *Cleopatra*. Shamroy overdoes the fog a bit, but he is very fond of reflection – the mirror kind. Surfaces are often highly polished, from the table Roland Young looks at to straighten his tie, to the ceiling of the nightclub showing the dancers in double vision. The nomination should stay.

As for the un-nominated films, two great choices were ignored.

Sol Polito's work on *Angels with Dirty Faces* couldn't be better, although I suspect director Michael Curtiz was behind many of the shots. As pointed out above (in Best Actor, Best Director, and Best Picture), the movie uses extensive shadows, dynamic camera moves, and stunning close-ups to create a unique look. The final scene on Death Row is a textbook example of how to film a scene with complexity and sophistication, while not sacrificing style for substance. If only the Academy had seen what was right in front of their faces, and nominated Polito.

But then again, they did ignore his work on *The Adventures of Robin Hood*. Somebody must have had it in for the Italians – Sol Polito and Tony Gaudio both got shafted. What glorious Technicolor! For the first time, we see what true colors are. Even a year later, in *Gone with the Wind*, Tara can't come close to this brashly beautiful, vibrant film. I compared the two restored versions on DVD, and honestly, there is no comparison. As Roger Ebert has said so pithily, "The result is a film that justifies the trademark Glorious Technicolor."[cxxxv] From the opening illuminated page of background, to our first sight of Basil Rathbone and Errol Flynn, to almost every single frame of the film, I could not help feeling as if I had been color blind before seeing it. The only logical explanation for why the Academy ignored it can only be that they were blind or blinkered by studio politics, which may have been the same thing when it came to artistic judgments. Sol Polito and Tony Gaudio not only should have been nominated; they should have won the Oscar for Best Cinematography.

Best Song: Ralph Rainger and Leo Robin's "Thanks for the Memory" won from *The Big Broadcast of 1938*, over Irving Berlin's "Now It Can Be Told" from *Alexander's Ragtime Band*, as well as Berlin's "Change Partners" from *Carefree*; Lionel Newman and Arthur Quenzer's "The Cowboy and the Lady" from *The Cowboy and the Lady*; Harry Warren and Johnny Mercer's "Jeepers Creepers" from *Going Places*; Ben Oakland and Oscar Hammerstein II's "A Mist over the Moon" from *The Lady Objects*; Edward Ward, Chet Forrest and Bob Wright's "Always and Always" from *Mannequin*; Phil Charig and Arthur Quenzer's "Merrily We Live" from *Merrily We Live*; Jimmy McHugh and Harold Adamson's "My Own" from *That Certain Age*; and Johnny Marvin's "Dust" from *Under Western Stars*

The Oscar went to "Thanks for the Memory," from *The Big Broadcast of 1938*. One hopes that Bob Hope sent very expensive birthday presents to Ralph Rainger and Leo Robin for giving him his signature song. I can see why the Oscar went to "Thanks for the Memory," and Hope's numerous (and variable) performances of the song continue to spark strong memories from my childhood. Every so often, I even find myself humming it. But we are in another one of those competitions where genius beats out excellence (as opposed to the times when mediocrity wins). If you've never seen *The Big Broadcast of 1938*, you're in for a treat; Hope is great, as are Martha Raye and W.C. Fields (even with the one racist joke he zings off at a seal and Raye). As a child, I loved the big Art Deco boats; as an adult, the comedy brings me back. "Thanks for the Memory" deserved a nomination – but I'm arguing the Oscar should have been saved for an even greater classic.

Berlin was nominated for "Now It Can Be Told," a second-rate song from *Alexander's Ragtime Band*. But even second-rate Berlin can be worth a listen now and then – although I prefer Ella Fitzgerald's 1958 version from *The Irving Berlin Songbook*. The nomination should stay for this minor work from the great Berlin.

Irving Berlin also received a nomination for "Change Partners" from Fred Astaire and Ginger Rogers' eighth pairing, *Carefree*. This time around, Astaire plays a psychiatrist who falls in love with his patient, played by guess who? Ralph Bellamy shows up drunk. Ginger Rogers hates Astaire at first, but then she makes up dreams so that he will keep treating her. "Change Partners" serves the story, as Astaire tries to get Rogers back after hypnotizing her into loving Bellamy instead. The song speaks of the longing for another's lover, a feeling most human beings experience without the successful resolution Astaire achieves. The nomination should stay.

"The Cowboy and the Lady," from the movie of the same name, was written by Lionel Newman and Arthur Quenzer. Fake cowboy music, so unimportant to the movie that they simply use it as background, and let the characters talk all over it. No nomination should have been given.

"Jeepers Creepers" by Johnny Mercer and Harry Warren from *Going Places* would go on to become a standard, unlike most of the songs the Academy nominated (in this, or any other year). The major reason for that? Merely the greatest musician of the twentieth century: Mr. Louis Armstrong. Infamously, *Going Places* has him singing this song to a horse to calm him down – the horse, not Satchmo. Sadly, Hollywood rarely used Armstrong effectively, due to racism. The nomination can stay, although I would recommend the performance Louis Armstrong gives with Jack Teagarden on a live TV performance in 1958.[cxxxvi]

Although I am no lady, I too seriously object to "A Mist over the Moon" from *The Lady Objects*. I suggest this is the worst song of the year – pompous, fake, and pseudo-romantic. I can't believe Oscar Hammerstein II wrote the lyrics to this; or maybe I can – I've long suspected Richard Rodgers was the reason we listen to any of Hammerstein's lyrics. No nomination should have ever been given for this. I need to go clean my ears out now; somebody crapped in there.

"Merrily We Live" from *Merrily We Live* tries to be merry, but all it is, is fake Hollywood swing, the musical equivalent of saying "have a nice day" and not really meaning it, or meriting a nomination.

"Always and Always" from *Mannequin* isn't served well by Joan Crawford, who isn't known for her singing (and for good reason, since it's an eminently forgettable voice). But more so, the song is just a piece of piffle about eternal love, with no memorable melody or lyrics. That MGM's music department thought this was the best they could do still makes me cringe out of embarrassment for them – for just one better example, how about Judy Garland singing "Zing Went the Strings of My Heart" for starters? No nomination should be given for bad taste.

Deanna Durbin strikes again with "My Own," from *That Certain Age* (the song was written by Jimmy McHugh and Harold Adamson). The song serves Durbin well; I doubt anybody has wanted to hear it since. "My Own" is another forgettable love song with no real redeeming values other than Durbin's voice. Not a good nomination.

"Dust" by Johnny Marvin shows up in the Roy Rogers film *Under Western Stars*. I have a childhood fondness for Rogers, not from watching his films, but from living near him on the weekends up in Apple

Valley in the high desert of Southern California. He was a true gentleman, who couldn't have been nicer to his young fans (my younger cousin had a massive crush on him that reduced her to speechlessness every time she saw him). The Roy Rogers Museum was a special treat, although seeing Rogers' horse Trigger and his dog Bullet stuffed was creepy at first. Here, he plays a cowboy running for Congress, trying to help his constituents deal with drought and corrupt water companies. "Dust" is a serious song outlining the troubles of the American farmer and rancher, in a prayer and lament for rain. The nomination should stay for this unusual, earnest song, even if I don't expect anybody to go about humming it.

As for the snubs, the Academy omitted some great songs, but part of the reason was the shift in nomination rules: in an attempt to be egalitarian, they limited each studio's music department to the submission of a single song. I'm all in favor of democracy in love, politics, and marriage, but when it comes to parenthood, teaching, and art, democracy has no place. Parenthood and teaching requires benevolent dictatorship, but art requires a meritocracy. This submission process lasted from 1938 to 1945, and succeeded in producing some real howlers, both in terms of what they nominated, and in what they omitted. Here's a few of what they left out, all three of which should have been nominated: Harry Warren and Johnny Mercer's "You Must Have Been a Beautiful Baby" from *Hard to Get*, Hoagy Carmichael and Frank Loesser's "Two Sleepy People" from *Thanks for the Memory* and (hold onto your jaws), the Gershwin's "Our Love Is Here to Stay" from *The Goldwyn Follies*.

Dick Powell stars in *Hard to Get*, and "You Must Have Been a Beautiful Baby" was written for him, with Mercer's amusing lyrics ("when you were only to startin', to go to kindergarten"). Powell's version was rapidly eclipsed by Bing Crosby's cover, which may explain why the studio bypassed this song (that, and Powell's film wasn't a hit).

Hoagy Carmichael, the composer of "Stardust" and many other classics, got together with Frank Loesser (best known for *Guys and Dolls*), and the amusing "Two Sleepy People" resulted for Bob Hope, the star of *Thanks for the Memory*. Gee, there's a surprise: Hollywood rushing out a film to capitalize on success; "Two Sleepy People" is also intended as a clone of "Thanks for the Memory." My feelings about "Two Sleepy People" are tied to a version Christopher Lloyd sang as the Reverend Jim on *Taxi*, so I keep hearing Lloyd's unmistakable voice whenever I think of this song; I freely admit I'm prejudiced because of how much that made me laugh. But the song has been covered numerous times as a standard, so clearly I'm not alone. The movie is completely forgotten except for this one song.

The same is not true of *The Goldwyn Follies*, a musical monstrosity Samuel Goldwyn concocted that is infamous for a number of reasons: this was George Gershwin's last assignment, as he died of a brain tumor during filming (Vernon Duke helped Ira finish); George Balanchine came in and choreographed a ballet for Gershwin's *An American in Paris*, only to have Goldwyn hate it and cut the piece before it was filmed; Goldwyn fell in love with Zorina, his leading lady, who fell in love with Balanchine instead; the Ritz Brothers had a ball creating mayhem; Edgar Bergen shows up with some other dummies. In the middle of it all, "Our Love Is Here to Stay" quietly made its fabulous way into the world, where it has remained as one of the greatest songs ever written. Kenny Baker introduced the song; Baker is best known today for rising to stardom on the Jack Benny show, as well as appearing in the Marx Brothers' *At the Circus*. He has a nice crooner voice, sounding mostly like Dick Powell, although Baker could sing opera (to a small degree). The song itself, and not the performance, should be the point, and this song has it all: a great melody and compelling lyrics, and that indefinable quality of grace and permanence that marks the classic American song: "But oh, my dear, our love is here to stay / Together we're going a long, long way / In time the Rockies may tumble, Gibraltar may crumble / They're only made of clay / But our love is here to stay." Enchanting! "Our Love Is Here to Stay" should have been nominated for Best Song, and should have won the Oscar as well.

Best Short Subject (Cartoon): Disney continued his domination of this category, picking up four out of the five nominations: *Ferdinand the Bull, The Brave Little Tailor, Good Scouts*, and *Mother Goose Goes Hollywood*. The Fleischer Studio got the last nomination with *Hunky and Spunky*.[62]

Disney couldn't have done any better this year. *The Brave Little Tailor* is one of the most famous Mickey Mouse cartoons, as Mickey has to slay the giant to win the hand of Minnie. Fun stuff, although Pluto talking bugged me. *Good Scouts* starred Donald Duck and his nephews; this is the one with the ketchup routine, the bear, and a geyser with Donald's rear end stuck in it.[63] *Mother Goose Goes Hollywood* parodies a number of Hollywood stars as Mother Goose characters: among them, Katharine Hepburn as Little Bo Peep; the Marx Brothers as Old King

---

[62] As for *Hunky and Spunky*: two cute donkeys, anybody, with really, really, really annoying voices? I didn't think so. No nomination for the Fleischers.
[63] Am I the only one who has ever noticed Disney's obsession with butt humor?

Cole's fiddlers three; Charles Laughton, Spencer Tracy, and Freddy Bartholomew as the three men in a tub; W.C. Fields as Humpty Dumpty; Laurel and Hardy as Simple Simons, and so forth. We do get some unfortunate blackface jokes, but the overall humor isn't at a particularly high level regardless. No nomination for that one, Mr. Disney, but you did win for *Ferdinand the Bull*, based on the classic children's book by Munro Leaf and Robert Lawson. One of the studio's most fully realized stories, the animators had fun using caricatures of themselves – and Walt Disney – as the bullfighters. The cartoon still works beautifully today, and fully deserved its Oscar...were it not for a little piece of revolution the Academy ignored.

Disney had invented the madcap style of animation, then largely abandoned it in the fruitful quest for realism and depth. The rest of Hollywood had to choose between those two paths as well, with varying degrees of success. But Warner Brothers' animation unit would eventually overtake Disney in the short cartoon category, precisely because they took up the manic flag and carried it as far as it could go under the leadership of men like Bob Clampett, Tex Avery, Friz Freleng and Chuck Jones. As Disney moved his true creativity into the features, Warners took over his leadership in the shorts, beginning with one groundbreaking cartoon.

In 1938, Clampett gave the world *Porky in Wackyland*, which broke every rule in the book in the search for zany humor. The opening credits get walked over by a newspaper boy, hawking the daily paper with news of Porky hunting for the do-do bird. Chuck Jones once said that the animation unit known as Termite Terrace wasn't making cartoons for kids; they were making them for themselves. Wackyland is a place for jokes that kids could laugh at, but only adults would truly get (the secret behind the durability of the classic Warner cartoons of the Forties and Fifties). Salvador Dali would have been proud to invent Wackyland, but Clampett got there first. Many of the classic Warner gags begin here; my favorite is the pencil that can draw real things. *Porky in Wackyland* should have been nominated, and as the harbinger of things to come, it should have won for Best Cartoon.

CHAPTER TWELVE: 1940 AWARDS
12th Show

Movies released in 1939

1939 is commonly thought of as the greatest year in Hollywood's history; at the very least, 1939 brought the studio system to its very heights. As historian Larry Swindell has put it, "Taken all together, the films of 1939 are the best argument for the studio system."[cxxxvii] We have an embarrassment of riches in this annus mirabilis, and the difficulties of nomination and awards radically increase when there are so many losing movies that in other years would have swept the Oscars. Want to know how great 1939 is? Here is a *partial* list of the films that were NOT nominated for Best Picture: *Beau Geste, Destry Rides Again, Drums Along the Mohawk, The Four Feathers, Gunga Din, The Hound of the Baskervilles, The Hunchback of Notre Dame, Only Angels Have Wings, The Private Lives of Elizabeth and Essex, The Roaring Twenties, The Women, You Can't Cheat an Honest Man,* and *Young Mr. Lincoln*.[64]

---

[64] One of the greatest films ever made, Jean Renoir's *The Rules of the Game*, was made and released in France in 1939, but it was not released in the United States until 1950 and not in restored form or widely until 1961. *Gone with the Wind* should be grateful for this.

The six-hundred-pound gorilla of 1939, of course, is *Gone with the Wind*, a problematic, sweeping, inescapable film masterpiece that has never ceased both to infuriate and fascinate viewers since it was first taken up by David O. Selznick as a project. But other movies, in their way, are just as influential (or even more so), including *Mr. Smith Goes to Washington* (the quintessential film about American politics and ideals), *Stagecoach* (the first modern Western), *The Wizard of Oz* (the best fantasy musical ever made), *Ninotchka* (a model for romantic comedy), and *Gunga Din* (a mold for the comic adventure tale). By any reckoning, however, *Gone with the Wind* remains the bedrock of the argument that 1939 is the greatest year ever, as the epic by which all other epics get judged. Truly a magnificent year – and one that caused me to tear out what little hair I have left trying to navigate safely through its many attractions.

THE SCENE OF THE CRIME:

On February 29, 1940, Hollywood gathered to celebrate their fabulous achievements of 1939. For a change of pace, they switched from the Biltmore back to the original venue, the Cocoanut Grove at the Ambassador Hotel. Bob Hope began the first of a record eighteen times as host of the Oscars. Frank Capra filmed the event for the first time; Warner Brothers had paid a cash-strapped Academy $30,000 for the rights.

The *Los Angeles Times* broke its word and released the names of the winners in its 8:45 edition. Since the awards weren't given out until 11:00 p.m., most of the nominees knew they had lost, forcing them to paste smiles on their faces. As a result, beginning the next year, all of the results would be kept secret by Price, Waterhouse.

1939 was David O. Selznick's night. As host Bob Hope joked, "What a wonderful thing, this benefit for David Selznick." Not only did *Gone with the Wind* sweep most of the awards, but Selznick received the Thalberg Award.

Judy Garland got a special Oscar for starring in *The Wizard of Oz*. She then sang "Over the Rainbow," which won for Best Song.

Legend has it the greatest outrage of the night was when Clark Gable was passed over for the role of his lifetime, Rhett Butler. When his wife Carole Lombard consoled him by saying they would bring one home next year, he said he would never get another chance. She then snapped back, "Not you, you self-centered bastard. I mean me!"

Several new awards appeared. Best Cinematography was split into separate categories for Color and Black & White (they would eventually do the same for Best Art Direction). The Academy also introduced Special Effects as a new category.

WHAT THEY GOT RIGHT:

Best Supporting Actress: Hattie McDaniel won for *Gone with the Wind*, over Edna May Oliver, *Drums Along the Mohawk*; Olivia de Havilland, *Gone with the Wind*; Maria Ouspenskaya, *Love Affair*; and Geraldine Fitzgerald, *Wuthering Heights*

For me, watching *Gone with the Wind* has been problematic, as the film both thrills and frustrates. Great art often does that, and apparently, I'm not alone in having trouble with the movie. Molly Haskell has written an insightful book about all things *Gone with the Wind*, called *Frankly, My Dear: Gone with the Wind Revisited*. Haskell makes the case for the universal experience of those who watch this movie: "For those of us who fell under its spell, the range of emotions attached to the film fluctuate over time with the predictable volatility of a love affair and its aftermath, in my own case what we might clinically designate as the Seven Stages of *Gone with the Wind*: Love, Identification, Dependency, Resentment, Embarrassment, Indifference, and then something like Half-Love again, a more grown-up affectation informed by a film lover's appreciation of the small miracle by which a mere 'woman's film' with a heroine who never quite outgrows adolescence was transfigured into something much larger, something profoundly American, a canvas that contains, if not Walt Whitman's multitudes, at least multiple perspectives."[cxxxviii]

The later disdainful stages come when we realize how racist the film is. To suggest that *Gone with the Wind* isn't inherently racist is to ignore the celebration of the antebellum world, in which slavery was a great goodness, and the loss of it a tragedy from which America supposedly never recovered – or so the movie would have you believe. *Birth of a Nation* trumpets the same argument, going so far as to make the Ku Klux Klan the heroes. The second half of *Gone with the Wind*, after the slaves are freed, is considerably harder to swallow in the ugly portrayals of those formerly in bondage who buy into the Republican political system, and in the hostility the film has for Yankee carpetbaggers. The primary, elemental force mitigating that racist argument is Hattie McDaniel. The figure of the Mammy in the film, and in southern history, remains as central as any other single factor in understanding race, prejudice, and the intensely misunderstood and interconnected hatreds and passions that grow the fouler weeds of this, our American life. As Haskell points out, "It's easy for someone who's never lived in the South to take a cynical view of this bond between black and white, but no one in good faith can believe it doesn't exist. Likenesses, in the form of rhythms, speech, a great many common virtues and defects, the caring that springs naturally from intimacy – these have to be acknowledged alongside the evils of slavery, chronic racism, and segregation. Under slavery, blacks and whites grew up alongside and intertwined with one another like vines on a tree, their roles mutually defined, their status mutually dependent." cxxxix

The Mammy was a real figure, as black slave women were entrusted with raising the children of the rich, and were often portrayed in literature as the important, influential women they were (see, for example, the character of Dilsey in Faulkner's works). Yet Mammy and the house slaves at Tara stick by Scarlett and the O'Hara family no matter what, reasserting their dominant role in the world of blacks, and supporting in turn white dominance over them. *Gone with the Wind*, for better or worse, continues to form many of these opinions in those who watch it, reinforcing and challenging prejudices simultaneously. To counter all that, you must watch Hattie McDaniel's eyes. As I heard one black commentator say years ago, what you see in them is "stupid white people." We can spot that from the very first sight and sound of McDaniel, sticking her head out of the upstairs window, ordering with a strong voice of command that Scarlett O'Hara come in, and reminding her of her social responsibilities. Throughout the movie, McDaniel's voice of authority is constant; she may at times be ignored, but she is rarely disputed as knowing what the right thing to do is. One of the most interesting facets of her performance lies in the flirtation with Clark Gable, in the scene with the red petticoats. Black civil rights activists protested against *Gone with the Wind*, and the black actors cast in it. But as Hattie McDaniel famously said, "I would rather make seven hundred dollars a week playing a maid than seven dollars being one." She also said, "What do you expect me to play? Rhett Butler's wife?"cxl Hattie McDaniel is every bit the match for Vivien Leigh and Clark Gable, and that is saying a great deal. As Haskell puts it, "Mammy is, of course, the presiding genius, the soul of the family, its jealous guardian, Scarlett's conscience and scold, the only one who understands *and* stands up to her."cxli Hattie McDaniel fully deserved a nomination, and the Oscar, for a strong, compelling performance that arguably is the best in *Gone with the Wind*.

As for Olivia de Havilland, I have always found Melanie to be a warm, loving human being, if perhaps a little too goody two-shoes for my full acceptance. Her constant sense of noble sacrifice, and of reading Scarlett's behaviors in a false positive light, provides a dramatic counterpoint to Scarlett's selfishness and passions. De Havilland would rarely play to this level of purity again, but she carries it off as few other actresses ever could. She deserved the nomination.

Drums Along the Mohawk was John Ford's Revolutionary War movie, depicting colonial frontier life in the wilds of New York. Ford was running on full throttle in 1939 and 1940, making *Stagecoach*, but also directing three films with Henry Fonda: *Young Mr. Lincoln* and *The Grapes of Wrath* sandwich *Drums Along the Mohawk*. *Drums* may be the weakest of those four films, and yet, it is the only one shot in color (see Best Cinematography (Color) below for more). Henry Fonda and Claudette Colbert are the young farmer and his wife; nominee Edna May Oliver, who was always a joy to watch, plays a crotchety old widow who takes them in after they lose their home. The scene where she bullies two drunken Indians burning her house down into carrying her bed out is memorable. Oliver also gets a great death scene to chew on, as she is shot down by an Indian arrow. The nomination should stay for this classic character actress.

Maria Ouspenskaya plays Charles Boyer's grandmother in *Love Affair* –the same role, as Warren Beatty's aunt, would be Katharine Hepburn's last turn on the screen. Ouspenskaya is still most famous today as the gypsy in *The Wolf Man*, but here, she is every bit the sweet little old lady we all wish our grandmothers could be. The joyous smile she gives Boyer at seeing him again has rarely been matched by any actress. Her character is the moral hinge of the movie, the voice of the well-lived life. She plays the minor but critical role beautifully, as she also does the tough old bird, the Maharina with a cigarette, in *The Rains Came*. I would have nominated her if the Academy hadn't.

In *Wuthering Heights*, Geraldine Fitzgerald plays Isabella, whom Heathcliff marries as a means of revenge against her brother and Catherine. Fitzgerald is convincing as the innocent young girl, turning to Heathcliff out of loneliness, a desire to defy her brother, and young infatuation. When she looks into the mirror after her first dance with Heathcliff, one can see the surprise at the love she feels without a single word from Fitzgerald. Her transformation from the giddy girl in love to the unhappy wife of Heathcliff is quietly effective. A very good nomination, for what may be the best acting in the movie (see below for more in Best Picture, Best Actor, Best Cinematography (Black & White), Best Writing (Screenplay) and Best Original Score).

As for those who should have been nominated, they include Greer Garson in *Goodbye, Mr. Chips* (see Best Actress below for why) and Margaret Hamilton for *The Wizard of Oz*. Hamilton had a face like a hatchet, and the capacity to hurl insolence and recrimination better than any other character actor of the Thirties. In the dual role of Elvira Gulch and the Wicked Witch, she personifies the evils of those with power asserting themselves merely because they can. Her evil laugh may be the best evil laugh ever. Her cries of "I'll get you, my little pretty, and your little dog too!" have haunted childhood nightmares for generations. Hamilton should have been nominated.

I would also add that Bette Davis could have easily received a nomination for Best Supporting Actress as the mad Empress Carlota in *Juarez*. Watching her go mental is a kooky treat. She really deserves a nomination (see Best Cinematography (Black & White) for more).

Best Supporting Actor: Thomas Mitchell won for *Stagecoach*, over Brian Donlevy, *Beau Geste*; Brian Aherne, *Juarez*; Harry Carey, *Mr. Smith Goes to Washington*; and Claude Rains, *Mr. Smith Goes to Washington*.

Thomas Mitchell won for *Stagecoach*, a richly deserved award for a role he had largely played already in *The Hurricane* two years before (and would play again elsewhere), but which this time works beautifully as the drunken doctor who carries the moral messages of the film. By evoking morality from the mouth of the drunkard, director John Ford places Mitchell in the same position as one of Shakespeare's fools, the ones who can speak the truth and get away with it. Mitchell is absolutely marvelous in the role, and nowhere more so than in the childbirth scene, wherein he has to sober up and become a doctor in more than name (see Best Picture and numerous categories below for more). Mitchell also delivers the final ironic summation of the film, as he and the sheriff send off the young lovers: "Well, they're saved from the blessings of civilization." Mitchell definitely deserved the Oscar, especially when you also consider the rest of his 1939 performances: his grounded flier in *Only Angels Have Wings*, the crazed father in *Gone with the Wind*, the king of beggars in *The Hunchback of Notre Dame*, and his touchingly comic reporter in *Mr. Smith Goes to Washington*.

Brian Donlevy was nominated for *Beau Geste*, directed by William Wellman, which stars Gary Cooper in this much-filmed tale of the French Foreign Legion. Donlevy plays Sergeant Markoff, a cruel sadist out to acquire a sapphire from the three Geste brothers. The movie opens with the arrival of a relief unit, to find a fort seemingly manned by nothing but dead men; a letter reveals the story in flashback. An enjoyable action film, *Beau Geste* does expect us to swallow a number of silly plot turns, not the least of which is that all three brothers would join the French Foreign Legion, that they would end up in the same unit, and that the Arabs would cooperate by attacking repeatedly (and stupidly). Donlevy performs intensely as Markoff, but it's rather a one-note performance not really worthy of an Oscar nod.

Brian Aherne was nominated for playing the Emperor Maximilian in *Juarez*, which stars Paul Muni as Benito Juarez and Bette Davis as the Empress Carlota. Aherne took a page from Muni's book, and put on a beard to play a historical figure; apparently, only one beard could be had, because Muni went without one playing Benito Juarez. Aherne had been playing romantic leads before this; Emperor Maximilian was an opportunity to prove he was capable of more, and he succeeded in capturing an Oscar nomination. Aherne dug playing the clothes horse; he preens like a peacock in the role. The film itself isn't that interesting, since we keep cutting back and forth between Muni and Aherne, with no interaction. John Huston worked on the screenplay, but it's hard to see his ironic touch here. Mostly, the film is memorable for Bette Davis going crazy. Aherne does a respectable job, particularly in the kind of quiet civilized tones he adopts; he should keep the nomination for the high point of his acting career.

Harry Carey had been a major silent film star, and a particular friend of John Ford, who later directed Carey's son repeatedly. By the sound era, Carey's craggy voice proved to be a match for his craggy face, and he moved into character parts with great success – and never more so than in *Mr. Smith Goes to Washington*, the most memorable moment of his later career. As the President of the Senate, Carey invests his role with an assumed dignitas, an inherent sense of justice and fair play – and a disguised sense of humor. As he watches over the unfolding events like a judge in a courtroom, Carey allows Jimmy Stewart's Jefferson Smith to have his day telling his story. Without Carey making that rather unlikely chance possible, nobody would believe this movie. Carey richly deserves his nomination, and were it not for Thomas Mitchell, he should have won the Oscar.

Claude Rains was also up for his role as the senator with the noble facade and the broken soul in *Mr. Smith Goes to Washington*. As Jimmy Stewart's hero, Rains is forced to confront his loss of ideals, and the blackness of his soul. Rains does the smooth-tongued orator beautifully, although I've always found his breakdown and attempted suicide at the end to be a bit too much deus ex machina, but other than that flaw due to the screenplay, Rains provides a subtle performance which deserved this nomination.

The Academy could have just as easily nominated others, including all four male supporting actors from *The Wizard of Oz*. Dorothy's three companions never made a more memorable performance or a better film: Ray Bolger as the Scarecrow, Jack Haley as the Tin Woodsman, and Bert Lahr as the Cowardly Lion. Each of them developed a distinctive dance style, movement, and vocal inflection for their characters, aided by the astonishing makeup and costumes. Bolger's "If I Only Had a Brain" and Bert Lahr's "If I Were King of the Forest" never fail to entertain. In addition, Frank Morgan had a perfect opportunity for his bumbling authority figure in the Wizard, as well as Professor Marvel. If for nothing else other than a gesture of respect, all four of them should have been nominated.

Bela Lugosi created his second unforgettable character in Ygor in *Son of Frankenstein*. Along with his Dracula, the broken-necked hunchback Ygor has proven to be a truly unique character, and one that may be a more effective cinematic performance than the Count. Ygor's broken, twisted face is a mirror of the German expressionist sets (see Best Art Direction below). The sheer malevolence of Lugosi's Ygor is only matched by his grotesqueness and desire for revenge; unlike many screen villains, Ygor is completely believable, to the point of stealing the film from Karloff, who is reduced to a giant shaggy hound at Lugosi's command. He also had a fine role in Ernst Lubitsch's *Ninotchka*, in what may be his last non-horror film, as Razinin, the Communist commissar. Lugosi should have received a nomination for Best Supporting Actor – and if you don't think so, try for a few minutes to walk and talk like Ygor, and see how hard it is not to descend into parody.

Best Writing (Original Story): Lewis R. Foster won for *Mr. Smith Goes to Washington*, over Felix Jackson, *Bachelor Mother*; Mildred Cram and Leo McCarey, *Love Affair*; Melchior Lengyel, *Ninotchka*; and Lamar Trotti, *Young Mr. Lincoln*

We're not likely to get a better story than *Mr. Smith Goes to Washington*, in this or many other years. While elements of the plot have been used before, notably in *Mr. Deeds Goes to Town*, in *Mr. Smith* they were brought to their peak. Actually, *Mr. Smith* was conceived as a sequel to *Mr. Deeds*, and only Cooper's unavailability prevented that, which helps explain the similarities and continuities between the two films. I've often told students that no one has the right to call themselves an American until they've seen *Mr. Smith Goes to Washington*, which shows better than any other single American creation the ideals for which we strive, even while it recognizes how often they are betrayed. Lewis Foster came up with an excellent examination of American political ideals clashing with political realities – and made the ideals the victor. I couldn't have chosen a better winner than the Academy did in this category. Foster would end up writing Disney's *Zorro* and other television adventure tales; never would he again reach these artistic heights.

Bachelor Mother, directed by Garson Kanin, stars Ginger Rogers as a single girl everyone thinks is the mother of an abandoned baby. *Bachelor Mother* was her first film after breaking off her partnership with Fred Astaire. David Niven co-stars as the romantic lead, finally finding his niche as an actor with comic qualities; Charles Coburn provides one of his many fine performances as Niven's father. Felix Jackson's story had already been made into a German film; Norman Krasna does a good job adapting it under the Production Code. Jackson is better known for writing the story and screenplay for *Destry Rides Again*; he later became a producer. *Bachelor Mother* takes a case of mistaken identity and spins it into a romance; the movie is fun, and well worth seeing. The nomination should stay.

Mildred Cram and Leo McCarey were nominated for *Love Affair*, the comic but weepy look at a love almost thwarted by fiancées and a car accident. Delmer Daves and Donald Ogden Stewart wrote the screenplay; Leo McCarey's remake of his own film as *An Affair to Remember* has been enshrined in our romantic consciousness by *Sleepless in Seattle*. What appears to be a light romance with lots of froth turns dark when the Irene Dunne/Deborah Kerr character gets hit by a car on her way to meet Charles Boyer/Cary Grant. True love triumphs, but the dilemma has always felt to me to be creaky, artificial and all too convenient. Because I have been threatened with bodily harm over this one, I will not take that statement to its logical conclusion. McCarey, like Shakespeare, was very fond of mixing tragedy with comedy; few writer-directors have ever matched him in that department. The nomination should stay for this durable romantic tale.

Melchior Lengyel's story of *Ninotchka* contains Greta Garbo's last great performance, and remains her only good comedy – and my favorite Garbo movie. Directed by Ernst Lubitsch, and co-starring Melvyn Douglas, *Ninotchka* may also be the best anti-Communist argument ever made: come to Paris, fall in love, and be alive – or return to Siberia and live a cold existence, literally and metaphorically. How do I know this to be true? The Soviet Union banned it immediately. Melchior Lengyel's original story touts the wonders of democracy and capitalism in the tangible freedoms the West nurtures; he pitched it in exactly three lines: "Russian girl saturated with Bolshevist ideals goes to fearful, Capitalistic, monopolistic Paris. She meets romance and has an uproarious good time. Capitalism not so bad after all."[cxlii] Lengyel was a Hungarian who rose to literary prominence in Germany, then fled to America in 1935, where his friend Lubitsch was waiting. Lengyel provided the stories for both this movie and *To Be or Not to Be*. Good friend, no? Lengyel deserved his Oscar nomination.

In *Young Mr. Lincoln*, the story is almost wholly constructed out of fictional and apocryphal events, rather than from the known events of Lincoln's life (other than that he ran a store, worked as a lawyer, and so forth). What we have here is not some pompous attempt to tell the truth (and then lie to us), but an exercise in mythic construction and the revelation of a great man's character. I think of *Young Mr. Lincoln* the same way I think of a folk tale about Paul Bunyan or Pecos Bill, told in the simplest human terms. Approaching the movie with that frame of reference, I have watched *Young Mr. Lincoln* with great joy and satisfaction throughout my life, and always found renewal in each viewing. I am particularly fond of the human images: Lincoln riding the mule with his stovepipe hat and his legs dangling; Lincoln judging the pie contest; Lincoln during the trial, telling his pointed jokes. The most influential scene of all may be when Lincoln prevents the mob from lynching his clients; I suspect *The Ox-Bow Incident* and *To Kill a Mockingbird* both trace their cinematic roots to here. Henry Fonda emphatically did not want to play the part; Ford had to bully him into it. At the heart of this film is Fonda's deeply fulfilled performance, and one I doubt any other actor could have pulled off in 1939. What touches my heart the deepest is the look of great glee on his face when Fonda learns of some books a traveling family would like to trade for some goods. Trotti's screenplay provided the basis for that performance, and a film the equal of anything Ford had made up to this point. Trotti should keep his nomination.

Best Score: Richard Hageman, Frank Harling, John Leipold, and Leo Shuken won for *Stagecoach*, over Roger Edens and George E. Stoll, *Babes in Arms*; Charles Previn, *First Love*; Phil Boutelje and Arthur Lange, *The Great Victor Herbert*; Alfred Newman, for both *The Hunchback of Notre Dame* and *They Shall Have Music*; Lou Forbes, *Intermezzo*; Dimitri Tiomkin, *Mr. Smith Goes to Washington*; Aaron Copland, *Of Mice and Men*; Erich Wolfgang Korngold, *The Private Lives of Elizabeth and Essex*; Cy Feuer, *She Married a Cop*; Louis Silvers, *Swanee River*; and Victor Young, *Way Down South*.

Like the Best Writing (Screenplay) category, what the Academy meant primarily in Best Score was adapting the works others have written for use on the screen – but it did not ban original work outright in this category.[cxliii] I have chosen to tighten up the divisions more than they did, to prevent the double entry of scores in both categories (which happened in 1938 with Franz Waxman's *The Young in Heart*, in 1939 with Aaron Copland's *Of Mice and Men*, and again in 1940 with Copland's *Our Town*). Eventually the Academy would divide the scores up between those for Drama/Comedy and Musicals, and try other categories, before settling into their present configuration, just as they would keep fiddling with the writing categories, due to many of the same issues of originality and adaptation.

Stagecoach has a score that cannot be equaled in its incorporation and extension of American folk songs: the hymn, "Shall We Gather at the River"; the Gold Rush song, "Joe Bowers"; the frontier ballad, "The Trail to Mexico"; Stephen Foster's "Gentle Annie"; bordello songs, including "She Is More to Be Pitied than Censured" and "Up in a Balloon, Boys"; and the 1923 Broadway musical number "I Love You" which plays as the love theme for John Wayne and Claire Trevor.[cxliv] Richard Hageman, Frank Harling, John Leipold, and Leo Shuken worked together, although Hageman seems to have been the primary creative force here, at least on the evidence that Hageman went on to score *The Long Voyage Home, Fort Apache, Three Godfathers, She Wore a Yellow Ribbon*, and *Wagon Master*. *Stagecoach* was the high point of Frank Harling's career, although I have a childish love for his *Flash Gordon* scores. John Leipold also scored Laurel and Hardy's *Flying Deuces* and DeMille's *Union Pacific*. Leo Shuken went on to a full career as an orchestrator, often uncredited, on many John Wayne films, as well as *Roman Holiday, The Magnificent Seven,* and *Butch Cassidy and the Sundance Kid*, among others. Louis Gruenberg was given credit in the film itself, but according to Rudy Behlmer, his contribution was deleted from the final score. Gruenberg composed a number of operas, including an adaptation of Eugene O'Neill's *The Emperor Jones* and many B-film scores, among them *Batman and Robin*, as well as the A-picture *All the King's Men*. Another composer, Gerard Carbonera, should have been included, according to Behlmer.[cxlv] The score for *Stagecoach* is an American classic, and rings in my ears whenever I think of the film. A perfect nomination and win for the Academy, who seem to be developing some taste at last in their musical choices. Nicely done, Academy!

Babes in Arms was adapted from a Rodgers and Hart musical by Roger Edens and George E. Stoll, which puts us once again in the situation of people receiving nominations for music they didn't write, which means it comes down to the invention and originality to which they put the source material. Roger Edens became an integral part of the famous

Arthur Freed production unit which made MGM's most famous musicals in the Forties and Fifties. George Stoll worked at MGM as well, particularly with Judy Garland. Edens and Stoll only kept a few of the Rodgers & Hart songs, and added two new numbers, one by Nacio Herb Brown & Arthur Freed, and the other by Harold Arlen & Yip Harburg. Directed by Busby Berkeley, *Babes in Arms* is the best of the "Hey, kids! Let's put on a show!" genre. Berkeley never really indulges himself with his usual geometric patterns and outrageous imagery. Judy Garland and Mickey Rooney lead this excuse for one musical number after another. Until we get to the show, we barely have a score; then the score exists to string the songs together (including an awful minstrel show). Edens and Stoll were apparently responsible for much of the show, so for that, and despite the minstrelsy, the nomination should stand – by adding the name of Richard Rodgers to the nominees.

Charles Previn was nominated for *First Love*, a Deanna Durbin vehicle retelling the Cinderella story. Durbin is an orphan, graduating from school and moving in with her rich uncle (Eugene Pallette) and aunt, and her beautiful, accomplished, snooty cousin. A very, very young Robert Stack plays the Prince Charming figure. Durbin had turned 18, and Universal wanted to market her as an adult, rather than a child star – so Stack gives her her very first onscreen kiss. Previn provides a bright, cheery, romantic score, which accommodates Durbin's singing, and keeps things moving along. The dance brings a sumptuous sound to the score – and the Strauss waltz medley is done well (although not by Previn). The highlight of the film is an outstanding rendition of "Un Bel Dia" from Puccini's *Madame Butterfly*. A good nomination for Previn.

Phil Boutelje and Arthur Lange rode *The Great Victor Herbert* on the back of Victor Herbert's operettas, played liberally throughout this mediocre biopic. Boutelje was the music director for Paramount and United Artists; Lange ran the MGM music department, and orchestrated both *High Sierra* and *The Maltese Falcon*. I don't find this nomination to be warranted, largely because the film itself is so forgettable; a musical for which the score doesn't convince us of the power of the music isn't worth a nomination. *Stagecoach* is the exact opposite, using existing folk songs and hymns to reinforce and build the narrative. No nomination should have been given for *The Great Victor Herbert*.

Alfred Newman had a very busy, successful year as a composer, including four Academy Award nominations for *The Rains Came, Wuthering Heights, They Shall Have Music*, and *The Hunchback of Notre Dame*. Now, when we consider that in 1939 he also scored *Beau Geste, Young Mr. Lincoln, Drums Along the Mohawk*, and *Gunga Din*, we begin to understand the tremendous range of this man's talent. Here, in the best version of *The Hunchback of Notre Dame*, he serves Charles Laughton's terrific performance and the achingly beautiful Maureen O'Hara in her first American film with a beautiful score. *Hunchback* has been filmed numerous times, most famously with Lon Chaney, Sr.'s silent version, but also with Anthony Quinn doing his best to keep up, and a disturbingly adult animated version from Disney.[65] Newman's score is rich in the music of the period, including the "Ave Maria" of Tomas Luis de Victoria, with church bells and choruses of angelic voices, as well as lively rhythms for the dances and romance. Perhaps the finest musical moments come with Esmeralda displaying mercy to the flogged hunchback by giving him water, in the great assault on Notre Dame, and for Quasimodo in his solitude at the end. Newman does an excellent job, and he deserved this nomination.[66]

In Newman's other nomination for this category, we get an offbeat movie, *They Shall Have Music*, which argues for the value of music schools in guiding young people towards a valued life. The plot, such as it is, brings a runaway to hear Jascha Heifetz; the runaway then joins a music school, and flourishes. William Wyler shot the concert with Heifetz at the end; to this day, the movie attracts devotees of the violinist. The story itself is badly acted and badly filmed otherwise, but Newman's score does an admirable job leading up to the Heifetz appearances, and proves another worthy nomination.

I have but two reasons to watch *Intermezzo* again: Ingrid Bergman, and the way cinematographer Gregg Toland photographs her (see Best Cinematography (Black & White) below). In her first American film, Bergman recreates her 1936 role in the same story, only this time with

---

[65] The sequence where the priest deals with his sexual desires has no place in a film nominally for children, but then, several Disney films, including *Bambi*, have no business being shown to children; many have still not recovered from seeing the death of the mother at too young an age.

[66] David Aspinall does a better job than I summarizing the gifts of this score: "...the brief but nobly understated main title which rises quietly through the fading choral statement of Tomas Luis de Victoria's Ave Maria, which opens the film; the intoxicating Esmeralda theme, introduced teasingly in the Gypsies' cue right after the main title, but receiving its most eloquent statement in the great scene of Quasimodo's flogging and Esmeralda's mercy mission (John Mauceri observed that no modern composer could, or would even try to, get away with Newman's string rubato and glissando for this sequence); the theme for Quasimodo himself, grotesque like the cathedral's gargoyles, yet somehow pathetic at the same time, never receiving a full treatment, but snaking throughout many of the cues; the Hallelujah which accompanies Esmeralda's rescue by Quasimodo (rumored to have been actually composed by Ernst Toch); the earnest and idealistic Gringoire theme; the evocations of Notre Dame cathedral itself, the Victoria Ave Maria intoned with grave sobriety by low strings. On the other hand, the Whipping cue (excised from the soundtrack) and the assault on Notre Dame are merely routine, both thematically and in their developments." [David Aspinall review of cd, http://www.audiophilia.com/software/Soundtracks/reviews/da13.htm]

Leslie Howard in the role of the married violinist with whom Bergman has an affair. The score for *Intermezzo* was nominated for an Oscar for Lou Forbes, but the music was composed and arranged by several others, including producer David O. Selznick's favorite Max Steiner, and Heinz Provost, whose 1936 theme centers the film. Taken as a whole, the score isn't much more than the classical pieces strung together until we get to the affair, when the score then perfectly supports the narrative, and enchantingly so. Lou Forbes worked for Selznick at the height of Selznick's glory, on *Gone with the Wind* and *Rebecca*, before going on to Samuel Goldwyn and several Danny Kaye films. The nomination should stay, since this category isn't for original work, but it still rankles when the people who actually wrote the music get no credit, so Steiner and Provost should have been added to the nomination.

As with *Stagecoach*, the score for *Mr. Smith Goes to Washington* is a catalog of Americana: among others, we get "Columbia, the Gem of the Ocean"; "Yankee Doodle Dandy"; "Our Country, 'Tis of Thee"; "Red River Valley"; "I Dream of Jeannie with the Light Brown Hair" (as the love theme); the requisite Sousa; and, inescapably, "The Star-Spangled Banner." The often-used "Auld Lang Syne" shows up too – and if you ever watch enough, it seems about every fourth movie from the Thirties works the tune in somewhere. Dimitri Tiomkin pulls out all the stops to build and reinforce Capra's morality tale of American hopes and ideals, against the villainy of corruption and cynicism. That is, when there's music. Vast stretches of *Mr. Smith* have no music whatsoever, as Capra and Tiomkin save their guns for the big scenes, and let the actors do their work in relative silence, which seems to make the music all the more effective when it does sound out. Tiomkin wrote a marvelous score here, and one that the Academy was right to nominate.

I am moving Aaron Copland's score for *Of Mice and Men*, which was nominated in both this category, and in Best Original Score, completely to the latter, where it belongs – again, I am being more stringent than the Academy, which didn't ban original compositions here.

While not the equal of his perfect accompaniment for *The Adventures of Robin Hood*, Korngold's score for *The Private Lives of Elizabeth and Essex* provides a powerful, rollicking, romantic experience, as his music so often did. His biographer Brendan G. Carroll believes it to be one of his best, calling it "one of Korngold's most resplendent scores, embellished with heroic fanfares and some of his most expressive melodic writing. The opening titles are superb, accompanied by a full, rich statement of Elizabeth's theme...This title music is conceived exactly like an overture, or operatic prelude...The title segues (complete with cannon fire) to the triumphal march of Essex through the streets of

London. Then the camera cuts to Elizabeth...and we hear a poignant theme to symbolize her doomed love for the younger man...The climax of the march blends into the heraldic Elizabeth's theme once more" before it stops when Elizabeth speaks.[cxlvi] Carroll makes a strong case for the score winning the Oscar, but I think *Stagecoach* the more innovative piece of work. What is more to the point, this is all original composition, and like Aaron Copland's score for *Of Mice and Men*, should be in that category, so it should be moved there.

Cy Feuer's score for *She Married a Cop* was put up by its poverty row studio as their slotted nominee in this category. Jean Parker plays the supervisor of an animation department doing a knockoff of Porky Pig, which makes sense, since the cartoon was done by Warner Brothers for Republic. The film only exists in incomplete form in UCLA's archive, but the clips I could find don't speak well of the score, or the movie, for that matter. No nomination should have been given.

Louis Silvers' work on *Swanee River* embellished the largely fictionalized biography of famous nineteenth century American songwriter Stephen Foster, played by Don Ameche. Like the Victor Herbert bio, *Swanee River* rides piggyback on Foster's songs, without making the kind of artistic use of source material at which *Stagecoach* excels. *Swanee River* also has Al Jolson's last role. Blackface abounds. Silvers organized the music of Foster and other members of his music department, then took the nomination for himself. I hate thieves and credit hogs; no nomination should exist for such chicanery.

Way Down South is another Bobby Breen vehicle, although an unusual one. The great black poet and playwright Langston Hughes wrote the script with black activist-actor Clarence Muse. Breen plays an antebellum Southern boy who has to defend his patrimony, a plantation from his dead father, from a scheming lawyer and the lawyer's mistress. Breen is helped by two slaves (called by the written introduction, "faithful Negro retainers"), played by "Stymie" from the Little Rascals and Muse himself. Victor Young's score works itself (minimally) around a number of spirituals, as well as songs by Hughes and Muse; the great spiritual composer Hall Johnson arranged the vocals. The movie opens with a spiritual, but Young anachronistically starts to swing it as a 1939 big band. This trend continues during the cane dancing, when suddenly jitterbugging seems to be occurring; perhaps the point is to suggest the connection for audiences between spirituals and big band swing, as well as slave and swing dancing. The movie puzzles me, what with all the happy slaves; perhaps Hughes and Muse wanted to show the humanity of these characters, since they act in full, rounded ways, not (much) like stereotypes, and they often speak openly and with little subservience to

Breen and his father. Still, the movie seems to suggest plantation life is a good life, until the nice master dies. Given the existence of slavery, perhaps they wanted to suggest the dangers in allowing a master in the first place; a good one might make it tolerable, but if there were no slavery, the risk of a bad master would never occur. Or perhaps by showing the good master, the writers felt they could then show the horrors of slavery to a white audience and get away with it. I'm genuinely confused, and I would argue the film needs considerably more attention than it has received, precisely because the messages seem so conflicted. After all, we are talking Langston Hughes here! And on another front, Breen would soon see his career end when his soprano voice was ruined by puberty; *Way Down South* was almost the end (maybe it was the 1939 suit he wears incongruously throughout this antebellum picture...). As for the nomination, Victor Young seems to be riding the back of the songs, as well as taking advantage of the one-nomination rule of the day; the score actually appears only in brief moments. I don't think Young alone deserves a nomination for this one; Hall Johnson should have been included, since so much of the music is obviously his work. The movie deserves a look – and a listen – if only for its perplexing qualities.

Best Song: In the easiest selection in Academy history in this category, Harold Arlen and E. Y. Harburg's "Over the Rainbow" won for *The Wizard of Oz*, over Ralph Ranger and Leo Robin's "Faithful Forever" from *Gulliver's Travels*; Buddy de Sylva's "Wishing" from *Love Affair*; and Irving Berlin's "I Poured My Heart into a Song" from *Second Fiddle*

Almost any single song from *The Wizard of Oz* could have won the Best Song of 1939. The richness of Harold Arlen's music combined with the matchless wit of E.Y. "Yip" Harburg's lyrics make *The Wizard of Oz* one of the handful of musicals which will be remembered centuries from now. That, and Judy Garland's unbelievably beautiful voice. Her rendition of "Over the Rainbow," a song Louis B. Mayer wanted cut from the movie as irrelevant and disruptive, has withstood the test of time to become the very definition of wistfulness and longing. Arlen and Harburg originally wrote it as an up-tempo number, then one day while they were noodling around with it, Arlen grew distracted and slowed down, and even they were stunned by its soul. I salute the Academy for their genius in both nominating and selecting "Over the Rainbow" as the Best Song of 1939.

Unfortunately, they didn't stop there. They picked three awful songs to nominate alongside it, and ignored some damn fine ones.

"Faithful Forever" is a completely forgettable song from the Fleischer Studio's *Gulliver's Travels*, doing its best to imitate the tunes of *Snow White* (and Jeanette MacDonald). No nomination should have been given for this mush – which is too bad, because *Gulliver's Travels* is worth at least one look, especially if you have children (okay, maybe only if you have children). The movie does little justice to Jonathan Swift's masterpiece of satire and human observation, but taken on its own terms, it holds up, particularly for children and aficionados of the Fleischers. As the Fleischers had throughout the Thirties, they desperately wanted to outdo Disney (this was true of most animation departments). Paramount gave them their chance with this film, although the Fleischers wouldn't match Disney until their first remarkable *Superman* cartoons, which took their animation in directions that have their roots in *Gulliver*. The opening shipwreck pales next to what Disney's animators were doing with water, but at this point, the Fleischers had little experience with realistic animation, what with their focus on Popeye and Betty Boop. When they needed realism, they used rotoscoping, an animation process invented by Max Fleischer in 1915, wherein human actions are filmed, then traced by the animators. What the film does have going for it is in Lilliput, where the expertise of the studio in caricatures could emerge fully and comically. We see the weakest animation in the prince and princess, who look like vaguely drawn kewpie dolls, but the kings, the servants, and all the other Lilliputians have amusing moments, and something of Swift's original intention emerges from the climactic war. One of the best bits, Gulliver's waking, has been imitated ever since. None of the warmth of Disney's dwarves comes out here, but an occasional (small) chuckle does. Worth a watch, if only to see what not to do if a major studio provides you with the funding for a full-length cartoon.

In *Love Affair*, Irene Dunne is a night club singer, but "Wishing" is the song she sings with orphans after her accident. Buddy de Sylva's song, unfortunately, is a forgettable mediocrity Leo McCarey dropped for the remake, along with everybody else who ever heard it. No nomination was deserved.

"I Poured My Heart Into a Song" is from *Second Fiddle*, which stars an odd pair: Sonja Henie and Tyrone Power, with a mediocre Irving Berlin score, and Power singing. A second-rate film at best, making fun of the search for Scarlett O'Hara, without much fun for the audience. Sonja Henie skates again, as well as ever. Only Berlin's name brought in this nomination – which should be taken away for this forgotten, and forgettable, song.

And what about the other songs they should have selected? As I've said above, almost any of the songs from *The Wizard of Oz* would have been superb choices, but the best are "Ding Dong, the Witch Is Dead"; "Follow the Yellow Brick Road"; "If I Only Had a Brain"; "We're Off to See the Wizard"; and the outrageously punning "If I Were King of the Forest." Has any other single musical ever had that many perfect songs specifically written for it?

1939 was the year of Arlen and Harburg. The only remaining song that should have been nominated is also by them: "Lydia, the Tattooed Lady," from the Marx Brothers' *At the Circus*. Groucho swung this one for the rest of his life.

Best Actress: Vivien Leigh won for *Gone with the Wind*, over Bette Davis, *Dark Victory*; Greer Garson, *Goodbye, Mr. Chips*; Irene Dunne, *Love Affair*; and Greta Garbo, *Ninotchka*.

Vivien Leigh's performance in *Gone with the Wind* is the engine that drives the entire film. Were ever eyes so green? Few actresses have been so stunningly beautiful; few actresses have been given a juicier, richer part, or been more perfect for it: "In truth, she was made for the movies, as Olivier never was, but *Gone with the Wind* was both the glorious peak and the beginning of the end of her movie career as a woman in full possession of her beauty."[cxlvii] Like many women in Thirties films, Leigh is far stronger than equivalent roles would be in the Forties and Fifties. The flash of fire in her eyes of defiance and righteous selfishness and individualism can only be matched by Bette Davis and Barbara Stanwyck in other Thirties performances. Leigh's sense of humor is one of the best parts of the character, even if more in the audience's reaction than to any intentional joking. Few actresses could have made believable the impulsiveness of the character, as she follows her passions and whims (and makes me long all the more for a *Wuthering Heights* with Vivien Leigh instead of Merle Oberon). As Scarlett grows in her own power and willingness to do whatever is necessary, Leigh's ability to convey that intensification grows accordingly. Leigh seems to have known film acting is primarily with the eyes, small gestures, and the short speech. The famous scene where she swears she will never be hungry again is an ideal example of this, backed up by a stunning camera move back into the darkness, as we see the gorgeous sunrise. When she offers herself to Gable in exchange for the tax money on Tara, the sheer hunger and honest greed comes through beautifully. Vivien Leigh deserved both her nomination and the Oscar.

Bette Davis continued her domination of this category with a tremendous performance in *Dark Victory* as a wild socialite who learns that she is going to die from a brain tumor. Davis milks this role for everything she can, which is considerable. One minor caveat: in both this film and *The Private Lives of Elizabeth and Essex*, she has developed this unfortunate twitch in her left hand, as if she was wringing it by itself. William Wyler, her director on *Jezebel*, would have noticed and stopped it; unfortunately, neither Edmund Goulding or Michael Curtiz were that observant, or willing to fight Davis (then again, unlike Wyler, neither of them were sleeping with Davis at the time). My problem with Bette Davis prior to watching this film is that she never seemed to be playing real people, but rather caricatures of real people. She learned tremendously in *Jezebel*; the fruits of that training by Wyler show her, for this viewer at least, playing a full human being: intelligent, willful, zesty, stubborn, warm and flawed. Watching Davis display a maturing, a deepening of human character, a growing of the human spirit is a real pleasure. Bette Davis reached her full powers in this movie, calling it a "jewel in my crown."[cxlviii] A fully-justified nomination, and one that very easily might have taken the Oscar here. When we consider that in 1939 Davis also starred as Queen Elizabeth in *The Private Lives of Elizabeth and Essex*, as well as the Empress Carlota and a self-sacrificing mother in *The Old Maid*, we can only applaud her achievement in *Dark Victory* as the best of the lot.

Greer Garson in *Goodbye, Mr. Chips* has to bring life to Mr. Chips, a teacher stuck in stagnation. Garson's stardom rests on her projecting a kind of matrimonial glow in her parts – as Mrs. Chips, and later as Mrs. Miniver. When she married the much younger actor who played her son in *Mrs. Miniver*, the contrast between this cougar and her screen image was so jarring even jaded reporters didn't believe it. What is more, she is on the screen in *Chips* for barely a third of the film, in what should really be a supporting role. The death of Mrs. Chips happens off-screen, with only the reactions of other characters to her loss. Garson misses the opportunity to die on-screen, which may have been due to dramatic construction, but may also have been a necessity due to her inability to act out a death. She doesn't belong in this category, as she should have been in the supporting category.

Irene Dunne's role in *Love Affair* as the woman in love with Charles Boyer uses her comic and dramatic talents equally. When she looks at Boyer for the first time, we can see her figuring him out instantly; when she begins to fall in love with him, we can see her trying to understand her own heart with considerably less acumen. Most of that is done with her eyes. A subtle, convincing performance, and well worth a nomination.

I absolutely love Greta Garbo in *Ninotchka*, and have willingly watched it many times; I cannot say that of any other Garbo movie. Ernst Lubitsch produced a first-rate comedy in *Ninotchka*, and gave Garbo her opportunity to prove she could be more than tragic: as the ballyhoo went, "Garbo Laughs!" But first, she plays a human robot of a Communist, someone cold as stone and hard as steel (hey, pick your own clichés, I'm running out of them…). Watching Garbo when she first laughs is one of the great joys of the cinema. Seeing her intoxicated and in love makes up for all those tortured characters she ever had to play (and I had to watch). Her talents for sadness and loss come into play as well, allowing her a full range of emotion. As a contemporary reviewer said, "1939 will go down in cinema history as the year that turned Greta Garbo from the screen's greatest dramatic actress into one of its first comediennes and that brought that great sleeping beauty of the screen, Marlene Dietrich, back to life [in *Destry Rides Again*]."[cxlix] As Andrew Sarris more recently opined, "From the moment she steps off a train in her commissar's costume, Garbo's exquisite gravity of expression and the metronomic doomsday delivery of her lines are as profoundly hilarious as anything in the history of talking pictures."[cl] Garbo absolutely earned this nomination.

Finally, how could the Academy have ignored Dorothy?

For *The Wizard of Oz*, Judy Garland deserved a nomination, as she portrayed with simple, quiet determination the innocence and wonder of childhood, and the fears of the evils of the adult world. Her stunningly beautiful rendition of the longing, aching glory that is "Over the Rainbow" alone should have earned her a nomination, as we can see the meaning of the lyrics in her eyes and face, as well as hear it in her voice. Garland would never be better.

I would also argue that Jean Arthur deserved a nomination for *Mr. Smith Goes to Washington*. She has to do the exact opposite, and in some ways, more difficult thing than James Stewart: as he goes from innocence to awareness, she has to go from cynical pessimism to regain her innocence and beliefs. Arthur is our viewpoint character, allowing Capra to comment on Stewart's naiveté and innocence before we can, disarming our own response in her more pointed one. Thus, by the time we get to the shift in Stewart's awareness, and the accompanying uphill battle, we accept the possibility because Arthur does. Arthur pulls off the cynicism with an understated disbelief, as well as a look in her eyes as if she can't believe anybody could be this dumb. Well, the Academy was, for ignoring Garland and Arthur.

1940

WHAT THEY GOT WRONG:

Less than usual, I must say. Either they're improving, or I'm just getting tired of telling them what they're doing wrong...nah, they just had a good year. It won't last.

Best Picture: *Gone with the Wind*
Best Actor: Robert Donat, *Goodbye, Mr. Chips*
Best Director: Victor Fleming, *Gone with the Wind*
Best Writing (Screenplay): Sidney Howard, *Gone with the Wind*
Best Cinematography (Black & White): Gregg Toland, *Wuthering Heights*
Best Cinematography (Color): Ernest Haller and Ray Rennahan, *Gone with the Wind*
Best Original Score: Herbert Stothart, *The Wizard of Oz*
Best Art Direction: Lyle Wheeler, *Gone with the Wind*
Best Special Effects: Edmund H. Hansen and Fred Sersen, *The Rains Came*
Best Short Subject (Cartoon): Walt Disney, *The Ugly Duckling*

Best Picture: *Gone with the Wind* won, over *Dark Victory*; *Goodbye, Mr. Chips*, *Love Affair*, *Mr. Smith Goes to Washington*; *Ninotchka*, *Of Mice and Men*, *Stagecoach*, *The Wizard of Oz*, and *Wuthering Heights*

The winner was a foregone conclusion; Bob Hope joked that Selznick "should have brought roller skates" to make coming up so many times easier. The presenter Y. Frank Freeman joked that "the only reason I was called upon to give this honor is because I have a Southern accent." Freeman then went on to lament "I never saw so many soldiers as were used in *Gone with the Wind*. Believe me, if the Confederate Army had had that many, we would have licked you damn Yankees."[cli] The film itself remains an inescapable part of film history and American culture. But as I've pointed out above in Best Supporting Actress, the racism of the film remains difficult to swallow. Even more disturbing is the second half of the film, once Scarlett is married to Rhett. After her first pregnancy, Scarlett decides she no longer wants to have sex; eventually, Rhett Butler ends up raping her – and she likes it. The scene remains difficult for me to accept, and has been since I first saw it in my adolescence. I can't blame Vivien Leigh for this scene, and I think she plays it to her audience's cultural expectations.[67] Many Gable films feature this kind of forceful dominance over his actresses, including more than one time when he hits the woman – and she likes it. But that doesn't mean I have to, any more than I have to accept racism. Is *Gone with the Wind* a great film? Yes, it is. But *Gone with the Wind* is also a film marred by the sexual and racial lessons it promotes as positive virtues. And yet, we continue to watch, as we work through these issues with each viewing. *Gone with the Wind* provokes constant reappraisal, as all great art does. Much as I am troubled, the nomination should stay – but not the Oscar.

Dark Victory is just a melodrama, but a melodrama with an absolutely brilliant, first-rate performance at its heart, as Bette Davis very nearly brought me to arguing the Oscar should have gone to her. George Brent is serviceable as the doctor and love interest. Humphrey Bogart is badly miscast as a groom with an Irish brogue (actually, it's the brogue that's the problem – Bogie can't do it). Geraldine Fitzgerald does beautiful work here, perhaps even more so than in *Wuthering Heights*. The plot of *Dark Victory* hinges on a rather ridiculous conception: that Davis' brain tumor will leave her completely unimpaired, until she goes blind and dies rather suddenly. If you can swallow that one (and I managed, somehow), you can enjoy this excuse for Bette Davis to soar. The nomination should stay.

Goodbye, Mr. Chips stars Robert Donat and Greer Garson in an adaptation of the book by James Hilton. Since I'm a teacher, you'd think this would be my favorite movie. Perhaps it's merely the depiction of the British educational system, filtered through some very thick rose-colored glasses, but I've never warmed to *Chips*. Yes, I appreciate the emotional connections Mr. Chips makes with his students, especially after his marriage, but I've never found him to be a credible teacher. We either get him cold and disconnected, or all warm and fuzzy. We see very little of his actual teaching, and what there is of it, doesn't really convince me he should be so beloved. *Goodbye, Mr. Chips* is telling us, rather than showing us. I'm inclined to argue for discarding the nomination entirely, but a few people find it heartwarming enough that *Chips* should stay.

Love Affair stars Charles Boyer and Irene Dunne in the thrice filmed tale of two shipboard lovers trapped by previous commitments and fate from remaining together. Add a wise old relative, a car accident, and one of the most sentimental endings ever filmed, and you've got ro-

---

[67] My father could never understand why I wasn't thrilled at the discovery that Scarlett liked sex. He didn't see it as rape; but then, he was born in 1930, when the virgin/whore complex was in full force in American male sexual channeling.

mance. More famous in Leo McCarey's Fifties remake of his own film – that one starring Cary Grant and Deborah Kerr – here we get Boyer as the French lover and Irene Dunne as his soon-to-be wheelchair bound beloved. Dunne is considerably more amusing than Kerr, and Boyer gives Grant a run for his money as well (the Warren Beatty remake has exactly one thing going for it: Katharine Hepburn). A decent movie, worth seeing, and a good nomination.

Mr. Smith Goes to Washington is one of Frank Capra's greatest films, as well as one of Jimmy Stewart's finest hours as an actor. That it is also the shining portrait of ourselves as a nation, and the summation of our political hopes and fears, only cements its place on this list of Best Picture nominees. *Mr. Smith* came within a hair's breadth of deserving the Best Picture; had the ending been less contrived, the Oscar should have gone there. Capra always had trouble with his endings; the only two that he ever really nailed were *Mr. Deeds Goes to Town* and *It's a Wonderful Life*. The lack of a proper ending ruined *Meet John Doe*. I have paid the movie its compliments above and below in numerous categories; the nomination by the Academy should be acclaimed.

Ninotchka is the only comedy the Academy nominated for Best Picture in this greatest of all years, and for good reason: *Ninotchka* is the best comedy of this miraculous year, and a romantic comedy at that, which still charms today. But the humor is a deep variety, the kind that leads us to laugh because it hurts too much not to laugh, the kind that causes us to reconsider those daily experiences we all too often take as standard issue, without realizing their true rarity in human history: the breath of freedom, the choice to love, the privacy of our own thoughts and surroundings. By first satirizing communism and celebrating the West, Lubitsch then throws us fully into the Soviet Union, all the while mixing the reality of its sordidness and brutality with the longing for what has been lost (and by that I do not mean imperial Russia – Garbo and Lubitsch are insistent on how one kind of dictatorship has been exchanged for another). Lubitsch would later go after the Nazis with *To Be or Not to Be* in something of the same manner, but *Ninotchka* is more perfectly balanced. A truly great film, and one which carries with it still this capacity to enlighten and enrich us in ways few comedies (or tragedies) ever do. An excellent nomination.

Many of John Steinbeck's works have formed the basis of truly great adaptations, among them *The Grapes of Wrath* and this, the best of all the many adaptations of the short, brilliant, and tragic *Of Mice and Men*. Starring Burgess Meredith and Lon Chaney, Jr., and directed by Lewis Milestone, this film eloquently captures the pain and suffering of the Great Depression, while evoking the crushed hopes for a better place and time that seems to drive most human beings to strive and suffer. Meredith and Chaney prove to be the perfect Lenny and George, and that neither one of them was nominated for any acting category, even in this amazing year, reflects poorly on the Academy (see Best Actor below). Few films have ever depicted male friendship more tenderly. An excellent nomination by the Academy, in this category, as well as in Best Original Score. Oddly, Copland was also nominated for Best Score for the same movie, due to the nominating rules, wherein each studio was allowed to put one film into the running; Hal Roach apparently decided to double his odds of an Oscar by tossing Copland into both. *Of Mice and Men* is Hal Roach's finest achievement outside of Laurel and Hardy.

Stagecoach is John Ford's first great sound Western; as Ford's best biographer Scott Eyman puts it, "*Stagecoach* remains the paradigmatic western...Ford would make deeper films than *Stagecoach*, and he would make more virtuosic films than *Stagecoach*, but he would never again make one so nearly perfect, more filled with an easeful grace, with perfectly inflected camera and characters. It's a film as pure and refreshing as deep breaths of mountain air. It's his *City Lights*, his *Rules of the Game*..." [clii] Peter Bogdanovich identifies *Stagecoach* as "the first adult Western."[cliii] I couldn't agree more with these two film mavens. I have watched *Stagecoach* dozens of times, and have always been deeply comforted by the level of art, ingenuity, grace, and nuance in what had always been a relatively shallow genre before Ford invested everything he knew into its making. As Claire Trevor, the lead actress in this energetic poem of a film, said so insightfully, "To me, it was a symphony, a marvelous piece of work that used the motion picture camera in the best way that I'd ever seen it done."[cliv] Ford made John Wayne into a star with this film, through the rolling close-up which introduces him. The most famous stunt in film history up to that point comes with Yakima Canutt's famous leap onto the stagecoach's horses, followed by the fall under the horses and out under the coach; few chase scenes have ever equaled it, much less surpassed it (Canutt did it in other westerns before and after). The final shootout, with the famous image of Wayne throwing himself to the ground, remains indelible. More than that, the story takes (or creates) most of the stereotypes of the genre, and presents them in a deep thematic discussion of the nature of civilization. The forces of society, with the hypocrisies and lies brilliantly castigated, are matched by those who are deeply human, with all their flaws and strengths. Society's outcasts carry the real weight of genuine morality, from Mitchell's drunken doctor to Wayne's outlaw to Claire Trevor's prostitute to John Carradine's gambler. Ford was never more subversive than in this film. A serious contender for Best Picture, *Stagecoach* was the movie Orson Welles watched obsessively when teaching himself the craft of filmmaking. The New York Film Critics couldn't decide between *Gone with the Wind* or *Mr. Smith Goes to Washington* for thirteen ballots, before finally choosing *Wuthering Heights* as a solution. But they never argued over Ford as Best Director, "because if ever direction stood out like a sore thumb, his work on *Stagecoach* was the greatest evidence of what fine direction could do for just an ordinary story."[clv] An excellent nomination, and a movie which should be seen repeatedly and often, and then some more (see Best Director and other categories above and below for more)

The Wizard of Oz is both a perfect musical and a perfect film. Few other movies have ever been cast this brilliantly; few others have ever been blessed by the songs this one has (see Best Song above), or captured the way a child sees the world, and the dangers that accompany the loss of innocence. Dorothy sits on the cusp of adolescence, and is faced by the evils of the world, lurking about the edges, personified by Ms. Gulch. The film opens with her running away from evil; it ends with her safely at home. One of the many ingenuities of the film lies in having the same cast play characters in the outside world, and the world of Oz, of the imagination. While this was pioneered in stage productions of *Peter Pan*, wherein the father and Captain Hook are generally played by the same actor, what this duality gives to *The Wizard of Oz* is a continuity of experiences, as well as the suggestion that it really has all been a dream, and it is time to wake up from that dream, and accept the responsibilities of adulthood. One of the reasons why "Over the Rainbow" remains so touching is because we know the fragility of escape, of imagination, and yet we cling to it, because after all, Oz is in Technicolor, and reality is sepia-toned. Fans of Oz tend to either read the books, or watch the movie; moving back and forth between them can be jarring, because the books never suggest that Oz is but a dream; they celebrate the imagination over reality. Produced in the final days of the Depression, the movie seems to sum up that endless drain on hope, and assert once again, that there's no place like home, reassuringly and realistically. Like all great films, *The Wizard of Oz* can be watched many times, and at each stage of our life, a new experience awaits us: as a child, we see the wonder; as a young adult, we love the songs; as a parent, we see the miracle in our children's faces; as we age, we come to the nostalgia for all the times we've watched it. I doubt if MGM ever made a better film (remembering they didn't make *Gone with the Wind*; Selznick did). If any film this year could be considered a finer one than *Gone with the Wind* in its mythic, enduring qualities, *The*

Wizard of Oz would be that film. In polling my friends and family, I found *The Wizard of Oz* easily overtook the voting this year (we'll have to see if I listened).

Widely regarded as the best adaptation of the classic Emily Brontë novel, this film of *Wuthering Heights* fails to encompass the fullness of the novel's brilliant structure, and utterly devastates the ending of the novel with its insipid ghost fade-out. Director William Wyler can't be blamed; Goldwyn tacked on the ending, using doubles for the leads. When we add into that a very inadequate Merle Oberon and the flaws of Laurence Olivier, whose greatness on the stage has always been a conundrum for those of us who can only view his largely mediocre film performances, what we get is a deeply troubled rendition, whose main delights are visual and not narrative (see Best Actor for more). Let us be honest: this movie isn't the novel. It isn't even close. *Wuthering Heights* is a decent melodrama, with some good sets, lovely costumes, and pretty people. No nomination should be given for what is a corpse of a film compared to that living, breathing miracle that is Emily Brontë's novel.

As for the movies passed over, allow me a lengthy coda in this best of all Hollywood years, to point at films which should be seen, many of which could have easily been nominated for Best Picture in other years.

The Adventures of Huckleberry Finn has Mickey Rooney doing a fine job with Huck, but the best part of this adaptation of Mark Twain's classic comes from the bit parts of the Duke and the King, brought to life by William Frawley and Walter Connolly with great gusto. Rex Ingram does a good job bringing out the nobility and frustration of Jim. Overall, although I think this one is far from perfect, we have never really had a better version of the novel.

For *Another Thin Man*, Dashiell Hammett wrote the story for the third in the series, which is fun, but not as much as previous entries. The baby dampens things, but does provide some cuteness; some of the bit players aren't cast well. The nightclub scene with the Latin lover is fun. In the end, we are in the gradually diminishing returns of series.

In *Confessions of a Nazi Spy*, Warner Brothers declares open war on the Nazis in this movie, as Edward G. Robinson stars in this harsh exposé of American Nazis, as well as Hitler. Paul Lukas, playing the leader of the American Bund, modeled his performance on Hitler. The movie is based on a real case of the FBI breaking a spy ring. Using a documentary style, *Confessions* depicts spies fairly accurately, if a bit simply. The movie provides lots of protection for the good German-Americans who are anti-Hitler. In the end, we have to give credit to Warner Brothers for being the first studio to take on the Nazis.

Destry Rides Again is Marlene Dietrich's comeback to box office success, and her first comedy; Jimmy Stewart hadn't had much of a chance to do comedy either. *Destry* is based on a Max Brand novel (Brand was the king of the pulps, writing millions upon millions of words). I'm not sure what Dietrich is doing, but it isn't singing...she's Lili von Shtupp from *Blazing Saddles*, singing flat, and forcing her voice to produce an even flatter note. Dietrich does have some sex appeal, but I think it's emerging mostly from that "screw-you" attitude she projects towards most men – it's the ice princess who's really smoldering underneath that appeals to the older generation of repressed American males. We get some beautiful shots of the stagecoach – one tracking alongside the horses, another watching the coach come into a small pass, bringing the dust up behind it, and another perched atop the stagecoach looking down. Mischa Auer has a comic romp of a part as the second husband of Callahan. But the best parts of the movie show Stewart and Dietrich just cutting loose and having fun with their characters – the catfight, the water bucket, their brawl. And for the love of manners, why is Dietrich chewing with her mouth wide open?!? Ultimately, the movie is about pacifism turning into armed activism, which could easily be a comment on the international situation. A fun movie, worth your time – just don't blame me when Dietrich goes on stage to sing.

Dodge City was Errol Flynn's first Western, co-starring Olivia de Havilland and Alan Hale in bright Technicolor, with some beautiful outdoor work. Directed by Michael Curtiz, with a big, fat bombastic score by Max Steiner, *Dodge City* is a good Western. A beautiful opening shot begins the film, pulling away from the train as it speeds toward the camera, followed by a race between the stagecoach and railroad. We get two dueling national anthems in "Dixie" vs. "Marching through Georgia," a concept which Curtiz would reprise with greater effect in *Casablanca*. Most famously, *Dodge City* has the bar fight to end all bar fights. Flynn does a nice pratfall *à la* Cary Grant. *Dodge City* wraps up with an exciting end on a burning train.

In *Each Dawn I Die*, James Cagney stars with George Raft; Cagney plays a crusading reporter who faces a framed charge of vehicular manslaughter, goes to jail, and gets hardened. A particularly ridiculous plot contrivance can't dull the fun of watching Cagney and Raft together. The prison breakout is filmed beautifully, as are the opening scenes in the rain. Pieces of the last twenty minutes of the movie are as good as any gangster film. Well worth the time for fans of Cagney, Raft, gangster pictures, or Warner Brothers.

The Hound of the Baskervilles began the immensely successful 14-film series with Basil Rathbone as Sherlock Holmes (the best we had until Jeremy Brett took on the role), and Nigel Bruce as Dr. Watson (As a child, I loved Bruce's Watson, until I read the original stories and saw how these films had turned the noble doctor into a buffoon). *The Hound* is a well-told version, with John Carradine and George Zucco, but the whole film ends rather abruptly, with Holmes telling Watson...to bring the needle!? I am still surprised that got by the censors. The same year, they also made *The Adventures of Sherlock Holmes,* this time with Zucco as Professor Moriarty; I actually enjoy *The Adventures* better, as it is a particularly fine rendition with beautiful dark cinematography, although Watson is considerably more of an idiot than in the first film.

The Hunchback of Notre Dame has one major advantage: the astonishing performance by Charles Laughton. See Best Actor for more.

For *Only Angels Have Wings*, look at the Best Cinematography (Black & White) category.

The Private Lives of Elizabeth and Essex needs to be seen for its color cinematography and brilliant art direction, as well as Bette Davis' fine performance. *Private Lives* tells the story of the supposed love affair between Queen Elizabeth (played by Bette Davis in one of her unattractive modes) and the rebellious Earl of Essex (Errol Flynn, doing his best to keep up with the best actress on the Warners lot). Neither Davis nor Flynn liked each other in the slightest. Flynn was never in a more highbrow film; Davis never played against a more charismatic male. The movie runs quite well today, even after all the other films we've seen since on the subject of Queen Elizabeth I. *The Private Lives of Elizabeth and Essex* is worth more than one viewing, for both the swashbuckling of Flynn, and the tremendous power of Davis' acting (although she does seem to be relying far too much on twitching and arm jerks).

The Roaring Twenties has James Cagney and Humphrey Bogart in an adaptation of a Mark Hellinger story, based on real people and events. Raoul Walsh directed, albeit very stiffly. The camerawork is mostly static, with only occasional mobility. *The Roaring Twenties* looks backward a decade and more, beginning with Cagney and Bogart fighting in WWI. The setup is awkward, with a bit of ridicule for the way things used to be. *The Roaring Twenties* uses a documentary newsreel style between sections. Cagney isn't as interesting here as in *Angels with Dirty Faces*, and is not investing his role with unique tics as he has before. The conflict lies between so-called normal life and the underworld. Cagney has a decent heart, and wants nice girl Priscilla

Lane, but he has to make his way through the criminal side to succeed. Gladys George is great as the underworld moll who loves Cagney without him knowing. The ending is almost the entire reason to watch the film; the look on Cagney's drunken face when he confronts Bogart, the look of satisfaction when he kills Bogart, and that long, luxurious, balletic death scene when Cagney staggers almost endlessly down the street to collapse on the church steps, to be capped by George's classic line: "He used to be a big shot."

The Women remains an interesting gimmick film, with a large cast, but not a single man. Norma Shearer appears in her last major role, along with Joan Crawford as a home-wrecker, Rosalind Russell as a gossiping "friend" to Shearer, and Paulette Goddard as a woman about to be divorced. George Cukor directed *The Women*, based on the play by Clare Luce, and adapted by Anita Loos and Jane Murfin. *The Women* takes a dim view of female behavior, as comprising mostly backstabbing, conniving, and gossiping. Two minutes into the movie, and Ecclesiastes is ringing in my ears: "Vanity, vanity, all is vanity." The women are all introduced as animals in the credits: Shearer is an innocent fawn, Joan Crawford is a leopard, Rosalind Russell is a cat, Mary Boland is a monkey (she of the pining cry, "L'Amour, L'Amour!"), Paulette Goddard is a fox, and so forth. What may be getting satirized here are the idle female rich, since the serving class is generally making fun of them, but the working class doesn't come off much better. Russell chews up her part with gusto. Shearer and her daughter are supposed to be the moral center of the film, with the happy healthy family – and once threatened, she must wear "Jungle Red" and fight back for your man, even if he's done her wrong! *The Women* provides a primary document of its time, ripe for scholars looking to pontificate on attitudes about women before WWII.

You Can't Cheat an Honest Man stars W.C. Fields, with Edgar Bergen and Charlie McCarthy, based on a story by Charles Bogle (another of Fields' pseudonyms). Fields plays Larson E. Whipsnade, one of his best names. I find it hard to believe Bergen had a movie career; although he was a funny man, he was a horrible ventriloquist. I could also do without the racist jokes. Fields does a great hat toss onto Charlie's head, and his battle with the wooden dummy never flags: "I shall send over a couple of pet beavers to romp with you." My problem with the movie is that it is really more a Bergen and McCarthy outing than a Fields vehicle. Fields does get in a few zingers, especially with the play off of Garbo's line about a whiskey and ginger ale on the side, then takes back the movie with the rattlesnake, the boa constrictor tires, and the ping pong game at the end. All in all, not Fields at his absolute top, but close.

As I've said in the Original Story category, *Young Mr. Lincoln* is my favorite movie about our greatest president. Henry Fonda's performance is first-rate; the mythic quality of the film persists in memory, as it should.

And now, the envelope for Best Picture please.

Now that I've suckered you into thinking I've denied *Gone with the Wind* the Academy Award for Best Picture, allow me to assuage your anger by announcing that we have, for the first time, a tie: *Gone with the Wind*, perhaps the greatest epic ever made, should have tied with *The Wizard of Oz*, perhaps the greatest musical and greatest fantasy ever made. The issues of racism and sexism in *Gone with the Wind* vied with those choruses of votes for *The Wizard of Oz*, and the way in which Oz can be seen throughout your life. Both films reach the level of great art, which is often problematic, provocative, and deserving of extended discussion. *The Wizard of Oz* contains the wonders of childhood, and *Gone with the Wind* presents the passions of when we grow up and discover love is not the simple thing we thought it was. Both films are cultural icons, inescapable parts of who we are as moviegoers, and we should not deny either. *Gone with the Wind* and *The Wizard of Oz* should have both been named the Best Picture of 1939.

Best Actor: Robert Donat won for *Goodbye, Mr. Chips*, over Mickey Rooney, *Babes in Arms*; Clark Gable, *Gone with the Wind*; James Stewart, *Mr. Smith Goes to Washington*; and Laurence Olivier, *Wuthering Heights*

The greatest shock of the Oscars this year was when Robert Donat won for *Goodbye, Mr. Chips*. The story that usually accompanies this is that everybody was flabbergasted that Clark Gable didn't win as Rhett Butler in *Gone with the Wind*. In reality, the odds were seen as rather in favor of James Stewart in *Mr. Smith Goes to Washington*, with Gable as a likely second choice. What seems to have happened is that the vote split between those two favorites, thus handing the Oscar to Donat. As a teacher, I suppose I should agree, but I've never met a teacher like Mr. Chips, and I find the story to be treacly and stifling in its depiction of the true life of the teacher. Donat hams it up in his old man makeup, but with a degree of humor and twinkle in his eye, dispensing warmth and wisdom. Playing the young, inexperienced teacher, Donat is appropriately fuzzy and out of control. As a middle-aged man with no particular success in his career, we can see the disappointment and sense of waste. As the lover and husband, we feel the warmth and surprise. As the old beloved mentor and giver of student teas, Donat plays Chips for all his doddering worth. But Best Actor?!? Not even close, although the look in Donat's face after the death of Mrs. Chips is first-rate acting. He should keep the nomination – hey, we teachers have to stick together! – but several other actors this year deserved the Oscar far more than Donat did.

Mickey Rooney wasn't one of them. He was nominated for *Babes in Arms*, his very first musical. Rooney, like his co-star Judy Garland, were child stars who made the transition to adult stardom; like her, Rooney was capable of nearly everything, from comedy to dancing to singing to drama. Watching Rooney in this film is like watching a coiled spring in action, always threatening to explode. Rooney himself couldn't quite believe he was nominated, and perhaps the MGM block voting had something to do with it (as it must have for Donat to win), but I'm going to go out on a limb here and suggest he deserved a nomination. I'm not saying there isn't a whiff of ham at times, but overall, Rooney does something I doubt few others could have, then or now. Who else could have been this effervescent, this intensely excited, and gotten away with it? What is more, he so overshadows Garland as to make her almost disappear at times. That takes talent, and deserves a nomination (if for nothing else, some drop-dead impersonations of Clark Gable and Lionel Barrymore).

Clark Gable in *Gone with the Wind* gets as good an introductory shot as John Wayne in *Stagecoach*, the camera soaring down the stairs into his leering grin. As Scarlett says of him, "Who is that nasty fellow? He looks like he knows what I look like without my shammy!" Gable has a ball being the disreputable, passionate, sexual Rhett Butler. I'm not sure it's acting so much as Gable being Gable, but he is amazingly effective: "You should be kissed and often, and by someone who knows how." Watching Gable is one of the great treats of the movie, as he plays the scoundrel of all scoundrels. The moment at which Gable moves deeper and more dangerously than ever before or since is when he threatens to kill O'Hara by crushing her skull. His capacity to evince passion was greater than any other American actor, as he does when he carries her upstairs. Problematic as that rape is, Gable's intensity cannot be questioned, since the whole scene relies on our belief that he would do it. His final exit, perhaps the most famous last scene in all of cinema, cannot be forgotten: "Frankly, my dear, I don't give a damn." Gable deserved his nomination.

Jimmy Stewart gave the first truly great performance of his career in *Mr. Smith Goes to Washington*. Consider what the role demanded of him, to project all of the following: the utter innocence of a naïve child;

the shining ideals instilled in him by his schooling, his parentage and the documents of the Founding Fathers; the soul-shattering discovery that those he has respected and nigh worshipped are not what he thought they were – and then the determination and pigheadedness to keep fighting for what he believes in, even when all of the odds (and the powers that be) are arrayed against him. I don't think another American actor could have brought us through all of those stages, at least not successfully. The innocence alone is beyond almost every actor I can recall; many trying it would have brought the awful nervous laughter of disbelief. Gary Cooper or Henry Fonda might have been able to pull it off, but I doubt it; for modern actors, Tom Hanks comes the closest in *Forrest Gump*. I have shown *Mr. Smith* to teenage males for nearly twenty years now, and not once has anybody not bought into Stewart's performance (trust me, teenagers have intense bullshit radars that ping insincerity in everything adults present to them; they just can't use it on themselves). Yes, Stewart had help to make his voice hoarse, and then a shattered whisper: first bicarbonate of soda, then later, mercuric chloride.[clvi] Later generations of method actors would duplicate these extreme lengths to produce an authentic performance (think of Robert De Niro's weight gain in *Raging Bull*). Few method actors would ever equal Stewart's performance in this film, regardless of their willingness to live the role. An outstanding nomination on the Academy's part.

Laurence Olivier received his first nomination for *Wuthering Heights*, a problematic one at best. Olivier rarely lived up to his immense stage reputation in his film performances; someone explained to me once that Olivier's ability to create a linear performance on the stage was unparalleled, as he built from A inexorably to Z. But in film, the production goes from Z to C to A to T, and so forth, as they shoot out of sequence; Olivier never quite learned how to work through that discombobulation. William Wyler did the best he could to bring Olivier to a better understanding of film acting, as he had for Bette Davis in *Jezebel*; the results are marginally acceptable. Olivier resented it, pronouncing "I suppose this anemic little medium can't take great acting"; Wyler and the crew laughed at this pompous ass.[clvii] Olivier eventually admitted he was wrong, and did his best to improve, but the problem with Olivier's Heathcliff is that there is very nearly nothing attractive about him. Why would Cathy be in love with him? Or for that matter, with the wimpish Edgar? In the original novel, Heathcliff has a wild, dark, romantic, dangerous side; he is the eternal bad boy, the Lord Byron of the piece. Olivier projects very little of these qualities, substituting instead a kind of churlish resentment. He is effective as the cruel old Heathcliff, and one wishes that Wyler had chosen to film more of the second half of the novel to emphasize this strength. When Olivier is called to be the lover, he goes for broad strokes, which would have worked very well on stage, but not so much in film. Oberon has difficulty as well projecting the wild passion that draws her to Heathcliff, the deep longing for freedom from social expectations and restraints (she is a petulant child of a woman, rather than the torn human being she should be). What is worse, I for one feel very little chemistry between the two of them; Olivier and Oberon didn't get along. They both need to stop posing. One longs for Vivien Leigh in the part, since she and Olivier were crazy mad in sexual desire and love. Occasionally, one gets flashes of what Olivier must have been like as a theatre god: the naiveté of the young Heathcliff comes across, although without the conviction of his desire for revenge which should accompany it; the hunger in his eyes when Cathy returns from the Lintons (done without Oberon in the shot); the scene where he hides behind the door and listens to Cathy talk of Edgar, but much of this is due to the editing and the cinematography (Olivier is in the dark; Oberon is in the light); the look of calm, evil satisfaction when he gives his former tormentor alcohol the doctor has ruled out. Olivier should keep the nomination, for these moments – that, and I'm not sure if any other actor in 1939 could have done the part any better. Most of the male stars of the period were either far too American (Jimmy Stewart), the wrong body type (Jimmy Cagney), or too suave (Cary Grant). Heathcliff, like Hamlet, may be one of those parts impossible to cast with complete satisfaction; that Olivier did his best and failed to fully satisfy in both roles speaks to his courage.

Many great performances were neglected by the Academy this year.

Foremost among them were Burgess Meredith and Lon Chaney, Jr., for their roles as George and Lenny in the Hal Roach production of *Of Mice and Men*. Chaney, Jr. in particular hit his artistic high point. His portrayal of the hulking Lenny prompted endless parodies, as so many of the great performances do, and typecast him for most of the rest of his career. As Lenny, the stupid, hopeful giant, Chaney, Jr. simply could not be better. Once you hear his vocal pattern, never again will any other Lenny do (although John Malkovich comes close). Meredith is quieter, and carries the despair of shattered hopes in his eyes. Both deserved nominations.

As did Henry Fonda for his intensely quiet, humorous turn as that young "jackleg lawyer" Abe Lincoln in *Young Mr. Lincoln*. For the first time, the depths Fonda could plumb out of stillness emerges, and from this movie on, his career was assured as one of our greatest actors. My favorite scene in the movie is a comic one, in the pie eating contest, which may seem like an odd choice, but we can see Fonda driving the anxious baking contestants into a frenzy while they wait his decision, while he continues delaying out of the joy of eating pie. Fonda is also electric when he stops the lynch mob, and I am fairly certain that a young Gregory Peck knew this scene by heart, as we see the same disarming of the crowd in *To Kill a Mockingbird* two decades later. Fonda should have been nominated.

Finally on my snubbed list, I present Charles Laughton, who created one of his finest performances in *Hunchback of Notre Dame*. Given that he believed himself to be a terribly ugly man (in his own words, "I have a face like the behind of an elephant"), and one torn by his homosexuality, for *Hunchback*, Laughton drew on his deepest inner conflicts to produce an emotionally devastating performance. Unlike the silent performance of Lon Chaney, Sr., where the makeup is primarily what you see, here the makeup is entirely secondary to the role. Laughton uses his mastery of vocal inflection and body language to wring every last drop of pathos out of the role, never once dipping into sentimentality or excess. Watch his face when the crowd first captures him, and wants to make him King of Fools – without a word, through his eyes and the smallest smile, Laughton brings the character's fears and hopes alive. During the flogging, the look of surprise, then quiet resignation, speak more volumes than all the howls ever could have (I suspect Denzel Washington knew this scene before he made *Glory*). The tender agony and grace Laughton displays when O'Hara brings him water has rarely been equaled by any actor before or since. His triumphant cries of "Sanctuary! Sanctuary!" have never been matched for sheer exultation in all of cinema. Laughton should have been nominated.

In the final summation, the Best Actor Oscar should have gone to James Stewart for *Mr. Smith Goes to Washington*. A handful of moments in American cinema define the perfection of acting; after the look on Chaplin's face and in his eyes at the end of *City Lights*, Stewart's fight on the Senate floor is the second, particularly when he sees the telegrams – every bit as emotionally shattering as *City Lights*, if not more so. I have seen Stewart's performance dozens of times; I have yet to see it with eyes unblurred. In any rational consideration of the craft of the actor, Stewart's look of disbelief at the evidence in front of him, followed by his continued defiance, must be seen as an American treasure. Gable was sexy, Donat was doddering, Laughton was heartbreaking, but Stewart seared and uplifted and cleansed the national spirit and body politic, and we need that reminder more today than we ever have before. In the greatest year of American cinema, James Stewart gave the greatest performance. Stewart should have won the Oscar for Best Actor.

Best Director: Victor Fleming won for *Gone with the Wind*, over Sam Wood, *Goodbye, Mr. Chips*; Frank Capra, *Mr. Smith Goes to Washington*; John Ford, *Stagecoach*; and William Wyler, *Wuthering Heights*.

Don't get me wrong; I think Victor Fleming did an outstanding job directing *Gone with the Wind*, as well as *The Wizard of Oz* – for which he should have received a second nomination, much as Michael Curtiz did in 1938 (the Academy changed the rules to allow only one film per nominee per category). Other directors did contribute, but overarching everything is David O. Selznick, popping Benzedrine and thyroid boosters while he composed endless memos, micromanaging the birth of this rare beast, *Gone with the Wind*. Like Hitchcock, who saw some of his best projects diddled to death by Selznick, Fleming should be congratulated for surviving the experience. He deserved a nomination, but Fleming isn't the one to whom we owe the existence and form of *Gone with the Wind*. David O. Selznick is. Still, any director who guided the majority of both *Gone with the Wind* and *The Wizard of Oz* deserves vast and weighty kudos, and nominations. He just doesn't deserve the Oscar in this particular year, because his contributions are not those specific ones which make those films great (with *The Wizard of Oz*, it's the music and the set designs and the performances, which Fleming didn't have much of a hand in by the time he came on the set).

Sam Wood was nominated for directing *Goodbye, Mr. Chips*. Wood was little more than a competent director, reliable in getting the movie finished on time and under budget, with little originality. The Marx Brothers used to torture him regularly; he had almost no sense of humor. *A Night at the Opera* succeeded in spite of Wood. Wood did direct a few other classics, including *The Pride of the Yankees* and *For Whom the Bell Tolls*, but none of them are remembered for any particular flair. His films succeeded because Wood had the resources of the studio system behind him, and not because he imposed any particular vision. He didn't draw out any compelling performances in *Goodbye, Mr. Chips*; everything seems very stiff and by the numbers. No nomination should be his.

Frank Capra, on the other hand, was working at his peak in *Mr. Smith Goes to Washington*, crafting one of his three best films (the other two being *Mr. Deeds* and *It's a Wonderful Life*). Capra's great strength as a director was in choosing story material that was significant, humorous, uplifting, very human – and then in casting the best actors for their roles. His endings were often weak, especially as he set himself higher goals, and the payoffs became harder to achieve. But his pacing, his sense of both the comic and the tragic, and his optimism make almost all his films worthwhile, even the weaker ones, until we get to the early Fifties and his collapse as a top-notch director into mediocrity. In *Mr. Smith*, watch how Capra sets up his audience to know what is going on, and then see him toss his innocent senator into an Eden full of snakes. Capra understood American reactions in the Thirties and Forties down to his core; I suspect the end of the studio system, his service in WWII, the rise of the Cold War, and the creation of the atomic bomb played significant roles in his declining sense of how close he could get to corn and get away with it. He was rarely better at walking that line than in *Mr. Smith*. Watch the scene in the Lincoln Memorial where the young boy reads from the Gettysburg Address; no true American could help having to fight off the tears during that recitation. Capra absolutely deserved this nomination.

William Wyler does the best he can with *Wuthering Heights*, and that best can be summed up in two words: Gregg Toland. Olivier is only just acceptable as Heathcliff; Oberon is insipid as Cathy; Niven is the poor man's Leslie Howard, and that's not saying very much. As it is, in terms of the story, I feel somewhat as if I were watching another practice run at *Gone with the Wind*, what with the young defiant woman caught between the cultured, mannered Niven and the outcast Olivier. Wyler was also betrayed by Goldwyn, who tacked on that ugly sop of an ending. Still, for why Wyler should keep his nomination, see Best Cinematography (Black & White)) below.

Stagecoach, as I've pointed out above in Best Picture, is John Ford's mature masterpiece, the film that marks his arrival at cinematic perfection (see Best Cinematography (Black & White) for more on his brilliant visuals). Ford created a microcosm of society aboard his stagecoach: the rich banker, the elegant lady, the salesman, the sheriff, the working man driver, the gambler, the drunken doctor, the whore with a heart of gold, the outlaw. From rich to poor, respectable to disrespected, from the upper crust to the dregs, Ford sets us off on a pilgrimage to Lordsburg, the City of God, wherein we will be delivered of our pretensions, shown the truth, taught the ways of genuine humanity, and shorn of the wicked. Ford then ironically inverts that name, by showing that Lordsburg is full of violence, sin, and injustice. *Stagecoach*, like *Gone with the Wind* and *Mr. Smith Goes to Washington*, is more than a movie: it is a genuine experience, teaching us what it means to be American. If *Gone with the Wind* shows us the racism and sexism and dreams that drive us, if *Mr. Smith* lifts us up to our highest political ideals, then *Stagecoach* reveals the heart of who we are in America: good people, doing the right thing, following our hearts, breaking the law where it needs to be broken, and never allowing social pretension to get in the way of honesty. All that, wrapped up in a helluva good story, with love, action, revenge, and rich characterization. Some minor nitpicking might include the ridiculous lack of evidence of pregnancy for the lady, as well as the overt buffoonish villainy of the banker, and the insanity of all those Indians dying to attack one measly stagecoach, but some flaws can make the diamond sparkle. In *Stagecoach*, Ford outdid himself and every other director this year, including Victor Fleming servicing David O. Selznick's monomaniacal obsession, Frank Capra reworking *Mr. Deeds* into something even better, and William Wyler sentimentalizing the great Emily Brontë masterpiece, *Wuthering Heights*. From this moment on in American filmmaking, until the middle Fifties, John Ford would be king of the hill, and the man who set the pace for stretching the craft of direction. Masterpiece after masterpiece would flow from his creative genius; *Stagecoach* gave Ford his dominance. Ford should have won the Oscar for Best Director.

But allow me one coda: how could the Academy not have nominated Ernst Lubitsch for *Ninotchka*?! Who else could have made Garbo appear so deliciously funny? Off to Siberia with the Academy! Academy, nyet! *Ninotchka* and Lubitsch, da!

Best Writing (Screenplay): Sidney Howard won for *Gone with the Wind*, over Eric Maschwitz, R.C. Sherriff, and Claudine West, *Goodbye, Mr. Chips*; Sidney Buchman, *Mr. Smith Goes to Washington*; Charles Brackett, Walter Reisch and Billy Wilder, *Ninotchka*; and Ben Hecht & Charles MacArthur, *Wuthering Heights*

Poor Sidney Howard was run over by his own tractor on his farm in Massachusetts and died before knowing he had won, thus marking the first posthumous Academy Award. That anybody could adapt a novel this long and succeed is a remarkable achievement. Howard did the best he could to cut the book down to a manageable size, and for that pruning alone, he should keep his nomination. But while many of the best parts of the book made it into the movie, and some of the dialogue snaps beautifully, I always find myself wishing they had tightened it further, and cut out some of the moonlight and magnolia swooning over how great the South was. I do think Howard deserves a nomination for the winnowing, but I don't find much about the writing that keeps me coming back to the movie.

Goodbye, Mr. Chips begins at the end, the better to facilitate the rosy, deceptive glow of sentimental nostalgia in this exceedingly slow film. The script has very little conflict, and gives Robert Donat almost nothing to do as the teacher. This is as much due to the original Hilton work as it is to Chips, an essentially passive character. The best parts of the film come from the romance and the rare moments when Donat becomes a bit active, before slipping back into passivity again. My complaints about the script have to do with the lack of evidence that Chips is a decent teacher (tea and cake do not a great teacher make); surely a film about teaching ought to show some actual, convincing, inspiring teaching going on? Instead, Mr. Chips is turned into a mascot of the school, like some old St. Bernard kept around for the students to pat on the head. The direction and the script are the reason this film falls down in the competition. No nomination should have been made for Maschwitz (this was his career high), R.C. Sherriff (*The Invisible Man, That Hamilton Woman*), and Claudine West (*Mrs. Miniver, Random Harvest*).

Sidney Buchman's script for *Mr. Smith Goes to Washington* turns the wonderful original into a deep examination of American ideals: "I want to make that come to life for every boy in this land. Yes, and all lighted up like that too! You see, you see, boys forget what their country means by just reading 'the land of the free' in history books. And they get to be men – they forget even more. Liberty's too precious a thing to be buried in books, Miss Saunders. Men should hold it up in front of them every single day of their lives and say: 'I'm free to think and to speak. My ancestors couldn't. I can. And my children will.' Boys want to grow up remembering that." The movie's theme is the need to never stop fighting for those things: "Dad always used to say the only causes worth fighting for were the lost causes." Buchman could also be funny, as when Stewart whistles at the backs of the Senators' heads: "I just wanted to find out if you still had faces." Buchman wrote the Elizabeth Taylor *Cleopatra* and *Billy Jack Goes to Washington*, which proves that he really should have stopped while he was ahead. He should keep this nomination as a reminder of when he was on top of his game.

Charles Brackett, Billy Wilder, and Walter Reisch[68] worked under Ernst Lubitsch on *Ninotchka*, their first truly great script. Reisch would go on to write *Gaslight*, but Brackett and Wilder would head much higher to craft two of the finest films of the coming decade: the groundbreaking *The Lost Weekend* and the miracle that is *Sunset Blvd*. Building off of the basic story created by Melchior Lengyel, some of the finest, funniest dialogue of the year emerges: Garbo: "We don't have men like you in my country." Douglas: "Thank you." Garbo: "That is why I believe in the future of my country." Perhaps the coldest line in the film: "The last mass trials were a great success. There are going to be

---

[68] Ed Sikov relates this story about Reisch in his marvelous biography of Billy Wilder, *On Sunset Boulevard*. Kurt Weill once said that Reisch "ought to be shot right after Hitler." P. 134.

fewer but better Russians." They even spoof Garbo's famous tagline, when they have the three envoys ask her if she wants to be alone, and she says, emphatically, no. Like most films that Lubitsch made, the dialogue is tantalizing and suggestive; Wilder in particular took up that banner, as he moved into directing his own scripts. An excellent nomination.

As an adaptation, *Wuthering Heights* filters this classic English novel through the mind of two very successful American screenwriters, Ben Hecht and Charles MacArthur. Like many Hollywood adaptations, less than half of the original book was used (*The Grapes of Wrath* stops about halfway through as well). We can't blame Hecht and MacArthur for the idiotic ending with the ghosts; that was Sam Goldwyn's heavy-handed botch. But Hecht and MacArthur seem to have missed much of the heart of the book, as well as only allowing themselves to submit to Brontë's stunningly original structure in the briefest possible way. What they focus on is the romance, bringing it away from the larger view of life Brontë drew out of her tale; they reduce one of the finest novels ever written to a melodrama. No nomination should have been given for butchering a literary masterpiece.

As for the scripts the Academy snubbed, I would like to point at one in particular: the Claudette Colbert/Don Ameche *Midnight*. Directed by Mitchell Leisen, from a screenplay by Billy Wilder and Charles Brackett, *Midnight* is a fine screwball comedy. Colbert plays a gold digger down on her luck; Ameche plays the taxi driver who picks her up. John Barrymore plays a rich man who hires Colbert to seduce his wife's lover away from her. The piano-playing prince is a hoot. Barrymore is an absolute wreck, but he's very funny. Billy Wilder was apparently so incensed by the changes Leisen made, he swore he would become a director. Thanks, Mitch! Watching the film, I have no idea what Wilder was upset about. *Midnight* should have been nominated for Best Screenplay.

In picking the best of this category, I came down to the one film whose screenwriters created the best dialogue, the most memorable lines, out of the story they were adapting – that, and which films were the most tightly plotted and paced. On those grounds, *Ninotchka* deserved the Oscar for Best Writing (Screenplay). Garbo: "Must you flirt?" Douglas: "Well, I don't have to, but I find it natural." Garbo: "Suppress it." Priceless. Wilder, Reisch and Brackett should have taken home the

Academy Award, with one proviso: Ernst Lubitsch's name should have been added.[69]

Best Cinematography (Black & White): in this new category, Gregg Toland won for *Wuthering Heights*, over Joseph Valentine, *First Love*; Gregg Toland, *Intermezzo*; Joseph H. August, *Gunga Din*; Victor Milner, *The Great Victor Herbert*; Tony Gaudio, *Juarez*; Norbert Brodine, *Lady of the Tropics*; Joseph Walker, *Only Angels Have Wings*. Arthur Charles Miller, *The Rains Came*; and Bert Glennon, *Stagecoach*

Gregg Toland won for *Wuthering Heights.* Wyler and Toland were a perfect working pair, merging "their ideas of lyrical, fluid camera movements, long takes, and deep-focus photography that would reveal backgrounds as clearly as characters and images close to the camera. Toland rejected the typical Hollywood soft-focus, one-plane depth and strove for razor-sharp black-and-white images. To achieve the maximum contrast between shadow and light on this film, he used high-powered Technicolor arc lamps and a film stock four times faster than customary without an appreciable increase in graininess. He set the mood Wyler wanted for the picture by using candlelike effects, keeping the characters partially in darkness before coming fully into the light at climactic moments, and shooting from a low angle to capture the ceilings of the sets, emphasizing the confining loneliness of Wuthering Heights."[clviii] I could not have said it better, for it is the cinematography that brings me back to this *Wuthering Heights*, and not the troubled performances of Olivier and Oberon, or the ruin they make of the novel. Still, Toland's work was gone one better by another director's partnership with a cameraman – but the nomination could not be more appropriate.

First Love is a very minor film, and the rationale for Joseph Valentine's nomination is not obvious. The movie opens with a nice panning shot, with a very economical camera, and lots of pretty shots of Durbin, all lit by bright, cheery, romantic lighting, just like the score. The film was probably nominated for the crowd disappearing scene, when Deanna Durbin dances with Robert Stack, and the entire crowd of dancers slowly fades away like ghosts. Some good special effects were shot in addition to the dance scene – Durbin's reflection sticks her tongue out at her real self; later, she argues with her reflection. When her cousin tries to keep her from going to the ball, Valentine gives us a

---

[69] The screenwriters had petitioned for Ernst Lubitsch's name to be added to the original credits, and MGM turned them down. See the details in Ed Sikov, *On Sunset Boulevard*, p. 135-36.

nice shot of her ascending the stairs, dejected, followed by her shadow. The nomination should stay.

Victor Milner shot *The Great Victor Herbert*, and while Milner, as I've noted before, was capable of first-rate work, often with Cecil B. DeMille, *The Great Victor Herbert* doesn't fall into that category. Milner seems to be phoning it in here. No nomination should have been given for this static, visually boring film.

Joseph H. August filmed *Gunga Din*, which stars Cary Grant, Victor McLaglen, and Douglas Fairbanks, Jr. in one perfect adventure film: fighting, comedy, sacrifice, spectacle, a great villain, and a little romance. Opening shots of the villains approaching the sleeping soldiers look great – especially the shot of the horses shying back in terror from the murders. Some of the unusual camera moves include the most extreme close-ups anybody has used up to this point, both for the purposes of romance with Fairbanks and his fiancé, and for the purposes of terror, with the head of the Kali cult glaring. Overall, August's highly competent cinematography, particularly for the action scenes, makes for a fine nomination.

In *Intermezzo*, Gregg Toland has faces dominating, with the fresh glory of Ingrid Bergman leading the pack. Toland even makes Leslie Howard bearable (although I wish he'd drop the damn pipe that obscures his diction). Toland's photography is clean and simple, with little of the depths he would soon reveal in *The Long Voyage Home* and *Citizen Kane*, or the kind of darkness he would attempt to imbue into *Wuthering Heights*. But when Ingrid Berman comes onto the screen, Toland tries to turn each and every frame of her into a portrait, of youth, of beauty, of raw talent and commitment. Bergman never looked better, even in *Casablanca*. The shots from inside the piano doubling Bergman's face are a nice touch, as are the images in the shop window when Bergman tries to end the affair (indicating the double lives adulterers lead). Later, when she realizes she must try again, she pulls back into the darkness from the bright window, fading into it (a scene stolen by countless films). Toland deserved this nomination, as well as the one for *Wuthering Heights*.

Juarez has occasional flashes of inventive cinematography from Tony Gaudio, and two excellent performances from Brian Aherne and Bette Davis. The battle scenes have a suitably chaotic, confused feel to them. One striking scene has soldiers running across a hill while the sun sets behind them. When the Emperor begins his repressions, the mourning and praying of women and their lamentations is done in deep shadows, with the lights coming down from some strange outside source, rendering the women as compositions of light and dark, rather than human beings. Certainly, the film isn't as impressive visually in comparison to the kind of work Toland and Glennon were producing this year, with the exceptions being the scenes above, and those with Davis as the Empress Carlota, peaking with the scene where she goes crazy. Davis pulls out the stops, since she insisted on this role simply to be able to go bonkers. When she collapses on the ground, she wakes to see Napoleon (Claude Rains) kneeling over her – and suddenly, all the lights of his face become darks, all darks become lights. Gaudio invented an unusual, compelling way to indicate insanity, aided and abetted by Davis' fine cuckoo fit. She then vanishes into utter darkness. Gaudio may not have been at the head of the pack in terms of what cinematographers were developing, but he wasn't sitting on his haunches scratching for fleas either. The nomination should stay.

Norbert Brodine's work on *Lady of the Tropics* can't really compare with the best this year – but then, neither can the movie, a truly abominable piece of work; Joseph Schildkraut has the worst role of his career. Brodine spent much of his career at the Hal Roach studios, and shot *One Million B.C.* and *Of Mice and Men*. *Lady of the Tropics* stars Robert Taylor as a rich playboy in love with Hedy Lamarr, a part-Asian woman; their love is blocked by institutionalized racism, as he can't extract her from French Indochina to go home with him (the movie seems to be based on *Manon Lescaut*, a 1731 French novel which has been remade into many films and a classic opera by Massenet). Brodine's camerawork is largely confined to making Lamarr and Taylor look pretty, and not much else. No nomination should ever be given for pretty pictures with no substance.

Joseph Walker's work on *Only Angels Have Wings* helps Howard Hawks in taking a hard, unvarnished look at men under pressure and the stoic culture of flying. Hawks understood that world well, having served in the Army Air Corps in WWI, and then losing his own brother in a freak flying accident during the filming of an aerial stunt. Cary Grant stars in a serious dramatic role, along with Jean Arthur, Thomas Mitchell, and a young Rita Hayworth, who definitely shouldn't have been asked to show real emotion at this point of her career; it introduces a note of falsehood in an otherwise brutally honest film. Hawks also gave silent film star Richard Barthelmess a chance at a comeback. Joseph Walker's cinematography is experienced and mature, as it should be; Walker had already shot *It Happened One Night*, *Mr. Deeds Goes to Town* and *The Awful Truth*. He would go on to his masterpiece, *It's a Wonderful Life*, after WWII. For *Only Angels Have Wings*, the opening scenes of the cargo ship coming into the Central American harbor reveal a rich knowledge of deep dark shadows, luminescent fog, and natural lighting. Mitchell's death scene is shot as if each frame were a Rembrandt painting. Most importantly for a film shot almost entirely on a soundstage, none of it looks like a soundstage, largely due to the excellent art direction and Walker's camera. A solid nomination, but the gorgeous flying scenes were shot by Elmer Dyer, and he should have shared in the honors.

The Rains Came was yet another big budget disaster melodrama: two men (Tyrone Power, George Brent), two women (Myrna Loy, Brenda Joyce), a monsoon, an earthquake, and plague! Power plays an Indian doctor (without a trace of accent) with whom married Myrna Loy tries to have an affair, while husband Nigel Bruce looks askance. Brent plays a dissolute aristocrat who once had an affair with Loy, and is now pursued by a too young and innocent Joyce (one of the very few unusual things about the plot is that the women are the aggressors). *The Rains Came* is more eye candy than anything, from the gorgeous costumes to the intensely detailed sets to the first-rate special effects (see the new category below) to the inventive cinematography. Arthur Miller performed some interesting tricks to produce the bright, glimmering look director Clarence Brown wanted, including spraying the furniture and tables at a dinner scene with oil to make it glisten, and having the silverware polished repeatedly. Miller claimed a special talent for shooting rain, having the rain come in at an angle, then "You have to backlight rain or you don't see it; it's just a blur. And all the way in my picture the rain shines; it was the theme of the film."[clix] From the opening shot of the camera floating through the trees and monkeys to dolly in on George Brent, Miller does his best to keep the picture floating, despite its bloat. In the final scene, he has this wonderful long dolly out backwards down the stairs as Tyrone Power comes marching towards the camera to assume his rulership of the restored city. An excellent nomination.

Bert Glennon's work on *Stagecoach* may be the best this wonderful cameraman ever produced – but the guiding hand of John Ford must be accorded its due. Glennon's best work was always with Ford (see Best Cinematography (Color) for more on Glennon). The camerawork on *Stagecoach* remains one of cinema's treasures, and its endless invention and clarity cannot be beaten – even by the brilliant Toland, who was moving into the artistic groundbreaking that would lead to *Citizen Kane* in two years. The opening credits stun with the solitary stagecoach, the lines of cavalry, and Indians moving through Monument Valley, the landscape Ford would inhabit for much of the next two decades in his westerns. When we get into the exposition, a number of moves do Glennon and Ford honor: the dollying camera as we watch

Claire Trevor being railroaded out of town; the glowing interior of a saloon, ironically rendered in the shafts of light of a church window (and the liquor salesman is called a "reverend"); the exit from town out onto the beautiful desolation of Monument Valley; the magnificence of John Wayne's instant stardom. Ford and Glennon provide an endless variety of shots of the movement through the landscape, simple and elegant, without showing off. Part of the reason why *Stagecoach* is such an important film lies in the poetry that finally emerges as a major component of Ford's films, without letting the action and characterization subside. The composition of individual scenes is economical and precise, as when Ford shows the reaction shot of the banker, the gambler, and the lady to the outlaw addressing the prostitute with the honorific of "Ma'am"; the look of shock on all three faces is conveyed at once, as is the milder surprise and amusement on the drunken doctor's face. Ford also uses his favorite framing device of the door, although obliquely; we are not yet at the end of *The Searchers*. But the chase scene across the dry river bed, and the gunfight at the end, remain cinematic tour de forces, almost entirely told visually, with very little dialogue. Masterful! Bert Glennon should have won the Oscar for Best Cinematography (Black & White).

Best Cinematography (Color): in this new category, Ernest Haller and Ray Rennahan won for *Gone with the Wind*, over Ray Rennahan and Bert Glennon, *Drums Along the Mohawk*; Georges Périnal and Osmond Borradaile, *The Four Feathers*; William V. Skall and Bernard Knowles, *The Mikado*; Sol Polito and W. Howard Greene, *The Private Lives of Elizabeth and Essex*; and Hal Rosson, *The Wizard of Oz*.

Ernest Haller and Ray Rennahan film *Gone with the Wind* in a Technicolor opulent and nostalgic for the beauty of the old South. The scene we remember, more than any other, is the great sweeping crane shot of the dead and dying Confederates in the street, pulling back and back and back to reveal the horrendous cost of the loss, until we finally reach a Confederate flag, shredded and fluttering in the wind. What follows almost immediately is the birth of Melanie's baby, shown in shadows. What both scenes have is absolute honesty, told almost entirely in visual terms, with little or no dialogue. We then move quickly to the burning of Atlanta, and the grand romantic gesture of the goodbye kiss against the burning oranges of the sky – true cinematic magic, followed by a grand slap from Scarlett for Rhett's impertinence. Like the direction, however, the cinematography is problematic, since Lee Garmes was fired, along with George Cukor, when Selznick wasn't getting what he wanted. In the end, the cinematography is impressive, but only at moments, rather than throughout, as should be the case. The nomination should stay, but I think another film is more visually impressive.

Drums Along the Mohawk is John Ford's first color film (as well as Claudette Colbert's). Ford would alternate between color and black and white for the rest of his career, depending on budgets, as well as the appropriateness of the medium for the story he wanted to tell. Can anyone seriously imagine *The Quiet Man* in black and white, without those glorious Irish greens, or *The Man Who Shot Liberty Valance* in color, without those endless shades of gray that reflect the dubious morality of the characters? Ray Rennahan and Bert Glennon did an excellent job on the film, under Ford's guidance. Rennahan had a long and illustrious career, including the first Technicolor full-length film, *Becky Sharp*, the Tyrone Power *Blood and Sand*, *For Whom the Bell Tolls*, and *Victory Through Air Power*. Glennon filmed even greater classics than Rennahan, including *Stagecoach, Young Mr. Lincoln* and *Rio Grande* for Ford; he also shot the first full length 3-D film with stereo, *House of Wax*. *Drums Along the Mohawk* opens with a wedding, widening out from the bride's bouquet into a full length shot of Henry Fonda and Claudette Colbert, looking serious and nervous. Unlike the British films nominated this year, the colors are rich, vibrant, and full. Although this may be due to film restoration more than the original intent, I doubt it; British films seem to have more pastels and restraint than American palettes at this point. Fonda's eyes have their intense blue revealed fully; no wedding gown was ever a brighter white than Colbert's seems to be here. Colbert actually has fuller eyebrows for a change, but one of the great flaws of this film lies in her makeup – which only prostitutes wore until the twentieth century. Edna May Oliver is wearing makeup too, looking even more ridiculous. Unfortunately, moments have grown embarrassing with the passage of time: Colbert grows hysterical at the first sight of an Indian, and Fonda strikes her; Fonda's Indian friend, Blue Back, is a bundle of stereotypes.[70] But considered strictly in terms of its cinematography, *Drums* is a beautiful film, and grows more interesting as Ford became surer of the new color medium. Perhaps the most memorable shot in the whole movie is when Fonda is running to get help against this glorious sunrise, with the three Indians chasing him against successive skylines. The Academy made a good choice with this one.

---

[70] Andrew Sarris is quite dismissive: "...the film never recovers from Claudette Colbert's whining performance at the outset of her ordeal in the wilderness." *You Ain't Seen Nothin' Yet"* p. 189.

The Four Feathers stars Ralph Richardson, John Clements, and C. Aubrey Smith in the best version of the classic adventure novel by A.E.W. Mason. An Alexander Korda production, *The Four Feathers* tells the story of a young soldier who resigns his military commission before a war begins which he opposes, only to find his three best friends and the woman he loves branding him a coward with four white feathers. The young man sets out to redeem himself through acts of bravery. Be warned that colonialism and racism are celebrated here even more than in *The Lives of a Bengal Lancer* and *Gunga Din*. The color photography has some of the vibrancy we associate with films like *The Adventures of Robin Hood* – the red of the soldier's coats has never been so red – but some of it has that washed-out British feel. A considerable amount of footage was shot live in the Sudan, overall, the outdoor scenes are considerably more vibrant in color and inventiveness than the interior scenes. The shots of the ships on the river are particularly striking, even more so than the ambitiously large battle scenes. Georges Périnal (*The Life and Death of Colonel Blimp*) and Osmond Borradaile (*I Was a Male War Bride*) split the duties, with Périnal taking the interior scenes, and Borradaile shooting in the Sudan. Both deserved this nomination.

William V. Skall and Bernard Knowles shot the first color version of Gilbert and Sullivan's *The Mikado*. Directed by Victor Schertzinger, this British version features the great members of the D'Oyly Carte opera company (still the best in the world for Gilbert and Sullivan). As an adaptation, this *Mikado* is surprisingly good, despite a number of songs being cut, and having to put up with the American radio star Kenny Baker as Nanki-Poo (I much prefer Kenny Baker as R2-D2...). As for the cinematography, we get a fairly lush palette as one would expect from Technicolor, although in those hushed color ranges one often finds in British color in this period. The whole thing looks like a hand-tinted picture postcard from late nineteenth century Japan. The camerawork isn't particularly interesting, remaining largely stationary, with only occasional movements of the sort American cinematographers had been moving beyond for several years at this point. Overall, though, an impressive production, and the nomination is worthy.

The Private Lives of Elizabeth and Essex was shot by Sol Polito and W. Howard Greene under the direction of Michael Curtiz. The color cinematography of *Elizabeth and Essex* comes close to matching that of *The Adventures of Robin Hood*. Great angles and strong close-ups build on the inventive use of shadows Curtiz had already made his trademark style. Sol Polito built on his fantastic work on *Robin Hood* and *Angels with Dirty Faces*; W. Howard Greene shot *Nothing Sacred* and *A Star Is Born*, and would go on to *Jungle Book*. All told, the camerawork is up to the usual high standards of Curtiz films, which is a very high one. The nomination is well earned.

The Wizard of Oz remains, for many, their first experience with what color film truly meant. As a child, we didn't have a color television for many years after others did, but when we finally did, and that yearly ritual of watching *The Wizard of Oz* anybody over the age of thirty grew up with came around, I recall vividly the shock of seeing Technicolor after the sepia tones of the Kansas scenes. Has a film ever used that bright, brilliant color more effectively to support the narrative? Yes, *Gone with the Wind* is stunning to look at, but *The Wizard of Oz* produces the very colors of childhood and imagination. Hal Rosson's mastery is most evident when we shift into Oz, and his camera floats out of the doorway into Oz, taking a wide, soaring slow sweep into the landscape and back around to Dorothy, so we can be fully immersed in the fantasy. Hal Rosson should have won the Oscar for Best Cinematography (Color).

Best Original Score: Herbert Stothart won for *The Wizard of Oz*, over Max Steiner for both *Dark Victory* and *Gone with the Wind*; Werner Janssen, *Eternally Yours*; Victor Young for three scores, *Golden Boy*, *Gulliver's Travels*, and *Man of Conquest*; Lud Gluskin and Lucien Moraweck, *The Man in the Iron Mask*; Anthony Collins, *Nurse Edith Cavell*; Aaron Copland, *Of Mice and Men*; and Alfred Newman for both *The Rains Came* and *Wuthering Heights*

Much as I hate to argue an Oscar should not have been given to *The Wizard of Oz*, I suspect this Oscar went to Stothart on the strength of the MGM block voting, and the genius of Harold Arlen and Yip Harburg's brilliant songs. MGM jiggered with the category, by nominating Stothart for Original Score, when the credits themselves label his contribution as "Musical Adaptation"! Stothart wrote the incidental music, so we can give him credit (and the nomination) for the terrifying theme that goes along with Elvira Gulch and the Wicked Witch whenever we see them, as well as other interstitial music, but in all honesty, another film deserved the Oscar more. I'm also not happy when any composer "borrows" music from another composer and fails to credit him; when Toto is running away from the Witch's castle, the music playing is Mendelssohn's Scherzo in E-Minor; Stothart also lifts from Mussorgsky's *Night on Bald Mountain* when the Cowardly Lion, the Scarecrow, and the Tin Woodsman approach the room where Dorothy is kept prisoner.[clx] We shouldn't give Oscars to thieves.

Let me just go ahead and say it first this time: Max Steiner deserved to win the Oscar for Best Original Score for *Gone with the Wind*. The majestic, sweeping "Tara's Theme" alone should have won him the Oscar. As Molly Haskell has pointed out in her brilliant study of GWTW, Steiner's score built on everything he had ever done, and went beyond: "Following his usual practice of writing 'themes,' there is one for Scarlett, another for Melanie, and of course the Tara melody that later became the popular single 'My Own True Love.' The rest was a brilliant assemblage of Civil War songs – 'Marching through Georgia,' 'Dixie,' 'The Bonnie Blue Flag' – and various Stephen Foster tunes. It was Hollywood prestige music, perfectly fitting Selznick's idea of a score that could soothe, excite, tranquilize, or quiver according to the demands of the situation."[clxi] Steiner should have won the Oscar. Cue the wind!

Max Steiner was also nominated for *Dark Victory*, with a softer, more subtle score for *Dark Victory* than he did for *Gone with the Wind*. While not the thrilling sweep that Tara's theme is, the lush violins and sentimental turns of the score are excellent, and more memorable than anything in the film other than Bette Davis' performance. "But the waspish Bette Davis occasionally broke through her docility. Getting ready to shoot her death scene, Davis jokingly asked the director, 'Well, Eddie, am I going to act this, or is Max?' meaning composer Max Steiner. Goulding assured her that the drama would be all hers, but Steiner's choirs of angels eventually did escort Judith into the hereafter, to Davis' dismay."[clxii] Davis may have been right, but the blurred fadeout of the camera was just as intrusive, rather than letting Davis act what was a beautiful death scene to a finish. The last few minutes of the score, with violins, harp and human chorus, is elegantly beautiful. Steiner deserved this nomination as well.

Eternally Yours stars David Niven and Loretta Young in a romantic melodrama. He plays a magician, fortune teller and escape artist; she marries him, then decides she wants a normal life without risk. Werner Janssen wrote the score, such as it is. One of the most wretched title songs ever written is sung over the credits. Janssen gives us typical soap opera music, and not much more. No nomination was merited.

Directed by Rouben Mamoulian, *Golden Boy* stars William Holden in his breakthrough picture as a violinist turned boxer. Barbara Stanwyck plays his love interest in this adaptation of the Clifford Odets play (which originally ended in a double suicide as a finale). Holden, like the rest of the cast, seems stuck in the play; everything is a bit stilted, and too talky, with a few exceptions (the big fight at the end is done with a wicked satiric touch). Stereotypes abound: the Italian father, the Jewish friend, the crooked fight promoter, the dumb daughter, the abusive son-in-law, the Italian gangster. Still, the movie works, mostly because Barbara Stanwyck anchors everything. The score by Victor Young remains one of his best, although he does incorporate Johannes Brahms' "Cradle Song" as a touchstone. At times, he restricts the instrumentation to a solo violin; given the role the instrument has in the story, the score does a fine job conveying and supporting the emotional turns in the script (Young was himself a violinist). Young once said, "Writing a movie score is like a boy sitting in the balcony seat with a girl. He must be forceful enough to impress the girl but not loud enough to attract the usher!"[clxiii] Young certainly does that here, and deserved his nomination.

Victor Young was also up for the Fleischer Studio' first full-length animated film, *Gulliver's Travels*. Young is credited for the "atmospheric music" (as opposed to the music and lyrics, for which see Best Song above, wherein the film is also discussed more thoroughly). While not the more personal, interesting score Young produced for *Golden Boy*, his music for *Gulliver's Travels* does everything one expects and more. Try just listening to the score, and hear how varied and constantly shifting the instrumentation and tonal qualities are. Young was rapidly developing into one of the best composers Hollywood had, if not yet one of the distinctive ones like Max Steiner. The nomination should stay for his inventiveness.

Victor Young was nominated yet again for *Man of Conquest*. The only reason this thing got a nod was that each studio got one nominee, and Young was on a roll for other film scores. Young must have been tired, as he gave us complete trash here – call the garbageman, because he should get no nomination.

The Man in the Iron Mask stars Louis Hayward in the dual role of Louis XIV and his imprisoned brother Philip, the one a bug-eyed lecherous creep, and the other a noble victim of cruelty. Warren Williams does a grand job of playing d'Artagnan in his older years; Joseph Schildkraut brings a foppish glee to the villain Foucault. The score is serviceable, but hardly worth an Oscar. I didn't even notice the score until the very end of the picture, when the organ music began playing for the wedding ceremony. All we get is predigested pap in an era of talented men like Copland, Newman, and Steiner. For the final chase scene, we get a crescendo of brass, topped by some soaring strings, then some descending scales – repeatedly and with only minor variation. No nomination for Lud Gluskin and Lucien Moraweck, who never came even close to this kind of recognition again (they went on to other B-pictures, then mostly forgettable television music).

Nurse Edith Cavell tells the story of the WWI nurse who helped prisoners of war escape. Starring Anna Neagle, Edna May Oliver, George Sanders, and May Robson, *Nurse Edith Cavell* is adamantly antiwar. The score by Anthony Collins is brassy and martial at times, then softly introspective at others. No dominant themes or connecting structure seems to exist, as Collins just jumps into whatever mood the scene seems to require. He has clearly listened to Korngold, and comes dangerously close to plagiarism from parts of *Robin Hood*. Collins never really broke into the A-picture level; he seems to have been a competent hired gun with little substance to his music. No nomination should ever have been given for this jumbled, hurried hodgepodge.

Aaron Copland's score for *Of Mice and Men* has remained in my memory since I first heard it in high school. One of the few truly great American composers, Copland also wrote a handful of movie scores that prove him to be the equal in that artistic form as well; *Of Mice and Men* was his first. Apparently, it was so good Hal Roach placed it in two different categories, Best Score and Best Original Score. The nomination belongs here in this Original Score category. Copland's music begins in the bright blare of trumpet calls, undergirded by ominous kettledrums and that moaning, pensive flute so distinctive in this score. Copland was a master of orchestral color, shifting his instrumentation to reflect the needs of the story on the screen, providing the perfect accompaniment. More importantly, Copland explored the pastoral qualities he was reaching for in his concert hall work, underscoring the longing for Eden which marks *Of Mice and Men* at its heart. A great nomination.

The Rains Came is mostly pseudo-Indian (lots of big fat brass, floating oboes, single drum percussion), along with what sounds like a reasonably accurate Indian band playing, interspersed by mundane, run of the mill adventure and romance music. But every so often, Alfred Newman returns to the authentic Indian instruments, even if they have been filtered through a western sensibility and compositional process. While not aurally memorable, *The Rains Came* is an early attempt at some level of authenticity, at least part of the time. The flute and tambourine combination is quite suggestive as well. The nomination should stay for that experimentation.

Newman was nominated again for the *Wuthering Heights* score, heavy with romantic strings. For less loving scenes, he uses the strings to suggest mystery and fearful outcomes in quite an effective way; the lonely woodwinds float through it. One of the most brilliant ideas in the score comes when Newman judiciously adds human voices, in preparation for the arrival of the ghostly voice of Cathy. Newman composes for almost every single scene, drawing out each emotional turn with a shift in instrumentation and tonal quality. Perhaps he does this a bit too much; we're not really allowed to decide how we feel before the score informs us. More than that, however, none of the score is particularly memorable, in the way that Steiner's score for *Gone with the Wind* or the horde's score for *Stagecoach* is. The nomination should stay for a good piece of work, but it isn't Newman's artistic peak.

As mentioned above, Korngold's score for *The Private Lives of Elizabeth and Essex* should be moved here from Best Score (see discussion there). Were it not for giving Max Steiner and *Gone with the Wind* the Oscar, Korngold should have won for this score, with the only other serious contender being Copland's *Of Mice and Men*.

Best Art Direction: Lyle Wheeler won for *Gone with the Wind*, over Hans Dreier and Robert Odell, *Beau Geste*; Charles D. Hall, *Captain Fury*; Jack Otterson and Martin Obzina, *First Love*; Van Nest Polglase and Alfred Herman, *Love Affair*; John Victor Mackay, *Man of Conquest*; Lionel Banks, *Mr. Smith Goes to Washington*; Anton Grot, *The Private Lives of Elizabeth and Essex*; William S. Darling and George Dudley, *The Rains Came*; Alexander Toluboff, *Stagecoach*; Cedric Gibbons and William A. Horning, *The Wizard of Oz*; and James Basevi, *Wuthering Heights*.

Lyle Wheeler won for *Gone with the Wind*. We should add William Cameron Menzies and David O. Selznick to the nominees for this category. Wheeler, Menzies, and Selznick do their best to recreate the antebellum South, but it's really a moonlight and magnolias South that never really existed except for in overactive Southern imaginations. The sets of the film aren't what we remember, so much as the costumes, the actors' faces, and the occasionally rich skylines that seem to mark the emotional turns of the narrative. Wheeler deserved a nomination, but another film's art direction was far more integral to the story, as well as to our memories of it.

For *Beau Geste,* Hans Dreier and Robert Odell give us a decent fort set, but essentially one we've seen dozens of times in other pictures, before and since. We do get some nice shots of an English country house in its upper class Edwardian glories, but *Beau Geste* really has no justification to be nominated.

Captain Fury tells of an Irish immigrant fighting against a dastardly rich landowner in mid-nineteenth century Australia. Hal Roach directed this enjoyable film starring Brian Aherne, Victor McLaglen, and Paul Lukas. Charles D. Hall provided the first-rate sets; Hall is more famous for his art direction on *All Quiet on the Western Front, Dracula, Frankenstein* and *Bride of Frankenstein*. Hall's ability to coax a solid look out of a low budget served him well with Roach; here, we get kangaroo, emu, a prison, a ranch and some outdoor sets. He should keep the nomination, especially given the limits he probably had.

Jack Otterson and Martin Obzina help Deanna Durbin out in *First Love* with a girl's school graduation; a rich mansion (the staircase of which looks recycled from another movie, although I couldn't say from where). I could hear Carrie Bradshaw gasp at the enormous closet for the spoiled cousin. We get a country club and horse paths, and a truly magnificent home where Durbin goes for her first dance (which she must leave by midnight). A decent nomination.

Van Nest Polglase and Alfred Herman do a nice job on parts of *Love Affair*. The best visual part of this film is the hilltop home of Maria Ouspenskaya, an enchanted place of terraces and lush vegetation. The chapel there is touched with a holy light as well. Other than that, we get a cruise ship, a nightclub, and a couple of apartments. Polglase and Herman were really nominated for that idyllic Shangri-La, which is enough to keep the nomination.

John Victor Mackay does his best for *Man of Conquest*, in which Richard Dix stars as Sam Houston. The movie feels like a warmed over attempt by poverty row studio Republic Pictures to remake *Cimarron*. MacKay spent his career in B-pictures, working on miniscule budgets; he was nominated three times for this category, but never won. He isn't going to this time either, but for trying hard, he can stay.

Lionel Banks (*The Awful Truth, His Girl Friday*) reproduced the U.S. Senate and many of its accoutrements for *Mr. Smith Goes to Washington*. The Senate floor was a nearly exact replica, and feels like the real thing (I used to wonder if they had simply gotten permission to film there). As for the other monuments, Capra took on-site footage illegally, as the government denied him the right to film at various monuments. Banks did a superlative job for this movie; for the main set alone, the nomination was well-deserved.

Anton Grot seems to have been born for Technicolor and *The Private Lives of Elizabeth and Essex*: "...his design...compliments and underscores the emotional nature of each scene. In Elizabeth's court, the gray walls and vast spaces underline her sense of isolation. Wooden doors with heavy carved patterns add to the sense of monumentality. Essex's residence has warmer, richer colors and a greater sense of intimacy to provide an effective contrast to the impersonality of the court... In the set of the Tower dungeon, especially striking are the heavy arches, which seem to weigh down upon the queen, and the staircase in the middle of the floor from which emerges not only the Earl of Essex, but the last rays of warm light before Elizabeth is sealed off permanently in her world of isolation and mistrust."[clxiv] Watching the movie is a visual delight matched only by the excellent acting of Bette Davis and the charm of Errol Flynn. Anton Grot well deserved a nomination in this category.

The Rains Came reproduces an Indian city, private residences, the palace and hospital – both before and after the disasters. William S. Darling and George Dudley do an excellent job detailing the world of India, looking beautiful, realistic, and romantic. The outdoor scenes in particular look very much like what similar sets look like in *A Passage to India* and *Gandhi*. One of the finest sets is the great gate to the city, with the ruins beyond, and elephants being used to clean up the flotsam and jetsam. Wonderful stuff, entirely deserving of an Oscar nomination (and in most other years, an easy win).

Alexander Toluboff was named for *Stagecoach*. Given that the major visual attractions of the film, other than the brilliant cinematography, are John Wayne and Monument Valley, I am not quite sure we can credit Toluboff with this nomination. His sets look like the typical western town, which we've seen in dozens of B-westerns. But they do have an authentic flavor, and we never feel as if we're not in the Old West. The nomination should stay.

Cedric Gibbons and William A. Horning went all out for *The Wizard of Oz*. Having seen the movie before reading the Oz stories, I never knew them as my first experience, although I have come to love the original book illustrations by John R. Neill as much, if not more, than the film, through my children's eyes. The movie remains something quite special, in a category by itself. From the opening of the film on the Kansas plain, to the Professor's wagon, to that incredible opening scene in Munchkin land, and to all of the rest of this remarkably visual film, we get what I think is the most imaginatively designed set of the entire studio era. A truly outstanding nomination.

For *Wuthering Heights*, James Basevi did the best he could turning a southern California hill into the heath: tumbleweeds masqueraded as heather; a giant rock sticks out of a field. Not exactly inspiring. The homes are reasonably done, but that should not have been enough for a nomination.

As for the films that the Academy neglected, I want to point out two horror films. *The Tower of London* is basically a version of Shakespeare's *Richard III* with Boris Karloff added as Mord the executioner. Basil Rathbone plays Richard. Vincent Price has a very early role as one of Richard's murder victims, drowned in a giant barrel of wine. Price hasn't developed his rich voice or acting style, substituting a set of nervous tics instead, except for the manic drinking and death scene, which is well done. Although the limited budget is obvious, the sets do justice to the medieval world in realistic detail, as horrific in the torture room as it is domestic in the living quarters. The little model throne room kept by Richard III on his murderous way to the throne room proves to be quite helpful in keeping the plot straight, as Richard bumps off each one in his way.

The other film is *Son of Frankenstein*, which gives us the last gasp of German expressionism in American film with its strikingly odd sets. The opening scenes of the town look like an updated, surreal *Cabinet of Dr. Caligari*. Look at the foyer of the Frankenstein castle, with its jagged staircase and marvelous shadows; I recall as a child how disturbing this film was, compared to the others in the series, and I have to conclude that the sets are the reason. I suspect the unusual nature of the sets also played a part in Mel Brooks choosing this movie as the largest part of his brilliant parody *Young Frankenstein*. The sulfur pits have also been imitated, most famously in the death scene in *Terminator 2*. The same innovative, budget-conscious art director did both *Son of Frankenstein* and *Tower of London*: Jack Otterson. *Son of Frankenstein* in particular should have garnered Otterson a nomination.

But of all the films made this year, the one whose sets are a part of the mental landscape of almost all moviegoers are those of *The Wizard of Oz*, which should have won the Oscar for Art Direction for Cedric Gibbons and William A. Horning. Follow the Yellow Brick Road!

Best Special Effects: Edmund H. Hansen and Fred Sersen won for *The Rains Came*, over *Gone with the Wind* (John R. Cosgrove, Fred Albin, and Arthur Johns); *Only Angels Have Wings* (Roy Davidson and Edwin C. Hahn); *The Private Lives of Elizabeth and Essex* (Byron Haskin and Nathan Levinson); *Topper Takes a Trip* (Roy Seawright); *Union Pacific* (Farciot Edouart, Gordon Jennings, Loren Ryder); and *The Wizard of Oz* (A. Arnold Gillespie and Douglas Shearer)

Best Special Effects is a brand new category, and one that my inner technocrat geek has always loved.

The Rains Came won the very first Oscar for special effects for creating the monsoon, the earthquake, and all the other disastrous touches to this big-budget spectacular. The rains are gorgeous – see Best Cinematography (Black & White) for more – but the earthquake outdoes *San Francisco* in its audaciousness. In one scene, a huge chunk of the street collapses with a crowd on it, below the level of the rest of the street, all while every part of the street is shaking and buildings are collapsing. Today, this would be minor CGI; in 1939, this was groundbreaking (pardon me while I duck...). We also get a spectacular dam collapse, and the ensuing flood over a bridge and through the streets of the city. Fox really poured money into *The Rains Came*, even if the story they used to get to the special effects isn't all that interesting (a problem Hollywood has avoided solving repeatedly over the decades). If it weren't for a more enduring film, with a far greater story, I would consider Edmund H. Hansen and Fred Sersen should keep their Oscar for their incredible work – but another set of special effects burned itself into our collective memory decades ago, and should have been the winner.

But before we get to that perennial favorite, allow me a quick look at the other nominees.

John R. Cosgrove, Fred Albin, and Arthur Johns came up for *Gone with the Wind*, with the burning of Atlanta at the heart of the special effects here. They torched the old wall from *King Kong*, with the great stuntman Yakima Canutt pretending to be Rhett Butler. The scene of the wall collapsing into burning debris while Rhett and Scarlett race in their carriage across the front of it is justly famous. In addition, the glass mattes used throughout the film to provide full views of Tara and other scenes provide support for this nomination.

Only Angels Have Wings earned a nod for Roy Davidson and Edwin C. Hahn. The special effects are for the model planes, which aren't bad; the crashes are done effectively. The model builder in me wants to cry when they break up those beautiful planes, but the nomination should stay.

Byron Haskin and Nathan Levinson found a way into this category with *The Private Lives of Elizabeth and Essex*, but I can't see why. The special effects seem limited to some fog and a few cannon fired and bows shot. No real reason exists for this film to be nominated in this category, so it should be removed from consideration.

Roy Seawright floated in with *Topper Takes a Trip*. Once again, we get the ghostly special effects of a Topper movie: a floating key, a riderless bicycle, a pencil writing by itself, appearing and disappearing ghosts, and so forth. First developed fully for *The Invisible Man*, these kinds of special effects have been used hundreds of times since for a variety of ghosts and invisible creatures. Seawright does a nice job; the nomination should stay.

Farciot Edouart, Gordon Jennings, and Loren Ryder rolled in with *Union Pacific*, Cecil B. DeMille's paean to the transcontinental railroad, starring Joel McCrea, Barbara Stanwyck, Brian Donlevy, and Robert Preston. Nobody has ever been able to direct a crowd scene better than DeMille, even to this day, and nobody has ever done epic spectacle better. DeMille did it by going the distance with the details – for this film, he acquired actual original railroads and designs, and he even got to use the original golden spike!^{clxv} Watching *Union Pacific* has its pleasures; among them, the railroads themselves, the western town rife with life, the railroad camp and the shooting. One comic touch comes at a long bar, when the whole line of workers drinking does a kind of double take when they hear there's gold at the end of the track. One fistfight scene is poorly staged and speeded up, giving it an unintentional look of falsehood, but the fight between McCrea and the big bearded bully at the advance camp is beautifully timed and staged – and funny. The portrayal of the Indians is particularly ugly: DeMille presents them as stupid, superstitious and childish. Ford was always far more respectful in his westerns. The main reason for this nomination is the excellent, detailed model work, on a level nobody could come close to today, because they'd simply use CGI: a water tower crashing on a train during an Indian attack, a train crossing a burning bridge, a train crashing in the snow. All good support for a valid nomination.

Finally, Arnold Gillespie and Douglas Shearer appeared courtesy of *The Wizard of Oz*. Prior to the rise of CGI, was there ever a more dramatic special effect than the twister in *The Wizard of Oz*? For that matter, has there really been any to match it since, for sheer impact and remembrance? Seeing the cyclone coming, and then Mrs. Gulch (and the Witch) circling about it, still haunts our collective dreams – as do so many other special effects in this movie: the witch writing "Surrender Dorothy!"; the crystal ball, with Auntie Em's face morphing into the Witch; the flying monkeys; the Great and Powerful Oz; the dying witch; the floating ball that brings Glinda the Good Witch. *The Wizard of Oz* should have easily won this category.

Best Short Subject (Cartoon): Disney won for *The Ugly Duckling*, and was also nominated for *The Pointer*, beating Warner Brothers for *Detouring America* and MGM for *Peace on Earth*

Walt Disney continued his dominance in this category, winning for *The Ugly Duckling*, and getting another nomination for *The Pointer*. *The Ugly Duckling* remains the best adaptation of this Hans Christian Anderson tale, and was the very last Silly Symphony Disney released. The look the father duck gives the mother duck when he sees the ugly duckling for the first time is unexpected in a Disney cartoon: duck adultery is such an ugly topic.

The Pointer is one of the very best of the Mickey Mouse cartoons, wherein Mickey attempts to train Pluto to be a hunting dog. The animation is rich and detailed; the relationship between master and mutt seems real and warm; the bear they flush is terrifying. Truly memorable!

I would also like to nominate *Goofy and Wilbur*, which has remained in my brain for its comedy and depiction of friendship since I first saw it as a child. Wilbur, if you don't know, is a grasshopper who willingly acts as bait for fish for Goofy. The relationship between the two is mutually beneficial, and emotionally resonant in a way few cartoon characters were prior to Disney's animators digging deep into their art in the late Thirties (as few have since). The numerous chases Goofy goes on to rescue his friend are marvelously inventive.

Unlike Warner's *Detouring America,* which is a travelogue, and an excuse to hang one silly joke after another with no consistent development (Tex Avery directed, and it isn't one of his best). The kind of cartoon most studios made repeatedly, *Detouring America* hasn't aged well, particularly with its racist jokes. No nomination should ever be given to mediocrity.

Peace on Earth is an MGM cartoon that remains in a class by itself: a post-apocalyptic world, in which men have completely wiped themselves out, is rebuilt by animals who actually do what the Bible says to do. A pacifist vision made on the edge of WWII breaking out, *Peace on Earth* retains the power of its simple homily. The animation is very near to the kind of beauty Disney was achieving, but in service to a higher purpose: universal peace. The scenes of war are as horrific as the home life of the animals is utopian. A great nomination; *Peace on Earth* should have won the Oscar for the gentleness with which it makes its point.

CHAPTER THIRTEEN: 1941 AWARDS
13ᵗʰ Show

Movies released in 1940

THE SCENE OF THE CRIME:

On February 27, 1941, back the Academy went to the Biltmore Bowl in the Biltmore Hotel, hosted by Walter Wanger (producer of *The Cocoanuts* and *Algiers*). President Roosevelt made a speech over the radio thanking Hollywood for its assistance in raising money to prepare defenses for a possible war. Judy Garland sang "America" to honor FDR. Bob Hope took over halfway through, and this year's joke about the table full of Oscars was "What's the matter, did Selznick bring them back?" Bob Hope received an honorary plaque for his humanitarian efforts.

Preston Sturges accepted his own Oscar by saying "Mr. Sturges isn't here this evening but I will be happy to accept the Award for him." Nobody laughed, because they didn't know what he looked like.

Price, Waterhouse successfully imposed secrecy on the winners through the sealed envelopes, a task they have performed ever since. *The Los Angeles Times* bitched about the secrecy, but nobody listened.

The fiddling with the categories continued, this time by splitting up Best Writing into Original Story, Original Screenplay, and Screenplay (by which they meant adaptations). The Best Art Direction category followed in the footsteps of Best Cinematography and separated into Color and Black & White.

WHAT THEY GOT RIGHT:

Surprisingly, a good deal. I wonder if it will last? Never fear – it won't. You'll have me around for at least a few sequels!

Best Director: John Ford won for *The Grapes of Wrath*, over Sam Wood, *Kitty Foyle*; William Wyler, *The Letter*; George Cukor, *The Philadelphia Story*; and Alfred Hitchcock, *Rebecca*.

When it came time to hand out this award, presenter Frank Capra recalled his own humiliation with *Lady for a Day* losing to *Cavalcade*, and decided to have all of the nominees come up and shake hands, to show there were no hard feelings, before he announced the winner. Naturally, the one director who didn't show up was the winner. Alfred Hitchcock, George Cukor, William Wyler and Sam Wood (three of the greatest directors of the twentieth century, and one of the most average) walked back alone. Ford was too busy fishing with Henry Fonda on his yacht to come. After Ford's death, Hitchcock was graciously generous in his praise of the man who beat him to his first Oscar: "A John Ford picture is a visual gratification – his method of shooting, eloquent in its clarity and apparent simplicity. No shots from behind the flames in the fireplace toward the room – no cameras swinging through chandeliers – no endless zooming in and out without any discernible purpose. His scripts had a beginning, middle and an end. They are understood all the world over and expand as a monument to a part of the land he loved: Monument Valley."[clxvi] Hitchcock should know; Ford won for *The Grapes of Wrath*, and rightfully so. When asked about the film, Ford demurred, as he so often did when asked questions about his work: "I was sympathetic to people like the Joads, and contributed a lot of money to them, but I was not interested in *Grapes* as a social study."[clxvii] What is left unsaid there is the fact that the Joads were constructed as a social study by Steinbeck, and Ford put that into visual terms every bit as visceral and poetic as the words Steinbeck chose. The one flaw in the film, the overly optimistic "We're the people" speech by Jane Darwell, has always struck me as deliriously stupid, given the film's somber, intense mood. Ford wanted the film finished with Fonda's departure, which is the proper ending to this adaptation (in visual terms, it completes the arrival of Fonda at the beginning of the movie; anything after that is extraneous and should not be there). Regardless of what was said later about it, Darwell's speech is just plain wrong for this movie. Perhaps it let the audience go home with a happy ending, but I cannot believe an artist like John Ford would end a masterpiece like *The Grapes of Wrath* with a happy face (more than that, visually the scene is clumsy, unlike the rest of the movie). I do not discount the sentimental streak in Ford, or his willingness to end films on a high note, as we can see in *The Battle of Midway* or *The Quiet Man*; I simply assert that he would not do so with this particular film. Rudy Behlmer's well-researched *America's Favorite Movies: Behind the Scenes* concurs; in an interview with Dorris Bowdon, the wife of screenwriter Nunnally Johnson, "She also recalls John Ford trying to convince Zanuck to use a different ending (she doesn't remember what exactly) from the one in Johnson's script."[clxviii] So I will not blame John Ford for the lukewarm vanilla pudding of a scene Zanuck plopped onto his plate after the gourmet meal was done; Ford deserved to win the Oscar for Best Director for *The Grapes of Wrath*.

Even nominating Sam Wood's direction of *Kitty Foyle* is, metaphorically, the same thing as suggesting that clothes bought at Wal-Mart should be seen to have the same fashion sense as something I will be wearing if this book sells well.[71] Never more than a talented hack, Wood was repeatedly nominated in this period because of studio block voting. I have no other explanation why such a dismally uninspired director repeatedly shows up in these nomination lists. Even worse than the hackwork is the deliberate misogynist framing this movie celebrates: we begin with a Victorian scene, in which the working girl is properly romanced and respected...but then she has the temerity to ask for the right to vote, and now, she is "rightfully" disrespected! We see this visually when men stand up on a streetcar and offer the girl a seat; once she has the right to vote, she is pushed and shoved out of the way. Wood's malevolent grin can be seen in his glee at her being denied, and all an enlightened audience can do is cringe. That vitriol returns throughout the film, as in the scene when the young doctor threatens

---

[71] Support the Fashion Police! Buy more copies for your friends today.

Our Heroine with exposure and a hypodermic if she doesn't date him. As we all know, bullying women is an acceptable dating tactic, right? No nomination should have been given for this boring troglodyte.

William Wyler's remake of *The Letter* proves to be one of the highlights of his collaborations with Bette Davis (see Best Actress below). Based on a Somerset Maugham story, *The Letter* had already been made with Jeanne Eagels in 1929. Wyler stakes out his claim in the famous opening shot of the film, a sinuous take beginning with the rubber dripping from a tree through the bunkhouse of workers, then up and around to look at the main house – and we hear a shot ring out and a man stumbling out pursued by a woman firing. Cut to the workers, then cut to the killing, with Davis' intense pursuit and repeated pulls on the trigger. Wyler understood the way to grab an audience's attention and keep it. As the camera pulls in on her face, and then on the workers, the moon clouds over, then reappears as we look down on the dead body. The motif of the moon and the guilt it brings to Davis effectively visualizes her internal drama. Tony Gaudio was nominated, and rightfully so, for the cinematography; as with many cinematographers, working with Wyler brought out their best. When Davis tells the story of the murder, the camera becomes her eyes, recreating her steps (Hitchcock does the same sort of thing in *Rebecca*). The rest of the movie continues on this high artistic level. Like Davis, Wyler was reaching a winning streak as an artist that had few rivals. He highly deserved this nomination for *The Letter*.

As for George Cukor, his gift for comedy emerged fully for the first time in *The Philadelphia Story*, guiding Cary Grant, Jimmy Stewart, and Katharine Hepburn to three of their best performances. The entire supporting cast is pitch-perfect, as is the pacing and framing of the entire film. No higher praise can be given to a director. Cukor definitely deserved this nomination.

Rebecca is important as Hitchcock's first American film, and for securing his reputation as someone who could be trusted to have his films make money – even as his battles with control freak David O. Selznick would become the bane of his existence until the end of their contract. One of the many ways Hitchcock fought to stay in charge of his film was to do what John Ford and a few other directors did: he cut in the can, shooting only what was needed, and leaving very little opportunity to edit the film in any way other than how the director wanted it. Selznick complained bitterly about it, but could do nothing; what we see on the screen is largely what Hitchcock wanted. But Selznick imposed control prior to filming, by demanding that Hitchcock stick to the novel as closely as possible, and at least early on, by sending orders that no scene was to be shot until he saw the run-through on the set.[clxix] Regardless, we are in the presence of a master enjoying his new American toys, which allowed Hitchcock to make his most elaborate, technologically advanced film thus far. The movie is drenched in the issues of memory and identity, life and death, murder and suicide, decisions and indecisions. The first character we hear is the nameless narrator, played by Fontaine; the first character we see is Maxim de Winter, played by Olivier. From the ruins of Manderley, we hear Fontaine's voice, haunted in dreams by what happened there; from the cliffs of the south of France, we see Olivier, contemplating suicide over his actions. The actions of the past haunt us forever in *Rebecca*. Love itself seems to be challenged in this film, as most poignantly visualized when Fontaine breaks the statue of love, and tries to hide the pieces – after we've seen her subjected repeatedly to the memory of Rebecca. We don't often think of Hitchcock as an actor's director, in the way we do George Cukor, for example; but given the need he could be excellent, as we can see from Joan Fontaine's unforgettable performance. Hitchcock himself later disparaged the film – saying it was "not a Hitchcock picture...It has stood up quite well over the years...I don't know why."[clxx] I suspect these comments were a means of distancing himself from Selznick: I do think *Rebecca* is a fine movie, but an unusual one in Hitchcock's canon. Despite Selznick's interference, Hitchcock deserved this nomination.

As for those directors who were snubbed, Howard Hawks should have been nominated for directing *His Girl Friday*. Comedies do not fare well with the Academy, then or now; it seems to be a permanent character flaw – for the Academy. I do give them credit for nominating George Cukor for the very funny *The Philadelphia Story*. I may not need to say much more than this for Hawks: *His Girl Friday* is almost as good, if not better in some ways, than *Bringing up Baby*. His decision to accelerate the dialogue, and to provide overlapping dialogue, was a brilliant one. Frenetic, intense, and consistently funny, he also guided Cary Grant to his first comic performance with a character who was more than a little dark, as well as giving Rosalind Russell her greatest role (see Best Actor and Best Actress for more). Hawks should have been nominated for Best Director.

Best Supporting Actor: Walter Brennan won for *The Westerner*, over Albert Bassermann, *Foreign Correspondent*; Jack Oakie, *The Great Dictator*; James Stephenson, *The Letter*; and William Gargan, *They Knew What They Wanted*

For the third time, Walter Brennan won in this category because the voters loved him. I appreciate Walter Brennan as an actor; I truly do.

But I don't think anybody should win an award based on popularity; they should win in terms of merit, and merit alone. I know the world doesn't work that way, but this book does – usually. For once, however, the Academy did the right thing, even if for the wrong reason. Director William Wyler brought out the best in Brennan, or rather, the worst, for Brennan is playing a villainous character, an odd fictional incarnation of Judge Roy Bean, a violent, impulsive man obsessed with the actress Lilly Langtry. Watch him as he hangs the farmer for the supreme crime of killing a cow. The farmer's defense? He was aiming at the cattleman. Brennan's face carries a cynicism and a sense of bewilderment at the same time, as he sifts through the world with his peculiar sense of justice. A salesman is kicked out of Brennan's bar for once having been in the same country as Lilly Langtry, but not having bothered to take the opportunity to go see her perform. When Cooper comes into town, the bizarre friendship begins – over Cooper's trial for horse-thieving; they banter and fool each other, and amuse the audience; eventually, things end badly. Brennan does more with just the look in his eyes and the shift in his facial features than in any other film he ever made; he tended to use that marvelous raspy voice and exuberance to make his way instead. As he had with Bette Davis, Wyler toned down Brennan's usual tricks, and Brennan responded with the best performance of his career thus far. Walter Brennan deserved the Oscar for Best Supporting Actor.

In Alfred Hitchcock's *Foreign Correspondent*, Albert Bassermann plays the diplomat Van Meer. Bassermann was perhaps the finest German actor of his generation; he fled Nazi Germany when they ordered him to divorce his Jewish wife. Bassermann spoke no English when he made this movie; every line was learned phonetically, which makes his subtle, gentle performance all the more remarkable. He has very little screen time, but the scene in the Dutch windmill as he fights off the drugs the spies have fed him, and the scene in the bed when he realizes what is happening, should be chapters in any handbook of the actor's craft. A most worthy nomination.

Jack Oakie never came off better as an actor than he did playing Chaplin's rival dictator Benzini Napaloni of Bacteria in *The Great Dictator*. He is obviously spoofing Benito Mussolini, and Oakie apes the chin thrust perfectly, as well as offering an atrocious Italian accent Chico Marx would be proud to claim. The dominance dance that ensues between the dictators is one of the highlights of the film, including the absurdity of dueling barber chairs. If the Academy hadn't nominated Oakie, I would have suggested him. Nice to see they get one right now and then, isn't it?

Playing the family attorney who slowly unravels the truth, James Stephenson in *The Letter* finally made his career move upwards with this performance. Sadly, he died of a heart attack within a short time, only completing a handful of other movies. Stephenson is excellent, a firm, quiet, but implacable presence in the movie. His voice alone adds a deeper dimension to the story, since he is often shot speaking as Davis or others react to him. Stephenson reads the letter to Davis, while the camera follows her reaction. Stephenson then becomes even more the active force in the movie, as well as entering into his own moral quandaries. A very fine nomination.

Garson Kanin directed Carole Lombard, Charles Laughton and Harry Carey in *They Knew What They Wanted*, a mismatched love story that lifts equal parts from *Cyrano de Bergerac* and any number of stories of sexual betrayal. Laughton falls in love with Lombard at first sight, and sets out to woo her through the mail; he makes the mistake of sending William Gargan's picture instead of his own. When Lombard accepts, she is horrified to discover Laughton is her intended. Bad things happen. Gargan later had turns in *The Canterville Ghost* and *The Bells of St. Mary's*, but this was his career high. He's not bad with Lombard, who is trying a serious role here. Laughton isn't at his best, hamming it up as an Italian immigrant, but he does a decent enough job igniting some heat with Lombard, which is surprising, given how dorky he looks. A minor, acceptable nomination, if forgotten, as the film generally is, as second-rate Laughton.

As for those the Academy should have nominated, the first should have been John Carradine for *The Grapes of Wrath*, as the ex-preacher Casey. Ford loved the look of Carradine's emaciated face and body, and used him frequently in his films. Carradine never had better roles than the ones Ford gave him, and *The Grapes of Wrath* is no exception. Carradine's capacity to project fervor and intensity was almost otherworldly, and explains why he ended up in so many horror films as he aged. Carradine is wonderful throughout the movie, especially when he slugs the cop and gleefully gets arrested to keep Fonda safe. His most famous scene, however, comes in the hollow, when Carradine preaches the truth about exploitation. Carradine was rarely better, and he should have been nominated.

From the same movie, and in one of the few times he didn't use his patented Swedish accent, John Qualen gives the performance of his career as Muley, the farmer crazed at the thought of losing his land, pounding out his frustrations in the dirt as he gives one of the major thematic speeches of *The Grapes of Wrath*, after asking the sheriff, "Who do we shoot?" for stealing his land: "There ain't nobody gonna push me off my land! My grandpa took up this land 70 years ago, my pa was born here, we were all born on it. And some of us was killed on it! And some of us died on it. That's what make it our'n, bein' born on it...and workin' on it...and dyin' on it! And not no piece of paper with the writin' on it!" Qualen should have been nominated.

As should Frank Morgan for *The Shop Around the Corner*, a remarkably restrained, nuanced performance from a man who usually went way over the top (appropriately so in *The Wizard of Oz*). Director Ernst Lubitsch pulled out a great role for Morgan, as the shop owner who mistakenly believes that James Stewart is sleeping with Morgan's wife. Lubitsch generally extracted excellent performances from his cast; Frank Morgan shows here he could do more than bumble and posture. He should have been nominated.

Finally, Conrad Veidt plays one of the great villains of the Forties, as Jaffar in *The Thief of Bagdad* is deliciously wicked and evil. The look of villainy in his eyes would rarely be equaled. Few could pull off this kind of melodramatic folderol successfully. Veidt's most famous roles were as the sleepwalker in the silent horror classic of German expressionism, in *The Cabinet of Dr. Caligari*, and as Major Strasser in *Casablanca*. Jaffar completes the trifecta, and Veidt should have been nominated.

Best Supporting Actress: Jane Darwell won for *The Grapes of Wrath*, over Barbara O'Neil, *All This, and Heaven Too*; Ruth Hussey, *The Philadelphia Story*; Marjorie Rambeau, *Primrose Path*; and Judith Anderson, *Rebecca*.

Jane Darwell won for playing Ma Joad in *The Grapes of Wrath*. Let me just say this: Darwell gives an excellent performance, fully deserving of the Oscar. When she looks at herself in the mirror, she is transformed by Gregg Toland's camera and John Ford's conception into one of the iconic images of American cinema history – and of the Great Depression itself. Allow me a caveat. Physically, she's wrong for the part; the rest of the family is bone thin, worn, and obviously on the edge of starvation. Darwell was carrying too much weight for those circumstances. Darwell is not at fault here; Ford cast her, despite all that, because he wanted her as the emotional heart of the film. That she is, many times over. Without her or Henry Fonda, the movie simply wouldn't work. An outstanding choice by the Academy.

Fresh from playing Scarlett O'Hara's selfless mother in *Gone with the Wind*, Barbara O'Neil moved to playing a completely lunatic jealous wife in *All This, and Heaven Too*. She must have enjoyed herself playing a much younger character with such flaws, rather than the perfect mother of *Gone with the Wind*: here, she is spoiled, selfish, vindictive, whiny, obsessed, and temperamental. These kinds of parts don't grow on trees. O'Neil made the most of it, even though at times the smell of ham wafts over her actions (right before she is killed I could swear it was Easter...). Ultimately, though, the problem with the character is that she has no redeeming qualities whatsoever, other than a surface beauty. The nomination should stay, but the lack of a third dimension holds her back.

Playing Katharine Hepburn's rival for Jimmy Stewart in *The Philadelphia Story*, Ruth Hussey manages to create an independent woman in many ways the equal of Hepburn – and that's not easy. Her character is a master of the wisecrack, but also of the threatened heart, and she comes across as easily the most realistic character of the entire film, as well as the pragmatic conscience of the story: "We all go haywire at times and if we don't, maybe we ought to." Hussey never had a better role, or a better movie; *The Philadelphia Story* was the peak of her career. She deserved her nomination.

Primrose Path is an odd film for Code Hollywood, since it's about three generations of women becoming prostitutes – grandmother, mother, and daughter. Ginger Rogers had her first chance to carry a drama as the sole female star in this movie, pinning her hopes on a career away from Fred Astaire and musicals; her Oscar for *Kitty Foyle* was at least partially won by her daring here in *Primrose Path*. Although the profession is only subtly hinted at in the movie, it's enough for Joel McCrea to reject her when he realizes what her mother does. Rogers never actually plays a prostitute, but she is on the road to becoming one, and pretends to the hilt before things get set right. The grandmother's unsavory character is a catalog of the ways unscrupulous females manipulate men; Rogers takes a page from the old strumpet's book early on and comes to regret it. Nominee Marjorie Rambeau plays Rogers' mother, who comes across as one of those tramps who made *The Jerry Springer Show* so slimy. Rambeau revels in the low-class life she leads; she hoots it up in a gas station, squirting people with the water hose, and embarrassing her daughter who is trying to live a straight life with McCrea. But Rambeau also tries to be a good mother, showing kindness and understanding to Rogers and to Rogers' alcoholic father. Then the trampiness comes out, as she shows Rogers how to walk like a wanton. She gets to act out a death scene, which the Academy always loves. Rambeau had a long career on the stage, in silents, and in pictures; in another kind of fame, the Reuben sandwich was apparently invented for her, although other claimants exist.[clxxi] Rambeau deserved her nomination.

Judith Anderson was nominated for *Rebecca*, playing the housekeeper, Mrs. Danvers, who is described in almost all the reviews as "menacing." More subtly than that, Anderson and Hitchcock successfully create the impression that Mrs. Danvers is a lesbian, and that her attraction for the dead Rebecca forms the motivation for much of the movie's plot. From the first moment we see Anderson, the Gothic aspects of the story emerge, and the tension returns from the opening scene (when Olivier was about to commit suicide off the ocean cliff). Anderson is perfect in the role, although I don't get the feeling that the implied lesbianism was the reason for the creep factor; rather, it is her monomania, her driving obsession, with the first Mrs. de Winter that instills such discomfort in us. Anderson keeps Rebecca in second wife Joan Fontaine's mind, from showing her the door to Rebecca's room, to using Rebecca's monogrammed dinner napkins and appointment books for Fontaine, to Rebecca's dog showing up wherever she used to be. All that, and so much more. The creep show only intensifies when Anderson finds Fontaine in Rebecca's bedroom, and proceeds to take her on a tour of the "museum." Anderson's eyes get wilder and more obsessed, and nowhere more so than when she starts fondling Rebecca's lingerie. The wickedness continues, as she sets up Fontaine to wear the same costume to the ball that Rebecca wore. Anderson later became Dame Judith Anderson, and justly celebrated, but she would never have a more famous or successful role in the movies. She richly deserved this nomination.

One omission must be mentioned: Ida Lupino's starmaking turn in the George Raft-Humphrey Bogart trucking movie, *They Drive by Night*. Raoul Walsh took this odd film of underdog truck drivers, romance, and social commentary and made a big hit out of it, helping Bogart to move up in his career, and giving Lupino a great start to hers. From the moment Lupino appears on the screen, we are in a very different kind of film, as she is an early example of the femme fatale that had been missing from the screen for a time, as Hollywood focused on the good girls. As a sexual temptress and murderer, Lupino points directly at film noir's future. Her court confession scene stunned audiences in 1940, and if over the top today, is still well worth seeing. She should have been nominated.

Best Original Score: Leigh Harline, Paul J. Smith and Ned Washington won for *Pinocchio*, over Victor Young for *Arizona*, *The Dark Command* and *Northwest Mounted Police*; Louis Gruenberg, *The Fight for Life*; Meredith Willson, *The Great Dictator*; Frank Skinner, *The House of the Seven Gables*; Richard Hageman for *The Howards of Virginia* and *The Long Voyage Home*; Max Steiner, *The Letter*; Alfred Newman, *The*

Mark of Zorro; Roy Webb, *My Favorite Wife*; Werner Heymann, *One Million B.C.*; Aaron Copland, *Our Town*; Franz Waxman, *Rebecca*; Miklós Rózsa, *The Thief of Bagdad*; and Herbert Stothart, *Waterloo Bridge*.

Of all the scores and songs from 1940, none will be as familiar to more ears than *Pinocchio*, by Leigh Harline, Paul J. Smith and Ned Washington. Part of this is due to the lock Disney has had on American childhoods for most of the last eighty years, for all that implies, good and bad (and I have some friends who equate his work on a par with satanic influences; I just smile at them and go back to Disneyland every chance I get). *Pinocchio* is simply the best of what Disney and his team did, because the immense profits from *Snow White and the Seven Dwarfs* allowed Walt and his animators to indulge themselves in every artistic manner possible. A huge part of the achievement that is *Pinocchio* rests on the music, particularly on "When You Wish upon a Star" (see Best Song), along with "Little Woodenhead," "Give a Little Whistle," and "Hi-Diddle-Dee-Dee." After a decade of Silly Symphonies, the Disney people understood the connection between music and narrative better than any other film studio. The music comes first in animation; the action follows. Perhaps the music is a bit too sweet, the reliance on human choirs a bit too much, but more than seventy years have now passed since *Pinocchio* was first released, and people are still humming away with each successive generation. Truly, for inventiveness, originality, integration with the narrative, and memorability, nothing outdoes the score for *Pinocchio* this year, and they well deserved the Oscar.

Victor Young was nominated for three scores this year: *Arizona*, *The Dark Command* and *Northwest Mounted Police*.

Arizona stars William Holden and Jean Arthur in an unusual western: Arthur is a tough chick, fast with the guns – a "female army" – and Holden is a wanderer who undoes Arthur's hardened exterior. The opening shots of the wagon train traveling through the desert show John Ford's influence on how to shoot the west: movement in the middle of the screen, with giant skies above, preferably with cloud formations piled atop one another. Holden is naturalistic, looking as comfortable as possible on screen at last; Arthur, on the other hand, is awkwardly out of sorts at times, although that may be the point of a character forced to take up violence even as she makes pies for a living. *Arizona* is a fascinating portrayal of gender reversal. Victor Young's score for *Arizona* announces itself with big fat kettle drums and brass, before moving into a more conventional set of strings playing western themes. Much of the music then pulls from traditional American tunes, including "I Dream of Jeannie with the Light Brown Hair," "Kiss Me

Quick," and a triumphant version of "Dixie." We also get some basic chase music when the safe is blown. Young has delivered another memorable score, particularly in the discordant variations on "Jeannie" used to indicate emotional downturns. The nomination should stay.

Raoul Walsh directed Claire Trevor, John Wayne and Roy Rogers in *The Dark Command*, a Republic western based loosely on Quantrill's Raiders from the Civil War era. Victor Young gave Republic some class with this broadly written western score, using mostly violins and brass to excite the audience, but also indulging his more melodramatic side, as when Rogers pulls a gun and murders a man who socked him one. I suspect this was Rogers' attempt to show he could act as more than a singing cowboy. Long stretches of the film go without music at all, which is not surprising given the budget restraints. The movie has some good pieces, but overall, Rogers should have stuck to singing and playing the good guy. Young did much better elsewhere this year; no nomination was deserved by this one.

For *Northwest Mounted Police*, Cecil B. DeMille directed Paulette Goddard and Gary Cooper (as the oddly named Dusty Rivers) in this tale of a manhunt that leads into a Canadian rebellion. Perhaps the worst film DeMille ever made in the sound era, *Northwest Mounted Police* is badly written, badly acted, and downright boring for most of its interminable length (and, apparently, not very accurate Canadian history). Paulette Goddard is a textbook case of how to advertise for Easter supper. Victor Young's score is often martial and jolly, asking us along on a great adventure, which we never really get. He sounds as if he had swallowed John Philip Sousa, then filtered Sousa through a few of Strauss' waltzes. Unusual combination for Young, who should keep his nomination.

The Fight for Life was directed by Pare Laurentz, who also made *The Plough That Broke the Plains* and *The River*. A government film crusading for more doctors to enter the field of obstetrics which borders on film noir for a time, *The Fight for Life* features a score by Louis Gruenberg, who is best known for *Stagecoach* and *All the King's Men*. Here is *The New York Times* reviewer Frank Nugent to relay a sense of the score: "Louis Gruenberg's score, dramatic as the film's imagery, has exploited that heartbeat magnificently, has used its rhythm with drums and strings to create a haunting symphony of birth and death and the long, suspenseful, muted passage between. Lorentz always has been fortunate in finding his composers, but never has he been more beautifully served than here."[clxxii] Although Gruenberg lets the bombast get a little out of hand at times, the nomination is worthy of that lyrical description at its best.

1940 369

Far better known for his phenomenal *The Music Man*, Meredith Willson was given credit for "Musical Direction" on *The Great Dictator*. The score relies heavily on brass for the scenes with the dictator Hynkel, and strings for the Jewish barber. Overweening at times, when more subtle music would have serviced the story better, Willson's score doesn't sound much like his own work. Willson himself disavowed much of the credit for the score: "I got the screen credit for *The Great Dictator* music score, but the best parts of it were all Chaplin's ideas, like using the *Lohengrin* "Prelude" in the famous balloon-dance scene."[clxxiii] What Willson seems to have done is take Chaplin's music and written it down. Certainly, much of the music sounds like other Chaplin scores. Overall, the score is not worthy of the company it was keeping this year. No nomination should have been given.

Vincent Price and George Sanders star in an adaptation of the Nathaniel Hawthorne classic, *The House of the Seven Gables*, for which Frank Skinner wrote the nominated score. Guilt, greed, brotherly hatred and love form the thematic core of the novel, and the movie does a poor job bringing the convoluted book to the screen. Price and Sanders take turns overacting. Frank Skinner's score sounds like any typical soap opera music, and adds little. Skinner himself does better in *Harvey* and *Saboteur*. Not much of this adaptation recommends it for more than one viewing, least of all the rare appearance of the score. No nomination was warranted.

When a movie is as bad as *The Howards of Virginia*, does even an Oscar-nominated score really matter, especially since the studio got a freebie automatically each year in this category? Frank Lloyd directed *The Howards of Virginia*; that alone should put the viewer on alert for a potentially awful film like his *Cavalcade*. On the other hand, he did direct *Mutiny on the Bounty*, and this is another historical picture, set in the cauldron of the American Revolution. Cary Grant, however, was never cast more awkwardly than in this film (unless you count his other costume blunder with Sophia Loren and Frank Sinatra, *The Pride and the Passion*). Richard Hageman goes overboard all too often. Then again, so does Cary Grant in what I think may be the worst movie he ever made. No nomination for this bile of Virginia, which is little more than a blatant rip-off of Korngold's score from *The Adventures of Robin Hood*.

Richard Hageman's other nomination for his work on *The Long Voyage Home* finds me scratching my head over how odd it is to put a score in an original category, when it begins with a citation of "Blow the Man Down" as its opening notes, and then moves into an adaptation of "Harbor Lights" for its romantic epigram to sailors (which is reprised several times later in the film, noticeably when they leave port). But then we get a long stretch of "native" music, which sounds Polynesian, even though the scene is in the West Indies; for that matter, the native girls look like refugees from Ford's *The Hurricane*. When a crewman escapes and is brought back, the score is a foreshadowing of the kind of thing we get in film noir a decade later. I don't find the score anywhere near as effective as Hageman's work on *Stagecoach*, but I found it unobjectionable. On the other hand, Paul Bowles violently hated the score for this movie, saying *The Long Voyage Home* is "the pure and good movie cruelly betrayed by the worthless score...Clouds of musical error keep rolling down across the beauty of the film." Bowles felt that Hageman repeatedly intruded himself in the exact opposite way from how he should have, such as after a man dies, Hageman uses a "Wagnerian brass comment, as jarring to the mood as the slamming of all the theatre's exit doors."[clxxiv] I'm not as disdainful as Bowles – but then, who is? – so we should let the nomination stay.

For *The Letter*, Max Steiner begins with an oriental-flavored instrumentation, as the movie starts in Singapore on a rubber plantation, but then it builds dramatically into the murder, and deep into the cellos, and back up the higher tonal range into violins and brass. Steiner by this point was a master at scoring, particularly when he wasn't urged over the top when working with David O. Selznick (although that could go well too, as in *Gone with the Wind*). Occasionally, he does add more volume than necessary, lending credence to Bette Davis' noted resistance to Steiner's scores. Overall, Steiner's music proves to be among his best, and an excellent nomination.

My Favorite Wife gives us Cary Grant as a husband who lost his wife in a shipwreck, and is just about to remarry, when his dead wife Irene Dunne appears, alive as ever, having survived on a deserted island – with Randolph Scott. A fine screwball comedy from director Garson Kanin, *My Favorite Wife* looked to re-capture the success of *The Awful Truth*, playing with many of the same issues of fidelity, jealousy, and love. The reason for that is Leo McCarey, who directed *The Awful Truth* and was nominated for Best Original Story for *My Favorite Wife*; McCarey was prevented from directing by a severe automobile accident. Kanin does a good job, but McCarey would have been better, breathing full life into this story, rather than the mere occasional flashes of comic genius we get. Watch the hotel manager's face when Grant installs his two wives in different rooms in the same hotel: "What a man!" As for the music, Roy Webb's score is quite good: upbeat and quick, comic and romantic. Webb proved to be a distinguished Hollywood composer, as a partial list of his scores should show: *Bringing up Baby, Notorious, Out of the Past,* and *Marty. My Favorite Wife* is one of his best scores, and I point your attention to the scene where Grant meets the other man as proof: the score lampoons the other man's name, undercutting with the sense of urgency Grant feels at investigating his first wife's possible adultery. One alone would be a tad too obvious; both together form a tension that is both humorous and stressful at the same time. Therefore, a solid nomination for Webb.

Other than the giant lizards, the outsized part of *One Million B.C.* remains the score. Werner Heymann also composed the music for *Ninotchka, The Shop Around the Corner, To Be or Not to Be* and many others. In some ways, the music is more complete than in films with more talking; this one hearkens back to silent picture days. I still remember pieces from my childhood. Heymann created an over-the-top score, because without the actors able to use speech more than grunts, the music had to carry much more of the meaning. Heymann does better when he relaxes, particularly with a haunting oboe in contrast to the big sweeping impacts of the orchestra. Heymann clearly did something right, and deserves his nomination for this extensive work.

Aaron Copland returned to the movies with his music for *Our Town*, which is a constant, gently lyrical score that acts almost like the narrator's voice in commenting on what is occurring. In the end, though, none of the soaring power of Copland's concert hall pieces nor the longeurs of his score for *Of Mice and Men* emerge – just a quiet, nostalgic, reassuring score, much like the film itself. A decent nomination, then.

Franz Waxman found David O. Selznick interfering as usual on *Rebecca*. Selznick shoved in some of Max Steiner's score for *A Star Is Born* where he felt like it, infuriating both Waxman and Steiner.[clxxv] Waxman's opening music has a tremendous appeal, establishing a portentous mood, touched by something awful about to happen with those imposing violins, sounding like the distant ancestors of the horror that is the *Psycho* score. The warmth of some romantic spring flows with the name "Rebecca" on the screen, and then a return to the more frightening themes. Waxman was more than capable of producing a masterful score; Selznick shouldn't have crammed in Steiner. On the other hand, even Waxman wrote corn, as when we see the door to Rebecca's room, and an organ chord worthy of *The Phantom of the Opera* is hit, followed by a few others. I am also fairly certain we get a theremin – that spooky science fiction instrument – quietly played as Fontaine enters Rebecca's bedroom for the first time, although nobody else seems to think so; the instrumentation may be different, but the effect is much the same. Great score, although I wish Steiner wasn't pried into it. The nomination should stay.

Miklós Rózsa would go on to a fabled career in movie music, hitting such peaks as *Double Indemnity, The Asphalt Jungle, Ben-Hur, King of Kings, The Private Life of Sherlock Holmes,* and *The Golden Voyage of Sinbad.* His work on *The Thief of Bagdad* has exquisite moments, particularly in the otherwise flaccid love scenes between the tepid romantic leads: the mixture of harp, human voice, bells, and strings is otherworldly. The overture thrills, with big sweeping gestures worthy of Max Steiner. Rózsa never makes the mistake of indulging in more than a flavor of the kind of Middle Eastern tones used by every desert picture ever made. His score shows subtlety and power in its restraints, as well as its excesses (moments emerge where we can hear the score for *Ben-Hur* prefigured). Much as I think *Pinocchio* deserves the Oscar, I was hard pressed to deny Rózsa for this score, as well as Korngold for *The Sea Hawk*. Few film scores can stand alone; listen to the suite of music for this film, which has been recorded several times – you won't be disappointed. *The Thief of Baghdad* would be the first of many great nominations.

Once again, Stothart is nominated in the Original Score category, when he's largely taking music from other men and reworking it for himself. This time, for *Waterloo Bridge*, he uses Tchaikovsky and the love theme from *Dracula*...er, *Swan Lake*. Vivien Leigh plays a ballerina who turns to prostitution, so ballet music seems appropriate source material, but is it original? We get ballet and military pieces pulled from a variety of places, as well as old love songs, but Stothart does modulate them to fit the mood, and often quite nicely – listen to the first sounds when Robert Taylor re-visits Waterloo Bridge at the opening of WWII, before he heads to France again, and the theme that plays then. Assuming I have not missed the classical source, for that minute of music alone, Stothart should keep this nomination – truly, a moment of beauty. Stothart also does an amazing piece of work when Leigh reads that Taylor has been killed (falsely reported), mixing Stephen Foster's touching "The Minstrel Boy" with that strain from *Swan Lake* effectively, building the horrific discovery. I especially enjoyed the old tunes that filter into certain scenes, like memories, then drift away. Stothart could just have easily been nominated for the adaptation category, but MGM used that slot for *Strike up the Band* (which is almost entirely original, and should have been nominated here instead). Thus far, *Waterloo Bridge* is my favorite Stothart score.

As noted below, several nominees should have been moved here from Best Score.

First of all, Georgie Stoll and Roger Edens' score for *Strike up the Band*; other than the title song, nothing has been adapted. *Strike up the Band* may have copied the formula for *Babes in Arms*, but the music outstrips the first outing, as does the inventiveness of the staging (illogical as much of it is). One odd but amusing accompaniment: Mickey Rooney and Judy Garland set up a fruit orchestra, which is then animated to play a song (this looks like the sort of thing George Pal would do in a few years with Duke Ellington's *Perfume Suite*). The "La Conga" number makes me wonder just how much amphetamine was being passed out on the set. "The Drummer Boy" is a barn-burner, with Rooney swinging like Gene Krupa on the drums. Mostly, the score is absent, except when we get songs. But the songs are more than enough to secure a nomination.

Korngold's score for *The Sea Hawk* should be moved here, as I explained in Best Score.

Franz Waxman's lively and unique score for *The Philadelphia Story* should also have been nominated. You've gotta love the xylophone poking its tinkle in where it's never really been before – and the saxophone, which hadn't often been used for symphonic scores. In fact, throughout the score, Waxman lets one instrument solo for a bar or so, to make a comic or dramatic point, before returning to the normal full string treatment that makes up the majority of scores in this period. The drum marching Cary Grant on his way to abuse Katharine Hepburn for breaking his golf clubs, for example. Waxman was trying out something new, and he succeeded. He deserved a nomination.

Best Song: Leigh Harline and Ned Washington's "When You Wish upon a Star" won from *Pinocchio*, over Harry Warren and Mack Gordon's "Down Argentine Way" from *Down Argentine Way*; Jules Styne and Walter Bullock's "Who Am I?" from *Hit Parade of 1941*; Chet Forrest and Bob Wright's "It's a Blue World," from *Music in My Heart*; James V. Monaco and Johnny Burke's "Only Forever" from *Rhythm on the River*; Artie Shaw and Johnny Mercer's "Love of My Life" from *Second Chorus*; Robert Stolz and Gus Kahn's "Waltzing on the Clouds" from *Spring Parade*; Roger Edens and Arthur Freed's "Our Love Affair" from *Strike up the Band*; and Jimmy McHugh and Johnny Mercer's "I'd Know You Anywhere" from *You'll Find Out*.

I'm just going to say it up front: "When You Wish upon a Star" may be a simple little ditty, but infectiously so. We're not talking the insidious ear worm that is "It's a Small World" – sorry about that – but Cliff "Ukulele Ike" Edward's rendition as Jiminy Cricket speaks to the same longing for a better world that "Somewhere Over the Rainbow" does. In a year when Irving Berlin or Cole Porter were producing something, perhaps we would be making a different decision – and Porter was indeed ignored for the very good "I Concentrate on You" from *Broadway Melody of 1940*, which I am herewith nominating for this category. As it is, no more memorable song emerged this year from Hollywood. The Oscar should stay with Jiminy.

Down Argentine Way is a harmless Betty Grable-Don Ameche programmer turned Technicolor extravaganza, with the great good sense to have the excesses of Carmen Miranda and the miracle of the Nicholas Brothers to spice up the pretty slop. During the Forties, the United States went crazy for all things Latin: the rumba, the conga, the cha-cha-cha, Desi Arnaz, Xavier Cugat, Carmen Miranda and more. Even Disney got into the act with *Saludos Amigos* and *The Three Caballeros*. Orson Welles wrecked his career by abandoning *The Magnificent Ambersons* at the cutting stage to head down to Rio for what was eventually released in 1993 as *It's All True*. The nominated title song, "Down Argentine Way" by Harry Warren and Mack Gordon, is of a piece with this fad, and one that cropped up throughout my childhood on various television shows. Like a large number of songs from before the Sixties, and precious few since, this attempt to paint a picture of a foreign land in rhythm and words was a common form of popular song. Catchy, yes; deep, no. A pleasant little ditty, and one that keeps its shelf life better than one would expect. The nomination should stay.

Hit Parade of 1941 is forgettable. "Who Am I?" by Jules Styne and Walter Bullock is one of those songs that speaks of the insecurity we may feel when outclassed by the one we have chosen to love. A gentle song, and now largely forgotten. I can imagine Frank Sinatra using it on one of those suicidal albums he recorded in the late Fifties – you need to be careful with his music! The nomination should stand for that alone. Styne would go on to write many songs for Sinatra, as well as "Diamonds Are a Girl's Best Friend," "Let It Snow! Let It Snow! Let It Snow!" and "Time after Time." Bullock wrote a number of forgotten songs.

"It's a Blue World," by Chet Forrest and Bob Wright, came out in *Music in My Heart*. Tony Martin sang the song; Rita Hayworth starred. The ballad isn't bad, and it has been covered by other artists as a kind of minor standard. Martin had a decent voice, even if he is almost completely forgotten today in the aftermath of Sinatra's revolution in singing in the Forties. Chet Forrest and Bob Wright also wrote "Stranger in Paradise" and "Baubles, Bangles and Beads." The nomination is a reasonable one.

Bing Crosby and Mary Martin croon their way along this little ballad, "Only Forever." *Rhythm on the River* has Basil Rathbone using ghostwriters to put his songs together; Crosby and Martin decide to break out on their own. "Only Forever" is the result. James V. Monaco is most famous for "You Made Me Love You," Johnny Burke for "Swinging on a Star" and "What's New?" "Only Forever" is pleasant enough, but if I remember it a year from now I will be shocked. No nomination should have been given to trifles.

Going in, I had high hopes for *Second Chorus*: Fred Astaire's feet dancing, Artie Shaw's swing band rocking, and Johnny Mercer's lyrics lyricking. Who could ask for anything more? It turns out I could. Paulette Goddard can't dance. Astaire himself named it "the worst film I ever made."[clxxvi] On the plus side, Artie Shaw's music and Fred Astaire's dancing fit together nicely. Somebody should have taught Burgess Meredith and Astaire how to play fake trumpet better, although Goddard must have been impressed with his ability to pucker up and blow, as she married Meredith in 1944. Mercer was one of the finest lyricists in musical history; Shaw led one of the top swing bands. Putting them together should have resulted in classics – but no, sometimes fire doesn't catch in the tinder. The song "Love of My Life" is brief, swinging, and hardly up to Johnny Mercer's best. An interesting sidenote for those of us who love Shaw and Mercer, but hardly anything other than a minor event. The nomination should stay, but only due to the generally weak competition this year.

When Robert Cummings meets Deanna Durbin on their first date (such as it is) in *Spring Parade*, "Waltzing on the Clouds" is the song he composes on the spot, with her help shushing everybody. Gus Kahn ("Makin' Whoopee") does his usual rhymes; Robert Stolz (he's world famous in Vienna) provides a decent waltz. Not a bad little ditty, but nothing to make you grab your strudel – or a nomination.

"Our Love Affair," from *Strike up the Band*, was written by MGM musical mavens Roger Edens and Arthur Freed. "Our Love Affair" couldn't be lovelier, when sung by Judy Garland. A memorable tune, and one that fit the needs of the musical perfectly, as the song proves capable of being orchestrated in a multitude of ways; "Our Love Affair" remains a minor classic, well worth the nomination.

Jimmy McHugh and Johnny Mercer wrote "I'd Know You Anywhere," for *You'll Find Out*, a truly odd nomination, which marks the only time a movie starring Boris Karloff, Peter Lorre and Bela Lugosi produced an Oscar-nominated song – and the only time those three were in a movie together. Given that Kay Kyser and his big band feature as well, the paradox seems even odder (and you may never get another chance to see Kay Kyser and His College of Musical Knowledge quite this extensively). The orchestra uncovers a plot against an heiress (the band is playing at her birthday). Of course, any time you can get Johnny Mercer lyrics and Jimmy McHugh music, you increase the chance that you've got a classic on your hands. Both of them are responsible, separately, for some of the greatest songs ever written; I leave it as an exercise for the class to discover which ones. Trust me, they're worth your time. "I'd Know You Anywhere" is sung by the band's canary, Ginny Simms. A love ballad of some charm, the song can stand with most of the typical sort that every big band produced. I found myself wondering why it never caught on as a minor standard, but that alone guarantees it a nomination.

In addition to Cole Porter's "I Concentrate on You" from *Broadway Melody of 1940*, starring Fred Astaire, "I Hear Music" by Burton Lane and Frank Loesser, should also have been nominated; the song is from *Dancing on a Dime*, an otherwise forgettable movie. Both have become solid standards of the American Songbook, and could easily replace almost all the songs the Academy did select.

Best Art Direction (Color): Vincent Korda won for *The Thief of Bagdad*, over Cedric Gibbons and John S. Dethe, *Bitter Sweet;* Richard Day and Joseph C. Wright, *Down Argentine Way*; and Hans Dreier and Roland Anderson, *Northwest Mounted Police*

Vincent Korda's sets for *The Thief of Bagdad* truly impress, even when they occasionally feel like they are on a sound stage. Korda designed the film, with the uncredited help of William Cameron Menzies, to evoke the look and feel of the original Arabian Nights stories. While I would have preferred a look drawn more from Maxfield Parrish or N.C. Wyeth, what we get is a treasure trove of images that have persevered in the memory of childhood. Much was lifted entirely for Disney's *Aladdin*, which also completely "borrowed" Jaffar and the Sultan, and turned Sabu into Abu the monkey. While Korda borrowed himself from the original silent version with Douglas Fairbanks, Sr., – a classic everybody should see – no other live action color film this year has proven more enduring: the palace, the temple, the toys (especially the flying horse), and the genie can still stun viewers. Korda highly merited this Oscar.

Cedric Gibbons and John S. Dethe designed *Bitter Sweet* for Nelson Eddy and Jeanette MacDonald, this time warbling in late nineteenth century Vienna. Oh, look – a beer garden! So what if they're worshipping wine, it's still a beer garden. Oh, and a concert hall. Boring, boring,

boring. Like many MGM productions, lush but dead on arrival. No nomination should be given to pretty corpses.

So what did Richard Day and Joseph C. Wright get the nomination for in *Down Argentine Way*? A loading dock; a New York nightclub; stables; hotel room; another nightclub; another nightclub; a horse ranch; an Argentine village; and yes, another night club. Yup – that's a Betty Grable pic. *Down Argentine Way* was her first starring role, and set the pattern for almost all the rest: repetitive, harmless, fluffy entertainment. The sets do what they're supposed to do, and little more. No nomination should ever be given for a lack of imagination.

Hans Dreier and Roland Anderson did the sets for *Northwest Mounted Police*. Given Cecil B. DeMille's obsession with detail, the surprise would be if one of his historical pictures wasn't nominated in this category. Dreier and Anderson were old hands at creating detailed, accurate sets, particularly Dreier, who had been doing this kind of work for more than twenty years by 1940; Anderson worked with DeMille on numerous films. The problem with this nomination, other than the general failure of the movie itself to gel is that Dreier and Anderson have little experience with color sets, and the air of falsehood hangs about. What would have worked in black and white simply helps foster the disconnection that undoes this film. No nomination is needed.

Best Special Effects: Lawrence Butler and Jack Whitney won for *The Thief of Bagdad*, over *The Blue Bird* (Fred Sersen, Edmund H. Hansen); *Boom Town* (A. Arnold Gillespie, Douglas Shearer); *The Boys from Syracuse* (John P. Fulton, Bernard B. Brown and Joseph Lapis); *Dr. Cyclops* (Farciot Edouart and Gordon Jennings, Loren Ryder); *Foreign Correspondent* (Paul Eagler, Thomas T. Moulton); *The Invisible Man Returns* (John P. Fulton, Bernard B. Brown and William Hedgecock); *The Long Voyage Home* (R.T. Layton and R. O. Binger, Thomas T. Moulton); *One Million B.C.* (Roy Seawright, Elmer Raguse); *Rebecca* (Jack Cosgrove, Arthur Johns); *The Sea Hawk* (Byron Haskin, Nathan Levinson); *Swiss Family Robinson* (Vernon L. Walker, John O. Aalberg); *Typhoon* (Farciot Edouart; Gordon Jennings; Loren L. Ryder); and *Women in War* (Howard J. Lydecker, William Bradford Ellis J. Thackery, and Herbert Norsch)

The Academy began splitting up the nominees into photography and sound slots, which makes a certain sense, but at this remove, I'm more inclined to drop the distinction and just applaud the group.

While *The Thief of Bagdad* has flaws with the human elements, the special effects were the state of the art in 1940, and it would be years before any other film came close to matching them. Watching *The Thief of Bagdad*, we can see the ancestor of the special effects blockbusters that have dominated American films since the Seventies, and with many of the same problems: a generally weak story, unlikely resolutions, ham-fisted acting, and a reliance on the spectacular to instill so much of what science fiction readers call a "sense of wonder" that viewers will ignore all the other problems. *The Thief of Bagdad* has a few effects that have aged badly, but most remain charming and unmatched in today's era of computer wizardry – among them, the flying horse, the images of the genie in the bottle, the genie being released, and the flying carpet. The movie well deserved this Oscar, which forms the main reason to see it today, unless you just happen to be a Sabu or Conrad Veidt fan. Consider that many of the techniques they developed, particularly for the added complexities of color, had never been done before, and still form the basis of today's special effects. *The Thief of Bagdad* remains a visual feast. As much as I want to fast forward past the truly deadening love scenes, the Oscar for Best Special Effects is well-deserved.

The Blue Bird has cheesy special effects, with little imagination. We do get one nice fade out scene with the fairy, as well as an ambitious forest storm and fire scene, though poorly executed when they combine the actors. The lightning strikes are done well. Shirley Temple saw her career crash to an end with this movie. No nomination should have been given for hurting a child!

Boom Town does have one great special effects scene. On top of the significant realism with which the wildcatting business is filmed, and Clark Gable's obvious joy in a role based on his own experience on oil rigs, the special effects of a spectacular oil well fire drove this nomination, which isn't a bad choice.

The Boys from Syracuse is a Broadway musical version of Shakespeare's *A Comedy of Errors*, with some great Rodgers and Hart songs – "Falling in Love with Love" and "This Can't Be Love" among them. Those songs go with the comedy of Martha Raye, Charles Butterworth, and Eric Blore. But we also have to put up with Allan Jones and Rosemary Lane as the leads. The special effects come from showing the actors doubling as two sets of twins. We've seen this before; we'll see it again. No nomination should ever be given for copycats.

Directed by Ernest B. Shoedsack of *King Kong* fame, *Dr. Cyclops* is an intricately designed film about a mad scientist using a ray to shrink animals and people. For its day, the special effects were the best in the business – and if it weren't for *The Thief of Bagdad*, would have easily been my choice for the Academy Award for special effects. The first major effect of the tiny horse still holds a certain magic, especially for those of us who watched movies before CGI came along. When the main characters are shrunk by Dr. Cyclops, the ability of Edouart and Jennings to have them interact on the same screen together still astonishes after seventy years, because we know how hard it was to achieve in hindsight. An excellent nomination for such painstaking work.

Foreign Correspondent gives us very elaborate model work, and a spectacular plane crash. William Cameron Menzies should have been included in the list of nominees, since the credits include him for "Special Production Effects." Hitchcock told Truffaut "there's one shot so unusual that it's rather surprising that the technicians never bothered to question how it was done. That's when the plane is diving down toward the sea because its engines are crippled. The camera is inside the cabin, above the shoulders of the two pilots who are trying to pull the plane out of the dive. Between them, through the glass cabin window, we can see the ocean coming closer. And then, without a cut, the plane hits the ocean and the water rushes in, drowning the two men. That whole thing was done in a single shot, without a cut...I had a transparency screen made of paper, and behind that screen, a water tank. The plane dived, and as soon as the water got close to it, I pressed the button and the water burst through, tearing the screen away. The volume was so great that you never saw the screen."[clxxvii] Hitchcock was in love with models and special effects; *Foreign Correspondent* deserves the nomination.

As part of Universal's return to the horror film that began with 1939's *Son of Frankenstein*, they resurrected the Invisible Man as well. *The Invisible Man Returns* suffers from the lack of Claude Rains and James Whale, but in exchange we get Vincent Price in the title role, trying to discover the murderer of his brother before he goes insane. The special effects by John P. Fulton, the same genius of the first film, are outstanding, particularly the undressing of the scarecrow, the smoke bomb effects, and the invisible returning to the visible. Good nomination.

The Long Voyage Home has some ships and fog. I can't really see why this movie was nominated.

Feel like seeing some iguanas with fins attached to make them look like dinosaurs? When I was eight, I couldn't get enough of *One Million B.C.* Victor Mature stars as Tumak, a caveman cast out by his father, Lon Chaney, Jr. Fake dinosaurs abound, shot large by the special effects team. Willis O'Brien did it far better in *King Kong*; after WWII, Ray Harryhausen would carry O'Brien's stop-motion animation into the same heights of genius. But outside of those two, when they wanted dinosaurs, they used lizards with parts God didn't make (not unlike most of the starlets today). Indeed, the footage from this film was endlessly recycled for other movies, as was the spectacular volcano explosion that wraps up the plot. A fine nomination.

Rebecca was nominated for the great burning house at the end, and merited one for that conflagration.

The Sea Hawk has first rate sea battles, with these 18 foot models in a studio tank. I suspect these may be the best naval special effects in pre-CGI film history (other contenders would include Disney's *20,000 Leagues Under the Sea* and *Captain Blood*). Watching Flynn's ship the *Albatross* take apart the Spanish galleon thrills every time I see it. A top-notch nomination.

I fell in love with the Disney version of *Swiss Family Robinson* as a child, with its magnificent tree house and the wondrous pirate attack. Imagine my disappointment when I tried to read the original, and the entire plot is more or less the family constantly praying. This 1940 version stars Thomas Mitchell and Freddie Bartholomew, and doesn't live up to the quality of the color Disney version. The nomination for this category is based primarily on the storm sequences, which are fairly well done and deserving of a nomination.

Typhoon has a typhoon, believe it or not. They also have Dorothy Lamour as a wild child. Toss in a forest fire, and the nomination is a good one. You go figure out for what. I'm betting it was for Lamour's sarong.

Women in War tells the story of a woman, Wendy Barrie, who accidentally kills a masher; she flees into nursing in a war zone to escape. The special effects nomination is probably for the war zone scenes; given that the film only exists in the UCLA nitrate archives and is not available for viewing, I have no way of admitting the nomination, so we will drop this one.

WHAT THEY GOT WRONG:

With the exception of Ginger Rogers and the cartoon this year, the Academy is at least not awarding too many stinkers any longer. The winners they chose are often quite good; they're just not the best. They really should have discussed this with me first…

Best Picture: *Rebecca*
Best Actor: James Stewart, *The Philadelphia Story*
Best Actress: Ginger Rogers, *Kitty Foyle*
Best Writing (Original Story): Benjamin Glazer & John S. Toldy,

Arise, My Love
Best Writing (Original Screenplay): Preston Sturges, *The Great McGinty*
Best Writing (Screenplay): Donald Ogden Stewart, *The Philadelphia Story*
Best Cinematography (Black & White): George Barnes, *Rebecca*
Best Cinematography (Color): *The Thief of Bagdad*
Best Score: Alfred Newman, *Tin Pan Alley*
Best Art Direction (Black & White): Cedric Gibbons & Paul Groesse, *Pride and Prejudice*
Best Short Subject (Cartoon): MGM, *Milky Way*

Best Picture: *Rebecca* won, over *All This, and Heaven Too*; *Foreign Correspondent*; *The Grapes of Wrath*; *The Great Dictator*; *Kitty Foyle*; *The Letter*; *The Long Voyage Home*; *Our Town*, and *The Philadelphia Story*

David O. Selznick was on a roll, winning the Best Picture Oscar two years in a row as an independent producer. In *Rebecca*, he scored another triumph, bringing Alfred Hitchcock to America for his first American picture, and despite interfering endlessly with Hitch, ending up with this film to his credit as a producer. Selznick was going to have Hitchcock film a story of the *Titanic*, and even purchased an entire ship to double for it! Instead, Selznick assigned Hitchcock to a property the director wanted anyways: Daphne du Maurier's Gothic novel, *Rebecca*. *Rebecca* is the "Cinderella story, gone terribly wrong," as well as a version of *Jane Eyre*, with Maxim de Winter (Laurence Olivier) as the Prince/Mr. Rochester, and the unnamed narrator (Joan Fontaine) as Cinderella/Jane.[clxxviii] Set in the mysterious mansion of Manderley, a home haunted by the memory of the first Mrs. de Winter (Rebecca) and the creepiest housekeeper in film history, *Rebecca* turned out to be wildly successful commercially and critically. Watching it today, I am struck by the depth and brilliance of the film, even as I am, after multiple viewings over the years, still unhappy with the butchered ending (as I have been with next year's *Suspicion*). Still, *Rebecca* is a wonderful movie, and well worth a nomination – in this category as in many others below. But the Oscar should have gone elsewhere.

Warner Brothers made *All This, and Heaven Too* as an attempt to outdo *Gone with the Wind*. Based on a bestselling novel, *All This* tells the true story of the murder of a Duchess in 1840s France; the governess (and possible murderer) is played by Bette Davis; her employer (and possible lover) is played by Charles Boyer. Davis does her usual masterly job in bringing her characters utterly to life, sinking herself into her roles intensely, this time with a quieter outing as a kind, gentle governess who falls in platonic love with the married Boyer. Directed by Anatole Litvak, and burdened by a far too predictable melodrama, *All This, and Heaven Too* doesn't really belong in this category, not in a year which completely ignored *His Girl Friday, The Bank Dick, The Mark of Zorro,* and *Pinocchio*. Without Davis, and to a lesser degree Boyer, few would bother watching this movie today, which should have received no nomination.

Foreign Correspondent was directed by Alfred Hitchcock for independent Walter Wanger (Hitch was on loan out after *Rebecca* was such a big hit). Joel McCrea got the chance to star after Gary Cooper turned down the part. *Foreign Correspondent* is a worthy successor to the kind of suspense thrillers on which the director had built his reputation in England, mixing spies, romance, humor, and brilliant cinematic technique into compelling films. But *Foreign Correspondent* was something more, a film that mattered to Hitchcock as a means of contributing to the war effort at home, as he struggled to find a way to wake America up out of its isolationism, and to encourage Britain to keep fighting. To that end, *Foreign Correspondent* ends with a plea to stay strong, to build weapons and ships, and to keep the lights burning that are going out in Europe: "Hello, America! Hang on to your lights! They're the only lights left!" Powerful propaganda, and a strong ending to the movie, which deserved its nomination for Best Picture.

The Grapes of Wrath epitomizes the Great Depression better than any other artistic response, in its tale of the Joad family losing its farm and having to go on the road, looking for work on the way to California. Nobel laureate John Steinbeck's masterwork isn't read as much as it used to be, outside of high school English classes and college courses that cover the Thirties. But *The Grapes of Wrath* instills in us an understanding of what the Depression meant on a deep emotional and experiential level. Heavily researched by Steinbeck, who traveled the road and lived in the camps as the Joads did, the novel makes an intense argument that the problem of the Depression was a problem of power structures, and not of anything intrinsically wrong with America outside of the overweening and overreaching influence that attaches itself to the ownership of property, and the potential to brutally exploit those who are not on top. Given the economic crisis that surrounded the writing of this very book you're reading now, I'm surprised Steinbeck's novel and Ford's film didn't get a rebirth of popularity. The movie doesn't encompass the entire novel, or some of its more radical aspects, and yet captures the very heart of the book. The movie ends on an awkward, uplifting note, as Ma Joad preaches Americana, but I doubt anybody could have filmed the actual ending then – or even, I suspect, now, when few Hollywood studios would invest this kind of project with any serious resources. Watching a grown woman suckling a dying man would have to be handled with extreme care to avoid nervous tittering in the audience – see what I mean? But what we do get on the screen, up until the last minute or so, is absolute honesty, with no reservations or shortcomings. Think of how few movies fit that description. We owe that miracle to the actors, writers, and crew involved, but even more so to producer Darryl F. Zanuck for embarking on this project, and for choosing the perfect director for *The Grapes of Wrath*: John Ford (see above). Had the Academy not nominated this movie, I would have personally tracked down each and every one of their graves and screamed at them in rage and frustration, "What the hell were you thinking?!?" An indispensable nomination for an indispensable film.

The Great Dictator is often thought of as Chaplin's last great film. I'm not so sure that isn't *Monsieur Verdoux*, but I am reasonably sure that *The Great Dictator* contains the finest parody of Adolf Hitler and Benito Mussolini outside of the Three Stooges' groundbreaking attack in *You Nazty Spy*, released nine months before *The Great Dictator*.[72] The one scene that remains with every viewer is the ballet with the giant globe, and from that moment on, Hitler's ambitions were doomed. It only took WWII to complete the prediction. Watching *The Great Dictator* has always been an odd mix of enjoying the inventive humor and tolerating the desperate earnestness. Chaplin wanted to be Important again; he never quite achieved that, except on the basis of his earlier work. The essential problem with the film lies in its tone: we begin with utter slapstick; we end with utter seriousness. That emotional transition can pay off (Robin Williams used to do so regularly in his standup), but the kind of delicacy required just isn't in Chaplin's grasp at this point in his career. Look at *City Lights*, and you can see him succeed in the same gambit, but in that far greater film, we are prepared from the first encounter with the blind girl for this to be a romance with comedy and sadness intertwined. Chaplin fails to establish the nature of *The Great Dictator* at any point in the movie, so the gags rarely reach any sublime effect. Even Hynkel's speeches are treated as pure parody, and the shift to the cruelty of watching Paulette Goddard being pelted by tomatoes is about the same as being pelted ourselves. Now, if that were

---

[72] If you've never seen *You Nazty Spy*, you really should, if only to hear the Stooges put Yiddish words into the mouths of Nazis – in fact, the Three Stooges should have been nominated for, and won, the Oscar for Best Short Subject (Comedy) for this daring film. Nyuk Nyuk!

the point, then all well and good – but we're expected to laugh at the stormtroopers and Hynkel as buffoons, but we've been too shocked for that to work any longer. I still appreciate the attempt to attack Hitler with humor, but overall, the effect has ceased to function, although apparently, it once did. Even Chaplin came to the point of wishing he hadn't made it, in the face of the Holocaust.[clxxix] Paulette Goddard could have easily been left out completely, as she adds little to the film, and her performance constitutes much of the weakness. For the sake of the ballet scene, the nomination should stay.

People remember *Kitty Foyle* for precisely one reason: Ginger Rogers won a Best Actress Oscar (see that category below). Were it not for that, nobody would watch this concoction of clichés and the hard choice poor, poor, poor pitiful Kitty has to make between a rich guy and a doctor – which isn't quite a real Lady and the Tiger scenario, is it? Choose door #1, and you have a rich guy! Choose door #2, and – gasp! – you have a doctor! This is a hard choice?! Granted, the decision is flavored by suggesting a grand passion for the wrong man, with a logical partnership with the right man, and passion generally wins out, but still *Foyle* is all about getting the audience sympathies and squeezing them until their cojones turn azul. Is this a great film? About as far from it as the last three *Star Wars* movies are from the first three real *Star Wars* movies. No nomination was needed for this talking twaddle.

The Letter is one of the great movies of the year. Melodrama though *The Letter* is, when the performances, direction, score and cinematography are this high grade, melodrama works as well as any other form in delivering a first-rate movie. Bette Davis and James Stephenson hit every mark, and Wyler extends his directorial talent in new directions with longer and longer shots. Granted, the film does indulge in some very common stereotypes, not the least of which is the inscrutable quality the West all too often ascribed to Asians – as well as the kind of devious trickery seen in movie serials of the period. The scene where the Eurasian wife (played almost silently by Gale Sondergaard) hands over the letter has proven to be the weakest part of the movie, despite the cinematographic skill with which Wyler and Gaudio shot it. Still, despite that, *The Letter* is well worth a nomination.

The Long Voyage Home never quite comes together as a great film. Putting John Wayne in a Eugene O'Neill play, and then expecting him to pull off an accent, may have been asking too much of this movie star. I'm not one of those who thinks John Wayne can't act – watch *Red River*, *She Wore a Yellow Ribbon*, or *The Quiet Man* and you'll see that he can – but as more than one movie producer and director has said, casting is everything in the movies. The bigger problem with Wayne is that he's already a star because of *Stagecoach* (and decades of watching his later films). Here, he isn't more than an ensemble cast member; we keep expecting him to stand out more, and the film disappoints because he doesn't. John Ford directed; Gregg Toland laid out the astonishing camerawork. The result is a visually compelling film, with a lackluster, episodic narrative. Ford did this as his follow-up to his smash hit, *The Grapes of Wrath*, and he seems to have decided to indulge his artistic side a bit too much. Either that, or he just wanted to spend time with actors pretending to be sailors, as they get drunk, whore, and fight their way through a war zone. If there's a false note in the movie, it's the imposition of the British flag over the dead body of an alcoholic ex-officer, after he's shot by an enemy plane; Ford already had him throwing an oarlock at the plane, falling backward into a lifeboat, and having the tarp for the boat blow back over him like a shroud; the flag and "Rule, Britannia" were just too much propaganda. Because of the visuals (see Best Cinematography (Black & White) for more), the nomination should stay.

Based on the famous Pulitzer Prize-winning play by Thornton Wilder, *Our Town* stars William Holden and Martha Scott, with an excellent supporting cast, including Fay Bainter, Beulah Bondi, Thomas Mitchell, and Guy Kibbee. Thornton Wilder co-wrote the screenplay, and it shows: the heart of his play is preserved (one of his co-writers was the narrator from the original play and film, Frank Craven). William Cameron Menzies designed the production. Sam Wood directed, and not in his usual anonymous way. Wilder preserved the unusual features of his play (the breaking of the fourth wall, and his narrator, which must have still preserved some of their surprise for audiences of 1940, but seems creaky today). My first problem with the film is that they changed the ending to a happy one, with Thornton Wilder's surprising cooperation (and why I will not be suggesting that the script receive any nominations, which it didn't originally either). He apparently felt film audiences wouldn't be able to handle the lead character's death, because they would be too close to her. Perhaps, but I still prefer original endings. My second problem is that the film is badly in need of substantial restoration, and since a major studio didn't make it, that isn't likely to happen. Still, *Our Town* is worth watching; I think it may be the one film Sam Wood made that leads me to suspect he was capable of more when not working in the studio system. For example, one nicely turned scene shows a country road from above, and then, as the boy leaves the top of the frame, we learn that he will die in France in WWI. Wood lingers just a moment on the empty road (of course, this could be the influence of cinematographer Bert Glennon, who made numerous movies with John Ford). The play's inventions are more interesting than the cinematic equivalents, since there is no bare stage here, but it's a good adaptation and deserved its nomination.

The Philadelphia Story has long been one of my favorite films, despite the misogynistic overtones, both overt and covert. After all, the movie starts with Cary Grant shoving Katharine Hepburn to the ground with an open palm in her face. The movie ends with Hepburn insisting that she will be *yar* (there, I've given away the ending, but only to those who have already seen it. Nifty, no?). In between, Hepburn gets blamed for her father's affairs, as well as hearing her mother forgive her father for having them, just so Mommy won't be alone.[73] A feminist tract, *The Philadelphia Story* isn't – except when it is. The misogyny is countered by Hepburn's overwhelming strength and power as an actress, as well as by investing her character with those same traits, along with sustaining an active role throughout in her destiny (unlike most female roles in this time period, when they are largely reactive). In short, *The Philadelphia Story* is a complex film about love, marriage, male and female roles, submission to marriage, resistance to submission, sex, self-control, self-denial, self-acceptance, and some of the funniest things ever said about any of those subjects. *The Philadelphia Story* remains a favorite, and a great nomination.

As for the omitted films this year, the most shocking oversights are *The Bank Dick*, *His Girl Friday*, *The Mark of Zorro* and *Pinocchio*.

Many W.C. Fields' fans regard *The Bank Dick* as the great comedian's finest hour, as he played Egbert Sousé ("accent grave over the E"). The Academy, logically, therefore ignored him completely (thus continuing their perfect losing streak with the great misanthropist). A first-rate screenplay from Mahatma Kane Jeeves (see Best Original Screenplay for his secret identity), some of W.C. Fields' best routines and snappers, an excellent supporting cast – what more could any lover of comedy ask for? For the first time, Fields got a chance to do what Keaton did at his height, and Chaplin alone managed to do for the bulk of his career: control the structure, tone, and outcome of an entire film. Fields had made so much money for Universal when co-starring with Edgar Bergen in *You Can't Cheat an Honest Man* and Mae West in *My Little Chickadee* that the head of Universal took a chance and gave Fields his head. Smart man. Now if only the Academy had paid atten-

---

[73] Shortly before going to press, I ran across Andrew Sarris saying much the same thing I had decided about Hepburn's films after her "box-office poison" decline: "*The Philadelphia Story* is quite simply the breaking, reining, and saddling of an unruly thoroughbred for the big races to come on Broadway and in Hollywood. It is Katharine Hepburn getting her comeuppance at long last and accepting it like the good sport she was." *"You Ain't Heard Nothin' Yet"* p. 451.

tion, because *The Bank Dick* most definitely deserved a nomination for Best Picture.

The Academy completely ignored *His Girl Friday* in every single category. The word "dumbfounded" is all I can muster. One of the funniest movies ever made, *His Girl Friday* broke new ground in strong female roles for Rosalind Russell, a deeper characterization for Cary Grant, and fast, overlapping dialogue for screenplays. Hawks' driving narrative never lets up, bringing the movie flying together at an amazing clip, and never letting up except when the audience needed a breather. I have seen it many times and never failed to laugh, or to appreciate more fully the artistry of all those involved. Once again, the Academy failed to recognize obvious genius, and should have nominated it for Best Picture, and so much more (see numerous categories below).

I'm not sure *The Mark of Zorro* is a work of genius, but swashbucklers don't get much more fun than this. By far, *The Mark of Zorro* is my favorite Tyrone Power film, and very nearly as good as the best Errol Flynn. The score by Alfred Newman is one of his very best, and clearly, he had been listening to Korngold, for the music shows that influence – but Newman brings out the glory of the adventure just as well as Korngold at his best, as well as the romance of it all. Like the score, the movie is highly influenced by *The Adventures of Robin Hood*: the outlaw fights for justice; his lady love is in the enemy camp; Basil Rathbone plays the villain's main henchman; Eugene Pallette plays a Friar Tuck figure; Rathbone and Power have a big sword fight at the end (cutting candles too). The crowd fight is muddled and unlikely at the end, but the duel is well done. Overall, even though the film imitates *Robin Hood*, *The Mark of Zorro* remains highly viewable, and should have been nominated.

Pinocchio represents Walt Disney and his animators at their absolute peak of perfection. No one has ever made a better animated film, in terms of the whole package. Other full length animated features may have a finer song or two, a catchier score, a more telling scene or two, a deeper theme, better comedy, or more experimentation – but none have ever gone beyond *Pinocchio* in all these categories together. Watching *Pinocchio*, above all else, is a visual extravaganza of the art of the animator (see below in Best Cinematography (Color)).[74] The story matters: we must learn to be true to ourselves, to take responsibility for our actions, to be real. The cast of supporting characters is as good, if

---

[74] As is much of *Fantasia*, particularly *The Nutcracker Suite* and *Night on Bald Mountain*.

not better, than those of any other movie this year: Geppetto, Honest John, Stromboli, Lampwick, and Monstro. The pacing and resolution of the film couldn't be more satisfying to a child – for those of you who are gagging, you might enjoy the original novel, where Pinocchio dies by hanging! The voice work is fine; the comedy gentle and persistently amusing. The score and songs are exceptional. The visuals are as good as they have ever been in American animation – or for that matter, for most of American cinematography. *Pinocchio* should have been nominated for Best Picture.[75]

Finally, we come to who should have won the Best Picture Oscar. Much as I respect *Rebecca*, a far more important film, made with an equal or surpassing level of artistry, and containing indelible scenes which form part of our national memory, deserves the award. As Steinbeck himself judged, *The Grapes of Wrath* is "a hard, straight picture in which the actors are submerged so completely that it looks and feels like a documentary film, and certainly it has a hard, truthful ring."[clxxx] *The Grapes of Wrath* should have won the Academy Award for Best Picture.

Best Actor: James Stewart won for *The Philadelphia Story*, over Raymond Massey, *Abe Lincoln in Illinois*; Henry Fonda, *The Grapes of Wrath*; Charlie Chaplin, *The Great Dictator*; and Laurence Olivier, *Rebecca*

I am always willing to watch Jimmy Stewart in *The Philadelphia Story*, but almost everybody at the time thought he was given the Oscar because he had been passed over for his phenomenal performance in *Mr. Smith Goes to Washington* the year before. I concur. His role as the reporter in *The Philadelphia Story* is joyful and wry, and the moment when he confesses his love for Katharine Hepburn may be one of the greatest declarations of passion in American cinema: "A magnificence that comes out of your eyes, in your voice, in the way you stand there, in the way you walk. You're lit from within, Tracy. You've got fires banked down in you, hearth-fires and holocausts." Stewart deserved the nomination, and in almost any other year, he should have won. But one man went beyond him, and ironically, it was his best friend – of which, more later.

---

[75] I might also point to Ernst Lubitsch and *The Shop Around the Corner*. The problem is, my expectations were so high due to years of hearing about it that I was inevitably disappointed. I can't work up much enthusiasm for this quiet story, so I'm not going to nominate it. See it yourself and let me know; I may change my mind for the second edition...which by the way, you didn't. and I didn't. So, try for the third edition!

Raymond Massey brought to the 1940 filmed version of Robert Sherwood's Pulitzer-Prize-winning Broadway play *Abe Lincoln in Illinois* all the experience and accumulated gravitas he had built up in the title role of the play's 472 performances. Following on the heels of John Ford's mythic *Young Mr. Lincoln* – which I still find the better film of the two – Hollywood butchered *Abe Lincoln in Illinois*, even though Sherwood himself co-wrote the screenplay. Massey is best remembered for his farewell scene, as he leaves to become president. Really, the sole reason to watch this movie is for Massey's performance, which is convincing, and remains the yardstick we use to measure other Lincolns. Hearing him intone Lincoln's speeches is probably better than the real thing; Lincoln himself had a high-pitched, reedy voice, with little of this resonance. The nomination should stay.

Without Henry Fonda's performance, *The Grapes of Wrath* simply wouldn't work as a film. As Scott Eyman insightfully observes, "Fonda's Tom Joad combines the Midwestern sincerity of his Lincoln with an ex-con's stone-cold paranoia. He's no victim, is, in fact, perfectly capable of making trouble. Fonda's lean equalizer is the reason the film never subsides into a morass of little-people sentimentality, the reason it still speaks with a surprising immediacy."[clxxxi] Fonda's body language is intensely controlled, as is his face. He's a man who refuses to bend to the world, jaw set. Watching him stand next to the animated twist that is John Carradine, I am put in mind of Buster Keaton facing into the wind, another indomitable man fighting against everything that opposes him. Fonda's quiet intensity must have influenced Clint Eastwood, especially in Eastwood's later films, when he gave up the Dirty Harry approach and sought deeper roles. As the film goes on, the depth of feeling in Fonda's performance unlocks itself, as his jaw unclenches and he allows himself to open up, most famously in the scenes with his mother, played by Jane Darwell. When he sees her for the first time in four years, Fonda breaks a grin as wide as the sky in joy, with just one word out of his mouth: "Ma." Steinbeck himself said Fonda's performance made him "believe my own words."[clxxxii] A first-class nomination.

I get the feeling the Academy was trying to make up for the snubbing Charlie Chaplin received in earlier years by nominating him for his portrayals of Adenoid Hynkel, dictator of Tomania, and a Jewish barber, in *The Great Dictator*. Chaplin had put off a full speaking role for over a decade after sound had entered the pictures. His portrayal of Hynkel is more interesting than that of the barber, and Danny Kaye must have been watching Chaplin during the first hate speech, because Kaye stole a number of facial expressions from Chaplin. As the barber, what we get is mostly second-rate Little Tramp (excepting the shave to the rhythms of the Brahms Hungarian Rhapsody #5); as Hynkel, we get Chaplin exploring a new kind of darker comedy, one that would lead to *Monsieur Verdoux*. For that half of the performance, and the globe scene, Chaplin should keep his nomination.

Laurence Olivier was nominated again for Best Actor, this time for *Rebecca*. As Maxim de Winter, Olivier goes far beyond his flawed Heathcliff, and playing much older than he was, produces a nuanced, restrained portrayal of a man under the tremendous burden of his past. I think de Winter is Olivier's best screen performance to date, and damn near his best one ever, and much of that is due to Hitchcock's brilliance. We can see the depths of feeling in Olivier's eyes, and the power of his voice seems to hit – for the first time – as it must have on stage, but modulated here for the screen. His greatest moment comes in his confession scene, a long, extended dialogue in which he keeps cornering himself on the set, moving about from one tight spot to the next, as he reveals his past to Fontaine. Olivier is simply riveting, and that scene alone secures his nomination here.

As for the omissions, the most glaring is the Academy's failure to nominate Cary Grant for two of his finest performances in his brilliant comedy work in *The Philadelphia Story* and *His Girl Friday* (not to mention his solid turn in *My Favorite Wife*). As C.K. Dexter Haven in *The Philadelphia Story*, Grant plays an upper crust has-been alcoholic, trying his best to regain his equilibrium, as well as the girl. As in *The Awful Truth*, Grant has a kick of a time playing the rejected lover, his eyes and voice conveying a range of bemusements, judgments, and innuendo. For *His Girl Friday*, Grant pulled on his somewhat unsavory role in Hawks' *Only Angels Have Wings*, and combined it with the lightheartedness he had made his own in comedies, to create a Machiavellian portrayal of love and career as Walter Burns. While Grant could have (and should have) been nominated for either of those roles, I prefer his performance in *His Girl Friday* for the Best Actor nomination.

In fact, I came very close to deciding he should have been named the Best Actor of 1940. But Henry Fonda's final moments in *The Grapes of Wrath* should have clinched the Oscar for his portrayal of Tom Joad. No other scene in the cinema before WWII better encapsulates an entire decade, of the hopes and fears of the Great Depression, and the staunch determination of the American character to continue fighting injustice and oppression. Fonda would not win an Oscar until the end of his life, for *On Golden Pond*. He should have won for this, his first nomination, for Best Actor in *The Grapes of Wrath*.

Best Actress: Ginger Rogers won for *Kitty Foyle*, over Bette Davis, *The Letter*; Martha Scott, *Our Town*; Katharine Hepburn, *The Philadelphia Story*; and Joan Fontaine, *Rebecca*

Ginger Rogers won the Oscar for *Kitty Foyle*, having sworn to give up the dancing shoes and only take dramatic roles. Possibly, she may have parlayed her more interesting performance in the risqué *Primrose Path* into this nomination (see Best Supporting Actress above for more). Rogers winning in this category can only be chalked up to her great popularity in Hollywood, and the fact that in the back of every comedian's head is a longing to play Hamlet. Watching *Kitty Foyle* is something like being forced to view one of those shows where rich girls have to decide which obscenely priced item to pick for their sweet sixteen parties, paid for by their daddies: every well-mannered, balanced human being should avert their eyes out of shame at the excesses of those with too many choices. Rogers isn't bad in the role; she just simply isn't anywhere near as good emoting as she is dancing or inspiring laughter. She tends to use staring off into space as her default expression in this movie. Where is Fred Astaire, anyways? He misses you too! Trust me on this one, Ginger: Paulette Goddard is no substitute for you as a dancing partner. I would even argue that this award is one of the worst ones in this category since Mary Pickford and *Coquette* – we're not talking that level of abomination, but that level of poor choice, compared with the rest of the competition. To be fair, Rogers has her moments. I especially liked the expression on her face and eyes when she accepts the doctor's proposal, even as I questioned what the movie is saying about women: is she only worth marrying because she looks good with a child? Rogers spends a great deal of time misty-eyed and confused, and she does it as well as anybody can. She is also quite good at staring at her lover with that kind of adoring gaze men would kill to see, as well as getting her back up when confronted with social snobbery. But Rogers could have done so much more, if only they had given her more to do other than go all noble whenever she doesn't get what she wants. Her character is simply too passive, too reactive to others, to provide any depth of interest – her repeated declarations of independence ring hollow, because they are just defensive maneuvers to protect her feelings, while she waits for Prince Charming to return. So, no Oscar should there be for Our Lady of the Two Choices, but for what she does manage to convey at times, she should keep the nomination.

When we first see Bette Davis in *The Letter*, she is murdering a man, viciously and gleefully. The next view of her face is in shadows, looking troubled. Following that, we see her face lit up by the moonlight, with a wistful look upon her face. All three of those expressions happen in under a minute of film. After that, she is guarded and fully in control, as she claims murder in self-defense against sexual assault. She plays the victim with great understatement, and we are all but finished with our impressions of her – and then the blackmail begins, with a letter incriminating her and completely destroying her carefully built façade. As Pauline Kael observed, "Davis gives what is very likely the best study of female sexual hypocrisy in film history."[clxxxiii] Davis fully deserved her Oscar nomination, and were it not for the incredibly powerful competition this year – a competition she did much in laying the groundwork for, and providing the spur to other actresses to achieve – I would gladly have seen her win the Oscar for this performance.

Martha Scott plays Emily, the young lead in *Our Town* who will fall in love and marry William Holden. Scott made her debut in this film, received her only nomination, and spent a long career slowly going downhill from this height (she also played Yochabel in *The Ten Commandments* and Miriam in *Ben-Hur*). She does an excellent job bringing out the confusions and conflicts of love, such as they are in the nostalgic *Our Town*. Like the play, hers is a quiet, restrained performance, and a good nomination.

As Katharine Hepburn had discovered, female audiences in the late Thirties and early Forties were changing, and while they enjoyed headstrong women, they also expected them to be tamed and controlled, if not punished. We see this pattern over and over again, from *Jezebel* to *Gone with the Wind* (hence the necessity of the rape scene, and Rhett Butler leaving) to Hepburn's *The Philadelphia Story* and especially, 1942's *Woman of the Year*, the ending of which was ruined by female audience demands that Hepburn be humbled. Hepburn did the best she could to satisfy her audience, and maintain an acting career playing strong, vibrant, independent women. But she had had to deal with being labeled as uncommercial by exhibitor Harry Brandt in 1938, who named several female stars as "box-office poison": Hepburn, Joan Crawford, Marlene Dietrich, Greta Garbo, and Mae West.[clxxxiv] *The Philadelphia Story* changed all that for Hepburn, restoring her to profitability, but exacting a price for a time on the outcomes of her characters. Playing Tracy Lord, Hepburn does a grand job playing a spoiled society girl about to marry a man of the people, who discovers how to be fully human and return to Cary Grant, but only after flirting with Jimmy Stewart. One of the ways out of the charges of misogyny is to look at Hepburn not as a woman, but as someone who has never accepted her own humanity, insisting on an unattainable perfection. By embracing flaws, and the need to work together, her character learns how to truly love (still a problematic reading, given the flaws she is expected to accept – alcoholism and infidelity). Hepburn is a marvel in the role. As evidence, I point to her drunken scene as one of the finest comic moments in film history, as it is for Jimmy Stewart. I never tire of hearing the shifts in her voice throughout the movie. A grand nomination.

Joan Fontaine received her first nomination in *Rebecca* playing the second Mrs. de Winter (the eponymous first wife's memory troubles the film). Fontaine couldn't have been better cast or handled by Hitchcock, who used her nervousness to help her create a terrified mouse of a performance, filled with an endless conflict between passivity and a desire to matter. Watching *Rebecca* can be an unpleasant experience, because all the main characters are deeply flawed – in other words, rich in human frailties. But we are pulled in by the power of Fontaine, for which I point to one scene in particular: watch when she dances with Olivier, and her face conveys the essence of romance, of the dreamy dissolving of self into the happiest emotions – but then she notices that he is watching her, and the traces of uncertainty reappear, only to dissolve once more with his smile. Beautifully done! When Fontaine finally stands up to the housekeeper, and begins to assert herself, we can only cheer at the mouse learning to roar. Fontaine's performance in this film was the finest of her career, and a far better one than in the following year's *Suspicion*, for which she received the Oscar – primarily, I would argue, to make up for passing over her performance in *Rebecca*. Let us rectify that decision, by granting that Joan Fontaine should have won the Best Actress Oscar for this film.

But before we start applauding Fontaine, one omission needs to be addressed.

His Girl Friday made Rosalind Russell a star, and her main role the tough, beautiful, smart career woman who wants a family as well. Decades before this would be the primary problem of American women, Russell was there first, dominating the screen in this film with Cary Grant, and never losing an inch to Grant, who was at the peak of his acting and comic abilities in this movie as well. Russell is every inch the fully realized individual, about to go to war with Grant, her ex-husband – a war she and Grant will eventually conclude with a truce and renewed alliance (over poor Ralph Bellamy, also trounced by Grant in *The Awful Truth*). Russell was not the first choice for the role – that was Carole Lombard – nor was she even in the top six (Katharine Hepburn, Claudette Colbert, Jean Arthur, Ginger Rogers, and Irene Dunne were the other five after Lombard). But Russell made the role her own, and cemented her place as a major fixture of classic Hollywood. Her performance is nuanced, powerful, sexy, and tangibly real, in a way few female stars were at the time. Watching Bette Davis, I have always felt a little like I was watching an artiste at work – I always feel that slight frisson of excitement at knowing she is pushing her art to the limit, but at the same time, we are almost always aware she is acting. Katharine Hepburn has something of that distancing going on as well, in that she always seems to me to be subtly calculating her next move, and we can see her thinking – the experience is always joyful. But here, with Rosalind Russell, in this role alone, I feel as if I'm watching someone truly immersed in the part, living it, breathing it – as if she were embodying the Zen concept of the archer being one with the bow. Russell was never better, never more completely herself on the screen. That she was not nominated for Best Actress is a crime, but that she did not win it is a slap in the face to every actor's dream of finding the perfect role. Rosalind Russell should have won the Oscar for Best Actress for *His Girl Friday*.

You didn't read that wrong. I am declaring one of the rare ties in this book series. The Academy did it a few times; I will restrain myself as well. But I simply can't choose between the two, as both are the quintessential dramatic and comic performances of this year (and many others as well) – and both make Ginger Rogers look like an amateur. Joan Fontaine and Rosalind Russell should have both won for Best Actress.

Best Writing (Original Story): Benjamin Glazer and John S. Toldy[76] won for *Arise, My Love*, over Walter Reisch, *Comrade X*; Hugo Butler and Dore Schary, *Edison, the Man*; Leo McCarey, with Samuel and Bella Spewack, *My Favorite Wife*; and Stuart N. Lake, *The Westerner*.

Benjamin Glazer and John S. Toldy won for *Arise, My Love*. We get an unusual way to start a romance: Ray Milland is a prisoner of war in a Spanish military prison; Claudette Colbert is a reporter who fakes being his wife in order to get a story. They escape – into romantic complications. Colbert's character was apparently based on Ernest Hemingway's third wife, journalist Martha Gellhorn.[clxxxv] *Arise, My Love* has a nice setup, and one of which screenwriters Charles Brackett and Billy Wilder take full advantage, working their Lubitsch training at every opportunity. The scene where Milland thinks Colbert has come up to be romantic is hysterical, as she proceeds to rush the setup for photos and an interview – and every line makes Milland think she's about to have some-

---

[76] John S. Toldy did not, in fact, exist. He was actually John Szekely, a Hungarian who had gone back to Europe and "stood the risk of facing severe repercussions for having...written this anti-Nazi story." Ed Sikov, *On Sunset Boulevard*, p. 149.

what kinky sex with him. Mitchell Leisen directed, which makes this something of a reunion for the team that made *Midnight,* also starring Colbert. Good nomination.

Walter Reisch's *Comrade X* stars Clark Gable and Hedy Lamarr, and isn't even remotely close to an original story: it's *Ninotchka* remade with Gable as an American and Lamarr in the Greta Garbo role. He marries her to help her escape the Soviets; the end is a chase scene in tanks. Very minor film, and not worth a nomination for story whatsoever.

Hugo Butler and Dore Schary gave us *Edison, the Man.* MGM created two films about Edison, one as a boy with Mickey Rooney, and one as an adult with Spencer Tracy. Watching Tracy play Edison is enjoyable, and watching him struggle with his inventions is believable. Hugo Butler ended up writing *Lassie, Come Home.* Dore Schary would one day run MGM (into the ground, according to Louis B. Mayer). *Edison, the Man* is worth seeing once, if only for Spencer Tracy, but shouldn't have been worth a nomination for the quality of the writing, which is mundane.

Leo McCarey worked with Samuel and Bella Spewack on *My Favorite Wife.* As noted above in Best Original Score, McCarey went looking for a vehicle to make another film in the same vein as *The Awful Truth.* Here, he and his two writing partners took Tennyson's poem "Enoch Arden" and reversed the genders of the main characters, and updated it to the modern world. So, how "original" is an original story when a poem is the source of the story? Tennyson wrote a tragedy, and McCarey turned it upside down and made it a comedy (a fairly standard gimmick). What is more, so much of this film feels like a carbon copy of *The Awful Truth* that I find myself wondering why it was nominated at all in this category – and then I remember the accident McCarey had, and the nomination becomes clear: Hollywood was saluting one of its own with a get well card. Well, McCarey got well, so the card worked – but that doesn't mean I have to agree. Much as it pains me to turn away from a good comedy like *My Favorite Wife,* I can't in good conscience agree with the nomination – it really isn't as funny or poignant or deep as *The Awful Truth.* Still, I recommend seeing it at least once, if only to watch Grant and Dunne having fun again.

Stuart N. Lake (*My Darling Clementine*) wrote the original story for the Gary Cooper film *The Westerner* (for more on which, see the Best Supporting Actor category above). Lake's story was more heavily focused on Judge Roy Bean than what was eventually filmed, but writers Jo Swerling and Niven Busch took Lake's original ore and mined it for dark gold. Lake deserved his nomination for that inspiration, and for providing the framework for one of the most influential westerns of all time.

The Academy once again ignored a better choice in *Road to Singapore*. The original story by Harry Hervey (*Shanghai Express*) would spawn a franchise of various Road pictures for Paramount, create a new genre of film with the buddy picture, and forever cement one of the great comedy teams of Hollywood: Bob Hope and Bing Crosby, as they compete for Dorothy Lamour. We've seen movies where two men vie for the same woman before – all those Spencer Tracy-Clark Gable pairings, for example – but never before had it been done with this level of bickering and biting humor, both insulting and self-deprecating at the same time. The series would hit its peak in *Road to Morocco* in 1942; here, the Road begins (with less bite and manic comedy than would accrue with time in the series). Like a great standard, Hervey's basic plot allowed Hope and Crosby to ring endless changes on it. Perhaps Hervey never expected it, since Hope and Crosby generally ignored the script and improvised (or used their gag men's ideas), but a frame is a frame, and Hervey produced a durable one – which should have given him a nomination, and the Oscar for Best Writing (Original Story), for inventing a genre and giving us a chance to laugh so much over the years.

Best Writing (Original Screenplay): Preston Sturges won for *The Great McGinty*, over Ben Hecht, *Angels Over Broadway*; Norman Burnside, Heinz Herald and John Huston, *Dr. Ehrlich's Magic Bullet*; Charles Bennett and Joan Harrison, *Foreign Correspondent*; and Charlie Chaplin, *The Great Dictator*

Preston Sturges began his remarkable and nigh unprecedented run of directing his own screenplays with *The Great McGinty*, starring Brian Donlevy as the hobo who becomes the governor with the help of political machine boss Akim Tamiroff. Watching the movie today, we get an initiation into the mechanics of how politics used to be played, as the homeless McGinty votes 37 times in a row in the same election to garner the two dollar fee per vote. Donlevy milks his reputation as a screen villain, putting over his character's unsavoriness with a considerable degree of savoir faire. Sturges fully displays his own characteristic qualities of pushing the edge of the envelope, of telling stories few others would even try, and of doing so with absolute deadpan seriousness for his characters (thus increasing our own laughter). Sturges succeeded in proving that the screenwriter could be the most effective director of his own stories; as others have pointed out before me, John Huston and Billy Wilder would soon follow the trail Sturges blazed. While *The*

Great McGinty is a compelling, cynical little tale, highly deserving of its nomination, one greater tale was told this year that deserved Oscar more.

Ben Hecht wrote *Angels over Broadway*, for which I provide one major caveat: unless your name is Orson Welles, don't put Rita Hayworth into a dramatic role. *The Lady from Shanghai* has her only decent acting; before you say *Gilda*, let's remember the only reason we watch that film is for the strip tease number. And while we're at it, Douglas Fairbanks, Jr. should only be seen in light comedy and adventure films. Now that we've straightened that out, let's go after the crookedness inherent in *Angels over Broadway*. The plot is far-fetched, but that never stopped a good film before: take four characters, one of them suicidal, then have the other three set aside their selfishness and work a con to save Captain Kamikaze's life. I won't go into the con, but I will point out that Ben Hecht wrote, produced, and directed this movie. Hecht was a very good playwright (*The Front Page*), screenwriter (among many others, *Notorious*) and the most highly paid script doctor in Hollywood (including *Gone with the Wind*). Hecht directed a total of seven films; *Angels over Broadway* would be his fifth, aided by the excellent cinematographer and co-director Lee Garmes (most famous for working with Josef von Sternberg). Elements of this film prefigure film noir, with the rain and the urban setting and the cynical voice-over. Perhaps the most interesting character (and one I suspect Hecht based on himself), is the one played by Thomas Mitchell, an alcoholic has-been playwright with a penchant for trenchant speeches: "Allow me to present my credentials as a fellow cadaver. I'm being divorced by my wife whom I love dearly in my own nasty way. I was disemboweled by another woman. I have written three bad plays in a row, and next year I'll write a worse one. I have neither a home, a single hope, nor a shred of curiosity left. Bankrupt and broke, I've destroyed myself, sir, in becoming famous. I am no longer a man, Mr. Engle, I'm an epitaph over an ash can! And now, sir, what's your story?" The problem with the movie centers on Fairbanks and Hayworth; their characters are as two-dimensional as the suicide is one-dimensional. Only Mitchell's character breathes fire. For that performance, the nomination should stay as an exploration of the mind of the playwright in action.

Heinz Herald and John Huston fired *Dr. Ehrlich's Magic Bullet*. I still find it hard to believe Hollywood actually managed to make a movie about curing syphilis. Part of overcoming the objections of the Breen Office had to do with fighting Hitler's hostility to Jewish scientists; Edward G. Robinson put his heart and soul into the role, as a way of giving the finger to the Nazis. Basing it heavily on the unpublished documents about Dr. Ehrlich's life and work, Heinz Herald crafted an honest look at the fight against syphilis, while John Huston came in and made it palatable.[clxxxvi] The result is a fairly intense biopic that still plays well today, both due to the screenplay, and to Robinson's solid performance. The nomination should stay.

Charles Bennett and Joan Harrison's supposedly original screenplay for *Foreign Correspondent* is based on a book, Vincent Sheean's *Personal History*. Fourteen writers worked on this one; I doubt Sheean would recognize any of it. Hitchcock was notorious for taking source material and so completely rewriting it nobody could recognize the origins of his story. Part of the reason Hitchcock and Selznick fought so intensely when he was filming *Rebecca* is that Selznick actually expected him to film the novel. *Foreign Correspondent* is a smoothly paced, somewhat comic, somewhat tense spy story, and while the dialogue doesn't have the kind of wicked leer Hitch's films so often have, that may be more due to Joel McCrea being too earnest a presence for that to work. A good nomination, as it almost always is for a Hitchcock film.

Charlie Chaplin wrote an entire script before filming *The Great Dictator*, contrary to his usual improvisational practices. He came up with some wonderful gags: the rotating dud shell; the grenade in the pants; the watch defying gravity; the ballet scene; the dueling barber chairs. At times, however, I wish Chaplin had thought of the verbal components of the script as inherent to the story, rather than as something he threw on top of the visuals because he had to have talking. Throughout *The Great Dictator*, the feeling of a jarring inconsequentiality emerges, and makes me wish Chaplin had simply defied the critics and continued making silents – or learned sooner how to be funny with words (he doesn't have this jarring quality in his later work). Exceptions exist, of course: the peremptory command, "Give me that stick!" followed by a dangling Chaplin's firm "Impossible." Best of all, the ridiculous German of Hynkel's speeches: "und die Sauerkraut!" But the serious aspects, especially Paulette Goddard's lines and the excruciating speech at the end, lead me to deny Chaplin should have a nomination for writing this flawed film. He was capable of so much more. The ending of the movie abandons his mastery of visuals completely, and what is worse, breaks the character of the Jewish barber (who is based on the Little Tramp) completely apart: what comes out of the character's mouth isn't remotely what that character could have said. One prime example: the supposedly Jewish character quotes, from memory, a passage from the New Testament, and he refers to "Saint Luke." The ending is heartfelt, but essentially, badly written and overacted. We needed images, Charlie; you gave us a static diatribe – and watching Paulette Goddard's face and hearing the ironic return of Wagner's *Lohengrin* isn't the answer. No nomination should have been made.

As is often the sad case, the Academy ignored the best work of the year.

In *The Bank Dick*, W.C. Fields reached his absolute peak of perfection in this satire on the middle class, and all it stands for: marriage, motherhood, children, possessions, respectability. Fields only got away with it because nobody took him seriously, which is why comedy and genre films often end up with the greatest durability; they willingly take risks that few straight films would dare, and doing so subtly and sneakily enough that nobody in power noticed. Writing as Mahatma Kane Jeeves, Fields goes all out, layering his performance with his best gags and lines, such as his teaching children smoking tricks. The dialogue crackles and whips around our expectations. When a child points out Fields' nose, the mother says, "You mustn't make fun of the gentleman, Clifford. You'd like to have a nose like that full of nickels, wouldn't you?" On hearing of his prospective son-in-law, Fields sums up: "Og Oggilby...sounds like a bubble in a bathtub!" When he thinks he has lost a twenty, only to confirm he spent it drinking, Fields sighs in relief: "Oh boy, what a load that is off my mind! I thought I'd lost it." In trying to shame his future son-in-law to embezzle, "Don't be a luddy-duddy! Don't be a mooncalf! Don't be a jabbering owl! You're not those, are you?" In discussing children, he reassures quietly: "I'm very fond of children. Girl children, around eighteen and twenty." As he's about to strike his daughter, he explains why: "She's not going to tell me I don't love her." And my favorite of all, that dreaded disease, mo-go on the ga-go-go. W.C. Fields should have been nominated for – and won – the Oscar for Best Writing (Original Screenplay). Sorry, Sturges fans – and I include myself here – you just can't beat Fields on this one. So please send around the Oscar to him, along with my hat, my cane, Jeeves. William Claude Dukenfield is in the house, and respect must be paid!

Best Writing (Screenplay): Donald Ogden Stewart won for *The Philadelphia Story*, over Nunnally Johnson, *The Grapes of Wrath*; Dalton Trumbo, *Kitty Foyle*; Dudley Nichols, *The Long Voyage Home*; and Robert E. Sherwood and Joan Harrison, *Rebecca*.

Donald Ogden Stewart's screenplay of *The Philadelphia Story* is a polished, comic, often poignant adaptation of the stage play – both of which are misogynistic (see Best Picture above). When Stewart won, he thanked himself.[clxxxvii] Apparently, Philip Barry didn't write the play for its Broadway run. Other than creating a prologue (perhaps the most misogynistic scene with the physical assault on Hepburn), and some transitional materials, Barry's dialogue is largely preserved. What exactly Stewart was being given the Oscar for, therefore, is not quite clear. I still think he deserved a nomination for preserving Barry's play intact, but work this easy shouldn't be worth an Oscar. Stewart would go on to other films, but his best was behind him: *The Prisoner of Zenda, Holiday,* and *Love Affair*.

Nunnally Johnson took an enormous novel, *The Grapes of Wrath*, and brought it down to manageable size while not sacrificing tone and depth. Steinbeck's economy of language, his refusal to blink away from the reality of the Depression, and the strange combination of anger, despair, hope, and mercy that fills the novel comes through in Johnson's adaptation. What gives me pause, and makes me question giving Johnson the Oscar immediately, is that damn ending, which is in his script.[clxxxviii] Johnson pulled it from the novel, but by placing it at the end, he privileges those words, and undercuts the essential quality of sadness and defiance which Fonda's departure should leave us with, replacing it with a sappy uplift that is not replicated in the novel. Granted, Hollywood could never have used the original ending, which involves a dead baby and suckling a grown man, but as is usual with art, less is more: Johnson should have trusted that Fonda and Ford could bring the film to its rightful close. Zanuck approved Johnson's script; nobody seems to know for sure if Ford directed the ending they used or not, but given that it looks very different from much of the rest of the film, and Ford himself denied shooting it, I tend to want to blame Johnson. In the end, however, I can't deny the power of Johnson's script, for bringing much of the greatness of the novel intact to the screen. The nomination should stay.

Dalton Trumbo would go on to be the most famous blacklisted writer of the Fifties. When Kirk Douglas insisted that he be credited for *Spartacus*, a decade of abuse and neglect began to come to an end. Trumbo infamously won an Oscar for Best Screenplay for *The Brave One* under an assumed name, Robert Rich, as he survived as best he could. Written before the McCarthy era, Trumbo's script for *Kitty Foyle* is based on a bestselling novel, and Trumbo does his best to adapt it to Code Hollywood. He moves the story away from the abortion line, for example, but he does offer Ginger Rogers a choice, of sorts: run away with the rich guy she loves, despite his being married to someone else, or marry the earnest, good-looking doctor. Given audience expectations in 1940 and the Code, only one outcome is really possible, but Trumbo milks the risks of becoming a social outcast for all he can. My problem is that he maneuvers the women into one category: husband hunters. I have no doubt that in a world where women were limited in their choices, that was the main game they pursued, but shouldn't great writing challenge the status quo, rather than celebrate it? The casting reinforces the script's ridiculing of the one woman who suggests that marriage isn't the be-all and end-all of female existence by selecting the least attractive woman in the elevator to proclaim her independence. But the entire structure of the film, centered on Kitty Foyle's need to choose between two men, also plays up this decision as the only important one in a woman's life. Granted, that story is still going on in today's Hollywood, but generally speaking, we see more balance in how they are told (although just once, I'd like to see a romantic movie that starts with the wedding day, and shows how tough marriage can be, rather than dumping us at the altar and swooping out with the happily- ever-afters). Trumbo's screenplay fails to craft a balanced choice between Foyle's two men, focusing on the rich guy, and all the pretty stuff that goes along with the rich, rather than the poor doctor (now there's an oxymoron we no longer see!). *Kitty Foyle* is simply fancied- up melodrama, and a rather shallow one at that, although I did find Rogers arguing with her reflection in the mirror to be useful as a dramatic tool, since it gives a solitary character dialogue instead of just monologuing. Still and all, the film's telegraphed ending, the wallowing in the sentimental excess, and the lack of some kind of admirable depiction of women leads me to argue Trumbo should have had no nomination.

Dudley Nichols adapted four Eugene O'Neill one act plays into *The Long Voyage Home*. Nichols didn't treat O'Neill as holy scripture, but then again, Nichols was friends with O'Neill, and O'Neill liked what he saw so much he kept a print of the film.[clxxxix] Nichols captures the essence of the O'Neill plays, bringing them together into what is admittedly an episodic film, and not one with the power of a single narrative. But he provides the framework for Toland and Ford to create a groundbreaking set of visuals, and for that alone, he deserves the nomination.

Robert E. Sherwood and Joan Harrison were nominated for adapting *Rebecca*, a then-famous novel by Daphne du Maurier. The dialogue is pointed, and rich in textual layering. For example, when Olivier and Fontaine sit down together for the first time to eat, she tells of her recently deceased beloved father; he then tells her he will take her somewhere, and to eat up "like a good girl" – playing up his age, and the need for a replacement for her lost father in the man who will become her husband. Hitchcock emphasizes that by including in the scene Olivier's graying temples, and Fontaine joins in the conversation as well, by eating as if she were a little girl, not quite able to hold her fork, or to take a big bite (later on, Olivier tells her to stop biting her nails in fatherly fashion). He asks her to marry him, in the most unromantic way possible – "I'm asking you to marry me, you little fool." The power relationship is clearly a submissive one for Fontaine. That will change – and Olivier knows it, because he tells her "It's a pity you have to grow up." Precisely when is the issue of much of the film. Until then, Olivier keeps ordering her about, telling her to put on her raincoat, because "you can't be too careful with children." What clearly emerges after their first fight is that he wanted only someone who would be totally under his control, who wouldn't defy him – and who would allow him to let the past go. Instead, as Faulkner said, "The past isn't dead; it isn't even past." The screenplay has multiple layering built on it throughout with the cinematography, direction, and acting, providing the kind of framework for this richness in ways so few screenplays ever do. The biggest problem is the shift away from Rebecca's death going from a deliberate murder to an accident, which seriously limits the depth of feeling which Fontaine has, and reduces the danger of Olivier to a fraction of what his character has in the novel. Code Hollywood would never have allowed a guilty man to go free, which is also what wrecks the ending of *Suspicion*, when Cary Grant's character turns out to be innocent, in a betrayal of everything Hitchcock laid out up to that point. Sherwood, one of America's most successful playwrights in the Thirties, had written *The Petrified Forest* and *Abe Lincoln in Illinois*; Harrison also wrote *Suspicion*. Both deserved a nomination for *Rebecca*.

Several screenplays were unjustly ignored by the Academy.

As noted in Original Story, they should have added Charles Brackett and Billy Wilder for *Arise, My Love*. They wrote a screenplay worthy of Lubitsch in their capacity to openly discuss sex without ever saying a word. They've also structured a story that goes from prison to freedom to commitment to grander things than romance, which is an unusual way to put things together – and one that *Casablanca* would emulate soon. Yes, the ending brings them back together in an interventionist plea, but the end of *Casablanca* makes something of the same call, with more élan. They deserved to be nominated in this category.

Also omitted was the adaptation of *Pride and Prejudice* by Aldous Huxley (*Brave New World*) and Jane Murfin (*Alice Adams*; *The Women*). The movie opens in a dress shop with the unmarried women and their mother, then Mr. Darcy and Mr. Bingley show up in a carriage outside. The hunt for husbands is on. My favorite line: "There's no one as dignified as a mummy." The adaptation shifts some of the social satire down a few notches, and Greer Garson is too old to play Miss Elizabeth, but the spirit of the novel is largely intact, and so should have been nominated.

In the end, the single best adaptation of the year is the unnominated *His Girl Friday*, Charles Lederer's brilliant revisioning of Ben Hecht and Charles MacArthur's classic play, *The Front Page*. Howard Hawks had the initial idea of making Hildy Johnson a woman; Ben Hecht worked on it with both Hawks and Lederer before moving on to other assignments. Lederer wrote a groundbreaking script, with overlapping dialogue and extremely fast delivery, in order to reproduce how people actually spoke. The movie laid the groundwork for entirely new ways of telling stories, and moved the cinema closer to the kind of realism Hemingway strove for in his lean writing. After you've seen it once, sit looking away from the screen and listen to it without looking. The crisp, pointed dialogue alone should convince you Lederer should have been nominated, and *His Girl Friday* should have won.

Best Cinematography (Black & White): George Barnes won for *Rebecca*, over James Wong Howe, *Abe Lincoln in Illinois*; Ernest Haller, *All This, and Heaven Too*; Charles B. Lang, *Arise, My Love*; Harold Rosson, *Boom Town*; Rudolph Maté, *Foreign Correspondent*; Gaetano Gaudio, *The Letter*; Gregg Toland, *The Long Voyage Home*; Joseph Valentine, *Spring Parade*; and Joseph Ruttenberg, *Waterloo Bridge*

George Barnes got the statue for *Rebecca*, but as with any Alfred Hitchcock film, that masterful controller of the look and feel of the entirety of his films must be taken into account, particularly for the cinematography. The cinematographer is omitted in most critical discussion of Hitchcock's work, as if he didn't exist at all. Barnes also shot *Spellbound* with Hitchcock, but Barnes had a substantial career apart from the director, including *Meet John Doe, Jane Eyre*, and *The War of the Worlds* among many other solid films. But *Rebecca* was his only win. From the opening shot, we are in a very special world, one of mists and memory, and the confusion of making sense out of past events (which we, as the audience, have never seen). Throughout the film, we can see why the Oscar went to Barnes, even as we wonder if Hitch was responsible. When Fontaine learns about Rebecca, the very next scene shows her in bed, twisting in her dreams, while the shadows from the window form prison bars over her (an image Hitchcock employed again in later films). The same image is then used when Fontaine and Olivier dance for the first time, and the camera pans from their romantic reflections in the pool, up to where they are within the cell-bar shadow of the trellis; the suggestion that the two of them falling in love will be a kind of prison is inescapable. As they work their way through the past, one of the great scenes of the film has Olivier confronting Fontaine about what she's heard about Rebecca, while the home movies showing the past literally screen across his chest as he stands in front of the home movie screen: one narrative chases another, one version of the past plays across a different past. Then, when he steps aside, and we see the happy Olivier of their courtship side by side with the angry Olivier, all we can do is marvel at the ingenuity of Barnes and Hitchcock in carrying it off so tellingly. In the confession scene, the camera becomes Rebecca, to avoid the problem of having to cast someone so impossibly beautiful.[cxc] I would also argue that Orson Welles saw the final scene, since something very like it occurs in *Citizen Kane*. *Rebecca* should keep the nomination, and definitely makes a case for being one of the most innovative, enduring examples of cinematography – but another film goes even farther, and should have won the Oscar instead.

James Wong Howe's career as a cinematographer was long and highly rewarded, but *Abe Lincoln in Illinois* shows him falling behind the curve. Compared to Gregg Toland, and even George Barnes, Howe is hopelessly old-fashioned in this *Abe Lincoln*, which looks as if it could have easily been shot five years before. Granted, the film as it is shown today is badly in need of restoration, but even so, the camerawork is stolid and rarely does more than sit there, with little poetry to it. Howe would make much better movies, but he didn't deserve the nomination here.

Ernest Haller's camerawork on *All This, and Heaven Too* is fluid. I love when he shoots Davis running down the staircase, although it's a move right out of the silent *Seventh Heaven*. Despite all the motion, something feels to me as if he's doing paint-by-numbers cinematography. Perhaps I shouldn't have come to this film directly after watching Gregg Toland's three masterly experimental movies, but competition is the name of the game here. The story requires some poetry, some sense that we are in the nineteenth century and in a romance of a noble variety, but Haller's cinematography isn't providing much of any of that. Things improve when the movie heads back further into the past, with some gentler lighting at times to go with the fluidity of the camera as well. Haller also begins to illuminate the scenes to emphasize the action more effectively, moving from darkness to light, or vice versa, depending on the narrative. Overall, I think what we're looking at has little inspiration, but much understated competence. One nice shot moves up to Davis' face after the candles get doused, and we see her smelling the flower given to her – and the wistful longing is matched nicely by the close-up and the lighting. Another nice shot is the Halloween in the woods, with that great foggy light that helps spook us. Haller does add some shading to the story in the chateau nearer to the end, but not with the kind of memorable imagery Toland was developing in film after film; then again, when you've got Bette Davis, I suspect the whole film rides on her acting more than any other factor. Haller also did the camerawork on *Gone with the Wind*, *Mildred Pierce*, and *Rebel without a Cause*. Anatole Litvak directed movies which, like this one, encouraged strong female performances, rather than cinematic tour de forces: *Sorry, Wrong Number*; *The Snake Pit*; and *Anastasia*. The two of them gave Bette Davis her stage, and not much more – but enough to keep the nomination.

Claudette Colbert and Ray Milland star in a screenplay from Charles Brackett and Billy Wilder. *Arise, My Love* starts in the aftermath of the Spanish Civil War, as a few "soldiers of fortune" await their fate in a military prison. Cinematographer Charles B. Lang has fallen in love with the crane camera, and uses it to swoop slowly into a prison courtyard, where an execution is about to take place. We then shift into a prison cell below the courtyard, and the light filtering in illuminates a card game between Milland and a priest. Milland is due to die at five, and as part of his last meal, he wants a bubble dancer for dessert. Note the lascivious hand of Brackett and Wilder at work; a bubble dancer is a kind of strip tease with a giant bubble obscuring things; the most famous of them was Sally Rand. Claudette Colbert shows up, pretending to be his wife so she can get a story for her paper. They escape – into Lubitsch territory, full of innuendo (surprising what they got away with in this one, but Brackett and Wilder learned well at the feet of their master). The cinematography after the opening is mostly just serviceable, with a few exceptions: the cobblestone street scene; the forest paradise; the attack on the boat, when the rocking back of the camera is done on a large scale. The nomination should stay for those scenes.

We've seen most of *Boom Town* before, in *San Francisco* and *Test Pilot*. This time, we also get oil. *Boom Town* is a big expensive mess of a movie. Gable and Tracy are friendly rivals; they compete over Claudette Colbert (in her first film with Gable since *It Happened One Night*); later, Hedy Lamarr shows up to complicate things. Harold Rosson filmed it with all the gloss a dirty oil town can take. Rosson's photography is straightforward and competent, but like so many nominated pictures this year in this category, nothing compared to Gregg Toland, or even George Barnes or Rudolph Maté. Rosson does some very nice lighting to produce a realistic tone to the interior scenes, and he films outdoors with confidence as well. The fight scene between Tracy and Gable near the end of the film, however, was so overcranked that it looks more like a Keystone Cops or Three Stooges outing, a ridiculous effect that destroys some of the film's credibility. The nomination should stay, if only because something of the look of *Giant* seems to hearken back to this movie.

Watching *Foreign Correspondent*, we are in the hands of a master storyteller; every image, every word, builds up suspense and delivers; this time, Alfred Hitchcock works with Rudolph Maté. The mystery of the foreign diplomat who disappears, then reappears, and is then assassinated in plain sight, drives the entire narrative forward. Visually, the image of the killer pushing his way through a crowd of open umbrellas in the rain, followed by reporter Joel McCrea, signals Hitchcock's unique way of finding a common image, and then making brand new use of it. As Karl Kraus once said, "My language is the universal whore whom I have to make into a virgin." Hitchcock renovates often. In the Dutch windmill, the constantly rotating machinery of the mill gives Hitchcock an endlessly moving pattern of light and shadow, as McCrea attempts to avoid being spotted (James Whale does something similar in *Frankenstein*). Another nicely composed shot is through the roof entrance, when McCrea re-enters the mill, and we see down the ladder into the dusty interior and watch the bad guys below. Hitchcock wasn't above using the camera for a bit of trickery, as when a man – our hero? – falls from the tower. An excellent nomination, as it almost always would be on a Hitchcock film.

Tony Gaudio's work on *The Letter* assures this to be an excellent nomination – see above in Best Director for more.

Joseph Valentine was nominated for *Spring Parade*, which attempted to replicate the success of Deanna Durbin's 1939 *First Love* (my favorite of the Durbin films); at least in part, they did so by bringing back the cinematographer, Valentine, and scorer, Charles Previn, who had gained Oscar nominations the previous year, and the same director, Henry Koster. Unfortunately, Durbin is returned to the kind of friendly scheming of her earlier pictures, rather than the somewhat more adult tone of *First Love*. Here, she falls in love with a young soldier who likes to write music, but is forbidden to do so in his military role; Durbin secretly sends one of his songs to the Austrian Emperor. Valentine provides decent camerawork, particularly during some fast dancing, where he maintains focus on action nearly as violent as a football game – with Durbin as the football. Overall, though, mostly what we get are pretty pictures, without any depth. No nomination should have been given.

Waterloo Bridge stars two very attractive people, Vivien Leigh and Robert Taylor, in a remake of the James Whale film about a love affair between a soldier and ballerina who turns to prostitution when her intention to marry Taylor is delayed by his leave being canceled. When she is fired from the ballet after missing a performance to see him before he goes, she has no other choice (remember, this is Code Hollywood). Leigh made this after *Gone with the Wind*, and being passed over for the leads in *Rebecca* and *Pride and Prejudice*; as beautiful as ever, she also dances ballet credibly (although we never see her feet). Taylor rated this movie his favorite: "It was the first time I really gave a performance that met the often unattainable standards I was always setting for myself."[cxci] Cinematographer Joseph Ruttenberg opens the film with a graceful sweeping crane shot that moves down a street filled with people listening to the declaration of war against Germany in 1939. Indeed, other than close-ups to show the pretty people, Ruttenberg uses the camera crane a number of times to excellent effect. The result is a romantic film that keeps the story moving along nicely. The most famous scene in the movie comes in the nightclub, when the lights go out, followed one by one by the candles, until we reach their first kiss, deep with shadows. The scene with Vivien Leigh looking directly into the camera while it rains is also memorable, but that one has been used before, but never as effectively. The second kiss in the rain isn't quite as good as the first one (in visual terms), but it's still a corker. Ruttenberg worked closely with director Mervyn LeRoy to craft these touching images, and along with the touching performances, the result makes for an exceptional romantic melodrama (yes, I'm approving of a melodrama! And no, I'm not drunk). Rutterberg deserved his nomination.

For me, Gregg Toland's stunning cinematography and Ford's compositional sense are the main reasons to watch *The Long Voyage Home*. Some of it is quite outrageous (I swear I can hear Ford chuckling evilly in the background): we start with this lush shot of the ocean, moonlight shimmering, and the cargo ship, then we cut to a frame of palm trees, through which we can see the ship – and native women, luxuriating in the moonlight, against the phallic palm trees, while the woman in the foreground on the left slowly moves down her top, caressing her breast, and looking orgasmic...while she smokes a cigarette. We also see more cleavage than in any other early Forties film I can think of; the Breen Office must have been sleeping. One striking scene has one of the crewmates jumping ship, then running down a long dock into a very bright light, only to be chased and taken down by police in more bright light and very long shadows; I suspect that film noir cinematographers paid attention to this scene, as it is of a piece of the kind of thing you see in late Forties/early Fifties film noir (the same can be said for the score when the runaway returns to the ship). One lovely, sad shot at the end shows a newspaper submerged in the flowing current, telling of a torpedoed ship, upon which one of their former shipmates has been shanghaied.

What surprises me is that Toland was nominated for *The Long Voyage Home*, and not for the more popular and artistically complete *The Grapes of Wrath*. Remember Jane Darwell silently trying on her jewelry in the mirror, nearly surrendering to nostalgia and the pain of lost youth? Just as fine is the scene in the tent, lit with what looks to be a match, but in reality, was a hidden wired light in Henry Fonda's hand. The great topper follows, with Fonda giving his unforgettable final speech as Tom Joad, with Toland lighting up the fires of his eyes. Not a single shot in *The Long Voyage Home* can equal them.

Consider as well that Toland shot a third film this year that goes beyond what anybody else was doing, *The Westerner*. We open with a shot of a wagon train moving west under a stunning western sky, every bit as panoramic and poetic as a John Ford western. Toland and director William Wyler follow that up with a dust-filled land full of cattle, the largest herd ever put on film up to that time.[cxcii] A fight breaks out between the farmers and the cattlemen in the midst of a corn field, and the imagery of the men on horseback searching through the field of dried corn hunting for their quarry may be the best shot in the whole film. I don't think anybody else ever captured just how graceful and powerful Gary Cooper was on the back of a horse (he'd grown up riding, and because of a broken hip when he was young, had had to learn how to be one with the horse and avoid any jarring). The stalks of corn form a motif throughout the film, and when the farmers bend down to pray, the stalks reach into this unbelievably beautiful sky like the hands of supplicants. The grave amongst the corn with the stoic woman on one end reading the service, and Cooper's long lanky form standing on the other end of the grave, looks almost like an impressionist painting.

So Gregg Toland should have been nominated for all three. *The Grapes of Wrath*, *The Westerner*, and *The Long Voyage Home* – three very different films, shot in three very different styles (although deep focus is the stylistic link among them), all masterfully. Toland was rapidly proving himself to be one of the small handful of cinematographers who are more than mere technicians. Toland was an artist.

In deciding the winner, looking back over the year, and Toland's great trifecta, I think Gregg Toland deserves the Oscar for *The Grapes of Wrath*. Start the film, and freeze it on the very first shot, the one of Fonda as a small figure moving from far away towards the camera, which is focused on a crossroads. Above the roads are telephone wires, stretching off into the distance; surrounding the roads are fields, the furrows evident of farmland. As a visual metaphor, Toland and Ford have placed us at that crossroads between technology and agriculture, between America's past and America's future, and immediately connected us to Fonda's character as the protagonist (which is why ending the film when Joad leaves is a perfect circle, completing the film, and makes Darwell's "We're the people" the false note that it truly is). Fonda then enters the Cross Roads Café, to reinforce the imagery. From that point on, Ford and Toland and Fonda never let up, forming a perfect triangle within which the story lays itself out, and all told in a mix of documentary realism and poetic genius (look at the night scene under the bridge, as beautiful as the haystack scene in *It Happened One Night*, and yet, a prelude to the brutal crushing of the strikers). Truly, *The Grapes of Wrath* is the most visually stunning film of the year, and Toland should have won the Oscar for it. Given Orson Welles' obsession with John Ford, I would argue that *The Grapes of Wrath* led directly to Welles hiring Toland for *Citizen Kane*, the apex of Toland's career as an innovative cinematographer. [77]

Best Cinematography (Color): Georges Périnal won for *The Thief of Bagdad*, over Oliver T. Marsh and Allen Davey, *Bitter Sweet*; Arthur C. Miller and Ray Rennahan, *The Blue Bird*; Leon Shamroy and Ray Rennahan, *Down Argentine Way*; Victor Milner and W. Howard Greene, *Northwest Mounted Police*; and Sidney Wagner and William V. Skall, *Northwest Passage*

For *The Thief of Bagdad*, the script is disjointed at times, and the romantic leads have all the charisma of wet toilet paper – but the cinematography is quite good, and the special effects were cutting edge for their day (see above). A British production moved wholesale to Hollywood due to the war, *The Thief of Bagdad* is most famous today for its special effects, for Sabu's antics with the genie played by Rex Ingram, and for Conrad Veidt's wicked Jaffar (yes, Disney was paying attention decades later). Georges Périnal had already filmed *À Nous la Liberté*; he would go on to the wartime classic *The Life and Death of Colonel Blimp*. His camerawork here is often as impressive as Technicolor got, particularly in the scenes with special effects and Conrad Veidt. Be-

---

[77] As Toland worked with these successful, maverick directors, and as he would finally achieve most fully with Orson Welles on *Citizen Kane*, he went directly counter to the dominant trend of Thirties cinematography by breaking free of the budgetary restraints on individuality. As Tino Balio puts it, "Once production had begun, tight schedules and budgets kept expensive retakes and experimentation to a minimum. Because the system forced cameramen to fall back on conventional forms of shooting, Hollywood cinematography during the Thirties all too often lacked individuality." *Grand Design*, p. 97.

cause of the need for a stationary camera for the matte shots[78] and other special effects, the film has a static quality that doesn't wear well today, but within those limits, Périnal did solid work worth a nomination. He just didn't deserve the Oscar.

Oliver T. Marsh and Allen Davey shot *Bitter Sweet*, a Noel Coward operetta turned into a Nelson Eddy and Jeanette MacDonald flop. Their first film in Technicolor doesn't help Eddy be any less wooden; I still feel bad for MacDonald being stereotyped into his partner (and her hair looks just like Lucille Ball's would in color). The cinematography is mundane at best. What's worse, color makes Eddy and MacDonald look really old. No nomination should have been given for embalming for Marsh, who died shortly after this film appeared, and Davey, best known for the far livelier *Cover Girl* with Rita Hayworth and Gene Kelly.

Arthur C. Miller and Ray Rennahan filmed *The Blue Bird*, trying to help Twentieth Century-Fox, who had a problem on their hands: Shirley Temple was rapidly growing up. The adorable mop-top would soon face what has always plagued child stars: adolescence and adulthood (not that they don't plague the rest of us, but most of us don't have audiences watching for zits and other new protuberances). Fox also wanted to match MGM in every way that it could, and *The Wizard of Oz* had shown that prestige could be minted out of classic children's stories. Turning to Maurice Maeterlinck for *The Blue Bird*, Fox chief Darryl F. Zanuck also brought the cinematographer from *Gone with the Wind*, Ray Rennahan, and Arthur C. Miller, best known for *How Green Was My Valley* and *The Ox-Bow Incident*. If anything, *The Blue Bird* put an incomprehensible, muddled end to Temple's fabled childhood career. She did make a good film with John Ford in *Fort Apache*, but she never really caught on as an adult, which is the usual fate of a child star. Watching *The Blue Bird* is excruciating, and nothing about it can really recommend any interest, save for those who enjoy watching train wrecks. The story is allegorical, the sets cheesy, the tone maudlin – all of it highly imitative of *The Wizard of Oz*, but boring. They even do the shift from black and white to color, but with little of the impact of *Oz*. No nomination should ever be given for being copycats, and bad copycats at that.

You might never recover from the first image of *Down Argentine Way*: a full screen shot of Carmen Miranda in full-blown Brazilian get-

---

[78] Matte shots were perhaps the single most important special effect prior to blue screen and CGI. As Dictionary.com so pithily explains, a matte shot is "a shot in which parts of the background and sometimes the foreground are masked so that a different background, foreground, image, etc., can be substituted during printing."

up, in this, her first American film. The phrase "over the top" may have been coined for Miranda. My eyes still reel. The images of Argentina preserve a lost moment like a time capsule. Betty Grable and Don Ameche look as pretty as they ever got, with glowing skin (and Grable shows a good deal of it). Nominees Leon Shamroy and Ray Rennahan shoot Grable dancing as Fred Astaire taught: full body, so the dancing can be seen uninterrupted. I suspect with Grable it was more about the full body (my father never stopped obsessing about her legs). The whole film, actually, is structured like an Astaire-Rogers musical, what with the to-ing and fro-ing between the intended lovers. The best part of the picture remains the Nicholas Brothers, whose standing flip into the splits and other acrobatics have to be seen to be believed – and even then I'm not so sure I trust my eyes. Ray Rennahan seems to be everywhere in these years, as he was likely the world's foremost expert of filming in Technicolor; Leon Shamroy had a long career, including *The King and I* and even *Planet of the Apes*. They did reasonable work for a piece of fluff, and should keep the nomination (for my father's sake, if nothing else).

Although Cecil B. DeMille had made segments in color before, *Northwest Mounted Police* was his first full foray into the medium – as it was for Gary Cooper. Victor Milner had done much better work in black and white; W. Howard Greene had worked on color before, in *Nothing Sacred* and *A Star Is Born* (none of which recommends him to me as a good color cinematographer). The color cinematography of the great outdoors is fine. Unfortunately, the rest is not, looking like a bad high school production of some melodramatic reject from Broadway. The nomination fairly begs to be dismissed, and so it is; never let it be said I don't pay attention to out and out groveling.

Northwest Passage features Spencer Tracy as a leader of men in the great outdoors during the French and Indian War. Directed by King Vidor, *Northwest Passage* is a good adventure story, spiced up by fights, starvation, and a crazed cannibal, and marked by particularly virulent hatred towards the Indians. Ironically, the title is where the movie ends, as Tracy and his men set out in pursuit of the fabled passage to the Orient through the North American wilderness. The blues of the sky frame the subdued greens of the trees and the soldiers' green garb, lending the whole affair a more somber tone than we expect from typical Technicolor. Sidney Wagner and William V. Skall were learning how to adjust the palette to match the needs of the story, and for that alone, they deserve the nomination. Skall went on to *Rope* with Hitchcock; Wagner later did *The Postman Always Rings Twice* (where he helped turn Lana Turner into a legendary sex symbol). Good work here on *Northwest Passage*.

And what did they leave out?

First of all, *Dr. Cyclops*. Once again, science fiction, fantasy and horror films tend to be ignored by the Academy, until fairly recently. *Dr. Cyclops* uses color brilliantly, to evoke mood, mystery, and suspense. The titles are distinctive (and a precursor to *The Thing*). From the opening shot, color and shadow create a unique look, with that sickly green of the radiation setting up a contrast with the more natural greens of the jungle we see later. The revealing of a skull from murder by radium still creeps me out from the childhood memories of it. Excellent matte work equals that of *The Thief of Bagdad*.[79] Cameraman Henry Sharp was in the midst of a long career in slow decline from the heights of *The Crowd*, *Duck Soup* and *It's a Gift*. The Academy should not have missed nominating *Dr. Cyclops*.

I am about to propose a radical concept: animated movies should be eligible for their cinematography. Indeed, no category of film may be more pure, as the entire image is under control of the animator, who decides precisely how every frame will be filmed. In 1940, the Walt Disney Studios reached the peak of their craft in *Pinocchio* and parts of *Fantasia*; we need to honor that achievement here. Watch *Pinocchio* and *Fantasia* again, in the restored versions, with a high quality television. I think you may find yourself agreeing with me (and if you don't, may I suggest some personal therapy to explore precisely what is wrong with you?). First of all, other than *The Adventures of Robin Hood*, no pre-WWII movie took greater advantage of the possibilities of Technicolor than these two did. Second, through the use of the multi-plane camera, true depth could be achieved. But more than anything else, we need to consider the sheer staggering beauty of the art of the animator in these two films. Think of *Pinocchio*'s finest artistic moments, purely in terms of their imagery, and the various uses of the multiplane camera for depth effects; throughout the film, anything having to do with water is done with delicacy and care (or with power and rage, as with Monstro); the shifts in the color palette, depending on the lighting source; the voyage of the steamboat in moonlight to Pleasure Island; throughout, the splendid verisimilitude of the backgrounds, even when rendered in fantastic terms; and the major showcase of the entire film,

---

[79] As is the art direction, which creates a fantastic pulp look throughout, and the greenest jungle you have ever seen – and I so accord it should have received a nomination in the category of Best Art Direction (Color), as a special secret bonus to those of you who like this movie from your childhood Creature Features matinees as much as I do!

Pinocchio's underwater journey looking for Monstro to rescue his father.

As for *Fantasia*, consider: the delicate nuances and colors of *The Nutcracker Suite*, particularly the dew of the morning fairies (and later the frost of the snow fairies); the flowers and their reflections falling upon the waters; the diaphanous qualities of the goldfish and their translucent fins; and the coming of the fall colors. Mickey has one of his greatest appearances ever in *The Sorcerer's Apprentice*, but the animation of shadows and water is intricate and impressive. The volcanoes and dinosaurs of *The Rites of Spring* charged my imagination for years, even as the demon of *A Night on Bald Mountain* haunted me. Bela Lugosi posed for the artists! I think Lugosi had the most expressive hands in the history of Hollywood, and the demon uses his gestures extensively.

Fantasia has its wondrous moments, but the ways in which the camera and the art serve *Pinocchio* should have won it the Oscar for Best Cinematography (Color).

Best Score: Alfred Newman won for *Tin Pan Alley*, over Victor Young, *Arise, My Love*; Cy Feuer, *Hit Parade of 1941*; Anthony Collins, *Irene*; Aaron Copland, *Our Town*; Erich Wolfgang Korngold, *The Sea Hawk*; Artie Shaw, *Second Chorus*; Charles Previn, *Spring Parade*; and Georgie Stoll and Roger Edens, *Strike up the Band*

Alfred Newman was chosen for the score of *Tin Pan Alley*, a nostalgic look back at WWI era popular music, with a romance starring Alice Faye and John Payne as the objects of affection; Jack Oakie and Betty Grable provide some minor comic relief. The mostly naked Nicholas Brothers have some great fun in their stereotyped number "The Sheik of Araby," which I am surprised got past the censors, since the Nicholas Brothers are surrounded by white women wearing almost as little as they are. Other than their top notch dancing, the score is by far the best part of this forgettable film, mixing "Harrigan," "K-K-K-Katie," "Honeysuckle Rose" and lesser hits from Tin Pan Alley, along with a mediocre patriotic song written for the film. Newman does a solid piece of work here, but let's be real: a film this forgettable having a great score is like getting your Ford Pinto detailed. No Oscar should have been given, but Newman deserved a nomination.

Victor Young turned in a competent if uninspired score for *Arise, My Love*. Lots of big bombastic, soaring notes in the opening, some violin and harp, some menacing music when the war begins – and little of it strikes the ear as more than aural wallpaper. We do get a couple of nice songs out of the orchestra at Maxim's, including "Dream Lover," from Ernst Lubitsch's *The Love Parade*, and a lovely romantic interlude in the forest. Otherwise, completely forgettable, and not worth a nomination.

Cy Feuer wrote the score for *Hit Parade of 1941*, yet another film set in a radio station in trouble; this time, they need to convert to television. Mostly boring forced shenanigans ensure; we have to put up with Kenny Baker, but we get Frances Langford, Phil Silvers and Ann Miller to compensate. Like so many of these musicals, the score is mostly the songs, as is the case here (see Best Song below). Republic Pictures slipped this one in on the one studio/one vote rule, because they never could have received a nomination otherwise.

Irene is a very minor film with Ray Milland and British musical star Anna Neagle, and a score by Anthony Collins. The music largely hides itself behind the songs, which are almost all forgettable. The movie is fluff, with little memorable going on, but nothing particularly objectionable either (although the makeup on the women may be the worst I've ever seen in a black and white movie). No nomination should have been allowed for this pablum.

Aaron Copland was nominated in both scoring categories for *Our Town*; as noted above, he belongs in the other one.

For *The Sea Hawk*, Erich Wolfgang Korngold produced his finest score after *The Adventures of Robin Hood* (some would reverse that ranking). From the opening moments, Korngold's music sets the thrilling, powerful tones for the movie. I still get chills watching it, even though I've seen it a dozen times. Korngold was so grand with trumpets and strings, few could match him. Often, we don't think of Korngold in quiet moments, but listen to the dinner conversation after the Spanish galleon is sunk, and you can hear Korngold being as subtle as could be in reinforcing the emotional swings of the scene. The entry music for Queen Elizabeth into court would make anybody believe in monarchy. One of the things Korngold does better than most film composers is shift tonal colors to match the scene – and quicker than many, serving Curtiz' fast pacing beautifully. Korngold would never again reach these heights as a film scorer, although what he did produce was usually quite good. An excellent nomination – but not in this category. Korngold's music was entirely fresh and new; he should have been nominated under Original Score.

In *Second Chorus*, seeing Artie Shaw and his big band play is the one highlight of the movie. Shaw's songs and music swing like few others did (see Best Song above for more). If only Shaw had been the focus of the movie, instead of the tepid rivalry between Burgess Meredith and

Fred Astaire. If they had just let Astaire dance to Shaw's music, perhaps they might have made a film worth watching. Shaw deserved his nomination, however.

Charles Previn scored *Spring Parade*, a fairy tale that may be set in Vienna, but every song has a bit of a swing to it. The waltz keeps threatening to break through, but so does the schmaltz. I mean, do we really need the goat? In the middle of the song? Previn provides some good marching music for the soldiers, which sounds as if Strauss met Sousa at times. Strauss gets quoted liberally. A reasonable musical score for the prolific Previn – and an acceptable nomination.

Georgie Stoll and Roger Edens wrote the score for *Strike up the Band*. After the smashing success of *Babes in Arms*, MGM brought back Busby Berkeley, Mickey Rooney and Judy Garland for another outing. *Strike up the Band* had been a hit musical for the Gershwins on Broadway; MGM tossed out all but the title song (weird people, throwing away Gershwin, but the musical is a political satire that produced no standards, other than "The Man I Love" in its original version). Once again, Rooney is a frustrated musician; Garland plays his friend who wants to be more; they get to hit the big time. As part of the general silliness of the nomination process for scores and songs in these years, almost all the music here is new, rather than adapted, and should have been placed in the Best Original Score category. We should move it there now.

As for films that were not nominated, the glaring omission for adapted score is Walt's grand experiment, *Fantasia*. Yes, classical purists (like me) find glaring faults in the way the music is shortened and, at times, visually represented. I am not sure we can blame Disney for the aural shortcuts, since he turned to the foremost American conductor, Leopold Stokowski, who could not have been more highly regarded in his day. Stokowski's score – and truly, he must be nominated for it, along with music director Edward Plumb – has probably been responsible for more children being turned on to classical music in the last seventy years than anything else ever has, with the possible exception of annual performances of *The Nutcracker Suite* (which is in *Fantasia* as well, and forms one of its animation highlights). A broad range of music is incorporated, from my favorite composer J.S. Bach (whose music H.L. Mencken described aptly as Genesis 1:1) to Beethoven to Tchaikovsky to Dukas to Mussorgsky. In 1940, including Stravinsky in a family film would have been cutting edge music.[80] I trace my lifelong love

---

[80] *Fantasia* premiered in New York, Argentina, and Brazil in late 1940, and in LA in early 1941; technically, this disqualified the film for Academy consideration in this year, but the IMDB lists it as 1940, so who am I to argue?

of classical music to this film, as do many others (the movie didn't find its audience, or profitability, until the Sixties). Edward Plumb and Leopold Stokowski should have won the Oscar for Best Score.

Best Art Direction (Black & White): Cedric Gibbons and Paul Groesse won for *Pride and Prejudice*, over Hans Dreier and Robert Usher, *Arise, My Love*; Lionel Banks and Robert Peterson, *Arizona*; John Otterson, *The Boys from Syracuse*; John Victor Mackay, *The Dark Command*; Alexander Golitzen, *Foreign Correspondent*; Richard Day and Joseph C. Wright, *Lillian Russell*; Van Nest Polglase and Mark Lee Kirk, *My Favorite Wife*; John DuCasse Schulze, *My Son, My Son*; Lewis J. Rachmil, *Our Town*; Lyle Wheeler, *Rebecca*; Anton Grot, *The Sea Hawk*; and James Basevi, *The Westerner*

Cedric Gibbons and Paul Groesse won for *Pride and Prejudice*, an 1813 novel pushed several decades into the middle of the nineteenth century for the costumes (as Pauline Kael once pointed out, more like Dickens than Austen). Gibbons and Groesse give us a decent recreation of village and costumes. The dance is nicely done, with some interesting camera moves – the withdrawing camera in front of the line of dancers advancing, the in and out as the dancers intertwined. The movie has perhaps the best fireplace ever in the mansion, and the garden party is lovely. Good nomination, but MGM's block voting won it for them, as it did so many times for Cedric Gibbons; Groesse would go on to *The Yearling, The Music Man,* and *In the Heat of the Night*. Nothing particularly spectacular merits *Pride and Prejudice* the Oscar in this category, so no award should have been given, but the nomination should stay for what they do give us.

Hans Dreier and Robert Usher designed *Arise, My Love*. The prison that opens the film is forbidding and cinematically attractive. The set for the famous Maxim's was as close to the real thing as possible.[cxciii] The Parisian cobblestone street glistens perfectly in the lamplight. Overall, effective work from Dreier, who had a long career from 1919 Germany to *Double Indemnity* and *Sunset Blvd.*; Usher also did *The Road to Morocco* and *This Gun for Hire*. The nomination should stay.

You have never seen filthier, uglier, more scabrous people and animals than those which inhabit the wagon train at the opening of *Arizona*, and the tiny hamlet of Tucson. The sets look like they simply found an old ghost town, picked up whatever was left from the last century, and put it back together with enough spit and adobe to keep it from falling apart before filming was done (actually, the set remains standing, and open to tourists). The effect is decades ahead of its time, looking much more like a late Sixties/early Seventies film. Lionel Banks had a fabulous career, including *Mr. Smith Goes to Washington* and *His Girl Friday*; Robert Peterson ended up on *Bewitched*. *Arizona* is a high point of their careers. Unfortunately, once Jean Arthur shows up, the effect of extreme realism is sometimes lost, given up for studio sets with a jarring sense of artificiality. Still, the movie delivers a first-rate look otherwise, so the nomination is a good one.

John Otterson designed *The Boys from Syracuse*: Togas, anyone? Otterson hits on the Greek setting, but the whole thing looks like a stage set, which should not have a nomination.

Given the low budget (despite being more than Republic usually spent), John Victor Mackay did his best for Republic's *The Dark Command*, a Civil War era western. But nothing cries out for our attention; on the contrary, given what was happening in *Arizona* and *The Westerner*, Republic should have stuck to their usual shoe strings, and they should not have received a nomination.

Alexander Golitzen gave *Foreign Correspondent* excellent sets, with a whole town, a Dutch windmill, and a plane crash. Few other directors were as involved with set design as Hitchcock. The Dutch windmill alone is a marvel of hidden corners and opportunities to film interesting angles (see Best Cinematography (Black & White) and Best Special Effects for more). Golitzen had a very long career, including *Touch of Evil* and *Play Misty for Me*. He deserved this nomination.

One of the surest bets to get a nomination in this category is to do a Victorian picture like *Lillian Russell*. If there's a bustle in it, the Academy will surely get excited. Must be from all those unlit gaslights. Alice Faye, Don Ameche, and Henry Fonda star in yet another musical from Twentieth Century-Fox's cookie cutter. This time, Faye plays Lillian Russell, the turn of the century singing star, with songs like "And the Band Played On" and "After the Ball" ringing the nostalgic cash register. The movie isn't bad, but certainly not true to Russell's real life. The sets by Richard Day (*A Streetcar Named Desire*) and Joseph C. Wright (*Guys and Dolls*) reproduce the stage successes, filtered through a 1940 set of expectations. For them, the nomination should stay.

So, what do we see in *My Favorite Wife*, other than Cary Grant and Irene Dunne playing their love games? A courtroom, an upper class home with a pool, a ritzy hotel in Yosemite, and a mountain lodge. All beautifully, appointed, and tasteful in that early Forties style. Nicely done, and in that mode of realism in which most films are rooted. The sets by Van Nest Polglase (*Citizen Kane* and too many classics to list) and Mark Lee Kirk (*The Grapes of Wrath*) make for a good nomination.

They don't come much weepier than *My Son, My Son!* A man born into hardship swears that he will raise a son the right way. He proceeds to spoil the son to the point of ruining any chance the boy has of having character and backbone. The son then proceeds to fall in love with the same woman as the father. Male weeping and much gnashing of teeth ensue, until WWI sets everything right again (yes, you read that right; isn't it nice to see that WWI had a good effect somewhere?). John DuCasse Schulze died not too long after designing this film, but he had already made his mark with *The Count of Monte Cristo* and *The Man in the Iron Mask*. Here, he produces everything from late Victoriana to a coal mine to World War I. A decent nomination, due to the necessary range.

The movie *Our Town*, like the play, is a reminiscence of small-town life at the turn of the century. William Cameron Menzies should have been included in this nomination, and he and Lewis J. Rachmil succeed in reproducing small details, such as the tool the milkman uses to dole out the milk in canisters; I've never seen it before or since. The detachable cuffs, the arm garters, and more costume details are all authentic (and confusing to a modern dresser). Rachmil eventually shifted to being a producer, making it all the way up to *Footloose* (there, I've helped you the next time you play *Six Degrees of Kevin Bacon*). A solid choice.

The primary reason for the nomination for *Rebecca* is that monstrous place, Manderley, the mansion of Maxim de Winter, and the first Mrs. De Winter, Rebecca. As in the best films and fiction, the setting is as much a character as the people in it, and here, we get a place as important as Tara is to *Gone with the Wind*, but explored more fully. The story begins with Manderley – "Last night I dreamt I went to Manderley again" – and ends with the burning of the place. Hitchcock indulges his love of miniatures with the opening long, mysterious move of the camera through the ruins of Manderley, and Lyle J. Wheeler does his part in allowing Hitchcock to roam with confidence through this particular model. Wheeler also did *Gone with the Wind* and *All About Eve*; he deserved this nomination.

After *Captain Blood* and *The Adventures of Robin Hood*, I think *The Sea Hawk* is Errol Flynn's best swashbuckler (and on some days, better than *Captain Blood*). Michael Curtiz directed all three of them, as well as what I often consider my favorite film, *Casablanca*, and a slate of other classics. Despite the title, the movie has little to do with the original novel. I love Flynn and his sidekicks, and Flora Robson's Queen Elizabeth is as fierce and intelligent as anyone could want. Anton Grot's set design helps lay the groundwork for the large themes of the movie: the individual and freedom, opposed to the threat of world conquest and conformity. As many commentators have noted, in 1940, Britain was fighting for its life against Hitler; imperial Spain served as a useful analog for Nazi Germany. Grot puts in the background of the first scene a grand map of the world, showing the stakes of that battle. When we move to the next scene, we are in the open sea, with a Spanish galleon – propelled by English slaves. The models are discussed above in Special Effects, but the shipboard sets are solid, detailed depictions of naval power and human degradation. Historical anachronisms crop up here and there, but overall, Grot spent his part of the big budget intelligently, and always with an eye to serve the story. Grot had a long career in Hollywood, from 1916 to 1950; *The Sea Hawk* formed a high point. An excellent nomination.

James Basevi's work on *The Westerner* was to create the first truly dirty Western film. Dirt and dust seems to coat everything except Gary Cooper's eyes. James Basevi's designs, both inside and outside, are remarkably realistic, and laden with meaning. Basevi's career went from the silent era through *Fort Apache* and *The Searchers*. He definitely deserved a nomination, for the town, the corn fields, and the opera house.

As for those not nominated, first and foremost must come Richard Day (*On the Waterfront, A Streetcar Named Desire*), Mark-Lee Kirk (*Young Mr. Lincoln*), and Thomas Little (*All About Eve, Miracle on 34th Street*) for *The Grapes of Wrath*. Recreating poverty is far harder than recreating wealth, because it takes more than money; it requires a worn quality to the possessions, a sense of intense living and few options. One can fake wealth on sets, with big staircases and fancy doodads; while many of the scenes in *The Grapes of Wrath* were filmed on location, others were reproduced on the sound stage, where Toland could control the lighting more effectively. Nowhere is this more apparent than in the scenes in the cabin, where the sense of loss and worry breathes out of the sets. Watch the scene where the Joads come into the transient camp, and the audience becomes the camera. If you want to know what the Depression looked like, this scene is the best evidence ever filmed. For that scene alone, Day, Kirk, and Little deserved a nomination – and should have won the Oscar for Best Art Direction (Black & White).

Best Short Subject (Cartoon): MGM won for *The Milky Way*, and earned another nomination for *Puss Gets the Boot*; Leon Schlesinger and Warner Brothers snuck in *A Wild Hare*

For the first time, the Disney studio animators not only didn't win, they weren't even nominated. The reason Disney lost its lock on this category has to do with Walt's decision to shift his best people, and most of his own attention, over to feature length films, including the pinnacle of animation, *Pinocchio*, and that magnificent experiment, *Fantasia*. The Disney Studio continued to produce animated shorts, and although many of them are worth a look, few of them contain anything we haven't seen before. MGM had been trying for years to catch up to Disney, and while they won their first Oscar in this category with Rudolf Ising's *The Milky Way*, and took another nomination in *Puss Gets the Boot*, they really shouldn't have. *The Milky Way* has three little kittens being punished for losing their mittens, so they make a balloon to go to the Milky Way, where they explore a universe made of milk. Nothing distinguishes the kittens from each other; the conceit of going to outer space drives the narrative, such as it is.

Puss Gets the Boot, on the other hand, would point the way to MGM's dominance of this category in the Forties, since it features a cat named Jasper and an unnamed mouse, who would in the next year be reincarnated as Tom and Jerry, which finally gave MGM a pair of characters to match other studios' name brand animated stars. William Hanna and Joseph Barbera would go on to make 114 Tom and Jerry cartoons before heading into television in the Fifties to dominate cartoons there the next twenty years. *Puss Gets the Boot* sets the basic plot for all the Tom and Jerries to come: Tom wants to eat Jerry, Jerry doesn't want to be eaten; they fight, repeatedly. The formula would be lifted for Sylvester and Tweety Bird, as well as the Coyote and Roadrunner, and many others (and reduced to its cruel bones in *The Simpsons* with Itchy and Scratchy). But Tom and Jerry pounded at the old sawhorse longer than any other duo. *Puss Gets the Boot* isn't particularly amusing, and we get saddled with a racist depiction of a black housekeeper (she spells out "O-U-W-T".) The nomination can stay, if only because of the cartoon's importance.

But over at Warner Brothers, a lunatic by the name of Tex Avery further developed an iconic character who would take the cartoon world by storm: Bugs Bunny made his first true appearance in *A Wild Hare*. Elmer Fudd began to look like Elmer Fudd (Chuck Jones had paired a rabbit and a hunter who would evolve into Bugs and Elmer earlier in 1940 in *Elmer's Candid Camera*). Two immortal catch-phrases were invented: "Be vewy, vewy quiet. I'm hunting wabbits" and "What's up, doc?" The difference between Warner Brothers at their best, and almost every other cartoon from other studios, is that the animators at Termite Terrace were almost completely unsupervised, and as Chuck Jones said, "We weren't making them for kids, or for adults. We were making them for ourselves." The result of that independence was a level of invention, utterly irreverent humor, and productive insanity that has never existed in any other animation studio. I respect Disney cartoons, but I live in a mental state informed by Warner Brothers. They are funny – wickedly, hysterically, drop-dead funny – in a way Disney abandoned in the middle of the Thirties as he pursued realism (not that he ever really had it before then). The Oscar should have gone to *A Wild Hare*. Watch the other two nominated cartoons, then watch *A Wild Hare*, and see the enormous difference.

CHAPTER FOURTEEN: 1942 AWARDS
14th Show

Movies released in 1941

THE SCENE OF THE CRIME:

Despite the war – which was at its lowest ebb in the dark days before the victory at Midway – the Academy met again on February 26, 1942, at the Biltmore Bowl in the Biltmore Hotel. Academy President Bette Davis wanted to shift it to a theater and open it to the public, but the Board of Governors stopped her. Davis quit over the issue. Eventually, even the Board had to tone down the celebration due to the war; they dropped the dancing and asked the ladies to donate their corsage money to the Red Cross.

Bob Hope returned. This time, Republican presidential candidate Wendell Willkie made a speech. Hope, a lifelong Republican, wore a Willkie button. People still showed up, despite the threats of Willkie's speech and an air raid scare (lampooned in Spielberg's *1941*). Hope joked the air raid was actually John Barrymore coming home from W.C. Fields' house. The big fight of the evening (other than staying awake while Willkie rattled on) was between sisters: Olivia de Havilland was up against little sister Joan Fontaine for Best Actress. Hope gave Jack Benny an Oscar in a wig and skirt, with a cigar in its mouth.

Disney had a huge night, with four Oscars: one for Best Cartoon, one for the score of *Dumbo,* and two special Oscars for *Fantasia,* one for Disney and one for Leopold Stokowski. The Academy was making up big time for ignoring the movie the year it premiered in New York and South America. He then received the Thalberg Award for producing *Fantasia.* Disney cried and apologized for making the movie, which had been a flop: "We all make mistakes. *Fantasia* was one but it was an honest one."

When Gary Cooper won, he forgot his Oscar on the lectern.

As part of the continuing process to refine the musical categories to better divisions, the Academy reworked the two music score fields into Best Dramatic Score and Best Musical Score. Like the writing awards, the music categories would change regularly over the decades to gain precision and avoid the kind of silly nominations we've seen in the past.

They also added a new category: Best Documentary. Unfortunately, I am going to have to ignore it, as the films are extremely difficult to find, or no longer in existence. The next year, they nominated 25 films and handed out four awards in the same category! Granted, one of them was Ford's masterful *The Battle of Midway,* but still, life is too short to spend years tracking down one obscure documentary after another, even if I do love the form.

Orson Welles was the biggest loser of the night, seeing the film most would name the greatest of all time – *Citizen Kane* – fail in all but the screenplay category. We'll have to see about that...

WHAT THEY GOT RIGHT:

Remarkably little, due to the willful refusal to recognize the genius of Orson Welles and *Citizen Kane,* among other misses.

Best Writing (Original Story): Harry Segall won for *Here Comes Mr. Jordan,* over Billy Wilder and Thomas Monroe, *Ball of Fire*; Monckton Hoffe, *The Lady Eve*; Richard Connell and Robert Presnell Sr., *Meet John Doe*; and Gordon Wellesley, *Night Train to Munich*

Harry Segall took home the Oscar for *Here Comes Mr. Jordan,* in which Edward Everett Horton takes Robert Montgomery's spirit a moment too soon. Horton's angelic boss Claude Rains – the titular Mr. Jordan – then has to help find Montgomery a new body to continue his life. Montgomery ends up in the body of a rich man with a wife who is trying to kill him. Segall's story was remade by Warren Beatty in 1978 as *Heaven Can Wait*, which remains one of the few Beatty films I think will survive into the next century. The original spurred a spate of angelic intervention films, including *Angels in the Outfield, A Guy Named Joe*, and *It's a Wonderful Life*. Of course, the *Topper* series is the grandparent of the genre. Segall wrote the play on which the movie is based, entitled *Heaven Can Wait*, which was also the title of an unrelated Don Ameche movie. Segall later wrote the story for *Monkey Business*, the one with Cary Grant and Marilyn Monroe, not Groucho, Chico, and Harpo. The story is quite original, and deserving of the Oscar; but the execution of that story in the screenplay? Not so good (see Best Writing (Screenplay) below).

Billy Wilder and Thomas Monroe put together a great idea with *Ball of Fire*, mixing a nightclub singer with a group of eccentric professors, with gangsters on the side. The result still pleases, and gave Barbara Stanwyck her sexiest role to date (Wilder would remember this when casting *Double Indemnity* a few years later). Any nomination for Wilder is generally a good idea; he deserved one for *Ball of Fire*. So did Thomas Monroe, who helped Wilder tweak the plot for director Howard Hawks; Monroe would never come up with anything as good again.

Monckton Hoffe gave *The Lady Eve* a very Shakespearean core: love turned inside out, hidden identity, the struggle for power, a setting of all things back to rights, bawdiness, and the dominance of women (if you think Shakespeare didn't often find women to be more capable and mature than men, you haven't read his plays very carefully). Hoffe had a career going back to the silents, but this was as good as anything he ever wrote. Of course, we are talking Preston Sturges here, so whatever he got from Hoffe was surely transformed by that genius. But the essentials of the tale, even if they served as a springboard for Hoffe, make the nomination here an excellent one.

Richard Connell and Robert Presnell, Sr. met John Doe, and it didn't turn out so well. Infamously, *Meet John Doe* represents Frank Capra at his darkest and most daring, while at the same time completely failing to deliver on the premise of this film: at the instigation of Barbara Stanwyck, Gary Cooper's character swears to commit suicide as a social protest, then doesn't follow through. Sometimes, writers (and filmmakers) paint themselves into inescapable corners. I've rarely met anybody who has seen *Meet John Doe* who didn't feel completely disappointed by the ending. The responsibility for that has to lie squarely with the writers who conceived the initial story and treatment. Richard Connell remains most famous for writing the inventive short story "The Most Dangerous Game"; Robert Presnell, Sr., reached his peak with this work. Despite the audacious setup, *Meet John Doe* is a failure, so I am inclined to suggest the nomination was not a good one.

For those fond of *The Third Man*, Carol Reed directed a Hitchcock-influenced spy film called *Night Train to Munich*, which stars Rex Harrison, Margaret Lockwood, and Paul Henreid. A scientist's daughter gets left behind in Czechoslovakia; Henreid helps her escape from the concentration camp. Gordon Wellesley wrote the novel on which the movie is based. At times, one could almost swear Hitchcock is directing. Reed uses miniatures in much the same way. Something of Hitch's dark humor shows up when a bookstore has copies of *Mein Kampf* for sale – right next to a copy of *Gone with the Wind*. The cricket nuts from *The Lady Vanishes* appear in this one as well. While not Hitchcock, *Night Train to Munich* is worth seeing once, if only to keep an eye out for Carol Reed on his way to *The Third Man*. Wellesley wrote a satisfactory suspense story; the nomination should stay.

Best Writing (Original Screenplay): Orson Welles and Herman J. Mankiewicz won for *Citizen Kane*, over Norman Krasna, *The Devil and Miss Jones*; John Huston, Howard Koch, Abem Finkel and Harry Chandlee, *Sergeant York*; Karl Tunberg and Darrell Ware, *Tall, Dark and Handsome;* and Paul Jarrico, *Tom, Dick and Harry*

The screenplay for *Citizen Kane* remains one of the touchstones of American cinema, despite the fact that in the light of what has come since, much of what made it revolutionary has become commonplace. We need to scrape off the patina, and try to see with fresh eyes what was unprecedented and fresh in this tale of a rich man's rise and fall through his own hubris. At its heart, *Citizen Kane* is a Greek tragedy, but one seen through twentieth century populist eyes: "If I hadn't been rich, I might have been a really great man." As the movie opens, we begin outside, forbidden to enter by fence and sign – we then violate those rules, those prohibitions, and move inwards. We begin at the end, to discover the meaning of a man's life. Just as his estate lies in ruins and disrepair, so too does this man, whoever he may be. After the moody, mysterious beginning, with the whispered word "Rosebud" and the shattered snow globe, we launch into a newsreel, loud, brassy, informative – and innovative. From that basic backstory, we delve into the witnesses to the mystery of Rosebud and Charles Foster Kane – and the problem of unlocking the interior life of another human being, even one as famous and public as Kane. Pauline Kael once made a famous argument that Orson Welles stole the credit from Herman J. Mankiewicz, but scholarly work with the archival papers show that Kael was wrong: Welles was an integral part of the writing. Mankiewicz eventually turned against Welles: "There but for the grace of God goes God."cxciv But Mank shouldn't have carped, because the pair deserved this Oscar for a brilliant screenplay.

Norman Krasna gave us *The Devil and Miss Jones*. Having been a horny teenager in the Seventies, I had to do a double take on the title of this film, which was spoofed as one of the most infamous porn films of the decade (hey, you can't blame me for mistaking a conjunction for a preposition! And if you don't get the grammar joke, clearly you never passed English). In this family-friendly film, a rich man (Charles Coburn) goes undercover as a shoe salesman in his own store to discover why his workers want a union; he meets Jean Arthur, who befriends him as a helpless old fuddy-duddy.[81] A mildly funny film with a kind of Capraesque feel for the needs of the rich to be more aware of the travails of the poor, *The Devil and Miss Jones* does have a good central conceit, as the rich man is taken under Arthur's wing. As he discovers the abuses of power, Coburn corrects them in a kind of righteous karma. Not a good nomination, as it is derivative of Capra, largely bordering on sheer fantasy in its ending, and with little snap to the dialogue.

John Huston, Howard Koch, Abem Finkel and Harry Chandlee banded together to give us *Sergeant York*, the biography of WWI's most celebrated American soldier. As World War II had begun for the United States less than three months before this year's Academy Awards show, we shouldn't be surprised to see the ultra-patriotic *Sergeant York* gathering so many nominations. Written in the light of isolationism, which is reflected in York's pacifism, *Sergeant York* shows one man choosing to fight himself, his poverty, and his principles to find a way to stop sinning, get some good bottomland, and shoot the evil Germans overseas. York cooperated in the making of the picture; perhaps that personal influence substantiates this nomination by doing some original research (they credit York's diaries as the source material). Regardless of the provenance, the screenplay does provide some set pieces for Cooper that have remained in our minds: finding salvation at the hands of one of Walter Brennan's best old coots; wetting the front sight of his rifle at the turkey shoot and again at the act of heroism at the end; locating the answer to his pacifism (and ours) in the Bible. The screenplay keeps things moving along, never dragging as so many biopics do. The nomination should stay.

Karl Tunberg and Darrell Ware wrote *Tall, Dark and Handsome*, which stars Cesar Romero as a gangster who makes up an identity as a

---

[81] Nothing is ever left unrecycled in Hollywood; in 2011, the same premise drove the show *Undercover Boss*.

family man to get a girl involved with him. Milton Berle is Romero's flunky. Mixing gangsters and fake children is an interesting idea, and a reasonably amusing movie results in a good nomination.

Paul Jarrico lined up *Tom, Dick and Harry* for Ginger Rogers, as she dreams about marrying these three different men (and acts like a fourteen-year-old girl, which may be her satiric take on this restrictive role). Jarrico's screenplay was brought to life by director Garson Kanin, with the dream sequences being particularly memorable, as they have absurdist tones. Phil Silvers shows up. Jarrico spoofs romantic conceptions of love, as he begins with a soppy movie's dialogue playing over Ginger Rogers' rapt attention; she learns better by the end. Jarrico should keep the nomination, if only because I don't know many films that would better serve to show the obsession with marriage and the sexist female limitations of the Forties.

As for those screenplays the Academy ignored, the best of the lot is Preston Sturges' top-rate *Sullivan's Travels*. Too bad *Citizen Kane* showed up this year, because *Sullivan's Travels* is one of the finest screenplays of the entire decade, with slapstick, romance and hardship, lifted by a belief in the power of laughter – and "with a little sex." The story of a comedy movie director who wants to make a serious picture entitled *O Brother, Where Art Thou?*[82] over studio objections, *Sullivan's Travels* stars Joel McCrea, Veronica Lake, and Pluto. Once again, Sturges punctures sexual expectations, by having McCrea chased by a middle-aged husband hunter (the deceased husband's picture changes to reflect his opinion from beyond the grave). More pointedly, Sturges skewers audiences who don't know how to be quiet during a picture by showing a very unattractive picture of the people as they watch a sob story. Funny inside joke: "Who's Lubitsch?" McCrea gets what he asks for: trouble. He ends up on a chain gang. Throughout the movie, Sturges shows one kind of enslavement after another: the studio system, marriage and spousal support, widows trying to trap new husbands, and the legal system's abuse of the poor. The point of the movie is finding the true freedom of helping others. Having accepted his gifts as a comic genius, McCrea is set free, to find a new life and love.

Best Cinematography (Color): Ernest Palmer and Ray Rennahan won for *Blood and Sand*, over Wilfred M. Cline, Karl Struss, and William Snyder, *Aloma of the South Seas*; William V. Skall and Leonard Smith, *Billy the Kid*; Karl Freund and W. Howard Greene, *Blossoms in the Dust*; Bert Glennon, *Dive Bomber*; and Harry Hallenberger and Ray Rennahan, *Louisiana Purchase*.

---

[82] Yes, that's where the Coen Brothers got their title.

In a remake of the silent Valentino classic, *Blood and Sand* features Tyrone Power in pants so tight you can tell what religion he is. As a Spanish bullfighter, Power appears the part, but even better, Rita Hayworth looks fabulous dancing the tango with Anthony Quinn, and tempting Power away from his wife (sadly, Hayworth still can't act). TV's Superman George Reeves shows up as Hayworth's boyfriend. Director Rouben Mamoulian, who had long been interested in tricking the eye through the camera, leaped at the chance to show what Technicolor could do. He designed each scene to copy the look of the great Spanish painters, including Goya and Titian. For the hospital, "I thought if El Greco had painted it, it wouldn't look white, it would look green and gray, so I sprayed all the sheets and painted shadows on the walls. It looked absolutely appalling to the eye, and it really shook me because I thought I'd really ruined the set, but it came out beautifully."cxcv Ernest Palmer and Ray Rennahan do their best to facilitate Mamoulian's experiments. Almost every single scene can be described as "painterly"; the shadows and patterns of shadows in this movie look alive with depth and feeling. A banquet for the eyes, *Blood and Sand* is only hampered by the secondary quality of the performances and the narrative. Unfortunately, the look is more or less all the film has, as the story is insipid and tortured; as *The New York Times* said in 1941, *Blood and Sand* decides "to posture beautifully."cxcvi Power getting ready for the ring, and the bullfight scenes, especially in the rooms beneath the stadium before the fight, are staged with some verve. Ray Rennahan was probably the "world's expert on Technicolor"; this film would be a forerunner for *Black Narcissus*.[83] No more influential or stylistic color film would emerge in Forties American cinematography. *Blood and Sand* deserved this Oscar.

In a kind of casting sequel to John Ford's *The Hurricane*, *Aloma of the South Seas* reunites Jon Hall and Dorothy Lamour with another natural disaster: instead of a hurricane, we get an exploding volcano. The cinematography by Wilfred M. Cline, Karl Struss, and William Snyder is competent, but hardly inspired, even with Dorothy Lamour's sarong. No nomination should apply.

We have to suffer through yet another Frank Borzage melodrama, this one with Robert Taylor as *Billy the Kid*. Pretty outdoor pictures of a

---

[83] The DVD commentary track for *Blood and Sand* discusses the extensive use of "hard lighting" in these early color films, a look that would persist until cinematography changed with *Butch Cassidy and the Sundance Kid* and *The Godfather* – "both films changed the ways movies looked" due to the shift from hard light to soft light (also known as bounced light).

pretty boy should not earn an Oscar nomination for William V. Skall and Leonard Smith.

Blossoms in the Dust is a biographical picture about Edna Gladney, the Texas child welfare advocate who campaigned against the stigma about illegitimacy, and succeeded in getting it removed from birth certificates: "There are no illegitimate children; there are only illegitimate parents." Hard to go wrong with filming Greer Garson and her hair, if color is available. Karl Freund and W. Howard Greene provide a fairly mobile camera when the opportunity presents itself; other than that, we get mostly portrait style photography. During one dance, the camera sways back and forth in time, which made me a little motion sick. Freund was nominated in both the black & white and the color categories this year, a rare achievement. Freund had a long career, from *Metropolis* to *Dracula* to *Key Largo*, before ending up on *I Love Lucy*. Greene was an early pioneer in color, including *A Star Is Born* and *Nothing Sacred*. They did a good job on *Blossoms in the Dust*, even if one still longs for a Toland to take a turn with Technicolor. They should keep their nomination.

Dive Bomber stars Errol Flynn, Fred MacMurray, and Ralph Bellamy in an overly melodramatic look at the risks of dive bombing, blackouts and altitude sickness, and the development of a pressure suit. Flynn isn't particularly heroic, which cuts against what audience expectations have always been for him, but he does a decent job handling the challenge. *Dive Bomber* has waaaaaay too much smoking, but it does have some decent sense of how medical research goes, although I suspect too much shorthand has been incorporated. And did I mention too much smoking? The main reason to watch this film today is for the live naval scenes, filmed by Bert Glennon in Technicolor from aboard the *USS Enterprise* and in flight, and all set to Max Steiner's bombastic score. Glennon succeeded in the massive challenge of shooting aerial scenes with a 600 pound Technicolor camera in another plane. I particularly loved the take offs and landings from the *Enterprise*, the beautifully precise formation flying, and one very crisp sight of a training plane flying past the Hotel Del Coronado in San Diego (famous from *Some Like It Hot*). If you love pre-WWII aircraft and want to see some beautiful flying, you should agree that *Dive Bomber* deserved its nomination.

Louisiana Purchase stars Bob Hope in his first color film, an Irving Berlin Broadway musical about graft in Louisiana (now there's a surprise...graft, in Louisiana...whoda thunk it? After all, Huey "The Kingfish" Long had only been dead a few years). Do we really need to see Ol' Ski Nose in color? Probably not. A large number of brightly dressed women try to make up for the fact that the musical has been drained of most of the bite of the original. The songs that remain are from the bottom of Irving Berlin's talent, and none have become standards. The only reason to watch this is for Hope's typical comedy of this period. The Technicolor is unleashed as it was in *The Adventures of Robin Hood*, but to less effect. The camerawork by Harry Hallenberger and Ray Rennahan is competent, but little more. Rennahan remains most famous for his work on *Gone with the Wind*; Hallenberger also did *Arizona*, but *Louisiana Purchase* remains his career high point. The nomination should stay for the bright colors.

Best Musical Score: Frank Churchill and Oliver Wallace won for *Dumbo*, over Edward Ward, *All-American Co-Ed*; Robert Emmett Dolan, *Birth of the Blues*; Charles Previn, *Buck Privates*; Herbert Stothart and Bronislau Kaper, *The Chocolate Soldier*; Cy Feuer, *Ice-Capades*; Heinz Roemheld, *The Strawberry Blonde*; Anthony Collins, *Sunny*; Emil Newman, *Sun Valley Serenade*; and Morris Stoloff, *You'll Never Get Rich*

Frank Churchill and Oliver Wallace took home the Oscar for *Dumbo*, which like *Bambi*, deals with real issues: conformity, prejudice, cruelty, friendship, and the importance of the individual to embrace his differences, and thereby thrive. And lest we forget, the essentially creepy quality of clowns (I suspect Stephen King saw this movie as an impressionable child). Ironically, then, that the film has been accused of having some of the most racist characters in a Disney film prior to *Song of the South*. Granted, the crows help Dumbo, but one of them is called Jim Crow...nothing like a joke about institutionalized segregation, right? I doubt any children have ever picked up on this, but any reasonably aware adult might think twice about the implications. On the other hand, the crows do display a degree of independence, individuality, and humor not known in the world which has abused and disdained Dumbo. If anything, Dumbo ends up acting more like them with their nonconformity than anybody else in the movie – flying being the visual representation of that. All in all, *Dumbo* is still worth watching, and I doubt any child today is going to associate the crows with racist depictions, given that no African-American talks that way anymore anyways (I shudder to think what hip-hop crows would be like, were the movie remade today). The score is predominantly made up of the songs, some of which are brilliant (see Best Song category below). The one unforgettable piece of animation is the "Pink Elephant" segment, with the roustabouts segment running a close second (even though the black workers are faceless, which is disturbing). The scoring of the songs remains one of the best parts of the movie, and a good choice for the Academy.

All-American Co-Ed is a very short Hal Roach movie which bends the gender of its entire male cast at one point, puts them all into drag, and then has the main love story between Frances Langford and a boy forced to be in drag to get into her college. Edward Ward had scored *Mr. and Mrs. Smith, Another Thin Man,* and would go on to score *Cobra Woman* and *Phantom of the Opera.* He's just asked to do so little here, he doesn't deserve a nomination.

Bing Crosby has a band that is present at *Birth of the Blues* in New Orleans – although it's more Dixieland than blues. The great jazz trombonist and vocalist Jack Teagarden shows up with his band (but not enough to save this movie). As for the music, we get "Memphis Blues," "Melancholy Baby," "Tiger Rag" and "St. Louis Blues" among others. The movie does tend to suggest that whites invented jazz, although some credit is given to black musicians. What is worse, most of the numbers have no real jazz feel, and even Crosby can't save the title song. "Memphis Blues" isn't bad. As for the score by Robert Emmett Dolan, the less said the better. A nomination?!? Did I not say the less said the better?

Buck Privates was the first film to star vaudeville greats Abbott and Costello; the massive success of the army comedy would launch them as the biggest comic team of the Forties. Abbott and Costello are quite funny as they skewer the military and each other. The score by Charles Previn keeps things bouncing along, with a nice touch when the rhythm of the song is matched to the train engine; Previn extends the songs into the instrumental score here and there, particularly when the Andrews Sisters show up for some swing numbers (see Best Song below). Previn deserved a nomination.

Herbert Stothart and Bronislau Kaper scored *The Chocolate Soldier*, which is neither about chocolate, or much soldiering. We get Oscar Straus[84] songs, couched in the usual MGM gloss and forgettability, but the original source material is uniformly fluff, and not superior fluff; the stuff in between is serviceable for a vehicle for Nelson Eddy, but not for an Oscar nomination.

Ice-Capades stars nobody you've ever heard of, in a skating extravaganza from Republic Pictures. The score by Cy Feuer is functional, but uninspired, except during a few of the different numbers in the ice-capades (which performers are by far the best part of the movie). For

---

[84] Straus dropped the second "s" of his last name to avoid confusion with the more famous waltzing Strauss. *The Chocolate Soldier* was the high point of his career, which isn't very high.

some of that inventiveness, the nomination should stay, but part of me wonders if the performers brought their own music with them.

James Cagney meets Rita Hayworth in *The Strawberry Blonde*: guess which one is more interesting to watch? Hayworth still hasn't learned how to do more than pose in a movie where she isn't dancing with Fred Astaire, but Cagney keeps things going reasonably well in this Victorian groan-fest. Olivia de Havilland has a thankless role as Cagney's wife. Heinz Romheld's score works the nostalgia trail of 1890s' hits, including "And The Band Played On," "Won't You Come Home, Bill Bailey," "Wait Till the Sun Shines, Nellie," "In the Good Old Summertime," and "In the Shade of the Old Apple Tree." Romheld composed for the movies from 1923 to 1959, from Lon Chaney, Sr.'s *The Hunchback of Notre Dame* to *The Mole People*. He should keep his nomination for *The Strawberry Blonde*.

We don't remember *Sun Valley Serenade* for Emil Newman's lightly connective score; we remember it for the Glenn Miller Orchestra's numbers, which I seriously doubt Newman scored. Emil Newman is the brother of Alfred Newman, and a much more honored music director than a composer. No nomination should be given to Emil for what is obviously Glenn Miller's show.

Sunny features Mardi Gras, a rich guy and a circus girl, and lots of complications. Ray Bolger and Edward Everett Horton liven it up somewhat, as do the Jerome Kern songs. But the score by Anthony Collins helps this mediocrity remain mediocre, so no nomination is needed.

You'll Never Get Rich stars Fred Astaire as the fall guy for Robert Benchley's shenanigans; Rita Hayworth is involved, thankfully more as a dancer than as an actress – and I can say nothing higher about her than that she is a match for Astaire, step for step! Astaire gets drafted. Morris Stoloff's overture stays bright and punchy, like a morning alarm going off that you almost don't mind because it's so friendly. Stoloff was ahead of the curve by integrating swing music into his score – a pathway that would be used by up-and-comers for the next decade and more as a way of getting around the domination of film music by European émigrés like Korngold and Steiner. Stoloff also scored *Mr. Smith Goes to Washington, His Girl Friday,* and *From Here to Eternity,* which shows his range and capacity – but here, the score isn't really very much Stoloff. Almost all of it is Cole Porter, whose songs automatically up the ante, but makes Stoloff's barely existing score a distant runner in our ears. The nomination should stay for the nice wake-up call, but the rest sent me back to bed.

WHAT THEY GOT WRONG:

The biggest problem of the year was what to do with *Citizen Kane*, a movie so unlike anything that had come before that the Academy members risked the censure of William Randolph Hearst in even nominating it – which, to their credit, they did repeatedly.[85] Granted, *Citizen Kane* only won one Oscar, but a nomination was a dangerous recognition in and of itself.

Even though I disagree with many of their final choices, 1941 was a year in which fewer bad movies were handed awards. They're still wrong; they're just not as wrong as they usually are.

Best Picture: *How Green Was My Valley*
Best Actor: Gary Cooper, *Sergeant York*
Best Actress: Joan Fontaine, *Suspicion*
Best Director: John Ford, *How Green Was My Valley*
Best Supporting Actor: Donald Crisp, *How Green Was My Valley*
Best Supporting Actress: Mary Astor, *The Great Lie*
Best Writing (Screenplay): Sidney Buchman and Seton I. Miller, *Here Comes Mr. Jordan*
Best Cinematography (Black & White): Arthur C. Miller, *How Green Was My Valley*
Best Dramatic Score: Bernard Herrmann, *All That Money Can Buy*
Best Song: Jerome Kern and Oscar Hammerstein II, "The Last Time I Saw Paris," *Lady Be Good*
Best Art Direction (Black & White): Richard Day, Nathan Juran, and Thomas Little, *How Green Was My Valley*
Best Art Direction (Color): Cedric Gibbons, Urie McCleary, and Edwin B. Willis, *Blossoms in the Dust*
Best Special Effects: Farciot Edouart, Gordon Jennings, and Louis Mesenkop, *I Wanted Wings*
Best Short Subject (Cartoon): Walt Disney, *Lend a Paw*

Best Picture: *How Green Was My Valley* won, over *Blossoms in the Dust*, *Citizen Kane*, *Here Comes Mr. Jordan*, *Hold Back the Dawn*, *The Little Foxes*, *The Maltese Falcon*, *One Foot in Heaven*, *Sergeant York*, and *Suspicion*

---

[85] Hearst attacked primarily through his powerful and feared entertainment reporter Louella Parsons at *The Los Angeles Examiner*. Louella would become such a legend herself as to merit Elizabeth Taylor playing her in a 1985 TV movie, *Malice in Wonderland*.

1941 represents one of the most difficult decisions for Best Picture, because of the masterpieces we have to deny in order to select one. John Ford's *How Green Was My Valley* is a delicate achievement, an emotional film about nostalgia, memory, perception and love, which retains a small but fanatical following. Orson Welles' *Citizen Kane* is a robust revolution; watching *Citizen Kane* has become a rite of passage for movie lovers (and film critics, two groups which don't necessarily overlap…). When young, we tend to be blown away by what seems to be absolutely unprecedented. After a time, we may come to see that much of the acting seems hammy, and decide that ultimately, we just may not care about Kane and his Rosebud. The film has no emotional center we can rely on; the pleasures of watching *Citizen Kane* remain primarily intellectual.[86] Watching it again, I have come to the conclusion that the movie often sounds better than it looks, particularly in terms of the acting; the voices are all marvelous, and perfectly pitched and cast, but the faces that go with the voices haven't always learned how to act. Watch the scene where Kane's guardian labels him a Communist, and you can see how bad the acting is; ditto for the Joseph Cotten scenes as an old man. Not surprising, given Welles' experience was primarily in the theater and radio, and most of his actors came from radio with him. On the other hand, once Welles and Toland and their set designers let themselves go, the imagery of the film shatters our conception of what is possible in the movies. Watch the scene of celebration when Kane succeeds in hiring the entire staff of the *Chronicle* to his own paper. Every last moment is a revolution in lighting, cinematography, set design and the patterns of narration. Ultimately, the criteria for picking the Best Picture for 1941 is this: do other movies quench our desires more effectively? *How Green Was My Valley* certainly fills a different hunger, as Peter Bogdanovich notes: "There's no question that *How Green Was My Valley* is the emotional film, and comes from the heart, whereas *Kane* comes from the head."[cxcvii]

What we want is a movie that satisfies both the heart and the head, a rare beast indeed.

How Green Was My Valley stars Walter Pidgeon, Maureen O'Hara, Donald Crisp, Sara Allgood, and Roddy McDowall, all under the forceful guidance of John Ford. Set in a Welsh mining town around the turn of the century, only one Welsh actor is actually in the movie, and most of them speak with an Irish accent. The theme of the movie announces

---

[86] Although not for everyone. The great Argentine writer Jorge Luis Borges dismissed the entire movie: "It suffers from grossness, pedantry, dullness." He also called it a "centreless labyrinth" – which he ought to know about as the author of *Labyrinths*. Qtd. in Andrew Sarris, *"You Ain't Heard Nothin' Yet"* p. 286.

itself with the opening narration: "There is no fence nor hedge around time that is gone. You can go back and have what you like of it, if you can remember. So I can close my eyes on my valley as it is today, and it is gone, and I see it as it was when I was a boy. Green it was, and possessed of the plenty of the Earth..." Like many great artistic experiences, the subject is loss and the unrecoverable past, save through the function of memory, and the process that allows the recreation of the past, if only momentarily. Still, the inescapable truth of the narrator looking back on his childhood is that he escaped that life. I'm not sure if survivor's guilt isn't driving this narration, this film, as much as anything. Emotionally, the movie is fraught with the death of the father, the mistakes others have made, and lost opportunities. The movie most definitely deserved a nomination for Best Picture, but the Oscar really should go elsewhere.

On a far lesser plane, but emotionally driven as well, *Blossoms in the Dust* brings us Greer Garson and Walter Pidgeon. This filmed biography of orphans' rights advocate Edna Gladney movie would begin a series of eight films that Garson and Pidgeon would make together; in some ways, the pairing undercut the actor Pidgeon might have become, had he been allowed to develop the kind of performances he had in *How Green Was My Valley*, and not been typecast as Mr. Greer Garson. Director Mervyn LeRoy tries to cram too much into a single movie, as is true of many biopics; almost every scene is squeezed for the tears (what do you expect from a movie about a crusader and persecuted children?). Overall, a heartwarming film, dedicated to a true servant of children, and worth a nomination for the noble intentions, and for those who like their movies reassuring with the milk of human kindness.

Citizen Kane, as I've said above, almost always ends up at the top of critics' lists for the greatest movie. For an intellectual, that may be so (I've often regarded it as such, although with reservations). Beyond any doubts, the movie deserves a Best Picture nomination. We shall see if it deserves more than it got originally.

Here Comes Mr. Jordan stars Robert Montgomery in the supernatural fantasy about a man taken too soon by an angel. The movie as a whole elusively charms, as Robert Montgomery's somewhat dunderheaded but stubborn boxer keeps pushing to get his body back, and helping the damsel in distress. Claude Rains as Mr. Jordan gives one of his best performances, matching Spencer Tracy for his capacity to project a knowing purity and spiritual innocence. Edward Everett Horton has a nice bit as the enthusiastic but bungling apprentice angel. *Here Comes Mr. Jordan* is an odd choice for the Academy to nominate, given their traditional hostility to genre films, but the movie proves to be unique enough to sustain their nomination. [87]

With *Hold Back the Dawn*, Charles Brackett and Billy Wilder crafted another unusual script for Mitchell Leisen (director of their screenplays for *Midnight* and *Arise, My Love*). Charles Boyer is a gigolo who flees from the Nazis to Mexico, on his way to the United States. In order to gain entry, he woos Olivia de Havilland, a shy schoolteacher who blossoms with love for Boyer – until she finds out his shady past, and thinks he married her solely to enter the U.S. Tortured melodrama ensues. One of the more interesting parts of the movie comes when Boyer sneaks onto the Paramount lot, and we get a behind the scenes look at Veronica Lake filming – including somebody reading lines to her while she's shooting a phone call, and the images from the camera viewfinder which frames the action (*Anchors Aweigh* steals this scene). Generally, behind the scenes shots don't get quite so specific, so enjoy the touch of insider piquing. Wilder would often work in commentary about Hollywood into his scripts, as we see most famously in *Sunset Blvd*. Here, too, love is not the simple thing Hollywood would have us take it as. Boyer is a scoundrel; Paulette Goddard has a good turn as the amoral woman who finds him irresistible as well. De Havilland has one of her best parts (see Best Actress). By the time *Hold Back the Dawn* is done, we've had just about everything we could ask for from a high quality romantic melodrama, and one which easily retains a nomination for Best Picture.

The Little Foxes stars Bette Davis and Herbert Marshall. William Wyler directed this Lillian Hellman script from her own play; Gregg Toland did the cinematography. With all that talent, how can you go wrong? Answer: by having Wyler and Davis end their partnership. Wyler disagreed so violently over Davis' interpretation of her character that he never cast her again. Given that all three of their collaborations are classics – the other two being *Jezebel* and *The Letter* – who knows what might have come? Watching *The Little Foxes* today, the movie seems broken at times, due to Davis and her refusal to follow Wyler's direction, and yet, even with the cracks (mostly Teresa Wright's performance and Davis' makeup decisions), *The Little Foxes* remains a fascinating display of the corruption of wealth, the machinations inherent in dysfunctional families, and the cruelty of selfish people. Not a perfect movie, but still a powerful one, and a good nomination.

---

[87] Thorne Smith's *Topper* books had carved out a place for these kinds of stories commercially.

Of all the films made this year, *The Maltese Falcon* remains my personal favorite, just in terms of sheer enjoyment and the pleasure of performance. Apparently, I am not alone, as the movie rapidly proved itself to be the popular favorite of friends and family. Rarely does a movie get so much right; even more rarely does it shift the careers of almost everybody involved. For John Huston, *The Maltese Falcon* was his directorial debut, launching him on one of the most varied careers in cinema history; for Bogart, this movie made him a star. *Casablanca* would then make him the most popular actor in the world, a position he would largely retain until his death, and even afterwards.[88] For Sydney Greenstreet, a film career would begin; for Peter Lorre and Mary Astor, careers would be capped. Dashiell Hammett never had a more faithful movie made of one of his books. One could argue that film noir itself was born here.[89] The Academy did itself proud nominating this movie!

Generally, a sign of a bad movie is when it's nominated for Best Picture, and nothing else. Fortunately this time, that isn't the case. *One Foot in Heaven* stars Fredric March and Martha Scott in an honest portrayal of the life of a minister and his wife. Realistic, with just touches of sentimentality, *One Foot in Heaven* shows the life of the pastor far more eloquently than later iterations such as the television series *Seventh Heaven*, based as *One Foot* is on the memoirs of the son of the subject. In today's world, when religious awakenings and motivations tend to be politically charged, highly suspect, or overly mawkish, *One Foot in Heaven* is a serious depiction of religious motivations and actions driven by a genuine desire to inspire and help others. A very fine movie, although not a great one. The nomination should stay for approaching an often maudlin subject with grace.

Sergeant Alvin York was the most highly decorated American soldier of WWI. He had famously begun as a pacifist before ending his war by singlehandedly killing 28 Germans, and capturing 132 soldiers with the

---

[88] The American Film Institute named him their #1 male star in 1999: http://www.afi.com/100years/stars.aspx

[89] Here are two concurring opinions I found after I made this statement:

"As he reengineered the source material for *The Maltese Falcon*, Huston pared away unnecessary characters and limited action to a few locations: Sam's office, Miss O'Shaughnessy's hotel room, Gutman's suite, Sam's apartment, a few others. The idea was to make Sam's world a rat's maze; constricted, frustrating, exhausting. . . In the process, Huston went about inventing what we now call film noir, showing other directors that in the urban crime drama, tight, claustrophobic spaces are as psychologically significant and as thematically profound as spacious outdoor vistas are to the Western." http://www.albany.edu/writers-inst/webpages4/filmnotes/fnf97n2.html.

Rudy Behlmer agrees: "*The Maltese Falcon* was the forerunner of a number of films over the next several years that were a direct, if somewhat belated, result of its influence: Hammett, Raymond Chandler, James M. Cain and similar authors of the hard-boiled school became fashionable in Hollywood." *America's Favorite Movies*, p. 152-53.

help of seven other Americans. *Sergeant York* was yet another entry in the continuing effort by Warner Brothers to get America to fight the Nazis. Casting the eternally likeable Gary Cooper as Sergeant York was a stroke of genius; if Gary Cooper wants to fight the Germans, who wouldn't? Part depiction of rural America, part romance, and part clarion call for an end to isolationism and pacifism, *Sergeant York* was a massive hit, and offered the Academy a reasonable alternative to handing awards to *Citizen Kane* when it gave Cooper the Best Actor Oscar (see below). *Sergeant York* remains one of the better biographies Hollywood has made, and an excellent depiction of rural evangelical Christianity, as well as a rousing piece of pro-American propaganda. The nomination should stay.

Watching *Suspicion* is like having amazing foreplay, fantastic intercourse – and the most disappointing climax ever. The ending is a travesty that nearly ruins everything that came before it. Cary Grant is terrific, bringing the kind of dark edge he had developed in Howard Hawks' *Only Angels Have Wings* and *His Girl Friday* even deeper into his characters, while retaining the suave romanticism nobody else has ever done better. Joan Fontaine is playing the same nebbish she did in *Rebecca*, which this time around leads me to want to see Cary Grant kill her (I suspect Hitchcock felt the same way). Hitchcock returns to his suspense roots, escaping from David O. Selznick's control, but not from the studio hacks who butchered *Suspicion*. I won't suggest stripping the movie of the nomination, simply because what precedes the ending is so perfect, but I wish Hitchcock had been able to film his real ending, so that we could have the restored film.

As for the movies the Academy omitted, their worst thud of judgment came when they ignored *Sullivan's Travels*, from the great Preston Sturges. *Sullivan's Travels* remains one of the best satires ever made on Hollywood, ex-wives, and pretentiousness. I can't think of another movie that's ever made a more blatant argument for the value of comedy over tragedy, while also pointing out the disparity between rich and poor. I also found the depiction of a black preacher and his parishioners to be dignified, warm, and unusually free of the stereotypes of the period. Joel McCrea and Veronica Lake never made a better movie – and an argument can be made that neither did Preston Sturges. *Sullivan's Travels* deserved a nomination for Best Picture.

Picking the Best Picture this year is almost as difficult as it was in the golden year of 1939, as any number of these movies could have easily won in another year with less competition. *How Green Was My Valley* and *Citizen Kane* are the obvious choices, but as I've noted above, neither one engendered any particular joy in the conversations I had with others about watching them. They are both formidable artistic achievements, and *Citizen Kane* remade the cinematic tool box for decades to come. But another film has proven to be just as influential, just as artistic – and filled with indelible performances that mark practically all the performers with their signature roles, which only grow richer with repeated viewings. Intellectually, the movie is an exploration of the evil of the world, and the place of a single man within it, as he must decide for himself the nature of good and evil, and where the dividing line exists. Emotionally, the movie provides us with love, friendship, betrayal, excitement, and the hard satisfactions of work well done. I speak of *The Maltese Falcon*, which should have been named the Best Picture of 1941.

Best Actor: Gary Cooper won for *Sergeant York*, over Walter Huston, *All That Money Can Buy* (aka *The Devil and Daniel Webster*); Orson Welles, *Citizen Kane*; Robert Montgomery, *Here Comes Mr. Jordan*; and Cary Grant, *Penny Serenade*

Gary Cooper won for *Sergeant York* mostly because he wasn't Orson Welles. Cooper's Sergeant York isn't much more than his typical aw-shucks performance, and feels very similar to other Cooper films in how he projects the character of York. I shan't begrudge Cooper his nomination, as he does carry the picture almost singlehandedly, but Cooper doesn't explore new territory here at all (and I've already rectified the Academy's neglect for him by showing he should have won an award for *Mr. Deeds Goes to Town*).

Walter Huston has an absolute ball playing the devil in *All That Money Can Buy*, better known today as *The Devil and Daniel Webster*. Gleefully scene-chewing his way through this sell-your-soul-to-the-devil tale, Huston invests the demonic as nobody has before or since. You've never seen a more wicked grin or gleam in the eye, or a more sinister whisper – or a pie devoured with more gluttony! I think this performance has to rank with Huston's greatest, that of the old prospector in *The Treasure of Sierra Madre*. An excellent nomination, full of brimstone and sulfur!

Seeing Orson Welles for the first time onscreen in *Citizen Kane*, he appears impossibly young, good-looking, and charismatic. Not a trace of the ham emerges until he has to play an older man, although one could argue that Welles deliberately plays those false notes into his character because Kane himself becomes untrue to his best self the older he gets. Nothing like Welles had ever been seen in the movies before; he was a true American original, and one whose career, both in front of and behind the camera, would never be less than problematic, yet compelling. Welles was a genuine film presence as a result of *Citizen Kane*; he deserved the nomination.[90]

Robert Montgomery didn't want to make *Here Comes Mr. Jordan* at Columbia. After breaking out of his light comic stereotyping with his psycho killer in *Night Must Fall* and getting his first Academy Award nomination, the last thing he wanted to do was go back into the happy box – but back Louis B. Mayer put him. At least at MGM, the box was plushly lined. The movie worked for him, as he received a second and final acting nomination for *Here Comes Mr. Jordan*. At the end of WWII and his service in the Navy, he made what is arguably his best film with John Ford, *They Were Expendable*, and his directorial debut with the Raymond Chandler adaptation, *Lady in the Lake*. Montgomery also had a nice turn in Alfred Hitchcock's odd foray into marital comedy, *Mr. and Mrs. Smith*. Montgomery's role here runs against his usual suave intelligence and charm, as he plays a boxer with a one track mind and a Brooklyn accent who needs a new body. The part is something of a one-note job, without a great deal of subtlety – but then, the part doesn't require that. Gossamer can't bear too much weight, after all. Montgomery should keep his nomination, just to encourage the Academy to look outside the heavy melodramas.

Cary Grant's nomination for *Penny Serenade* is yet another one of those secondary nods for far better work done the previous year (in Grant's case, for *The Philadelphia Story* and *His Girl Friday*). Grant was reunited with Irene Dunne by director George Stevens. Marx Brothers' writer Morrie Ryskind produced the screenplay. Everybody involved turned serious, including one miscarriage and a dead adopted baby. Get out the hankies. The movie is decidedly secondary to the kind of witty and wicked comedies Grant and Dunne had made before. Everyone seems so committed to being serious that the film never really takes off, except in spurts, partly due to the flashback construction of the film, and partly due to the arbitrary occurrences, including an earthquake designed primarily to kill a baby. The section with the adopted baby flows better, but then it gets even more maudlin. I don't know how else to put this, except to say that Cary Grant seems to have lost most of his Cary Grant-ness. He's mundane in the role, and that should never be good enough for a nomination.

Several actors deserved nods who did not receive them.

---

[90] I don't expect this book to settle many arguments, although I hope it starts quite a few pleasant ones. Andrew Sarris notes "Welles himself was the biggest histrionic explosion on the movie scene, but to this day people differ on whether he was all that good and revelatory or all that bad and hammy purely as a performer." *"You Ain't Heard Nothin' Yet,"* p. 288.

Why the Academy failed to nominate Walter Pidgeon for his role in *How Green Was My Valley* is further evidence of their blindness. Pidgeon never again reached these heights of delicate nuance and heart-wrenching shifts in the turns of his voice. Look into his eyes when he explains why he can't marry Maureen O'Hara, and you will see the very definition of regret. Ford brought out the best in Pidgeon, and the Academy owed him a nomination at the least. Unfortunately, he would spend the next decade cast in largely thankless roles as the on-screen husband of Greer Garson, and never fulfill the promise shown here.

I also believe that Cary Grant deserved a nomination for *Suspicion*, playing a villain for the first time. I don't care what the fake ending shows; Grant is a cur and a bounder who deserves damnation. What joy there is in *Suspicion* comes from Grant playing a cad. He should have been nominated for this role, rather than the lackluster *Penny Serenade*.

But to show how completely the Academy had no clue, how could they not have nominated Humphrey Bogart for his brilliant performance as Sam Spade in *The Maltese Falcon*? Bogart is relaxed and poised, and yet he brings an unprecedented intensity, comic bite, and drive to the role of the hard-boiled detective, just as Hammett did when he wrote the original book. Bogart *is* Sam Spade in this movie, with the same amoral quality, balanced by and against the personal code of ethics which is all that separates good and evil in the world of *The Maltese Falcon*. Bogart's face has aged, the wrinkles and worries of his life etching into what had been a boyish canvas the deep knowledge of precisely how badly the world can go – and yet, how important it is to maintain a personal stand on what is right and wrong. Huston knew Bogart could be far more than a villain, but Huston also knew that the audience brought into the movie all those years of watching Cagney and Edward G. Robinson killing Bogart for his perfidies and betrayals. Bogart was also building from his fine performance in *High Sierra* this year, which had already challenged audience expectations. Like John Garfield, Bogart was exploring the possibilities of the flawed hero, if not the antihero. Never before had an entire film hinged on this kind of protagonist, a man who was willing to break everybody else's rules but his own. *The Maltese Falcon* shows us the Bogart we have never been able to forget, and succeeded in doing what *The Petrified Forest* and *High Sierra* had never quite achieved: bringing Humphrey Bogart to the forefront of American actors, and granting the Forties of film noir and the end of American innocence a name and a face to remember them by. Bogart should have been nominated for Best Actor for *The Maltese Falcon* – and he should have won.

Best Actress: Joan Fontaine won for *Suspicion*, over Barbara Stanwyck, *Ball of Fire*; Greer Garson, *Blossoms in the Dust*; Olivia de Havilland, *Hold Back the Dawn*; and Bette Davis, *The Little Foxes*

Joan Fontaine almost certainly won for *Suspicion* because she didn't win for *Rebecca*. In nearly every area of consideration, Fontaine's performance in *Rebecca* vastly outshines her work in *Suspicion*, a film deeply flawed by the false ending forced onto it by the Production Code. I find her portrayal to be very imitative of her previous role, one that she never really escaped. She should not have a nomination for doing the same thing over again, much less the Academy Award.

Barbara Stanwyck cuts loose in *Ball of Fire*. Stanwyck makes the entire film come alive with her portrayal of Sugarpuss O'Shea. As the housekeeper says of her, "That is the kind of woman who makes whole civilizations topple." Sexy, assured, smart and incandescent, Stanwyck never had a better comic role. Watch her work Cooper into a froth, and compare that to the famous scene in the dark bedroom when all we see are her eyes, as Cooper returns the favor. Stanwyck most assuredly deserved this nomination (even though she lip-syncs to Martha Tilton), especially when you consider she also starred in *Meet John Doe* and *The Lady Eve*, which must comprise one of the most successful years ever for any American actress.

Greer Garson in *Blossoms in the Dust* spends most of her time looking pretty, then behaving nobly – to quote Pauline Kael, "at her most sickeningly prissy."[cxcviii] The one crying scene she has she does with her back to the camera, which seems to me to be a dodge. Once her character is on her own, and fighting for the children, Garson does a credible job bringing out the passion the real Mrs. Gladney must have had for the children she helped. When she has to say goodbye to one little boy, dry eyes are nowhere to be found. The nomination should stay.

When we first see Olivia de Havilland in *Hold Back the Dawn*, she is driving a small pack of schoolchildren from America into Mexico to celebrate the Fourth of July (if that's not irony, I don't know what is). One of the brats is dropping firecrackers at the feet of Charles Boyer, who gets distinctly unpleasant when de Havilland tries to have the boy apologize. The pattern of initial dislike, followed by de Havilland being charmed by a rogue, is lifted straight out of her pictures with Errol Flynn (most famously in *The Adventures of Robin Hood*). De Havilland does a beautiful job with her portrayal of a schoolteacher who finds love, and then finds Boyer has been using her to gain entry to the United States. De Havilland is playing out one of her strengths, the ability to project sweetness and innocence. Look at her eyes after Boyer has enchanted her with a tale of a former love turned bad; without saying a word or changing her facial expression, de Havilland shows she is puzzled and excited by the attention. Her expectations of marriage, particularly of the wedding night, are done with great subtlety and hidden passion, along with the usual shyness. When she discovers Boyer's intent, again de Havilland responds mostly with her eyes. De Havilland gives a performance which is a textbook example of movie acting, as opposed to stage acting – and one which fully merits the nomination.

Bette Davis turned in a performance in *The Little Foxes* that shows her at her rock hard bitchy best – or worst, depending on your point of view. Wyler wanted her to add human touches; I believe he was right. Much of this goes back to my problems with Davis in *Of Human Bondage*, wherein her character has no redeeming human qualities whatsoever, and remains two-dimensional as a result. She also seems to be channeling Tallulah Bankhead, rather than inhabiting the role herself (many sources suggest she based her performance on the Broadway play; others suggest she felt she couldn't use anything Tallulah did, which made the part more disjointed than it should have been). As a result, Davis occasionally drops from what she can do so brilliantly on the screen, to a stagier performance that plays falsely. Watching her face while she knows her husband is dying, and she is choosing not to help him, doesn't work as well as it might, because Davis had insisted on wearing a mask-like make up, nominally to make her look older; the effect is to point forward to *Whatever Happened to Baby Jane?* On the other hand, the earlier scene where she looks in the mirror, comparing her present face with that in a picture of her younger self, couldn't be better acted. And perhaps best of all, the look of grim satisfaction on Davis' face when she defeats her brothers is matched only by her realization of the impending loss of her daughter – and Davis does it almost entirely with her eyes. Davis definitely earned her nomination this year, for that scene alone.

Yet again, the Academy ignored worthy performances.

Where the hell is Maureen O'Hara for *How Green Was My Valley*? As Angharad, the one daughter of the Morgans, Maureen O'Hara is beyond beautiful. Any man would kill to have a woman look at him the way O'Hara looks at Walter Pidgeon when she sees him for the first time in church. She and Walter Pidgeon form the relentless heart of the film, the pain of life's choices and the restrictions of society acted out in their faces, and their eyes, and the sound of longing they have for each other. O'Hara should have been nominated.

As should Joan Crawford, for *A Woman's Face*. Crawford plays a criminal whose face is disfigured; she then gets plastic surgery and has her beauty restored. George Cukor directed from a script by Donald Ogden Stewart and Elliott Paul. *A Woman's Face* has good cinematography, best shown in the shadowy walk down the prison tunnel. Conrad Veidt gives a fine performance, particularly in the scene where he seduces Crawford by completely ignoring her scar, and manipulating her feelings of insecurity by helping clear something from her eye. When she has the bandages removed, Crawford finally proves herself worthy of being nominated for an Oscar. One of the best shots in the film is of her looking in a mirror reflecting into itself into infinity – and Crawford's face multiplied as well. Crawford gives a beautifully restrained performance like no other in her career.

The final decision isn't an easy one, and had Bette Davis allowed William Wyler to help her maintain control over her character, I think her performance in *The Little Foxes* would easily have won, and been perhaps her best. [91] As it is, the flaws prevent me from doing so. Barbara Stanwyck is quite good in *Ball of Fire*, but she does have a fairly limited role to play; she was capable of far more. Greer Garson has her moments, but she too wears thin after awhile. De Havilland comes close to winning, but melodrama only goes so far. Had Crawford been given a better screenplay for *A Woman's Face*, she could have easily taken the Oscar with Cukor's guidance. In the final decision, I found myself returning to watch Maureen O'Hara in *How Green Was My Valley*. Her performance is largely within her eyes, as she is socially constrained in so many ways that she simply cannot break free physically; her one attempt ends in failure. O'Hara often played very strong women who have to work out those strengths through the straitjacket of the cultures her characters inhabit – think of her in *The Quiet Man* – and here, she provides perhaps the strongest performance in *How Green Was My Valley*. Watch her scene in the parsonage with Walter Pidgeon, and her wedding day to a man she does not love, and tell me she doesn't deserve the Oscar. She does, despite the competition. Maureen O'Hara should have won for Best Actress.

Best Director: John Ford won for *How Green Was My Valley*, over Orson Welles, *Citizen Kane*; Alexander Hall, *Here Comes Mr. Jordan*; William Wyler, *The Little Foxes*; and Howard Hawks, *Sergeant York*.

---

[91] One of the surprises of writing this book is how often Bette Davis didn't deserve Oscars. She was definitely one of our greatest actresses, but many of her fabled performances haven't aged as well as her fans would like. On the other hand, she does have many more years to keep trying to convince me, now, doesn't she?

John Ford considered *How Green Was My Valley* to be his finest work, and part of me grieves for this greatest of all American directors. I mourn, because in this moment of Ford's artistic triumph, one of his students surpassed him, before heading into a rocky decline of brilliant failures and trampled dreams. John Ford did subtle, profound work on the nature of memory and love in *How Green Was My Valley*, but what Orson Welles did was to remake the entire toolbox of the director, aided by the brilliant cinematography of Gregg Toland and the layered, puzzle-like screenplay Welles wrote with Herman Mankiewicz. Given that Welles directly credited Ford with everything he ever knew about directing, the lineage of master to student is clear. Watching *How Green Was My Valley*, one can only marvel at the subtleties and poetic genius of this emotionally devastating film. The scene that lodges longest in memory is when Maureen O'Hara leaves the church after marrying another man, and her true love Walter Pidgeon emerges from the church in the distance, in a very long shot, then turns and walks away from the life he could have had with her, back into the church. No other director would have managed to stop himself from shifting to a close-up. But by keeping Pidgeon at a distance, Ford visually reinforces the emotional gaps Pidgeon's character has imposed on himself, out of a noble desire to save O'Hara from a life of poverty as a minister's wife. Ford definitely deserved the nomination here – but as you may have guessed, Orson Welles was in his way.

When Welles arrived at RKO, he famously remarked: "This is the biggest toy-train set any boy ever had." He had an unprecedented contract, granting him "total artistic control" over his films (which he signed away to be allowed to make *The Magnificent Ambersons*). In *Citizen Kane*, Orson Welles forged a movie that looked like nothing else ever done before in Hollywood. That alone qualifies him for this nomination. If the film succeeds on as many levels as so many people think it does, we have to credit Welles as a director (on top of his contributions to the screenplay, his acting, and, at the very least, his allowing Gregg Toland to try anything he wanted as a cinematographer). Among other radical decisions, Welles shot most of the film in long, continuous takes, laying out the action and blocking as he would have in the theater, and then rehearsing the dialogue as if on radio. Welles would then cut to a close up for the payoff. Toland clearly helped in the visual aspects, which is one of many reasons Welles had Toland getting his credit on the same card as Welles himself, but Welles was the one who set the pacing and tone of the film.[cxcix] As Jean-Luc Godard said about Welles, "Everyone will always owe him everything."[cc] Even the contemporary critics recognized the unique nature of the film. *The New York*

Post raved: "The interlocking jigsaw puzzle of human personalities and their relationships to each other simply doesn't appear in other American motion pictures. *Citizen Kane* has the field to itself."[cci] Welles deserved this nomination, and the Academy's bravery in naming him in the face of Hearst's disapproval is still remarkable.

Alexander Hall had a forty year career as a director, beginning in 1916. He never made a better movie than *Here Comes Mr. Jordan*. What we get is competent, but not gifted. He did guide his cast and crew to a number of nominations, and given that the studio was Columbia, and not MGM, block voting had to play a smaller part (of course, with Montgomery having an MGM contract, some of that may have spilled over). Hall should keep his nomination for bringing this gentle little fantasy to success.

William Wyler lost control of *The Little Foxes* when he couldn't rein in Bette Davis. As a result, his fine work on this film is pushed away from the ambiguities he had begun to build into his work with *The Letter* and other films, and becomes a much less shaded creation, which mars *The Little Foxes* considerably. Still, what remains is worth seeing – and a nomination.

Howard Hawks was nominated for *Sergeant York*, but I strongly suspect this nomination to be yet another where the Academy makes up for past sins by honoring a lesser work. After all, they had snubbed Hawks so many times, most recently for *His Girl Friday*. *Sergeant York* was one of his most successful films, yet one of his least innovative. Hawks does keep the action going, juggling the different strands of York's life story; Hawks deserves a nomination for making a biopic that doesn't have serious dead spots.

As for those directors the Academy ignored, first and foremost must be Preston Sturges and John Huston.

Sturges wrote and directed both *The Lady Eve* and *Sullivan's Travels* in 1941, as good as any director ever achieved in the same year, crafting two classic American comedies with economy, wit, and verve. Of the two, I have always found *The Lady Eve* to be slightly less compelling than *Sullivan's Travels*, mostly because I always laugh out loud when the producer demands that the director make his tragedy "with a little sex." This satire on pretensions, Hollywood, and the general tendency on the part of the critical establishment to prefer tragedy (or melodrama) over comedy never fails to speak to my inherent belief that laughter is a more profound human need than crying. Sturges should have been nominated for directing *Sullivan's Travels*.

John Huston produced a tour-de-force with his debut as a director: *The Maltese Falcon*. Told with absolute economy, humor, and biting suspense, *The Maltese Falcon* is the visual equivalent of Hammett's taut, tough prose. Watch the scene after his partner is shot, as Bogart is framed and almost trapped in a profile in his bedroom as he learns what has happened. I can't recall anything like it in film before, where the star is reduced to a part of a mise en scene, rather than being the focal point. Throughout, Huston uses unusual camera angles, often from behind Bogart's head, to encourage our identification with Bogart, who might otherwise have continued to be distanced from the audience due to all those villains he played. Huston helped to alter those associations, subverting them to add a darker dimension to the hero than ever before in movies. Huston's choices for camera angles, cutting, and pacing simply could not be more original or effective. I want to highlight, in particular, the ending, when Humphrey Bogart has handed Mary Astor over to the police. As she descends in the elevator, he heads down the stairs; more than one commentator over the years has suggested both are going to hell – he's just getting there more slowly than she is. This kind of cinematic virtuosity comes rarely to us. For that scene alone, Huston should have earned a nomination for Best Director.

Even so, Orson Welles should have won the Oscar for Best Director. Nobody in the Forties was more revolutionary or more insightful into the possibilities of filmmaking. Welles would spend the rest of his life trying to live up to the genius of this film – and failing.

Best Supporting Actor: Donald Crisp won for *How Green Was My Valley*, over Charles Coburn, *The Devil and Miss Jones*; James Gleason, *Here Comes Mr. Jordan*; Sydney Greenstreet, *The Maltese Falcon*; and Walter Brennan, *Sergeant York*

Donald Crisp is indeed wonderful as the Welsh father in *How Green Was My Valley*. At the first family dinner, quite early in the picture, watch Crisp's grimace of disapproval at Roddy MacDowell when he tries to take a piece of bread before prayers, followed by a wry grin of bemusement when the boy puts it back. All wordless, all done with economy and style, as befits a man who had been acting in the movies for thirty years (Crisp played General Grant in *The Birth of a Nation*). My favorite scene with Crisp is when he turns from fawning toady to proud patriarch, when he realizes that the mine owner has come to get permission for his son to court O'Hara. Crisp deserved the nomination, but other actors this year turned in milestone performances.

Charles Coburn was nominated for *The Devil and Miss Jones*. Coburn increasingly gained the attention of the Academy in the early Forties, playing role after role as an older eccentric, primarily in comic films like *To Be or Not to Be, The Lady Eve, The More the Merrier* –

and this movie. As the rich tycoon who owns the department store he subsequently infiltrates under an assumed name, Coburn has a ball playing grumpy and conspiring. He deserves a nomination for this role, even if he does seem like a refugee from a Frank Capra film, because he is the major reason to watch *The Devil and Miss Jones*.

Which is also true for James Gleason, for his role in *Here Comes Mr. Jordan*. Gleason is one of my favorite character actors, showing up with his sourpuss in dozens of movies, including *Arsenic and Old Lace*, *The Bishop's Wife* and *The Night of the Hunter*. *Here Comes Mr. Jordan* gave him his only Oscar nomination. Gleason is his usual comic self, but at some point, he becomes the audience, helping us through to a willing suspension of disbelief that the fantastic events around him are happening. The look on his face when Gleason realizes his best friend is in a rich man's body is a wonder of eyes and voice. Claude Rains could just as easily have received a nomination for playing Mr. Jordan, the angelic helper; run this movie, then watch next year's *Casablanca*, and this great actor's range reveals itself all the more. As it is, we will leave James Gleason his nomination, as he well deserved it for this warm performance.

Warm is not what I would call Sydney Greenstreet, who comes close to taking *The Maltese Falcon* away from Humphrey Bogart. As the Fat Man, Casper Gutman, Greenstreet brought malevolence and intelligence to the part of a villain, as few ever had before. What he also brings is a sense of humor, with his zest for a jest, and his evil twisting of the knife of betrayal. Huston aids Greenstreet by shooting from below him, to emphasize his girth and dominance, but Greenstreet adds far more with his facial expressions and that unmistakable voice: rich, suggestive, with a touch of gravel and a pint of snake oil. Greenstreet spent the rest of his career trying to outdo himself in this, his first performance; he never succeeded. He fully deserved this nomination.

In *Sergeant York*, Walter Brennan is once again playing an old coot, this time as a storekeeper/preacher who converts Gary Cooper. Brennan sports the wildest eyebrows, like two black furry caterpillars under a tangled crop of white hair. Brennan brings the power of a true backwoods revivalist to bear, as he gathers Cooper into the fold at long last. Brennan deserves a nomination for that scene alone.

Two more actors should have been nominated.

First, the Academy should have recognized Charles Dingle, as Bette Davis' older brother in *The Little Foxes*, the most scheming, ambitious, and amoral human being in the film – except for Davis herself. He's a breath of fresh air, as much as Greenstreet in *The Maltese Falcon*, making villains into fully human characters.

Second, Peter Lorre's turn as the sexually suggestive Joel Cairo in *The Maltese Falcon* is unforgettable. His appearance is the first real sign we have that something more than murder has occurred in the tale. His scenes with Bogart are riveting, as they would be again in *Casablanca*. Lorre successfully implies the forbidden aspects of the character – Cairo is clearly gay in the novel – without stereotyping or downplaying the character's innate danger or craftiness. Lorre does choose to portray homosexuality in feminine terms, in crying and emotional outbursts, when he doesn't get what he wants, but we've seen contemporary Hollywood make the same choices. Lorre should have been nominated.

Out of all these wonderful performances, Sydney Greenstreet remains the most indelible supporting character of the year. Greenstreet redefines menace, while undercutting the stereotypical attitudes the movies had towards jolly fat men (which he uses as a masquerade). Greenstreet should have won the Oscar for Best Supporting Actor – now there was a statue he could have kept!

Best Supporting Actress: Mary Astor won for *The Great Lie*, over Sara Allgood, *How Green Was My Valley*; Patricia Collinge, *The Little Foxes*; Teresa Wright, *The Little Foxes*; and Margaret Wycherly, *Sergeant York*

Mary Astor had an extremely long career, and 1941 was her absolute peak of success, as she won the Oscar for *The Great Lie* and starred as the femme fatale in *The Maltese Falcon*. *The Great Lie* stars Bette Davis as the true love of a flier, played by George Brent; Mary Astor is the bitchy pianist the flier marries (when Astor won, she thanked Tchaikovsky and Davis.) The marriage turns out to be invalid, a baby is involved, and Astor and Davis have a fine soapy time arguing over everything. Watching *The Great Lie*, I could only find any interest when Astor and Davis let loose, and even then, Mary Astor goes overboard too much to deserve the Oscar – especially when she gave a far better performance in *The Maltese Falcon*. As Brigid O'Shaunessy, Astor gained movie immortality, for which she has been remembered ever since. As the manipulative, secretive criminal, Astor gives the kind of subtle, restrained performance that holds our interest past one viewing. She should have been nominated for *The Maltese Falcon* instead of this overwrought soap opera. I will end the suspense and announce that she should have been victorious in this category for *The Maltese Falcon*.

As for the others, Sara Allgood in *How Green Was My Valley* plays the mother who never stops working. Her great scene comes when she confronts the striking miners, and defends her husband against their false attacks. The look of quiet despair when she realizes two of her sons will be going to America, and gone forever from her home, haunts me still. As the film progresses, Allgood reveals her power as an actress, and in her role, as the one wielding the true power in the family, putting Donald Crisp in his place with small gestures and utterances. She deserved the nomination.

Patricia Collinge and Teresa Wright were both nominated for *The Little Foxes* as the over-talkative aristocratic aunt, and the overshadowed daughter of Bette Davis. Teresa Wright is playing the same sweet, simple girl she does in almost all her movies; with the exception of *The Pride of the Yankees* and *Shadow of a Doubt*, her performances seem less than adequate these days. Wright does try to wring some anger and darker emotion out of her role, but she really doesn't have it in her. Given that the whole narrative hinges on her dawning self-awareness of what her family is truly like, the movie suffers accordingly. No nomination should have been given.

Patricia Collinge reproduces her role from the Broadway production of *The Little Foxes*, and she comes out of the movie nicely, as the slightly dunderheaded, sweet, musically inclined aunt who is abused by her husband. Collinge provides the first evidence that all is not well in this family; her performance remains the most memorable in the film, along with Davis when she isn't being too stagy, and Charles Dingle, playing the crafty oldest brother. Collinge would go on to minor roles in *Shadow of a Doubt* and *The Nun's Story*, but this remained her signature moment. She deserves to keep her nomination.

In *Sergeant York*, Margaret Wycherly brings a grim intensity lightened by a spark of humor to her role as Mrs. York (she would later go over the top as Jimmy Cagney's mother in *White Heat*). Wycherly roots *Sergeant York* into a sense of the poverty and stubbornness most of the hill people carried with them; without her, Cooper would have had to work much harder to keep the film centered on a feeling for reality. Wycherly is the Howard Hawks heroine at the end of her life: indomitable, committed, and still with a vibrancy missing from many other female performances in much of Hollywood's output in the Forties. She definitely deserved her nomination.

In case you missed it, Mary Astor should have been given the Oscar for Best Supporting Actress for *The Maltese Falcon*. You really should be paying more attention.

Best Writing (Screenplay): Sidney Buchman and Seton I. Miller won for *Here Comes Mr. Jordan*, over Charles Brackett and Billy Wilder, *Hold Back the Dawn*; Philip Dunne, *How Green Was My Valley*; Lillian Hellman, *The Little Foxes*; and John Huston, *The Maltese Falcon*

Sidney Buchman and Seton I. Miller won for *Here Comes Mr. Jordan*. The idea is truly original; the execution surely could have used the kind of snap that the Epstein brothers or Billy Wilder could have lent it. If *Here Comes Mr. Jordan* has a fault, it's the dialogue. Robert Montgomery's character speaks in very limited ways, and yes, that does befit a boxer – but Muhammad Ali was a boxer too, and his dialogue sparkled. Sidney Buchman never really did much of value after this, becoming a producer, and ending his career writing *Billy Jack Goes to Washington*; Seton I. Miller's life is very similar, heading down into less and less interesting films. Perhaps they should have learned that words should float like a butterfly and sting like a bee. Neither nomination nor award should have been given for this slight script.

Charles Brackett and Billy Wilder wrote *Hold Back the Dawn*, which begins in Hollywood. Charles Boyer needs money, so he offers to sell his story to a Hollywood director he met once in France (played by the director of *Hold Back the Dawn*, Mitchell Leisen). As Boyer tells his story, we head back into the past. I suspect Wilder decided to work in some commentary about the restricted quota system used to control immigration to the United States. We allowed almost no admittance from anywhere other than Mexico and northwestern Europe from the Twenties through the Forties, which is one of the reasons the Holocaust claimed more victims than it might have. Wilder himself had been forced to leave the United States and apply for re-entry; he later lost his mother and step-father to Auschwitz. A darkly comic moment comes when Boyer manages to get a room when a German hangs himself (a suggestive jab at the Nazis, perhaps?). That Wilder and Brackett can go from that dark humor to Boyer's deeply romantic and rapid seduction of Olivia de Havilland is a sign of their range as writers.[92] Some of the dialogue is incisive and biting, as when Paulette Goddard explains why she divorced a jockey: "A woman wants a man, not a radiator cap." The movie turns on a ridiculous accident, which almost led me to denying the nomination was a good one. Wilder wasn't happy with the movie. Infamously, Boyer's refusal to play a scene with a cockroach which Wil-

---

[92] Wilder was a liberal; Brackett was a Republican. They were very different personalities whose fighting produced excellence. Miklós Rózsa said of them, "The volatile Wilder was all jokes and wit and wouldn't sit still for a moment. They were like solid iron and quicksilver." Qtd. in Ed Sikov's biography of Billy Wilder, *On Sunset Boulevard*, p. 189.

der and Brackett thought essential, and Leisen's refusal to stick to the script, drove Wilder into directing in order to protect his scripts. Despite the false turn and this buggy omission, Brackett and Wilder deserved the nomination here for *Hold Back the Dawn*.

Philip Dunne's screenplay for *How Green Was My Valley* admirably condenses the original novel by Richard Llewellyn, but as the film moves past the emotional denials of Maureen O'Hara and Walter Pidgeon, and past the boy's recovery, the screenplay turns episodic to a small but noticeable degree. Throughout, however, the sense of poetry is maintained in the dialogue, especially in some of the narrative passages, including the famous "There is no fence nor hedge around time that is gone. You can go back and have what you like of it, if you can remember." Dunne should be congratulated for the use he made of Llewellyn's original sentences, which he drew together for much of that famous voiceover from the film, and for preserving Llewellyn's voice and intent. What else are adaptors intended to do? Granted, Dunne left out the labor strike from the book, but that was done at Darryl F. Zanuck's insistence. Dunne would go on to adapt other works, including a number of biblical epics; he never reached greater artistic heights than he did with *How Green Was My Valley*. He deserved this nomination.

Lillian Hellman adapted her own Broadway play, *The Little Foxes*, for William Wyler. For the most part, she provided a faithful rendition, and one that still plays well today. One of the finest speeches comes from the dying husband: "There must be better ways of getting rich than building sweatshops and pounding the bones of the town to make dividends for you to spend. You'll wreck the town, you and your brothers. You'll wreck the country, you and your kind, if they let you. But not me, I'll die my own way, and I'll do it without making the world worse. I leave that to you." Hellman deserved a nomination for keeping her deprecatory vision of those in power intact.

John Huston began as a screenwriter, and his success led him to both writing and directing *The Maltese Falcon*. Ironically, the version Huston ended up filming was a transcription of the novel, almost word for word, which his secretary had prepared. Huston did cut some odd corners out of Hammett's book, including Casper Gutman's daughter and a long reminiscence by Sam Spade about a man named Flitcraft, who almost dies in an accident, abandons his life, and then ends up recreating the exact same life somewhere else. The Breen Office also forced Huston to give up the seduction scene; to a significant degree, the demonic quality of Bogart's Sam Spade is implied, rather than foregrounded, as it is in the original book. Huston also changed the end of the novel, adding the line about "the stuff that dreams are made of" –

which is the one everybody remembers. But overall, few adaptations have ever been so faithful, while still maintaining the integrity of a film's narrative drive, which is quite different from a novel. I wish I knew the name of the secretary; she should receive credit for this excellent adaptation, along with Huston.

But the Academy completely ignored the best adapted screenplay of the year: Preston Sturges' script for *The Lady Eve*, loosely using Monckton Hoffe's story as its basis. Sturges has so much fun playing with allusions to the Garden of Eden: the title; the snake (Fonda is reading a book entitled, *Are Snakes Necessary*?); the jungle; the sexual innuendos; Fonda's innocence; "Eve" tripping him; and finally, the fall from "grace" (love) when he learns of her past. When Barbara Stanwyck (Eve) turns against Fonda, and returns as the British lady, the subterfuge is as ridiculously transparent as any in Shakespeare. The whole idea of the movie is to undercut sexual and romantic mores; the first half of the film is all infatuation and enchantment; the second half turns to sexual hypocrisy, destroying the very idea of romantic love. Watch the engagement scene with the horse to see what I mean. The ending finds Stanwyck returning to the first half's emotional terms; having wrung her revenge, she remembers the love she originally had for Fonda, and restores that relationship. Sturges seems to be suggesting that after we've accepted our shortcomings, love becomes, once again, the best game in town – once adults are playing it, with honesty. *The Lady Eve* isn't the kind of film that evokes much loud laughter; the tone is more of an insider's grin. Sturges should have been grinning with the Oscar, because he deserved it so highly. How the Academy could have ignored *The Lady Eve* can only be blamed on Satan.

Best Cinematography (Black & White): Arthur C. Miller won for *How Green Was My Valley*, over Karl Freund, *The Chocolate Soldier*; Gregg Toland, *Citizen Kane*; Joseph Ruttenberg, *Dr. Jekyll and Mr. Hyde*; Joseph Walker, *Here Comes Mr. Jordan*; Leo Tover, *Hold Back the Dawn*; Sol Polito, *Sergeant York*; Charles Lang, *Sundown*; Edward Cronjager, *Sun Valley Serenade*; and Rudolph Maté, *That Hamilton Woman*

Arthur C. Miller won for *How Green Was My Valley* with his simple and poetic cinematography, which served John Ford's artistic vision elegantly. Watch the scene in the parlor when Bronwen comes to visit, and look at the shadows upon the ceiling and wall, framing the mother and the prospective bride, while the boy Huw looks on. When Walter Pidgeon takes Roddy McDowall up the hill to the daffodils, to where he will walk once more, the framing is achingly beautiful. The most famous scene in the movie comes after Maureen O'Hara is married, and her veil is blown up and out repeatedly, filling the screen with that pristine whiteness. Miller and Ford planned every step of O'Hara's way, with hidden fans blowing the veil where they wanted it to go. Miller did a fine job on this film – but the greatest genius of American cinematography turned in his finest work in the same year, so Miller shouldn't keep the Academy Award.

Karl Freund shot *The Chocolate Soldier*. Freund was a master cameraman, but when you have to shoot Nelson Eddy, you have your work cut out for you. Granted, Freund also got to have Risë Stevens, one of the century's greatest opera singers, for this musical version of George Bernard Shaw's *Arms and the Man* mixed with *The Guardsman* (which had been made with Lunt and Fontaine). Freund lavishes most of his ability on Stevens, creating bright musical numbers, as well as moody close-ups, but even Eddy comes off better than he has before. A decent nomination.

We should approach this next nomination with something of hushed awe – and if that gives my selection away, so much the better.[93] Feel free to genuflect, for we are in the presence of one of the handful of achievements in cinematography that will last into the centuries: Gregg Toland's finest achievement, his camerawork on *Citizen Kane*. How Gregg Toland failed to win the Oscar for cinematography can only be chalked up to the hostility towards Welles, from the fear of what William Randolph Hearst might do to Hollywood. Every single frame of *Citizen Kane* bears the mark of the greatest cinematographer studio Hollywood ever employed; if there is a reason to watch this film over and over, Toland's camerawork is it. The acting is often hammy; the story, once unlocked, loses some of its wonder. But Toland's cinematography simply continues to marvel, as does Rembrandt's obsession with the effects of light and shadow. Toland's extensive use of deep focus, unusual camera angles, dissolves and fades, and groundbreaking use of darkness and shadows serve to highlight the narrative. He should have won the Oscar – particularly when we consider his work on *The Little Foxes* this year, which the Academy ignored as well. Some beautiful shots to keep an eye out for during *The Little Foxes* would include: the mirroring of the carriage in the brass plaque on the building; the magnificent shot of Herbert Marshall's face collapsing into pain while we can see Davis over his shoulder, fully in focus, and trying to cope with the restrictions he's laid upon her; Davis and her brothers in the foreground, where she lays down the law – and framing her daughter com-

---

[93] I don't seem to be able to restrain myself to the end of the categories this year; I don't usually let my kids open Christmas presents early...

ing down the stairs; and the final shot of the young lovers leaving in the rain framed by the balcony and the weeping willow. Gregg Toland died young, at the age of 44, from coronary thrombosis. Had he lived, who knows what might have resulted, especially if he had ever turned his eye to color (more than just his unexpected credit for Disney's *Song of the South*). Toland's mastery of the extremely difficult technique of deep focus (wherein all objects in the frame remain sharply focused) lends *Citizen Kane* much of its terrible beauty. Toland most definitely deserved the Oscar for Best Cinematography (Black & White).

As for those he so utterly outclassed, some deserve mentioning, and some deserve obituaries for the artistic death they suffer after watching Toland's work.

Joseph Ruttenberg received a nomination for filming Spencer Tracy, who never wanted to make *Dr. Jekyll and Mr. Hyde*; hiding behind makeup ran directly opposite to the instincts and abilities of this actor's actor. Tracy gives in to tendencies of overacting (which he rarely did), with his eyes going too wide and his voice becoming too strident – and that's as Jekyll. I'm not sure one can overact as Hyde, but Tracy evinces little of the menace necessary as Hyde. I am fairly sure that asking the Swedish Ingrid Bergman to use a cockney accent falls into the category of "not a good idea" (thankfully, she drops it much of the time, and she does project an intense sexuality as the bad girl Ivy). In some ways the most lavish of the different adaptations of the Robert Louis Stevenson story, this particular *Dr. Jekyll and Mr. Hyde* takes advantage of MGM's resources to such a high degree that the story gains too much gloss and polish. They could have used some of the low-down dirty feel of Warner Brothers, although Tracy and Ingrid Bergman try to bring out the sadism of Mr. Hyde. Ruttenberg's cinematography may simply be too pretty as well, since the story needs to wallow in the dark side. As is so often true of MGM films, the movie is damaged by the studio insistence that everything be beautiful all the time. MGM never should have delved into horror films; the results were almost always mixed at best. On the other hand, the transformation scene is done in a series of extreme close-ups, quick cuts, and surreal images; this segment doesn't look like the rest of the film at all. As Tracy whips two horses, they turn into a naked Ingrid Bergman and Lana Turner (who plays Tracy's good girl fiancée). The nomination can stay, for that scene, and for some of the atmospheric shots of the final chase, but somebody should have taught Victor Fleming and MGM how to make a real horror film. Can you imagine what James Whale, for instance, would have done?[94]

Joseph Walker handled *Here Comes Mr. Jordan*, which opens with a beautiful shot of a lake, in a forest, with cows drinking, and fulfilling every dream a city boy might have ever had of the countryside – and then we cut to a boxing match. Walker's photography fully supports the writers' ironic shift. As we pass into what is meant for heaven, Walker provides first a long shot, then a medium shot, then a mobile camera backing up as the characters come into view, all so that we can get accustomed to the idea of being in the afterlife. Other than that, the camerawork is mostly mundane and not worth a nomination – so this one should go away.

Leo Tover's work on *Hold Back the Dawn* benefits from the quick editing of Doane Harrison (I don't usually comment about the editing, but the movie's pace seems unusually fast in its cuts, and economical). Tover uses a wide variety of camera setups, and lighting schemes. Look at how Veronica Lake glows in her brief cameo, as opposed to the harder lighting for Boyer. Director Mitchell Leisen's films rarely have this kind of artistic tone to them, so I have to credit Tover with much of this improvement. Notice the regular use of foreground objects to frame and direct the viewer's attention on the main action, which is not something Leisen generally does. In the Mexican bar, while Paulette Goddard ogles Charles Boyer, Tover produces a great shot of Boyer in the mirror behind the bar, which reveals the general raucous party going on behind Boyer. When Boyer begins to put the moves on de Havilland, Tover lights their eyes up to signify their spark. Later, when Boyer and de Havilland are about to spend their wedding night in the back of the station wagon in the midst of a small Mexican town, Tover sets up Boyer's view of her in the rear view mirror: I am fairly convinced de Havilland was never more beautiful. I don't think American cinema ever showed a woman reclining quite like this before. While I'm sure the idea came from writers Billy Wilder and Charles Brackett, Tover delivers the goods with the aid of de Havilland – and for that shot alone, he should keep the nomination (although the whole movie merits the nod).

For *Sergeant York*, Sol Polito gives us some beautiful outdoor work, with shadows framing the moonlighted characters. At times, the backdrops for the studio shots needed far better lighting to make them ap-

---

[94] Whale's movie career was by and large over by this point, the victim of a variety of circumstances. See James Curtis' excellent biography, *James Whale: A New World of Gods and Monsters* for more. While you're at it, Curtis' biographies of W.C. Fields and Spencer Tracy simply could not be better.

pear as anything other than artificial; after the use of so many excellent locations, to not create the impression that what was done inside at least match somewhat is disconcerting. Director Howard Hawks was rarely interested in artistic shots; he just liked to use whatever would keep the story moving ahead, and would reveal the characters at their greatest impact. Orson Welles once told Peter Bogdanovich that "Hawks is great prose; Ford is poetry."[ccii] Polito helps Hawks keep the story moving along, by keeping the visuals lean and no-nonsense. Polito deserved this nomination (as he did so many others).

Charles Lang took us through *Sundown*, which stars Gene Tierney as a fifth columnist helping the Allies fight the Germans in Africa. An adventure film, *Sundown* works some of the same territory as other colonial pictures, along with a flavor of Marlene Dietrich and *Trader Horn* (Harry Carey even shows up playing a clone white hunter from that awful film). Unexpectedly, *Sundown* also promotes the concept of telepathic premonitions. The film has a social agenda, to protest the kind of discrimination endemic to colonialism; in that, *Sundown* is considerably ahead of the times. The ending speech almost cripples the movie with portentousness. As for the photography, Lang has a habit of moving to soft focus and elaborate lighting every time we get a shot of Gene Tierney's face and belly button; after a while, the tactic starts to annoy, as if we had taken off our glasses repeatedly. He does photograph the brilliant skies of the desert well, as if John Ford had snuck over to direct here and there. The nighttime murder attempt is done with tracer bullets, which create a stunning effect. A good nomination, for a film that deserves to be known better.

Edward Cronjager shot *Sun Valley Serenade* – lightweight fluff, but filmed crisply. The primary reason for this nomination remains the innovative work on the musical numbers, including shadows cast behind the musicians, shots that place us almost inside Glenn Miller's trombone, and the great images of the Nicholas Brothers. The outdoor scenes of snow and skiing and skating also sparkle. A good nomination, especially for big band buffs.

Rudolph Maté did some of his usual fine work on *That Hamilton Woman*. Detailing the life and affairs of Lord Nelson and his lover, Lady Hamilton, *That Hamilton Woman* finally gave Laurence Olivier and Vivien Leigh the chance to act together in a big romantic film, after they were kept from doing *Wuthering Heights*, *Pride and Prejudice* and several other projects together. Leigh and Olivier do their best to pump life into this sometimes stiff historical romance. The Napoleonic wars, with England standing alone against a worldwide threat, are obviously intended to resonate with the world situation at the start of WWII – Napoleon and Hitler, together again, for the first time. Reminding the English of their greatest victory against tyranny in the time of their struggle against Hitler was good for morale (and it couldn't hurt to remind the Americans of British indomitability). Maté provides a beautiful sheen to Vivien Leigh and the rest of the cast, filling the set full of soft light and gentle shadows. The camera keeps the action going, moving quite ably. Leigh looks nearly as beautiful in black and white as she does in the colors of *Gone with the Wind*. Repeatedly, Maté proves his excellence as a cinematographer, and the worth of this nomination.

As for cinematography the Academy ignored, perhaps the most interesting is *All That Money Can Buy* (aka *The Devil and Daniel Webster*), with camerawork by Joseph August. August does excellent work, as the use of shadow and light is quite artistic. The scenes where the farmer sells his soul to the devil are done beautifully: Walter Huston strides out of the seeming smokes of hell into the barn. Clearly, the influence of *Citizen Kane* is extensive here, in the innovative angles and narrative tactics, but also in the use of chiaroscuro (darkness to hide characters and light to reveal them). The trial scene alone is an exercise in unusual lighting and tone. A highly unusual movie, and not one that should be missed – and one that deserved a nomination.

In case you missed it, Gregg Toland should have won the Oscar for Best Cinematography (Black & White). You know, you really should be paying more attention. There will be a quiz later.

Best Dramatic Score: Bernard Herrmann won for *All That Money Can Buy*, and was also nominated for *Citizen Kane*, over Frank Skinner, *Back Street*; Alfred Newman for both *Ball of Fire* and *How Green Was My Valley*; Edward Ward, *Cheers for Miss Bishop*; Franz Waxman for both *Dr. Jekyll and Mr. Hyde* and *Suspicion*; Victor Young, *Hold Back the Dawn*; Edward Kay, *King of the Zombies*; Morris Stoloff and Ernst Toch, *Ladies in Retirement*; Meredith Willson, *The Little Foxes*; Miklós Rózsa, getting two nominations for *Lydia* and *Sundown*; Cy Feuer and Walter Scharf, *Mercy Island*; Max Steiner, *Sergeant York*; Louis Gruenberg, *So Ends Our Night*; Edward Ward, *Tanks a Million*; Werner Heymann, *That Uncertain Feeling*; and Richard Hageman, *This Woman Is Mine*

Bernard Herrmann won for his score for *All That Money Can Buy* (better known today as *The Devil and Daniel Webster*). Or, as I like to call it, the "damn that new kid Herrmann can compose, but we don't want to give it to him for *Citizen Kane*" award. Herrmann's score for *The Devil and Daniel Webster* is first-rate stuff – a kind of crazed square dance music alternates with low threatening rumbles, dizzying shifts in emotional qualities, and comic commentary on the events –

but not the revolutionary work that *Citizen Kane* is, with Herrmann's very first film score. *Citizen Kane* begins with the sign "No Trespassing" and a fence that never seems to end – matched by the ominous sounds of Bernard Hermann's score, all low strings and deep brass, etching itself into our minds as a wall all its own, forbidding us from entering (even while both sign and sound essentially kick into that basic human instinct, the curious drive to go where we're not supposed to be). When the newsreel begins, the music mimics the typical loud, brassy, self-important sound. When the narrative returns to the earliest known days of Kane's childhood, the romantic, wistful longing of the music matches the snow globe of the beginning, and the joys of childhood play – which the movie casts as what has been lost in exchange for all that money and power. After the portentousness of the Thatcher episode, Hermann's final explosion of what I can only describe as brass farts form the perfect raspberry to the pretensions of the rich which the movie skewers. At the newspaper office, with the dancing girls, a vaudeville singer belts out a song celebrating Charles Foster Kane; Hermann later works the same song into the campaign for governor. In addition, he wrote all the opera segments, which reveals yet another aspect of his immense talent. Herrmann should have won the Oscar for Best Dramatic Score for *Citizen Kane*, not *The Devil and Daniel Webster*.

Back Street stars Charles Boyer and Margaret Sullavan as a couple in love – even though he's married, and she sacrifices everything for him (the original novel is by Fannie Hurst, who wrote *Imitation of Life*, which ought to be enough to warn you things aren't going to end well). The movie is a tear-jerking melodrama that had to get the topic of adultery past the Breen Office by showing how miserable Boyer and Sullavan become because of their illicit affair. I found myself wanting to gag at Sullavan's willingness to give up everything for the man she loves. A little thing called "self-respect" kept intruding on my attention. Frank Skinner's score proclaims itself as classy by quoting classical piano and then diving headlong into syrupy violins. It never really does anything else but help milk the tear ducts. No nomination was deserved, but Skinner went on to score *Abbott and Costello Meet Frankenstein* and *Harvey*, so we'll forgive him for this one (hey, can I help it if I loved those movies as a child?).

Given that the musical moments we remember from *Ball of Fire* are the two Gene Krupa numbers and the conga number with the professors, we might be forgiven when we realize Alfred Newman provided the score. For the swing-tinged *Ball of Fire,* Newman has introduced the saxophone and other swinging brass into his scores, layering them over the strings in a bouncy syrup. Newman rarely turned in any score that wasn't Oscar worthy; *Ball of Fire* is no exception. But placed next to Gene Krupa's drums and "Drum Boogie," we tend to forget the quieter music behind it. Newman still deserved the nomination, although I would love to have heard what Krupa could have done if he were ever given a chance to score an entire film. I suspect we'd all be dizzy and on fire afterwards.

Alfred Newman was also nominated for *How Green Was My Valley*, crafting a score modeled on the use of folk songs in *Stagecoach*, in that a number of traditional Welsh hymns and songs string together to reinforce the actions and feelings of the story (one of the best of which is "Arglwydd, Arwain Trwy'r Anialwch" / "Lord, Lead Me Through the Wilderness," commonly known in English as "Guide Me, O Thou Great Jehovah.")[cciii] Where Newman's own work begins to fall into place is in the quiet moments, especially between Walter Pidgeon and Maureen O'Hara, as Newman's sweet, plaintive strings begin to underline the lovers as they break apart, and the sadness inherent in their refusal to complete their attraction with a life together. The score swells at the last few moments, building to a crescendo of trumpets and the triumph of memory – and cementing the nomination in place for Newman.

In *Cheers for Miss Bishop*, Martha Scott (*Our Town*) plays out a feminine version of *Goodbye, Mr. Chips* to very little effect (despite work on the adaptation by Stephen Vincent Benét). Edward Ward's score, appearing only occasionally, doesn't do much more, other than occasionally mark a change of scene or tempo, and generally in the most obvious way possible. Once in a while he does touch a note of lyricism, but he never develops a consistent melodic line – or any justification for a nomination.

In *Dr. Jekyll and Mr. Hyde*, Waxman seems to be recycling some of the music from his brilliant score for *Bride of Frankenstein*, even if only in the stylistic gambits he ran to increase the tension and suspense. During the transformation scene, he provides music every bit as strange and wild as the images. Other than that, only occasional flashes appear to underscore the overacting, but the music shows Waxman's usual talent. The nomination should stay, if somewhat grudgingly.

Waxman was also nominated for *Suspicion*, in which he "moves from very broad sweeping melodies and very romantic, operatic kinds of gestures to steadily more contained, repetitive, claustrophobic kinds of formulations."[cciv] The score is quite effective in reinforcing the emotional states Joan Fontaine has to project. At times, however, Waxman can be a little obvious, as in the scene where Fontaine is pining for Cary Grant, and a telegram finally comes. As she opens it, the violin goes very low and insistent, thump-thump-thumping its way along like a heart in tremendous anxiety; when Fontaine finds out Grant is coming, the music swells romantically. Effective, yes, but clichéd today (of course, the tactic may be clichéd precisely because Waxman made it so popular). Waxman also uses a waltz by Johann Strauss as a leitmotif for the lovers, turning it into something creepy when Grant whistles it. An excellent nomination for Waxman.

Victor Young's music over the opening credits for *Hold Back the Dawn* announces that we are about to enter into a romantic melodrama, with a big, lush, romantic embrace. Young has rarely been this overt, but he may have decided the material required it as an introduction. However, once the movie starts, we get almost no music until we enter into the bar in Mexico, and we are awash in the sounds of south of the border (including the usual bullfight themes, and a saint's day festival with church music, and the fiesta afterwards). We don't return to the opening themes until the very end, and then incompletely. He should keep the nomination por la musica.

One of the most bizarre nominations ever in this category, *King of the Zombies* was meant to star Bela Lugosi, but he avoided this schlock for once. The place responsible for this truly bad film, Monogram Studios, was even smaller than Republic, and rarely produced anything of lasting value. *King of the Zombies* is not one of those rare finds; a German-speaking scientist in the Caribbean seems to be raising zombies for fun and profit. He gets stopped. There: I've saved you from a fate worse than death; now you don't have to watch the movie. Minor caveat: bug-eyed Manton Moreland has a small but rabid following who find him amusing. I am not one of them. Let's not even talk about the music. Edward Kay scored himself five Oscar nominations for his Z-grade work, under the ridiculous one nomination per studio rule. No nomination here for Kay and his big, bad voodoo drums and trumpeted cries, which I don't think makes up more than ten minutes all told of the running time.

The score for *Ladies in Retirement* by Morris Stoloff and Ernst Toch helps maintain the suspense fairly well – when the score shows up. Vast stretches of the film have no music at all. In one way, that increases the tension, because until the film turns dark, we are in silence; the violins then begin to moan and suggest the dark turn the story is about to take into murder. The score then becomes intermittent, except in moments of conflict. The music is rather obvious when it does show up, but effective nonetheless. The nomination should stay – barely.

For such a dark film as *The Little Foxes*, the opening of the score is setting all the wrong tone, with its moonlight and magnolias chorus trying to make us nostalgic for what is to come. Perhaps composer Meredith Willson meant it ironically, but I suspect he just felt a movie set in the Deep South around 1900 needed some of that spiritual flavor. I actually think one of the problems with this movie is the score, which seems to not quite match the sinister tones Wyler keeps weaving into the images of bourgeois life. Willson doesn't seem to have the same level of ambiguity Wyler does, and that hurts the overall effect of the film. One of the interesting aspects of his score is the use of one long, low stringed instrument being played during Herbert Marshall's death scenes. That helped me overcome my feeling that the score isn't quite up to the level of the rest of the film, so the nomination should remain.

Miklós Rózsa scored *Lydia*, which gives us Merle Oberon as an old woman trying to relive her past by contacting four men who proposed marriage to her. A lavish production from Oberon's husband Alexander Korda, *Lydia* also has a script by Ben Hecht and the last appearance of Edna May Oliver. The movie, however, tends to be a crashing bore, and that thud is mostly due to Merle Oberon, who has been vastly overrated as a star. Rózsa's score was the film's only nod from the Academy, and that due to the one score per studio automatic entry. Rózsa still hasn't found his own distinctive voice, and seems to be content recycling other people's ideas, including waltzes. A largely forgettable score, which should not be worth a nomination.

Rózsa's other nod, *Sundown*, opens with the worst sort of African pastiche, and it never really ascends from there. Miklós Rózsa works every musical cliché from every Tarzan and desert movie ever made, and with little originality. Again no nomination should have been given.

Mercy Island is another Republic low-budget thriller, this one involving a doctor hiding from justice, a crazed husband, and a giant alligator, although this one has a decent score by Cy Feuer and Walter Scharf that supports the action. The nomination should stay.

Max Steiner always provided a variety of music for his scores, and *Sergeant York* is no exception. What pleases about this score is the quiet restraint he brings to scenes for which a producer like Selznick would have encouraged Steiner to go overboard. The instrumentation is simple, but effective – a few strings for the most part, with some occasional brass for power surges, or a little angelic choir to inspire faith. Steiner is not above pushing patriotic buttons by playing "The Star-Spangled Banner" and "My Country 'Tis of Thee" behind the major's attempt to convert York from his pacifism, but Steiner does it very quietly. On the other hand, "Yankee Doodle Dandy" is worked for all that it can be in the first attack scenes. Steiner helps keep the pace and attraction of this movie at a high level; he should keep the nomination.

Louis Gruenberg scored *So Ends Our Night*, which stars Margaret Sullavan, Fredric March, Glenn Ford, and Erich von Stroheim. March and Ford have escaped from a concentration camp. *So Ends Our Night* was an attempt to make Americans aware of the horrors of the Nazis, in those days before our entry into WWII. The movie is quite effective at certain moments, particularly when Fredric March trails behind his wife saying goodbye to her while she can't turn around, as she is being watched. At other times, as with the voiceovers, the movie is too earnest and obvious. The movie looks like a bad live performance from Fifties television, even though it's been restored for DVD; the camera chooses very odd angles, and the actors tend to overact regularly. The score is functional, if uninspired (much of it sounds like a typical movie serial: overblown, frenetic, suspenseful). Drums beating in the background to organ doodling worthy of a Z-grade horror film do not an Oscar caliber score make. The movie should be seen once as an example of the kind of warning a few films were trying to make about the Nazis before we officially entered the war, but the score is not worth a nomination.

Tanks a Million is one of Hal Roach's short features, this one starring William Tracy and James Gleason in the first of a series about a soldier with a photographic memory. Edward Ward's score takes some military tones and stridently pours them into our ears now and then, when the mood takes him. No nomination should have been given for something this minor.

Ernst Lubitsch directed Burgess Meredith, Merle Oberon and Melvyn Douglas in *That Uncertain Feeling*, a tale of hiccups, psychiatrists, and a marriage on the rocks. Werner Heymann's score is all very romantic, and somehow Viennese in the waltz-like tones Heymann enjoys. Long stretches of the film have no score at all. Lubitsch is still playing with the forbidden, and nudging against the Production Code whenever possible; here, it's an unhappy marriage and potential adultery. Sometimes the movie works, sometimes it doesn't. The score does pop a bit comically now and then – enough to keep the nomination.

Franchot Tone and Walter Brennan star in *This Woman Is Mine*; the woman is the now forgotten Carol Bruce, who stows aboard a ship in the mid-nineteenth century. A typical staid romance about two men in the love with the same woman, *This Woman Is Mine* features a score too good for the poor story, by Richard Hageman (*Stagecoach*), although that's not saying much for this piece of slop. No nomination need apply.

Other films should have been nominated as well.

How could they have omitted *The Maltese Falcon*?! Adolph Deutsch provides a tremendous score with a wonderful sense of humor, using brass overlays, with an underpinning of strings, and a flute-harp-xylophone overlay that is truly unique, along with some thrumming brass when needed. One nice touch: when Peter Lorre's character is introduced, a kind of vaguely Turkish strain of music enters the picture, suggesting the Orient. I suspect the Academy hid the nomination, like the black bird. Where is Sam Spade when you need him?

Finally, Erich Wolfgang Korngold put in a unique score for *The Sea Wolf*, which his biographer calls a "sinister, brooding score, quite unlike anything he had done before, reflecting the cruel personality of Larsen. Apart from an exquisite love theme of bare rising fourths scored unusually but appropriately for harmonica, the music is unrelenting in its harshness and is spiced with brutish, dissonant harmonies. Korngold was much more sparing in his use of music in the film, and this is one of his shortest scores."[ccv] Who am I to argue? Let Korngold have another nomination he should have received in the first place.

Do you remember who should have won this year? If you do, fifty points! If you don't, you need to stay after school and clean the chalkboards.

Best Song: Jerome Kern and Oscar Hammerstein II's "The Last Time I Saw Paris" won from *Lady Be Good*, over Lloyd B. Norlin's "Out of the Silence" from *All-American Co-Ed*; Harold Arlen and Johnny Mercer's "Blues in the Night" from *Blues in the Night*; Hugh Prince and Ron Rave's "Boogie Woogie Bugle Boy of Company B" from *Buck Privates*; Frank Churchill and Ned Washington's "Baby Mine" from *Dumbo*; Louis Alter and Frank Loesser's "Dolores" from *Las Vegas Nights*; Gene Autry and Fred Ross's "Be Honest with Me" from *Ridin' on a Rainbow*; Harry Warren and Mack Gordon's "Chattanooga Choo Choo" from *Sun Valley Serenade*; and Cole Porter's "Since I Kissed My Baby Goodbye" from *You'll Never Get Rich*

The biggest protest over the Oscars this year came over giving Jerome Kern and Oscar Hammerstein II the Academy Award for a song that had been publicly performed in 1940, and therefore, was clearly not written for *Lady Be Good*. I suspect that situation has been true more often than the Academy has admitted, but in this case, almost nothing from that movie was original ("You'll Never Know" – not the famous one – and "Your Words and My Music" by Nacio Herb Brown and Arthur Freed being the exceptions). *Lady Be Good* stars the tapping feet of Eleanor Powell, the geniality of Robert Young and Ann Sothern, and the clowning of Red Skelton – and more importantly, the music of the Gershwins, Kern and Hammerstein. "The Last Time I Saw Paris" is an act of mourning for the loss of Paris to the Nazi invasion, and probably explains the Oscar more than anything. The song is an excellent one, however, and deserves its nomination, even though it wasn't written for the film. I would argue the fact that it hadn't been used in another film or play by that point should allow it to squeak by; after all, how many unused songs do composers keep in their trunks, then pull them out when needed?

In *All-American Co-Ed*, Frances Langford stars as a young college girl; the boy who falls in love with her is disguised in drag as another student. "Out of the Silence" is a forgettable tune sold big by Langford, with little melody and lyrics that are interchangeable with dozens of other love songs. No nomination was merited for songwriter Lloyd B. Norlin.

"Blues in the Night," by the profoundly gifted Harold Arlen and Johnny Mercer, gave the title to the Priscilla Lane musical, *Blues in the Night*. Thankfully, we don't have to listen to Lane singing the tune (as Gary Giddins pithily said, she "couldn't swing from a trapeze").[ccvi] Instead, we get William Gillespie singing it in jail (Gillespie also plays Porgy in the biopic *Rhapsody in Blue*). Other than the brilliance of the title song, we get a one-shot scene of Jimmy Lunceford's band (who need to be as well known as Count Basie and Duke Ellington, since they swung as hard as any band ever did). The movie itself is a dark story of gangsters and booze, which probably fit with Hollywood's idea of the blues (and they aren't far wrong). *Blues in the Night* is worth seeing, although awkwardly paced at times, due to being conflicted between the happy go lucky scenes and the melodrama. The title song is an excellent nomination.

Hugh Prince and Ron Rave produced one of the most memorable WWII songs in "Boogie Woogie Bugle Boy of Company B." I've loved this song since the first time I saw the Andrews Sisters sing it in *Buck Privates*, starring Abbott and Costello. Infectiously fun, "Bugle Boy" still gets the toes tapping after all this years. The nomination should most definitely stay.

"Baby Mine," from *Dumbo*, is a paean to motherly love, and rarely leaves a dry eye in the house. The animation gently shows a series of animal moms and their babies. On an Eighties collection revisioning of Disney music, *Stay Awake*, Bonnie Raitt delivers a killer version of this song. Whenever a song can be recorded by different artists in artistically rich ways, that song begins to gain traction in the race for permanence. "Baby Mine" is the emotional center of *Dumbo*, and an excellent nomination. "Pink Elephants" should also have been nominated as the most experimental and adventurous piece of music – and animation – ever released by the Disney Studio.

Louis Alter and Frank Loesser penned "Dolores," from *Las Vegas Nights*. "Dolores" is sung by the vaudevillian Bert Wheeler, but became a bigger hit when Tommy Dorsey recorded it with his regular singer, Frank Sinatra. *Las Vegas Nights* is yet another story about trying to make it big in show business, and stars Constance Moore and Bert Wheeler. Tommy Dorsey appears, with a flash of Sinatra. The song isn't bad in Sinatra's handling, but forgettable otherwise – now, if they'd only forgotten to give this song a nomination…

Gene Autry and Fred Ross gave us "Be Honest with Me," from *Ridin' on a Rainbow*. I have a great fondness for Autry, growing up as I did with his Christmas album, and as an Angels fan in the Seventies when he owned the team. I had no idea he had scored an Oscar nomination – a big upgrade for a singing cowboy from B-westerns! His song with Fred Ross, "Be Honest with Me," comes in *Ridin' on a Rainbow*, which has Autry going undercover on a showboat to recover his friends' stolen cattle money. "Be Honest with Me" has a touch of cowboy swing, and the blues that lie at the heart of the best country and western music. Autry puts it across well, and the nomination should stay.

"Chattanooga Choo Choo" is by Harry Warren and Mack Gordon. Glenn Miller and his band play it in *Sun Valley Serenade*, a celebration of swing, skating and skiing starring Sonja Henie, John Payne, and Milton Berle. The Nicholas Brothers show up in the middle of the song and join in with their acrobatics. A huge hit for Glenn Miller,[95] "Chattanooga Choo Choo" is one of the hallmark songs in the orchestra's repertoire, and perhaps the most iconic song of the swing era, although not one that inspires any deep response. We just love tapping our toes to it – and that's more than enough for a solid nomination.

Cole Porter gave us "Since I Kissed My Baby Goodbye," in *You'll Never Get Rich*. Fred Astaire dances with Rita Hayworth, and sings to her. Need I say more? A small handful of composers wrote both music and lyrics; of them, the choice for the best always comes down to either Irving Berlin or Cole Porter. Both men preferred Fred Astaire to introduce their songs, since Astaire sang like he danced, with impeccable rhythm and a respect for the music. As Gary Marmorstein so aptly reminds us about Astaire in *Hollywood Rhapsody*, "Dancing alone or with a partner, the man was his own master. When singing, however, the greatest screen interpreter of popular songs had the inestimable help of our greatest songwriters."[ccvii] "Since I Kissed My Baby Goodbye" finds Astaire accompanied by the black group, The Four Tones, who

---

[95] "Chattanooga Choo-Choo" hit #1 on December 7th, 1941 – and became the first gold record by February, 1942, with 1.2 million in sales.

also starred with Herb Jeffries in some black westerns.[96] Too bad they never got more famous; they're quite good. Oddly enough, Astaire not only doesn't sing the song, he gets out of beat with the performers, all so Hayworth can point it out to him. The Four Tones and Astaire truly go to town with "A-Stairable Rag" later on. While *You'll Never Get Rich* may not be top drawer Cole Porter, like Hemingway and Twain, even second-rate output by these masters is better than first-rate stuff from almost anybody else. The nomination for "Since I Kissed My Baby Goodbye" should stay.

While I do think "The Last Time I Saw Paris" is a classic, "Blues in the Night" has proven to be a more enduring, more widely recorded song, and more deserving of the Oscar for Best Song.[97]

Best Art Direction (Black & White): Richard Day, Nathan Juran, and Thomas Little won for *How Green Was My Valley*, over *Citizen Kane* (Perry Ferguson, Van Nest Polglase, Al Fields and Darrell Silvera); *The Flame of New Orleans* (Martin Obzina, Jack Otterson, and Russell A. Gausman); *Hold Back the Dawn* (Hans Dreier, Robert Usher, and Sam Comer); *Ladies in Retirement* (Lionel Banks and George Montgomery); *The Little Foxes* (Stephen Goosson and Howard Bristol); *Sergeant York* (John Hughes and Fred MacLean); *The Son of Monte Cristo* (John DuCasse Schulze and Edward G. Boyle); *Sundown* (Alexander Golitzen and Richard Irvine); *That Hamilton Woman* (Vincent Korda and Julia Heron); and *When Ladies Meet* (Cedric Gibbons, Randall Duell, and Edwin B. Willis)

Richard Day, Nathan Juran, and Thomas Little won for *How Green Was My Valley*. The Welsh mining town is truly a wonder, built onto the hillside in Malibu Beach, California (on the Twentieth Century-Fox ranch, where many years later, the TV series *M*A*S*H* would also be filmed nearby). Throughout the picture, except for the rare studio rear projection shot, we never lose the feel that we are in a real place. Day, Juran, and Little do fine, quality work, and John Ford and his actors take full advantage of their gift of this place and time seemingly stolen from forty years before. They deserved the nomination – but the Oscar should have gone elsewhere.

Perry Ferguson, Van Nest Polglase, Al Fields and Darrell Silvera helped create the revolution that is *Citizen Kane*. While the sets for *How Green Was My Valley* remain the best realistic achievement of the

---

[96] Jeffries, who also sang with Duke Ellington, was known as the "Bronze Buckaroo."
[97] Looking over the major jazz and pop singers of the Twentieth century, the Arlen-Mercer song shows up roughly three times as often, in my admittedly unscientific count; feel free to do your own count and start an argument online – I'm hoping yours isn't the only one. Controversy encourages books sales, or hadn't you heard?

year, the sets for *Citizen Kane* are really sui generis. From ruined Xanadu to the sad nightclub to the ponderous memorial vault of Thatcher, we are in a set of very odd places indeed. One of the innovations of *Citizen Kane* are the ceilings of many of the sets, which had largely been ignored by movies before. Look at the newspaper office, with its curiously low ceilings and support columns. Perhaps the most famous mise-en-scene in the film comes from the successive series of breakfasts, where the table grows longer, to reflect the distance between the spouses. Another great scene wherein the decoration signals everything is when Welles sits in a chair listening to his future wife and mistress singing, and the scene fades from her shabby place into an elegantly appointed room, showing how she has become Welles' kept woman. Or the scene where the camera moves up and up and up into this cavernous opera house, to show the stagehand holding his nose to indicate how much the second wife stinks as a singer. And the jigsaw puzzles in the endless cavern that is Xanadu, revealing the need to kill time, as well as pointing ironically at the entire plot of the film (I always wonder which crew member had to put all those puzzles together). While the nomination list should stand as is, the credit should really go to Perry Ferguson, who did most of the real work on *Citizen Kane*.[ccviii]

Martin Obzina, Jack Otterson, and Russell A. Gausman lit up *The Flame of New Orleans*, in which Marlene Dietrich meets Bruce Cabot, while French émigré René Clair directs this attempt to be funny and romantic; Dietrich pretends to be two different women (and she is more amusing and less wooden than she had been in the Thirties, except for *Destry Rides Again*). The nomination is for recreating nineteenth century New Orleans, which it does fairly well (I could do without the highlighted black stereotypes). For the sets, both indoor and outdoor, the nomination should stay.

Hans Dreier, Robert Usher, and Sam Comer do an excellent job on *Hold Back the Dawn*. Much of the setting for this movie is a border town in Mexico, recreated in grubbiness and dirt streets and all the paraphernalia an American audience would expect from such a place. We also see backstage on a Hollywood studio, and inside a sound stage, which doesn't require much art direction (turn the camera around!). Dreier and company do a good job, particularly in the Mexican sets, and should keep the nomination.

Lionel Banks and George Montgomery helped with *Ladies in Retirement*, which gives us Ida Lupino as a housekeeper who must care for her crazed sisters (one of them played by Elsa Lanchester). Lupino murders her employer rather than let her sisters go to the insane asylum. Add in a thief, and we've got a nifty little suspenseful picture, although not one with much staying power. Fans of Lupino and Lanchester are today's target audience. As for the sets, we stay mostly in a country home of some means, which seems reasonably well done. The nomination should stay.

Stephen Goosson and Howard Bristol designed *The Little Foxes*, replete with a southern mansion, town, and bank, all nicely done. Star Bette Davis bitched about the sets, for being overly opulent, but then, Davis bitched about many things on this set.[ccix] Goosson and Bristol deserved the nomination.

John Hughes and Fred MacLean give us some of the worst sets of the year for *Sergeant York*; I've already blamed Sol Polito for failing to film them properly, but Hughes and MacLean seem content with some of their sets looking like a college production of the Hatfield-McCoy feud. At other times, the realism is inspiring, as in the plowing scenes, which convey a strong sense of how hard it was to farm a hillside. The battle scenes are dressed fairly well, lending an air of realism to an inherently fairy tale kind of history (who could believe one man would capture so many enemies?). A difficult decision, this mix of good and bad – but we should let it stand, because they never quite tear through the whole cloth of the film.

John DuCasse Schulze and Edward G. Boyle worked on *The Son of Monte Cristo*, starring Louis Hayward, Joan Bennett, and George Sanders. *The Son of Monte Cristo* is a sequel to the more famous *Count of Monte Cristo*. The sets are conspicuously present in this costume swashbuckler, flashy and ornate. The whole thing reminds me more of the Selznick *Prisoner of Zenda* than any other movie. The palace is done up beautifully. The nomination should stay.

Alexander Golitzen and Richard Irvine recreated Africa in the American desert for *Sundown*, and a fairly impressive job they did too. Mostly, we are focused on the colonial government outpost, on the outbuildings set against the desert sky, and a cave complex that would make any movie serial proud to have it. A good job, on what looks like a limited budget, for a good nomination.

Set in the Napoleonic era, *That Hamilton Woman* brings out a variety of settings for Vincent Korda to work on with his detailed, imaginative abilities. Korda does beautiful work reproducing a palace, in ways MGM never quite got right. I always suspect nobody at MGM ever actually went into a palace; one gets the feeling Korda grew up in one. I would have loved a Korda design for an Errol Flynn swashbuckler. Korda and fellow nominee Julia Heron do a fabulous job on *That Hamilton Woman*, and deserve the nomination.

Cedric Gibbons, Randall Duell, and Edwin B. Willis overdid *When Ladies Meet*, in which Joan Crawford plays a novelist in love with a married man, played by Herbert Marshall. Robert Taylor is in love with Joan Crawford, and introduces her to Marshall's wife, Greer Garson, in the hopes of convincing Crawford so she will see how hopeless her love for Marshall is. Confusing, isn't it? The sets seem to occupy that special province called MGM-land, wherein everybody lives in a beautiful, spacious home, decorated perfectly, and never allow anything other than glamour to thrive in their environs. *When Ladies Meet* is a dreadful, endlessly talkative film, wherein all involved are trying way too hard, including the art direction, which should not have been nominated.

In any final summation, no greater art direction exists in this phenomenal year than that of *Citizen Kane*, which should have received the Oscar for Best Art Direction (Black & White). Who knew ceilings could be so important?

Best Art Direction (Color): Cedric Gibbons, Urie McCleary, and Edwin B. Willis won for *Blossoms in the Dust*, over *Blood and Sand* (Richard Day, Joseph C. Wright, and Thomas Little) and *Louisiana Purchase* (Raoul Pene du Bois and Stephen A. Seymour)

Cedric Gibbons, Urie McCleary, and Edwin B. Willis won for *Blossoms in the Dust*: as always, if you make a film in the Victorian era, you are almost guaranteed a nomination in this category. *Blossoms in the Dust* is no exception. We start in turn of the century Wisconsin, in a richly appointed mansion. We then go to Texas, to a richly appointed mansion. Toss in a couple of mills, an office or two, and some children, and you've got yourself a weepy melodrama (the crew on the movie referred to it as *Bugs in the Mud* for all the children running about).[ccx] Gibbons and McCleary never really move beyond the mundane, and certainly show little imagination in these appointments. Even after bankruptcy, Garson and Pidgeon live in a house beyond their apparent means; what was needed here was some of the realism over at Warner Brothers. No Oscar was deserved, but the nomination should stay for the pretty stuff.

Richard Day, Joseph C. Wright, and Thomas Little help make *Blood and Sand* look like Spanish paintings, rather than a real village. The effect, facilitated by the camerawork and director Mamoulian's intent, is far better than the narrative and acting. The sets are inventive, especially Power's home as a child, which looks like a painting rather than a real place (and I mean that in the highest terms of flattery). The chapel looks like an El Greco painting.[ccxi] The bullring is shot live in Mexico, but the preparation rooms behind the scenes are nicely done. Rita Hayworth's spectacular dining hall and rooms in her mansion glow and shimmer as if they were made of solid water. An excellent nomination.

As *Louisiana Purchase* was nominated for color cinematography, so too was it nominated for this category – so few color films were being made, even this made the list. Eye candy is what we get – like the Goldwyn Girls would be in Danny Kaye movies in a few years – along with the typical political settings. No particular pattern emerges, because the story has little depth, existing mostly as an excuse for showgirls and Hope's wisecracks. Raoul Pene du Bois did the art direction; Stephen A. Seymour did the sets. Du Bois never worked on a true classic, but Seymour did *Going My Way, The Miracle of Morgan's Creek, Hail the Conquering Hero,* and *The Uninvited.* The sets are impressive for what they are there for: to look good in color. Du Bois and Seymour deserve the nomination on that count.

Of the three, *Blood and Sand* shows the most creativity and ability, and should have won the Oscar.

Best Special Effects: Farciot Edouart, Gordon Jennings, and Louis Mesenkop won for *I Wanted Wings*, and were also nominated for *Aloma of the South Seas;* they beat *Flight Command* (Arnold Gillespie and Douglas Shearer); *The Invisible Woman* (John P. Fulton and John Hall); *The Sea Wolf* (Byron Haskin and Nathan Levinson); *That Hamilton Woman* (Lawrence Butler and William H. Wilmarth); *Topper Returns* (Roy Seawright and Elmer Raguse); and *A Yank in the R.A.F.* (Fred Sersen and Edmund H. Hansen)

I Wanted Wings is a run of the mill Army Air Corps recruiting poster mixed with a complicated good girl-bad girl romance and mystery, starring Ray Milland, William Holden and Veronica Lake (as the femme fatale). The special effects Oscar was for the first-rate model work on the flying and night raid sequences, which incorporated some cloud effects that were well done, as well as a fine model of Los Angeles for the blackout scene. The movie deserved this nomination, but these kinds of effects were becoming run of the mill with the slew of military pictures being made. Another, greater film deserved this Oscar for its groundbreaking, brilliant work with visual effects – as we shall see.

Exploding Technicolor volcano, anybody? Technicolor made special effects much harder, and *Aloma of the South Seas* succeeds fairly well in coping with the challenge, so the nomination should stay.

Flight Command has Robert Taylor as a wannabe pilot, with Walter Pidgeon as his commander. The real flying sequences look decent, but the special effects are murky and less than convincing, and deserve no nomination.

Universal Studios milked all of its horror film monsters with multiple sequels, and *The Invisible Woman* was the next morning at the dairy. For this third entry in the Invisible Man series, they pulled a gender switch (as they had with *Dracula's Daughter*) and chose a woman to vanish. John Barrymore (who would soon be dead in 1942 from the ravages of alcoholism) was brought in to play the professor who invents the means to go nude and still pass the Production Code. Barrymore digs into the role of the absent-minded professor with plumminess and joy. As for the special effects, some of the great equipment from the Frankenstein movies shows up. The majority of the effects, of course, are the invisible ones: a floating mirror and other mobile objects; a walking dress; a brandy snifter that empties in mid air; a smoking cigarette...and so on. Fairly well done, in all, in this light comic take on this series.

The Sea Wolf features Edward G. Robinson as a sadistic, Nietzsche-reading sea captain (the Sea Wolf of the title), in philosophical and physical combat with his crew, some shipwreck survivors, and his brother – and his own growing blindness. The nomination for special effects is a weak one, however, as it is limited to fog and one cannonball shot, as well as producing, on a sound stage, a sense of being on the open sea. So no nomination, but the movie is worth seeing, especially if you have a fondness for anti-fascist films and Jack London – and Robinson going deeper into evil than ever before in his roles.

Napoleonic sea battles bring the nomination for *That Hamilton Woman*. Warner Brothers did it with more panache, but *That Hamilton Woman* does a reasonable job with the big ships of the line, burning and exploding several. A good nomination.

The third in the Topper series, *Topper Returns* boils up a plot, complete with a would be assassin in black hat, mask and cape, instead of the screwball hijinks. Joan Blondell takes on the ghostly role for the first time, but Roland Young returns for his third and final outing as Topper. To a degree, the movie spoofs *Rebecca*, complete with the creepy housekeeper. Eddie "Rochester" Anderson makes his usual side comments (including one about going back to Mr. Benny), but he does seem to be playing the apparently standard role in the ghost stories of the frightened black man. As for the special effects: we get the obligatory spirit leaving the body; things moving by themselves (as Blondell manipulates them), including one nice effect of Blondell getting into bed; a line of footprints next to Young walking; a cigarette lighting and smoking itself; clothes putting themselves on; a boat rowing itself, and so forth. We've seen many of these things before, in the Invisible Man series, as well as the other two Topper films – but they're well done, so the nomination should stay.

A Yank in the R.A.F. has Tyrone Power, Betty Grable, and some flying with the Royal Air Force. What is worse, much worse, is the continued demonstration in Power's movies that regardless of how much women say no, if Power keeps forcing himself on a woman, she will eventually say yes (*The Black Swan* does much the same). An entire generation of males must have had its ideas of female attitudes reinforced when they saw that no didn't really mean no, if they kept pushing the issue. *A Yank in the R.A.F.* should never be shown as entertainment, although I could see it being used as a historical artifact in a class on sexist attitudes of the Forties. As for the visual effects, the model work is very poor, almost amateurish at times, so no nomination.

As for those films the Academy ignored, we should not forget *Citizen Kane*, which, as Roger Ebert points out, has as many special effects as *Star Wars*.[ccxii] The matte shots and optical printing shots are especially fine. Vernon Walker was the man responsible here, and he should have received a nomination here for his indispensible work.[98]

But of all the special effects done this year, the most memorable, the most mythic, come from a film the Academy ignored in all respects: *The Wolf Man*, starring Lon Chaney, Jr. and Claude Rains. Chaney brings pathos to the role, one he would repeat over the years, although rarely with the believability of this outing. The script is cogent, and one passage has remained in my memory for decades: "Even a man who is pure in heart and says his prayers at night, can become a wolf when the wolfbane blooms, and the autumn moon is bright." Perhaps it's just the way Maria Ouspenskaya says it, or my childhood fears that I would sprout hair and fangs, but I still enjoy the movie. The transformation scenes with the makeup of Jack P. Pierce and the visual effects of John P. Fulton weren't equaled until the coming of computer graphics (even now, I find the original more affecting than the 2010 remake, as it reflects true craft and patience, and the suffering of Chaney). Pierce and Fulton should have been nominated, and they should have won the Oscar for Best Special Effects.

Best Short Subject (Cartoon): Disney won for *Lend a Paw*, and was also nominated for *Truant Officer Donald*, over *Boogie Woogie Bugle Boy of Company B*; Leon

---

[98] "Another key collaborator was Vernon Walker, who handled the special effects and optical printing (layering and assembling of images, etc.) which were more extensive on *Kane* than on any other RKO picture since *King Kong* in 1933." Thomas Schatz, *Boom and Bust: Hollywood in the 1940s*, p. 93.

Schlesinger, *Hiawatha's Rabbit Hunt* and *Rhapsody in Rivets*; Columbia, *How War Came*; MGM, *The Night Before Christmas* and *The Rookie Bear*; George Pal, *Rhythm in the Ranks*; and Max Fleischer, *Superman*

After finally missing a year in this category, Disney came charging back, winning an Oscar for *Lend a Paw* and another nomination for *Truant Officer Donald*. *Lend a Paw* stars Pluto saving a cat from being drowned in a sack, and reflects the mastery the animators had developed on the feature length pictures: multiplane camera use, stronger pacing and dramatic effect, better comic timing, and more effective musical scoring. Mickey shows up too, making this the only Mickey Mouse cartoon to win an Oscar. The appearance of a devilish Pluto and an angelic Pluto has a feel like Tex Avery's work to me, which suggests the Disney animators were starting to pay attention to the competition from Warner Brothers. A good cartoon, yes, but the best of the year? No. The nomination should stay, of course.

Truant Officer Donald has Donald making his nephews Huey, Dewey, and Louie go to school. Donald is as amusing as ever, especially when he loses his temper. A good nomination, although not as technically accomplished as *Lend a Paw*.

Walter Lantz, the future creator of Woody Woodpecker, was up for *Boogie Woogie Bugle Boy of Company B*. A black band swings the night away; some have objected to the animation as being racist, but the music is hot, the images are caricatures similar to those used on white figures, and I suspect Lantz was being about as respectful as any white man could in that era. I certainly find it less objectionable than the typical Hollywood use of blackface. The nomination should stay.

Warners and Leon Schlesinger were nominated for *Hiawatha's Rabbit Hunt* and *Rhapsody in Rivets*. *Hiawatha's Rabbit Hunt* features Bugs reading Longfellow's once widely known poem (my maternal grandmother had to memorize reams of it for elementary school recitals). Occasionally viewed as promoting Indian stereotypes, *Hiawatha's Rabbit Hunt* remains largely unseen due to this complaint. Hiawatha speaks like Lenny from *Of Mice and Men*, so the sense of stupidity attributed to the character might be offensive to some; then again, Elmer Fudd and Yosemite Sam acted the same way, so perhaps not. Many of the routines became standard gags in later cartoons (the bath tub, among others), so for sheer influence, the nomination should stay.

Set to Franz Liszt's "Hungarian Rhapsody #2," *Rhapsody in Rivets* shows us a building built to the manic little tune. Very gentle humor, but a harbinger of all the great Looney Tunes to come which will spoof classical music, including *What's Opera, Doc*? For that grand lineage, the nomination can stay. By the way, if you don't know the musical genius that was Carl Stalling, I refer you to the recordings on *The Carl Stalling Project*; he guided Disney through many of the Silly Symphonies before heading to the rest of his career at Warner Brothers.

Columbia finally got into this category with the black and white cartoon *How War Came*, which is completely forgotten today; I could not locate a copy. I only found one mention of it anywhere, in Michael S. Shull and David E. Wilt's history of wartime cartoons, *Doing Their Bit*, a "sort of animated political lecture released through Columbia."[ccxiii] Doesn't sound promising, so let's drop the discussion.

In the Fifties, George Pal became the producer of science fiction epics like *Destination Moon, The War of the Worlds,* and *When Worlds Collide*; he got his first recognition with *Rhythm in the Ranks*. One of Pal's Puppetoons, *Rhythm* tells the story of a toy soldier who watches a beautiful ice skater instead of doing his duty; he gets a chance to make up for it in the war. The Puppetoons featured stop motion animation, which apparently qualified in this category. Unfortunately, the short was not available at any time during the writing of the book, but we should let the nomination stand for the reputation Pal has.

MGM picked up two nominations, for *The Night Before Christmas* and *The Rookie Bear*. *The Night Before Christmas* gives us another Tom and Jerry smashup, this time during yuletide. Nicely drawn, but like most Tom and Jerry cartoons, extremely repetitive. One scene leaves Tom and Jerry a lot...friendlier than ever expected. And because it's Christmas, they end up on a peaceful note for a change.

The Rookie Bear shows that MGM animators may have built their own multiplane camera. A spoof of the draft, *The Rookie Bear* stars Barney Bear, who isn't quite sure what's hit him. A good example of the kind of humor that would sustain Hollywood through the war years, *The Rookie Bear* should keep the nomination.

Finally, Max Fleischer received a nomination for the first superhero cartoon, *Superman*. At last, Fleischer got the financing to do a cartoon to the best of the studio's ability. Paramount wanted the Fleischers to do a Superman series; Max Fleischer responded by quoting a ridiculously high amount of money, $100,000 – which Paramount then negotiated down to merely triple what Fleischer had been spending on each of the Popeye cartoons.[ccxiv] Fleischer couldn't say no, and he embarked on what many regard as one of the highlights of the golden age of animation. Watching *Superman* today, along with the dozen-plus sequels, still gives us a kick, and shows us the development of the Man from

Krypton into an American icon.[99] The animation is superb, leaning towards film noir shadows and glorious Technicolor. *Superman* gives us the origin story (no Ma and Pa Kent, as they hadn't been invented yet), and then one of the multitudes of mad scientists who populated the early Superman stories in the newspapers, comics, and movies (Lex Luthor would become the representative for these villains eventually). The problem with writing Superman stories has always been coming up with credible threats; unlike Batman, whose villains typically were more flawed and therefore more interesting, Superman's villains quickly ran into giant dinosaurs, apes, robots, and super-science. The cartoon was highly influential. The regular introduction to the series would later be mimicked for the George Reeves television series; the great Batman and Superman animated series of the Nineties, which most see as the best ever done, drew much of their inspiration from the Fleischer cartoons. Before this series, Superman couldn't fly; as the series went on, flying proved easier to animate, and looked better on screen. The Fleischers did better human animation in this film, as well as better action scenes, as can clearly be seen in this first *Superman*, which should have won the Oscar for Best Cartoon in 1941.[100]

One other suggestion: this year, the Fleischers also released their second full length feature, *Mr. Bug Goes to Town* (also known as *Bugville* and *Hoppity Goes to Town*). Surprisingly, Hoagy Carmichael and Frank Loesser provided three songs. Leigh Harline, who worked for Disney as well, did the score. Like *Superman*, *Mr. Bug* shows that the Fleischers were reaching for their own style; had they not lost their studio to Paramount, the Fleischers might have eventually produced their own masterworks, as Disney did with *Pinocchio*.

---

[99] An argument could be made that the Fleischer cartoons are responsible for the Superman that became the American myth, rather than the original comic books, which feature a very different Superman.
[100] My personal favorite is the second in the Fleischer *Superman* series, *The Mechanical Monsters*, with the iconic giant robots. With WWII, the series descended into propaganda as it switched production to Famous Studios, and was particularly virulent towards the Japanese. I use the cartoon "Japoteurs" when teaching about the Japanese internment camps in WWII.

CHAPTER FIFTEEN: 1943 AWARDS
15th Show

Movies released in 1942

THE SCENE OF THE CRIME:

The Academy went back to the Cocoanut Grove on March 4, 1943. The war was in full bloom, and Hollywood was out to win it. Why not? They were making their biggest profits in more than a decade. Despite that, the Oscars were made of plaster, because of the wartime metal shortages (the Academy later replaced them). Bob Hope was back. Jeanette MacDonald sang the national anthem. FDR sent a congratulatory telegram to be read over the radio broadcast; California Governor Earl Warren showed up to make a speech.

Irving Berlin gave the Oscar for Best Song to himself: "It's someone I've known for a good many years. He's a nice kid and I think he deserves it."

When Gary Cooper presented the Oscar for Best Actor to James Cagney, and started to back away, Cagney threw his arms around Cooper and cried, "Please don't leave me!"

Hollywood did its best to acknowledge the foreign contingents, giving special Oscar certificates to Noel Coward and Charles Boyer, and later reading a telegram from Madame Chiang Kai-shek. Just to keep things American, though, they gave another special Oscar certificate to Louis B. Mayer for the Andy Hardy series.

The Writing awards were slightly adjusted again, as Original Story became Best Writing (Original Motion Picture Story).

The ceremony went on for almost three hours, and the tradition of complaining about boredom and length began. Greer Garson got a raw deal when what was only a five-and-a-half minute speech came to be remembered as an hour-long snooze fest, along with the quip: "Her acceptance speech was longer than her part!" Others complained that letting the extras vote was skewing the results away from excellence towards popularity.

Silly people. They should have just asked me.

WHAT THEY GOT RIGHT:

Surprisingly, the Academy got two out of three musical awards right this year, including a rare best Song choice. They also continued to pick the correct original screenplays two years in a row! Now if they could just work on the rest of these categories...

Best Writing (Original Screenplay): Michael Kanin and Ring Lardner, Jr. won for *Woman of the Year*, over Michael Powell and Emeric Pressburger, *One of Our Aircraft Is Missing*; Frank Butler and Don Hartman, *Road to Morocco*; W.R. Burnett and Frank Butler, *Wake Island*; and George Oppenheimer, *The War Against Mrs. Hadley*

Michael Kanin and Ring Lardner, Jr.'s screenplay for *Woman of the Year* contains so much promise, only to end in so much disappointment. The setup is perfect: Katharine Hepburn is a powerful columnist, smart, sexy, fully engaged in the pursuit of her career. She meets Spencer Tracy, who is a sportswriter, masculine, amusing, and charming. The two fall in love, and then their marriage goes on the rocks over the issue of equity, of affording space and respect towards the other partner. Hepburn's character doesn't really understand people; her flaw is self-absorption (some of this film drew off of the dynamic of *The Philadelphia Story*). Tracy tries, gently at first, to get her to see his needs, without expecting her to sacrifice herself. The original ending has her offering to give it all up, but Tracy delivers the same line as in the version we have now: he doesn't want her to be the little wife – he just wants her to be his partner, as he is hers. The difference between the released version and the original version[101] lies in the humiliation Hepburn undergoes in the released version, and the ways in which her character loses the full dimensions she had worked so hard to create in the first place. We can't blame Kanin and Lardner for the horrible ending; they didn't write it. They protested, got the right to edit out some of the more offensive lines (the mind boggles at what could be more offensive), and were otherwise ignored, as writers so often are in Hollywood. They still should get the Oscar, for the same reason I think the Academy gave it to them in the first place: the script is truly original, and enough people knew what had been stolen to make this a protest against violating the intent of the authors.

One of Our Aircraft Is Missing shows the fate of the crew of a British bomber shot down over the Netherlands, and how they got back home. The movie was written and directed by Michael Powell and Emeric Pressburger – the same team as *The Invaders* (*49th Parallel*). David Lean was the editor. A very young Peter Ustinov plays a Dutch priest. Essentially, the movie reverses the situation of *The Invaders*, only now, the escaping men are the heroes, not the Nazi villains. Shot in a documentary style, with an insistence on realism, *One of Our Aircraft* doesn't follow the typical Hollywood gambits, and really comes alive when the crew has to bail out, and interact with the Dutch as the men try to escape from the Nazis. Powell and Pressburger would go on to a fabled career together, including *Black Narcissus* and *The Red Shoes*. They deserve this nomination, for this detail-rich screenplay.

Road to Morocco has proven to be the best of the road pictures, although since so much of it is improvised, or written by Bob Hope and Bing Crosby's gag writers, I am not sure how much W.R. Burnett and Frank Butler deserve credit. The famous camel spitting scene just happened on the set, and Hope and Crosby went with it, especially Crosby, who patted the camel on the neck and said "good girl, Susie!" after Hope got spit in the eye by the camel. Burnett and Butler must be given credit for some of this wonderful movie, or at the very least, providing the framework for the improvisation. They should keep the nomination for that alone.

Wake Island takes the actual events of the battle – the Japanese attacking the Marines in overwhelming numbers – then completely

---

[101] Available in various places on the internet as an excerpt from the treatment Kanin and Lardner wrote.

makes up the ending by stealing Custer's last stand. *Wake Island* formed the template for almost every combat movie made since, as film historian Jeanine Basinger has so convincingly argued.[ccxv] I have to imagine this story was well-received by audiences, given how much of the film is devoted to the vicarious pleasures of killing the enemy, as well as to the intensities of watching Americans die to preserve liberty. I'm not sure I would ever bother watching the movie again, but for its influence, W.R. Burnett (*Scarface*) and Frank Butler (*Road to Morocco*) should keep their nomination.

The War Against Mrs. Hadley stars Edward Arnold and Fay Bainter. Bainter digs into her role as an upper crust Washingtonian who finds the coming of WWII to be tiresome and personally offensive; basically, WWII is apparently out to ruin her life, and how dare the war intrude? Never fear; she comes around and becomes a proper patriotic supporter. George Oppenheimer's script does a decent job with this kind of reversal, although in somewhat predictable melodrama. The enjoyable parts come from watching Bainter grow indignant, as when the Japanese attack Pearl Harbor on HER birthday, of all the impertinence! For that audacity, Oppenheimer should keep his nomination (he also wrote *Libeled Lady* and *A Day at the Races*).

Best Dramatic Score: Max Steiner won for *Now, Voyager*, over Frank Skinner, *Arabian Nights*; Frank Churchill and Edward Plumb, *Bambi*; Alfred Newman, *The Black Swan*; Dimitri Tiomkin, *The Corsican Brothers*; Victor Young, for *Flying Tigers*, *Silver Queen* and *Take a Letter, Darling*; Max Terr, *The Gold Rush*; Roy Webb, *I Married a Witch* and *Joan of Paris*; Miklós Rózsa, *Jungle Book*; Edward Kay, *Klondike Fury*; Leigh Harline, *The Pride of the Yankees*; Herbert Stothart, *Random Harvest*; Richard Hageman, *The Shanghai Gesture*; Frederick Hollander and Morris Stoloff, *The Talk of the Town*; and Werner Heymann, *To Be or Not to Be*

Now, Voyager is one of the very best Bette Davis films, allowing her to go from ugly duckling to swan. Max Steiner rightfully won the Oscar for Best Dramatic Score, and once again showed his mastery by producing what may be his most romantic music after *Gone with the Wind*. Beginning with a mixture of strings, brass, and deep kettle drums, and moving on to more quiet tones, Steiner's score reinforces one of Bette Davis' best performances. At times, I felt like Steiner was the only one matching the level of Davis' work. Claude Rains and some of the other actors try hard, and Sol Polito's camerawork is at times as lyrical as the score. Oddly, Steiner has the pianist quote Cole Porter's "Night and Day" when Davis meets Paul Henreid again. Odd, because the warmth of the love theme that swells from time to time is every bit as memorable as the "Tara" theme. Steiner definitely deserved the Oscar for *Now, Voyager*.

Arabian Nights stars Sabu, Jon Hall and Maria Montes in a film clearly intended to duplicate the success of *The Thief of Bagdad*. Oddly, Shemp Howard is cast as Sinbad, of all people (his buddy Aladdin rubs every lamp in sight). The movie is watchable, although with little of the charm of *The Thief of Bagdad*. Frank Skinner provides a typical score for this kind of movie, and one we've heard many times before, but done with a great deal of energy and verve. For the swordfights, Skinner has been paying attention to Erich Wolfgang Korngold, although without the inventiveness of Korngold. Skinner also provides a score throughout the entire film, and his music, while not all that original, never wears out its welcome. The nomination should stay.

Bambi remains the most emotionally devastating animated feature Walt Disney ever made (my brother and my college mentor both reported never recovering from it). I recall seeing *Finding Nemo* in the theaters; when the mother clown fish is killed in the first few minutes, the gasps and shocks of the audience (mostly mothers and small children) were palpable, and the silence that ensued was broken only by one child wailing, "What happened to the mommy?" At that moment, I knew Pixar was out to return animation to real emotions, but nobody has ever equaled *Bambi* for the wholesale devastation wrought upon its audiences when the mother is slain by the hunters (and other than the owl, the unseen humans are the only predators in the film). The secret to that lies in the fact that it all happens off-screen, and all we know are the sounds, the look on Bambi's face, and the sound of his voice when he searches for her. The score by Frank Churchill and Edward Plumb does its best to match that maturity, particularly since *Bambi* has so few words; the score has to do much more work than usual. After the credits, we begin with pastoral music, soft and gentle: violins, a harp, flute and a wordless human chorus. The pace picks up, rhythmically accelerating and adding other instruments to reflect the changes. Frank Churchill (who committed suicide before the film was released) and Edward Plumb never look back, adding musical nuances to match whatever was occurring on the screen. Much of it sounds like Tchaikovsky and other late nineteenth century Romantics – and that's a compliment (provided it's not plagiarism, which it may be; one of the themes of repeated notes sounded familiar). The nomination is highly deserved.

The Black Swan stars Tyrone Power and Maureen O'Hara in Fox's attempt to make an Errol Flynn/Olivia de Havilland swashbuckler (even using another novel by Rafael Sabatini, the author of *Captain*

Blood). They were mildly successful, although I could have done without Power forcing himself on O'Hara and then hitting her when she fought back. Alfred Newman's score sounds like Korngold was looking over his shoulder the whole time – but then, of what swashbuckler has that not been true? Lots of trumpet fanfares, driving brass accompanying the action, and so forth. Good stuff, but Korngold still did it better. Newman was a chameleon of a composer, capable of producing anything needed at high speed and high quality – but I am beginning to wonder if he is ever going to develop a signature sound the way that Korngold did in *The Adventures of Robin Hood*, or Max Steiner in *Gone with the Wind*.[102] Newman should keep his nomination.

Douglas Fairbanks, Jr. took up the swashbuckling tradition with his version of *The Corsican Brothers*, based on the novel by Alexandre Dumas about the Siamese twins separated at birth, one of whom still shares the sensations and feelings of the other telepathically. Fairbanks is quite good in the roles, although the action elements are better than the rest of the movie. Dimitri Tiomkin's score does a good impression of Korngold, rendering the action scenes even more enjoyable; plaintive violins with a touch of organ lift up the dramatic scenes. A good nomination, although Tiomkin was capable of much more than this.

Victor Young received three nominations for score this year, beginning with *Flying Tigers*, in which John Wayne flies against the Japanese in China in the coolest paint job ever seen on a fighter plane. Young's score helps Wayne along fairly well, mixing the typical sounds we associate with China (we all know those chords) with martial tones, fairly successfully. He also provides some somber music for the moments of sorrow and difficulty. A decent nomination.

I can't say the same for Young's *Silver Queen*, which has Priscilla Lane stuck between the good George Brent and the dastardly Bruce Cabot in nineteenth century *San Francisco* – why does this movie sound so familiar? How about *Barbary Coast*? Overall, *Silver Queen* isn't a bad film, but it sure isn't a good one. The score rings all the expected changes, but as always with this composer, he only really exerts himself occasionally, and this isn't one of those occasions. Dull, dull, dull. Nominations should really be for sharper material.

Finally, Young put himself in a better place with *Take a Letter, Darling*, an interesting role reversal comedy, with Fred MacMurray as a male secretary hired by Rosalind Russell, who then proceeds to use him to deflect other men. As is the rule with such movies, the two will fall in

---

[102] Odd to talk about this in the present tense, I know, but I am watching all of these movies in chronological order.

love. A nude portrait plays a role in the denouement. The score is romantic when need be, but with comic woodwinds and flute to play up the absurdities. Young provides one of his more inventive compositions for *Take a Letter, Darling*, and deserved his nomination this time.

Charlie Chaplin re-released *The Gold Rush* in 1942, with a new musical score, for which Max Terr was nominated. The score, like most of Chaplin's movies, was based on Chaplin's own musical ideas, and reflect his music hall origins with its sentimentality. I don't see why a movie released nearly twenty years before would be eligible for an Oscar; will we be nominating each new iteration of George Lucas' *Star Wars* movies whenever he adds something new? Chaplin clearly used the one studio, one nomination rule to eke out another nod for his movie. No nomination should be yours, Charlie. Besides, *The Gold Rush* was supposed to be a silent picture...

René Clair, one of the best of the French directors, guided Fredric March and Veronica Lake in *I Married a Witch,* a forerunner of such later films as *Bell, Book, and Candle* and the television series *Bewitched*. A social satire – at a witch burning, they have an intermission and a vendor sells pop-maize – *I Married a Witch* was produced by Preston Sturges. The studio went along with it so they could show off Veronica Lake's hair. Much of the film seems informed by the Topper series as well, with those kinds of special effects – but then, author Thorne Smith was the common source for the material. Roy Webb's score sounds comic, but also lifted from Mussorgsky's *A Night on Bald Mountain*. Webb provides most of the spooky musical effects we have grown accustomed to hearing in these sorts of movies, and he's been imitated ever since. Remarkably little of the film has a score, however, as is often the case with low-budget pictures. Webb deserves a nomination for what we do hear, however, for its originality.

Webb was also nominated for *Joan of Paris*, a patriotic piece of romance about a young Frenchwoman helping downed RAF pilots get home. Paul Henreid is good as the noble French flier; Laird Cregar is better as the Nazi bad guy. Joan is played by Michele Morgan. An anti-Nazi movie which was finished before Pearl Harbor and released shortly afterward, *Joan of Paris* actually has some decent acting and dialogue, and is a rewarding movie that deserves to be better known, even if it does drag a bit in the middle. Roy Webb's score is very lively, with lots of tonal shifts. The opening credits sounds like we ought to be walking very fast to catch up with it. Webb also provides French nightclub music at the opening. When we meet the downed fliers, things get quiet and serious, only to erupt with their actions. The score gets sinister with the Nazis (as well it should). The church music proves to be quiet and simple. Webb seems to be trying to have as much music as possible emerge from natural sources. While not a consistent themed score, what we get works well enough to deserve a nomination.

Alexander Korda adapted Rudyard Kipling's *Jungle Book*, which stars Sabu as Mowgli. Miklós Rózsa produced his first great score for this Technicolor extravaganza. A flavor of India touches the score, but mostly, we are in a riot of horns and adventurous strings. My ten-year-old son loved the music. I did too, and would recommend this movie to anybody wanting something different than the Disney version. The nomination is deserved.

Klondike Fury deserves to be forgotten, completely and utterly. The plot involves a neurosurgeon, a plane crash, a woman, and two operations, none of which could have taken more than a low C-average fourth grader's ability to write. A zero-grade production from a no-name company – King Brothers – the entire film could easily be a candidate for the worst film of the Forties. As for the so-called score, the less said the better. Edward Kay gave us the less-than-immortal *King of the Zombies* last year; *Klondike Fury* is worse. The one studio, one nomination rule saddles us with yet another unworthy candidate.

Leigh Harline's score on *The Pride of the Yankees* keeps circling back to the one piece of music we remember from it: Irving Berlin's "Always," which forms the beating heart of the score. Harline also works in other familiar tunes, including "Take Me Out to the Ball Game" and "Auld Lang Syne." The score does what it's supposed to do, reinforcing the humor, the love, and the tragedy, through the familiar songs, as well as Harline's use of "Always." A good nomination.

In *Random Harvest*, Ronald Colman plays an amnesiac married to Greer Garson, based on a novel by James Hilton (*Lost Horizon*; *Goodbye, Mr. Chips*). Herbert Stothart's score for the weeper *Random Harvest* is full of violins and strings, like most melodramas (and a threatening cello lurking beneath). Stothart does a reasonable job, but nothing memorable emerges, which is generally true of his scores. You know what else is almost always true of Stothart? He doesn't deserve any nominations.

Josef von Sternberg tries to turn Gene Tierney into Marlene Dietrich in *The Shanghai Gesture*. The Sternberg magic has nearly vanished; Richard Hageman's score isn't much better. Both needed to be even more outrageous than they were, but the Production Code wouldn't allow it. A cult film that appeals to a small but fanatic following, *The Shanghai Gesture* is a collection of kinks and oddities that follows – weakly – the Sternberg of *The Scarlet Empress*. Personally, I found the movie to be nearly unwatchable in its clichés, but I can see the attraction for people who enjoy going to dive bars to watch the drunken wrecks teeter and totter along. Both Hageman and Sternberg have seen much better days. As Pauline Kael so succinctly put it, *The Shanghai Gesture* is "hilariously, awesomely terrible...a gorgeous travesty. Some of this effect is probably intentional, but the total effect couldn't have been."[ccxvi] None of that is worth a nomination.

The Talk of the Town gives us Cary Grant as a man wrongly accused of arson and murder, Jean Arthur as his former childhood classmate in whose attic Grant hides, and Ronald Colman as a law professor and prospective Supreme Court Justice stuck in the middle of all this. George Stevens directed this very odd duck of a film, which garnered a hatful of Oscar nominations, including one for its score, by Frederick Hollander and Morris Stoloff. The credits overture reflects the strange mixture of emotional tones this movie pursues, from pompous seriousness to romantic longing to the impending danger of social unrest. The score rarely intrudes after that. One comic note: when Grant pantomimes hunger, the music provides his "voice" in squawking brass. When Colman learns he is to be appointed to the Supreme Court, warm and supportive strings appear. The music at the Supreme Court at the end is considerably fine, hitting a noble, uplifting note. For what is there, the score can remain.

Ernst Lubitsch's final masterpiece, *To Be or Not to Be*, attacks the Nazis through Lubitsch's love of the theater, marital infidelity, outrageous juxtapositions and satiric comment. Jack Benny and Carole Lombard in her last performance star as married thespians; he is playing Hamlet, and his wife's lover (is he?) keeps getting up and leaving during the famous soliloquy. The overture by Werner Heymann reminds me of nothing so much as Mendelssohn's music for Shakespeare's *A Midsummer Night's Dream*. The music only appears infrequently, but effectively. When Poland is attacked, Heymann resorts to a few sad violins. We get some more music that sounds very like Mendelssohn later. What is there, works, but I cannot support a nomination that is derivative and sporadic (as is almost all of Werner Heymann's work).

As for those scores the Academy omitted, the one that should not have been ignored is that of Erich Wolfgang Korngold for *Kings Row* (the picture where Ronald Reagan loses his legs – see Best Picture for more). Perhaps the best reason to nominate it is to make people more aware of a thief. John Williams has been the most famous composer in Hollywood since the Seventies. While his music is uplifting, he really needs to be castigated for shoplifting. Listen to the opening segments of *Kings Row*, and you will hear much of the original *Star Wars* music, only slightly tweaked; if you want to hear the rest of where Williams "borrowed" it from, go listen to Gustav Holst's *The Planets*, particularly *Mars, the Bringer of War*. Part of William's theme for *Raiders of the Lost Ark* is lifted wholesale from an old Kent cigarette commercial. As Jim Svejda has so aptly pointed out in his wonderful book, *The Insider's Guide to Classical Music*, a dissertation for a Ph.D. could easily be written by any graduate student looking at Williams' scores. Korngold's own score impresses, as his music almost always did; here, the score is in many ways the best part of this over the top melodrama. Korngold should have been nominated.

Best Song: Irving Berlin's "White Christmas" won from *Holiday Inn*, over Ernesto Lecuona and Kim Gannon's "Always in My Heart" from *Always in My Heart*; Burton Lane and Ralph Freed's "How About You?" from *Babes on Broadway*; Frank Churchill and Larry Morey's "Love Is a Song" from *Bambi*; Edward Ward, Chet Forrest and Bob Wright's "Pennies for Peppino" from *Flying with Music*; Gene de Paul and Don Raye's "Pig Foot Pete" from *Hellzapoppin'*; Harry Revel and Mort Greene's "There's a Breeze on Lake Louise" from *The Mayor of 44th Street*; Harry Warren and Mack Gordon's "I've Got a Gal in Kalamazoo" from *Orchestra Wives*; Jules Styne and Sammy Cahn's "It Seems I Heard That Song Before" from *Youth on Parade*; and Jerome Kern & Johnny Mercer's "Dearly Beloved" from *You Were Never Lovelier*

Irving Berlin, a Jewish American, wrote the greatest Christmas song of all time. Now if that's not irony, I don't know what is. Bing Crosby sang his heart out on the song, which spoke to the longing many soldiers had of being back home for Christmas. A wistful song of reminiscence, "White Christmas" remained the bestselling song of all time until Elton John's remake of "Candle in the Wind" honoring the memory of Lady Diana outsold it in a frenzy of grief. I suspect "White Christmas" will someday end up back on the top with its annual return to the airwaves. Regardless, Berlin wrote a perfect song, evoking a very special time. "White Christmas" was used in *Holiday Inn*, a Bing Crosby-Fred Astaire movie which features songs for every major holiday of the year. Berlin well deserved this Oscar, even with the strong competition he faced this year from "It Seems I Heard That Song Before," "I've Got a Gal in Kalamazoo," "How About You?" and even "Pig Foot Pete" – and the great song they omitted entirely, "I Remember You."

Always in My Heart stars Kay Francis and Walter Huston in a tale of a convict returning home to discover he has been completely forgotten. The song was written for a fifteen-year-old Deanna Durbin clone, the now-forgotten Gloria Warren. "Always in My Heart" is a complete throwaway song, and not worth a nomination for Ernesto Lecuona and Kim Gannon, who are as forgotten as you would expect from this song.

Judy Garland belts out the classic "How About You?" by Burton Lane and Ralph Freed in the third of her movies with Mickey Rooney, *Babes on Broadway*. I have loved this song ever since I was a child, having seen Lucille Ball and Van Johnson do it on *I Love Lucy* (I was vaguely disappointed when Rooney didn't do the exact same comic patter, although the somersaulting was a decent substitute). An inventive song, "How About You?" is hampered only by the topical references, which can be confusing to unaware listeners. Still, a classic, and most deserving of a nomination.

Perhaps the weakest part of the most adult cartoon Walt Disney ever made, "Love Is a Song" brings *Bambi* to a screaming halt, almost drowning it in schmaltz before it begins. Fortunately, the film recovers. No nomination should have been given for this overbearing use of chorus – I felt like I was being drowned in an avalanche of wet marshmallows.

Flying with Music is a silly knock-off Latin rumba musical from Hal Roach. The song "Pennies for Peppino" was dead on delivery, as was the score. No nomination or remembrance should there be for Edward Ward, Chet Forrest and Bob Wright.

I know "Pig Foot Pete" from Martha Raye's boogie woogie version in Abbott & Costello's *Keep 'Em Flying* (yet another sign of my television-drenched childhood). *Hellzapoppin'* starts in hell, incorporates invisibility and the Frankenstein monster, Shemp Howard, Martha Raye, talking animals, and two main characters who break the fourth wall and begin harassing the screenwriter as to what is going to happen next. The only thing *Hellzapoppin'* doesn't have is a rendition of "Pig Foot Pete" – the Academy goofed on this one, and credited the wrong film![103] "Pig Foot Pete" is a fun song, although "Boogie Woogie Bugle Boy of Company B" sounds remarkably similar at times. So we should let the nomination stay for Gene de Paul and Don Raye, while recognizing that it comes from *Keep 'Em Flying* – except that we can't, since the movie came out the year before.

The Mayor of 44th Street stars nobody anybody remembers, in a trite plot about a dance band manager keeping out gangsters. "There's a Breeze on Lake Louise" by Harry Revel and Mort Greene is a sickeningly sweet song with little to recommend it for repeated listening. Let's just agree to forget both the film and the song, and get on with our lives, shall we?

---

[103] The Academy database recognizes this, and they can't explain what happened either.

The second movie to star the Glenn Miller Orchestra, *Orchestra Wives* has some fairly unpleasant things to say about women who marry. Harry Warren and Mack Gordon's song "I've Got a Gal in Kalamazoo" quickly emerged as another big band standard for Miller, and still gets the feet tapping – and when the Nicholas Brothers come out dancing, the eyes popping! The lyrics, like most of those for Miller's standards, are mostly inane. The sound and the beat are what attract – and earn it the nomination.

Youth on Parade stars nobody you've ever heard from before or since; only this song has survived the Republic B-picture set in a college – but "It Seems I Heard That Song Before" quickly became a WWII classic (songwriters Jules Styne and Sammy Cahn would go on to write for Frank Sinatra). The song remains deserving of its nomination for its depiction of romantic longing, and the sadness of disappointment.

You Were Never Lovelier stars Fred Astaire as – surprise! – a dancer; Rita Hayworth thinks he is sending her secret presents. Romance and hijinks ensue, and some damn fine dancing with Astaire and Hayworth, all to a Latin beat (and a fifteen-year-old Fidel Castro shows up in the cast, reportedly).[ccxvii] "Dearly Beloved," oddly enough, is perhaps the weakest song in the entire movie, a mediocre throwaway song practically nobody has ever bothered singing ever again. What is incomprehensible is that the movie also features a definite classic, "I'm Old-Fashioned"! They should have switched out the boring fluff out for a real song, and nominated "I'm Old-Fashioned" – which may have not received a nomination because Rita Hayworth lip-synced to it, whereas Hayworth did a kind of striptease to "Dearly Beloved."

As for the other songs they omitted, the glaring holes are Irving Berlin's "I Remember You" from *Holiday Inn* and "Tangerine" from *The Fleet's In*, composed by Victor Schertzinger and Johnny Mercer. *The Fleet's In* stars William Holden, Dorothy Lamour, and Eddie Bracken in a remake of a Clara Bow silent flick about a sailor trying to get a singer to kiss him. "I Remember You" works a romantic sweetness into its lyrics and tones; "Tangerine" instills the Latin flavor into a song of longing for a gorgeous woman. Both were worth a nomination.

Best Short Subject (Cartoon): Disney won for *Der Fuehrer's Face*, over *All Out for V* (Terrytoons/20th Century); *Blitz Wolf* (MGM – Tex Avery); *Juke Box Jamboree* (Walter Lantz / Universal); *Pigs in a Polka* (Warner Bros.); and *Tulips Shall Grow* (George Pal / Paramount)

For years, seeing *Der Fuehrer's Face* was next to impossible, since Donald Duck plays a Nazi worker. Orchestrated to a song originally released by the incomparable Spike Jones, *Der Fuehrer's Face* is audacious, and very much in the line of comic attacks on Hitler like *The Great Dictator, You Nazty Spy*, and *To Be or Not to Be. Der Fuehrer's Face* was kept out of circulation until 2004, when Disney finally relented. Watching it today, you can see why Disney was hesitant. Rampant stereotypes abound: the Japanese are bucktoothed and short-sighted; bad dialects are heard for all; there's even a gay Nazi. One could argue that these cringe-worthy stereotypes were defensible in context: we were at war, caricature naturally relies on stereotypes for all its targets, and (the weakest argument) everybody else was doing it too. But once the band has moved on, and we turn to Donald, living in a land which is itself transformed into swastikas, the cartoon takes on a surreal intensity. My favorite gag is when Donald salutes the Fuehrer with his behind (Disney was inordinately fond of butt humor). No other cartoon equaled its inventiveness or devotion to fighting the war through humor. *Der Fuehrer's Face* deserved the Oscar.

As for the other nominations, we get a completely forgotten title from Terrytoons *All Out for V*. The cartoon has left absolutely no significant footprint on the internet, and while I can guess it's a propaganda cartoon from the title, other than that, I'm clueless (yes, I'm aware some of you already thought that. Sit down and shut up.) No nomination should ever stay for not being remembered.

Blitz Wolf, on the other hand, attacks Hitler with humor, just as *Der Fuehrer's Face* did. A spoof of *The Three Little Pigs*, with Adolf Wolf invading Pigmania, *Blitz Wolf* was Tex Avery's first cartoon at MGM. Watching it today, we can see why Tex Avery was such a genius at parody. The smart pig is named Sergeant Pork, his house bristling with artillery; the swastika is crossed sausage. The wolf's car says "Der Fewer Der Better"; he holds up a sign that says "Go on and hiss! Who cares." I care! The nomination should stay.

Juke Box Jamboree, directed by Walter Lantz, has a mouse getting drunk and dancing with crazy "spirits" from liquor bottles. Sound a little familiar? Right – *Dumbo* and the "Pink Elephants" number. *Juke Box Jamboree* is derivative and not particularly amusing. The butt in the hot mustard scene was as goofy as it got, but even that steals from Disney. No nomination should ever be given for theft.

Pigs in a Polka, like *Blitz Wolf*, retells the story of the Three Little pigs, this time set to several of Brahms' Hungarian Dances (conducted by the Big Bad Wolf). *Pigs in a Polka* is a forerunner of the opera spoofs Chuck Jones would perfect in the Fifties. Enjoyably silly, and all perfectly synchronized to a classical pastiche by the unduly ignored genius, Carl Stalling. A good nomination.

Tulips Shall Grow is one of George Pal's Puppetoons, this one showing the Dutch boy and girl resisting a mechanical invasion, clearly meant to represent the Nazis. The invasion succeeds, only to be turned back by nature itself. And yes, tulips grow. An odd little film, and more affecting than I expected it to be. The nomination should stay.

As for those cartoons which were passed over, perhaps the most innovative of all was *The Dover Boys*, directed by Chuck Jones – who almost lost his job when he broke some conventions to make this spoof of the early twentieth century Rover Boys series, which featured young lads getting into trouble at a military academy. *The Dover Boys* isn't as funny as it once must have been, because nobody reads the source material it spoofs, but what remains is still vintage Chuck Jones, and should have been nominated.

WHAT THEY GOT WRONG:

Patriotism should never be allowed to interfere with artistic judgment. Seriously.

Best Picture: *Mrs. Miniver*
Best Actor: James Cagney, *Yankee Doodle Dandy*
Best Actress: Greer Garson, *Mrs. Miniver*
Best Director: William Wyler, *Mrs. Miniver*
Best Supporting Actor: Van Heflin, *Johnny Eager*
Best Supporting Actress: Teresa Wright, *Mrs. Miniver*
Best Writing (Original Motion Picture Story): Emeric Pressburger, *The Invaders*
Best Writing (Screenplay): George Froeschel, James Hilton, Claudine West, and Arthur Wimperis, *Mrs. Miniver*
Best Cinematography (Black & White): Joseph Ruttenberg, *Mrs. Miniver*
Best Cinematography (Color): Leon Shamroy, *The Black Swan*
Best Musical Score: Ray Heindorf and Heinz Roemheld, *Yankee Doodle Dandy*
Best Art Direction (Black & White): Richard Day, Joseph C. Wright, and Thomas Little, *This Above All*
Best Art Direction (Color): Richard Day, Joseph C. Wright, and Thomas Little, *My Gal Sal*
Best Special Effects: Farciot Edouart, Gordon Jennings, William L. Pereira, Louis Mesenkop, *Reap the Wild Wind*

1942 493

Best Picture: *Mrs. Miniver* won, over *The Invaders, Kings Row, The Magnificent Ambersons, The Pied Piper, The Pride of the Yankees, Random Harvest, The Talk of the Town, Wake Island,* and *Yankee Doodle Dandy*

Mrs. Miniver proved to be the first chance the Academy had to show how patriotic it could be; they handed it every award they could, falling over themselves to show how much dear old England and Mrs. Miniver's stiff upper lip meant to them. Supposedly, the Minivers are middle class – it says so in the opening titles – but the enormous home they live in seems to undercut that. That disparity between the claims the movie makes, and the reality that certainly existed in England in 1942, cannot be reconciled except as propaganda – or typical MGM folderol. As an historical document of the war, and as an example of propaganda, *Mrs. Miniver* should be seen and appreciated. But as an artistic achievement, *Mrs. Miniver* is certainly not the best picture of the year – Pauline Kael went so far as to call it a "generally offensive picture" and "scandalously smug."[ccxviii] The nomination should stay, for the impact it had, but not the Oscar.

Also known as *49th Parallel*, *The Invaders* stars Leslie Howard and Laurence Olivier in small roles, but the main focus is on a group of stranded Nazi submariners who are attempting to escape Canada. An unusual story, as it is told from the point of view of the Nazis (see writing awards below), *The Invaders* has some stunning outdoor cinematography of Canada, an impressive submarine set (which they blow up), and some of the pudgiest pilots you've ever seen. Okay, so that last one doesn't matter much, but just between you and me, the actors playing the pilots all look like they're trying to impersonate Curly of the Three Stooges or Oliver Hardy. Odd casting – almost as odd as seeing Laurence Olivier as a bearded French fur trapper taking a bath. Leslie Howard plays another of his effete intellectuals, then does something incredibly stupid by walking directly into gunfire, which seriously diminishes the hard-won realism of *The Invaders*. The pleasures of the movie, other than the nature photography, lie in abhorring the brutality of the Nazis, then watching them fall apart and get their comeuppance, one righteous death at a time. Overall, the movie is a fairly effective piece of propaganda, both in its paean to Canadian beauty, custom, and diversity, as it is in its condemnation of the Nazis. We do get a piece by Ralph Vaughan Williams in the score. The cinematography was done by Freddie Young, and the editing was by David Lean. The two would go on to *Lawrence of Arabia* and *Dr. Zhivago* (Lean switched to directing soon after *The Invaders*). As for being one of the best pictures of the year, and in terms of its continuing value as a work of art rather than propaganda, the nomination is only barely deserved – and that mostly for the idea and the cinematography, as the acting is minimally interesting at best.

All we remember of *Kings Row* today is Ronald Reagan looking under the blanket and crying out in anguish, "Where's the rest of me?!?" A kind of *Peyton Place* of the Forties, *Kings Row* aims to undercut the image of small town Victorian life as wholesome and pure. Much of the original novel by Henry Bellamann was excised, including the issues of incest and homosexuality, but what is left is enough to titillate and upset bourgeois sensibilities. If the film has a unifying theme, it would be the need to treat the problems of our life in psychological terms, to root out the causes of our behaviors, and through understanding them, heal. We tend to see this as a matter of fact in this age of readily available therapists, but in 1941, when psychiatry was seen as a fad by most Americans, and dangerous hoopla at that, *Kings Row* was a brave film. *Kings Row* isn't perfect (see Best Director below for more), but still worth watching – particularly for Reagan's shining moment. The nomination is deserved.

The Magnificent Ambersons remains the great could-have-been-the-best-movie-ever-made in American sound film history. The opening is a great montage of nostalgia, of the ever-shifting ways of fashion and the slower pace of life. Director Orson Welles has chosen an unusual technique of extreme close-ups of the town's citizens, a kind of Greek chorus commenting upon the doings of the Ambersons. What strikes me at this particular viewing of *Ambersons* is how much the movie is constructed like a radio show. We simply don't need to watch the movie to experience most of its pleasures, particularly at the beginning of the movie, which seems fairly close to Welles' original conception, as Welles' narration looks to be complete and interrelated with the action. RKO studio, however, derailed Welles' plan for the movie (detailed in Robert L. Carringer's indispensable *The Magnificent Ambersons: a Reconstruction*). The studio cut the movie from two and a half hours to eighty-eight minutes and released it as a double feature with Lupe Velez' *Mexican Spitfire Sees a Ghost*. One of the great lost treasures of the cinema is the rough cut of Welles' version of *Ambersons* that was sent to him in Brazil, where he was on a good will tour; perhaps somewhere it still exists, waiting to be found. As it is, *The Magnificent Ambersons* is a study in ruined perfection. According to at least one report, Welles claimed the first hour of the film was largely as he shot it; everything after that, was not.[ccxix] I would agree; the movie starts so well, and ends so badly. For what remains of Welles' vision, the movie richly deserved the nomination.

In *The Pied Piper*, crusty old Monty Woolley plays an Englishman who decides to help Roddy McDowall and a growing tribe of children escape the Nazis in France. Based on a novel by Nevil Shute (*On the Beach*), and directed by Irving Pichel (*Destination Moon*), *The Pied Piper* also features Otto Preminger as a Nazi interrogator. Clearly a picture made to support WWII – and nothing is quite so effective as showing innocent children being hurt by such monsters as the Nazis – the film rises above its propaganda purposes to inspire and amuse. The nomination should stay for this unusual movie.

One of the best sports films ever made, *The Pride of the Yankees* presents the inspiring, heart-rending story of Lou Gehrig, who may have been the best baseball player ever (and had his eponymous disease not stricken him down, might have shattered many more records). Gary Cooper is perfectly cast as Gehrig, with Teresa Wright as his wife, and Walter Brennan as his sportswriter advocate. Most famous for the "Luckiest Man" speech at the end – a speech Cooper memorized and used to entertain troops in WWII – *The Pride of the Yankees* was, by far, the sentimental favorite of my friends and family. Watching the film objectively, one can see the schmaltz working, particularly in the scenes with the overbearing German mother. Appearances by Gehrig's real teammates include Babe Ruth in his best movie turn. Sam Wood's direction is stodgy, and the pacing could use some tightening, but the ending never fails to start the waterworks. A very fine nomination, mostly due to Gary Cooper.

Random Harvest strikes a somber tone, as Ronald Colman plays a WWI veteran stricken by amnesia – not just once, but twice! Greer Garson is a theatrical entertainer who has to find a way to lift Colman out of his pain as a broken soldier, then help him find his way back to her as a victim of a second round of amnesia, without simply telling him (some folderol about the shock being too much keeps the plot going). Ultimately, however, I feel much the same as Bosley Crowther did in 1942: "But, for all its emotional excess, *Random Harvest* is a strangely empty film. Its characters are creatures of fortune, not partisans in determining their own fates. Miss Garson and Mr. Colman are charming; they act perfectly. But they never seem real. And a sense of psychiatric levels is not conveyed in either the script or direction. One might also inquire mildly why it is that the wife in this case never persuaded her aberrant husband to consult a doctor in an effort to regain his lost life. Personally, we had the feeling that there was nothing wrong with him which couldn't be cured by a psychiatrist—or maybe a whack on the head."[ccxx] No nomination should have been made for this falsehood of a film.

That *The Talk of the Town* was nominated for best picture is a sure sign of the Academy loving pictures that take themselves too seriously (and not in a good way). Cary Grant is still hunting for an Oscar by taking on roles with very dark sides; it would take Hitchcock for that blend to finally work well, for which see *Suspicion* and, especially, *Notorious*. Jean Arthur and Ronald Colman seem lost in this mishmash of a film, which is part screwball comedy, part philosophic debate, and part social awareness lesson. The film manipulates us into taking Grant's side from the first moments, trading on the experiences we've had with Grant in other films to assure us he isn't guilty, and then forcing us to identify with Grant through the visuals (see Best Cinematography (Black & White) below for more). All too soon, the comic Grant is back, and we've forgotten the anguish of his escape – so what was the point in escalating the tension and setting up expectations of a serious film? Those expectations only return when the movie needs to come to a satisfactory end of some kind. Overall, the movie is in desperate need of a major script rewrite (see Best Writing (Screenplay) below) and the kind of brilliance given by Frank Capra at his height. No nomination should have been given.

One of the very first combat films of WWII, *Wake Island* would be imitated throughout WWII and afterwards as the model for this genre. Beginning before Pearl Harbor and ending with a patriotic fervor, *Wake Island* remains an enjoyable film, mixing a recreated island at California's Salton Sea, combat footage, special effects and lots of explosions. As a piece of propaganda, *Wake Island* proved very effective. As a work of art, not so much, as it is limited by two-dimensional characters. The nomination should stay, for the influence it had on the genre.

To protect himself against charges of communism, James Cagney went out of his way to find the most patriotic film that he could. More importantly, he was always looking for a chance to sing and dance again. Cagney found both in the life story of the patron saint of patriotic song and dance, George M. Cohan (fortunately for him, Fred Astaire turned the part down first). *Yankee Doodle Dandy* is a lollapalooza of a songfest, all red white and blue and full of Cagney's special intensity and energy, layered over with a thick emotional investment on Cagney's part (watch his farewell to his father, played by Walter Huston). *Yankee Doodle Dandy* remains one of Cagney's best films – although the narrative frame is a bit creaky – and perhaps his best musical. A delight to watch when many patriotic films have lost some of their appeal to age and false notes played for propaganda, *Yankee Doodle Dandy* richly deserved this nomination.

1942 497

As for those films not nominated, I would first like to mention *Holiday Inn*. I don't think Bing Crosby ever made a better musical (although some prefer the remake, *White Christmas*); Fred Astaire was only better when he was with Ginger Rogers. The musical outshines almost every other made this year, including the more patriotic *Yankee Doodle Dandy*. The recursive quality, in which the movie we are watching is remade into a movie the characters are watching, and the "real" love story ends up back on the "set" which was used as the "real" inn, has always struck me as a comment about the ways in which our sense of life has come to be determined by the pictures we see, and the songs we sing.[104] A very fine film indeed, and one that should have been nominated for Best Picture.

But even more, *To Be or Not to Be* seems to be the major omission of the year. Lubitsch went for the Nazi jugular on this one, by way of the funny bone (the actor playing Hitler says, "Heil, myself!"). Jack Benny gives a fine comic performance, his best on film; Carole Lombard does as well as she ever did, which is saying a great deal (and this was her last role). The script is brilliantly funny: "What a husband doesn't know won't hurt his wife." The tone, pace and shifts from comic to tragic are deft and swift (see Best Director for more). The movie remains one of the peaks of director Ernst Lubitsch's career. That it was ignored for everything but its score (a minor one at best) is criminal. The Academy should have recognized it with more nominations – and the Oscar for Best Picture of 1942.

Best Actor: James Cagney won for *Yankee Doodle Dandy*, over Walter Pidgeon, *Mrs. Miniver*; Monty Woolley, *The Pied Piper*; Gary Cooper, *The Pride of the Yankees*; and Ronald Colman, *Random Harvest*

James Cagney won for *Yankee Doodle Dandy*, and were it not for one single performance the Academy completely ignored, I would be happy to agree. Cagney is an absolute delight as George M. Cohan, and his unique dancing style has never been on better display, as was his sense of humor. Perhaps the emotional highlight of the movie is Cagney's farewell to his father, which should rend the heart of any person who owns one. An excellent nomination.

Having ignored his masterly performance in *How Green Was My Valley*, the Academy proceeded to nominate Walter Pidgeon for *Mrs. Miniver*, in the role for which he would be stereotyped for the next dec-

---

[104] A brilliant friend of mine suggests I am speaking of Baudrillard's theory of the simulacra here; apparently, I paid more attention in those literary theory classes than I realized.

ade: Mr. Greer Garson. Pidgeon would gaze adoringly at Garson, and get paid quite well to do it; given how lovely Garson was, I wouldn't call that acting. No nomination should have been given to this patriotic fooferaw.

Putting professional griper Monty Woolley with cute adorable children in *The Pied Piper* was a stroke of genius. When admonished to be kind to the children, Woolley quipped: "I shall pat each of the little darlings on their heads until they drop dead."[ccxxi] Woolley is at his best when he's being indignant and interacting with the children, but at times, he does go over the top. What we should not accept is this nomination, instead of his iconic performance in this year's *The Man Who Came to Dinner*, as Woolley was far better there. While he gives an interesting, enjoyable performance here, in *The Man Who Came to Dinner*, he made his claim to permanence in our cultural memory. There, Woolley plays Sheridan Whiteside (based on theater critic Alexander Woolcott), the greatest curmudgeon of the American theater, forced to stay in a local home when he hurts his hip. Woolley has the time of his life taking over the house, bullying and cajoling everybody, and generally having his way no matter what. Woolley should have been nominated for this brilliant turn. You will simply never see an actor enjoying a role more.

In *The Pride of the Yankees*, Gary Cooper brings a gentle strength to the role of Lou Gehrig, showing respect and reverence for the great first baseman. Cooper also adds a comic touch when needed, as well as providing some romance with Teresa Wright and the pathos of the onslaught of disease. Cooper's version of Gehrig's "luckiest man" speech ranks with his courtroom defense in *Mr. Deeds Goes to Town*, making his nomination a most worthy one.

In *Random Harvest*, Ronald Colman got a chance to play an amnesiac and WWI veteran who has to find his way in the world, after having his mental health shattered by his wounds. Colman's voice is as rich as ever, and his capacity to act has deepened over the years. Colman's best scenes come in the first part of the film, when he brings out the damage from the war in his eyes (Colman himself was wounded in WWI). He does the best he can with this material, but loses the focus of the movie (as it turns to Greer Garson), until the very end. Colman can keep the nomination for what he does get the chance to do.

Three performances were omitted by the Academy (in addition to picking the wrong Monty Woolley performance).

The first is Ronald Reagan for *Kings Row*, in his one great turn as an actor. As Bette Davis once said to David Letterman after Ronald Reagan was president, "I suppose we have to give him that one." For fifteen seconds, Reagan proved himself to be an actor of the finest caliber. I have rarely experienced the kind of chill down my spine as I did the first time I saw him realize his legs were gone. Some would say his greatest performance was as president; I say it's this moment in *Kings Row*, and he should have been nominated.

An early film noir, *This Gun for Hire* stars Alan Ladd as a cold-blooded killer out to get the enemy agent employer who betrayed him; Veronica Lake comes along for the ride. Few actors had ever portrayed such cold menace on the screen before; like Hitler, Ladd's psychopath lavishes attention on animals and tolerates children, but coldly kills anybody who gets in his way, or who crosses him (he does protect those who've been good to him). We've seen actors attempt this kind of role before, most famously with Robert Montgomery and *Night Must Fall*, but Montgomery never had that unforgiving gleam in his eye. Like Humphrey Bogart in *The Maltese Falcon*, Alan Ladd moves the conception of a protagonist further away from the goody two-shoes of the Thirties and deeper into the darker realms of human behavior. The movie itself feels like a bridge is being crossed from the goofy whodunits of the *Thin Man* series into the world of film noir. Robert Preston as a cop and Veronica Lake as a magician/singer/undercover agent have the kind of loving banter we find in many Thirties movies about couples; Alan Ladd takes Lake as a hostage, and heads her deep into another kind of movie altogether. The hybrid film doesn't always work because of the tonal shifts and the overblown ending, but for the daring of Alan Ladd at throwing himself into his character, he should have been nominated for Best Actor.

And finally, in a stunning neglect of the nation's most consummate actor, the Academy failed to recognize Spencer Tracy's performance in the butchered but compelling *Woman of the Year*. Tracy had won two previous Oscars for roles that were, in turn, showy and mannered (*Captains Courageous*), and sanctimonious and one-dimensional (*Boys Town*) – which is why he should not have won for those roles. Since that time, he had worked hard on further developing an absolutely natural style that evoked the deepest level of human emotion and complexity. With *Woman of the Year*, Spencer Tracy reached the pinnacle of his craft. Except when he took on unadvised roles that required accents, Tracy would mine this innately American character he projected on the screen in his very best roles. Watching his sportswriter character in *Woman of the Year*, we know we are watching a very real human being. One piece of evidence to show this acquisition of full mastery over all aspects of the human condition: for the very first time, Spencer Tracy played a man in love and didn't look ridiculous. Take a look at him wooing Lana Turner, or abusing Ingrid Bergman, in *Dr. Jekyll and Mr. Hyde*, and then tell me if he doesn't look more than a little false. Of course, on one level, Tracy wasn't acting at all: he was falling deeply in love with Katharine Hepburn. But when he did so, we fell in love with Hepburn all the more, which is what makes the revised ending of the movie as much of a betrayal of the story's construction and themes as Hitchcock's faked ending for *Suspicion* (for more, see Best Actress below). For Tracy, his capacity to project more and more by stripping away and paring down his mannerisms and responses was the secret to his craft. Watch his face in his close-ups with Katharine Hepburn, and tell me when you've ever seen more real passion. Want rueful glee? Watch when he calls up his fighter friend and has him bring up the bar crowd to counter the diplomats who have ruined his wedding night. Throughout, Tracy gives us a picture of a masculine character, but one capable of great sensitivity, warmth and compassion. *Woman of the Year* showed the best acting he had ever done – or anybody else did in this year. Spencer Tracy should have been nominated for Best Actor – and he most definitely should have won.

Best Actress: Greer Garson won for *Mrs. Miniver*, over Rosalind Russell, *My Sister Eileen*; Bette Davis, *Now, Voyager*; Teresa Wright, *The Pride of the Yankees*; and Katharine Hepburn, *Woman of the Year*

Greer Garson won for *Mrs. Miniver*. Well, Louis B. Mayer had already crowned her the new queen of MGM; the Oscar was just her scepter. Unfortunately, she didn't really deserve the Oscar for this role. She had a good performance in *Random Harvest* this year, getting to be a music hall dancer, a young woman who rescues a broken man, and a selfless sacrifice to her amnesiac husband's life. Watching Garson's face and eyes, we can see her wordless suffering. While I still think her performance in that film is ultimately a little shallow in its depiction of humanity, she still outdoes her part in *Mrs. Miniver* as a kind of walking Union Jack. Her scene with the downed Nazi pilot is the most unlikely in the film, and the most melodramatic (which is the same thing, quite often). She can't even slap the German right. She does do well in the bombing scenes, conveying fear and resolve at the same time. Regardless, I don't think Garson deserves the Oscar for either performance, but I would prefer her to have a nomination for *Random Harvest* as the more interesting of the two.

The Academy nominated Rosalind Russell this year for *My Sister Eileen* – perhaps to make up for ignoring her magnificent performance the previous year in *His Girl Friday*. In fact, *Eileen* reminds me a bit of

His Girl Friday, as Russell plays another writer on the way up – except with a screwy sister in tow this time. *My Sister Eileen* isn't a bad movie; it's just an obvious one (the only surprise comes in the cameo at the end). Russell is all right in the role – just not inspired, and not working on the level of the other nominees this year, so she should not have received this nod.

Bette Davis was nominated – yet again – for her superb acting, this time in the romantic melodrama *Now, Voyager*, co-starring Paul Henreid. Davis had been dipping into roles where she played a nebbish who suffers nobly (and sometimes not so nobly); she had also been playing very strong women who demand their own way. With *Now Voyager*, Davis got the chance again to show a human being changing and evolving. This time, instead of being tamed as she was in *Dark Victory* and other films, *Now, Voyager* shows Davis as a woman taking charge of her own life. She plays a daughter dominated and crushed by her Boston Brahmin mother, as Davis labors under her maternal impositions and the restrictions on behavior imposed by her class. *Now, Voyager* is a very subversive film that teaches young women to defy their mothers, pursue their own individual selves, have affairs with married men, and provide loving, healthy role models to children not their own. Idiotically, it also encourages smoking, and may have been more responsible than any other movie in showing cigarettes to be damn sexy. Paul Henreid's trick of lighting two cigarettes then passing one over must have been practiced by a generation of males as the smoothest move ever. While I can't approve of the smoking, this particular Bette Davis role is one of her finest. She brings to this richly rewarding part everything she had learned in her decade of acting, particularly the lessons of William Wyler (although I doubt he would have approved of the caterpillar eyebrows, which disappear when she emerges as the butterfly). If there is a flaw in her performance, it lies in the voiceovers somebody felt necessary, as if we couldn't see those thoughts in Davis' eyes. In the end, she even surmounts the female call to sacrifice that dooms so many of these films, by being the one to decide what her life will be; surprisingly, the source material for this movie is from the same writer who gave us *Stella Dallas*, which should cause all right-thinking human beings to shudder. Davis most definitely deserved this nomination.

Teresa Wright's performance in *The Pride of the Yankees* is at her best, because she follows Gary Cooper's lead and provides a warm, underplayed performance as Lou Gehrig's wife. She exerts an unexpected strength at times, as well as an emotional richness absent from most of her roles. Wright deserved this nomination, even if the role largely calls on her to be a spectator and respond to Cooper, rather than initiating her own actions.

Katharine Hepburn turned in another magnificent performance in *Woman of the Year* – then betrayed every aspect of that performance by shooting a revised ending, where she humiliated her character by taking up the stereotypical expectations of the typical male, and female, of 1942. Hepburn was forced to show herself to be an utter incompetent in those daily tasks of cooking which were the expectations of the housewife. Granted, Tracy added his own blotch to an otherwise flawless turn as her husband by participating, but he didn't have to do much more than sit there watching – and he makes it clear before the end that he doesn't want her to sacrifice herself. The original ending simply had her recognizing that she had to make space for Tracy in her rich, rewarding life of intellectual and diplomatic efforts. But rather than a meeting of equals, the revision made her show that she was willing to give up everything she was for her man. One of the greatest sins of love is to sacrifice character and individuality to satisfy somebody else's expectations. As Emerson put it in his great affirmation *Self-Reliance*, "I must be myself. I cannot break myself any longer for you, or you." What hurts even more comes from the fact that up until that ending, Hepburn and Tracy were turning in the most open and honest emotional performances of their careers[105] – hell, for practically anybody else's careers as well. Watch the scene in the taxi where they tell each other that they love each other, and tell me that's not the most touching and convincing moment in American cinema since Chaplin's face at the end of *City Lights*. For that, Hepburn deserves the nomination – and very nearly, the Oscar.

But in the end, the more impressive performance comes from Bette Davis in *Now, Voyager*. She never played a more complete human being, or one who taught a better lesson: never let other people define you. Always seek your best self. The Oscar should have gone to Bette Davis for the finest performance of the year.

Best Director: William Wyler won for *Mrs. Miniver*, over Sam Wood, *Kings Row*; Mervyn LeRoy, *Random Harvest*; John Farrow, *Wake Island*; and Michael Curtiz, *Yankee Doodle Dandy*.

William Wyler won the Best Director Oscar, after years of striking out. Films he directed had also been nominated for Best Picture every year since 1936; *Mrs. Miniver* was the first to win that category. Unfor-

---

[105] As well as beginning three decades of movie pairings, and a lifelong love affair.

tunately, *Mrs. Miniver* didn't deserve it – and neither did Wyler. In fact, I suspect Wyler set out to make the most crowd-pleasing movie he could in order to capture the elusive statuette, at long last. Finally working for MGM, who had the most organized studio block voting, couldn't have hurt either. The main story, with Greer Garson and Walter Pidgeon, is as blasé and bourgeois as can be; Garson and Pidgeon could have just as easily been Mr. and Mrs. America (which may have been the point, as the movie seems primarily propaganda rather than art). The secondary plot, the love story between the young Miniver son and Teresa Wright's aristocrat, bears little weight, as the son (played by the actor who briefly married his "mother" Greer Garson) has all the acting potential of a flea. One of the most interesting segments of the film comes during one of Lord Haw-Haw's pro-Nazi broadcasts, where the common Englishman keeps right on with his daily activities, unfazed by Haw-Haw's blatherings. The great rescue of the British army in the miracle of Dunkirk is told from the view of the men who sailed the ships back and forth across the channel that night, and remains the most distinctive part of the movie. The film is made well, but after the artistic heights Wyler reached with *The Letter* and *The Little Foxes*, *Mrs. Miniver* is a distinct comedown. Wyler would make a far greater, more personal film about the war in *The Best Years of Our Lives*. He should keep his nomination because of the competence, but he should not have won the Oscar.

In the Forties, Sam Wood always seemed to be trying his hardest to make an Important Picture. He should have relaxed; maybe the stodginess and pretension would have gone away. He never succeeded in making a truly great serious movie, but *Kings Row* may have come closest. The movie begins well, but once the romance ensues, the film begins to stumble, particularly when Robert Cummings begins to woo Betty Field. Her psychiatrist father (Claude Rains) has isolated her since childhood (in the novel, the cause is incest; here, congenital insanity from the mother, which absolves all moral stains for her father). The faults with pacing and motivation really should lie at the feet of Wood, who never really understood such things (Groucho Marx always said Wood never laughed at the jokes in *A Night at the Opera*). Field's performance should have been reined back in, and made more subtle, but Wood wouldn't recognize subtle if it snuck up and cut off his legs. As the movie shifts over to focus on Ronald Reagan and Ann Sheridan, the narrative solidifies again and Wood regains control over his material – but loses that drive when the movie returns to the Robert Cummings story arc, and the ending is clichéd and shorthanded. Wood should keep his nomination, even though the movie has these problems, because anybody who can pull the kind of performance Wood got from Reagan deserves this particular nod.

Clearly, Mervyn LeRoy had seen *Rebecca* before directing *Random Harvest*. The opening mimics that of *Rebecca*, with a camera dollying in towards an asylum instead of Manderley, but the voiceover resembles that of *Rebecca* as well. A serious melodrama, for *Random Harvest* makes some very interesting choices early on, among them the use of shadowy figures in the fog to replicate Colman's terrifying memories of the war. LeRoy does his habitual best to milk every chance for tears. *Random Harvest* is a competent, glossy MGM film, of a piece with the kind of pretty hackwork MGM put out regularly. LeRoy can keep his nomination, for doing the best he could with the kind of material he was given, and for the early, more artistic scenes.

John Farrow (Mia's father) turned to *Wake Island* after being injured during service in the Royal Navy. He crafted a propaganda piece which brings home the loss soldiers feel, as well as the bravery and sacrifices soldiers make. Farrow does get Brian Donlevy to dig a little deeper than that overbearing actor generally did, particularly in the scene where he explains to another soldier that his wife was killed at Pearl Harbor. Farrow doesn't show much imagination in his direction otherwise, and I strongly suspect the nod was a patriotic one, rather than an artistic decision. No nomination should have been given for mere flag-waving.

Michael Curtiz did a first-rate job on *Yankee Doodle Dandy*, keeping the musical songs coming, without dragging down the narrative of Cohan's life, or forgetting the need to root the story in an emotional depth few musicals have. Yes, corny it may be at times, but honest corn grown in honest manure. Much of that verve, efficiency and purity of purpose comes from the direction of Michael Curtiz, who knew how to tell a story more effectively than almost any other director (much of it by focusing on Cagney, but also through staging the musical numbers as inventively as Curtiz staged fights). A good nomination.

As for those directors who were omitted, Orson Welles might have received a nomination for *The Magnificent Ambersons* had he remained in the United States until his film was complete, rather than gallivanting off down to Rio for a party. The animosity in Hollywood was balanced against the respect for his genius, as we can see from the multiple nominations his first two films received, despite Hearst's enmity. Personally, I can see the innovations of *The Magnificent Ambersons*: the Greek chorus, the set design, the continued use of sound and narrative cuts to keep the story moving from *Citizen Kane*, the attempt to move American film further into social commentary without losing the essential quality of telling a story first and foremost, and the desire to have tragedy become a viable form of American cinema. These things are what the butchering of the film by RKO's masters endangered. Welles still should have been nominated.

Sadly, one more director is painfully absent: Ernst Lubitsch, for his last truly great film, *To Be or Not to Be*. Lubitsch deftly mixed satire, broad humor, pointed sexual commentary and infidelity, a ridiculing of actors and their egos, a spy adventure, a caper, and marital politics with an attack on the Nazis – and not just any attack, but the best one that Hollywood ever created. As Lubitsch himself said, "What I have satirized in this picture are the Nazis and their ridiculous ideology. I have also satirized the attitude of actors who always remain actors regardless how dangerous the situation might be, which I believe is a true observation."[ccxxii] *To Be or Not to Be* weaves its way from the silly to the serious to the satirical and back again with the deftest touch of any director working any style of film this year. Like many great films, *To Be or Not to Be* shocked people, who didn't quite know what to make of it. We do now: Ernst Lubitsch should have won the Oscar for Best Director, just as *To Be or Not to Be* should have won the Oscar for Best Picture.

Best Supporting Actor: Van Heflin won for *Johnny Eager*, over Henry Travers, *Mrs. Miniver*; Frank Morgan, *Tortilla Flat*; William Bendix, *Wake Island*; and Walter Huston, *Yankee Doodle Dandy*

Van Heflin won for *Johnny Eager*, or as I like to call it, MGM pretends they are really Warner Brothers, but with better looking people. *Johnny Eager* stars Robert Taylor and Lana Turner in a knockoff gangster flick, along with Taylor sporting Errol Flynn's mustache. Unless Taylor and Turner get the juices flowing for you, the only reason to watch this film is to see Van Heflin in one of his best roles, that of Taylor's alcoholic smartass of a best friend. When Van Heflin is on the screen, the movie comes alive; otherwise, *Johnny Eager* is just a run-of-the-mill gangster picture. At the end, Van Heflin does something that a male actor rarely did in the movies in 1942: he cries, openly, honestly, and effectively. For that alone he should keep his nomination, but the Oscar should have gone to a more exuberant turn.

Henry Travers is best known today for playing the angel Clarence in *It's a Wonderful Life*. In *Mrs. Miniver*, he is a railway employee who is friends with Greer Garson and shares with her his hobby of breeding roses – the best of which he names after her. A whole subplot of class warfare hinges on the rose contest, between the lower class Travers and the aristocratic Dame May Whitty. Ultimately, he exists to adore Greer

Garson, to espouse quiet support for England, and to increase the sentiment. Given all that, Travers still comes across with quiet dignity, and he deserves a nomination.

Frank Morgan played without his usual boisterous fumbling in *Tortilla Flat*, based on the Steinbeck novel, and starring John Garfield, Hedy Lamarr, and Spencer Tracy. This story of poor Mexican-Americans proves painful to watch with the reductive stereotypes of simple people and simple pleasures. Morgan plays the Pirate, an old bearded homeless man with a pack of dogs and a kindly face. When Tracy brings him into their home, intending to rob him of the quarters he has saved for years, Morgan plays the doddering aspects nicely, with a saintly look in his eyes. When Tracy discovers Morgan has saved nearly a thousand quarters in order to buy a gold candlestick for the church to honor St. Francis of Assisi, Tracy melts – and Morgan looks very much like St. Francis himself. Morgan gets cleaned up and takes a place of modesty in the church while the candlestick is presented – then his dogs show up. Of all the characters in the film, he's the most eccentric, and the least racist, showing the nobility of spirit in action. Morgan actually reminds me of a kind of a male St. Bernadette, the holy simpleton. He deserves his nomination (for a role very different from his iconic Wizard of Oz).

As he would in his long-running radio and television series *The Life of Riley*, William Bendix typically played comic supporting roles, often those with a temper. Here, in *Wake Island*, he plays the same kind of role, darkened with the need to portray a time of war. Bendix is a combative, dopey Marine, who gets out of the Corps just in time to watch WWII begin – and immediately re-enlists. Bendix had to have earned this nomination out of the patriotic surge for such performances; he really didn't deserve one for a role he generally played over and over again. But he did deserve a nomination for his role as the vicious thug in *The Glass Key*, starring Alan Ladd, Veronica Lake, and Brian Donlevy. After their surprise success in *This Gun for Hire*, Alan Ladd and Veronica Lake were quickly reteamed for this adaptation of Dashiell Hammett's novel. When William Bendix makes his first appearance, his eyes could kill. When Bendix spits on the floor to show his contempt, it may be the single ugliest thing ever put on the screen in America...until he beats the crap out of Alan Ladd, while Bendix calls Ladd "Baby" and "Sweetie-Pie" the entire time. For this role, Bendix deserved the nomination.

Walter Huston picked up another nomination for *Yankee Doodle Dandy*, after his excellent turn as Mr. Scratch in *The Devil and Daniel Webster*. Playing George M. Cohan's father, Huston hams it up on stage and off, showing off his singing and dancing skills (who knew?). His finest scenes come towards the end, as he and Cagney share honest raw emotion. A good nomination.

In the end, the most startling and memorable performance by an actor in a supporting role was that of William Bendix in *The Glass Key*. A more gleeful sadist could not be found in the Forties; Bendix played completely against the kind of light comic roles he would make his bread and butter. He deserved the Oscar...Baby.

Best Supporting Actress: Teresa Wright won for *Mrs. Miniver*, over Agnes Moorehead, *The Magnificent Ambersons*; Dame May Whitty, *Mrs. Miniver*; Gladys Cooper, *Now, Voyager*; and Susan Peters, *Random Harvest*

Teresa Wright won for playing the aristocratic granddaughter in *Mrs. Miniver*. She would go down in history as Mrs. Lou Gehrig in *The Pride of the Yankees*. Wright and the Miniver son fall in love, and marry, after some class warfare debates. Wright is pleasant enough in this movie, but I suspect voters gave her this as a consolation prize for not winning for her more personal performance in *The Pride of the Yankees*. That, and she gets a death scene, which the Academy always loves, but I rarely find convincing. No Oscar should have been given to her.

Dame May Whitty, nominated for playing the local aristocrat in the same movie, keeps her nose properly up in the air, even after she shows her human side. Wright didn't even deserve the nomination for this movie, for what is a very shallow performance, but Dame Whitty did.

Agnes Moorehead had given a very brief but intense performance in *Citizen Kane* as Kane's mother; in *The Magnificent Ambersons*, she is gifted a more extended part, and does just as well with it. As Aunt Fanny, a spinster who has set her hat on Joseph Cotten, Moorehead projects an intense, neurotic quality that builds off of the kind of emotional unsettling pioneered by Judith Anderson's housekeeper in *Rebecca*, and extends it into a true American archetype of the Victorian era (Aunt Pitty-Pat in *Gone with the Wind* is the comic version). In later generations, that group would make Miltown and Valium best selling drugs. The shrillness, plotting and emotional collapse of Moorehead's character remains a powerful performance, and a good nomination.

In *Now, Voyager* Gladys Cooper creates one of the meanest bitches on wheels in all of film history – literally on wheels, as her manipulative, smothering, destructive character is in a wheelchair. Bette Davis had pioneered this kind of character in *Of Human Bondage*; now, she had the opportunity to fight against the monster herself. Cooper sits herself on the parlor chair like a queen upon a throne, and only when

Davis declares her independence does Cooper find herself replaced. Gladys Cooper would later go on to play this same role elsewhere, notably in *The Bishop's Wife* – but she earned this nomination.

In *Random Harvest*, Susan Peters plays Kitty, the second object of Ronald Colman's romantic affections. Peters has a thankless role, since we know perfectly well that Colman will remember his wife Greer Garson, and that Peters will lose. Perhaps the Academy felt sorry for her, but I have no sympathy. Peters tries for perky; she comes off as aggressive then simpering; she is given the most ridiculous speech made in any movie this year. Peters died of complications from a gun accident at a very young age; even before that, she never managed another decent film. MGM studio block voting must have brought her this nomination, which isn't worthwhile.

In the end, Agnes Moorehead – who would end her career on TV playing the catty mother on *Bewitched* – offers the most impressive performance, building off the two minutes of excellence in *Citizen Kane* the previous year, and heading herself off to a career playing women who did not follow the usual expectations. Moorehead should have won the Oscar for *The Magnificent Ambersons*.

Best Writing (Original Motion Picture Story): Emeric Pressburger won for *The Invaders*, over Irving Berlin, *Holiday Inn*; Paul Gallico, *The Pride of the Yankees*; Sidney Harmon, *The Talk of the Town*; and Robert Buckner, *Yankee Doodle Dandy*

Emeric Pressburger was a Jewish refugee; *The Invaders* (aka *49th Parallel*) was a masterly attack on the Nazis for their brutality and danger. By depicting a group of Nazi submariners sunk off the coast of Canada who attempt to escape to the United States, Pressburger came up with a truly unique way to tell a story. He and director Michael Powell were also nominated for the screenplay of another collaboration this year; they would go on to make *Black Narcissus* and *The Red Shoes*; Pressburger was also nominated for the screenplay of this movie, making him a nominee in all three writing categories in a single year, a unique achievement. Pressburger deserved a nomination for the concept, but not the Oscar.

Irving Berlin was given credit for the story idea for *Holiday Inn*, another retrospective of his songs. Bing Crosby opens an inn only on various holidays; fourteen Berlin songs fill those celebrations. Crosby and Astaire fight over a woman (Crosby wins, as he almost always did in this repetitive formula). Remade later as the slower-paced *White Christmas*, *Holiday Inn* features one of Fred Astaire's best dance numbers (the one with the firecrackers) and Bing Crosby's biggest hit,

"White Christmas." Not much of a story, but enough to let Astaire dance and Crosby sing in one of the best films either one of them ever did (despite the blackface scene and the stereotyped black children). The nomination should stay for Mr. Berlin.

Paul Gallico's story for *The Pride of the Yankees* isn't particularly original, and neither is the way he tells it. How is it an original idea to tell the life of Lou Gehrig, who was all over the news with the onslaught of his disease and impending death? Depending on how the material is presented, perhaps – but this is the least original way to tell a story: start in adolescence, and then show his rise and fall episodically. Gallico would go on to a certain kind of fame by writing the novel *The Poseidon Adventure*, but no nomination should there have been for what is essentially a scrapbook of Gehrig's life, and not a very revealing one.

The idea of a kind of love triangle between an escaped man, an esteemed law professor, and a pretty girl seems fairly rife with possibilities. Unfortunately, *The Talk of the Town* never digs fully into them. Sidney Harmon never really went beyond writing, then producing, some minor Hollywood films. No nomination should have been given for this failed opportunity.

Robert Buckner's idea for *Yankee Doodle Dandy* isn't all that original: tell the story of George M. Cohan, and do so from cradle to (almost) grave. Mostly, it's an excuse to let Cagney dance, which is always a good idea, and he does come up with a unique frame by working President Franklin Roosevelt into the story – so we'll agree Buckner should keep his nomination.

The most original story of the year went un-nominated: *Cat People*, from an original story by DeWitt Bodeen. The horror is grounded in the sexual terrors of a young woman, a very potent well indeed in 1942, when such things were denied by most Americans even to exist. Bodeen and his friend, producer Val Lewton, realized very quickly that they could do things in low-budget B-pictures that they simply couldn't get away with elsewhere. The same was true of science fiction throughout the Forties and Fifties, for which illustration I suggest the short works of Robert Heinlein, Ray Bradbury, and Theodore Sturgeon from the period, as well as others. How else could anybody have made a fear and longing for sexuality on the part of a beautiful woman into such a suggestive film? Granted, some of the execution of that idea isn't done brilliantly – the male lead has all the emotional depth of a puddle – but the concept itself is groundbreaking. DeWitt Bodeen would go on to write *The Curse of the Cat People, I Remember Mama*, and *Billy Budd* – but he should have won the Best Writing (Original) Oscar in 1942 for *Cat People*.

Best Writing (Screenplay): George Froeschel, James Hilton, Claudine West, and Arthur Wimperis won for *Mrs. Miniver*, over Rodney Ackland and Emeric Pressburger, *The Invaders*; Herman J. Mankiewicz and Jo Swerling, *The Pride of the Yankees*; George Froeschel, Claudine West and Arthur Wimperis, *Random Harvest*; and Sidney Buchman & Irwin Shaw, *The Talk of the Town*

George Froeschel, James Hilton, Claudine West, and Arthur Wimperis won for *Mrs. Miniver*, adapting the book by Jan Struther. I think they could have taken *Burke's Peerage* and made a movie and still won the award in this year of patriotic fervor. The writers start by getting the women in the audience to sympathize with Greer Garson by showing her rushing to buy a hat she can't afford – but can't resist. She is being depicted as a "typical female" – one dressed to the nines and looking like a beauty parlor follows her around. The writers then get the sympathy of the males by showing Garson as worried about what her husband will think of the expense, and then by showing her accepting male adoration from the safely old Henry Travers. The only flaw the writers allow to either Garson or Walter Pidgeon is a slight economic extravagance, which is only there to provide a little comic relief, and allow the two leads to give things up when the war begins. My favorite scene in the script comes in the bomb shelter, when they are reading from *Alice in Wonderland* as the children sleep and Garson knits, and the tension builds and builds – and the gentle memories of Lewis Carroll's classic reminds us all of better days. The ending of the film, with the sermon in the bombed out church, is very well-written propaganda. For those two scenes, the nomination can remain. Overall, however, *Mrs. Miniver* is not the best adaptation of the year.

For *The Invaders*, Rodney Ackland and Emeric Pressburger shared the nomination – Pressburger for adapting his own story, which won the Oscar in that category (although he didn't deserve it). Unfortunately, much of the execution doesn't live up to the audacity of the original idea. *The Invaders* is episodic, uneven, and focused on positions rather than character development. No nomination was warranted.

Herman J. Mankiewicz and Jo Swerling took a hackneyed form in *The Pride of the Yankees*, and turned it out fresh, with good dialogue and real emotion. They even took Gehrig's original speech and made it work even better. Now that takes some doing. They were so good, nobody remembers what Gehrig actually said: they just remember Cooper doing the script version. A solid nomination, even if director Sam Wood does it as little justice as possible.

Adapting James Hilton's novel *Random Harvest*, the crew of writers did their best to set aside the issues of bigamy by erasing Ronald Colman's first wife. They crafted a romantic melodrama rife with opportunities for Colman to be sadly noble, for Greer Garson to be bubbly and optimistic and compassionate, and for the audience to weep copiously. They shifted the focus of the story away from the mystery of who Colman is, to the romance and emotional conflicts MGM preferred. All in all, I suspect the original was more interesting, but the film has its moments. The nomination should stay, begrudgingly.

Sidney Buchman and Irwin Shaw's script for *The Talk of the Town* (and the direction) has significant problems. We begin all too seriously with a jailbreak and an intensity of purpose; within minutes, we are jarred from that expectation into a comedy of hiding, hunger, and deception. The plot is so full of holes Swiss mice look at it hungrily. Want an example? Cary Grant has injured his ankle so seriously, Jean Arthur can't move him. By the next morning, Grant is up and doing calisthenics, begging for food through the window and mugging outrageously for the camera. What is also unbelievable is the suggestion that Grant and Colman become so deeply involved in each other emotionally (friendship? something more?) in under twenty-four hours that they feel like brothers. Another scene fairly deep into the picture truly puzzles me: when Ronald Colman decides to shave off his beard, why does his manservant Rex Ingram look like somebody has just murdered his first born son? The camera lingers for what seems like forever while Ingram cries. Why is never explained. Perhaps I am missing some subtext, but I suspect the crying is a heavy-handed attempt to get us to think of the sacrifice of the beard in more emotional terms than we have been prepared for by the film. At times, the movie expects us to be incredibly dumb (what screenwriter William Goldman calls a "make stupid" plot). Prime example: Grant goes back to hide in the exact same spot he hid before, and the police never think to look there again. The romance between Grant and Arthur has almost no groundwork laid for it either. In other words, the screenplay is a sloppy mess, which relies entirely on star power to sell it, with help from the director and cinematographer. A more intelligent screenplay would have made this mess work somehow. As it is, no nomination was deserved by Sidney Buchman (*Mr. Smith Goes to Washington*) and Irwin Shaw (more famous as a novelist).

The finest adaptation this year went unrecognized by the Academy: Julius and Philip Epstein's screenplay of George S. Kaufman and Moss Hart's *The Man Who Came to Dinner*. Some of the greatest lines of the movies this year zinged from the mouth of Monty Woolley: "My great aunt Jennifer ate a whole box of candy every day of her life. She lived to be 102 and when she was dead three days she looked better than you do now"; "Will you take your clammy hand off my chair? You have the touch of a love-starved cobra"; "Is there a man in the world who suffers as I do from the gross inadequacies of the human race?" Brilliant stuff! They should have been nominated, and they should have won the Oscar for Best Writing (Screenplay). The Epsteins, by the way, are also responsible for two other adaptations: *Casablanca* and *Arsenic and Old Lace*.

Best Cinematography (Black & White): Joseph Ruttenberg won for *Mrs. Miniver*, over James Wong Howe, *Kings Row*; Stanley Cortez, *The Magnificent Ambersons*; Charles G. Clarke, *Moontide*; Edward Cronjager, *The Pied Piper*; Rudolph Maté, *The Pride of the Yankees*; John Mescall, *Take a Letter, Darling*; Ted Tetzlaff, *The Talk of the Town*; Leon Shamroy, *Ten Gentlemen from West Point*; and Arthur C. Miller, *This Above All*

Joseph Ruttenberg won for *Mrs. Miniver*, in the usual sort of MGM gloss and respectability. The film is very economically shot, with only a few scenes where we can see Wyler and Ruttenberg pushing the limits of MGM respectability. When the young Miniver goes to his room to gather his belongings, the camera is focused on the empty space of the staircase, emphasizing the impending absence and loss. One of the best visuals comes when Walter Pidgeon returns from the Miracle of Dunkirk, and we see Garson rushing along the dock, framed by an overarching tree as her husband's boat approaches. Given the sense of the Minivers having a kind of paradise threatened by the war, I suspect some intent of suggesting the Garden of Eden may not be too far-fetched. The scene in the bomb shelter is filmed quite effectively, in close up shots that allow for the actors to do their best for once in this movie. The shifts in lighting are done very well. Ruttenberg deserved a nomination for this work, but not the Oscar – as another film would use the camera as an integral part of the narrative, rather than the kind of pretty but empty approach MGM nearly always emphasized.

James Wong Howe does some fine work in *Kings Row*, although when Sam Wood is directing, any cinematographer has to carry more weight than is reasonable. The opening pan shot across the welcoming sign to the town, across the school letting kids out for the day, and then the dissolve into the idyll of the forest is nicely done. The small paradise of the swimming hole is elegantly shot by Howe. We can see the influence of Gregg Toland and *Citizen Kane*, repeatedly. As the grandmother lay dying, a large water pitcher fills the foreground while the bed, the door and the grandson all remain sharp through Toland's deep focus techniques. The same setup occurs with the medicine bottles instead of the pitcher, and again later, with "Happy New Century" written in the snow in the foreground. Howe learned quickly, and deserved a nomination.

Stanley Cortez collaborated with Orson Welles on *The Magnificent Ambersons*, providing the camerawork. For Welles' second film, Cortez was filling the enormous shoes of the best cinematographer in the world, Gregg Toland, who had taught Welles how a film should look with *Citizen Kane*. Nobody seems to know why Toland wasn't brought in for *Ambersons*; I suspect Welles wanted to show that the student he had been could now handle things himself; certainly, Cortez was nowhere near the artist or technical innovator Toland was, and in fact, would be moved out of principal photography after he failed to meet Welles' expectations.[ccxxiii] Welles simply expected Cortez to facilitate his vision, rather than act as the mentor Toland must have been; when Cortez either couldn't, or wouldn't, comply, Welles moved him out of the way. The question of whether or not Cortez deserves this nomination thus emerges as an unsolvable riddle; I am inclined to say no, given the generally less-than-stellar shape of most of the rest of his career (except for *The Night of the Hunter*!).

Fritz Lang began directing *Moontide*, an early film noir; French star Jean Gabin drove him out of the movie very early on, to be replaced by director Archie Mayo (some say Lang wasn't happy on the project anyways). Thomas Mitchell, Ida Lupino and Claude Rains co-star in this very odd film. Gabin had never made a movie in America before, and he hand-picked this story of murder, prostitution, suicide, and blackmail (which had to be radically changed to pass the Breen Office). Charles G. Clarke was brought in with Archie Mayo; Clarke replaced Lucien Ballard, who set the tone and look of the movie with Fritz Lang. The cinematography justly deserves the nomination. Everything was done in sound stages, allowing for absolute control over the cinematography, especially in the actual dream sequences, which were originally designed by Salvador Dali.[ccxxiv] The whole film looks like sketches from the Ashcan School of American art, but *Moontide* as a whole simply doesn't hang together very well. We have here an example of style with little substance. What we remember is the look of the movie, and some vague disappointment that the solid pieces don't add up to anything. Gabin never really moves his performance anywhere; Mitchell is cast against expectations of his usual role, and doesn't satisfy; Ida Lupino does quite well, suggesting more to the character than she can put into words; Claude Rains seems completely wasted. The nomination should stay for the ways in which Clarke and crew experiment with filming with shadows, but others did it far better this year (as we shall shortly see).

The Pied Piper features competent interior photography and some effective outdoor work as well, all by nominee Edward Cronjager. As the story grows darker and more desperate, so does the cinematography; the camerawork reflects the narrative most effectively. The nomination should stay.

Two reasons exist for Rudolph Maté to merit his nomination for *The Pride of the Yankees*: first, he makes the forty-one-year-old Gary Cooper look much younger; and second, he (or somebody else in the production) made Cooper look left-handed by costuming him in reverse lettering and numbering, having him run to third base, and then flipping the negative. Overall, *The Pride of the Yankees* has a somewhat stodgy appearance, although lit and filmed well. Maté should keep his nomination.

Clearly, cinematographer Ted Tetzlaff and director George Stevens have seen *Citizen Kane*, as the opening montage of *The Talk of the Town* pulls on the same newsreel/newspaper stratagem of *Kane* to get the story rolling along quickly, with surreal images of a giant gavel coming down on the audience as Cary Grant looks sullen and put-upon, and the judge points directly at the audience. We are, by this visual gambit, supposed to put ourselves in Grant's place as the accused and sympathize with him. Tetzlaff isn't interested in Toland's deep focus (he may not have been capable of it, as very few other than Toland were), but he does know how to bring out the pathos in Grant's face as he is filmed in the rain and dark during Grant's jailbreak and pursuit. At the end, Tetzlaff returns to a more artistic approach, framing Ronald Colman and Jean Arthur in their farewell nicely. When Tetzlaff is pushing himself, the cinematography is Oscar caliber. For those few scenes, the nomination should stay. I just wish it was in service to a more polished screenplay and a less confused execution.

John Mescall's work on *Take a Letter, Darling* is a distinct decline from his far more interesting cinematography on *Bride of Frankenstein* and *The Black Cat*. But then, Boris Karloff is far more photogenic than either Fred MacMurray or Rosalind Russell. The camerawork is competent but completely uninspired, which isn't surprising, given that the director is Mitchell Leisen, who was always more interested in sets and sexist misogyny. No nomination should ever be given for mundane work.

Ten Gentlemen from West Point stars Maureen O'Hara as the love interest of two cadets at West Point, who go off to fight Tecumseh in early nineteenth century America. Unfortunately, the movie was completely unavailable at the time of this writing, despite having been briefly released on DVD. Leon Shamroy would go on to do outstanding work in color, particularly in *Leave Her to Heaven*. We will have to set aside this nomination for now, but Shamroy will receive his just rewards later.

This Above All stars Tyrone Power as a deserter who learns what the war is truly about, and returns to service – all because of Joan Fontaine. Arthur C. Miller's cinematography is functional, and occasionally inspired. One beautiful shot in the dark leaves all the actors' faces in shadows, and only the edges of their clothes and hats glow in the moonlight – all to keep Tyrone Power a mystery. *This Above All* imitates *Rebecca* and *Suspicion* in that the male lead has a dark secret. The camerawork helps to move it along, mostly with standard set shots, but every so often, they get inventive, as with a shot down a dumbwaiter shaft. Overall, Miller deserved this nomination, even if the film gets overheated at times (Fontaine's paean to England goes on far too long, and with much false emoting).

One film that the Academy ignored for cinematography needs attention, as it has for decades been acclaimed for its incredibly suggestive lighting and camerawork. *Cat People*, starring Simone Simon, came from the phenomenal team of director Jacques Tourneur (*Out of the Past*) and producer Val Lewton, who produced a string of innovative B-pictures for RKO in the Forties, including *I Walked with a Zombie* and *The Body Snatcher*. *Cat People* proves the importance of limitations for the artist; without them, ingenuity and imagination aren't forced to devise new answers. Working on very low budgets, Lewton's team had to be inventive, and *Cat People* has more sheer suspense and tension than any half-dozen slasher flicks. The cinematographer was Nicholas Musuraca, who helped Tourneur and Lewton fill the screen with darkness, so that the audience could create their own terror in that rich blackness. Watch the famous scenes of the nighttime swim, and the walk through the park, to see how marvelous suggestion can be. I also found the effects of the engineering light tables to be innovative, as were the brief scenes of animation in the dream sequence. Musuraca would go on to shoot *The Curse of the Cat People* and the film noir classic, *Out of the Past*. The Academy tended to ignore B-pictures, which would soon take on a deeper life as film noir developed in the Forties. They should have nominated Nicholas Musuraca for *Cat People*, who easily should have won the Oscar in this category (had *The Magnificent Ambersons* not been butchered, the competition would have been much harder).

Best Cinematography (Color): Leon Shamroy won for *The Black Swan*, over Milton Krasner, William V. Skall, and W. Howard Greene, *Arabian Nights*; Sol Polito, *Captains of the Clouds*; W. Howard Greene, *Jungle Book*; Victor Milner and William V. Skall, *Reap the Wild Wind*; and Edward Cronjager & William V. Skall, *To the Shores of Tripoli*

Leon Shamroy won for *The Black Swan*, a swashbuckler starring Tyrone Power and Maureen O'Hara (look for swords, not tutus, if you get confused by the 2010 film of the same name). The color cinematography comes across at times as a touch too pastel and subdued for me, and at others, garish, but seeing Maureen O'Hara in color is always a pleasure. I strongly suspect Walt Disney and his Imagineers watched this movie before designing the *Pirates of the Caribbean* ride at Disneyland, as the looks are considerably similar at times. In the end, the movie has none of the intensity and crackle of *The Adventures of Robin Hood*, or even *The Mark of Zorro*. They even cheated by speeding up the final swordfight between Power and George Sanders. The camerawork is largely mundane. No Oscar was deserved, but Shamroy should keep the nomination for O'Hara's eyes, which he brings out as well, if not better, than anybody else ever did.

Arabian Nights has beautiful title cards, reminiscent of children's books of the Forties. The camerawork reflects the ponderousness of the Technicolor cameras, but during the fights, they do use some unusual angles. The close-ups are crisply shot as well. Technicolor and the scanty costumes remain the big draws of this flick, since it has none of the magical events of others of its type. Throughout, the matte shots are excellent; one particularly fine one mixes movement across the sand dunes with a shot of the entire Arabian city. The great cavalry charge over the sand dunes at the end is done well. Milton Krasner, William V. Skall, and W. Howard Greene get a worthy nomination.

Captains of the Clouds is Cagney's first Technicolor film, filmed by Sol Polito. For the first time, the colors all look very realistic, with absolutely beautiful nature photography. One of the worst aspects of the movie comes in the very bad model plane work. Brenda Marshall, on the other hand, is quite beautifully filmed. Polito can keep the nomination.

W. Howard Greene does a beautiful job on *Jungle Book*, with astounding live animals and jungle scenes. To the best of my knowledge, this movie contains the first Technicolor footage of all the animals we see here: wolves, a tiger, a bear, black panthers, leopards, monkeys, and so forth. Some of the forest scenes look like Maxfield Parrish painted them. The orange of Shere Khan seems to be the platonic ideal of orange, matched only by the roaring fires consuming the temple at the end. The film has been restored; if you've never watched the cleaned-up version, you haven't seen this movie properly. An excellent nomination for Greene, who was one of the pioneers of color cinematography, filming *A Star Is Born* and *Nothing Sacred*; my only caveat here is that Lee Garmes should have been included in the nomination, as he was given screen credit as well.

In *Reap the Wild Wind*, Cecil B. DeMille sends John Wayne and Ray Milland to tackle each other – and a giant squid. Paulette Goddard gets in the way (having watched enough of her movies now, I can tell you she usually does, and not in interesting ways). Victor Milner and William V. Skall serve DeMille in shooting some of the best underwater footage ever on color film – except for the fact that it was actually Dewey Wrigley who did that, and he wasn't nominated for the very thing that merited the nod this time. Wrigley was a special effects man, mostly working with DeMille. He should have been added. The nomination should stay, with him included.

The only real reason to watch *To the Shores of Tripoli*, a paean to the Marines, is to see Maureen O'Hara in Technicolor for the first time. She is, as always, an earthly (and earthy) beauty with intelligence and warmth – and stubborn fires deep in her eyes. Unfortunately, she is trapped in a story that repeatedly argues men should force themselves on women, even when they say "no" loudly. Admittedly, the on-location training footage of real soldiers on the Marine base in San Diego right before Pearl Harbor is also worthwhile, as is the footage aboard naval warships. Overall, the color cinematography by Edward Cronjager and William V. Skall looks more realistic than most of what Hollywood had shown so far, so the nomination should stay – especially for Maureen O'Hara's eyes.

Finally, the Oscar should go to the movie which has retained its magic, and bears repeated watching. Maybe I just love animals, but *Jungle Book* seems to have the finest color cinematography of the year, and W. Howard Greene and Lee Garmes should have won the Oscar for Best Cinematography (Color).

Best Musical Score: Ray Heindorf and Heinz Roemheld won for *Yankee Doodle Dandy*, over Edward Ward, *Flying with Music*; Roger Edens and Georgie Stoll, *For Me and My Gal*; Robert Emmett Dolan, *Holiday Inn*; Charles Previn and Hans Salter, *It Started with Eve;* Walter Scharf, *Johnny Doughboy*; Alfred Newman, *My Gal Sal*; and Leigh Harline, *You Were Never Lovelier*.

Ray Heindorf and Heinz Roemheld took the statue for *Yankee Doodle Dandy*, so then why do the credits give George M. Cohan the title card, "Lyrics and Music By..."? More importantly, why isn't Cohan listed for the nomination? Heindorf did the orchestration; Roemheld is nowhere to be found in the credits (he helped with the orchestrations, according to the IMDB). For *Yankee Doodle Dandy* the Oscar seems to have gone to the use made of Cohan's songs (in much the same way that *Stagecoach* used folk songs and such as source material). The score does make very inventive use of themes from Cohan's music, as well as "Yankee Doodle Dandy" and a flurry of other patriotic warhorses. Unlike so many of these nominations, Heindorf crafted something unique and original out of Cohan's simple tunes. For that he deserved the nomination. So why do I have this winner in the "wrong" department? Because George M. Cohan should be part of the nomination – and part of the Oscar, for *Yankee Doodle Dandy* truly is the Best Musical Score of 1942.

As I said above in the Best Song category, *Flying with Music* is best forgotten, unless you really have an obsession for third-rate Latin-tinged musicals from Hal Roach with Edward Ward's scores. The movie has almost completely disappeared from existence, with TCM only rarely showing it; I now wish I had missed it. No nomination was necessary.

Busby Berkeley directed Judy Garland and Gene Kelly – in his film debut – in *For Me and My Gal*, set during vaudeville and WWI, but clearly supporting our involvement in WWII. As one online reviewer so pithily put it, "this movie's patriotic message is about as subtle as a knee in the Kaiser's groin."[ccxxv] Garland had her first major opportunity to play an adult role; Kelly had to overcome an unsympathetic character (he breaks his hand to dodge the draft). Both get the chance to sing songs from the WWI era. Garland's turn on "After You've Gone" is particularly memorable. Roger Edens and Georgie Stoll string together a whole slew of melodies the audience would have known into a comfortable homage to vaudeville. Overall, their score is little more than linking the songs together; this piecemeal approach works because of the talent involved, although the overall effect of the movie is lackluster. For that reason, the nomination should never have been made. A musical lives on its score and songs; *For Me and My Gal* fails to come to life.

Robert Emmett Dolan got credit for giant Irving Berlin's musical footsteps in *Holiday Inn*, benefitting once again as the music director rather than the composer. He doesn't deserve the nomination here; Berlin does. Dolan would go on to compose the music for a passel of Bob Hope pictures, as well as *The Bells of St. Mary's* and *The Three*

Faces of Eve. Irving Berlin should keep the nomination for the music for *Holiday Inn*.

Yet another Deanna Durbin movie gets nominated for the score. *It Started with Eve* has Durbin once again involved in shenanigans, this time as the pretend fiancée of Robert Cummings. One guess as to what happens by the end! A genuine surprise: Charles Laughton plays the supposedly dying father of Cummings, which adds some real class to this Durbin programmer. Laughton deliciously bites into playing a rich old reprobate; Durbin and Cummings delight as well. Best scene? Charles Laughton doing the conga! Hans Salter wrote the score; Charles Previn is included as the music director. Salter was one of the best composers working at Universal, if not the best; he wrote scores for some of their horror films that have gained traction in respectability in the last decade or so: *The Wolf Man, House of Frankenstein,* and *The Creature from the Black Lagoon* remain memorable. For this Durbin entry, Salter plays with strings, harp and horns to create a compelling accompaniment. Durbin gets to sing "When I Sing" (Tchaikovsky, *Sleeping Beauty*), "Clavelitos," and "Goin' Home." Salter's score thus actually doesn't show up very often, but what is there gives enough quality to have earned the nomination.

Bobby Breen returns again in a musical. Gee, there's a surprise. Hasn't this boy hit puberty yet? Actually, he has, and his remarkable voice is gone. *Johnny Doughboy* isn't even about him, but child stars growing up is the theme in this utterly forgettable film from Republic Pictures. Alfalfa and Spanky show up too, and they are the only reason I can recommend seeing this movie, from morbid curiosity. The score certainly isn't a reason to see it, and yet another dud comes from the Academy's rules for this category, which nomination should be summarily cast out.

Alfred Newman was recruited again to string together old hits and make a score, this time for *My Gal Sal*. "On the Banks of the Wabash," anybody? Or the title song? What's that you say? You've never heard of them? Well, nobody else has any more either, and for good reason: they're mundane. The source material lacks depth, and so does this movie – although the score tries very, very hard to bring the flick to life. For the effort, Newman (barely) secures this nomination (and I love the Victorian trumpet style, which nobody uses anymore).

Leigh Harline moved from animation (*Pinocchio, Mr. Bug Goes to Town*) into live action in 1942, including this Fred Astaire musical, *You Were Never Lovelier*, co-starring Rita Hayworth. Setting all the music to a Latin beat, including Jerome Kern's tunes, *You Were Never Lovelier* has some wonderful music, songs, and dancing (although not at the level of Astaire and Hayworth's first pairing, *You'll Never Get Rich*). Mostly what we hear are the tunes from Jerome Kern and Johnny Mercer, but in between are lovely interstices by Harline, with a soft romantic touch. He deserved his nomination.

Remember now: *Yankee Doodle Dandy* got the Oscar. You're welcome, Mr. Cohan.

Best Art Direction (Black & White): Richard Day, Joseph C. Wright, and Thomas Little won for *This Above All*, over *George Washington Slept Here* (Max Parker, Mark-Lee Kirk, and Casey Roberts); *The Magnificent Ambersons* (Albert S. D'Agostino, Al Fields and Darrell Silvera); *The Pride of the Yankees* (Perry Ferguson and Howard Bristol); *Random Harvest* (Cedric Gibbons, Randall Duell, Edwin B. Willis and Jack Moore); *The Shanghai Gesture* (John B. Goodman, Jack Otterson, Russell A. Gausman and Boris Leven); *Silver Queen* (Ralph Berger and Emile Kuri); *The Spoilers* (Edward R. Robinson); *Take a Letter, Darling* (Hans Dreier, Roland Anderson, and Sam Comer); and *The Talk of the Town* (Lionel Banks, Rudolph Sternad, and Fay Babcock)

This Above All doesn't do all that much special to start with – a small mansion, a training camp, a barracks – but once the movie moves into the romance, some of the outdoor scenes are nicely done (especially since they're all studio sets). We then get a variety of hotels and drinking establishments, as well as a supposed medieval church which looks all too modern. Finally, we do get an effective scene during the blitz, in a shattered, burning street, and a hospital. Ultimately, I believe this Oscar is for the wartime topic, and the angst the movie tackles. The nomination should stay, but the Oscar really belongs elsewhere.

Jack Benny never had much of a movie career, as his real forte was on the radio, but between *George Washington Slept Here* and Ernst Lubitsch's *To Be or Not to Be*, he did manage to create two movies worth watching more than once. Based on a Broadway hit by George S. Kaufman and Moss Hart, *George Washington Slept Here* uses the plot device of renovating a house (which has been stolen for many other movies, such as *Mr. Blandings Builds His Dream House* and *The Money Pit*). The sets of the old house were those used on Frank Capra's *Arsenic and Old Lace*, which had been filmed and set aside for later release.[ccxxvi] The nominees then proceeded to trash it for the set on *Washington*. Apparently, recycling is not a new idea. *George Washington Slept Here* deserves this nomination.

In terms of the sets, what everybody remembers from *The Magnificent Ambersons* is the stupendous staircase from the mansion, a staircase (and house) designed to move and unfold so the camera could freely roam in and out of it. But more than that, the turn of the century small-town America that *The Magnificent Ambersons* occupies has never been more lovingly recreated, from the modes of transportation to the fashions to the endless bric-a-brac. An excellent nomination, despite the butchering of the film by RKO executives.

How hard is it to find a ball park? For *The Pride of the Yankees*, we get some apartments, hotel rooms, a train or two – and ball parks. The nomination should stay, but barely.

Random Harvest has an insane asylum; music hall; tavern; an English village; a country cottage with trees in blossom; an English manor; business offices; a grand ballroom in the manor; an ironworks. Nice variety, for a good nomination.

The Shanghai Gesture fails to provide either a realistic suspension of disbelief or the kind of outrageous over-the-top style of films like Sternberg's *The Scarlet Empress*. The main set of the casino is interesting, particularly the carved railings, but Sternberg never really does anything worth watching in that set (except with the early crane shot when we first see the place). Lady Gin Sling's costume and hair have to be seen to be believed. Sternberg apparently directed this while lying down on a cot; it shows, in the lack of purposeful inventiveness. No nomination should be given for wasted opportunities.

I can just imagine the thinking on *Silver Queen*: Barbary Coast film? Ok. Gambling hall? Check. Big skirts and low cut gowns? Check. Saloons to fight in? Check. Oscar? No, but keep placing your bets, gentlemen. *Silver Queen* does well enough to stay in the game, though.

For *The Spoilers*, John Wayne is the good guy; Marlene Dietrich is the woman he loves. Randolph Scott, against expectations, is the bad guy. Gold mines, Alaskan snows, gambling halls – it's the Klondike, in the 1890s! We've never seen this picture before, have we? Much as I want to deny it, the nomination is worthwhile, the sets are decorated to stuffing with the kind of touches that make a movie work better (Dietrich's room has more Victorian bric-a-brac than a dollhouse). The fight scene at the end gets to wreck most of the sets, and brings the movie to an exciting finish. The nomination is a good one.

Let's consider the sets of *Take a Letter, Darling*. Yup, that's an office set. Oooh, the joy. Very standard stuff, with nothing other than what is necessary to tell the story. Not the fault of Hans Dreier and Roland Anderson, who were capable of much more, but they did what they were asked, and competently. They should keep their nomination for serving the story, such as it is.

The Talk of the Town happens in a prison, a country home, a small town, a courthouse, and the Supreme Court. All reasonably well done, and convincing. The nomination should stay.

The best sets of the year were built for *The Magnificent Ambersons*, which were endlessly reused in some of Val Lewton's great movies of the Forties. The staircase alone deserved the Oscar for Best Art Direction (Black & White).

Best Art Direction (Color): Richard Day, Joseph C. Wright, and Thomas Little won for *My Gal Sal*, over *Arabian Nights* (Alexander Golitzen, Jack Otterson, Russell A. Gausman, and Ira S. Webb); *Captains of the Clouds* (Ted Smith and Casey Roberts); *Jungle Book* (Vincent Korda and Julia Heron); and *Reap the Wild Wind* (Hans Dreier, Roland Anderson, and George Sawley)

My Gal Sal won for color art direction. The movie stars Rita Hayworth and Victor Mature in a highly fictionalized biography of Paul Dresser, the songwriter brother of novelist Theodore Dreiser. Gay Nineties, anyone? We've seen this kind of picture before, including *Alexander's Ragtime Band* and *Lillian Russell*. Hayworth is fun to watch dance, but she generally lip-syncs to other singers in her musicals. The art direction is all you'd expect from a prettified version of the 1890s. As I've said repeatedly, if you want an Oscar, do a piece in the 1890s. I'm getting tired of it, so no Oscar, or nomination, for that matter, should there be. Copycats shouldn't get Oscars (unless they do it better, of course...).

Arabian Nights has some wonderful matte shots of the palace, to go with a marketplace, a finely designed throne room, a private residence, a torture chamber, a slave auction, a smithy, tents, and pools. A curiously flat quality typical of the Universal Technicolor films inhabits most of the sets, although they are colorful. The nomination should stay for what works, but much of it is empty of grace.

Captains of the Clouds gives us Jimmy Cagney versus the Royal Canadian Air Force, with Michael Curtiz directing. The movie as a whole feels disjointed, as it begins as a competition among pilots for a young woman and then turns into a combat training movie. Very weak narrative arc, and one that lifts much of what is interesting from *Angels with Dirty Faces* and other Cagney movies (the whole need to learn to care about others before yourself comes from *Angels*). The sets include some trading posts, a mining camp, a fancy hotel, a coffee shop, and some military bases, And Canada. Lots of Canada. And planes. Lots of planes, which are the real attraction of this film, at least to aviation buffs. Some simulated outdoors scenes look well. The nomination should stay, to make Canada happy.

The sets for *Jungle Book* outdo *The Thief of Bagdad* by far. The jungle seems to be right out of Eden, but it was constructed at Lake Sherwood in Los Angeles from scratch.[ccxxvii] They also built the village and an abandoned temple that Disneyland wants back. A very good nomination indeed.

Cecil B. DeMille goes wild underwater in *Reap the Wild Wind*; Hans Dreier and company are his enablers above the waterline. 1840s America comes to life – or at least in Key West. As is usual in a DeMille film, the art direction is superb. *Reap the Wild Wind* is no exception, although with Paulette Goddard trying her best to be Scarlett O'Hara and Hattie McDaniel's sister pretending to be Mammy, and the giant squid, the movie feels like the illicit love child of *Moby Dick* and *Gone with the Wind*. The typical DeMille spectacular eye candy, which merits the nomination – and which should have won the Oscar for Best Art Direction (Color).

Best Special Effects: Farciot Edouart, Gordon Jennings, William L. Pereira, and Louis Mesenkop won for *Reap the Wild Wind*, over *The Black Swan* (Fred Sersen, Roger Heman and George Leverett,); *Desperate Journey* (Byron Haskin and Nathan Levinson); *Flying Tigers* (Howard Lydecker and Daniel J. Bloomberg); *Invisible Agent* (John P. Fulton and Bernard B. Brown); *Jungle Book* (Lawrence Butler and William H. Wilmarth); *Mrs. Miniver* (A. Arnold Gillespie, Warren Newcombe, and Douglas Shearer); *The Navy Comes Through* (Vernon L. Walker and James G. Stewart); *One of Our Aircraft Is Missing* (Ronald Neame and C.C. Stevens); and *The Pride of the Yankees* (Jack Cosgrove, Ray Binger, and Thomas T. Moulton)

So, here's the basic rule: if you use a giant squid, you get an Oscar in this category. Just ask Walt Disney a few years from now with *20,000 Leagues Under the Sea*. The squid in question in *Reap the Wild Wind* is nowhere near as good as the one that fights Captain Nemo, but for 1942, the fake invertebrate will do. Few things had ever been seen like it before, and certainly not while underwater. Some great shipwrecks also form a justification for this nomination – but not the Oscar, which should have gone elsewhere.

The Black Swan has some beautiful model ships, of the sort done to perfection by Warner Brothers in their swashbucklers, but with the added pleasure of gorgeous sunsets. We also get a burning city, and in one innovative scene, they matted in live sailors onto one of the attacking ships in the final combat scene. The nomination should stay.

In *Desperate Journey*, downed airmen Errol Flynn and Ronald Reagan face off against Nazi Raymond Massey, as they attempt to escape Germany with secret plans. Reagan comes off well in this movie, especially in his double-talk nonsense with Massey. As for the special effects, more flying scenes, but done about as poorly as any major studio did. No nomination should have been given.

Flying Tigers has more flying special effects, this time in large groups of model planes. Republic Pictures had the best flying models in the business – absolutely realistic, sweeping curves that don't defy the laws of physics, and cloud backgrounds. And lots of explosions! Republic had learned how to make flying work through their serials, particularly *The Adventures of Captain Marvel* (one of the best of the serials, from 1941). They richly deserved this nomination.

For the fourth dip into the Invisible Man series, *The Invisible Agent*, Universal sent him up against the Nazis. Peter Lorre and Sir Cedric Hardwicke play the bad guys. The model plane work is very weak, but the invisibility effects are still fairly good (John P. Fulton could probably do these in his sleep by now). As Hall parachutes into Germany, he strips as he plummets to the ground; a floating cup of coffee from which Hall drinks; a smoking cigarette; a particularly good scene where he takes a bath, the soap making his feet and hands visible; a piece of chicken eats itself; cold cream makes hands and a face appear; a desk and filing cabinet drawers get rifled through; a car drives itself. The nomination makes sense, especially given the occasional new effect this series is given by Fulton.

Jungle Book has a big fake alligator; the talking snakes are really silly; the giant snake in the water isn't done badly. The real animals just outclass the special effects, so no nomination was merited.

Mrs. Miniver has a nomination, mainly for the miracle at Dunkirk, when every ship available went across the English Channel to rescue the British Army from certain destruction at the hands of the Nazis. A plane crash and explosion are nicely done as well. They should keep this one.

The Navy Comes Through is a kind of David vs. Goliath film, as a freighter takes on the German navy. We also get a test of character, as a man accused of causing a gunnery explosion tries to redeem his reputation. The nomination was for a dive bomber attack, as well as the freighter fighting off two submarine attacks. Not badly done, so the nomination should stay.

One of Our Aircraft Is Missing has special effects which consist of a plane crash into an electrical tower, followed by an explosion – and one well-done nighttime bombing raid over a giant model of a city rigged for explosions, which is as good as this sort of thing ever got at this stage of the development of special effects. A good solid nomination for that alone.

For *The Pride of the Yankees*, see black and white cinematographer above for why these guys got nominated. It's a good trick.

Of all the special effects, Republic Pictures really deserves the Oscar this year for *Flying Tigers*, for those amazing flying models. Nothing like them had been seen in the big studios ever before.

CHAPTER SIXTEEN: 1944 AWARDS
16th show

Movies released in 1943

THE SCENE OF THE CRIME:

War requires sacrifices. The Academy thus sacrificed dinner, saving any number of rubber chickens. They moved the show to Grauman's Chinese Theatre on March 2, 1944. A giant Oscar dominated the stage. Jack Benny hosted. Speeches were short; awards were handed out.

The Oscars were still made out of plaster. So were most of their decisions.

Jack Warner ran to the stage first, and grabbed the Oscar for Best Picture for *Casablanca* before producer Hal Wallis could get there; Wallis got some face back when they gave him the Thalberg award.

No drinking occurred, since the public was allowed in; two hundred sailors and soldiers were the Academy's guests. This means the Academy handed out these awards sober, which may explain certain things…

WHAT THEY GOT RIGHT:

The Academy picked *Casablanca*; this wisdom covers such a multitude of sins, I'm almost inclined to forgive them for so many bad choices.
Almost.

Best Picture: *Casablanca* won, over *For Whom the Bell Tolls, Heaven Can Wait, The Human Comedy, In Which We Serve, Madame Curie, The More the Merrier, The Ox-Bow Incident, The Song of Bernadette,* and *Watch on the Rhine*

Finally, the Academy got the Best Picture right again by choosing *Casablanca,* the Best Picture of Hollywood's golden age, in my opinion, and many others – even among my friends and family, no movie produced more agreement with the Academy's choice. Never has so much been right in what Andrew Sarris called "an eternal treasure-trove of pleasure."[ccxxviii] The cast, the story, the direction, the dialogue – everything combines to make the most enjoyable, meaningful movie of the golden age of Hollywood. Nobody expected it; little of it seems to have been planned. But *Casablanca* may be the cinematic equivalent of serendipity: everything came together unexpectedly into the single best picture the studio system ever made. I would also argue that what occurred was people of talent and experience took their opportunity and made the most of it. The studios offered a maximum of ability and training, then placed those assets in service to an assembly line. By 1943, in the midst of WWII's immense drain on that system, *Casablanca* represents the purest expression of what would so soon be shattered by the end of the studio system: story, stars, setting, and style, none of which would ever be equaled again. Hollywood would never quite be Hollywood again, as it fractured (along with the decay of the Production Code) into a lesser incarnation of itself, while also spawning a multitude of independent producers and star-driven productions (as we will see in the next volume of this series). *Casablanca* is about many things, for many people: an exploration of love, friendship, patriotism, disappointment, recovery, intrigue, good, evil, betrayal, isolationism, engagement, self-sacrifice, and the salvation of one's soul and identity. No other movie has ever had better dialogue. No other movie has ever meant more to more people. If I could only watch one movie for the rest of my life, *Casablanca* would be it.

For Whom the Bell Tolls is the best adaptation of Ernest Hemingway Hollywood has ever made, but don't get too excited – that isn't saying much. Note that I do think a very fine film exists of a Hemingway title – *To Have and Have Not* – but that adaptation by William Faulkner has very little to do with the original novel. *For Whom the Bell Tolls* has some good performances, by Gary Cooper, Ingrid Bergman and Katina Paxinou, but we also have to deal with turgid direction by Sam Wood (the most aptly named director of all) and a screenplay that misses the more subtle points of Hemingway's warning about the dangers of fascism. I'm fairly sure making it in color was not the best choice, as it makes the characters look too clean and prefab for this story of guerrilla fighters in the Spanish Civil War. The makeup may be the worst ever done for a Forties Technicolor film; the Spaniards all look dark greys and false browns. But the greatest problem of all is the lack of pacing and narrative drive. The movie is at least watchable, if you ignore how it looks. Gary Cooper and Ingrid Bergman are fairly good, as are some of the supporting cast. For them, the nomination should stay.

In *Heaven Can Wait*, Don Ameche stars as a philanderer who tries to finagle his way into Hell by convincing Satan of the naughty life Ameche has led. Ernst Lubitsch made his only Technicolor production late in his career. Slightly less-than-naughty jokes are strung together in the life of a lady-killer – or as much as Don Ameche can be one). An essentially boring film, with none of the unexpected humor we expect from Lubitsch, and certainly not deserving of this nomination, which I think they gave him for ignoring the first-rate *To Be or Not to Be* the year before. So this nomination should be gone for Lubitsch.

The Human Comedy is MGM's stab at making an Important Picture. Louis B. Mayer commissioned Pulitzer Prize winning playwright William Saroyan to write an original story, which Saroyan turned into a novel when MGM rejected his screenplay. A dead man narrates, in the style of *Our Town*. The film occupies much of the same emotional territory as the later television series *The Waltons* and *Little House on the Prairie*, or if you prefer, a more thoughtful Andy Hardy entry. By the end, I felt as if I'd walked through this little town, seen a few people, and left – without finding any sense of true knowledge or lasting impression. *The Human Comedy* simply isn't a great movie, because the thing makes all the mistakes beginning writers make: they do character studies with no real narrative and no connective thematic structure to provide the glue to hold a slice-of-life story together. We just keep starting and stopping. A few of the vignettes are touching: I found the rendition of the hymn "Leaning" to be affecting, even with the awkward callout to the theater audience to join in. As a whole, *The Human Comedy* doesn't hold together – and shouldn't have a nomination.

In Which We Serve is a tour-de-force for Noel Coward, who wrote the screenplay, composed the score, starred and co-directed with David Lean, who moved up from editing with this film. Humphrey Bogart quipped, "Obviously, Noel Coward is the guy Orson Welles thinks he is."ccxxix Like *Citizen Kane*, *In Which We Serve* uses flashbacks to trace the paths by which we reach the present – in this case, the life histories of a few of the men, whose warship has been sunk by the Nazis. A propaganda film of high quality, *In Which We Serve* does what *Mrs. Miniver* wanted to do and failed: the film gives us a portrait of the British people and their national character. Watching it, I am struck again by how different American and British culture is, and how the phrase "stiff upper lip" remains a correct stereotype for that generation. On another level, I don't think I've ever seen another film that better depicts the creation and workings of a ship of war. Clearly, the Royal Navy fully co-operated in the making of this film. A quiet elegance and understatement suffuses the film, particularly at the end, when Coward says farewell to his remaining men. Overall, the movie stands up well, regardless of the propaganda purposes, and so, the nomination should stay.[106]

Madame Curie is a reasonable portrayal of the scientific and marital partnership of Marie and Pierre Curie, who explored radioactivity and discovered radium (among other accomplishments). The experiments and equipment are based on fairly accurate reproductions, and the Curies' intensity of purpose comes across clearly. If the science is reduced to simplistic approximations, the excitement of discovery still burbles. Greer Garson and Walter Pidgeon do a reasonable job, although Garson shows almost no emotional affect throughout, except for her trademark noble suffering. I find *Madame Curie* to be the least objectionable of her starring pictures, although not one I was interested in watching again until writing this book. The nomination should stay, for the pleasure of having a scientific pursuit at the heart of a film.

The More the Merrier stars Joel McCrea, Jean Arthur, and Charles Coburn in an amusing look at the wartime housing shortage (the movie would later be remade as Cary Grant's last film, *Walk, Don't Run*). Everyone concerned seems to be having a good time. Jean Arthur owns a large apartment; in WWII, she chooses to rent out part of it. Charles Coburn, a millionaire volunteering his time to the war effort, takes half. He then decides to rent part of his area to Joel McCrea. Romance and comedy follow, along with some side business about McCrea being con-

---

[106] The Academy pushed the eligibility deadline back from January 12 to December 31, which knocked *In Which We Serve* out of the previous year's running and put it in this year. The rule change also nudged *Shadow of a Doubt* out of 1942 (*Inside Oscar*, p. 124-25).

fused for a spy. Some of the humor is a bit forced, such as Jean Arthur's obsession with schedules – which is why the topic gets dropped from her character after it's milked, without any justification at all otherwise. But *The More the Merrier* is an amusing picture, and a good nomination.

The Ox-Bow Incident proves to be one of those rare moments when Hollywood takes on something uncomfortable, serious, and important – and makes it work. In the middle of WWII, the last thing we expect to find is a diatribe against lynching and the mob mentality, at a time when we had incarcerated every Japanese-American on the West Coast, were experiencing race riots around several military bases as well as in some of our inner cities, and were fighting a war largely on the basis of pulling together as one group (we were constantly admonished to set aside our individual concerns for the good of the group). Part of the reason director William Wellman and star Henry Fonda got away with it has to do with their choice of a genre that was not seen as important enough to pay attention: like science fiction and horror, the western has been used to make scathing indictments against mainstream American culture, and succeeded, because the powers that be didn't deign to impose restrictions that would have been standard on a more mainstream, contemporary setting. Watching *The Ox-Bow Incident* is like being knocked flat on your ass by the truth. One of the telling clues as to what Wellman and Fonda were shooting for can be found in the character of Reverend Sparks, a black man played with great dignity by Leigh Whipper (most famous for "Crooks" in *Of Mice and Men*). Sparks asks to go along, as he feels prayer might be needed; he also refuses to raise his hand and be deputized, with a dour look on his face when they swear to follow majority rule. Sparks also recalls seeing his older brother lynched, which explicitly connects the movie to the recurrent lynching of blacks. This kind of quiet understatement anchors the more obvious hysteria of the mob, and continues through Fonda's fine performance (which has some comic notes at first, to pull in the audience). The movie isn't perfect (hey, they can't all be *Casablanca*), particularly as some of the supporting players overact even in the quiet scenes, but taken as a whole, *The Ox-Bow Incident* is William Wellman's best film, and a definite candidate for Best Picture.

The Song of Bernadette is set in mid-nineteenth century France, telling the story of a young peasant girl who has visions of the Virgin Mary. Jennifer Jones played the saint; off-screen, she was David O. Selznick's obsession and eventual second wife. Vincent Price and Lee J. Cobb also appear. In the middle of WWII, *The Song of Bernadette* must have been comforting to watch, as a refuge into simpler times and faith (and it launched a whole series of inspirational religious pictures, not the least of which was *Going My Way*). Watching it today, much of the fascination remains, due to the intense hostility shown by the authorities, and the satiric comments made on the weaseling behavior of the typical bureaucrat when confronted with a problem that lies outside of their comfort zone. Not everybody liked it, least of all Bosley Crowther of *The New York Times*: "With all due respect, this writer feels that a better film could have been made...if it had been done at less ponderous length. Faith has the strength to move mountains, but it is sorely taxed in sustaining this mountainous film."[ccxxx] Perhaps, perhaps not. But the nomination should stay for trying something new in Hollywood.

Watch on the Rhine means so very well as an anti-Nazi picture, starring Bette Davis and Paul Lukas. Based on a Broadway play by Lillian Hellman, *Watch on the Rhine* has a script co-written with her long-time lover Dashiell Hammett, who had tragically stopped writing novels in 1934, after perfecting the hard-boiled genre. The main flaws of the film are the director, Herman Shumlin, who brings too much of the staging of the play with him, and the script, which forgets how people should talk in movies. All too often, the characters make speeches. Compare this with *Casablanca*, where the characters trade quips and barbs and small talk, all while getting across many of the same points without battering them into the audience's head with obvious and forthright earnestness. I can appreciate the movie, especially the performances of Davis in her restrained mode, Lukas in the best role of his career, and Lucile Watson as Davis' quirky, cranky mother. But like so many of Hellman's plays and screenplays, the characters are all too often cardboard types instead of three-dimensional people. The children in this movie are particularly egregious examples of false representations; only someone who has never had their own children would think these offspring would exist in any kind of real world. They display none of the suffering or deprivation being raised by parents participating in underground resistance movements would show, as they are insufferably noble, with almost no sense of the kind of resentment, however muted, that might come from having their childhoods and security stripped away from them. The movie might work better had they removed the children, to show the kind of sacrifices Davis and Lukas made for their mission to stop the fascists. Overall, the movie seems aimed at waking up an isolationist America; so too does much of *Casablanca*. The difference is that *Casablanca* is a work of art; *Watch on the Rhine* is mere propaganda. The nomination should stay, for the performances we get from Davis, Lukas, and Watson, but *Watch* cannot top *Casablanca*.

As for those films not nominated for Best Picture, the one glaring omission is *Shadow of a Doubt*, directed by Alfred Hitchcock and starring Joseph Cotten and Teresa Wright. Cotten plays a man who murders widows for their fortunes. He comes to visit his sister, and his favorite niece, played by Wright – all while the police are chasing him down. Wright becomes suspicious, and the Hitchcock touch ensues. Hitchcock provides an ironic undercutting of the Hollywood myth of the essential goodness of small town life in America: evil can come from anywhere. Hitch was able to focus on Cotten and Wright, and allowed the suspense to breathe out of their relationship, until the whole film gets closer and closer, as the space for them to maneuver around each other grows less and less. *Shadow of a Doubt* is one of Hitchcock's best Forties films, and deserved a Best Picture nomination.

Best Director: Michael Curtiz won for *Casablanca*, over Ernst Lubitsch, *Heaven Can Wait*; Clarence Brown, *The Human Comedy*; George Stevens, *The More the Merrier*; and Henry King, *The Song of Bernadette*

Michael Curtiz is the most underrated of all the classic directors, and he has never received the kind of attention deserved by a man who directed *The Adventures of Robin Hood, Angels with Dirty Faces, Captain Blood, Dodge City, The Private Lives of Elizabeth and Essex, The Sea Hawk, Yankee Doodle Dandy*, and dozens of other movies – including a little thing called *Casablanca*. Given the endless series of disasters that could have occurred on a movie with an unfinished script, we can only give credit to Curtiz for the outstanding completion of *Casablanca*. The movie has essentially no action; all of the tension lies in characters, their hunger for escape, the risk of discovery, the dangers of love, and the geopolitical fires keeping everything at a boil. Michael Curtiz really was one of the top directors the movies ever had, with *Casablanca* his finest hour, and this Oscar his most just reward.

Once again, we get a nomination for a secondary film after the Academy ignored a greater work the year before. This time, Ernst Lubitsch was nominated for the mildly amusing *Heaven Can Wait*, after being passed over for the masterpiece *To Be or Not to Be* in 1942. *Heaven Can Wait* has a great setup: a man defends his life's actions to Satan to earn his way into Hell, but the payoff is all too often staid and even boring. The director's famous "Lubitsch Touch" is sadly absent throughout much of the picture. Part of this may come from Don Ameche, who rarely engenders the kind of passionate excitement that the role requires; Errol Flynn would have been a more interesting casting choice. The grandfathers, played by Charles Coburn and Eugene Pallette, are by far the most interesting characters in the movie. They have most of the snap and crackle dialogue in the film – but we need far more of it to earn a nomination.

Working with an essentially formless screenplay – just one heartwarming vignette after another – Clarence Brown does his best to keep *The Human Comedy* going along. He evokes fine performances out of Mickey Rooney (see Best Actor), Van Johnson and Frank Morgan, as well as the child actor Jack "Butch" Jenkins. Visually, Brown seems to be trying too hard (see Best Cinematography (Black & White)), but when he focuses on the relationships between people, he produces a simple closeness that is quite effective. In the end, however, the weak screenplay dooms the whole thing to a pile of dough rather than a pie, and Brown simply can't succeed in baking it. Brown does deserve a nomination, if only for getting Mickey Rooney to give his best performance ever in a serious film.

George Stevens directed a number of classics – *Gunga Din*, *Woman of the Year*, *Giant*, *Shane*, and *A Place in the Sun* among others. *The More the Merrier* takes up his comic side, which must have been a relief after the maudlin *Penny Serenade* and the odd duck *The Talk of the Town*. The movie plays out with humor and a coziness absent from Stevens' previous two pictures, although some rough corners still remain. Did we really need the plot arc about the binoculars? Stevens brings out the naughtiness of the situation without losing the cozy sensibilities of Code Hollywood; when McCrea kisses Arthur on the neck, the eroticism is palpable. Stevens should keep his nomination.

Directing a film about religious visions can't be easy. Just ask Martin Scorsese, whose films always seem to be hovering about this kind of experience, even when God isn't mentioned explicitly. Henry King strikes the appropriate tone throughout *The Song of Bernadette*, which is set by the opening placard: "For those who believe in God, no explanation is necessary. For those who do not believe in God, no explanation is possible." King keeps the tension going between Bernadette's simple faith, and the disbelief of the authorities. He deserved a nomination.

Two other directors were ignored for recognition in this category.

Alfred Hitchcock was unjustly passed over for a nomination for *Shadow of a Doubt*, in which he presents the claustrophobia of family and small town life. Hitch's unique sense of the camera's eye begins in the scenes of the police manhunt for killer Joseph Cotten, which are shot from very high up. Hitchcock also uses some extreme close-ups, particularly with Cotten. The film's romance between the young Teresa Wright and the police detective hunting down Cotten is flawed, in that it happens with so little preparation, emerging as an arbitrary plot device with little depth. But Hitchcock also directs both Cotten and Wright to the most genuine performances of their careers up to that point, and keeps the tension ratcheting up throughout the film. He should have been nominated.

I also think William Wellman deserved a nod for Best Director for *The Ox-Bow Incident*. The most striking scene in the movie comes when watching the three men being lynched on the hilltop setting: the use of three victims, the shafts of light coming down from heavens, and the shadows of the hanged men upon the praying black preacher on his knees before them, comprise the best composed scene of Wellman's substantial career. He never made a more artistic film. See Best Picture above for more.

Best Supporting Actress: Katina Paxinou won for *For Whom the Bell Tolls*, over Gladys Cooper, *The Song of Bernadette*; Anne Revere, *The Song of Bernadette*; Paulette Goddard, *So Proudly We Hail!*; and Lucile Watson, *Watch on the Rhine*

Playing one of the finest female characters in all of American literature, Katina Paxinou's Pilar from *For Whom the Bell Tolls* is a highly effective performance. Watching her is like being in Hemingway's brain when he invented the character; she is the very personification of dignity, grace, and earthy strength. I can praise her no higher than this: when reading the novel, I find pleasure in letting Paxinou fill my mind when Pilar is on the page (unlike the general resentment I feel about most literary adaptations, which is why I generally refuse to see movies based on books I love). Paxinou emerged out of the theater in Greece, fleeing the Nazis and making her way to Hollywood – for this, the role of her lifetime. No better recipient for the Best Supporting Actress Oscar could be found than the mighty Paxinou.

In *The Song of Bernadette*, Gladys Cooper builds on the reputation she earned in *Now, Voyager* as a portrayer of harsh, cruel, older women. Here, she plays a nun who feels deep resentment that the Virgin Mary has appeared to a simpleton like Bernadette, instead of to her (the same plot device drives Salieri against Mozart in *Amadeus*). Cooper provides a selfish intensity that plays against Bernadette effectively. Cooper would go on to end her career playing Mrs. Higgins in *My Fair Lady*. She fully deserved this nomination.

As Bernadette's mother, Anne Revere puts across the passion of motherhood with the wistfulness of age, as well as the incredulity and embarrassment one would naturally feel when a teenage daughter begins claiming a vision of a divine lady. Revere's best scene in the film comes when she comforts Bernadette in the night, beside a soft firelight, and tells her what her life will be like when Bernadette becomes a woman: she will get married, have children, and grow old. For that scene alone, she deserved this nomination for *The Song of Bernadette*.

So Proudly We Hail! stars Claudette Colbert, Veronica Lake, and the nominated Paulette Goddard as three nurses serving in the Pacific theater during WWII. George Reeves (TV's Clark Kent) shows up as Colbert's love interest; he never had a better part in the movies. Goddard plays a flirty nurse who can't say no; she has two fiancés who show up to see her off, then picks up a third admirer on her way up the gangplank. Later, she gets to work through a variety of darker emotions, including guilt and expiation. Of all Paulette Goddard's movies, *So Proudly We Hail!* is the first that made me feel she had learned how to act. Perhaps the Academy nominated her out of shock, at discovering her inhabiting a role effectively for the first time. The movie does go overboard at times, including what seems an unnecessary slapping and fighting match between Lake and Goddard primarily there for the usual reason Hollywood has cat fights. The movie develops a certain compelling quality, as we get deeper and deeper into the war. Goddard deserved her nomination for what she contributes.

For *Watch on the Rhine*, Lucile Watson plays a domineering, eccentric mother who likes her own way and doesn't care who knows it. Watson brings across a huge ego, driven by equal parts selfishness and generosity, for what has to be the only truly human character in the entire movie. Bette Davis pursues the sacrificial undertones she liked to explore from time to time; Paul Lukas puts on nobility and the struggle for freedom like masks. Only Watson survives as a full human being, and remains the main reason to see *Watch on the Rhine* more than once.

Best Writing (Original Screenplay): Norman Krasna won for *Princess O'Rourke*, over Dudley Nichols, *Air Force*; Noel Coward, *In Which We Serve*; Lillian Hellman, *The North Star*; and Allan Scott, *So Proudly We Hail!*

Princess O'Rourke features Olivia de Havilland as a princess with whom flier Robert Cummings falls in love. Diplomatic nonsense complicates things in this tale of mistaken identity and romance, with mildly risqué touches throughout. Norman Krasna made a living out of this kind of glorious fluff. Watching the movie today after seeing the derivative (but far better) *Roman Holiday* can be a bit of a letdown, but de Havilland is enchanting. One wonderful line comes from Cummings, when de Havilland is almost unconscious on his shoulder from too many sleeping pills: "Are you lucky I was raised right." The wife of Robert Cummings' co-pilot is awoken and told to get dressed, for this apparently shocking reason: "Eddie wants you to undress a girl for him." The princess wakes, to discover a series of signs telling her where to go after getting dressed, culminating in the titillating "What a place to have a birthmark!" Later, we get a very sexy bathing scene with de Havilland doing her best to outdo Claudette Colbert in *Cleopatra*. The film rolls out as one exposure of the truth after another, with the leads finding out as much about themselves as they do about each other. The ending couldn't be more patriotic – or amusing. Norman Krasna directed his own screenplay, and deservedly won this Oscar.

Dudley Nichols wrote *Air Force*, a patriotic, driven look at the lives of combat pilots for Howard Hawks, who had already made *The Dawn Patrol* and *Only Angels Have Wings* on similar subjects. William Faulkner contributed as well, although he is uncredited. Among Faulkner's contributions was a pivotal death scene and some sharp bits of dialogue including Tobias' assessment of California: "The sun shines and nothing ever happens, and before you know it you're 60 years old."[ccxxxi] *Air Force* relies on John Garfield for its emotional center, as a character who washed out of aviation school and has to learn how to function within the group. As propaganda, the film must have inspired audiences; as a movie in and of itself, *Air Force* does much the same, and reminds me more of John Ford's *They Were Expendable* than any other war movie (Nichols wrote Ford's *Stagecoach*). Nichols' script is an excellent one, and well worth listening to for the dialogue, which is crisp and to the point, even as it works the sentiment effectively. A good nomination for Dudley Nichols.

Noel Coward is being ambitious in the war film *In Which We Serve*: he wants to give us the character of the British people through this intertwining of the lives of different officers and crewmen of a British warship. He shows the reality of life aboard that vessel, informed throughout by the desire to inspire the British to continue to fight Hitler and the Nazis. Unlike most American war films (*They Were Expendable* and *Wake Island* being exceptions), *In Which We Serve* lets us see the casualties of war, as we know the ship has been lost. Not a trace of false bravado exists in this movie. Noel Coward had been a playwright of drawing room comedies and controversial satires, and also a songwriter; later in life, he took to performing musical revues of his own songs. *In Which We Serve* was a major departure from his usual fare, and a very successful one – Coward even won an honorary Oscar for the film. The nomination should stay.

Lillian Hellman must have found this nomination for *The North Star* bittersweet: she was so incensed at what Goldwyn and director Lewis Milestone had done with her script, she bought out her contract with Goldwyn and never worked for him again.ccxxxii Watching this mess, I would have agreed with her, and to make her rest easy, let's concede this nomination should have never been given, in recognition of how often Hollywood ignores the script and produces crap (see Best Cinematography (Black & White) below for more on this fouled-up movie).

Allan Scott wrote the screenplay for *So Proudly We Hail!* The problem lies in the category: he based the story of wartime nurses trapped behind enemy lines on real events, including the records of the Army nurses – which the preface to the film acknowledges! So let's move this discussion over to the adapted category, where it belongs.

Best Writing (Screenplay): Julius J. Epstein, Philip G. Epstein, and Howard Koch won for *Casablanca*, over Nunnally Johnson, *Holy Matrimony*; Richard Flournoy, Lewis R. Foster, Frank Ross, and Robert Russell, *The More the Merrier*; George Seaton, *The Song of Bernadette*; and Lillian Hellman & Dashiell Hammett, *Watch on the Rhine*

Julius J. Epstein, Philip G. Epstein, and Howard Koch won for *Casablanca*, and if they hadn't, I would have refused to watch the Oscars ever again. Besides a pleasing plot, intriguing characters, real subjects, and the perfect ending (which resists the happy one most of Hollywood would have used), we get the snappiest dialogue of all American films up to that date (and for most dates afterwards, as well). Consider these classic lines: Peter Lorre, to Humphrey Bogart: "You know, Rick, I have many a friend in Casablanca, but somehow, just because you despise me, you are the only one I trust." Bogart, to Lorre: "I don't mind a parasite. I object to a cut-rate one." Bogart, to Ingrid Bergman: "Tell me, who was it you left me for? Was it Laszlo, or were there others in between? Or aren't you the kind that tells?" Claude Rains, to Bogart: "How extravagant you are, throwing away women like that. Someday they may be scarce." Bogart, about Bergman: "Of all the gin joints, in all the towns, in all the world, she walks into mine." Bogart, to Bergman: "Here's looking at you, kid." And again: "I've got a job to do, too. Where I'm going, you can't follow. What I've got to do, you can't be any part of. Ilsa, I'm no good at being noble, but it doesn't take much to see that the problems of three little people don't amount to a hill of beans in this crazy world. Someday you'll understand that." No better written script emerged in this entire period. The Oscar is a brilliant decision.

Nunnally Johnson adapted Arnold Bennett's novel *Buried Alive* as *Holy Matrimony*, which stars Monty Woolley as a painter who fakes his own death, takes up marriage, then begins painting again. A sweet little knot of irascibility of a film, driven by amusing performances by Woolley and the rest of the cast, *Holy Matrimony* should be far better known than it is. Johnson's script carries the movie forward step by interesting step, with the charm never flagging. Johnson had already written the screenplay for *The Grapes of Wrath*; he would go on to write and produce *How to Marry a Millionaire* among others. A fine nomination for a forgotten treasure.

The gang adapted *The More the Merrier* from an original story by two of them. Take a young woman, have her home invaded by a crafty old man, who then plots to make her happy by finding a young man suitable for her. Work in some vulgarity, as in the mantra of the film, "Damn the torpedoes! Full speed ahead!" Toss in some romance, a buffoonish fiancé, some wartime jokes, and perhaps a bit too much slapstick, and *The More the Merrier* is the fine result. The nomination should stay for Richard Flournoy, Lewis R. Foster, Frank Ross, and Robert Russell.

Franz Werfel's bestselling brick of a book, *The Song of Bernadette*, represents the same kind of adaptation nightmare as *Anthony Adverse* and *Gone with the Wind*. George Seaton did a good job bringing this book under control, even if the movie does drag on longer than is comfortable. Werfel was a Jewish refugee from Nazi Germany who stopped by Lourdes on the way to America, making a promise to tell Bernadette's story should he reach freedom. Part of the subtext to the novel explores the hostility of authorities to anything that defies their routine answers; I suspect Werfel wrote the novel as a slap against the dictatorial Nazis. Seaton's screenplay deserved a nomination.

Lillian Hellman and Dashiell Hammett's adaptation of *Watch on the Rhine* has a number of weaknesses. The children are stiffly written and acted, particularly the know-it-all middle son. Bette Davis is nicely underplaying, as is Lukas. Davis' family isn't badly done. Their guests, including the Nazi sympathizer, seem too broadly drawn. The conversation on the train between the Italian and Lukas seems stiff and awkward, as it is there to show that not all Germans and Italians are fascist – but instead of dramatizing that, we get speeches telling us that. I seriously doubt any man with underground connections would tell a stranger he just met "I fight against fascism." Only badly written fictional characters talk like that. As I've pointed out in Best Picture above, the script is perhaps the main reason the movie fails as anything other than propaganda. No nomination should have been given for such a weak piece of adaptation.

As for films not nominated, we've moved the discussion of Allan Scott's screenplay for *So Proudly We Hail!* over to this category, as it is based on real-life events, and credit is given to the official records. A fairly gritty story of the suffering of these nurses at the hands of the Japanese, *So Proudly We Hail!* grabs our sympathy by showing us the nurses after their travails, then in a flashback at play on the convoy, replete with romantic involvements. One very surprising scene, given the squeamishness of the production code, has one nurse being brutally honest about the Japanese soldiers raping female captives. The word rape is never used, but the discussion is as straightforward as any film ever got in 1943 about the horrors of war. Veronica Lake's character chooses a brutal death, one that must have shocked wartime audiences. Scott does a shameless bit of stealing from Ronald Reagan's famous scene in *Kings Row*, effectively weakening his script, which had been building towards something more than plagiarism. He also achieves a kind of pastoral longing on the night of the wedding of Claudette Colbert and George Reeves. Reeves never had a better film role, deepening the mystery over why he never managed a bigger movie career as a leading man. The ending rings false, because of the forced hope; rather than allowing the messages to emerge from the action, we get a canned letter. Overall, however, Scott did a good job, and deserved the nomination.

WHAT THEY GOT WRONG:

Despite choosing *Casablanca*, and making me want to hold a séance to give their spirits all a big congratulations and a reason to rest easier, they went on to make some truly boneheaded choices for some of the other categories. Two steps forward, one step back...again. Their dunderheaded decisions include:

Best Actor: Paul Lukas, *Watch on the Rhine*
Best Actress: Jennifer Jones, *The Song of Bernadette*
Best Supporting Actor: Charles Coburn, *The More the Merrier*
Best Writing (Original Motion Picture Story): William Saroyan, *The Human Comedy*
Best Cinematography (Black & White): Arthur C. Miller, *The Song of Bernadette*
Best Cinematography (Color): Hal Mohr and W. Howard Greene,

The Phantom of the Opera

Best Dramatic or Comedy Score: Alfred Newman, *The Song of Bernadette*

Best Musical Score: Ray Heindorf, *This Is the Army*

Best Song: Harry Warren and Mack Gordon, "You'll Never Know," *Hello, Frisco, Hello*

Best Art Direction (Black & White): James Basevi, William S. Darling, and Thomas Little, *The Song of Bernadette*

Best Art Direction (Color): Alexander Golitzen, John B. Goodman, Russell A. Gausman and Ira S. Webb, *Phantom of the Opera*

Best Special Effects: Fred Sersen and Roger Heman, *Crash Dive*

Best Short Subject (Cartoon): MGM, *Yankee Doodle Mouse*

Best Actor: Paul Lukas won for *Watch on the Rhine*, over Humphrey Bogart, *Casablanca*; Gary Cooper, *For Whom the Bell Tolls*; Mickey Rooney, *The Human Comedy*; and Walter Pidgeon, *Madame Curie*

In *Watch on the Rhine*, Paul Lukas plays an anti-Nazi freedom fighter newly come to America, the home of his wife Bette Davis. Lukas approaches the role with understatement, and a kind of quiet grace he had never really exhibited in American movies, where he mostly played the villains in B-pictures. While the script continually forces him to make speeches, Lukas does the best he can to carry them off; that he almost succeeds in doing so is a testament to his ability as an actor, an ability all too poorly used in Hollywood. His other major role would be in Disney's *20,000 Leagues Under the Sea*, in which his Professor Aronnax proves to be the movie's biggest flaw. Lukas deserved the nomination, but only a wartime audience could have ever given him the Oscar – particularly when they passed over the finest career performance of a far greater actor.

Watching Humphrey Bogart in *Casablanca* is like watching the perfection of the actor's craft as it stood in the golden age of Hollywood. Bogart builds off the anti-hero he had embraced in *The Maltese Falcon* to give the outstanding performance of his life, that of the embittered Rick. Bogart embodied the very idea of isolationism and selfishness, and in the course of his performance, embraced the activism America had fought to hold off for as long as it could. What is more, Bogart became, for the very first time, a figure of deep romantic dimensions – a fact he credited to Ingrid Bergman looking at him, but he does much the same with Lauren Bacall in *To Have and Have Not* and *The Big Sleep*. One of the insider touches Bogart brought to his character was his own obsession with chess. When we meet him for the first time in *Casablanca*, the chessboard is set up as a stalemate, which is precisely the position in life Bogart's character occupies – and not just in the movie, as he was trapped in a violent, alcoholic, abusive relationship with his wife Mayo Methot as "The Battling Bogarts." Bogart's face, voice, and posture are endlessly variable at this point of his career, and in service to a story worthy of those abilities. The Academy's nomination is an outstanding one.

As Robert Jordan in *For Whom the Bell Tolls*, Gary Cooper may be a little long in the tooth, but the dignity and dedication of the character comes through fine. The romance with Bergman has one sexy moment, with the first night in the sleeping bag, but much of the rest of it is lifeless. I do think Cooper deserves the nomination, for bringing out so much of the Hemingway code of honor and grace under pressure, but like so many literary adaptations, something is missing. This time, it's the cinematography and the direction, which could have deepened this movie considerably. Cooper does the best he can, and should keep his nod.

In *The Human Comedy*, Mickey Rooney tones down his usual exuberance, serving the material effectively. In particular, the scene wherein he gives an improvised speech on the role of the human nose in history comes off well, as does his mooning over the school girl, and his relationship with his younger brother. Even if the film as a whole never comes together, Rooney deserved this nomination, avoiding almost all trace of the ham he sometimes indulged.

In *Madame Curie*, Walter Pidgeon plays Pierre Curie, but more or less, he is once again cast as Mr. Greer Garson. He does have some nice scenes as the emotional one of the pair, and his proposal of marriage is as eccentric as they come. When he leaves the picture, much of the vitality departs as well. He gives a more interesting performance than Garson does by far, although still not quite living up to the promise he showed in *How Green Was My Valley*. Perhaps his finest moment is when he buys the earrings, and honest love and devotion fills his voice and eyes and face. The nomination is a good one.

As for those the Academy should have nominated, at the top of the list goes Henry Fonda in *The Ox-Bow Incident*. Along with his work of genius in *The Grapes of Wrath* and his excellent turn as Lincoln in *Young Mr. Lincoln*, his role as the cowboy who speaks out against lynching in *The Ox-Bow Incident* is the very definition of nuance. Watch his face as he listens to the new husband of his former girlfriend's prolix speech; the eyebrows and the eyes say it all. Listen to the final reading of the dead man's letter, and hear how Fonda's voice alone conveys shadings other actors would have missed. Fonda also brings touches of darkness to his character which were unexpected in the supposed protagonist of this morality lesson, and which rescues the film from the kind of preachiness that might have doomed *Ox-Bow*. Fonda brings weight and believability to most of his movies, and he should have been nominated.

Close behind Fonda comes the Merry Widow Murderer, Joseph Cotten, from Hitchcock's *Shadow of a Doubt*. Cotten always had a trace of the ham about him in his early movies, but Hitchcock seems to have helped him learn how to act more cinematically. Cotten plays the role with a very low-key intensity, and the scene wherein he talks about widows spending money chills us as thoroughly as any villain could have. Cotten should have been nominated.

So who truly should have won the Best Actor Oscar for 1943? The answer should be obvious: Humphrey Bogart, for *Casablanca*. Let me offer the best argument I can: who else could have convinced an audience that he would willingly give up Ingrid Bergman? Case closed.

Best Actress: Jennifer Jones won for *The Song of Bernadette*, over Joan Fontaine, *The Constant Nymph*; Ingrid Bergman, *For Whom the Bell Tolls*; Greer Garson, *Madame Curie*; and Jean Arthur, *The More the Merrier*

Jennifer Jones didn't make her first film appearance in *The Song of Bernadette*, the publicity machinations of Svengali David O. Selznick to the contrary (she made some B-pictures before, under another name). But *The Song of Bernadette* made her a star. Although at 24 she was already the mother of two and in a troubled marriage to actor and alcoholic Robert Walker, she played the young Bernadette with simple grace and a kind of serenity that must have been hard to maintain due to her personal struggles. But after a time, Jones is simply playing the same scene over and over, with little change or growing depth; a certain degree of boredom settles into the experience of watching her. Jones also proves incapable of displaying sorrow, hiding her face in her hands and being shot from behind, rather than showing tears or sadness honestly. She should keep the nomination, for doing as well with the role of an untroubled saint as anybody could have, but the performance is a one-note wonder, and she wears out her welcome by the end.

Joan Fontaine's performance in *The Constant Nymph* reveals her moving away from the kind of namby-pamby roles that made her famous. Playing a young teen, she comes across with all the gawkiness, plotting, and excitement of the age, and showing more emotional range than she has in other movies. Fontaine is in love with the much older

Charles Boyer, obsessively so, like some Lolita in reverse; the age difference doesn't seem to disturb the filmmakers in the slightest. Boyer plays a composer (the music we hear is that of Erich Wolfgang Korngold) who falls in love with another woman, Alexis Smith, thus creating the emotional tension of the story (such as it is). Fontaine's character has heart trouble, which provides the rest of the tension (such as it is). The movie hadn't been seen in decades owing to copyright issues; TCM and the Library of Congress came together in 2011 to make the film available in a beautifully restored print. The pace is entirely too leisurely at times, and could have used some judicious cutting. I would have enjoyed seeing George Cukor or even Michael Curtiz direct this film instead of Edmund Goulding. Boyer doesn't seem to be interested in the part, and Smith comes across as so cold and uncaring that we don't feel her pain for Boyer's unhappiness with her. Fontaine does a fine job with the role, which is the only real reason to watch *The Constant Nymph*; she does deserve her nomination, particularly in this surprisingly weak year for actresses.

In *For Whom the Bell Tolls*, Ingrid Bergman's portrayal of Maria, the young victim of brutal rape in the Spanish Civil War and the lover of Gary Cooper, simply could not be better. Nobody in Hollywood could have done more with the character, especially given the restrictions placed on the details of her past by the Production Code. She suggests so much more than can be explicitly told of her pain, and of her desire for Cooper. Bergman was definitely riding high this year. Her role as Ilsa in *Casablanca* has endured even longer than the performance for which she was nominated, in *For Whom the Bell Tolls*. She should have been nominated for *Casablanca* instead; that performance has become her claim to permanence (along with *Notorious*).

In *Madame Curie*, Greer Garson plays Marie Curie, a scientist of the first order, regardless of gender. Curie won Nobel Prizes in both physics and chemistry, a rare achievement. Garson's portrayal of Curie focuses on her single-mindedness and looking noble while struggling. The performance is one-dimensional at best, and has all the interest of watching a straight line being drawn with a ruler. She does throw a bit of a temper tantrum when the radium doesn't crystallize, but by that point, it seems more like a sexist depiction of a woman losing her cool rather than a legitimate response. No nomination should have been given for a performance that could have been nuanced and exceptional, but Garson as a star rarely tried for anything below the surface of her aquiline beauty.

Jean Arthur provides yet another comic role in *The More the Merrier*, a very light-hearted romantic comedy in which she holds her own against the plotting of Charles Coburn (her co-star from *The Devil and Miss Jones*) and the poor man's Gary Cooper, Joel McCrea. She brings a kind of bewildered befuddlement at the predicaments she opens herself up to when she meets Coburn, who levels his own comic exasperation back at her, especially when she resists his matchmaking. I did find her crying a bit too much at the end, although I suspect Lucille Ball was watching. While not the match of her earlier performances, particularly for Frank Capra, she does well enough to justify her nomination.

As for those the Academy ignored, I would like to suggest Teresa Wright, for her performance as the niece who discovers her favorite uncle is a serial killer, in Alfred Hitchcock's *Shadow of a Doubt*. Wright gives true, honest emotion, and has never been more convincing in a role. She should have been nominated for Best Actress.

The final decision can only have one answer: Ingrid Bergman for *Casablanca*, thus completing the sweep of five of the biggest Oscar awards for the first time since *It Happened One Night* (or so it should have been). Bergman utterly convinces as a woman trapped between her heart (Bogart) and her responsibilities (Paul Henreid). Perhaps the lack of knowing which man she would end up with helped that portrayal (nobody knew the ending until the picture was almost finished). Regardless, watching Ingrid Bergman with Humphrey Bogart in *Casablanca* remains one of the most satisfying movie-going experiences ever – and an experience that deepens itself with each viewing. Bergman should have won the Oscar for *Casablanca*.

Best Supporting Actor: Charles Coburn won for *The More the Merrier*, over Claude Rains, *Casablanca*; Akim Tamiroff, *For Whom the Bell Tolls*; Charles Bickford, *The Song of Bernadette*; and J. Carrol Naish, *Sahara*

Charles Coburn won for *The More the Merrier* because of the body of work he had been displaying for the past several years, as the sadistic doctor in *Kings Row* (he chops off Ronald Reagan's legs), the gambler in *The Lady Eve*, the father-in-law in *The Constant Nymph*, the millionaire in *The Devil and Miss Jones*, and the devil-may-care grandfather in *Heaven Can Wait*. While I enjoyed his performance in *The More the Merrier*, and believe he earned this nomination, I cannot help but be dumbfounded at the performances that were passed over in his favor.

Chief among those is that of Claude Rains as the French police inspector in *Casablanca*, forced to work with the Nazis in pursuit of the infamous letters of transit. Rains provides, paradoxically, most of the comic relief, and a good deal of the menace, in *Casablanca*. His womanizing and gambling are matched only by his cynicism and secret patriotism. Rains simply never had a better role, and his performance remains one of the many great pleasures of watching *Casablanca*.

One of the main flaws of *For Whom the Bell Tolls* remains Akim Tamiroff's often hammy performance as Pablo. He does have a couple of fine moments, particularly when he allows himself to be struck while drunk, but overall, Tamiroff plays the part far too broadly, and without the sense of despair that has to inhabit the character. No nomination should have been given for the ludicrous overacting (the bad makeup didn't help either).

In *The Song of Bernadette*, Charles Bickford plays Father Peymarale, the skeptical local priest who had to confront the visions of Bernadette. Played with gruffness by Bickford, the character comes across as needlessly harsh at times, but overall, a thoughtful man emerges. Bickford would go on to play troubled authority figures for much of his career, with that rumbling bass and craggy face. He deserved the nomination for this early role.

Like Bickford, J. Carrol Naish grabbed a great deal of attention for his breakout role. *Sahara* stars Humphrey Bogart in his best war picture, as the sergeant in charge of a solitary tank defending a dried up well from the Nazis who think it is full. *Sahara* is one of the few WWII era movies about WWII that plays beautifully still, not least in part due to Bogart's fine performance, and those of the ensemble cast. J. Carrol Nash is the friendly Italian POW. Doing an Italian accent in the Thirties and Forties ran a terrible risk of sounding like Chico Marx; Nash manages to avoid that comparison completely, bringing compassion and a deep emotional tension to his role as a POW. Unfortunately, Nash is also burdened with the film's one propaganda speech that comes out as little more than forced ideology. The ideas are great, but they are expressed so baldly, and so out of character, that they ring somewhat hollow today as part of a movie with an otherwise understated brilliance. For what came before, Nash can keep his nomination.

But the finer performance in *Sahara* may be the un-nominated Rex Ingram, who really should have been named in the category. Ingram – the genie from *The Thief of Bagdad* – plays a very noble African soldier, countering the prevailing American stereotypes of blacks. He has a quiet, steady wisdom, and he stands up for himself against the POW and the Nazi. Perhaps a little too subservient in the colonialist mode, Ingram keeps that all in perspective with good will and a sense of zest – and the gleeful fury with which he shoots Nazis, and then strangles and suffocates one by burying his face into the sand. I believe this to be the very first time Hollywood allowed a black character to kill a white character, and portray it as an act of heroism. I can just imagine the screams of outrage from KKK members in the South seeing this movie; many of the race riots in the period came from southern whites who were angered at the government training blacks to fight. Rex Ingram deserved a nomination for this, his finest hour.

So too did Peter Lorre for his turn as Ugarte in *Casablanca*. Lorre has his last great performance, playing a human worm who simply cannot be trusted. His interactions with Bogart may be as fine a duet as those in *The Maltese Falcon*. When he screams for help, my heart breaks for him, despite the fact that I know he is a very poor excuse for a human being. That's superb acting, to make us care for a scumbag, and Lorre should have received a nomination for Best Supporting Actor.

In the final reckoning, the choice really comes down to Peter Lorre or Claude Rains. Of the two, Rains' performance is more nuanced and sophisticated, and the entire movie swings on his character. Claude Rains should have won the Best Supporting Actor Oscar for *Casablanca*.

Best Writing (Original Motion Picture Story): William Saroyan won for *The Human Comedy*, over Guy Gilpatric, *Action in the North Atlantic*; Steve Fisher, *Destination Tokyo*; Robert Russell and Frank Ross, *The More the Merrier*; and Thornton Wilder, *Shadow of a Doubt*

William Saroyan won for *The Human Comedy*; I'm not sure why. Saroyan hasn't really crafted any kind of story. All we get is one disconnected scene after another, bringing us some nostalgia for small town life. This kind of slice-of-life tale can work, but something has to hold it all together, and nothing really does. Saroyan is a writer whose reputation has almost completely collapsed over the last several decades. His wife Carol Grace, who later married Walter Matthau, claimed he was abusive, which hasn't helped his status. Saroyan didn't really deserve this Oscar – I suspect his Pulitzer Prize and MGM's block voting brought it to him – but he should keep his nomination for the few moments that are original.

Guy Gilpatric's story for *Action in the North Atlantic* gives us a respectful nod to the merchant marine. Humphrey Bogart and Raymond Massey star as officers on a liberty ship carrying cargo to the Soviet Union for the war effort. The movie isn't bad, but the narrative doesn't really gel until the second half, when their ship get separated from the convoy, and singled out by a sub. I was surprised by Bogart playing the secondary character. By this point in Bogart's career, you'd think he'd have the lead. The nomination should stay, if only for giving the merchant marine their due.

Steve Fisher's *Destination Tokyo* is one of the best of the WWII films, in its casting (Cary Grant and John Garfield, with an excellent supporting crew), direction (Delmer Daves), special effects (see below), and its audacious story of a submarine mission into Tokyo Bay. One of the particular graces of this movie is the way in which we are brought into every stage of the submarine mission, from the initial orders, through the preparation, and so forth. But we are never far away from the human aspects, which open up to us first and foremost through Grant's attempts to contact his wife to say goodbye, then through his care for his men serving under him as captain of the sub. The pace of the film remains suspenseful and constant. Even with a few false touches of the minor characters acting like stereotypes, the story for *Destination Tokyo* remains compelling and an excellent nomination.

As for Robert Russell and Frank Ross, *The More the Merrier*, see Best Adapted Screenplay above for more on this nomination, which can stay, as *The More the Merrier* is built on a doozy of an idea: one woman, two men, and one apartment.

Thornton Wilder received the credit for the original story on *Shadow of a Doubt*. The problem is, it wasn't his original story. That honor belongs to Gordon McDonell, to whom the credits actually give credit as well (as credits should). The real sense of small-town Americana does owe something to Wilder, as it was his bailiwick ever since *Our Town*. Bringing a serial killer into a small town family, and having the young niece have to solve the problem, does prove to be a compelling story – for which Thornton Wilder should hand over the Oscar to Gordon McDonell.

Best Cinematography (Black & White): Arthur C. Miller won for *The Song of Bernadette*, over James Wong Howe, Elmer Dyer and Charles A. Marshall, *Air Force*; Arthur Edeson, *Casablanca*; Tony Gaudio, *Corvette K-225*; John F. Seitz, *Five Graves to Cairo*; Harry Stradling, *The Human Comedy*; Joseph Ruttenberg, *Madame Curie*; James Wong Howe, *The North Star*; Rudolph Maté, *Sahara*; and Charles Lang, *So Proudly We Hail!*

Arthur C. Miller won in 1943 for *The Song of Bernadette* because he took a studio set of a small, foreign village and made it real and believable – just as he had done for John Ford's *How Green Was My Valley* in 1941. His cinematography is absolutely convincing – and shows us that the experiences of common everyday people have all the profundity of the high and the mighty. I would go so far as to say that the film simply wouldn't work without the camerawork of Miller. Although the performances are affecting, Miller's visuals keep what is essentially a wordless experience believable, grounding a spiritual transcendence in tangible sights. Miller and director Henry King keep the camera moving from person to person, rarely keeping a shot for long; this kind of quick cutting and interesting camera shots help an essentially static story move along – the most interesting parts of the movie come from the resistance to Bernadette, rather than her repetitive religious visions. Miller deserved the nomination, but not the Oscar.

James Wong Howe was nominated for his cinematography on Howard Hawks' *Air Force*, a WWII love letter to the B-17 Flying Fortress, one of the truly great aviation advances. Watching *Air Force* reminds one of the power of propaganda, especially when a master filmmaker crafts it. I once saw Leni Riefenstahl's *Triumph of the Will* in an auditorium at UCLA, and the urge to join in was honestly felt by the audience, as the discussion afterwards surprisingly proved. Hawks is on the same level of artistry, although the reprehensibility of the Nazis is largely absent from *Air Force* (some understandable hostility towards the Japanese erupts). James Wong Howe was one of the great cinematographers, and he and his team seamlessly merge primary camerawork with special effects and some combat footage into one of the finest war films (see Best Special Effects for more), as well as providing an intense level of audience participation in what it felt like to be in aerial combat for a bomber crew. Watching *Air Force* matches with Howard Hawks' best films about the value of teamwork and the discipline of men under pressure (see Best Writing (Original Screenplay) for more). The early flying scenes where they are transporting the bombers to Pearl Harbor on December 6th, 1941 are beautifully filmed against the night and morning skies. Another great shot is from under the wing, as the enemy planes are attacking and they try to start the engines, which blow a furry of leaves up and past the camera. The nomination should stay.

Corvette K-225 is an atypical naval war film, with Randolph Scott, Barry Fitzgerald, and a very young Robert Mitchum. Much of its quality comes from the production of Howard Hawks (the movie feels like one of his), the direction of Richard Rosson, and the extensive onboard location shooting of Tony Gaudio. The emphasis is on how things are done aboard convoy duty, and on how a ship works. Ignore the substandard romance, and enjoy the historically informative footage (including the live combat footage Gaudio didn't shoot). The cinematography is effective, and deserved a nomination.

Written and directed by Billy Wilder, *Five Graves to Cairo* stars Franchot Tone and Erich von Stroheim in this tale of resistance against the Nazis in an Egyptian hotel during the battles between Rommel and the British. The movie is a thriller that plays with a touch of comedy as well; Von Stroheim has one of his best parts as Rommel. Cinematographer John F. Seitz worked extensively over the next few years with Billy Wilder (*Double Indemnity, The Lost Weekend, Sunset Blvd.*). Seitz films sand and desert more beautifully than in any picture before *Lawrence of Arabia*. He and Wilder craft an opening intriguing in its setup: a lone tank, heading over dunes, filled with dead men...and a wounded Tone. The image of Tone chasing after the tank makes this nomination a worthy one, but the use of low-key lighting and high contrasts between light and dark produces a chiaroscuro effect that is effective.[ccxxxiii] My second favorite shot is when Tone and the German officer fight – and all we see is a flashlight in the dark, glaring at the audience. An excellent nomination for Seitz, who would be Billy Wilder's best cinematographer, and a partner in the greatness to come.

Unlike most MGM films, *The Human Comedy* isn't just a pretty picture trying to be glamorous. Not that that's easy, but I'm surprised how quickly I've become jaded and bored with most MGM films. *The Human Comedy* starts off with scenes trying too hard to shout, "We're arty! Be impressed!" We get a sky full of clouds, an aerial view, a child watching a gopher dig a hole, the scene of a young boy running through a field and waving to a train as it goes by, filming through the harp while the Mom gives her homily to the little boy, and so forth. After a while, cinematographer Harry Stradling and director Clarence Brown shift to a more mundane but serviceable style of photography, to allow the human stories to come through. The MGM gloss isn't really here, and that aids the story as well. While I don't think Stradling is ever going to give Gregg Toland or other first-rank cinematographers any competition, he does well enough to squeak through with a nomination.

The cinematography of *Madame Curie* is largely dedicated to making Greer Garson look good, but moments exist in the film which seem to be bringing impressionist paintings come to life, particularly on the Curies' bicycling honeymoon in the countryside of France. Joseph Ruttenberg should keep the nomination for those scenes.

In *The North Star*, a small Ukrainian village, led by Dana Andrews, Anne Baxter, Walter Brennan and Walter Huston, fights off the Nazis and Erich von Stroheim. Like *Mission to Moscow*, *The North Star* was so pro-Soviet as to cause trouble during the Red Scare of the late Forties and early Fifties. Watching it today, the picture of peasants is laughable, in their happiness and joy of farm life. They all act like typical Americans, around the bourgeois breakfast tables, as if they had all escaped from the Andy Hardy series and were putting on a show about

Soviet peasants. Nothing whatsoever is wrong with this little paradise...until the Nazis show up, the evil, blood-sucking bastards! Well, they were, but the Soviets weren't the Stepford peasants this movie makes them out to be either. James Wong Howe provides his usual solid cinematography; several striking dolly shots impress. The combat footage is very well done. But overall, the movie has a tone of falsehood, from the balmy cheerfulness of the peasants to the vitriol applied to the Nazis (while the Soviets are nothing but good people, who've never harmed a fly). I can see the historical necessity of presenting the Allies in the best light possible, but as an artistic creation, Howe's work is rendered false by the content his substantial style is presenting. No nomination should have been given for this pack of lies.

Rudolph Maté's camerawork on *Sahara* meets this fine cinematographer's usual high standards – economical yet with a touch of lyricism, which shows the beauty of the desert sky and the desolation of endless sands. As in *Five Graves to Cairo*, the desert locations film beautifully in black and white. One particularly well-framed shot shows the anguish on J. Carroll Nash's face as he's being left behind in the desert, the treads of the tanks spewing dirt into his face, and the camera shifts to show the tank pulling away, creating a long track in the virgin sands of the desert. The next scene showing Nash at the top of a small dune, against the clear desert sky, the long tracks ahead of him, is just as poignant. Maté earned this nomination, as he so often did.

For the most part, Charles Lang's cinematography on *So Proudly We Hail!* is functional, but not memorable. One nice scene gives us Veronica Lake in the shadows, a darkness as troubled as her character. Once we get to the hospital camp (a foreshadowing of the Seventies television series *M*A*S*H*), Lang's work gets more atmospheric as he shoots one night scene after another. Later on in the film, when Claudette Colbert and George Reeves steal away for their honeymoon, Lang fills the screen with a light of longing on their faces. Lang does deserve this nomination, for the highlights.

Once again, however, the most inventive cinematography of the year came from a low-budget horror film the Academy ignored, Val Lewton and Jacques Tourneur's *I Walked with a Zombie*. Despite the ridiculous title, the movie is a lush, brilliantly imagined adaptation of *Jane Eyre*, with the most striking images of any film this year (I would also suggest watching *The Leopard Man* and *The Seventh Victim* for two other Val Lewton films with memorable cinematography). The visual heart of the film is the night walk through the sugar cane fields on the way to the voodoo ritual – the images are indelible, and deserved to win the Oscar for Best Cinematography (Black & White) for cameraman J. Roy Hunt, who would go on to shoot the film noir classic *Crossfire*.

Best Cinematography (Color): Hal Mohr and W. Howard Greene won for *Phantom of the Opera*, over Ray Rennahan, *For Whom the Bell Tolls*; Edward Cronjager, *Heaven Can Wait*; Charles G. Clarke and Allen Davey, *Hello, Frisco, Hello*; Leonard Smith, *Lassie Come Home*; and George Folsey, *Thousands Cheer*

In 1943, Universal decided to make their first Technicolor horror film, reworking their biggest hit of the Twenties, *Phantom of the Opera*, casting Claude Rains as the Phantom. Sadly, they also loaded us down with Nelson Eddy and a forgettable cast, hoping that color and Rains could carry the film. Rains does the best that he can with what little they give him to do, but compared to the original Lon Chaney, Sr. version, everything is a letdown, from the tone and pacing of the film, to Rains' inferior makeup. Part of the problem is placing Nelson Eddy as the main character, and giving him billing over Rains; it's as if they made a Sherlock Holmes film with a wooden Dr. Watson as the protagonist. The movie swept up the color awards, but given the competition, that isn't difficult – and besides, the Academy prefers costume pictures for cinematography and art direction. The cinematography begins beautifully, with a dolly shot of the orchestra, starting with a pre-accident Claude Rains then panning right; we then pull out and up to see the opera house and the all-important giant chandelier. Hal Mohr and W. Howard Greene have accessed the tools powerful enough to make the massive Technicolor cameras more mobile, and it pays off handsomely, as the cinematography is at least fluid. For that, they deserve the nomination, but the Oscar should have gone elsewhere.

Color was not a good idea for this adaptation of Hemingway's last masterpiece, *For Whom the Bell Tolls*.[107] Ray Rennahan has moments of attempts at art, but with color, they just look faked. Black and white film, and proper lighting, might have aided the adaptation substantially. Color also makes the makeup look like a cheap high school production. The outdoor shots do look good, but they simply show up the studio work. I do appreciate the shots done in shadow profiles, as they are the most striking in the film. Overall, however, the nomination simply isn't deserved.

For *Heaven Can Wait*, Edward Cronjager gives us fairly static camerawork on a rich color palette of the Victorian era. Nothing more can

---

[107] *The Old Man and the Sea* is good, but it's not on the same level as his work from the Twenties and Thirties, despite generations of high school teachers using it as an excuse not to read anything longer.

be said, because nothing more was done – so no nomination was warranted. I don't think it was Cronjager's fault – take a look at his work this same year with Busby Berkeley on *The Gang's All Here* to see a camera that never stops moving unless it's time for stopping.

In the case of *Hello, Frisco, Hello*, we have seen this film all too often before: Barbary Coast San Francisco in the Gay Nineties – and yes, that's Alice Faye and John Payne once again trapped in a tortured love story, with songs and a happy ending. This time, they're suffering and romancing in Technicolor, with a decent song (see Best Song below). The cinematography really is first-rate, actually, despite the fact that it's in service to a retread. The movie remakes, often scene for scene, *The King of Burlesque* from 1936. The colors are crisp and rich, filling the eyes with all that Technicolor could offer. The camera movement is stagnant, however, except for what the editors do in cutting between shots. The roller skating scene proves interesting, wherein the camera does pan back and forth a bit, and zoom in and out a touch, as they skate. The shots of Europe stun, but where did they get them in the middle of WWII? They had to be stock shots, but the Technicolor makes me wonder. The nomination should stay.

In *Lassie Come Home*, Roddy McDowall is forced to sell Lassie; she finds her way back to him. Elizabeth Taylor makes an appearance as well, as do Elsa Lanchester and Nigel Bruce. Along the way, the audience suffers from dehydration from the vast amount of tears shed. I had to keep a box of tissues close at hand. Part of this is manipulation, but *Lassie Comes Home* is at the very least an honest manipulation of believable situations. We cry because we care about the dog and her boy – or his boy; Lassie was a female character, but always played by male dogs, as they did what they were told more readily (my wife says this was right and proper, and to pay attention...). Leonard Smith's cinematography was nominated for capturing the beauty of nature as Lassie returns home across hundreds of miles of open terrain. Sunrises, beaches, waterfalls, forests, meadows, lakes, rainbows, and country glens are all shown beautifully, and make for a very good nomination.

We've seen *Thousands Cheer* before, since the earliest days of the Hollywood musical. A romance provides the excuse for the movie, but the real reason to watch this musical isn't to see Gene Kelly wooing Kathryn Grayson, but because MGM throws in the kitchen sink and has almost everybody they could drag into this thing do a bit. I won't spoil the surprises (such as they are), but I do want to applaud Lena Horne and the top-rate Benny Carter and His Orchestra, as well as Gene Kelly doing his famous dance with a mop, some brooms, and a couple of buckets. I also cannot understand why anybody thought José Iturbi was a good idea (and I love classical music, so even as a bald man, I'm a long hair...). George Folsey keeps the ball rolling with interesting camera angles and a moving camera eye as he copes with this mostly lifeless film. Folsey also captures a glorious sunrise while the bugle calls reveille. He deserved a nomination.

The best color cinematography wasn't even nominated: Edward Cronjager's work on *The Gang's All Here*, directed by Busby Berkeley. A more mobile, involved, or integral camera couldn't possibly be found in color cinema this year. Just go watch Carmen Miranda in all the fruit and you will agree: Edward Cronjager deserved the Oscar for Best Cinematography (Color) in 1943 for *The Gang's All Here*.

Best Dramatic or Comedy Score: Alfred Newman won for *The Song of Bernadette*, over Hans J. Salter and Frank Skinner, *The Amazing Mrs. Holliday*; Max Steiner, *Casablanca*; Louis Gruenberg and Morris Stoloff, *Commandos Strike at Dawn*; C. Bakaleinikoff and Roy Webb, *The Fallen Sparrow*; Victor Young, *For Whom the Bell Tolls*; Hanns Eisler, *Hangmen Also Die*; Walter Scharf, Philip Boutelje, *Hi Diddle Diddle*; Walter Scharf, *In Old Oklahoma*; Leigh Harline, *Johnny Come Lately*; Gerard Carbonera, *The Kansan*; Arthur Lange, *Lady of Burlesque*; Herbert Stothart, *Madame Curie*; Dimitri Tiomkin, *The Moon and Sixpence*; Aaron Copland, *The North Star*; and Edward H. Plumb, Paul J. Smith, and Oliver Wallace, *Victory Through Air Power*

For *The Song of Bernadette*, Alfred Newman's score won and for good reason: he conveys the religious fervor and wonder of the story brilliantly. Listening to the music, I would argue that the scores of all the biblical epics of the Fifties and Sixties which Hollywood produced in its fight against television trace their descent back to Newman's score for this picture: the sweeping chords, the swelling human chorus, the uplift of the visions of the spiritual. For a few moments, the score becomes overbearing and doesn't seem to match the action on screen, but I wonder if this was Newman, who wasn't known for hitting us over the head this way. Perhaps it is simply the sound mix. Overall, the score is quite effective, and as I've said, seminal in its influence on other religious pictures. The nomination should stay – but the Oscar should have gone to an even greater score.

Deanna Durbin strikes again in *The Amazing Mrs. Holliday* as a missionary trying to smuggle Chinese children into the U.S. Strangely enough, Jean Renoir had a hand in directing this musical, but he was replaced. The only thing anybody remembers from this movie is Durbin doing battle with a cherry. The score by Hans J. Salter and Frank Skinner is typical fare for a Durbin musical: lightweight, pleasant, and largely forgettable – so no nomination should there be for something we've heard a dozen times before this, and better.

Max Steiner's score for *Casablanca* is one of his very best, despite his resentment at having to use "As Time Goes By." He wanted to write his own song, both for the integrity of his score, but also for the royalties – but he proceeded to ring so many changes on it, it was almost like writing a new song. Steiner also incorporated "Le Marseillaise" into the score, like a great poet making use of allusions to other poems, connecting what is new with the traditional. Try listening to *Casablanca* without seeing the screen once, and two things emerge: one, that the dialogue is the best ever, and two, that Max Steiner's score is as much a character in the movie as Bogart or Bergman (actually, listening to great movies without looking at them can be an instructive exercise; I've done it with good results with other flicks). What Steiner does in his score is to completely remake the sounds of African and Arabian film themes. He starts afresh with his wonderful booming kettledrums and triumphant brass – and that impertinent use of the triangle! – then merges those freshly minted sounds into a discourse on the nature of romance and adventure, through his use of the strings and woodwinds. Not a single color of the modern orchestra was left untouched; Korngold's lessons on the pacing of action music are fully incorporated, and made Steiner's own. Steiner ties everything together by using percussion instruments – particularly the snare drum and kettle drum – to maintain the rhythmic pulse so central to the story, like the beating of the human heart. When Bogart sees Bergman again for the first time, the striking of a chord with low strings and woodwinds is like the breaking of that heart. Steiner also wrote the jazzy music of Rick's Place, with the swing touches which keep the voice of Dooley Wilson so complemented and vibrant. The piano – supposedly played by Wilson, but he faked it throughout – is the dominant instrument for vast stretches of the score, underlining the loneliness of Bogart when we first meet him, a solitary sound for a solitary man. When Bogart sits with Claude Rains, the score shifts into a duet of piano and horn, and perhaps a foreshadowing of the ending of the movie. That kind of commentary on the movie is rare in film scoring, requiring as it does a sense of the overarching narrative of the movie, and a willingness to do more than simply turn in a perfunctory set of sounds. The Paris flashback provides an interlude of great longing and beauty, in the variations Steiner invents from "As Time Goes By." Like Steiner's score for *Gone with the Wind*, I cannot imagine *Casablanca* without Steiner's contribution – which makes the Academy look very wise indeed for nominating him.

In *Commandos Strike at Dawn*, Paul Muni fights the Nazis in Norway – bravely, without his usual beard or much of his usual ham. Lillian Gish had her first film role in a decade. Irwin Shaw wrote the screenplay from a story by C.S. Forester. The attack by the soldiers – most of whom were real commandos – is staged with incredible stupidity, rather than the cunning and ability one expects (they attack in broad daylight, and announce their attack with bagpipes...apparently, nobody ever considered positioning and stealth). Overall, the music is the weakest part of the movie, with typical patriotic tones and clichéd scoring by Louis Gruenberg and Morris Stoloff, although some of the village wedding music is pleasant, and spots of the attack music are rousing, but both are negligible. Even more egregiously, the producers didn't pursue the score they commissioned from Igor Stravinsky, later published as *Four Norwegian Moods*.[ccxxxiv] Apparently, real music wasn't good enough for them – and crappy music isn't good enough for me, so no nomination should have been given for this bad substitution.

The Fallen Sparrow is a strange film, starring John Garfield as a refugee from a Spanish prison camp who is trying to solve the death of his friend in New York; Nazi spies are chasing him for the McGuffin he carries. Maureen O'Hara plays Garfield's love interest. The score by Bakaleinikoff and Roy Webb is suitably intense, if bluntly overstated at times. Garfield's character has psychological issues; I would have preferred something more subtle and reflective of that complexity, so no nomination was merited.

Victor Young's score fills *For Whom the Bell Tolls* like the stuffing in an old used couch: it keeps spilling out of the cracks. Overly present, and constantly commenting bluntly on whatever is happening on screen, the score serves to push the characterizations and direction of this adaptation further into simplistic good vs. evil. Listen when Akim Tamiroff shows up on screen, and the score goes all chilling and foreboding, from the first moment we meet him. When Ingrid Bergman is visible, the strings frolic lushly. We're never allowed to make up our own minds about these characters, who are never allowed to develop subtleties; much of this is due to Sam Wood's mediocre direction, but the score only reinforces the two-dimensional nature of much of this movie. To be fair, the music does entertain, and at moments, uplift the movie, but so much of it fills our ears, distracting us from what good there is on the screen. I think this is a case of too much of a not so good thing, which could have used some paring and selectivity. No nomination should ever be given for overbearing us.

Fritz Lang directed *Hangmen Also Die!*, which stars Brian Donlevy and Walter Brennan in a tale of Czech freedom fighters protecting the killer of a Nazi officer from pursuit and capture, despite the Nazis holding and killing hostages against the killer's surrender. Bertolt Brecht helped write the screenplay, but he and Lang had a disastrous falling out. James Wong Howe's cinematography is fine indeed. Hanns Eisler's score reflects an old world sensibility, with a Hollywood sense of melodrama. Long stretches of the film have no music at all, and what little there is imitates the period's typical music for these kinds of thrillers. Eisler had been a collaborator with Brecht in Germany; he became a refugee in Hollywood. After the war, he was accused of being a Communist spy and was deported in 1958.[ccxxxv] His nomination for *Hangmen* isn't a good one, as it has too much silence and imitation.

Adolphe Menjou and Billie Burke have a romp in *Hi Diddle Diddle*, a forgotten minor screwball comedy about con men, marriage, and parental responsibilities (or lack thereof). The tone of this movie is playful, particularly about movie conventions; the opening credits wish the audience good luck in finding a purpose; a beautiful blonde shows up throughout the movie, and Billie Burke finally explains her by saying she's a 'friend' of the director. Watching *Hi Diddle Diddle* has the flavor of watching the moments in a Bugs Bunny cartoon when Bugs breaks the fourth wall and addresses the audience, even though none of the characters in the movie ever make that move. A certain teasing of audience expectations emerges regularly, as one convention after another is ribbed. The movie is very much tongue in cheek, and so is the score, which takes a particular delight in making fun of the music of Richard Wagner, even while most of the rest is simply pleasant (and minor) swing music. Composer Philip Boutelje came out of the Paul Whiteman Orchestra; although he was nominated twice for an Academy Award, he never got the chance to work on a major film. I enjoyed his score for *Hi Diddle Diddle*; he deserved this nomination.

Also known as *The War of the Wildcats*, *In Old Oklahoma* features John Wayne fighting Albert Dekker over oil and a girl in the early twentieth century. Walter Scharf's score has some brassy flourish to it, building off the swelling violins in a blustery sweep – but like many B-pictures, especially from Republic, little actual music shows up during the movie. What we do hear is a typical western score with some Gay Nineties can-can music tossed in, and some nice romantic swooping when Wayne kisses the girl. I do love his use of the brass section, however. For that Scharf's nomination should stay (Scharf ended his career with *Willy Wonka and the Chocolate Factory*).

With *Johnny Come Lately*, James Cagney stars in his first independently produced film (which helps explain the rarity of the movie today). Cagney plays a vagrant turned newspaperman fighting political corruption in a late nineteenth century rural American hamlet. *Johnny Come Lately* is a good deal of fun, as Cagney is clearly enjoying his freedom from the studio system. The score by Leigh Harline (*Pinocchio*) offers up a warm palette of strings in the typical small town music style, with a touch of flute and woodwinds now and then for variation and a whisper of harp to close down scenes. Given the low budget, producer William Cagney did the best he could to provide his brother with all the accoutrements of a high-class production. Harline was part of that, and he delivers a good score, if a little over-recorded and pushy at times. He deserves this nomination.

The Kansan is yet another knockoff of the love triangle between a corrupt rich guy, the poor but noble man (Richard Dix going downhill in show business), and a girl. The movie feels very similar to *In Old Oklahoma*, but that just may be because Albert Dekker plays pretty much the same part in both. Gerard Carbonera spent his entire career scoring low-budget westerns, but it's doubtful that "scoring" is the right word for what he did with *The Kansan*: there is so little actual music – only a minute here and there – that there is no real basis for the nomination, which should be gone in the dust of Dix's fading career.

William Wellman directed *Lady of Burlesque* from a novel by Gypsy Rose Lee; Barbara Stanwyck plays the title role. Arthur Lange gives us a swinging score set in a burlesque house, with lots of bump and grind and sound effects. Competent, but hardly inspired, and not deserving of a nomination.

Herbert Stothart produced a serviceable, string-heavy score for *Madame Curie*. As is so often the case with Stothart, nothing memorable emerges; he simply provides the necessary accompaniment for whatever is on the screen, with little imagination and no depth. Stothart always seems to me to be the hairspray on the MGM coif; he just keeps every hair in place, allowing little room for any kind of movement or life in these pretty portraits in which MGM specialized. No nomination should ever be deserved for standard boredom.

In *The Moon and Sixpence*, based on W. Somerset Maugham's novelized life of Paul Gauguin, George Sanders plays the painter. Sanders abandons all middle class English respectability, to move first to Paris, and then to Tahiti, using anyone he can to produce his art. Except for fans of Sanders and Herbert Marshall, the movie is almost devoid of charm, and rampant in its misogyny. Also, no attempt is made to show us the kind of art for which Sanders is sacrificing everything (other than a tablecloth doodle) until the end, and the expectation isn't matched by the art that is offered. Dimitri Tiomkin's score couldn't be more conventional, which is odd, given the nonconformist nature of the material.

All we get are some overly sweet, plaintive strings, rising and falling, with little melodic interest – and not really deserving of an Oscar nomination (Tiomkin was capable of so much more).

For *The North Star*, Aaron Copland produced the score and a few folk songs, working with lyricist Ira Gershwin (Ira's brother George Gershwin had passed away in 1937). *The North Star* is not one of Copland's better efforts. The music doesn't fit the Ukrainian setting very well; nor does it have a Coplandesque tone to it for much of it (although others disagree, seeing some of his compositional techniques from other pieces working here).[ccxxxvi] Gershwin's lyrics are truly execrable, and the less said the better. The problem with the score here is it has none of the Copland uplift or sparkle. Serviceable, yes, but in service to a film that has an awful lie about the nature of the Soviets and peasant life built into its core. The music is forgettable propaganda, just like the movie – so no nomination.

Walt Disney threw almost his entire studio into WWII, with most of his output dedicated to propaganda and training films for the government and the military. The most famous of these is *Victory Through Air Power*. The 1942 bestseller of the same name by Russian ace Alexander de Seversky had advocated heavily for large scale, long-distance strategic bombing as the best way to win the war. Disney's animators went all-out themselves to demonstrate dynamically the soundness of strategic bombing, to the point of swaying FDR's mind over to the concept (if Leonard Maltin's assertion is taken as fact).[ccxxxvii] Some of the aerial combat animation, especially during the Battle of Britain segment, is quite inventive. As for the score by Edward H. Plumb, Paul J. Smith, and Oliver Wallace, the kindest word would be predictable. The score suffices, at best. But a few touches exist to secure the nomination, including the ironic use of "Rule, Britannia" as the Nazis sink two British warships.

In the final decision, I can definitely appreciate the influence of Alfred Newman's spiritual score for *The Song of Bernadette* – but I cannot do without the absolute ingenuity and sheer musicality of Max Steiner's score for *Casablanca*, which truly should have won the Oscar for Best Dramatic or Comedy Score.

Best Musical Score: Ray Heindorf won for *This Is the Army*, over Alfred Newman, *Coney Island*; Walter Scharf, *Hit Parade of 1943*; Edward Ward, *Phantom of the Opera*; Edward H. Plumb, Paul J. Smith, and Charles Wolcott, *Saludos Amigos*; Leigh Harline, *The Sky's the Limit*; Morris Stoloff, *Something to Shout About*; Frederic E. Rich, *Stage Door Canteen*; Robert Emmett Dolan, *Star Spangled Rhythm*; and Herbert Stothart, *Thousands Cheer*

Ray Heindorf won for *This Is the Army*. Once again, I ask: where is the credit for Irving Berlin? The music is his; the songs are his; heck, he even shows up to sing "Oh, How I Hate to Get up in the Morning" in his surprisingly weak voice! The credits once again state he wrote the "music and lyrics" – and yet, the nomination goes to Ray Heindorf, who did the orchestrations. I have no objection to Heindorf sharing credit – these things don't show up on clefs by themselves after all – but the Academy needed to consider these things more fairly. Irving Berlin should have been included here in the nomination, even if many of the songs are mediocre, and the movie drags on a good half hour too long (what passes for "humor" isn't, and the minstrel number is as offensive as ever). The Oscar, therefore, should be going to a more fascinating score.

Coney Island stars Betty Grable as the object of desire between George Montgomery and Cesar Romero, all set in Gay Nineties New York. The omnipresent Alfred Newman provides the score, which strings together a number of songs new and old into a light little confection. As Grable's movies were almost always empty fluff, this may not be a surprise; my father had two reasons to love her movies, and Grable flashed both of them whenever possible. The tonal colors are a bit shrill, but that may have been the sound track in general, which seemed more harsh than necessary. The orchestrations for standards of the period like "Cuddle up a Little Closer" are well done, suiting Grable's voice comfortably. Newman should keep his nomination for this often brash, but sometimes cozy, light entertainment.

Hit Parade of 1943 is a piece of piffle with Susan Hayward, Eve Arden and John Carroll, a Clark Gable wannabe. Fortunately, the movie also contains a cameo by Count Basie, and an early appearance by Dorothy Dandridge. Too much of this film is obsessed with the kind of sickeningly sweet swing and faked Latin beats we've almost managed to forget completely, particularly from the two third-string white bands they pull into this movie. Fortunately, much is forgiven when Basie shows up. Walter Scharf really can't be given credit (or blame) for this mess, since it remains unlikely that he wrote the band's orchestrations; the bands more than likely came in with their own charts. No nomination is deserved, but you should all go out and buy some of Count Basie's music (*Atomic Basie* and the Decca boxed set are a good place to start!).

Like many nominations in this category, classical music gets shoehorned into the score – sometimes legitimately, but generally through the rampant plagiarism endemic to Hollywood composers. For *Phantom of the Opera,* Edward Ward does adapt three operas, including music by Chopin and Tchaikovsky, but he also contributes the main musical theme of the score, the lovely and touching lullaby Claude Rains remembers from his childhood, which Rains has turned into music for his unrequited young love to sing. For a movie that spends so much of its time desperately wanting to be a Nelson Eddy-Jeanette MacDonald MGM extravaganza, rather than the horror film it should be, Ward should be congratulated on keeping the music fresh and worth hearing at least once. He deserved his nomination.

Disney was asked by the State Department, along with Orson Welles and many other filmmakers, to create projects that would help produce good will in Latin America during WWII as a means of fighting off Nazi influence. Disney responded with *Saludos Amigos* and *The Three Caballeros* (1945). *Saludos Amigos* is a collection of four segments of animation interspersed with live footage from the good will tour Walt Disney and his animators made of Latin America. Unfortunately, the collection never really picks up any speed or drive, as it is mostly disjointed observations and jokes, most of them not very amusing. The Goofy gaucho episode is the best of the lot, along with parts of the Brazil segment. As a travelogue, *Saludos Amigos* shows us some inviting aspects of Latin American culture, but as a movie we might watch, once is generally enough. The score has its points, particularly when in Brazil, which is written by musicians other than those nominated. Overall, however, the score by Edward H. Plumb, Paul J. Smith, and Charles Wolcott is one of the weakest of any Disney film. No nomination was deserved, as Disney can do much better than this.

The Sky's the Limit has Fred Astaire playing a pilot who falls in love with Joan Leslie while on leave. He expresses his rage at the unfairness of fate's timing and the war itself by smashing a slew of glasses in the brilliant song and dance number, "One for My Baby." Leigh Harline's orchestration of "My Shining Hour" sounds like it was intended for *Snow White* (although Joan Leslie is supposedly singing, she was lip-syncing). Sweet, syrupy, and forgettable, the song really took life outside of the movie, although not to the degree that "One for My Baby" did (see Best Song below). Harline's setting for Arlen and Mercer's masterpiece is jazzy, dark, and deep, and reflects all three of these gifted craftsmen at their best. The rest of the score of the film alternates between these two extremes, but overall, Harline deserves this nomination.

A second-rate musical starring Don Ameche and Jack Oakie, *Something to Shout About* isn't at all. The sole claim to fame for this convoluted and lackluster film is the song which appeared in it, "You'd Be So Nice to Come Home To" (see Best Song below). Stoloff's score isn't worthy of an Oscar nomination, as Columbia Pictures used their slot this year to crowbar it in to this category.

Stage Door Canteen is a relic of a film, wherein we get a wonderful series of snapshots of stars of the time, as they gave time to making servicemen happy. The stars did the same in real life, volunteering at the Broadway and Hollywood canteens for servicemen – and in 1944, they made *Hollywood Canteen* specifically to emulate the success of this New York film. If you love the classic film and stage stars of the Forties, *Stage Door Canteen* can be a fun time (at least once). It would probably be easier to list everybody who doesn't show up, rather than who does. My favorites are Peggy Lee singing "Why Don't You Do Right?" with Benny Goodman, and Ethel Waters singing "Quick Sands" with Count Basie. The movie's profits financed other canteens. Frederic E. Rich's score doesn't really exist, outside of the musical numbers – which I suspect had arrangements from the various bands already – so no nomination.

In *Star Spangled Rhythm*, Eddie Bracken's father tries to con Bracken into thinking that dear old dad runs the movie studio; we end in an all-star musical revue, including cameos by Bob Hope, Bing Crosby, Fred MacMurray, Ray Milland, Dorothy Lamour, Veronica Lake and almost everybody else under contract to Paramount at the time. The movie remains best known for giving us "That Old Black Magic" (see Best Song below). My favorite bit of the movie is Rochester in "A Zoot Suit" and the trio of Paulette Goddard, Dorothy Lamour, and Veronica Lake poking fun at Hollywood and the travails of the star's life in their musical number. Robert Emmett Dolan puts together the score to support the songs of Harold Arlen and Johnny Mercer, who really should have been nominated here as well.

Herbert Stothart, the house composer at MGM, provides a stodgy, furtive, clichéd score for the cameo-driven musical, *Thousands Cheer*. He does have some high points, as in the Gene Kelly dance number with the cleaning implements, but I suspect Benny Carter supplied his own charts for "Honeysuckle Rose," as even Kay Kyser must have with "I Dug a Ditch in Wichita." Stothart was occasionally capable of writing organized, interesting scores (think of *Waterloo Bridge*), but this isn't one of them. No nomination was deserved.

Finally, two all-black musicals should have been nominated. *Cabin in the Sky* is Vincente Minnelli's directorial debut. One of Hollywood's occasional all-black movies, *Cabin in the Sky* stars Ethel Waters, Lena Horne, Eddie "Rochester" Anderson, Louis Armstrong, Duke Ellington, and practically every other major black star of the period, outside of Hattie McDaniel. The story of the struggle for Eddie Anderson's soul,

Cabin in the Sky is mostly an excuse to string one musical number together after another, to our eternal benefit, since many of these acts had far less film time than their white counterparts. The plot and characterization haven't aged well, but the score largely has. Vernon Duke wrote the music for the original play (including "Taking a Chance on Love"); Roger Edens and Georgie Stoll adapted the music for the movie; Duke Ellington contributed one song; and Yip Harburg and Harold Arlen added three new songs (see Best Song category for more). The score is sweet, restrained (except when it swings), and appropriate for this fable. Duke Ellington is excellent, but not filmed as well as one would wish for this greatest of all American bandleaders; the music he plays is almost certainly his. Vernon Duke, Roger Edens, and Georgie Stoll – and Duke Ellington – should have been nominated for *Cabin in the Sky*.

The success of *Cabin in the Sky* led to *Stormy Weather*, a highly fictionalized biography of Bill "Bojangles" Robinson (who stars with Lena Horne) with excellent appearances by Cab Calloway, Fats Waller, and the Nicholas Brothers – which is why we watch the movie, and not for the almost non-existent plot (and the idiotic touches of minstrelsy and blackface). "Stormy Weather" was a decade old by this point, but Lena Horne made the song her own. Emil Newman was given the nomination for the musical direction, but the IMDB credits Benny Carter as well as others, including Fanchon, Arthur Morton, Gene Rose, and Cyril J. Mockridge. I suspect Fats Waller and Cab Calloway managed their own charts. Even though the story is a bare wisp of a thread, what is hung upon it shines it up like the Christmas tree in the Charlie Brown special. No other musical this year swung and sparkled like *Stormy Weather*. We get the finest musical performances ever put on celluloid for Fats Waller, Cab Calloway, Lena Horne, and especially, the Nicholas Brothers at the peak of their astonishing grace. This is the one with the staircase, the alternating splits, and the slide down at the end. *Stormy Weather* should have been nominated, and the list of nominees should have included Emil Newman, Fats Waller, Cab Calloway, and the others above – and they all should have shared in the Oscar for Best Musical Score.

Best Song: Harry Warren and Mack Gordon's "You'll Never Know" won from *Hello, Frisco, Hello*, over Harold Arlen and E.Y. Harburg's "Happiness Is a Thing Called Joe" from *Cabin in the Sky*; Jimmy McHugh and Herb Magidson's "Say a Pray'r for the Boys over There" from *Hers to Hold*; Jules Styne and Harold Adamson's "A Change of Heart" from *Hit Parade of 1943*; Charles Wolcott and Ned Washington's "Saludos Amigos," from *Saludos Amigos*; Harold Arlen and Johnny

Mercer's "My Shining Hour" from *The Sky's the Limit*; Cole Porter's "You'd Be So Nice to Come Home To" from *Something to Shout About*; James Monaco and Al Dubin's "We Mustn't Say Goodbye" from *Stage Door Canteen*; Harold Arlen and Johnny Mercer's "That Old Black Magic" from *Star Spangled Rhythm*; and Arthur Schwartz & Frank Loesser's "They're Either Too Young or Too Old" from *Thank Your Lucky Stars*

"You'll Never Know" won, from *Hello, Frisco, Hello*. A very good song indeed, but one that *Hello, Frisco, Hello* pounds on one too many times. "You'll Never Know" has a very simple lyric and melody, but fittingly speaks of the kind of deep emotional longing so many found difficult to express in the Forties in America – and often still do today, although I don't think it's a cultural experience as it was with my parent and grandparent's generation. Alice Faye puts it across fairly well. A very good song and nomination, but the song just is not the best of the year.

In "Happiness Is a Thing Called Joe," from *Cabin in the Sky*, Ethel Waters sings a paean to her sinner husband, Eddie "Rochester" Anderson. A confusing thing at best, and while not one of this brilliant team's best creations, the song still lets us know how important (and blind) love can be. The nomination should stay for Harold Arlen and Yip Harburg.

Hers to Hold is yet another Deanna Durbin vehicle, this one has her fully as an adult, and romancing Joseph Cotten, of all people. The nominated song, "Say a Pray'r for the Boys over There," means well, in patriotic support of the war and our soldiers, but does so in solemn forgettability. The song does have an occasional resurgence in choirs needful of a song to laud our troops, but that shouldn't be enough for a nomination.

"A Change of Heart" from *Hit Parade of 1943* is a completely nonentity of a song. No nomination is deserved for this syrupy mix of chorus oohing and sappy lyrics.

"My Shining Hour," by Harold Arlen and Johnny Mercer from *The Sky's the Limit* was nominated, but how could they have omitted "One for My Baby?" (see Best Musical Score above for more). The saccharine "My Shining Hour" should have been dumped in favor of the far better, richer, and more nuanced "One for My Baby," which later reached its apotheosis in the hands of Frank Sinatra, who, like Fred Astaire, knew this song's capacity to express the ennui and rage at the failure of love. Arlen and Mercer reached deep for this one, and they should have been nominated for it.

Saludos Amigos has the sad distinction, like *Bambi*, of having a really bad song nominated for this category. The title song is utterly forgettable claptrap, without a trace of musical snap to it. No nomination should have been given for this musical hokum.

Cole Porter provided the wonderful standard "You'd Be So Nice to Come Home To" for the not so wonderful *Something to Shout About*. Porter's song didn't make the impact it might have, being sung by Janet Blair and Don Ameche, but they do a fair job bringing the song to the audience. A paean to domestic love, written in the midst of war breaking up and separating many couples, "You'd Be So Nice to Come Home To" has persisted to resonate, despite the shifts in domestic expectations since its composition. A very fine nomination indeed.

"We Mustn't Say Goodbye," from *Stage Door Canteen* is a completely forgettable song. I had just finished watching this movie when I turned to this category, and I had absolutely no memory of it from the previous two hours. No nomination should have been given for causing amnesia.

A very good nomination, however, for "That Old Black Magic," from *Star Spangled Rhythm*, by Harold Arlen and Johnny Mercer. The only thing wrong with this song is the nobody they ask to sing it: Johnny Johnston. No, I'd never heard of him either; although he has a pleasant enough baritone, his complete lack of rhythm wrecks the song. Somehow, Johnston did have a big hit in 1944 with "Laura." After the vocal, they bring in a dance by Vera Zorina, who is best known today for her stage work and being married to George Balanchine at the time. She's not bad, but doesn't add much to the performance. Giving the song to Crosby might have won it the Oscar.

Like so many other WWII musicals, *Thank Your Lucky Stars* has only enough plot to justify showing us as many Warner Brothers stars as possible, including Humphrey Bogart, Eddie Cantor, Bette Davis, Errol Flynn, Olivia de Havilland and others. The proceeds went to support the Hollywood Canteen. We also get some great footage of Spike Jones and His City Slickers. Believe it or not, Flynn does a comic song and dance in Cockney dialect, and Davis actually belts out "They're Either Too Young or Too Old." She doesn't do a bad job, but we just don't expect her to sing. The lyrics have a touch of humor that helps Davis put it across, and for those moments, the song is worth nominating (that, and seeing Davis mug).

But not so fine as the song which should have won the Oscar. Of all the songs nominated this year, "That Old Black Magic" by Harold Arlen and Johnny Mercer should have narrowly won over Cole Porter's "You'd Be So Nice to Come Home To," as well as Arlen and Mercer's

"One for My Baby." All three are outstanding classics; but of the three, "That Old Black Magic" just has a slight edge in the sophisticated lyrics and the sense of intense desire it projects.

Best Art Direction (Black & White): James Basevi, William S. Darling, and Thomas Little won for *The Song of Bernadette*, over *Five Graves to Cairo* (Hans Dreier, Ernst Fegte, and Bertram Granger); *Flight for Freedom* (Albert S. D'Agostino, Carroll Clark, Darrell Silvera and Harley Miller); *Madame Curie* (Cedric Gibbons, Paul Groesse, Edwin B. Willis and Hugh Hunt); *Mission to Moscow* (Carl Weyl and George J. Hopkins); and *The North Star* (Perry Ferguson and Howard Bristol)

The Song of Bernadette gives us the nineteenth century French village of Lourdes, feeling very medieval in its roots. The poverty of the area is conveyed well. Even though all of the sets were manufactured in Hollywood, they have a look of age and long living. The French baker set was so believable, I could almost smell the loaves as they came out of the oven. The grotto where the Virgin Mary appears to Bernadette was manufactured wholesale on the studio back lot, providing a realistic grounding for the visions of Bernadette. A very good nomination – but *Bernadette* is not the best of the year, and should not have won the Academy Award.

Five Graves to Cairo has the best desert scenes of the year. Can we give a nomination for sand? For once, yes – but added to that is the partially destroyed inn the Nazis occupy, which affords director Billy Wilder and cinematographer John Seitz some marvelous angles, darkness and light with which to play. The nomination is a fine one.

Rosalind Russell, Herbert Marshall and Fred MacMurray star in *Flight for Freedom*, a fictionalized biography of Amelia Earhart; the movie pretends she's someone else, but most of the events are clearly from Earhart's life. The movie tries to claim we were able to fight the Japanese because of what Earhart did. At times, *Flight for Freedom* seems forced and by the numbers, with little other than melodramatic expectations, and a noble ending. The sets include airports, restaurants, a beach, offices, a flight simulator, mechanics shops, hangars, and landing fields. The look of the film isn't bad, although clearly things have been done as cheaply as possible. One very nice shot pulls back and back and back from Herbert Marshall standing on the tarmac as he sees Rosalind Russell for the last time; in another touch, the lighting gets very film noir in the hotel towards the end. *Flight for Freedom* is worth watching once, if only because of the suggestions it implanted in the public mind about Earhart. The nomination should stay.

Madame Curie gets a nod for reproducing the extensive laboratory experiments, the streets of turn of the century Paris, and the great hall of the University of Paris at the end. Good nomination.

Mission to Moscow is the single most notorious pro-Soviet film made by the Hollywood studios, presenting the Stalin regime in the best possible light, even going so far as to suggest the purges of the late Thirties were based on real confessions, and justified. Michael Curtiz directed Walter Huston as the second Ambassador to the Soviet Union (a real person, who wrote the 1941 bestselling book on which the film is based). The sets are as well done as anybody could ask for in a Potemkin village. In the end, watching this film must have given Stalin a massive erection. No nomination for this dangerous movie, which should be watched by every American at least once, preferably side by side with the Nazi *Triumph of the Will*, to see how movies can manipulate reality into the kinds of lies that lead to holocausts.

And speaking of Potemkin villages, *The North Star* gives us another fake Soviet village full of fake Soviet happy peasants. How about a fake Oscar? Or a fake nomination? How about none of the above for this fake?

The missing nomination is for *Casablanca*, for Rick's Place alone. Is there a more iconic bar in all of cinema history? The airport at the end with its forced perspective and midget workmen (go watch the special features on the DVD) remains as unforgettable as Rick's Place. Carl Jules Weyl (*The Adventures of Robin Hood, The Big Sleep*) should have been nominated – and he should have won – for *Casablanca*.

Best Art Direction (Color): Alexander Golitzen, John B. Goodman, Russell A. Gausman and Ira S. Webb won for *Phantom of the Opera*, over *For Whom the Bell Tolls* (Hans Dreier, Haldane Douglas, and Bertram Granger); *The Gang's All Here* (James Basevi, Joseph C. Wright, and Thomas Little); *This Is the Army* (John Hughes, Lt. John Koenig, and George J. Hopkins); and *Thousands Cheer* (Cedric Gibbons, Daniel Cathcart, Edwin B. Willis and Jacques Mersereau)

The Paris opera house wasn't original to the 1943 version of *Phantom of the Opera*; it remains even today, as the longest surviving set from Hollywood's silent era, when it was built for Lon Chaney, Sr.'s original 1925 silent version of *Phantom*. Given that it is the major focus of the movie, why give an Oscar for recycling? Other than that, we get the conductor's office, a lonely garret, lushly appointed rooms, several operas, and, of course, the sewers and catacombs. No real need for a nomination, I'm afraid – and certainly not the Oscar.

On *For Whom the Bell Tolls*, many of the indoor sets look false, and so ridiculously bad that they shatter the suspension of disbelief necessary for any narrative to succeed. The outdoor scenes are done well, but somehow, I don't think Dreier and company created the Sierra Nevadas, or deserve a nomination.

Busby Berkeley directed his first color musical, *The Gang's All Here*, starring Alice Faye, who is generally better here than elsewhere. Some other reasons exist to watch this movie: their names are Benny Goodman, Carmen Miranda at her greatest excess ("The Lady in the Tutti-Frutti Hat"), and the always amusing Edward Everett Horton. For the Carmen Miranda number alone, the art direction gang deserves this nomination.

This Is the Army is driven by the music and songs of Irving Berlin, who crafted the original stage show in order to raise money for the Army Emergency Relief Fund. Real soldiers were used in the cast of the show, and the movie. Michael Curtiz directed this songfest. The movie is badly in need of restoration, but what remains is colorful, with one stage set after another intertwined with the backstage business – or back-barracks business. Kate Smith shows up on a radio show to sing "God Bless America" (I confess – I got chills down my spine when she hit the chorus). World heavyweight champion Joe Louis shows up, in what I suspect may be the only Technicolor footage of him in existence. A good nomination, even with the poor print.

Thousands Cheer? I think not. To aid and abet this throw-in-the-kitchen-sink movie, the designers give us stages and theaters, army bases, some rooms, and whatever backdrop is needed for the numbers. Nothing particularly special highlights this movie's art direction, so no nomination should have been given.

The Gang's All Here should have won. Have you seen that fruity hat?

Best Special Effects: *Crash Dive* won for Fred Sersen and Roger Heman, over *Air Force* (Hans Koenekamp, Rex Wimpy, and Nathan Levinson); *Bombardier* (Vernon L. Walker, James G. Stewart and Roy Granville); *The North Star* (Clarence Slifer, R. O. Binger, and Thomas T. Moulton); *So Proudly We Hail!* (Farciot Edouart, Gordon Jennings, and George Dutton); and *Stand by for Action* (A. Arnold Gillespie, Donald Jahraus, and Michael Steinore)

Crash Dive stars Tyrone Power and Dana Andrews in a dual struggle for Anne Baxter and a submarine. The special effects of this hokum haven't aged well, nor do they reflect any kind of realistic warfare, mostly due to the Technicolor revealing the nature of the models far more bluntly than black and white film did. Some of the underwater scenes are done as well as anybody could ask before modern special effects. For those, the nomination should stay.

For *Air Force*, the flying scenes occasionally use models, very similar to those used in *Only Angels Have Wings*. We get some takeoffs, some landings, and one emotionally rich scene using a model is an aerial recreation of the destruction of Pearl Harbor. The aerial combat uses models for the most part, and looks very good, even all these years later; the nomination is a good one.

Yet another pro-US war picture, *Bombardier* has a struggle for a woman between Pat O'Brien and Randolph Scott. This time, we learn about bombing runs, and the possibilities of high-altitude precision bombing. The special effects consist mostly of poorly modeled bombing runs and some aerial combat, mixed in with real footage. In other words, what everybody else was getting nominated for this year, with little distinguishable from other war films. No nomination was necessary.

And what of *The North Star*?: Lots of explosions! Aerial strafing and bombing runs! Tanks! And all of it in service to a film that denies the reality of the Soviets, who were just as brutal, if not more so, than the Nazis who were attacking them. No nomination should have been given for this lying tripe.

So Proudly We Hail! has a few special effects, but mostly of the exact same variety we are seeing in all the nominated films this year: a model ship, an exploding convoy, and so forth. But when the Japanese bomb the hospital camp, we switch from models to the kinds of explosions so commonly seen in contemporary film, and so rarely (if ever) seen back in 1943. A level of realism is reached that the rest of the film has been building towards (mostly successfully). The attack on the docks during the evacuation is even more spectacular. Overall, an excellent nomination.

In *Stand by for Action,* Robert Taylor learns how to be a naval officer under Brian Donlevy and Charles Laughton. *The New York Times* viciously dismissed the film: "This is the sort of mock heroics which insults our fighting men."[ccxxxviii] My suspicion is that the reviewer didn't approve the silliness brought on by rescuing almost twenty babies and having two women give birth on board the destroyer. Laughton also plays his role with comic overtones. The special effects are limited to model warships and some explosions, but are effective in the scene of a naval combat pursued through the fog, for which the nomination should stay.

Once again, an un-nominated film deserved attention. *Destination Tokyo* has excellent model work, and the ocean has very realistic wave action. The shift from model to live footage is often seamless, and sometimes you have to look twice to be sure; the lighting effects are first-rate, and help the deception. The diving scenes are particularly well done, and the submarine work would set the standards for decades to come, along with those on *Crash Dive*, although the color film hasn't aged as well as this black and white take on submarines. We also get a beautiful camera move, as the lens dollies in after a PBY seaplane approaching the surfaced submarine; we would see this sort of thing perfected decades later with *Star Wars*. The centerpiece special effect is when the sub passes through the minefields and submarine net of Tokyo Bay, going in beneath Japanese warships for cover. The final attack on the aircraft carrier and the escape from Tokyo Bay works well still, and in some ways, formed the model for countless sub movies afterwards. The Academy should have nominated Lawrence W. Butler and Willard Van Enger for this movie, and they should have handed them the Oscar for Best Special Effects instead of *Crash Dive*, which never maintains this level of excitement and variation.

Best Short Subject (Cartoon): *Yankee Doodle Mouse* won for MGM, over George Pal's *The 500 Hats of Bartholomew Cubbins*; Walter Lantz's *The Dizzy Acrobat*; Friz Freleng and Warner Brothers' *Greetings Bait!*; Columbia's *Imagination*; and Disney's *Reason and Emotion*

Yankee Doodle Mouse won for MGM, and their cartoon stars Tom and Jerry. One of the better entries in this long series, *Yankee Doodle Mouse* casts Tom into a more villainous role than usual. Jerry is the good little American fighting off the attacks from his cat raid shelter. One of the most inventive gags is when Jerry's parachute turns out to be a bra. Overall, my problem with Tom and Jerry is that the entire series is one act of violence after another, not unlike the Three Stooges. Eventually, one tires of this very low level of comedy, and wants something more inventive, if not sublime. The nomination should stay for what we do get, but fortunately, we get a far better candidate for the Best Cartoon of the year!

Paging Dr. Seuss! *The 500 Hats of Bartholomew Cubbins* was based on Theodore Geisel's 1938 story of the same name, done as a Puppetoon by George Pal. Like many of the Puppetoons, however, this one was completely unavailable, although it has been shown at film festivals and Dr. Seuss celebrations upon occasion. I will have to set aside any consideration of this nomination, given its inaccessibility.

The Dizzy Acrobat stars Woody Woodpecker as he causes mayhem at a circus. The kind of divine fool gags that start the cartoon off are amusing; the conflict with the circus keeper really isn't. The nomination should stay for the first half.

Greetings Bait! came out from Fritz Freleng and Warner Brothers. A worm with the voice of Jerry Colonna is used as bait for a series of gags. Much of this has been done before with Goofy and his pet grasshopper in *Goofy and Wilbur*. Freleng would go on to much better than this imitative piece, although the voice and the two-eyed crab are amusing enough that the nomination should remain.

Imagination was released by Columbia Pictures, as a "Color Rhapsody" cartoon. *Imagination* retreads every Popeye cartoon ever made, with rag dolls and toys as the characters, and features third-rate animation, with fourth-rate rhymes and a fifth-rate song. No nomination was deserved.

Reason and Emotion came out from Disney, and what an odd little cartoon it is. We step inside the human brain, to find emotion in charge, until reason appears to keep it under control. The movie plays with this, to the point of making some silly arguments about women being overweight because their reason can't control their emotions. Then we jump into a Nazi brain, and see how emotion runs everything. I'm not quite clear what the Disney studios thought they were accomplishing with this overstated propaganda, but the nomination should be gone for this second-rate pop psycho-babble.

Two wonderful cartoons were omitted this year from consideration.

The first of these, Bob Clampett's *A Corny Concerto*, takes *Fantasia* and classical music in general and skewers them all. The real star of this cartoon is music director Carl Stalling, who crafts the two waltzes by Strauss perfectly for Porky Pig, Bugs Bunny and a baby Daffy Duck to trash. *A Corny Concerto* has very little dialogue, which is unusual for a Warner Brothers cartoon. If we had to pick only one from this best of all animated short studios, I would take *A Corny Concerto* over *Greetings Bait* any day – but the Academy should have nominated them both.

But far more revolutionary, and influential, was the cartoon designed by Tex Avery for more adult audiences, including the armed forces: *Red Hot Riding Hood*. An iconic character, the Wolf, gets updated, along with Red and her Grandma. Avery breaks the fourth wall and challenges the whole idea of narrative itself in a self-reflexive parody and send-up of every fable ever made up to that point. The wolf's reactions to Red may be the funniest depiction of lust in the history of American cinema; Jim Carrey in *The Mask* simply lifts the Wolf's entire performance. Perhaps the Academy was uncomfortable with the topic, or maybe MGM just didn't want this image associated with its Tiffany status, but *Red Hot Riding Hood* should have been nominated for the Oscar – and won easily.[108]

---

[108] I do realize that Bob Clampett's often highly regarded *Snow White and de Sebben Dwarfs* came out this year as well, and while I can appreciate the music, the caricatures of blacks (particularly the enormous lips) are just too painful to watch as anything other than a historical lesson.

AFTERWORD

So we come to our first stop on this journey. The studios are at the height of their power and profitability, as America fought WWII and Hollywood reveled in the glory that is still *Casablanca*.

I would say it's all downhill from here, except that it's not. American cinema would begin to change radically in 1944, as we shall see in the next book in this series, which will cover the years from 1944-1952. You should be able to get your grubby little mitts on that book by the summer of 2013 – or now, if you're reading this book after that. Go get the other volumes now! Go on, you know you want to!

The studios may have gone into decline, but the movies, both here in America and around the world, did not. As we shall see in the second book, the movies went dark – in film noir, in subject matter, and in tone. One might even say cinema began to mature, although not without growing pains. Spectacle would raise its gloriously ugly head, as Hollywood tried to find ways to defeat that young whippersnapper television. As the Production Code began to break down, things got more vulgar and less inventive – a trend that would accelerate and shows no signs of stopping yet. As before, some years for Hollywood would produce a slew of magnificent films, while others saw a less than stellar set. As usual, the Academy would get some things right – but more often than not, they would get things wrong, just as they did in the years we just got done talking about.

Actually, I hope we're not done talking about them. Nothing would please me more than to have further discussion of these movies. Please visit my blog, rjameswhowon.wordpress.com, join my Facebook page at https://www.facebook.com/WhoWonAnIrreverentLookattheOscars?ref=hl, or send me an email at rjameswhowon@gmail.com. One of the great pleasures of writing this book has been revisiting movies I thought I knew, and seeing new things, as well as discovering new treasures. If you think I've missed a better choice, please feel free to write me and make another suggestion. Please don't write me and suggest I perform anatomically impossible acts; let's keep this on a civil, physically possible plane. But I truly look forward to having you clue me into a wonderful movie I missed.

One new note for the Second Edition: out of guilt and my usual obsessive, burning need to complete anything I ever start, on my blog (rjameswhowon.wordpress.com) under Special Features I've recorded my attempts to cover every category I've omitted here. I want to be able to say when I'm done with this book series that I have seen EVERY available Oscar-nominated film, from the documentaries to the shorts. So feel free to pop in and watch me make a fool of myself some more.

We'll see you next time!

ROLL THE CREDITS!

First of all, I'd like to thank myself, for finishing this book. I couldn't have done it without me.

But seriously, I have to thank my wife, for having the strength, foresight, and patience not to kill me whenever I took time away from her in order to watch more old movies she didn't like, or to do yet another rewrite. Catherine, you deserve more than I could ever possibly give you – but I'll keep trying!

I'd like to thank my children and friends for watching these movies with me, and for telling me what they honestly thought. Serena, remember, you no canna foola me. There is no Sanity Clause. And two hard-boiled eggs. In particular, I'd like to give praise to my son for always being enthusiastic about his dad writing a book, as well as for taking the time to sit through yet another old movie. Ben, watching movies with you has been part of the family tradition my father started with me when I was younger than you. I hope you remember the laughter and the popcorn you share with me as much as I do about those times with my father.

Next, much gratitude to my film circle on Facebook, who played with a yearly list of possible best movies, and gave me their honest opinions. Among others, I would like to call attention to those who never failed to participate: Geo Rule, who was always willing to tell me I was wrong, but always made me feel smarter when he did it; David Freeman, whose taste is not limited to madras and Guinness, despite the rumors; William Koon, who redefines the term iconoclast; Marie Guthrie, whose graceful suggestions nearly always ended up leading me to the right choices; Galen Wilson, who could always be counted on to point out another angle; Anne Sidell, whose enthusiasm for the musical was boundless; Scott Neil Laster, who became my friend through these discussions; Michelle and Lisa Edmonds, for always taking the unbeaten path; and to any others who stuck their nose in where it belonged over the past two years. Thank you!

To my fellow teachers at Cathedral High, many thanks for your continued camaraderie, friendship and love – and particular gratitude goes to early readers and supporters of this project, including Helen Moses, Beverly Stavely, and the indomitable Terry Catlin.

For service above and beyond the usual responsibilities of feeding my addiction to books and movies, I would like to lead a rousing round of applause for my local Orange County Public Library and librarians, without whom I could not live a happy life. Thanks to David Elliott, Stephanie Engel, Patsy Langevin, Maria Enamorado and so many others who greeted me with a smile and a pile of requested materials week after week. Drug dealers have nothing on you fine folks. Every-body should support their local libraries and check out books regularly.

I cannot begin to recognize every book I've ever read about the movies, as I simply don't have a list that long going back to childhood. So, many thanks to many unnamed authors. I would, however, like to specifically thank a few. The late Damien Bona and Mason Wiley spent years researching and writing the one essential book for anybody interested in the Academy Awards, *Inside Oscar*. All of the information about what happened each year at the ceremony, and especially the behind-the-scenes comments about insider vote trading and backroom politics, can be found there; for other takes, try three other salacious but well-researched volumes: Anthony Holden, *Behind the Oscar*; Emmanuel Levy, *All About Oscar*; and Peter H. Brown & Jim Pinkston's wonderfully titled *Oscar Dearest: Six Decades of Scandal, Politics, and Greed Behind Hollywood's Academy Awards, 1927-1986*. Film critics and historians Andrew Sarris, Jeanine Basinger, David Thomson, Pauline Kael, Molly Haskell, and Roger Ebert were all welcome reads, although I very carefully avoided their thoughts until after I had made up my own mind about the films. Occasionally, they changed my mind. I enjoyed "talking" to them. Biographers are the workhorses of the non-fiction world, finding out the facts before they disappear. I found particular pleasure in the biographies by James Curtis and Scott Eyman, whose works cannot be praised enough. Scott Eyman was continually gracious enough to answer emails from a stranger, and encourage me to pursue my writing. Scott, I hope you enjoy my book half as much as I've enjoyed each of yours.

High kudos goes to my first editor and publisher, Deb Houdek Rule, whose intelligence, foresight, and stubborn delight in the project never wavered. Her standards of excellence made this a much better book than anybody else ever could have. When the time came to part, she sent me off with gracious generosity and continued friendship.

Finally, to Bill Patterson, my friend, occasional collaborator, mentor, bon vivant, and the best dressed man I know, I owe immeasurable thanks for his constant support and conversations about this book and every other subject under the sun. Bill was my first reader and first editor, and he taught me how to write better with every chapter. Thanks for getting rid of the unfortunate consequences of a failed public school education, and for helping me through life its ownself. We lost Bill in 2014; I cannot help but feel diminished every day that goes by without him. Bill, we love you still – and always will. *Recquisat in pace.*

INDEX

1
1941, 423

2
20,000 Leagues Under the Sea, 380, 523, 541

3
39 Steps, The, 175, 181

4
40-Year-Old Virgin, 2
42nd Street, 115, 117, 118, 136
49th Parallel, 481, 493, 508

5
500 Hats of Bartholomew Cubbins, The, 570

A
À Nous la Liberté, 104, 105, 409
Aalberg, John O., 377
Abbott and Costello, iii, 159, 432, 466, 489
Abbott and Costello Meet Frankenstein, 460
Abbott, George, 60
ABC Afterschool Special, 212
Abdullah, Achmed, 183
Abe Lincoln in Illinois, 389, 402, 403, 404
Academy of Motion Picture Arts and Sciences, i, iv, 1, 2, 5, 6, 7, 9, 10, 11, 12, 13, 14, 17, 18, 22, 23, 28, 30, 34, 35, 36, 37, 38, 40, 41, 46, 47, 49, 50, 53, 54, 56, 66, 69, 79, 83, 84, 85, 90, 91, 92, 93, 94, 96, 97, 98, 105, 108, 109, 110, 113, 114, 115, 119, 123, 125, 130, 133, 135, 136, 137, 140, 142, 148, 149, 151, 152, 153, 154, 155, 156, 157, 160, 161, 164, 165, 166, 174, 175, 180, 182, 191, 193, 194, 196, 197, 198, 200, 201, 202, 212, 214, 217, 218, 219, 223, 224, 225, 226, 228, 233, 234, 235, 237, 241, 247, 250, 251, 252, 253, 255, 256, 257, 261, 262, 265, 268, 269, 271, 272, 274, 276, 277, 279, 280, 281, 284, 285, 286, 292, 294, 295, 297, 300, 301, 303, 306, 307, 308, 309, 310, 312, 314, 318, 321, 322, 328, 330, 331, 333, 335, 337, 338, 343, 351, 357, 361, 362, 363, 364, 365, 376, 377, 378, 380, 383, 386, 387, 388, 389, 390, 394, 396, 399, 402, 412, 415, 417, 423, 424, 427, 428, 432, 434, 436, 438, 439, 440, 441, 442, 444, 447, 448, 449, 454, 455, 459, 463, 465, 474, 479, 480, 481, 487, 489, 493, 496, 497, 498, 499, 500, 507, 508, 511, 515, 519, 527, 528, 530, 533, 536, 542, 545, 551, 552, 555, 557, 560, 570, 572
Ackland, Rodney, 510

Action in the North Atlantic, 547
Adam's Rib, 134
Adamson, Harold, 216, 217, 293, 294, 563
Admirable Crichton, The, 174
Adrian, 57, 220
Adventures of Captain Marvel, The, 524
Adventures of Don Quixote, The, 122
Adventures of Robin Hood, The, 209, 215, 246, 247, 256, 258, 261, 265, 266, 268, 269, 270, 271, 274, 278, 279, 282, 287, 291, 292, 312, 344, 369, 387, 412, 414, 418, 431, 443, 484, 516, 533, 567
Adventures of Sherlock Holmes, The, 326
Adventures of Tom Sawyer, The, 109, 261, 262
Affair to Remember, An, 144, 307, 315, 321
Affairs of Cellini, The, 150, 151, 159, 161, 162
Affron, Charles, 39
Africa, 68, 458, 470
After the Thin Man, 211, 212
Aherne, Brian, 304, 305, 339, 349
Air Force, 536, 537, 548, 549, 568, 569
Aladdin, 222, 376, 483
Albin, Fred, 352, 353
Alcott, Louisa May, 113, 119, 130
Alexander's Ragtime Band, 259, 261, 262, 265, 266, 270, 284, 293, 522
Alfalfa, 68, 519
Algiers, 261, 262, 272, 280, 281, 288, 289, 357
Ali Baba Goes to Town, 226
Alibi, 31, 32, 35, 46
Alice Adams, 169, 177, 178, 278, 402
Alice in Wonderland, 109, 111, 121, 136
Alice in Wonderland (1949), 111
Alice in Wonderland (2010), 111
Alice in Wonderland (Lewis Carroll), 111, 136, 510
All About Eve, 178, 418, 419
All Out for V, 490, 491
All Quiet on the Western Front, 10, 24, 50, 51, 52, 59, 60, 61, 105, 128, 135, 277, 349
All That Money Can Buy, 440, 459, See *Devil and Daniel Webster, The*
All the King's Horses, 188, 189
All the King's Men, 309, 368
All This, and Heaven Too, 364, 381, 403, 404
All-American Co-Ed, 431, 432, 465, 466
Allen, Gracie, 226
Allgood, Sara, 435, 450
Allyson, June, 277
Aloma of the South Seas, 428, 429, 472
Alter, Louis, 216, 217, 465, 467
Always in My Heart, 488
Amazing Mrs. Holliday, The, 554
Ambassador Hotel, 29, 49, 83, 107, 300
Ambrose Wolfinger, 183
Ameche, Don, 231, 313, 337, 374, 411, 417, 425, 529, 533, 561, 565
America's Favorite Movies: Behind the Scenes, 359
American Film Institute, 31, 127, 438
American in Paris, An, 296
American Madness, 121, 124

American Newspaper Publishers Association, 65
American Revolution, 128, 303, 369
Amos n' Andy, 189
Anastasia, 405
Anchors Aweigh, 437
And Then There Were None, 104
Anderson, Eddie "Rochester", 269, 473, 562, 564
Anderson, Hans Christian, 354
Anderson, Ivie, 227
Anderson, Judith, 364, 366, 507
Anderson, Maxwell, 60, 156, 215, 220
Anderson, Roland, 135, 191, 192, 251, 252, 376, 377, 520, 521, 522
Andrews Sisters, The, 432, 466
Andrews, Dana, 550, 568
Andrews, Del, 60
Andy Hardy series, 480, 529, 550
Angel and the Badman, 261
Angels baseball team, 467
Angels in the Outfield, 425
Angels over Broadway, 397
Angels with Dirty Faces, 266, 270, 272, 273, 275, 278, 279, 284, 292, 326, 344, 522, 533
Anglophilia, 116, 128
Animal Crackers, 69, 76
Anna and the King of Siam, 220
Anna Christie, 50, 51, 56, 57, 58, 59, 66, 96
Another Thin Man, 324, 432
Anthony Adverse, 196, 197, 209, 213, 214, 215, 219, 539
Anti-Semitism, 145, 229, 244
Anytime Annie, 117
Applause, 53, 60
Apple Annie, 109, 119
Apple Valley, 295
Arabella, 170, 179
Arabian Nights, 376, 482, 483, 516, 522
Araner, 183
Arbuckle, Fatty, 32
Arden, Eve, 232, 560
Are Snakes Necessary?, 454
Arise, My Love, 381, 394, 402, 403, 405, 413, 416, 437
Aristocats, The, 168
Aristotle, 72
Arizona, 33, 42, 366, 367, 416, 417, 431
Arkansas, 65, 131
Arlen, Harold, 310, 314, 316, 345, 465, 466, 468, 561, 562, 563, 564, 565
Arlen, Michael, 43
Arliss, George, 49, 52, 54, 61, 145, 191, 199, 202, 219
Arms and the Man, 455
Armstrong, Louis, 11, 93, 173, 174, 216, 221, 279, 294, 562
Army Air Corps, 340, 472
Army Emergency Relief Fund, 568
Army Girl, 256, 257, 288, 290
Arnaz, Desi, 374
Arnold, Edward, 206, 244, 265, 287, 382
Arnold, John, 45
Arrowsmith, 85, 87, 88, 98, 101, 105, 131
Arsenic and Old Lace, 154, 449, 512, 520
Art Deco, 47, 80, 162, 293

Arthur, Jean, 61, 194, 206, 244, 265, 318, 340, 367, 393, 417, 427, 487, 496, 511, 514, 530, 531, 543, 544
Artists and Models, 250
As You Like It, 178, 214, 216
Ashcan School, 513
Asphalt Jungle, The, 372
Aspinall, David, 311
Asquith, Anthony, 269
Asta, 212, 224
Astaire, Fred, 31, 101, 117, 121, 144, 151, 174, 181, 188, 189, 190, 191, 200, 216, 218, 219, 226, 232, 234, 251, 252, 260, 263, 266, 291, 293, 294, 307, 365, 375, 376, 391, 411, 415, 433, 467, 468, 488, 490, 496, 497, 508, 509, 519, 520, 561, 564
Asther, Nils, 125
Astor, Mary, 76, 203, 240, 434, 438, 448, 450, 451
At the Circus, 296, 316
Atlanta, 8, 342, 353
Atomic Basie, 560
Atwill, Lionel, 170
Auer, Mischa, 200, 206, 207, 210, 232, 265, 325
August, Joseph H., 167, 338, 339
Aunt Pitty-Pat, 507
Auschwitz, 452
Austria, 276, 281
Autry, Gene, 465, 467
Avery, Stephen, 182
Avery, Tex, 297, 355, 420, 475, 490, 491, 571
Awakening, The, 46
Awful Truth, The, 224, 229, 235, 237, 238, 239, 243, 245, 251, 340, 350, 370, 390, 393, 395
Ayres, Lew, 77

B

B-17 Flying Fortress, 549
Babcock, Fay, 520
Babes in Arms, 308, 309, 328, 329, 373, 415
Babes in Toyland, 162
Babes on Broadway, 488, 489
Baby Face, 110, 121, 122
Bach, J.S., 213, 256, 415
Bachelor Mother, 306, 307
Back Street, 277, 459, 460
Bacon, Lloyd, 117, 118
Bad Girl, 87, 88, 97, 101
Baer, Max, 132
Bainter, Fay, 265, 275, 277, 282, 385, 482
Bakaleinikoff, C., 554, 556
Baker, Kenny, 296, 344, 414
Balanchine, George, 296, 565
Balboa Theater, ii
Balderston, John L., 102, 183, 185
Balio, Tino, 106, 409
Ball of Fire, 100, 239, 424, 425, 443, 445, 459, 460
Ball, Lucille, 37, 232, 410, 489, 545
Ballard, Lucien, 513
Bambi, iv, 235, 431, 482, 483, 488, 489, 565
Bancroft, George, 33, 35, 38
Band Concert, The, 168
Bank Dick, The, 382, 386, 387, 399
Bankhead, Tallulah, 444

Banks, Lionel, 261, 263, 349, 350, 416, 468, 469, 520
Baravalle, Victor, 259, 260
Barbary Coast, 166, 262, 484, 521, 553
Barbera, Joseph, 420
Barnes, George, 7, 44, 381, 403, 404, 405
Barney Bear, 476
Barretts of Wimpole Street, The, 142, 143, 151, 152
Barrie, James, 174, 216, 249
Barrie, Wendy, 380
Barry, Philip, 75, 263, 399
Barry, Tom, 41, 42
Barrymore, Ethel, 133
Barrymore, John, 8, 17, 55, 79, 89, 108, 128, 129, 133, 149, 151, 155, 199, 264, 276, 337, 423, 473
Barrymore, Lionel, 17, 19, 39, 40, 57, 68, 70, 122, 133, 156, 171, 209, 229, 265, 329
Barthelmess, Richard, 16, 39, 76, 340
Bartholomew Freddie, 171, 199, 229, 262, 380
Basevi, James, 240, 349, 351, 416, 419, 541, 566, 567
Basie, Count, 466, 560, 562
Basinger, Jeanine, 482
Bassermann, Albert, 361, 362
Bassett, Rex, 160
Bat Whispers, The, 32
Batman, 32, 76, 477
Batman and Robin, 309
Battle of Britain, 559
Battle of Midway, The, 359, 424
Battleground, 22, 284
Baudrillard, 497
Baxter, Anne, 550, 568
Baxter, Warner, 30, 35, 117, 208, 252
Bean, Judge Roy, 362, 395
Beard, Matthew "Stymie", 269
Beaton, Cecil, 47
Beatty, Warren, 303, 321, 425
Beau Geste, 299, 304, 310, 349
Beaumont, Harry, 39, 40
Beauty and the Beast, 182
Beavers, Louise, 146, 153
Becky Sharp, 177, 178, 343
Beery, Noah, 8, 260
Beery, Wallace, 53, 54, 55, 66, 87, 88, 92, 97, 103, 122, 147, 156
Beethoven, Ludwig van, 415
Beggars of Life, 33, 40
Behind the Oscar, 15, 629
Behlmer, Rudy, 256, 287, 309, 359, 438
Behrman, S.N., 200
Beiderbecke, Bix, 51
Belgium, 178
Bell, Book, and Candle, 485
Bellamann, Henry, 494
Bellamy, Ralph, 239, 245, 260, 293, 393, 430
Bells of St. Mary's, The, 363, 518
Bendix, William, 505, 506, 507
Benét, Stephen Vincent, 461
Ben-Hur, 372, 392
Bennett, Arnold, 539
Bennett, Charles, 396, 398
Bennett, Constance, 103, 240, 264
Bennett, Joan, 252, 470
Bennett, Russell, 256, 258

Benny Carter and His Orchestra, 553
Benny, Jack, 32, 170, 296, 423, 487, 497, 520, 527
Berg, Alban, 53
Bergen, Edgar, 224, 296, 327, 386
Berger, Ralph, 520
Bergman, Ingrid, 311, 339, 456, 500, 529, 538, 541, 543, 544, 545, 556
Bergner, Elizabeth, 177, 178, 216
Berkeley Square, 128
Berkeley, Busby, 80, 117, 118, 144, 187, 188, 189, 190, 217, 218, 226, 227, 310, 415, 518, 553, 554, 568
Berle, Milton, 428, 467
Berlin, Irving, 146, 174, 187, 188, 217, 250, 259, 266, 284, 293, 314, 315, 374, 430, 431, 467, 479, 486, 488, 490, 508, 518, 519, 560, 568
Berra, Yogi, 272
Best Actor, 9, 16, 18, 30, 35, 36, 52, 54, 56, 68, 70, 72, 84, 87, 90, 92, 94, 95, 114, 124, 128, 129, 130, 131, 149, 150, 168, 169, 174, 175, 176, 194, 196, 199, 200, 201, 202, 203, 207, 228, 229, 235, 237, 265, 266, 269, 270, 272, 275, 279, 292, 303, 319, 322, 324, 326, 328, 329, 332, 361, 380, 388, 390, 434, 438, 439, 440, 442, 479, 492, 497, 499, 500, 534, 540, 541, 543
Best Actress, 7, 9, 10, 16, 17, 18, 21, 30, 36, 37, 38, 39, 43, 50, 52, 56, 57, 66, 67, 75, 87, 90, 94, 96, 97, 108, 109, 111, 125, 142, 144, 151, 152, 154, 168, 169, 177, 193, 194, 196, 204, 206, 225, 228, 230, 237, 239, 265, 268, 269, 275, 276, 277, 304, 316, 360, 361, 380, 384, 391, 393, 394, 423, 434, 437, 443, 445, 492, 500, 540, 543, 545
Best Art Direction, 8, 30, 46, 47, 50, 51, 68, 79, 87, 105, 114, 157, 161, 169, 191, 192, 197, 219, 221, 251, 253, 261, 301, 306, 319, 349, 358
Best Art Direction (Black & White), 381, 416, 419, 434, 468, 471, 492, 520, 522, 541, 566
Best Art Direction (Color), 376, 412, 434, 471, 492, 522, 523, 541, 567
Best Assistant Director, 108
Best Cartoon, 84, 113, 141, 157, 163, 167, 197, 221, 227, 265, 296, 297, 319, 354, 381, 419, 434, 474, 477, 490, 541, 570
Best Cinematography, 7, 14, 30, 44, 45, 50, 68, 78, 85, 114, 134, 135, 157, 160, 166, 173, 197, 213, 214, 229, 245, 246, 265, 293, 358
Best Cinematography (Black & White), 301, 303, 304, 311, 319, 326, 334, 338, 342, 352, 381, 385, 403, 417, 434, 454, 456, 459, 492, 496, 512, 534, 538, 540, 548, 552
Best Cinematography (Color), 301, 303, 319, 341, 342, 345, 381, 387, 409, 413, 428, 492, 516, 517, 540, 552, 554
Best Dance Direction, 166, 169, 174, 188, 191, 197, 201, 217, 219, 226, 252
Best Direction (Comedic Picture), 6, 9, 24
Best Direction (Dramatic Picture), 6, 9, 21, 24

Best Director, 6, 9, 21, 22, 23, 24, 30, 39, 41, 52, 59, 60, 68, 73, 85, 87, 90, 97, 98, 100, 108, 113, 114, 124, 125, 130, 132, 142, 149, 154, 155, 168, 175, 179, 182, 185, 194, 195, 196, 200, 211, 224, 229, 251, 265, 270, 271, 278, 280, 292, 319, 323, 333, 335, 358, 359, 361, 406, 434, 445, 448, 492, 494, 497, 502, 505, 533, 535
Best Documentary, 424
Best Dramatic or Comedy Score, 541, 554, 559
Best Dramatic Score, 424, 434, 459, 460, 482
Best Film Editing, 141
Best Musical Score, 424, 431, 492, 517, 518, 541, 559, 563, 564
Best Original Score, 256, 259, 261, 303, 312, 319, 322, 345, 346, 348, 366, 395, 415
Best Picture, 6, 9, 10, 14, 21, 22, 24, 30, 31, 32, 33, 34, 35, 38, 39, 45, 51, 52, 54, 60, 68, 69, 70, 75, 84, 87, 90, 92, 97, 98, 100, 108, 110, 111, 112, 113, 114, 115, 119, 127, 128, 131, 132, 142, 144, 145, 149, 151, 152, 155, 168, 169, 170, 173, 175, 185, 194, 195, 196, 197, 200, 201, 202, 225, 228, 229, 232, 233, 234, 235, 251, 265, 266, 268, 269, 271, 272, 278, 279, 286, 292, 299, 303, 304, 319, 321, 323, 324, 328, 334, 380, 381, 382, 387, 388, 399, 434, 435, 436, 437, 438, 439, 487, 492, 493, 497, 502, 505, 527, 528, 531, 533, 535, 539
Best Score, 141, 157, 160, 161, 168, 186, 187, 197, 214, 229, 246, 247, 250, 255, 256, 259, 290, 308, 322, 348, 349, 372, 373, 381, 413, 416
Best Short Subject, 255
Best Short Subject (Comedy), 84, 115, 157, 164, 169, 192, 383
Best Short Subject (Novelty), 85, 114
Best Song, 80, 141, 145, 157, 161, 169, 174, 187, 188, 197, 201, 216, 229, 250, 256, 259, 260, 263, 265, 293, 296, 300, 314, 323, 347, 367, 373, 414, 431, 432, 434, 465, 468, 479, 488, 518, 541, 553, 561, 562, 563
Best Sound Recording, 50, 52, 62, 68, 84, 115
Best Special Effects, 319, 352, 377, 378, 417, 434, 472, 474, 492, 523, 541, 549, 568, 570
Best Supporting Actor, 173, 177, 194, 196, 199, 203, 206, 208, 209, 228, 230, 239, 241, 258, 265, 280, 304, 306, 361, 362, 395, 434, 448, 450, 492, 505, 540, 545, 547
Best Supporting Actress, 196, 209, 210, 224, 228, 230, 241, 242, 264, 265, 282, 284, 301, 319, 364, 391, 434, 450, 451, 492, 507, 535
Best Writing, 30, 41
Best Writing (Adaptation), 9, 24, 68, 73, 76, 87, 101, 155, 156, 185
Best Writing (Original Motion Picture Story), 480, 492, 508, 540, 547
Best Writing (Original Screenplay), 358, 381, 386, 396, 399, 426, 480, 536, 549
Best Writing (Original Story), 9, 26, 28, 68, 76, 78, 87, 103, 105, 114, 132, 134, 157, 166, 168, 182, 183, 196, 200, 210, 211, 212, 228, 242, 243, 257, 265, 267, 284, 306, 328, 358, 370, 380, 394, 396, 402, 424, 480
Best Writing (Screenplay), 168, 183, 194, 196, 198, 211, 213, 229, 243, 245, 265, 270, 286, 288, 303, 308, 319, 335, 337, 358, 381, 399, 425, 434, 452, 492, 496, 510, 538
Best Writing (Title Cards), 7
Best Years of Our Lives, The, 503
Betty Boop, 114, 221, 315
Beulah, 146
Bewitched, 417, 485, 508
Bible, The, 213, 355, 427
Bickford, Charles, 545, 546
Big Broadcast of 1936, The, 188, 189
Big Broadcast of 1938, The, 265, 293
Big Business, 33, 43
Big City, The, 17
Big House, The, 52, 53, 54, 55, 60, 61, 62, 75, 92
Big Parade, The, 23, 279
Big Pond, The, 54, 55
Big Sleep, The, 100, 262, 541, 567
Big Trail, The, 123
Bill of Divorcement, A, 108
Billy Budd, 509
Billy Jack Goes to Washington, 336, 452
Billy the Kid, 97, 428, 429
Biltmore Bowl, 141, 165, 193, 223, 255, 357, 423
Biltmore Hotel, 65, 141, 165, 193, 223, 255, 357, 423
Binger, R.O., 377, 568
Binger, Ray, 523
Biro, Lajos, 26
Birth of a Nation, 13, 46, 74, 301, 448
Birth of the Blues, 431, 432
Bishop's Wife, The, 96, 449, 508
Bitter Sweet, 376, 409, 410
Bitter Tea of General Yen, The, 121, 124, 125, 207
Black Cat, The, 158, 159, 162, 192, 514
Black Legion, 242
Black Narcissus, 214, 429, 481, 508
Black Swan, The, 287, 474, 482, 483, 492, 516, 523
Black Swan, The (2010), 516
Blackmail, 22, 53, 60
Blair, Janet, 565
Blake, Michael, 18
Blazing Saddles, 67, 325
Blitz Wolf, 490, 491
Blockade, 256, 257, 284, 285
Block-Heads, 256, 257
Blondell, Joan, 73, 118, 218, 473
Blood and Sand, 343, 428, 429, 471, 472
Bloomberg, Daniel J., 523
Blore, Eric, 378
Blossom Room, 5
Blossoms in the Dust, 428, 430, 434, 436, 443, 471
Blue Angel, The, 16, 67, 69, 73, 85, 90, 97
Blue Bird, The, 377, 378, 409, 410
Bluebeard's Eighth Wife, 287
Blues in the Night, 465, 466
Bluto, 222
Bob Cratchit, 281
Bodeen, DeWitt, 509

Body Snatcher, The, 292, 515
Boer War, 115
Bogart, Humphrey, 70, 75, 99, 120, 204, 230, 240, 242, 270, 320, 326, 366, 442, 448, 449, 499, 530, 538, 541, 543, 545, 546, 547, 565
Bogdanovich, Peter, 288, 322, 435, 458, 629
Bogle, Charles, 148, 183, 327
Böhme, Margaret, 62
Bojangles number, 189, 217, 218, 221, 563
Boland, Mary, 327
Boleslawski, Richard, 167, 172
Bolger, Ray, 197, 306, 433
Bombardier, 568, 569
Bombshell, 111, 121, 150
Bona, Damien, 7, 37
Bonaparte, Napoleon, 150, 197, 236, 340, 459
Bondi, Beulah, 209, 210, 282, 283, 385
Boogie Woogie Bugle Boy of Company B, 474, 475
Boom Town, 377, 378, 403, 405
Booth, Edwina, 68
Booth, John Wilkes, 208
Borges, Jorge Luis, 435
Born to Dance, 216, 217
Borradaile, Osmond, 342, 344
Borzage, Frank, 9, 19, 21, 40, 87, 88, 97, 116, 144, 277, 429
Boston Blackie, 35
Bottom, 173
Boudu Saved from Drowning, 121, 122
Boutelje, Phil, 308, 310
Boutelje, Philip, 554, 557
Bow, Clara, 9, 10, 20, 23, 43, 58, 490
Bowdon, Dorris, 359
Bowles, Paul, 370
Box-office poison list, 392
Boyd, William, 24
Boyer, Charles, 179, 215, 235, 236, 272, 303, 307, 317, 320, 381, 437, 443, 452, 457, 460, 480, 544
Boyle, Edward G., 468, 470
Boyle, Johnny, 249
Boys from Syracuse, The, 377, 378, 416, 417
Boys Town, 203, 256, 265, 266, 270, 272, 278, 279, 284, 286, 499
Bracken, Eddie, 490, 562
Brackett, Charles, 287, 335, 336, 337, 394, 402, 405, 437, 452, 457
Bradbury, Ray, 509
Bradford, William, 377
Brady, Alice, 209, 210, 224, 228, 231, 241, 283
Brahms, Johannes, 347
Brand, Max, 325
Brando, Marlon, 24, 112, 176, 281
Brandt, Harry, 392
Brats, 51
Brave Little Tailor, The, 296
Brave New World, 402
Brave One, The, 400
Brazil, 415, 494, 561
Breaking the Ice, 256, 257
Brecht, Bertolt, 557
Breen Office, 139, 285, 397, 407, 453, 460, 513
Breen, Bobby, 248, 257, 313, 519

Breen, Joseph L., 31, 139, 163
Brennan, Walter, 167, 196, 206, 265, 280, 361, 362, 427, 448, 449, 464, 495, 550, 556
Brenon, Herbert, 21, 22
Brent, George, 117, 320, 341, 450, 484
Bride Came COD, The, 207
Bride of Frankenstein, 13, 94, 99, 100, 102, 105, 159, 175, 181, 182, 185, 186, 192, 264, 349, 461, 514
Bridge of San Luis Rey, The (1929), 30, 46
Brigadoon, 289
Bright, John, 76, 77
Brigid O'Shaughnessy, 450
Bringing up Baby, 100, 109, 143, 224, 271, 274, 278, 280, 284, 286, 288, 361, 370
Bristol, Howard, 468, 470, 520, 566
Broadway, 30, 31, 36, 37, 39, 40, 67, 109, 117, 170, 178, 182, 188, 208, 210, 217, 236, 265, 309, 378, 389, 396, 400, 411, 415, 430, 444, 451, 453, 520, 532, 562
Broadway Hostess, 188
Broadway Melody of 1936, 169, 170, 182, 188, 189
Broadway Melody of 1940, 374, 376
Broadway Melody, The, 30, 31, 36, 37, 39, 40, 45, 117
Broadway Rhythm, 170, 189
Brodine, Norbert, 288, 291, 338, 340
Broken Blossoms, 16
Brontë, Emily, 324, 335
Brook, Clive, 27, 98, 109
Brooks, Louise, 33, 40, 53, 54, 58, 61, 62, 76
Brown, Bernard B., 377, 523
Brown, Clarence, 38, 59, 73, 95, 341, 533, 534, 550
Brown, Joe E., 114, 173
Brown, Lew, 250, 251
Brown, Nacio Herb, 31, 310, 465
Brown, Rowland, 76, 77, 284
Browning, Elizabeth Barrett, 143, 152
Browning, Robert, 143, 152
Browning, Tod, 23, 72, 124
Bruce, Carol, 464
Bruce, Nigel, 326, 341, 553
Bruce, Virginia, 216, 261
Bryan, Robert Alan, 37
Buccaneer, The, 288, 290
Buchman, Sidney, 335, 336, 434, 452, 510, 511
Büchse der Pandora, Die, 53
Buck and Bubbles, 227
Buck Privates, 431, 432, 465, 466
Buck Rogers, 80
Buck, Pearl S., 230
Buckner, Robert, 508, 509
Bugs Bunny, 420, 557, 571
Building a Building, 113
Bulldog Drummond, 51, 54, 55, 61, 65
Bullet, 295
Bullock, Walter, 216, 217, 373, 374
Bunin, Louis, 111
Buñuel, Luis, 70
Buried Alive, 539
Burke, Billie, 122, 197, 259, 264, 282, 283, 557
Burke, Edwin, 87, 101
Burke, Johnny, 216, 373, 375

Burke, Marcella, 284, 285
Burke's Peerage, 510
Burnett, W.R., 75, 480, 481, 482
Burns, Bob "Bazooka", 223
Burns, George, 226
Burns, Robert E., 111
Burnside, Norman, 396
Burroughs, Edgar Rice, 101
Burton, Tim, 111
Busch, Niven, 242, 395
Busy Bodies, 137
Butch Cassidy and the Sundance Kid, 309, 429
Butler, Frank, 480, 481, 482
Butler, Hugo, 394, 395
Butler, Lawrence, 377, 472, 523, 570
Butterworth, Charles, 378
Byington, Spring, 265, 282, 283
Byrd, Admiral Richard, 50, 51
Byron, Lord, 17, 185, 330, 353

C

Cabaret, 54
Cabin in the Sky, 562, 563, 564
Cabinet of Dr. Caligari, The, 158, 352, 364
Cabot, Bruce, 136, 469, 484
Caesar, Arthur, 157
Cagney, James, 27, 70, 71, 77, 118, 119, 145, 173, 205, 249, 270, 272, 273, 275, 325, 326, 331, 433, 442, 451, 479, 492, 496, 497, 522, 557
Cagney, William, 558
Cahn, Sammy, 488, 490
Cain and Mabel, 217, 218
Calico Dragon, The, 167, 168
California, 166, 191, 295, 351, 382, 468, 479, 496, 537
Calloway, Cab, 114, 221, 226, 252, 563
Camel spitting, 481
Cameraman, The, 12, 32, 44
Cameron, James, 105
Camille, 57, 237, 238
Campbell, Alan, 244
Canada, 368, 493, 508, 522
Cansino Dancers, 218
Canterville Ghost, The, 363
Cantor, Eddie, 80, 226, 565
Canutt, Yakima, 322, 353
Cape Fear, 236
Capone, Al, 10, 75, 93, 102
Capp, Al, 173
Capra, Frank, 95, 96, 100, 102, 108, 109, 111, 115, 124, 130, 142, 143, 154, 165, 180, 194, 195, 198, 206, 213, 231, 251, 255, 263, 265, 266, 278, 290, 300, 321, 333, 335, 358, 425, 449, 496, 520, 545
Capracorn, 154
Captain Bligh, 176, 184
Captain Blood, 80, 169, 170, 171, 179, 187, 380, 418, 484, 533
Captain Fury, 349
Captain Nemo, 523
Captains Courageous, 228, 229, 235, 244, 272, 499
Captains of the Clouds, 516, 522
Carbonera, Gerard, 309, 554, 558
Cardiff, Jack, 214

Carefree, 259, 260, 261, 263, 293
Carey, Harry, 69, 99, 304, 305, 363, 458
Caribbean, 462
Carl Stalling Project, The, 476
Carmichael, Hoagy, 295, 477
Carnera, Primo, 132
Carradine, John, 208, 216, 240, 283, 322, 326, 363, 389
Carrey, Jim, 571
Carrie Bradshaw, 350
Carroll, Brendan G., 312
Carroll, John, 560
Carroll, Lewis, 111, 136, 510
Carroll, Madeleine, 181, 285
Carroll, Nancy, 56, 57, 77
Carson, Robert, 229, 242, 244
Carter, Benny, 553, 562, 563
Casablanca, iii, 262, 266, 287, 325, 339, 364, 402, 418, 438, 449, 450, 512, 527, 528, 531, 532, 533, 538, 540, 541, 543, 544, 545, 547, 548, 554, 555, 559, 567, 573
Case of Sergeant Grischa, The, 62
Casella, Alberto, 156
Casper Gutman, 449, 453
Casper, Drew, 278
Cast of Killers, A, 23
Castro, Fidel, 490
Cat and the Canary, The, 186
Cat People, 122, 200, 509, 515
Catalina Island, 169
Catharine of Aragon, 129
Cathcart, Daniel, 567
Catherine the Great, 163
Cavalcade, 108, 109, 110, 114, 115, 119, 120, 126, 130, 135, 180, 358, 369
Cavens, Fred, 170
CGI, 221, 233, 352, 354, 378, 380, 410
Chaliapin, Feodor, 122
Champ, The, 84, 87, 88, 92, 93, 97, 103, 104, 156, 220
Chandlee, Harry E., 102, 426, 427
Chandler, Raymond, 438, 441
Chaney, Jr., Lon, 1, 183, 321, 331, 379, 474
Chaney, Sr., Lon, 1, 17, 18, 20, 32, 36, 42, 47, 55, 93, 130, 311, 332, 433, 552, 567
Chang, 14, 50, 232, 240
Chaplin, Charles, 8, 9, 16, 24, 26, 27, 28, 59, 69, 70, 72, 73, 78, 84, 85, 97, 104, 105, 114, 122, 181, 201, 202, 285, 332, 362, 369, 383, 384, 386, 388, 389, 390, 396, 398, 485, 502
Charge of the Light Brigade, The, 214, 215
Charig, Phil, 293
Charles Foster Kane, 426, 460
Charlie Brown, 563
Charlie McCarthy, 224, 327
Charlotte's Web, 111
Chatterton, Ruth, 36, 37, 56, 57
Cheers for Miss Bishop, 459, 461
Chevalier, Maurice, 54, 55, 60, 89, 104, 126, 148, 236
Chicago, 10, 231, 241, 242, 243, 246, 247, 266, 269
Children of Divorce, 20
Children's Hour, The, 210
China, 16, 85, 90, 98, 125, 207, 230, 238, 245, 484, 527, 554
Chocolate Soldier, The, 431, 432, 454, 455

Christmas, 33, 119, 141, 162, 281, 287, 455, 467, 488, 563
Christmas Carol, A (1938), 281, 287
Churchill, Douglas W., 102
Churchill, Frank, 246, 250, 251, 431, 465, 482, 483, 488
Cimarron, 61, 66, 68, 70, 73, 74, 78, 79, 191, 206, 350
Cinderella, 182, 310, 381
Circus, The, 9, 17, 24, 26, 27, 28
Citadel, The, 265, 267, 272, 273, 278, 279, 286
Citizen Kane, 86, 167, 246, 263, 339, 341, 404, 409, 417, 424, 426, 428, 434, 435, 436, 439, 440, 445, 446, 454, 455, 459, 468, 471, 474, 504, 507, 508, 512, 513, 514, 530
City Girl, 58
City Lights, 17, 24, 27, 69, 70, 71, 73, 78, 84, 131, 201, 322, 332, 383, 502
City Streets, 79
Civil War, 12, 31, 159, 283, 346, 368, 417, 544
Clair, René, 104, 469, 485
Clampett, Bob, 297, 571, 572
Clark Kent, 536
Clark, Carroll, 161, 191, 251, 252, 566
Clarke, Charles G., 512, 513, 552
Clarke, Mae, 91
Classics of the Horror Film, 124
Clawson, Elliott, 41, 42
Clements, John, 344
Cleopatra, 112, 142, 144, 151, 157, 159, 167, 537
Cleopatra (1963), 144, 292, 336
Clift, Montgomery, 281
Cline, Wilfred M., 428, 429
Clive, Colin, 91, 99, 124
Clock Cleaners, The, 228
Cobb, Lee J., 531
Cobra Woman, 432
Coburn, Charles, 307, 427, 448, 530, 533, 540, 545
Cocoanut Grove, 29, 300, 479
Cocoanuts, The, 56, 62, 357
Coffee, Lenore, 286, 287
Cohan, George M., 496, 497, 504, 506, 509, 518, 520
Cohn, Alfred, 24
Cohn, Harry, 143, 166, 231
Colbert, Claudette, 134, 136, 142, 143, 144, 146, 151, 153, 155, 177, 179, 234, 288, 303, 337, 343, 393, 394, 405, 536, 537, 540, 551
Cold War, 334
Coldeway, Anthony, 24
Collinge, Patricia, 450, 451
Collings, Pierre, 196, 210, 211
Collins, Anthony, 345, 348, 413, 414, 431, 433
Colman, Ronald, 54, 55, 61, 62, 98, 99, 199, 231, 232, 233, 264, 281, 486, 487, 495, 496, 497, 498, 508, 511, 514
Colombo, Alberto, 246, 249
Colonna, Jerry, 571
Colton, John, 183
Columbia Pictures, 143, 149, 150, 163, 166, 228, 231, 260, 263, 441, 447, 475, 476, 562, 570, 571

Comandini, Adele, 210, 211
Come and Get It, 196, 206
Comedy of Errors, A, 378
Comer, Sam, 468, 469, 520
Commandos Strike at Dawn, 554, 556
Communist, 17, 45, 306, 307, 318, 435, 557
Compson, Betty, 36, 38
Comrade X, 394, 395
Condemned, 55
Coney Island, 24, 559, 560
Confessions of a Nazi Spy, 324
Congress, 295
Connell, Richard, 424, 425
Connolly, Bobby, 188, 217, 218, 226, 227
Connolly, Marc, 244
Connolly, Walter, 324
Connotations, "gay", 274
Conquest, 236, 251, 252
Conrad, Con, 157, 161
Conrad, Joseph, 196
Constant Nymph, The, 543, 544, 545
Conway, Jack, 147, 200
Coons, Maurice, 102
Cooper, Gary, 20, 67, 79, 116, 126, 127, 136, 159, 172, 186, 194, 202, 203, 204, 207, 252, 258, 287, 288, 304, 330, 368, 382, 395, 408, 411, 419, 424, 425, 434, 439, 440, 449, 479, 495, 497, 498, 501, 514, 529, 541, 542, 544, 545
Cooper, Gladys, 507, 508, 535
Cooper, Jackie, 66, 70, 73, 88, 92, 97, 103, 156, 277, 279
Cooper, Merian C., 14, 188
Cop, The, 41, 42
Copland, Aaron, 308, 309, 312, 313, 322, 345, 347, 348, 349, 367, 371, 413, 414, 554, 559
Copperfield, David, 61, 169, 171, 176, 177, 185, 199, 200, 234, 262
Coquette, 30, 36, 391
Cormack, Bartlett, 75
Corny Concerto, A, 571
Corsican Brothers, The, 482, 484
Cortez, Ricardo, 75
Cortez, Stanley, 512, 513
Corvette K-225, 548, 549
Cosgrove, John R., 352, 353, 377, 523
Cotten, Joseph, 435, 507, 533, 534, 543, 564
Count of Monte Cristo, The, 418
Country Cousin, 197, 221, 222
Coward, Noel, 110, 115, 126, 182, 410, 480, 530, 536, 537
Cowardly Lion, 306, 345
Cowboy and the Lady, The, 256, 258, 293, 294
Coyote and Roadrunner, 420
Crabbe, Buster, 80
Cram, Mildred, 306, 307
Crandall, Roland, 114
Crane, Mack, 111
Crash Dive, 541, 568, 570
Craven, Frank, 385
Crawford, Joan, 17, 42, 47, 49, 87, 135, 209, 214, 294, 327, 392, 444, 471
Creature Features, iii, 412
Creature from the Black Lagoon, The, 519
Creelman, James A., 133
Criminal Code, The, 73, 75

Crisp, Donald, 434, 435, 448, 451
Criterion Collection, 290
Cronin, A.J., 286
Cronjager, Edward, 78, 454, 458, 512, 514, 516, 517, 552, 554
Crosby, Bing, 11, 31, 51, 93, 168, 174, 189, 216, 227, 251, 295, 375, 396, 432, 481, 488, 497, 508, 562
Crosby, David, 78
Crosby, Floyd, 68, 78
Crosman, Henrietta, 110
Crossfire, 552
Crowd, The, 14, 15, 16, 21, 23, 34, 97, 123, 279, 412
Crowther, Bosley, 495, 532
Crusades, The, 166, 167, 192
Crying Game, The, 182
Cthulhu, 128
Cugat, Xavier, 374
Cukor, George, 69, 89, 115, 119, 121, 129, 130, 171, 199, 200, 206, 220, 238, 262, 327, 342, 358, 360, 361, 445, 544
Cummings, Irving, 39, 40
Cummings, Robert, 375, 503, 519, 536, 537
Cunningham, Jack, 148
Curie, Marie, 530, 544
Curie, Pierre, 530, 542
Curse of the Cat People, The, 509, 515
Curtis, Charles, 65
Curtis, James, 61, 186, 457, 629
Curtiz, Michael, 170, 213, 266, 270, 278, 280, 292, 317, 325, 333, 344, 418, 502, 504, 522, 533, 544, 567, 568
Custer's last stand, 482
Cyrano de Bergerac, 363
Czechoslovakia, 426

D

D'Abbadie D'Arrast, Harry, 76
D'Agostino, Albert, 219, 220, 520, 566
D'Oyly Carte Opera Company, 344
Daffy Duck, 571
Dali, Salvador, 263, 297, 513
Dalrymple, Ian, 265, 286, 287
Damsel in Distress, A, 226, 250, 251, 252
Dancing on a Dime, 376
Dancing Pirate, 217, 218
Dandridge, Dorothy, 58, 560
Dangerous, 177, 276
Daniels, Bebe, 76, 117
Daniels, William, 50
Dark Angel, The, 169, 177, 178, 191
Dark Command, The, 366, 367, 368, 416, 417
Dark Passage, 144
Dark Victory, 316, 317, 319, 320, 345, 346, 501
Darling, William S., 114, 135, 219, 220, 251, 253, 349, 351, 541, 566
d'Artagnan, 347
Darwell, Jane, 359, 364, 389, 408
Dashiell, Chris, 267
Dave the Dude, 109, 119
Daves, Delmer, 144, 307, 548
Davey, Allen, 409, 410, 552
Davidson, Roy, 352, 353
Davies, Marion, 28, 97, 159, 218

Davis, Bette, 37, 76, 142, 152, 153, 166, 168, 173, 177, 178, 193, 210, 255, 260, 265, 268, 269, 275, 282, 291, 304, 305, 316, 317, 320, 326, 330, 339, 346, 351, 360, 362, 370, 381, 384, 391, 394, 405, 423, 437, 443, 444, 445, 447, 449, 450, 451, 470, 482, 498, 500, 501, 502, 507, 532, 536, 539, 541, 565
Dawn Patrol, The (1930), 68, 76, 128, 537
Day at the Races, A, 185, 226, 227, 482
Day, Doris, 149
Day, Richard, 47, 79, 105, 161, 162, 169, 191, 197, 219, 251, 252, 261, 263, 376, 377, 416, 417, 419, 434, 468, 471, 492, 520, 522
de Grasse, Robert, 288, 292
de Havilland, Olivia, 170, 173, 179, 197, 265, 301, 303, 325, 423, 433, 437, 443, 452, 483, 536, 565
de Lesseps, Ferdinand, 258
de Mille, Agnes, 5
de Mille, William, 5, 6, 29
De Niro, Robert, 53, 94, 330
de Palma, Brian, 91
de Paul, Gene, 488, 489
de Sylva, Buddy, 314, 315
de Victoria, Tomas Luis, 311
de Vinna, Clyde, 30, 44
Dead End, 229, 230, 240, 241, 242, 245, 246, 251, 252, 270
Death of a Salesman, 15
Death Takes a Holiday, 46, 156
Dee, Frances, 182
Deep focus, 86, 408, 456, 512, 514
Deep Throat, ii
Dekker, Albert, 557, 558
del Ruth, Roy, 76
Delgado, Marcel, 135
Delmar, Viña, 243, 245
Deluge, 199
DeMille, Cecil B., 5, 25, 46, 72, 134, 136, 144, 151, 163, 165, 167, 290, 339, 353, 368, 377, 411, 517, 523, 629
Dempsey, Jack, 132
Der Fuehrer's Face, 490, 491
Design for Living, 120, 121, 126, 132, 204
Desperate Journey, 523, 524
Destination Moon, 476, 495
Destination Tokyo, 547, 548, 570
Destry Rides Again, 299, 307, 318, 325, 469
Dethe, John S., 376
Detouring America, 354, 355
Deutsch, Adolph, 464
Devil and Daniel Webster, The, 225, 440, 459, 460, 506
Devil and Miss Jones, The, 426, 427, 448, 449, 545
Devil Dancer, The, 7
Devil's Holiday, The, 56, 57
Devil's Island, 55, 252
Devine, Andy, 225, 238
Diary of a Lost Girl, 54, 58, 61
Dick Tracy, 256
Dickens, Charles, 62, 176, 262, 287
Dieterle, William, 173, 224, 225
Dietrich, Marlene, 16, 66, 67, 69, 79, 85, 87, 90, 95, 97, 98, 163, 167, 215, 291, 318, 325, 392, 458, 469, 486, 521

Dillinger, John, 157
Dilsey, 302
Dingle, Charles, 449, 451
Dinner at Eight, 100, 121, 129, 130
Dinosaurs, 413
Dirigibles, 145
Dirty Work, 137
Disney, Walt, 14, 51, 84, 108, 111, 113, 114, 141, 157, 162, 163, 164, 167, 168, 193, 197, 211, 221, 222, 227, 228, 232, 234, 235, 243, 250, 255, 265, 296, 297, 307, 311, 315, 319, 354, 355, 367, 374, 376, 380, 387, 409, 412, 415, 419, 420, 421, 424, 431, 434, 466, 474, 475, 476, 477, 483, 486, 489, 490, 491, 516, 523, 541, 559, 561, 570, 571
Disney's True Life Adventure, 14
Disneyland, 40, 367, 516, 523
Disraeli, 52, 54, 60, 61
Dive Bomber, 428, 430
Divine Lady, The, 30, 36, 37, 39, 44
Divine Woman, The, 38, 41
Divorcee, The, 52, 56, 57, 59, 60, 61
Dix, Richard, 70, 191, 350, 558
Dixieland, 432
Dixon, Harland, 249
Dixon, Lee, 227
Dizzy Acrobat, The, 570, 571
Docks of New York, The, 33, 36, 38, 40, 45, 171
Dodge City, 325, 533
Dodsworth, 194, 197, 200, 202, 203, 209, 211, 212, 219
Doing Their Bit, 476
Dolan, Robert Emmett, 431, 432, 517, 518, 559, 562
Donald Duck, 221, 228, 296, 490
Donaldson, Walter, 216, 217
Donat, Robert, 181, 267, 272, 273, 319, 320, 328, 335
Donlevy, Brian, 304, 353, 396, 504, 506, 556, 569
Doorway to Hell, 76, 77
Dorsey, Tommy, 467
Doty, Douglas, 76
Double Indemnity, 44, 110, 239, 372, 416, 425, 550
Douglas, Haldane, 567
Douglas, Kirk, 400
Douglas, Melvyn, 205, 307, 464
Dove, The, 8
Dover Boys, The, 492
Down Argentine Way, 373, 374, 376, 377, 409, 410
Dr. Cyclops, 377, 378, 412
Dr. David Huxley, 274
Dr. Ehrlich's Magic Bullet, 99, 396, 397
Dr. Evil, 9
Dr. Frankenstein, 91, 182
Dr. Jekyll and Mr. Hyde (1931), 60, 65, 84, 85, 92, 96, 99, 101, 103
Dr. Jekyll and Mr. Hyde (1941), 87, 92, 454, 456, 459, 461, 500
Dr. Mudd, 208
Dr. Praetorius, 185
Dr. Seuss, 570
Dr. Van Helsing, 72
Dr. Watson, 326, 552

Dr. Zhivago, 493
Dracula, 17, 23, 59, 69, 71, 72, 79, 102, 105, 124, 306, 349, 372, 430, 473
Drag, 39
Dreier, Hans, 46, 51, 79, 80, 135, 163, 191, 251, 252, 261, 264, 349, 376, 377, 416, 468, 469, 520, 521, 522, 523, 566, 567
Dreiser, Theodore, 20, 522
Dresser, Louise, 18, 20
Dresser, Paul, 20, 522
Dressler, Marie, 37, 66, 94, 95, 109, 119, 121, 122
Dreyer, Carl Theodor, 34, 40, 41, 86
Dreyfus Affair, 229, 239
Drums Along the Mohawk, 299, 301, 303, 310, 342, 343
du Bois, Raoul Pene, 471, 472
du Maurier, Daphne, 381, 401
Dubin, Al, 169, 187, 250, 564
Dublin, 171, 176, 183
Duck Soup, 115, 121, 124, 127, 133, 148, 412
Dudley, George, 349, 351
Duel in the Sun, 23
Duell, Randall, 468, 471, 520
Dukas, Paul, 415
Duke Mantee, 204
Duke, Vernon, 296, 563
Dumas, Alexandre, 484
Dumbo, 221, 424, 431, 465, 466, 491
Dumont, Margaret, 133, 205
Duncan, Mary, 58
Dunkirk, 503, 512, 524
Dunne, Irene, 66, 188, 204, 205, 208, 224, 235, 237, 238, 239, 245, 307, 315, 316, 317, 320, 321, 370, 393, 417, 441
Dunne, Philip, 452, 453
Durbin, Deanna, 200, 232, 243, 247, 255, 257, 260, 264, 285, 291, 294, 310, 338, 350, 375, 406, 488, 519, 554, 564
Dutton, George, 568
Duvivier, Julien, 282
DVD, ii, iii, 9, 79, 86, 292, 429, 464, 514, 567, 629
DVR, iii
Dyer, Elmer, 341, 548
Dylan, Bob, 173
Dynamite, 46

E

Each Dawn I Die, 325
Eagels, Jeanne, 36, 37, 125, 360
Eagle and the Hawk, The, 128
Eagler, Paul, 377
Earhart, Amelia, 566
Earl of Essex, 326, 350
East Lynne, 68
Eastern Europe, 162
Eastman, George, 84
Eastwood, Clint, 264, 389
Easy Living, 244
Ebert, Roger, 93, 150, 151, 163, 274, 278, 292, 474
Ebsen, Buddy, 170, 189
Ecclesiastes, 327
Eddy, Nelson, 149, 173, 248, 252, 261, 376, 410, 432, 455, 552, 561

Edens, Roger, 308, 309, 373, 375, 413, 415, 517, 518, 563
Edeson, Arthur, 44, 50, 548
Edison, the Man, 394, 395
Edison, Thomas, 49, 65, 83
Edouart, Farciot, 352, 353, 377, 434, 472, 492, 523, 568
Educated Fish, 227, 228
Edwards, Cliff, 32, 217, 373
Egbert Sousé, 386
Egypt, 550
Eisler, Hanns, 554, 557
El Brendel, 79
El Greco, 429, 471
Eliscu, Edward, 161
Ellington, Duke, 107, 108, 227, 373, 466, 468, 562, 563
Elmer Fudd, 420, 475
Elmer Gantry, 97
Elmer's Candid Camera, 420
Eloi, 13
Elvira Gulch, 304, 345
Emerson, Ralph Waldo, 21, 502
Emma, 94, 95
Emperor Jones, The, 309
Emperor Maximilian, 305
Empress Carlota, 304, 305, 317, 340
Engineering Effects, 7
Epstein, Julius J., 286, 287, 538
Epstein, Philip, 511, 538
Erdgeist, 53
Erwin, Stuart, 206, 207
Escape Me Never, 177, 178
Estabrook, Howard, 60, 61, 68, 73, 171, 185
Eternally Yours, 345, 346
Europe, 145, 194, 203, 219, 271, 382, 452, 553
Evans, Madge, 122
Everson, William K., 124
Every Day's a Holiday, 251, 252
Expressionism, 23, 105, 158, 352, 364
Eyman, Scott, 40, 115, 126, 134, 171, 180, 322, 389, 629

F

Fain, Sammy, 250, 251
Fairbanks, Jr., Douglas, 75, 76, 233, 259, 339, 397, 484
Fairbanks, Sr., Douglas, 5, 376
Fairmont Hotel, 262
Falconetti, Renee Maria, 34, 38
Fallen Sparrow, The, 554, 556
Fanchon, 563
Fantasia, 235, 387, 412, 413, 415, 420, 424, 571
Far and Away, 74
Faragoh, Francis, 73
Farewell to Arms, A, 111, 114, 115, 116, 120, 134, 135, 136, 137
Farmer, Frances, 206
Farnham, Joseph, 7
Farrell, Charles, 9, 11, 19, 22
Farrow, John, 502, 504
Farrow, Mia, 504
Fascism, 529, 539
Faulkner, Ralph, 170

Faulkner, William, 41, 117, 302, 402, 529, 537
Faye, Alice, 189, 231, 253, 266, 413, 417, 553, 564, 568
Federal Bureau of Investigation, 157, 324
Fegte, Ernst, 566
Felix, Seymour, 197, 217
Femme fatale, 366, 450, 472
Ferber, Edna, 73, 121, 206, 244
Ferdinand the Bull, 265, 296, 297
Ferguson, Norm, 163
Ferguson, Perry, 219, 220, 468, 469, 520, 566
Feuer, Cy, 259, 260, 308, 313, 413, 414, 431, 432, 459, 463
Field, Betty, 503
Fields, Al, 468, 520
Fields, Dorothy, 187, 188, 197, 216, 217
Fields, W.C., 119, 127, 136, 143, 148, 171, 176, 183, 199, 202, 224, 293, 297, 327, 386, 399, 423, 457
Fiesta Room, 49, 83, 107
Fight for Life, The, 366, 368
Film noir, 43, 110, 246, 285, 366, 368, 370, 397, 407, 438, 442, 477, 499, 513, 515, 552, 566
Finding Nemo, 483
Finkel, Abem, 426, 427
Finlayson, James, 33, 234
First Love, 308, 310, 338, 349, 350, 406
First National, 62
Fisher, Steve, 547, 548
Fitzgerald, Barry, 549
Fitzgerald, Ella, 188, 284, 293
Fitzgerald, F. Scott, 47, 277
Fitzgerald, Geraldine, 301, 303, 320
Five Graves to Cairo, 548, 549, 551, 566
Five Star Final, 87, 89
Flaherty, Robert, 78
Flame of New Orleans, The, 468, 469
Flash Gordon, 80, 309
Fleet's In, The, 490
Fleischer Studio, 114, 221, 227, 228, 296, 315, 347
Fleischer, Max, 221, 315, 475, 476
Fleming, Victor, 156, 229, 270, 283, 319, 333, 335, 457
Flesh and the Devil, 43
Fletcher Christian, 169, 176
Flight Command, 472
Flight for Freedom, 566
Flirtation Walk, 142, 143, 144
Flitcraft, 453
Florence, 159
Flournoy, Richard, 538, 539
Flowers and Trees, 84
Flying Deuces, 309
Flying Down to Rio, 117, 121, 161
Flying Dutchman, 182
Flying Tigers, 482, 484, 523, 524, 525
Flying with Music, 488, 489, 517, 518
Flying Wombat, 259
Flynn, Errol, 42, 76, 170, 179, 215, 246, 265, 274, 292, 325, 326, 351, 387, 418, 430, 443, 470, 483, 505, 524, 533, 565
Folies Bergere, 188, 189
Follow the Fleet, 217
Folsey, George, 134, 159, 213, 214, 552, 554

Fonda, Henry, 125, 268, 285, 303, 308, 328, 330, 331, 332, 343, 358, 359, 363, 364, 388, 389, 390, 400, 408, 409, 417, 454, 531, 542, 543
Fontaine, Joan, 226, 361, 366, 381, 391, 393, 394, 423, 434, 439, 443, 461, 515, 543
Fontanne, Lynne, 92, 94, 95
Footlight Parade, 80, 117, 118, 249
Footloose, 418
For Me and My Gal, 517, 518
For Whom the Bell Tolls, 116, 333, 343, 528, 535, 541, 542, 543, 544, 545, 546, 552, 554, 556, 567, 568
Forbes, Lou, 308, 312
Forbidden Planet, 102
Forbstein, Leo, 214, 215
Ford, Glenn, 464
Ford, Henry, 80
Ford, John, 8, 22, 25, 27, 45, 59, 70, 87, 88, 98, 110, 125, 131, 143, 148, 160, 162, 168, 175, 179, 180, 183, 240, 242, 247, 252, 278, 279, 285, 290, 303, 304, 305, 322, 333, 334, 335, 341, 343, 358, 359, 360, 364, 367, 383, 385, 386, 389, 408, 410, 424, 429, 434, 435, 441, 445, 446, 454, 458, 468, 537, 548
Foreign Correspondent, 27, 86, 361, 362, 377, 379, 381, 382, 396, 398, 403, 406, 416, 417
Forester, C.S., 556
Forrest Gump, 330
Forrest, Chet, 293, 373, 374, 488, 489
Fort Apache, 309, 410, 419
Forty-Year Old Virgin, The, 2
Foster, Lewis R., 306, 538, 539
Foster, Stephen, 309, 313, 346, 372
Four Daughters, 265, 267, 270, 278, 279, 280, 281, 282, 286, 287
Four Devils, 44
Four Feathers, The, 299, 342, 344
Four Norwegian Moods, 556
Four Tones, The, 467, 468
Fra Diavolo, 137
Fractured Fairy Tales, 126
France, 20, 252, 264, 299, 361, 372, 381, 385, 452, 495, 531, 550
Francis, Kay, 132, 488
Francke, Caroline, 111
Frankenstein, iii, 12, 17, 71, 72, 87, 89, 90, 94, 98, 99, 100, 102, 103, 105, 123, 124, 129, 162, 175, 181, 264, 306, 349, 352, 406, 473, 489
Franklin, Sidney, 144, 224, 225
Frankly, My Dear: Gone with the Wind Revisited, 301
Frau im Monde, Die (Woman in the Moon), 80
Frawley, William, 324
Freaks, 23, 87, 91
Free Soul, A, 56, 57, 66, 67, 68, 70, 73, 120
Freed, Arthur, 31, 310, 373, 375, 465
Freed, Ralph, 488, 489
Freedonia, 133
Freeman, Y. Frank, 319
Freleng, Friz, 297, 570
French Foreign Legion, 304
French Indochina, 340

Freund, Karl, 8, 72, 124, 229, 245, 428, 430, 454, 455
Friar Tuck, 209, 266, 387
Froeschel, George, 492, 510
From Here to Eternity, 433
Front Page, The, 26, 68, 69, 70, 73, 75, 95, 397, 403
Frye, Dwight, 59, 70, 72, 76, 77, 249
Fulton, John P., 123, 185, 377, 379, 472, 474, 523, 524
Fulton, Maude, 76
Furthman, Jules, 111, 183, 184
Fury, 195, 203, 210

G

Gabin, Jean, 268, 272, 281, 513
Gable, Clark, 39, 55, 57, 70, 95, 142, 143, 150, 157, 165, 169, 175, 176, 199, 203, 211, 218, 231, 270, 300, 302, 328, 329, 378, 395, 396, 560
Gallico, Paul, 508, 509
Gandhi, 351
Gang's All Here, The, 553, 554, 567, 568
Gannon, Kim, 488, 489
Garbo, Greta, 38, 41, 43, 56, 57, 58, 66, 87, 88, 95, 96, 110, 114, 123, 153, 236, 237, 238, 307, 316, 318, 321, 327, 335, 336, 337, 392, 395, 629
Garden of Allah, The, 214, 215
Garden of Eden, 454, 512
Garfield, John, 267, 280, 281, 287, 442, 506, 537, 548, 556
Gargan, William, 361, 363
Garland, Judy, 207, 284, 294, 300, 310, 314, 318, 329, 357, 373, 375, 415, 489, 518
Garmes, Lee, 78, 79, 85, 95, 98, 120, 291, 342, 397, 517
Garrett, Oliver H.P., 117
Garson speech, 480
Garson, Greer, 304, 316, 317, 320, 402, 430, 436, 442, 443, 445, 471, 480, 486, 492, 495, 498, 500, 503, 505, 506, 508, 510, 511, 530, 542, 543, 544, 550
Gaslight, 289, 336
Gaudio, Tony, 50, 197, 213, 292, 293, 338, 339, 340, 360, 384, 403, 406, 548, 549
Gauguin, Paul, 558
Gausman, Russell A., 468, 469, 520, 522, 541, 567
Gay Deception, The, 182
Gay Divorcee, The, 101, 142, 144, 157, 160, 161, 162, 263
Gaynor, Janet, 7, 9, 11, 14, 18, 19, 21, 22, 44, 121, 153, 226, 233, 237, 238, 259
Gehrig, Lou, 495, 498, 501, 507, 509
Gellhorn, Martha, 394
General Died at Dawn, The, 206, 207, 213, 214, 215
General, The, 12, 213, 215
Generation of Vipers, A, 112
Gentlemen Prefer Blondes, 290
George Washington Slept Here, 520
George, Gladys, 204, 205, 327
Geppetto, 388
Germany, 23, 46, 87, 104, 145, 149, 162, 277, 308, 362, 407, 416, 419, 524, 539, 557

Gershwin, George and Ira, 226, 250, 251, 260, 266, 295, 296, 415, 465, 559
Gershwin, Ira, 296
Gettysburg Address, 174, 176, 334
Ghost Breakers, 186
Giant, 73, 206, 406, 534
Gibbons, Cedric, 30, 46, 135, 157, 161, 162, 219, 220, 251, 252, 261, 264, 349, 351, 352, 376, 381, 416, 434, 468, 471, 520, 566, 567
Giddins, Gary, 466
Gidget, 285
Gigi, 289
Gilbert and Sullivan, 344
Gilbert, John, 32, 43, 123
Gilda, 86, 397
Gillespie, A. Arnold, 352, 354, 377, 472, 523, 568
Gillespie, William, 466
Gilligan's Island, 42
Gilpatric, Guy, 547
Girls' School, 259, 260
Gish, Lillian, 18, 34, 38, 39, 43, 556, 629
Gladiator, 112
Gladney, Edna, 430, 436
Glasmon, Kubec, 76, 77
Glass Key, The, 506, 507
Glazer, Benjamin, 9, 24, 380, 394
Gleason, James, 257, 448, 449, 464
Glenn Miller Orchestra, 433, 458, 467, 490
Glennon, Bert, 338, 341, 342, 343, 385, 428, 430
Gliese, Rochus, 8
Glorious Betsy, 24
Glory, 332
Gluskin, Lud, 345, 347
Glyn, Elinor, 20
G-Men, 287
Go into Your Dance, 188, 189
Godard, Jean-Luc, 446
Goddard, Paulette, 259, 327, 368, 375, 383, 384, 391, 398, 399, 437, 452, 457, 517, 523, 535, 536, 562
Godfather II, The, 72
Godzilla, ii
Goebbels, Joseph, 13, 145
Going My Way, 472, 532
Going Places, 293, 294
Gold Diggers of 1933, 117, 118, 136
Gold Diggers of 1935, 169, 187, 188, 189
Gold Diggers of 1937, 217, 218
Gold Rush, 166, 309
Gold Rush, The, 24, 26, 27, 28, 482, 485
Golden Boy, 345, 346, 347
Golden Voyage of Sinbad, The, 372
Goldman, William, 511
Goldwyn Follies, The, 259, 261, 263, 295, 296
Goldwyn Girls, The, 472
Goldwyn, Samuel, 62, 80, 88, 98, 206, 296, 312
Golitzen, Alexander, 416, 417, 468, 470, 522, 541, 567
Gone with the Wind, 8, 79, 120, 150, 153, 171, 198, 230, 260, 262, 268, 291, 292, 299, 300, 301, 302, 304, 312, 316, 319, 323, 328, 329, 333, 334, 335, 342, 345, 346, 349, 352, 353, 364, 370, 381, 392, 397, 405, 407, 410, 418, 426, 431, 459, 482, 484, 507, 523, 539, 555
Good Earth, The, 207, 224, 225, 228, 229, 230, 237, 245
Good Neighbor Policy, 147
Good Scouts, 296
Goodbye, Mr. Chips, 112, 231, 304, 316, 317, 319, 320, 328, 333, 335, 461, 486
Goodman, Benny, 562, 568
Goodman, John B., 261, 264, 520, 541, 567
Goodrich, Frances, 155, 211, 212
Goofy, 69, 228, 355, 561, 571
Goofy and Wilbur, 355, 571
Goosson, Stephen, 79, 229, 251, 261, 263, 468, 470
Gordon, Mack, 373, 374, 465, 467, 488, 490, 541, 563
Gorgeous Hussy, The, 209, 213, 214
Gould, David, 169, 188, 189, 217, 226
Goulding, Edmund, 317, 544
Goya, 429
Grable, Betty, 207, 374, 377, 411, 413, 474, 560
Grace, Carol, 547
Grand Hotel, 87, 96, 98, 105, 121
Grand Illusion, 122, 265, 268, 271
Granger, Bertram, 566, 567
Grant, Cary, 26, 67, 75, 93, 120, 128, 136, 217, 224, 235, 237, 238, 239, 240, 245, 263, 271, 274, 278, 280, 282, 284, 288, 307, 321, 325, 331, 339, 340, 360, 361, 369, 370, 373, 386, 387, 390, 392, 393, 402, 417, 425, 439, 440, 441, 442, 461, 487, 496, 511, 514, 530, 548
Grant, Lawrence, 65
Granville, Bonita, 209, 210
Granville, Roy, 568
Grapes of Wrath, The, 172, 180, 191, 246, 303, 321, 337, 358, 359, 363, 364, 381, 382, 383, 385, 388, 389, 390, 399, 400, 408, 409, 417, 419, 539, 542
Grashin, Mauri, 157, 158
Grass, 50
Grayson, Kathryn, 553
Great Britain, 37, 53, 62, 63, 77, 112, 115, 119, 122, 129, 149, 155, 169, 171, 172, 174, 176, 178, 181, 184, 191, 196, 200, 204, 219, 220, 253, 260, 269, 273, 286, 290, 320, 343, 344, 382, 385, 409, 414, 418, 454, 458, 459, 481, 493, 503, 506, 515, 524, 530, 537, 550, 559
Great Depression, 66, 97, 101, 113, 117, 118, 121, 122, 125, 127, 143, 195, 201, 202, 230, 321, 323, 364, 382, 390, 400, 419
Great Dictator, The, 285, 361, 362, 366, 369, 381, 383, 388, 389, 396, 398, 491
Great Expectations, 171, 269
Great Lie, The, 434, 450
Great McGinty, The, 381, 396, 397
Great Victor Herbert, The, 308, 310
Great Waltz, The, 265, 282, 283, 288, 289
Great Ziegfeld, The, 194, 195, 196, 197, 198, 200, 201, 202, 203, 204, 210, 211, 217, 219, 220, 237
Greatest Story Ever Told, The, 253
Greece, 535
Green Goddess, The, 54
Green Hat, The, 43

Green, Howard J., 111
Green, Paul, 110
Green, Richard, 280
Greene, Mort, 488, 489
Greene, W. Howard, 225, 342, 344, 409, 411, 428, 430, 516, 517, 540, 552
Greenstreet, Sydney, 76, 438, 448, 449, 450
Greetings Bait, 570, 571
Grey, Lita., 27
Gribney, Sheridan, 196, 210, 211
Griffin, Eleanore, 265, 284
Griffith, Corinne, 36, 37
Griffith, D.W., 16, 34, 46, 165
Groesse, Paul, 381, 416, 566
Grot, Anton, 79, 80, 219, 251, 252, 349, 350, 351, 416, 418
Grove, Frank, 106
Groves, George, 62
Gruenberg, Louis, 309, 366, 368, 459, 464, 554, 556
Guardsman, The, 92, 94, 95, 455
Gulliver's Travels, 53, 314, 315, 345, 347
Gunga Din, 184, 299, 300, 310, 338, 339, 344, 534
Guy Named Joe, A, 425
Guys and Dolls, 295, 417
Gwenn, Edmund, 197
Gypo Nolan, 171

H

Hackett, Albert, 155, 211, 212
Hageman, Richard, 256, 258, 308, 309, 366, 369, 459, 464, 482, 486
Haggard, H. Rider, 68, 188
Hahn, Edwin C., 352, 353
Hail the Conquering Hero, 244, 472
Hal Roach Studios, 105, 162, 261, 264, 322, 331, 340, 348, 349, 432, 464, 489, 518
Hale, Alan, 42, 266, 325
Haley, Jack, 207, 306
Hall, Alexander, 445, 447
Hall, Charles D., 105, 162, 192, 261, 264, 349
Hall, David S., 251, 253
Hall, James Norman, 184, 240
Hall, John, 472
Hall, Jon, 240, 429, 483
Hallelujah, 58, 59, 97, 311
Hallenberger, Harry, 428, 431
Haller, Ernest, 166, 288, 291, 319, 342, 403, 404
Hallmark Cards, 239
Halperin Brothers, 122
Hamilton, Margaret, 304
Hamilton, Neil, 76
Hammeras, Ralph, 79
Hammerstein II, Oscar, 293, 294, 434, 465
Hammett, Dashiell, 147, 155, 212, 324, 438, 442, 448, 453, 506, 532, 538, 539
Handel, George Frederick, 213, 256, 277
Hangmen Also Die, 554, 556
Hanks, Tom, 330
Hanna, William, 420
Hannibal Lecter, 71
Hansen, Edmund H., 319, 352, 353, 377, 472
Hansen, Franklin, 62, 136
Harbach, Otto, 188

Harburg, E.Y. "Yip", 310, 314, 316, 345, 563, 564
Hard to Get, 295
Harding, Ann, 66, 67, 186
Hardwicke, Sir Cedric, 220, 524
Hardy, Oliver, 493
Hardy, Sam, 183
Harem, 24
Harline, Leigh, 246, 250, 366, 367, 373, 477, 482, 486, 517, 519, 554, 558, 559, 561
Harling, Frank, 247, 249, 308, 309
Harlow, Jean, 45, 73, 95, 96, 100, 111, 120, 121, 122, 198, 214, 217
Harman-Ising, 167, 221
Harmon, Sidney, 508, 509
Harris, Robert, 183
Harrison, Doane, 457
Harrison, Joan, 396, 398, 399, 401
Harrison, Rex, 273, 426
Harryhausen, Ray, 379
Hart, Lorenz, 161
Hart, Moss, 182, 265, 511, 520
Hartman, Don, 182, 480
Harvey, 369, 460
Harvey Girls, The, 284
Haskell, Jack, 217, 218
Haskell, Molly, 301, 346
Haskin, Byron, 352, 377, 472, 523
Hatch, Eric, 211, 212
Hatfield-McCoy feud, 470
Hathaway, Henry, 179, 180
Hatley, Marvin, 247, 249, 256, 257, 259, 261
Hawks, Howard, 45, 76, 91, 99, 100, 129, 143, 147, 149, 151, 155, 166, 171, 203, 206, 270, 271, 278, 279, 280, 340, 361, 387, 390, 403, 425, 439, 445, 447, 451, 458, 537, 549
Hawthorne, Nathaniel, 369
Haydn, Joseph, 258
Hayes, Helen, 87, 94, 116
Hays Office, 19, 26, 31
Hays, Will, 49
Hayward, Louis, 347, 470
Hayward, Susan, 560
Hayworth, Rita, 218, 340, 374, 397, 410, 429, 433, 467, 472, 490, 519, 522
Hearst, William Randolph, 28, 434, 447, 455
Heath, Percy, 101
Heathcliff, 303, 330, 334, 390
Heaven Can Wait (1943), 425, 528, 529, 533, 545, 552
Heaven Can Wait (1978), 425
Heaven Can Wait (original play), 425
Hecht, Ben, 9, 26, 69, 75, 102, 126, 149, 155, 156, 166, 168, 182, 233, 263, 335, 337, 396, 397, 403, 463
Hedgecock, William, 377
Heerman, Victor, 110
Heflin, Van, 492, 505
Heindorf, Ray, 492, 517, 518, 541, 559, 560
Heinlein, Robert, 509
Hell, 50, 51, 61, 118, 529, 533
Hell's Angels, 50, 51, 61
Hellinger, Mark, 326
Hellman, Lillian, 178, 210, 230, 437, 452, 453, 532, 536, 538, 539
Hello, Frisco, Hello, 552, 553, 563, 564
Hellzapoppin', 488, 489

Helm, Brigitte, 21
Heman, Roger, 523, 541, 568
Hemingway, Ernest, 41, 116, 117, 280, 394, 403, 468, 528, 529, 535, 542, 552
Henie, Sonja, 218, 227, 315, 467
Henreid, Paul, 426, 482, 485, 501, 545
Henry VIII, 129
Hepburn, Katharine, 67, 75, 95, 108, 110, 114, 119, 169, 170, 174, 177, 232, 238, 241, 249, 263, 271, 277, 278, 280, 282, 284, 288, 296, 303, 321, 360, 365, 373, 386, 388, 391, 392, 393, 394, 480, 500, 502
Herald, Heinz, 229, 242, 243, 396, 397, 398
Herbert, Victor, 162, 173, 261, 310, 313, 338, 339
Herczeg, Geza, 229, 242, 243
Here Comes Mr. Jordan, 424, 434, 436, 440, 441, 445, 447, 448, 449, 452, 454, 457
Here Comes the Navy, 142, 145
Herman, Alfred, 349, 350
Herman, Jan, 275
Hermia, 179
Heroin, 38
Heron, Julia, 468, 470, 522
Herrmann, Bernard, 434, 459
Hers to Hold, 563, 564
Hervey, Harry, 396
Herzbrun, Bernard, 261, 262
Heymann, Werner, 367, 371, 459, 464, 482, 487
Hi Diddle Diddle, 554, 557
Hiawatha's Rabbit Hunt, 475
Hide-Out, 157
High Sierra, 310, 442
Hildy Johnson, 403
Hill, Elizabeth, 286, 287
Hiller, Wendy, 269, 273, 275, 277
Hilton, James, 231, 320, 486, 492, 510
His Girl Friday, 26, 69, 93, 100, 160, 239, 264, 280, 350, 361, 382, 386, 387, 390, 393, 403, 417, 433, 439, 441, 447, 500
Hit Parade of 1941, 373, 374, 413, 414
Hit Parade of 1943, 559, 560, 563, 564
Hitchcock, Alfred, 22, 27, 53, 55, 59, 60, 70, 102, 112, 143, 149, 151, 155, 175, 181, 196, 214, 234, 237, 271, 278, 279, 280, 291, 333, 358, 360, 361, 362, 366, 379, 381, 382, 390, 393, 398, 401, 402, 403, 404, 406, 411, 417, 418, 426, 439, 441, 496, 500, 533, 534, 535, 543, 545
Hitler, Adolf, 13, 16, 149, 184, 229, 271, 324, 336, 383, 384, 397, 418, 459, 491, 497, 499, 537
Hoffe, Monckton, 424, 425, 454
Hoffenstein, Samuel, 101, 160
Hold Back the Dawn, 434, 437, 443, 452, 454, 457, 459, 462, 468, 469
Holden, Anthony, 15, 629
Holden, William, 346, 367, 385, 392, 472, 490
Holiday (1930), 66, 67, 73, 75
Holiday (1938), 163, 164, 261, 263, 264, 282, 400
Holiday Inn, 488, 490, 497, 508, 517, 518, 519
Holiday Land, 163, 164
Hollander, Frederick, 250, 482, 487
Holliday, Judy, 238

Hollywood, i, ii, iii, 2, 5, 6, 7, 8, 9, 14, 17, 18, 20, 23, 25, 26, 27, 29, 31, 35, 40, 42, 50, 53, 55, 57, 67, 68, 69, 71, 75, 83, 84, 86, 89, 103, 104, 105, 108, 111, 112, 113, 116, 122, 124, 125, 130, 132, 133, 135, 139, 140, 143, 145, 150, 152, 154, 166, 171, 172, 173, 178, 179, 180, 186, 192, 199, 203, 207, 210, 212, 220, 225, 231, 235, 236, 237, 239, 242, 243, 244, 249, 250, 252, 257, 258, 262, 264, 266, 268, 269, 283, 285, 294, 295, 296, 297, 299, 300, 324, 337, 338, 346, 347, 353, 357, 365, 366, 370, 374, 383, 386, 389, 391, 393, 395, 396, 397, 400, 402, 407, 409, 413, 419, 427, 437, 438, 439, 446, 447, 450, 451, 452, 455, 466, 467, 469, 474, 475, 476, 479, 480, 481, 487, 504, 505, 509, 517, 528, 531, 532, 533, 534, 535, 536, 538, 541, 544, 546, 553, 554, 557, 560, 562, 565, 566, 567, 573, 576
Hollywood Bowl, 173
Hollywood Canteen, 562
Hollywood Canteen, the, 565
Hollywood Hotel, 251
Hollywood Revue, 31, 32, 45
Hollywood Rhapsody, 467
Hollywood Ten, The, 285
Holmes, Brown, 76, 111
Holst, Gustav, 488
Holy Matrimony, 538, 539
Honest John, 388
Honeymoon, The, 41
Hope, Anthony, 233
Hope, Bob, 186, 255, 293, 295, 300, 319, 357, 396, 423, 430, 479, 481, 518, 562
Hope, Frederic, 161, 162, 219
Hopkins, George J., 566, 567
Hopkins, Miriam, 96, 126, 158, 166, 167, 177, 178, 210
Hopkins, Robert, 210, 211
Horne, Lena, 553, 562, 563
Horning, William A., 251, 252, 349, 351, 352
Horror movies, 18, 91
Horton, Edward Everett, 126, 136, 145, 174, 231, 232, 282, 424, 433, 436, 568
Hotel Del Coronado, 430
Hound of the Baskervilles, The, 291, 299, 326
House of Frankenstein, 519
House of Rothschild, The, 142, 143, 145
House of the Seven Gables, The, 366, 369
House of Wax, The, 291, 343
How Green Was My Valley, 410, 434, 435, 436, 439, 442, 444, 445, 446, 448, 450, 452, 453, 454, 459, 461, 468, 497, 542, 548
How to Marry a Millionaire, 539
How War Came, 475, 476
Howard, Curly, 493
Howard, Leslie, 57, 120, 128, 153, 186, 199, 204, 269, 272, 273, 312, 334, 339, 493
Howard, Ron, 74
Howard, Shemp, 483, 489
Howard, Sidney, 88, 101, 211, 212, 319, 335
Howards of Virginia, The, 366, 369
Howe, James Wong, 86, 246, 262, 288, 289, 403, 404, 512, 548, 549, 551, 557
HUAC, 285

Hubbard, Lucien, 76, 77, 103
Huckleberry Finn, 74, 181, 207, 324
Hughes, Howard, 10, 51, 61, 75, 139
Hughes, John, 468, 470, 567
Hughes, Langston, 313, 314
Hugo, Victor, 184
Hula, 20
Hull, Henry, 183
Human Comedy, The, 528, 529, 533, 534, 540, 541, 542, 547, 548, 550
Humbert Humbert, 71
Hume, Cyril, 101
Humpty Dumpty, 136, 297
Hunchback of Notre Dame, The (1923), 18, 433
Hunchback of Notre Dame, The (1939), 225, 299, 304, 308, 310, 311, 326, 332
Hunky and Spunky, 296
Hunt, Hugh, 566
Hunt, J. Roy, 552
Hunte, Otto, 8
Hurlbut, William, 185
Hurricane, The, 27, 208, 239, 240, 246, 247, 304, 370, 429
Hurst, Fannie, 287, 460
Hussey, Ruth, 364, 365
Huston, John, 305, 396, 397, 398, 426, 427, 438, 447, 452, 453
Huston, Walter, 75, 124, 191, 194, 202, 203, 440, 459, 488, 496, 505, 506, 550, 567
Huxley, Aldous, 402
Hynkel, 369, 383, 389, 398
Hypnotist, The, 23

I

I Am a Fugitive from a Chain Gang, 93, 111, 115, 118, 128, 136
I Am a Fugitive from a Georgia Chain Gang, 111
I Love Lucy, 245, 430, 489
I Married a Witch, 104, 482, 485
I Remember Mama, 509
I Walked with a Zombie, 200, 515, 551
I Wanted Wings, 434, 472
I Was a Male War Bride, 344
I'm No Angel, 120
Ice-Capades, 431, 432
If I Had a Million, 127
If I Were King, 256, 258, 261, 264, 280, 281
Ihnen, Wiard, 251, 252
Illegitimacy, 430
Ilsa, 538, 544
Imagination, 570, 571
Imazu, Eddie, 219
Imitation of Life, 142, 146, 151, 153, 287, 460
Imitation of Life (1959), 146
In Old Arizona, 30, 31, 33, 35, 39, 40, 41, 42, 44
In Old Chicago, 228, 229, 231, 241, 243, 266
In Old Oklahoma, 554, 557, 558
In the Heat of the Night, 416
In Which We Serve, 528, 530, 536, 537
India, 172, 184, 191, 252, 351, 486
Indiscreet, 158
Informer, The, 166, 167, 168, 169, 171, 175, 179, 180, 181, 183, 186, 192, 223
Ingram, Rex, 324, 409, 511, 546, 547

Inside Oscar, 7, 37, 530
Insider's Guide to Classical Music, The, 488
Inspector Javert, 172, 176, 184
Intermezzo, 308, 311, 338, 339
Internet Movie Database, 163, 260, 261, 415, 518, 563
Invaders from Mars, 8
Invaders, The, 481, 492, 493, 508, 510
Invisible Agent, 523, 524
Invisible Man Returns, The, 377, 379
Invisible Man series, 240, 473, 474, 524
Invisible Man, The, 99, 100, 112, 113, 115, 121, 123, 124, 129, 130, 336, 353
Invisible Woman, The, 472, 473
Irene, 413, 414
Irvine, Richard, 468
Irving Berlin Songbook, The, 284, 293
Ising, Rudolf, 420
Island of Lost Souls, The, 112, 121, 124, 129
It Girl, 9, 20
It Happened One Night, 90, 124, 130, 142, 143, 148, 150, 151, 152, 154, 155, 160, 180, 199, 234, 261, 340, 405, 409, 545
It Started with Eve, 517, 519
It's a Gift, 148, 412
It's a Wonderful Life, 40, 102, 119, 125, 154, 160, 231, 283, 287, 321, 333, 340, 425, 505
It's All True, 374
Italy, 143, 219
Itchy and Scratchy, 420
Iturbi, José, 553
Iwerks, Ub, 113

J

Jack the Ripper, 62
Jackson, Andrew, 209
Jackson, Felix, 306, 307
Jackson, Horace, 73
Jackson, Joseph, 76, 77
Jackson, Peter, 14, 136
Jaffar, 364, 376, 409
Jaffe, Sam, 163, 232
Jahraus, Donald, 568
Jane Eyre, 268, 381, 403, 551
Jannings, Emil, 9, 16, 31, 69
Janssen, Werner, 214, 215, 256, 257, 345, 346
Japan, 344
Japanese, 249, 477, 481, 482, 484, 491, 531, 540, 549, 566, 569, 570
Jar Jar Binks, 180
Jarrico, Paul, 426, 428
Jazz Singer, The, 6, 11, 24, 31, 80, 112, 193, 258
Jean Lafitte, 290
Jean Valjean, 172, 184
Jeeves, Mahatma Kane, 386, 399
Jeffries, Herb, 468
Jenkins, Jack "Butch", 534
Jennings, Gordon, 352, 353, 377, 434, 472, 492, 523, 568
Jennings, Talbot, 183, 184
Jerry Springer Show, The, 365
Jessel, George, 193
Jesus, 25, 74, 240
Jevne, Jack, 243

Jewell, Richard, 190
Jezebel, 177, 259, 260, 265, 268, 275, 282, 288, 291, 317, 330, 392, 437
Jim Crow, 431
Jiminy Cricket, 32, 217, 373
Jimmy Lunceford Band, 466
Joan of Arc, 34, 41
Joan of Paris, 482, 485
Joel Cairo, 450
Johnny Come Lately, 554, 557
Johnny Doughboy, 517, 519
Johnny Eager, 492, 505
Johns, Arthur, 352, 353, 377
Johnson, Hall, 313, 314
Johnson, Nunnally, 145, 359, 399, 400, 538, 539
Johnson, Van, 489, 534
Johnston, Arthur, 216
Jolly Little Elves, 163, 164
Jolson, Al, 6, 31, 189, 313
Jones, Allan, 378
Jones, Charles M. "Chuck", 113, 273, 281, 297, 420, 491, 492
Jones, Grover, 103, 112, 183
Jones, J.R., 150
Jones, Jennifer, 531, 540, 543
Jones, Spike, 491, 565
Jons, Newt, 136
Joplin, Janis, 173
Josephson, Julian, 60
Joyce, Brenda, 341
Juarez, 304, 305, 338, 339
Juarez, Benito, 305
Juke Box Jamboree, 490, 491
Juliet, 109, 177, 199, 205, 280
June, Ray, 85, 166
Jungle Book, 345, 482, 486, 516, 517, 522, 523, 524
Jungle Jim in Pygmy Island, 260
Juran, Nathan, 434, 468
Just Imagine, 79

K

Kael, Pauline, 142, 188, 271, 276, 392, 416, 426, 443, 487, 493
Kahn, Gus, 80, 157, 160, 161, 373, 375
Kahn, Madeline, 67
Kai-shek, Madame Chiang, 480
Kalmar, Bert, 76, 133
Kane, Bob, 32
Kanin, Garson, 307, 363, 370, 428
Kanin, Michael, 480
Kansan, The, 554, 558
Kansas, 285, 345, 351
Kaper, Bronislau, 431, 432
Karloff, Boris, iii, 12, 17, 55, 71, 72, 75, 78, 89, 90, 93, 94, 99, 102, 124, 126, 129, 130, 145, 147, 148, 158, 162, 175, 191, 192, 245, 306, 351, 375, 514
Kaufman, George S., 62, 76, 121, 185, 244, 265, 511, 520
Kawin, Bruce, 6
Kay Kyser and His College of Musical Knowledge, 376
Kay, Edward, 459, 462, 482, 486
Kaye, Danny, 243, 263, 312, 389, 472
Kean, Edmund, 225

Keaton, Buster, 12, 20, 24, 27, 32, 44, 114, 386, 389
Keeler, Ruby, 117, 118, 144, 189, 227
Keep 'Em Flying, 489
Keighley, William, 278
Kelly, Gene, 31, 410, 518, 553, 562
Kelly, Queen, 58
Kennedy, Edgar, 225
Kennedy, Margaret, 178
Kennedy, Rose, 58
Kent cigarette commercial, 488
Kentucky, 265, 280
Kern, Jerome, 187, 188, 197, 216, 217, 433, 434, 465, 488, 519, 520
Kerr, Deborah, 307, 321
Kettlehut, Erich, 8
Key Largo, 430
Key West, 523
Keystone Cops, 405
Kibbee, Guy, 111, 118, 385
Kid, The, 97
King and I, The, 292, 411
King Brothers, 486
King Kong, 14, 35, 115, 121, 127, 133, 135, 136, 160, 186, 188, 353, 378, 379, 474
King of Burlesque, 188, 189, 553
King of Jazz, 51
King of Kings, 25, 240, 372
King of the Zombies, 459, 462, 486
King, Henry, 533, 534, 549
King, Stephen, 431
Kings Row, 487, 493, 494, 498, 502, 503, 512, 540, 545
Kingsley, Sidney, 230
Kipling, Rudyard, 229, 244, 252, 486
Kirk, Mark Lee, 416, 417, 419, 520
Kirkpatrick, Sydney, 23
Kiss of Death, 291
Kitty Foyle, 358, 359, 365, 380, 381, 384, 391, 399, 400
Klaffki, Roy H., 45
Klondike, 482, 486, 521
Klondike Fury, 482, 486
Knowles, Bernard, 342, 344
Koch, Howard, 426, 427, 538
Koenekamp, Hans, 568
Koenig, Lt. John, 567
Kohner, Frederick, 284, 285
Ko-Ko, 114
Korda, Alexander, 119, 130, 344, 463, 486
Korda, Vincent, 220, 376, 468, 470, 522
Korjus, Miliza, 282
Korngold, Erich Wolfgang, 173, 187, 197, 214, 215, 247, 249, 256, 257, 258, 266, 308, 312, 348, 349, 369, 372, 373, 387, 413, 414, 433, 465, 483, 484, 487, 488, 544, 555
Koster, Henry, 406
Krakatoa, 114
Kraly, Hans, 30, 41, 242, 243
Krasna, Norman, 157, 158, 210, 211, 307, 426, 427, 536, 537
Krasner, Milton, 516
Kraus, Karl, 406
Krupa, Gene, 373, 460, 461
Krypton, 477
Ku Klux Klan, 242, 301, 547
Kuri, Emile, 520

Index

Kyser, Kay, 375, 376, 562

L

L'Atalante, 150
La Cava, Gregory, 150, 179, 194, 195, 224, 225
La Cucaracha, 157
La Ronde, 248
La Traviata, 238, 247
Ladd, Alan, 124, 499, 506
Ladies in Retirement, 186, 459, 462, 468, 469
Ladies of Leisure, 97
Lady and Gent, 103
Lady Be Good, 434, 465
Lady Eve, The, 167, 244, 424, 425, 443, 447, 448, 454, 545
Lady for a Day, 100, 108, 109, 110, 115, 118, 124, 130, 358
Lady from Shanghai, The, 397
Lady Hamilton, 37, 458
Lady in the Lake, 441
Lady Objects, The, 293, 294
Lady of Burlesque, 554, 558
Lady of the Tropics, 338, 340
Lady Vanishes, The, 271, 279, 280, 426
L'Âge d'Or, 70
Lagerstrom, Oscar, 62
Lahr, Bert, 306
Lake Sherwood, 523
Lake, Stuart N., 394, 395
Lake, Veronica, 428, 437, 439, 457, 472, 485, 499, 506, 536, 540, 551, 562
Lamarr, Hedy, 272, 340, 395, 405, 506
Lamour, Dorothy, 240, 261, 380, 396, 429, 490, 562
Lampwick, 388
Lancaster, Burt, 18, 112
Lanchester, Elsa, 185, 469, 553
Lane, Burton, 376, 488, 489
Lane, Priscilla, 267, 327, 466, 484
Lane, Rosemary, 378
Lang, Charles, 78, 134, 186, 403, 405, 454, 458, 548, 551
Lang, Eddie, 51
Lang, Fritz, 8, 12, 13, 80, 130, 131, 162, 173, 195, 203, 211, 513, 556
Lange, Arthur, 308, 310, 554, 558
Langford, Frances, 170, 414, 432, 466
Langtry, Lilly, 362
Lantz, Walter, 113, 114, 163, 475, 490, 491, 570
Lapis, Joseph, 377
Lardner, Jr., Ring, 233, 480
Larson E. Whipsnade, 327
Las Vegas, 221, 467
Las Vegas Nights, 465, 467
Lassie Come Home, 552, 553
Last Command, The, 9, 16, 26, 45
Last Days of Pompeii, The, 171, 199
Last of Mrs. Cheyney, The, 41, 42
Laszlo, Aladar, 112
Latin America, 147, 561
Laugh, Clown, Laugh, 17, 22
Laughter, 71, 76, 77, 629
Laughton, Charles, 39, 108, 112, 114, 115, 119, 124, 127, 128, 129, 143, 149, 151, 152, 169, 171, 172, 174, 175, 176, 185, 204, 269, 297, 311, 326, 332, 363, 519, 569
Laura, 101, 565
Laurel and Hardy, iii, 2, 21, 32, 33, 43, 51, 56, 57, 84, 105, 114, 124, 127, 137, 158, 162, 163, 164, 192, 224, 234, 243, 249, 257, 261, 297, 309, 322
Laurentz, Pare, 368
Lawrence of Arabia, 78, 148, 269, 493, 550
Lawson, John Howard, 284, 285
Lawson, Robert, 297
Layton, R.T., 377
Leach, Archibald, 237
Leaf, Munro, 297
Lean, David, 78, 171, 269, 481, 493, 530
Leatherneck, The, 41, 42
Leave Her to Heaven, 292, 515
Lecuona, Ernesto, 488, 489
Lederer, Charles, 75, 403
Lederer, Francis, 182
Lee, Gypsy Rose, 558
Lee, Peggy, 562
Lee, Robert N., 73
Lee, Sammy, 188, 189, 226
Leeds, Andrea, 241
Legion of Decency, 139, 163
Lehar, Franz, 160, 161
Lehman, Gladys, 156
Leigh, Vivien, 37, 302, 316, 319, 331, 372, 406, 407, 458, 459
Leipold, John, 247, 249, 308, 309
Leisen, Mitchell, 46, 136, 156, 244, 337, 395, 437, 452, 457, 514
Lend a Paw, 434, 474, 475
Lengyel, Melchior, 306, 307, 336
Leonard, Robert Z., 59, 194, 195
Leonhardt, Rudolf, 62
Leopard Man, The, 551
LeRoy, Mervyn, 89, 117, 118, 407, 436, 502, 504
Les Misérables, 166, 167, 169, 172, 176, 184, 200
Leslie, Joan, 561
Letter, The (1929), 36, 37, 125, 360
Letter, The (1940), 37, 358, 360, 361, 363, 366, 370, 381, 384, 391, 403, 406, 437, 447, 503
Leven, Boris, 261, 262, 520
Leverett, George, 523
Levien, Sonya, 110
Levinson, Nathan, 136, 137, 352, 353, 377, 472, 523, 568
Lewis, Cecil, 265, 286
Lewis, Russell, 217, 218
Lewis, Sinclair, 88, 194, 195, 212
Lewton, Val, 122, 200, 509, 515, 522, 551
Libeled Lady, 197, 198, 203, 212, 482
Library of Congress, 42, 67, 544
Life and Death of Colonel Blimp, The, 344, 409
Life of Emile Zola, The, 224, 225, 228, 229, 235, 236, 239, 242, 243, 244, 246, 248, 251, 252
Life of Riley, The, 506
Lifeboat, 27
Lili von Shtupp, 67, 325
Lillian Russell, 416, 417, 522
Lilliputians, 315

Lincoln, Abraham, 31, 208, 283, 308, 331, 334, 388, 389, 404, 542
Linden, Edward, 135
Lindsay, Raymond, 106
Lipscomb, W.P., 184, 200, 265, 286
Liszt, 475
Liszt, Franz, 247
Little Bo Peep, 296
Little Caesar, 69, 71, 72, 73, 75, 78, 80, 89, 91, 93, 102
Little Egypt, 219
Little Foxes, The, 434, 437, 443, 444, 445, 447, 449, 450, 451, 452, 453, 455, 459, 462, 468, 470, 503
Little House on the Prairie, 529
Little John, 266
Little Match Girl, The, 227, 228
Little Rascals, 68, 286, 313
Little Women, 109, 110, 113, 115, 119, 122, 130
Little, Thomas, 419, 468, 471, 492, 520, 522, 541, 566, 567
Litvak, Anatole, 382, 405
Lives of a Bengal Lancer, The, 112, 169, 172, 179, 180, 183, 191, 192, 344
Lloyd, Christopher, 295
Lloyd, Frank, 30, 39, 108, 114, 130, 179, 180, 281, 369
Lloyd, Harold, 24, 228
Lloyds of London, 219, 258, 259
Lockhart, Gene, 280, 281
Lockwood, Margaret, 271, 426
Loesser, Frank, 295, 376, 465, 467, 477, 564
Lohengrin, 369, 399
Lolita, 37, 544
Loman, Willy, 15
Lombard, Carole, 128, 149, 154, 155, 195, 202, 204, 205, 233, 300, 363, 393, 487, 497
London, 1, 17, 112, 128, 178, 219, 313, 351
London After Midnight, 1, 17, 23, 112
London, Jack, 473
Lone Ranger, The, 248
Long John Silver, 156
Long Voyage Home, The, 246, 309, 339, 366, 369, 370, 377, 379, 381, 384, 399, 401, 403, 407, 408
Long, Huey "The Kingfish", 430
Longfellow Deeds, 194, 204, 206, 213
Longfellow, Henry Wadsworth, 194, 203, 204, 206, 213, 475
Loos, Anita, 61, 211, 327
Lord Haw-Haw, 503
Lord Nelson, 37, 458
Lord, Robert, 114, 132, 242
Lordsburg, 334
Lorefice, Mike, 159
Loren, Sophia, 369
Lorre, Peter, 76, 124, 130, 131, 149, 151, 236, 375, 438, 450, 465, 524, 538, 547
Los Angeles, 29, 169, 193, 300, 472, 523
Los Angeles Examiner, The, 434
Los Angeles Times, The, 358
Losee, Harry, 226, 227
Lost Horizon, 154, 229, 231, 239, 240, 246, 248, 251, 486
Lost Patrol, The, 143, 148, 159, 160
Lost Weekend, The, 44, 336, 550

Louis XI, 264, 281
Louis XIV, 347
Louis XVI, 276, 281
Louis, Joe, 568
Louisiana, 428, 430, 471, 472
Louisiana Purchase, 428, 430, 471, 472
Lourdes, 539, 566
Love Affair, 301, 303, 306, 307, 314, 315, 316, 317, 319, 320, 349, 350, 375, 400
Love Affair (1994), 303, 321
Love Parade, The, 50, 51, 52, 54, 55, 59, 60, 62, 414
Love, Bessie, 36, 37
Lovecraft, H.P., 128
Lovett, Josephine, 41, 42, 43
Loy, Myrna, 132, 142, 146, 152, 157, 197, 198, 212, 270, 341
Lubitsch, Ernst, 31, 39, 40, 52, 59, 60, 62, 87, 89, 90, 112, 120, 125, 126, 127, 132, 134, 143, 148, 149, 158, 160, 161, 162, 167, 199, 287, 288, 306, 307, 308, 318, 321, 335, 336, 337, 364, 388, 394, 402, 405, 414, 428, 464, 487, 497, 505, 520, 529, 533, 629
Lucas, George, 59, 485, 629
Luce, Clare Booth, 327
Lugosi, Bela, iii, 17, 23, 55, 59, 71, 72, 79, 122, 124, 135, 158, 191, 192, 306, 375, 413, 462
Lukas, Paul, 271, 324, 349, 532, 536, 540, 541
Luke Skywalker, 172
Lulu, 53, 58, 76
Luna Park, 16, 24
Lunt, Alfred, 92
Lupino, Ida, 366, 469, 513
Lydecker, Howard, 377, 523
Lydia, 459, 463

M

M, 115, 121, 124, 130, 131, 132, 236
M*A*S*H, 468, 551
Ma and Pa Kent, 477
Ma and Pa Kettle, 111
Ma Joad, 364, 383
MacArthur, Charles, 26, 69, 75, 132, 149, 166, 168, 182, 335, 337, 403
MacDonald, Jeanette, 58, 90, 148, 173, 199, 231, 243, 248, 261, 315, 376, 410, 479, 561
Mackay, John Victor, 251, 252, 349, 350, 416, 417
MacLean, Fred, 468, 470
MacMahon, Aline, 132
MacMurray, Fred, 169, 430, 484, 514, 562, 566
Mad About Music, 259, 260, 261, 264, 284, 285, 288, 291
Madame Butterfly, 310
Madame Curie, 528, 530, 541, 542, 543, 544, 548, 550, 554, 558, 566, 567
Madame De Farge, 200
Madame X, 36, 37, 39, 40, 58
Maeterlinck, Maurice, 410
Magic Flame, 7
Magidson, Herb, 157, 161, 563

Magnificent Ambersons, The, 374, 446, 493, 494, 504, 507, 508, 512, 513, 515, 520, 521, 522
Magnificent Brute, The, 219, 220
Magnificent Seven, The, 309
Mahin, John Lee, 111, 156, 244
Mahler, Gustav, 257
Maid Marian, 261, 265
Main, Marjorie, 260
Major Strasser, 364
Make a Wish, 246, 248
Make Way for Tomorrow, 224
Malibu Beach, 468
Malice in Wonderland, 434
Maltese Falcon, The (1930), 75
Maltese Falcon, The (1936), 76
Maltese Falcon, The (1941), 75, 205, 310, 434, 438, 440, 442, 447, 448, 449, 450, 451, 452, 453, 464, 499, 541, 547
Maltin, Leonard, 559
Mammy, 168, 301, 302, 523
Mamoulian, Rouben, 53, 60, 79, 85, 99, 123, 178, 346, 429
Man for All Seasons, A, 129
Man in the Iron Mask, The, 345, 347, 418
Man of Conquest, 345, 347, 349, 350
Man on the Flying Trapeze, The, 183
Man Who Came to Dinner, The, 182, 498, 511
Man Who Knew Too Much, The (1934), 143, 149, 151, 155, 191
Man Who Shot Liberty Valance, The, 343
Man with a Movie Camera, 45
Manderley, 361, 381, 418, 504
Manhattan Melodrama, 151, 157, 211, 270
Manhattan Merry-Go-Round, 251, 252
Mankiewicz, Herman J., 121, 426, 446, 510
Mankiewicz, Joseph L., 73, 111, 277
Mannequin, 293, 294
Manon Lescaut, 340
Marc Antony, 144, 167
March of the Wooden Soldiers, The, 162
March, Fredric, 46, 70, 71, 77, 84, 85, 87, 92, 120, 126, 128, 143, 150, 152, 156, 172, 178, 197, 233, 235, 236, 238, 261, 290, 438, 464, 485
Marchioness of Queensbury, 221
Mardi Gras, 433
Margo Channing, 178
Marie Antoinette, 256, 258, 261, 264, 275, 276, 280
Marion, Frances, 43, 52, 60, 61, 87, 88, 103, 121, 132
Mark of Zorro, The, 43, 209, 266, 367, 382, 386, 387, 516
Marley, J. Peverell, 288, 291
Marmorstein, Gary, 160, 467
Marquardt, Paul, 161
Marquis St. Evremonde, 171, 200, 207
Mars, the Bringer of War, 488
Marsh, Marian, 89
Marsh, Oliver T., 409, 410
Marshall, Brenda, 516
Marshall, Charles A., 548
Marshall, Herbert, 70, 126, 285, 437, 455, 463, 471, 558, 566
Martin, Mary, 375
Martin, Tony, 374

Martinelli, Arthur, 135
Marty, 371
Marvin, Johnny, 293, 294
Marx Brothers, iii, 56, 62, 69, 76, 93, 104, 105, 119, 127, 133, 134, 175, 185, 215, 226, 244, 296, 316, 333, 441
Marx, Chico, 56, 76, 127, 133, 175, 362, 425, 546
Marx, Groucho, 56, 76, 104, 133, 226, 227, 316, 425, 503
Marx, Harpo, 56, 62, 76, 133, 168, 227, 235, 425
Mary Magdalene, 25
Mask of Fu Manchu, The, 147
Mask, The, 147, 571
Mason, A.E.W., 344
Mason, Sarah Y., 110
Massenet, Jules, 340
Massey, Raymond, 220, 240, 247, 388, 389, 524, 547
Mast, Gerald, 6
Master and Commander, 169
Mata Hari, 96
Maté, Rudolph, 86, 403, 405, 406, 454, 458, 459, 512, 514, 548, 551
Matthau, Walter, 547
Mature, Victor, 379, 522
Maugham, W. Somerset, 26, 360, 558
Maxim de Winter, 361, 381, 390, 418
Maxwell, Charles, 161
Mayer, Louis B., 6, 15, 16, 34, 122, 147, 150, 156, 171, 194, 196, 199, 202, 284, 314, 395, 441, 480, 500, 529
Mayo, Archie, 513
Mayor of 44th Street, The, 488, 489
Maytime, 246, 248
McCarey, Leo, 43, 127, 174, 224, 235, 245, 251, 274, 306, 307, 315, 321, 370, 394, 395
McCarthy, Mary, 205
McCartney, Paul, 120
McCleary, Urie, 434, 471
McCrea, Joel, 158, 166, 179, 206, 210, 230, 241, 246, 353, 365, 382, 398, 406, 428, 439, 530, 545
McDaniel, Hattie, 153, 170, 301, 302, 523, 562
McDonell, Gordon, 548
McDowall, Roddy, 435, 454, 495, 553
McGill, Barney "Chick", 78
McGilligan, Patrick, 271
McGuffin, The, 556
McGuire William Anthony, 210, 211
McHugh, Frank, 118, 132
McHugh, Jimmy, 187, 188, 293, 294, 373, 375, 376, 563
McKinney, Nina Mae, 58
McLaglen, Victor, 99, 148, 168, 171, 175, 179, 220, 339, 349
McLeod, Norman, 148
McNutt, William Slavens, 103, 183
McPherson, Aimee Semple, 96
Me and My Pal, 137, 138
Mechanical Monsters, The, 477
Meehan, John, 60, 286
Meerson, Lazare, 105
Meet Joe Black, 156

Meet John Doe, 154, 278, 287, 321, 403, 424, 425, 443
Mein Kampf, 426
Mencken, H.L., 415
Mendelssohn, Felix, 173, 345, 487
Menjou, Adolphe, 67, 69, 70, 116, 122, 189, 232, 243, 263, 557
Menzies, William Cameron, 8, 32, 46, 51, 111, 136, 220, 221, 262, 349, 376, 379, 385, 418
Mercer, Johnny, 217, 251, 293, 294, 295, 373, 375, 376, 465, 466, 468, 488, 490, 520, 561, 562, 564, 565
Mercy Island, 459, 463
Meredith, Burgess, 215, 321, 331, 375, 414, 464
Meredyth, Bess, 41, 43
Merman, Ethel, 189, 266
Merrily We Live, 261, 264, 282, 283, 288, 291, 293, 294
Merry Old Soul, The, 113, 114
Merry Widow, The, 112, 143, 148, 149, 157, 160, 161, 162
Mersereau, Jacques, 567
Mescall, John, 512, 514
Mesenkop, Louis, 434, 472, 492, 523
Mesopotamia, 148
Messel, Oliver, 220
Messiah, 277
Methot, Mayo, 542
Metropolis, 8, 12, 13, 21, 25, 35, 79, 430
Mexican Revolution, 147
Mexican Spitfire Sees a Ghost, 494
Mexican-Americans, 506
Mexico, 8, 147, 156, 261, 437, 443, 452, 457, 462, 469, 471
MGM, 15, 31, 32, 34, 44, 49, 50, 52, 57, 62, 68, 71, 87, 94, 109, 115, 120, 121, 123, 127, 132, 134, 135, 147, 149, 150, 156, 158, 159, 167, 168, 169, 170, 172, 173, 175, 177, 184, 196, 200, 206, 207, 214, 219, 220, 221, 225, 231, 252, 264, 266, 272, 276, 281, 282, 284, 286, 289, 294, 310, 323, 329, 345, 354, 355, 372, 375, 377, 381, 395, 410, 415, 416, 419, 420, 432, 441, 447, 456, 470, 471, 475, 476, 490, 491, 493, 500, 503, 504, 505, 508, 511, 512, 529, 541, 547, 550, 553, 558, 561, 562, 570, 572
Michener, James, 197
Mickey Mouse, 84, 162, 163, 168, 221, 228, 296, 354, 475
Mickey's Parade of Nominees, 84
Middle East, 24, 215, 372
Midnight, 23, 137, 337, 395, 437
Midnight Patrol, 137
Midsummer Night's Dream, A, 80, 166, 169, 173, 179, 187, 199, 487
Mikado, The, 342, 344
Mildred Pierce, 405
Milestone, Lewis, 9, 10, 24, 52, 59, 69, 73, 207, 321, 538
Milky Way, 381
Milky Way, The, 419, 420
Milland, Ray, 200, 244, 245, 246, 261, 394, 405, 414, 472, 517, 562
Miller, Ann, 232, 414
Miller, Arthur, 15

Miller, Arthur C., 338, 341, 409, 410, 434, 454, 512, 515, 540, 548
Miller, Ernest, 288, 290
Miller, Harley, 566
Miller, Seton I., 73, 287, 434, 452
Million Dollar Movie, The, iii
Milner, Victor, 50, 134, 135, 157, 159, 166, 167, 213, 288, 290, 338, 339, 409, 411, 516, 517
Miltown, 507
Min and Bill, 66, 92
Minnelli, Vincente, 562
Minnie Mouse, 69, 113, 121
Mintz, Charles, 163, 227
Mintz, Sam, 73
Miracle of Morgan's Creek, The, 244, 472
Miracle on 34th Street, 419
Miracle Woman, The, 96, 100, 110
Miranda, Carmen, 374, 410, 554, 568
Miss Elizabeth, 403
Mission to Moscow, 550, 566, 567
Mitchell, Sidney, 216, 217
Mitchell, Thomas, 208, 231, 239, 304, 305, 340, 380, 385, 397, 513
Mitchum, Robert, 549
Moby Dick, 523
Mockery, 17
Mockridge, Cyril J., 563
Modern Times, 104, 105, 201
Mohr, Hal, 166, 173, 540, 552
Mole People, The, 433
Moloch, 13
Monaco, James V., 373, 375, 564
Money Pit, The, 520
Monkey Business, 104
Monkey Business (1952), 425
Monogram Studios, 462
Monroe, Marilyn, 425
Monroe, Thomas, 424, 425
Monsieur Verdoux, 383, 390
Monstro, 388, 412
Montes, Maria, 483
Monteverdi, Guilo, 146
Montgomery, George, 468, 469, 560
Montgomery, Robert, 53, 157, 235, 236, 241, 424, 436, 440, 441, 452, 499
Monument Valley, 341, 351, 358
Moon and Sixpence, The, 554, 558
Moontide, 512, 513
Moore, Grace, 146, 151, 152
Moore, Jack, 520
Moorehead, Agnes, 507, 508
Moraweck, Lucien, 345, 347
Mord, 351
More the Merrier, The, 448, 528, 530, 531, 533, 534, 538, 539, 540, 543, 544, 545, 547, 548
Moreland, Manton, 462
Morey, Larry, 251, 488
Morgan, Frank, 77, 150, 159, 218, 306, 364, 505, 506, 534
Morgan, Helen, 53
Morgan, Michele, 485
Morley, Robert, 264, 276, 280, 281
Morlocks, 13
Morning Glory, 108, 109, 122, 150, 170, 232
Morocco, 66, 67, 73, 78, 79, 80, 85, 90, 97, 416, 481

Morris, Chester, 32, 35, 53, 56
Morros, Boris, 259, 261
Morton, Arthur, 563
Mother Goose, 162, 296
Mother Goose Goes Hollywood, 296
Mother Hubbard, 162
Motion Picture Magazine, 26
Moulin Rouge, 238
Moulton, Thomas T., 377, 523, 568
Mouse, Mickey, 113
Mozart, Wolfgang Amadeus, 258, 535
Mr. and Mrs. Smith, 432, 441
Mr. Bingley, 402
Mr. Blandings Builds His Dream House, 520
Mr. Bug Goes to Town, 477, 519
Mr. Darcy, 402
Mr. Deeds Goes to Town, 154, 194, 197, 198, 202, 203, 206, 211, 213, 306, 321, 340, 440, 498
Mr. Dodd Takes the Air, 250
Mr. Jordan, 424, 436, 441, 449, 452
Mr. Memory, 181
Mr. Micawber, 171, 176
Mr. Rochester, 268, 381
Mr. Scratch, 506
Mr. Smith Goes to Washington, 154, 160, 206, 231, 264, 287, 300, 304, 305, 306, 308, 312, 318, 319, 321, 323, 328, 329, 332, 333, 334, 335, 336, 349, 350, 388, 417, 433, 511
Mrs. Danvers, 366
Mrs. Higgins, 535
Mrs. Miniver, 112, 317, 336, 492, 493, 497, 500, 502, 505, 507, 510, 512, 523, 524, 530
Multi-plane camera, 227, 228, 412
Mummy, The, 115, 121, 124, 245
Muni, Paul, 35, 36, 93, 128, 196, 199, 202, 212, 219, 229, 230, 235, 236, 244, 305, 556
Murder!, 70
Murder, My Sweet, 263
Murfin, Jane, 327, 402
Murnau, F.W., 7, 8, 19, 22, 23, 44, 58, 78, 83, 131, 159, 162
Muse, Clarence, 313
Museum of Modern Art (New York), 16
Music Box, The, iii, 84, 137, 138
Music in My Heart, 373, 374
Music Man, The, 369, 416
Mussolini, Benito, 127, 362, 383
Mussorgsky, Modest, 345, 415, 485
Musuraca, Nicholas, 515
Mutiny on the Bounty (1935), 39, 150, 168, 169, 172, 175, 176, 179, 180, 183, 186, 240, 281, 369
Mutiny on the Bounty (1962), 24
My Fair Lady, 182, 269, 277, 535
My Favorite Wife, 263, 367, 370, 390, 394, 395, 416, 417
My Favorite Year, 171
My Gal Sal, 492, 517, 519, 522
My Little Chickadee, 386
My Little Margie, 9
My Man Godfrey, 105, 147, 150, 174, 194, 195, 201, 202, 204, 205, 206, 207, 208, 209, 210, 211, 212, 214, 225, 241, 283
My Sister Eileen, 500

My Son, My Son, 416, 417

N

Nagel, Conrad, 49, 83
Naish, J. Carrol, 545, 546
Nana, 229
Nancy Drew, 210
Nanki-Poo, 344
Nanook of the North., 78
Napoleon of Broadway, 150
Napoleonic Wars, 37, 220, 458, 470, 473
Nash, J. Carroll, 551
National Geographic, 14, 51
Naughty Marietta, 169, 173
Navarro, Ramon, 96
Navy Comes Through, The, 523, 524
Nazi, 13, 16, 25, 46, 69, 104, 173, 186, 196, 268, 321, 324, 362, 383, 397, 419, 437, 439, 452, 464, 465, 481, 485, 487, 490, 492, 493, 495, 497, 500, 503, 505, 508, 524, 530, 532, 535, 537, 539, 541, 545, 546, 549, 550, 551, 556, 557, 559, 561, 566, 567, 569,571
Neagle, Anna, 348, 414
Neame, Ronald, 523
Nero, 129, 134, 136
Netflix, 1
New England, 119
New Orleans, 432
New Year's Eve, 195
New York, 15, 16, 43, 70, 109, 149, 178, 188, 197, 199, 246, 249, 271, 277, 303, 323, 368, 377, 415, 424, 556, 560, 569
New York Film Critics, 271, 323
New York Mirror, The, 43
New York Post, The, 447
New York Times, The, 15, 178, 188, 197, 277, 368, 429, 532, 569
Newcombe, Warren, 523
Newman, Alfred, 246, 247, 256, 258, 259, 308, 310, 345, 348, 366, 381, 387, 413, 433, 459, 460, 461, 482, 484, 517, 519, 541, 554, 559, 560
Newman, Emil, 431, 433, 563
Newman, Lionel, 293, 294
Newport Beach, California, ii
Niblo, Jr., Fred, 73
Nicholas Brothers, The, 189, 374, 411, 413, 458, 467, 490, 563
Nichols, Dudley, 166, 168, 180, 183, 223, 288, 399, 401, 536, 537
Nicholson, Jack, 267
Nick and Nora Charles, 155, 212
Nick Scarsi, 10
Nietzsche, Friedrich, 123, 473
Night at the Opera, A, 127, 175, 185, 186, 333, 503
Night Before Christmas, The, 475, 476
Night in Casablanca, A, 215
Night Must Fall, 235, 236, 241, 441, 499
Night of the Hunter, The, 449, 513
Night on Bald Mountain, 345, 387, 413, 485
Night Train to Munich, 424, 426
Nightmare Alley, 266
Ninotchka, 57, 238, 300, 306, 307, 316, 318, 319, 321, 335, 336, 337, 371, 395
Niven, David, 200, 203, 233, 307, 346

Niven, Larry, 220
Noah's Ark, 32
Nobel Prize for Literature, 88, 230, 260, 269, 382
Nobel Prize for Peace, 120
Nobel Prizes for Chemistry and Physics, 544
Noose, The, 16
Nordhoff, Charles, 184, 240
Norlin, Lloyd B., 465, 466
Norsch, Herbert, 377
North Star, The, 536, 538, 548, 550, 554, 559, 566, 567, 568, 569
Northwest Mounted Police, 366, 367, 368, 376, 377, 409, 411
Norway, 556
Nosferatu, 23, 78
Not So Dumb, 97
Nothing Sacred, 22, 226, 233, 235, 237, 344, 411, 430, 517
Notorious, 27, 214, 370, 397, 496, 544
Novello, Ivor, 101
Now, Voyager, 210, 482, 500, 501, 502, 507, 535
Nugent, Frank, 368
Nun's Story, The, 451
Nurse Edith Cavell, 345, 348
Nutcracker Suite, The, 387, 413, 415

O

O Brother, Where Art Thou?, 428
O'Brien, Pat, 69, 144, 145, 270, 272, 279, 569
O'Brien, Willis, 135, 136, 379
O'Connor, Una, 123, 171, 182
O'Hara, Maureen, 311, 435, 442, 444, 445, 446, 453, 454, 461, 483, 514, 516, 517, 556
O'Neil, Barbara, 364
O'Neill, Eugene, 57, 309, 384, 401
O'Sullivan, Maureen, 79, 157
O'Toole, Peter, 170
Oakie, Jack, 361, 362, 413, 561
Oakland, Ben, 293
Oberon, Merle, 177, 178, 210, 258, 316, 324, 463, 464
Oberth, Hermann, 81
Obzina, Martin, 349, 350, 468, 469
Ocean's Eleven, 24
Odell, Robert, 349
Odets, Clifford, 207, 346
Of Human Bondage, 142, 152, 153, 177, 276, 444, 507
Of Human Hearts, 282, 283
Of Mice and Men, 24, 291, 308, 309, 312, 313, 319, 321, 331, 340, 345, 348, 349, 371, 475, 531
Okey, Jack, 51
Oklahoma, 73, 239
Oland, Warner, 90, 183
Old King Cole, 297
Old Maid, The, 317
Old Mill Pond, The, 221
Old Mill, The, 221, 227, 228
Oliver, Edna May, 119, 136, 171, 199, 200, 301, 303, 343, 348, 463
Oliver, Harry, 8, 46
Olivier, Laurence, 11, 37, 178, 216, 275, 324, 328, 330, 381, 388, 390, 458, 493

On Sunset Boulevard, 338
On the Avenue, 250
On the Beach, 495
On the Waterfront, 191, 419
One Foot in Heaven, 434, 438
One Hour with You, 87, 89
One Hundred Men and a Girl, 229, 232, 242, 243, 246, 247
One in a Million, 217, 218
One Million B.C., 105, 340, 367, 371, 377, 379
One Night of Love, 142, 143, 146, 151, 152, 154, 157, 160
One of Our Aircraft Is Missing, 480, 481, 523, 524
One Way Passage, 114, 132
Only Angels Have Wings, 270, 299, 304, 326, 338, 340, 352, 353, 390, 439, 537
Operator 13, 159
Ophüls, Max, 248
Oppenheimer, George, 212, 480, 482
Orchestra Wives, 488, 490
Oswald the Lucky Rabbit, 114
Otis B. Driftwood, 185
Otterson, Jack, 219, 220, 251, 253, 261, 264, 349, 350, 352, 416, 417, 468, 469, 520, 522
Our Dancing Daughters, 41, 42, 44, 47
Our Town, 309, 367, 371, 381, 385, 391, 392, 413, 414, 416, 418, 461, 529, 548
Ouspenskaya, Maria, 209, 301, 303, 350, 474
Out of the Past, 371, 515
Outlaw, The, 139
Outstanding Production, 6, 9, 14
Owens, Harry, 229, 250
Ox-Bow Incident, The, 22, 308, 410, 528, 531, 535, 542

P

Pablo, 546
Pabst, G.W., 22, 54, 60, 61, 122
Pacific Liner, 256, 258
Pack up Your Troubles, 137
Pal, George, 373, 475, 476, 490, 492, 570
Pallette, Eugene, 208, 232, 261, 266, 310, 387, 534
Palm Beach Story, The, 167
Palm Spring, 9
Palmer, Ernest, 44, 428, 429
Pan, Hermes, 174, 181, 188, 190, 217, 218, 219, 226
Pandora's Box, 22, 33, 53, 58, 60, 61, 122, 182
Paramount, 15, 68, 80, 84, 115, 120, 127, 134, 136, 186, 214, 261, 310, 315, 396, 437, 476, 477, 490, 562
Parent Trap, The, 211
Paris, 104, 219, 307, 434, 555, 558, 567
Parker, Dorothy, 225, 233, 244
Parker, Jean, 313
Parker, Max, 520
Parrish, Maxfield, 376, 516
Parsons, Louella, 434
Passage to India, A, 351
Passion of Joan of Arc, The, 34, 35, 38, 40, 41, 86
Pasteur, Louis, 236
Patent Leather Kid, The, 16

Patriot, The, 30, 31, 35, 39, 40, 41, 46
Paul Bunyan, 308
Paul Whiteman Orchestra, 557
Paxinou, Katina, 529, 535
Payne, John, 413, 467, 553
Peace on Earth, 354, 355
Peach, Kenneth, 135
Pearl Harbor, 145, 482, 485, 496, 504, 517, 549, 569
Peck, Gregory, 332
Pecos Bill, 308
Pennies from Heaven, 216
Penny Serenade, 440, 441, 442, 534
Pepe le Moko, 272, 289
Pepe le Pew, 273
Pereira, William L., 492, 523
Perelman, S.J., 104
Perfume Suite, 373
Périnal, Georges, 342, 344, 409
Perrin, Nat, 133
Perry, Harry, 50
Personal History, 398
Peter Ibbetson, 186
Peter Pan, 216, 323
Peters, Susan, 507, 508
Peterson, Robert, 416, 417
Petrified Forest, The, 120, 204, 240, 402, 442
Peyton Place, 494
Phantom of the Opera (1943), 432, 541, 552, 559, 560, 567
Phantom of the Opera, The (1925), 18, 42, 567
Philadelphia Story, The, 77, 93, 95, 263, 289, 358, 360, 361, 364, 365, 373, 380, 381, 386, 388, 390, 391, 392, 399, 441, 480
Phillips, Michael, 173
Philo Vance, 151
Piccadilly Square, 196
Pichel, Irving, 495
Pickfair, 37
Pickford, Mary, 9, 30, 36, 37, 391, 629
Pidgeon, Walter, 435, 436, 442, 444, 445, 446, 453, 454, 461, 472, 497, 503, 510, 512, 530, 541, 542
Pied Piper, The, 493, 495, 497, 498, 512, 514
Pierce, Jack, 192, 474
Pigmania, 491
Pigs in a Polka, 490, 491
Pigskin Parade, 206, 207
Pilar, 535
Pilgrimage, 110, 121, 125, 131
Pinocchio, 235, 366, 367, 372, 373, 382, 386, 387, 412, 413, 420, 519, 558
Pirates of the Caribbean ride, 516
Pitcairn Island, 184
Pitt, Brad, 156
Pixar, 483
Place in the Sun, A, 534
Plan Nine from Outer Space, 257
Planet of the Apes, 411
Planets, The, 488
Platinum Blonde, 87, 90, 93, 95, 96, 100, 102, 213
Play Misty for Me, 417
Playful Pluto, 163
Plough That Broke the Plains, The, 368

Plumb, Edward H., 415, 416, 482, 483, 554, 559, 561
Pluto, 163, 296, 354, 428, 475
Poe, Edgar Allen, 158
Poetry Titles
  "Enoch Arden", 395
Pointer, The, 354
Poland, 252, 487
Polglase, Van Nest, 161, 191, 261, 263, 349, 350, 416, 417, 468
Polito, Sol, 292, 293, 342, 344, 454, 457, 470, 482, 516
Polynesia, 370
Pomeroy, Roy, 8
Pontius Pilate, 171
Popeye, 221, 315, 476, 571
Popeye the Sailor Meets Sindbad the Sailor, 221
Poppaea, 134
Porgy, 466
Porky in Wackyland, 297
Porky Pig, 313, 571
Porter, Cole, 144, 145, 160, 161, 174, 216, 250, 374, 376, 433, 465, 467, 468, 482, 564, 565
Portia on Trial, 246, 248
Poseidon Adventure, The, 509
Postman Always Rings Twice, The, 411
Poverty Row, 143, 154, 248
Powell, Dick, 117, 118, 144, 173, 187, 189, 218, 295, 296
Powell, Eleanor, 170, 189, 216, 217, 252, 465
Powell, Michael, 480, 481, 508
Powell, William, 61, 119, 132, 146, 150, 151, 157, 195, 197, 198, 202, 205, 211, 212
Power, Tyrone, 43, 219, 231, 258, 266, 276, 315, 341, 343, 387, 429, 474, 483, 515, 516, 568
Pragmatism, 16
Preminger, Otto, 495
Presley, Elvis, 209
Presnell, Sr., Robert, 424, 425
Pressburger, Emeric, 480, 481, 492, 508, 510
Preston, Robert, 353, 499
Pretty Woman, 18
Previn, André, 260
Previn, Charles, 246, 259, 260, 308, 310, 406, 413, 415, 431, 432, 517, 519
Price, Vincent, 291, 351, 369, 379, 531
Price, Waterhouse, 30, 165, 300, 358
Pride and Prejudice, 402, 407, 416, 458
Pride and the Passion, The, 369
Pride of the Yankees, The, 86, 102, 333, 451, 482, 486, 493, 495, 497, 498, 500, 501, 507, 508, 509, 510, 512, 514, 520, 521, 523, 525
Primrose Path, 364, 365, 391
Prince and the Pauper, The, 182
Prince Charming, 310, 391
Prince John, 261, 265, 282
Prince, Hugh, 465, 466
Princess O'Rourke, 536
Prinz, Leroy, 188, 189, 226, 227
Prisoner of Shark Island, The, 208
Prisoner of Zenda, The, 77, 233, 234, 235, 246, 247, 251, 253, 281, 400
Private Life of Henry VIII, The, 114, 115, 119, 128, 129, 131

Private Life of Sherlock Holmes, The, 372
Private Lives of Elizabeth and Essex, The, 287, 299, 308, 312, 317, 326, 342, 344, 349, 350, 352, 353, 533
Private Worlds, 177, 179
Prizefighter and the Lady, The, 132
Production Code, 52, 57, 71, 89, 110, 117, 122, 123, 127, 139, 144, 149, 163, 209, 239, 307, 365, 400, 402, 407, 443, 464, 473, 486, 528, 534, 544, 573
Professor Henry Higgins, 269
Professor Marvel, 306
Provost, Heinz, 312
Psycho, 236, 371
Public Enemy, The, 22, 69, 70, 71, 72, 73, 76, 77, 78, 91, 93, 96, 273, 275
Puccini, Giacomo, 257, 310
Puck, 173
Pulitzer Prize, 88, 169, 385, 529, 547
Puppetoons, 476, 492, 570
Puss Gets the Boot, 419, 420
Pygmalion, 265, 269, 272, 273, 275, 277, 286

Q

Qualen, John, 363
Quality Street, 246, 249
Quantrill's Raiders, 368
Quartermaine, Leon, 214
Queen Christina, 57, 110, 121, 123
Queen Elizabeth, 317, 326, 414, 418
Quenzer, Arthur, 293, 294
Quiet Man, The, 249, 343, 359, 384, 445
Quinn, Anthony, 290, 311, 429

R

R2-D2, 344
Raab, Leonid, 161
Rachmil, Lewis J., 416, 418
Racket, The, 9, 10
RAF, 485
Raffles, 62, 272
Raft, George, 75, 91, 249, 252, 325, 366
Raging Bull, 53, 330
Raguse, Elmer, 377, 472
Raiders of the Lost Ark, 488
Raine, Norman Reilly, 243, 287
Rainer, Luise, 196, 204, 228, 230, 237, 245, 282, 283
Rainger, Ralph, 161, 265, 293
Rains Came, The, 303, 310, 319, 338, 341, 345, 348, 349, 351, 352, 353
Rains, Claude, 43, 123, 128, 129, 197, 213, 265, 267, 277, 282, 287, 304, 340, 379, 424, 436, 449, 474, 482, 503, 513, 538, 545, 547, 552, 555, 561
Raitt, Bonnie, 466
Raksin, David, 258
Ralph, Jessie, 171
Rambeau, Marjorie, 364, 365
Rand, Sally, 405
Random Harvest, 336, 482, 486, 493, 495, 497, 498, 500, 502, 504, 507, 508, 510, 520, 521
Ranger, Ralph, 314
Raphaelson, Samson, 112
Rasch, Albertina, 189

Rasputin and the Empress, 132, 133
Rathbone, Basil, 42, 76, 170, 171, 199, 200, 206, 207, 246, 248, 264, 265, 280, 281, 282, 291, 292, 326, 351, 375, 387
Rave, Ron, 465, 466
Raven, The, 191, 192
Rawhide, 264
Raye, Don, 488, 489
Raye, Martha, 227, 261, 293, 378, 489
Ready, Willing and Able, 226, 227, 251
Reagan, Ronald, 487, 494, 498, 503, 524, 540, 545
Reap the Wild Wind, 492, 516, 517, 522, 523
Reason and Emotion, 570, 571
Rebecca, 312, 358, 360, 364, 366, 367, 371, 377, 380, 381, 382, 388, 390, 391, 393, 398, 399, 401, 403, 407, 416, 418, 439, 443, 473, 504, 507, 515
Rebel without a Cause, 291, 405
Red Cross, 423
Red Dust, 95
Red Hot Riding Hood, 571
Red River, 100, 312, 384
Red Shoes, The, 481, 508
Redgrave, Michael, 271
Rée, Max, 68, 79
Reed, John, 147
Reeves, George, 429, 477, 536, 540, 551
Reinhardt, Max, 162, 166, 173
Reisch, Walter, 335, 336, 394, 395
Remarque, Erich Maria, 61, 277
Rembrandt, 79, 341, 455
Rembrandt (movie), 204
Renaissance, 159, 162
Renaissance Fair, 159
Rennahan, Ray, 319, 342, 343, 409, 410, 411, 428, 429, 431, 552
Renoir, Jean, 122, 224, 268, 299, 554
Republic Pictures, 248, 249, 257, 260, 290, 313, 350, 368, 414, 417, 432, 462, 463, 490, 519, 524, 525, 557
Republicans, 65, 154, 301, 423
Reuben sandwich, 365
Reunion in Vienna, 134
Revel, Harry, 488, 489
Revere, Anne, 535
Reverend Jim, 295
Reverend Sparks, 531
Rhapsody in Blue, 466
Rhapsody in Rivets, 475
Rhett Butler, 150, 282, 300, 302, 319, 328, 329, 342, 353, 392
Rhythm in the Ranks, 475, 476
Rhythm on the Range, 217
Rhythm on the River, 373, 375
Rich, Frederic E., 559, 562
Rich, Robert, 400
Richard III, 351
Richardson, Ralph, 220, 267, 273, 344
Richest Girl in the World, The, 157, 158
Richman, Arthur, 245
Ridin' on a Rainbow, 465, 467
Riefenstahl, Leni, 46, 549
Right to Love, The, 78, 79
Rio Grande, 249, 343
Riskin, Robert, 102, 110, 111, 142, 155, 211, 213, 231, 265, 286, 287
Rites of Spring, The, 413

Rittau, Gunther, 8
Ritz Brothers, 296
River, The, 368
RKO, 15, 62, 115, 117, 136, 137, 142, 157, 187, 188, 191, 214, 219, 266, 446, 474, 494, 505, 515, 521
RKO Story, The, 190
Road to Morocco, 396, 480, 482
Road to Singapore, 396
Roaring Twenties, The, 205, 299, 326
Roberta, 187, 188
Roberts, Casey, 520, 522
Roberts, Julia, 18
Robeson, Paul, 208
Robin, Leo, 161, 250, 265, 293, 314
Robinson, Bill "Bojangles", 189, 563
Robinson, Edward G., 10, 27, 71, 72, 75, 77, 89, 166, 167, 324, 397, 442, 473
Robinson, Edward R., 520
Robson, Flora, 418
Robson, May, 108, 109, 284, 348
Rocky and Bullwinkle, 126, 181
Roder, Milan, 247, 249
Rodgers and Hammerstein, 258
Rodgers and Hart, 309, 378
Rodgers, Richard, 294, 310
Roemheld, Heinz, 431, 492, 517, 518
Rogers St. John, Adela, 103
Rogers, Charles, 243
Rogers, Charles "Buddy", 9
Rogers, Ginger, 117, 121, 144, 174, 200, 216, 218, 219, 226, 232, 241, 260, 263, 291, 293, 307, 365, 380, 384, 391, 393, 394, 400, 428, 497
Rogers, Howard Emmett, 212
Rogers, Roy, 294, 368
Rogers, Will, 20, 108, 111, 114, 119, 121, 180
Rogue Song, The, 54, 56
Roland, Gilbert, 8
Roman Holiday, 27, 309, 536
Romance, 57, 59
Romeo, 32, 198, 204, 206, 207, 220, 276, 280
Romeo and Juliet, 32, 197, 198, 204, 206, 207, 219, 220, 276
Romero, Cesar, 427, 560
Romheld, Heinz, 433
Rookie Bear, The, 475, 476
Rooney, Mickey, 157, 173, 255, 267, 284, 286, 310, 324, 328, 329, 373, 395, 415, 489, 534, 541, 542
Roosevelt Hotel, 5
Roosevelt, Franklin Delano, 113, 147, 357, 479, 509, 559
Roosevelt, Theodore, 120
Rope, 27, 411
Rosalie, 251
Rose Tattoo, The, 246
Rose, Gene, 563
Rose, Ruth, 133
Rosebud, 426, 435
Rosher, Charles, 7, 159
Ross, Frank, 538, 539, 547, 548
Ross, Fred, 465, 467
Rosse, Herman, 51
Rosson, Harold, 45, 214, 342, 345, 403, 405
Rosson, Richard, 99, 549
Rotoscoping, 315

Rotwang, 21
Roy Rogers Museum, 295
Royal Air Force, 474
Royal Canadian Air Force, 522
Royal Family of Broadway, The, 70, 110
Royal Navy, 504, 530
Rózsa, Miklós, 367, 372, 452, 459, 463, 482, 486
Ruby, Harry, 76, 133
Ruggles of Red Gap, 169, 174, 176
Ruggles, Wesley, 73
Rumors of celebrity homosexuality, 274
Runyan, Damon, 111, 118
Ruric, Peter, 158, 159
Russell, Jane, 139
Russell, Robert, 538, 539, 547, 548
Russell, Rosalind, 26, 236, 267, 273, 327, 361, 387, 393, 394, 484, 500, 514, 566
Russia, 26, 31, 321
Russian Revolution, 8, 17
Ruth, Babe, 24, 495
Ruttenberg, Joseph, 265, 288, 289, 403, 407, 454, 456, 492, 512, 548, 550
Ruttman, Walther, 8
Ryder, Loren, 352, 353, 377
Ryder, Loren L., 377
Ryskind, Morrie, 62, 76, 185, 211, 212, 244, 441

S

Sabatini, Rafael, 483
Sabotage, 196
Saboteur, 369
Sabu, 376, 378, 409, 483, 486
Sadie Thompson, 7, 17, 18, 19, 21, 26
Safety Last, 228
Sahara, 545, 546, 548, 551
Sal of Singapore, 41, 42
Sala D'Oro, 65
Salieri, Antonio, 535
Sally, 51
Salter, Hans J., 517, 519, 554
Saludos Amigos, 374, 559, 561, 563, 565
Sam Spade, 76, 442, 453, 465
Sambo's restaurant, 146
San Diego, 430, 517
San Francisco, 132, 194, 195, 197, 199, 201, 202, 203, 207, 210, 211, 230, 231, 240, 243, 262, 269, 270, 272, 352, 405, 484, 553
Sanctuary, 117
Sanders, George, 348, 369, 470, 516, 558
Sandrich, Mark, 174
Santa Claus, 162, 175
Sarah and Son, 56, 58
Saroyan, William, 529, 540, 547
Sarris, Andrew, 31, 45, 78, 91, 149, 163, 289, 318, 343, 386, 441, 528
Satan, 76, 454, 529, 533
Satan Met a Lady, 76
Saunders, John Monk, 68, 76, 77
Saving Private Ryan, 52
Sawley, George, 522
Scarborough, Dorothy, 43
Scarecrow, 306, 345
Scarface, 10, 79, 87, 90, 93, 99, 100, 102, 103, 128, 171, 271, 287, 482

Scarface (1983), 91
Scarlet Empress, The, 163, 486, 521
Scarlett O'Hara, 268, 302, 315, 364, 523
Scharf, Walter, 459, 463, 517, 554, 557, 559, 560
Schary, Dore, 265, 284, 286, 394, 395
Schertzinger, Victor, 154, 157, 160, 247, 249, 344, 490
Schickel, Richard, 57
Schildkraut, Joseph, 228, 239, 276, 340, 347
Schlesinger, Leon, 419, 475
Schoedsack, Ernest B., 14, 15
Schoenberg, Arnold, 186
Schulze, John DuCasse, 416, 418, 468, 470
Schwartz, Arthur, 564
Scorsese, Martin, 59, 71, 73, 93, 97, 534, 629
Scotland Yard, 53
Scott, Allan, 536, 538, 540
Scott, George C., 274
Scott, Martha, 385, 391, 392, 438, 461
Scott, Randolph, 124, 188, 370, 521, 549, 569
Scoundrel, The, 182
Scram!, 137
Screen Actors Guild, 152, 193
Screen Writers Guild, 77, 166, 183
Screwball comedy, 77, 143, 151, 157, 198, 205, 224, 233, 245, 271, 272, 280, 291, 337, 370, 496, 557
Sea Hawk, The, 215, 372, 373, 377, 380, 413, 414, 416, 418, 419, 533
Sea Wolf, The, 465, 472, 473
Searchers, The, 59, 342, 419
Seaton, George, 538, 539
Seawright, Roy, 352, 353, 377, 472
Second Chorus, 373, 375, 413, 414
Second Fiddle, 314, 315
Secret Agent, The, 196
Segall, Harry, 424
Seitz, John F., 44, 548, 550, 566
Self-Reliance, 502
Selznick, David O, 8, 61, 121, 122, 147, 165, 171, 172, 198, 199, 200, 214, 215, 233, 234, 242, 253, 259, 262, 268, 271, 300, 312, 319, 323, 333, 335, 342, 346, 349, 357, 360, 361, 370, 371, 381, 398, 439, 463, 470, 531, 543
Sennett, Mack, 84, 85, 224
Sergeant York, 100, 426, 427, 434, 439, 440, 445, 447, 448, 449, 450, 451, 454, 457, 459, 463, 468, 470
Sersen, Fred, 319, 352, 353, 377, 472, 523, 541, 568
Seventh Heaven, 7, 8, 9, 10, 11, 18, 19, 21, 24, 40, 88, 404, 438
Seventh Victim, The, 551
Seymour, Stephen A., 471, 472
Shadow of a Doubt, 264, 451, 530, 533, 534, 543, 545, 547, 548
Shakespeare, William, 96, 113, 144, 166, 173, 199, 203, 214, 216, 304, 307, 351, 378, 425, 454, 487
Shall We Dance, 226, 250
Shamroy, Leon, 288, 292, 409, 411, 492, 512, 514, 516
Shane, 534
Shanghai Express, 67, 79, 85, 86, 87, 90, 95, 97, 98, 396

Shanghai Gesture, The, 482, 486, 487, 520, 521
Shanghai Lily, 90
Shangri-La, 231, 240, 251, 350
Sharp, Henry, 412
Shaw, Artie, 373, 375, 413, 414
Shaw, George Bernard, 265, 269, 286, 455
Shaw, Irwin, 510, 511, 556
Shaw, Winifred, 187, 188
She, 68, 188
She Done Him Wrong, 115, 119
She Loves Me Not, 161
She Married a Cop, 308, 313
She Wore a Yellow Ribbon, 309, 384
Shearer, Douglas, 50, 52, 62, 68, 352, 354, 377, 472, 523
Shearer, Norma, 42, 49, 50, 52, 54, 56, 66, 67, 94, 109, 120, 121, 144, 151, 152, 153, 194, 198, 204, 206, 264, 275, 276, 327
Sheean, Vincent, 398
Sheekman, Arthur, 104, 133
Shelley, Mary, 102, 185
Shelley, Percy Bysshe, 185
Shere Khan, 516
Sheridan Whiteside, 498
Sherlock Holmes, 181, 281, 326, 552
Sherriff, R.C., 112, 335, 336
Sherwood, Robert, 389, 399, 401
Shilkret, Nathaniel, 214, 216
Ship Comes In, A, 18, 20
Shipman, David, 153
Shirley, Anne, 241
Shoedsack, Ernest B., 378
Shop Around the Corner, The, 113, 277, 364, 371, 388
Short Story Titles
  "Black Cat, The", 158
  "Most Dangerous Game, The", 425
  "Rain", 26
  "Caballero's Way, The", 42
Short Subjects, 194
Show Boat, 73, 100, 208
Shuken, Leo, 308, 309
Shull, Michael S., 476
Shumlin, Herman, 532
Shute, Nevil, 495
Siam, 14
Siamese twins, 484
Siberia, 307, 335
Sidney, Sylvia, 79, 230
Sierra Nevadas, 568
Sight and Sound, 45
Sign of the Cross, The, 112, 129, 134, 136, 144
Sikov, Ed, 21, 98, 143, 336, 338, 394, 452
Silent Movie Theatre, 12
Silly Symphonies, 84, 168, 221, 228, 250, 354, 367, 476
Silver Queen, 482, 484, 520, 521
Silver, Louis, 246, 247
Silvera, Darrell, 468, 520, 566
Silverheels, Jay, 248
Silvers, Louis, 160, 256, 258, 308, 313
Silvers, Phil, 414, 428
Simms, Ginny, 376
Simon, Michel, 122
Simon, Simone, 515
Simple Simons, 297
Simpsons, The, 420

Sims, George Carol, 158
Sims, John, 15
Sinatra, Frank, 161, 216, 261, 369, 374, 467, 490, 564
Sinbad, 483
Sing Baby Sing, 216
Singapore, 370
Singin' in the Rain, 32, 111
Sins of Madelon Claudet, The, 94
Sir Guy, 265, 282
Six Degrees of Kevin Bacon, 418
Sjöström, Victor, 34, 38, 41
Skall, William V., 342, 344, 409, 411, 428, 430, 516, 517
Skelton, Red, 465
Skinner, Frank, 259, 260, 366, 369, 459, 460, 482, 483, 554
Skippy, 66, 68, 70, 73, 75, 97
Sky's the Limit, The, 559, 561, 564
Skyscraper, 41, 42
Sleeping Beauty, 519
Sleepless in Seattle, 307
Slifer, Clarence, 568
Smart Money, 76, 77
Smilin' Through, 115, 120, 128
Smiling Lieutenant, The, 87, 89, 149
Smith, C. Aubrey, 122, 123, 167, 172, 246, 344
Smith, Kate, 568
Smith, Leonard, 428, 430, 552, 553
Smith, Paul J., 246, 250, 366, 367, 554, 559, 561
Smith, Ted, 522
Snake Pit, The, 405
Snow White (Fleischer version), 114
Snow White and the Seven Dwarfs, 114, 168, 234, 235, 246, 250, 251, 255, 315, 367, 561, 572
Snyder, William, 428, 429
So Ends Our Night, 459, 464
So Proudly We Hail!, 535, 536, 538, 540, 548, 551, 568, 569
Some Like It Hot, 430
Something to Shout About, 559, 561, 564, 565
Something to Sing About, 247, 249
Son of Flubber, 207
Son of Frankenstein, 65, 352, 379
Son of Monte Cristo, The, 468, 470
Son of Paleface, 290
Sondergaard, Gale, 196, 209, 384
Song of Bernadette, The, 528, 531, 533, 534, 535, 536, 538, 539, 540, 541, 543, 545, 546, 548, 554, 559, 566
Song of the Flame, 62
Song of the South, 431, 456
Song Titles, 188, 189
 "After the Ball", 417
 "After You've Gone", 518
 "All God's Children Got Rhythm", 226
 "Always and Always", 293, 294
 "Always in My Heart", 488
 "America", 357
 "Arglwydd, Arwain Trwy'r Anialwch", 461
 "As Time Goes By", 555
 "A-Stairable Rag", 468
 "Auld Lang Syne", 312, 486
 "Ave Maria", 285, 311
 "Baby Mine", 465, 466
 "Band Played On, And the", 417, 433
 "Baubles, Bangles and Beads", 374
 "Be Honest with Me", 465, 467
 "Blow the Man Down", 369
 "Blues in the Night", 465, 466, 468
 "Boogie Woogie Bugle Boy of Company B", 465, 466, 489
 "Broadway Melody", 31
 "Carioca", 161
 "Change of Heart, A", 563, 564
 "Change Partners", 293
 "Chattanooga Choo Choo", 465, 467
 "Cheek to Cheek", 187, 188, 190
 "Clavelitos", 519
 "Columbia, the Gem of the Ocean", 312
 "Continental, The", 145, 157, 161
 "Cowboy and the Lady, The", 293, 294
 "Cradle Song", 347
 "Cuckoo Song, The", 249
 "Cuddle up a Little Closer", 560
 "Dearly Beloved", 488, 490
 "Diamonds Are a Girl's Best Friend", 374
 "Did I Remember", 216, 217
 "Ding Dong, the Witch Is Dead", 316
 "Dixie", 325, 368
 "Dolores", 465, 467
 "Down Argentine Way", 373, 374
 "Dream Lover", 414
 "Drum Boogie", 461
 "Drummer Boy, The", 373
 "Dust", 293, 294, 295
 "Elephant Number", 188, 189
 "Faithful Forever", 314, 315
 "Falling in Love with Love", 378
 "Fine Romance, A", 217
 "Foggy Day, A", 250
 "Follow the Yellow Brick Road", 316
 "Gentle Annie", 309
 "Give a Little Whistle", 367
 "God Bless America", 568
 "Goin' Home", 519
 "Hall of Kings", 188
 "Happiness Is a Thing Called Joe", 563, 564
 "Harbor Lights", 369
 "Harrigan", 413
 "Heat Wave", 266
 "Hi-Diddle-Dee-Dee", 367
 "Honeysuckle Rose", 413, 562
 "Hooray for Hollywood", 251
 "How About You?", 488, 489
 "Hungarian Rhapsody #2", 475
 "I Can't Give You Anything But Love", 286
 "I Concentrate on You", 374, 376
 "I Dream of Jeannie with the Light Brown Hair", 312, 367
 "I Dug a Ditch in Wichita", 562
 "I Hear Music", 376
 "I Love You", 309
 "I Only Have Eyes for You", 161
 "I Poured My Heart into a Song", 314, 315
 "I Remember You", 488, 490
 "I Won't Dance", 188
 "I'd Know You Anywhere", 373, 375, 376
 "If I Only Had a Brain", 306, 316

"If I Were King of the Forest", 306, 316
"I'll Be Hard to Handle", 188
"I'm an Old Cowhand", 217
"I'm in the Mood for Love, 161
"I'm Old Fashioned", 490
"In the Good Old Summertime", 433
"In the Shade of the Old Apple Tree", 433
"In the Still of the Night", 251
"Isn't This a Lovely Day?", 187, 190
"It Seems I Heard That Song Before", 488, 490
"It's a Blue World", 373, 374
"It's a Small World", 373
"I've Got a Feelin' You're Foolin'", 169, 188, 189
"I've Got a Gal in Kalamazoo", 488, 490
"I've Got My Love to Keep Me Warm", 250
"I've Got You Under My Skin", 216
"Jeepers Creepers", 293, 294
"Joe Bowers", 309
"Keep the Home Fires Burning", 102
"Kiss Me Quick", 368
"K-K-K-Katie", 413
"La Conga", 373
"Lady in the Tutti Frutti Hat, The", 568
"Last Time I Saw Paris, The", 465, 468
"Latin from Manhattan", 188, 189
"Le Marseillaise", 555
"Leaning", 529
"Let It Snow! Let It Snow! Let It Snow!", 374
"Let's Be Common", 60
"Let's Face the Music and Dance", 217
"Little Woodenhead", 367
"Lon Chaney's Gonna Get You If You Don't Watch Out", 33
"Love in Bloom", 161
"Love Is a Song", 488, 489
"Love of My Life", 373, 375
"Lovely Lady", 188, 189
"Lovely to Look At", 187, 188
"Lullaby of Broadway", 169, 187, 188, 190
"Lydia, the Tattooed Lady", 316
"Makin' Whoopee", 80, 375
"Man I Love, The", 415
"Marching through Georgia", 325
"Melancholy Baby", 432
"Melody from the Sky, A", 216, 217
"Memphis Blues", 432
"Merrily We Live", 293, 294
"Minstrel Boy, The", 372
"Mist over the Moon, A", 293, 294
"My Country 'Tis of Thee", 463
"My Own", 293, 294
"My Shining Hour", 561, 564
"Never Gonna Dance", 219
"Nice Work If You Can Get It", 250
"Night and Day", 145, 161, 482
"Now It Can Be Told", 293
"O Sole Mio", 126
"Oh, How I Hate to Get up in the Morning", 560
"Ol' Man River", 208
"On the Banks of the Wabash", 519
"On the Good Ship Lollipop", 161
"One for My Baby", 561, 564, 566
"Only Forever", 373, 375

"Our Country, 'Tis of Thee", 312
"Our Love Affair", 373, 375
"Our Love Is Here to Stay", 295, 296
"Out of the Silence", 465, 466
"Over the Rainbow", 300, 314, 318, 323
"Pennies for Peppino", 488, 489
"Pennies from Heaven", 216
"Piccolino", 188, 190
"Pick Yourself Up", 217
"Pig Foot Pete", 488, 489
"Pink Elephants", 431, 466, 491
"Playboy from Paree", 188
"Pretty Girl Is Like a Melody, A", 197, 217
"Quick Sands", 562
"Red River Valley", 312
"Remember Me", 250, 251
"Remember My Forgotten Man", 118
"Ride of the Valkyries", 259
"Rule, Britannia", 52, 385, 559
"Say a Pray'r for the Boys over There", 563, 564
"Shadow Waltz, The", 118
"Shall We Gather at the River", 309
"She Is More to Be Pitited than Censured", 309
"Sheik of Araby, The", 413
"Since I Kissed My Baby Goodbye", 465, 467, 468
"Singin' in the Rain", 32
"Smoke Gets in Your Eyes", 188
"Somewhere Over the Rainbow", 373
"St. James Infirmary Blues", 114
"St. Louis Blues", 432
"St. Louis Woman", 123
"Star-Spangled Banner, The", 312, 463
"Stiff Upper Lip", 226
"Stormy Weather", 563
"Stranger in Paradise", 374
"Sweet Leilani", 229, 250, 251, 256
"Sweet Mystery of Life", 173
"Swing Is Here to Stay", 226
"Swingin' the Jinx", 217
"Swinging on a Star", 375
"Take Me Out to the Ball Game", 486
"Taking a Chance on Love", 563
"Tangerine", 490
"Thanks for the Memory", 265, 293, 295
"That Old Black Magic", 562, 564, 565, 566
"That Old Feeling", 250, 251
"There's a Breeze on Lake Louise", 488, 489
"They All Laughed", 250
"They Can't Take That Away From Me", 250, 251
"They're Either Too Young or Too Old", 564, 565
"This Can't Be Love", 378
"Tiger Rag", 432
"Time after Time", 374
"Too Good to Be True", 188, 189
"Too Marvelous for Words", 226, 251
"Top Hat, White Tie and Tails", 187, 190
"Trail of the Lonesome Pine", 249
"Trail to Mexico, The", 309
"Two Sleepy People", 295
"Un Bel Dia", 310
"Up in a Balloon, Boys", 309

"Viennese Waltz", 188, 189
"Wait Till the Sun Shines, Nellie", 433
"Waltz in Spring Time", 218
"Waltzing on the Clouds", 373, 375
"Way You Look Tonight, The", 197, 216
"We Mustn't Say Goodbye", 564, 565
"We're in the Money", 117, 118
"We're Off to See the Wizard", 316
"What'll I Do", 146
"What's New?", 375
"When Did You Leave Heaven", 216, 217
"When I Sing", 519
"When You Wish upon a Star", 367, 373
"Whispers in the Dark", 250, 251
"White Christmas", 488, 509
"Who Am I?", 373, 374
"Who's Afraid of the Big Bad Wolf?", 113, 162
"Why Don't You Do Right?", 562
"Wishing", 314, 315
"Won't You Come Home, Bill Bailey", 433
"Words Are in My Heart, The", 188, 190
"You Made Me Love You", 375
"You Must Have Been a Beautiful Baby", 295
"You'd Be So Nice to Come Home To", 561, 564, 565
"You'll Never Know", 465, 541, 563, 564
"Your Words and My Music", 465
"You're Getting to Be a Habit with Me", 117
"Zing Went the Strings of My Heart", 294
"Zoot Suit, A", 562
Songs for Swingin' Lovers, 216
Sons of the Desert, 121, 124, 137, 234
Sorcerer's Apprentice, The, 413
Sorrell and Son, 21, 22
Sorry, Wrong Number, 405
Sothern, Ann, 465
Souls at Sea, 247, 249, 251, 252
Sousa, John Philip, 312, 368, 415
South America, 424
Spanish Armada, 119
Spanish Civil War, 285, 405, 529
Spanky, 68, 519
Spartacus, 400
Speed of Sound, The, 40, 629
Speedy, 24
Spellbound, 263, 403
Spewack, Samuel and Bella, 394, 395
Spielberg, Steven, 423
Spoilers, The, 520, 521
Spoto, Donald, 88, 143
Spring Parade, 373, 375, 403, 406, 413, 415
St. Francis of Assisi, 506
Stack, Robert, 310, 338
Stafford, Jeff, 146
Stage Door, 224, 225, 229, 232, 241, 244
Stage Door Canteen, 559, 562, 564, 565
Stagecoach, 180, 240, 242, 249, 262, 300, 303, 304, 308, 309, 310, 312, 313, 319, 322, 329, 333, 334, 338, 341, 343, 349, 351, 368, 370, 385, 461, 464, 518, 537
Stahl, John M., 151
Stalling, Carl W., 476, 491, 571
Stand by for Action, 568, 569

Stanwyck, Barbara, 96, 110, 122, 125, 237, 238, 241, 316, 346, 347, 353, 425, 443, 445, 454, 558
Star Is Born, A, 103, 224, 225, 229, 233, 234, 235, 237, 238, 242, 244, 345, 371, 411, 430, 517
Star Spangled Rhythm, 559, 562, 564, 565
Star Wars, 384, 474, 485, 487, 570
Star Witness, 103
Starr, Frances, 89
State Department, 561
State Fair, 110, 111, 115, 121
Stay Awake, 466
Steamboat Bill, Jr., 12
Steamboat Round the Bend, 180
Steamboat Willie, 168
Steinbeck, John, 321, 359, 382, 388, 389, 400, 506
Steiner, Max, 160, 168, 186, 187, 214, 215, 246, 248, 259, 260, 312, 325, 345, 346, 347, 349, 366, 370, 371, 372, 430, 459, 463, 482, 484, 554, 555, 559
Steinore, Michael, 568
Stella Dallas, 237, 238, 241, 277, 283, 501
Stephenson, James, 361, 363, 384
Stepin Fetchit, 180, 221
Sternad, Rudolph, 520
Stevens, C.C., 523
Stevens, George, 169, 200, 291, 441, 487, 514, 533, 534
Stevens, Risë, 455
Stevenson, Robert Louis, 101, 156, 456
Stewart, Donald Ogden, 61, 76, 77, 307, 381, 399, 445
Stewart, James, 93, 149, 209, 212, 217, 265, 283, 291, 305, 318, 321, 325, 328, 329, 331, 332, 360, 364, 365, 380, 388, 392, 393
Stewart, James G., 523, 568
Stokowski, Leopold, 232, 243, 247, 415, 416, 424
Stoll, George E., 308, 309, 310, 373, 413, 415, 517, 518, 563
Stoloff, Morris, 246, 248, 259, 260, 431, 433, 459, 462, 482, 487, 554, 556, 559
Stolz, Robert, 373, 375
Stone, Gregory, 259, 260
Stone, Lewis, 35
Storm over Bengal, 259, 260
Stormy Weather, 563
Story of Louis Pasteur, The, 99, 196, 197, 199, 202, 210, 211
Story of Temple Drake, The, 117
Stothart, Herbert, 161, 186, 246, 248, 256, 258, 259, 261, 319, 345, 367, 431, 432, 482, 486, 554, 558, 559, 562
Stradling, Harry, 548, 550
Straus, Oscar, 246, 248, 432
Strauss, Johann, 282, 283, 289, 310, 368, 415, 432, 462, 571
Strauss, Richard, 257
Stravinsky, Igor, 556
Strawberry Blonde, The, 431, 433
Streep, Meryl, 93
Street Angel, 7, 9, 18, 19, 44, 46
Street of Chance, 60, 61
Streetcar Named Desire, A, 191, 417, 419
Strickfaden, Kenneth, 106

Strike up the Band, 372, 373, 375, 413, 415
Stromboli, 388
Struss, Karl, 7, 85, 134, 428, 429
Struther, Jan, 510
Stuart, Gloria, 189
Sturgeon, Theodore, 220, 509
Sturges, Preston, 46, 150, 167, 244, 281, 357, 381, 396, 425, 428, 439, 447, 454, 485
Styne, Jules, 373, 374, 488, 490, 563
Sudan, 344
Suez, 256, 258, 288, 291
Suez Canal, 258
Sugarpuss O'Shea, 443
Sullavan, Margaret, 275, 277, 460, 464
Sullivan, Wallace, 212
Sullivan's Travels, 111, 244, 428, 439, 447
Sun Valley Serenade, 431, 433, 454, 458, 465, 467
Sundown, 454, 458, 459, 463, 468, 470
Sunny, 431, 433
Sunrise, 7, 8, 9, 10, 14, 15, 16, 18, 19, 22, 23, 45, 58, 78, 86, 159
Sunset Blvd., iv, 44, 80, 240, 268, 336, 416, 437, 550
Superman, 477
Superman (Fleischer series), 221, 315, 475, 476, 477
Superman (television version), 429
Supreme Court, 487, 522
Susan Vance, 278
Suspicion, 112, 381, 393, 402, 434, 439, 442, 443, 459, 461, 496, 500, 515
Suzy, 216, 217
Svejda, Jim, 488
Svengali, 70, 78, 79, 80, 89, 133
Swan Lake, 372
Swanee River, 308, 313
Swanson, Gloria, 18, 19, 21, 26, 56, 58, 66
Sweden, 34
Sweethearts, 259, 261
Swenson, Karen, 38
Swerling, Jo, 102, 395, 510
Swift, Jonathan, 53, 315
Swindell, Larry, 299
Swing Time, 197, 200, 216, 217, 218, 219
Swingin' Affair, A, 161
Swiss Family Robinson (1940), 377, 380
Swiss Family Robinson (1960), 380
Switzerland, 219, 285
Sydney Carton, 199
Sylvester and Tweety Bird, 420

T

Tabu, 51, 68, 78
Tahiti, 44, 78, 169, 184, 558
Take a Letter, Darling, 482, 484, 512, 514, 520, 521
Tale of Two Cities, A, 171, 184, 197, 199, 200, 207
Talk of the Town, The, 482, 487, 493, 496, 508, 509, 510, 511, 512, 514, 520, 522, 534
Tall, Dark and Handsome, 426, 427
Talmadge, Norma, 8
Tamiroff, Akim, 206, 207, 290, 396, 545, 546, 556
Tanks a Million, 459, 464

Tarkington, Booth, 169, 170
Tarzan, 68, 463
Tarzan the Ape Man, 87, 91, 101
Taurog, Norman, 66, 68, 73, 97, 262, 278, 279
Taxi, 295
Taylor, Elizabeth, 144, 336, 434, 553
Taylor, Frederick, 13
Taylor, J.O., 135
Taylor, Robert, 135, 170, 238, 277, 340, 372, 406, 429, 471, 472, 505, 569
Taylor, William Desmond, 23
Tchaikovsky, 247, 248, 372, 415, 450, 483, 519, 561
Teagarden, Jack, 294, 432
Technicolor, 25, 32, 80, 84, 145, 178, 218, 261, 262, 266, 269, 292, 323, 325, 338, 342, 343, 344, 345, 350, 374, 409, 410, 411, 412, 429, 430, 431, 472, 477, 486, 516, 517, 522, 529, 552, 553, 568
Tecumseh, 514
Telepathy, 458
Tell It to the Marines, 18
Tempest, 8, 17
Temple, Shirley, 37, 141, 142, 234, 252, 255, 378, 410
Ten Commandments, The, 159, 392
Ten Gentlemen from West Point, 512, 514
Tennyson, Alfred Lord, 395
Terminator 2, 352
Termite Terrace, 297, 420
Terr, Max, 482, 485
Terrytoons, 490, 491
Test Pilot, 265, 270, 284, 285, 405
Tetzlaff, Ted, 214, 512, 514
Thackeray, William Makepeace, 178
Thackery, Ellis J., 377
Thailand, 14
Thalberg Award, 194, 224, 255, 300, 424
Thalberg, Irving, 34, 41, 42, 49, 94, 127, 169, 185, 198, 199, 206, 230, 238, 276, 629
Thank Your Lucky Stars, 564, 565
Thanks for the Memory, 295
That Certain Age, 293, 294
That Hamilton Woman, 37, 336, 454, 458, 468, 470, 472, 473
That Uncertain Feeling, 459, 464
Their First Mistake, 137
Their Own Desire, 56
Them Thar Hills, 164, 192
Theodora Goes Wild, 204, 205, 208
There Goes My Heart, 259, 261
These Three, 209
Thesiger, Ernest, 175, 185
They Drive by Night, 366
They Knew What They Wanted, 361, 363
They Shall Have Music, 308, 310, 311
They Were Expendable, 441, 537
Thief of Bagdad, The (1940), 364, 367, 372, 376, 377, 378, 381, 409, 412, 483, 523, 546
Thin Ice, 226, 227
Thin Man, The, 142, 143, 146, 147, 150, 151, 152, 154, 155, 156, 195, 499
Thing, The, 100, 412
Things to Come, 8, 220
Third Man, The, 426
This Above All, 492, 512, 515, 520

This Gun for Hire, 416, 499, 506
This Is the Army, 541, 559, 560, 567, 568
This Woman Is Mine, 459, 464
Thomson, David, 171, 214
Thoreau, Henry David, 6
Thousands Cheer, 552, 553, 559, 562, 567, 568
Three Caballeros, The, 374, 561
Three Comrades, 275, 277
Three Faces of Eve, The, 519
Three Godfathers, 309
Three Little Pigs, 113, 162, 491
Three Orphan Kittens, 167, 168
Three Smart Girls, 197, 200, 210, 211
Three Stooges, iii, 205, 383, 405, 493, 501, 570
Three's Company, 162
Thru the Mirror, 221
Thunderbolt, 35
Tibbett, Lawrence, 54, 56
Tierney, Gene, 458, 486
Tilton, Martha, 443
Time Machine, The, 13
Timothy Mouse, 221
Tin Pan Alley, 381, 413
Tin Woodsman, 306, 345
Tiomkin, Dimitri, 246, 308, 312, 482, 484, 554, 558
Tit for Tat, 192
Titanic, 105, 115, 190, 381
Titian, 429
To Be or Not to Be, 86, 308, 321, 371, 448, 482, 487, 491, 497, 505, 520, 529, 533
To Have and Have Not, 100, 529, 541
To Kill a Mockingbird, 308, 332
To the Shores of Tripoli, 516, 517
Toch, Ernst, 186, 258, 311, 459, 462
Todd, Thelma., 32
Toland, Gregg, 86, 166, 167, 245, 246, 311, 319, 334, 338, 339, 364, 385, 403, 404, 405, 407, 408, 437, 446, 454, 455, 456, 459, 512, 513, 550
Toldy, John S., 380, 394
Toluboff, Alexander, 251, 252, 261, 262, 349, 351
Tom and Jerry, 420, 476, 570
Tom Joad, 389, 390, 408
Tom Powers, 71, 273
Tomania, 389
Tone, Franchot, 169, 172, 175, 176, 177, 277, 464, 549
Tong, 12
Tonto, 248
Top Hat, 169, 174, 175, 181, 187, 188, 190, 191, 263
Topper, 239, 240, 243, 259, 264
Topper Returns, 472, 473
Topper series, 425, 473, 485
Topper Takes a Trip, 352, 353
Tora! Tora! Tora!, 162
Tortilla Flat, 505, 506
Tortoise and the Hare, The, 141, 157, 163
Touch of Evil, 417
Tourneur, Jacques, 200, 515, 551
Tover, Leo, 454, 457
Towed in a Hole, 137
Tower of Babel, 13
Tower of London, 352

Tracy Lord, 392
Tracy, Lee, 147
Tracy, Spencer, 70, 92, 99, 195, 196, 198, 199, 202, 203, 207, 212, 228, 229, 231, 235, 243, 255, 265, 266, 270, 272, 275, 297, 395, 396, 411, 436, 456, 457, 480, 499, 500, 506
Tracy, William, 464
Trader Horn, 68, 458
Trail of Tears, 74
Trail of the Lonesome Pine, 216, 217
Trail, Armitage, 102
Transatlantic, 86, 87, 105, 191
Travers, Henry, 505, 510
Treasure Island, 156
Treasure of Sierra Madre, The, 440
Trespasser, The, 56, 58
Trevor, Claire, 230, 240, 241, 242, 322, 342, 368
Trigger, 295
Trilby, John, 62
Triumph of the Will, 46, 549, 567
Tropic Holiday, 259, 261
Trotti, Lamar, 306
Trouble in Paradise, 112, 120, 121, 126, 127, 132, 134, 135, 143, 167
Truant Officer Donald, 474, 475
Trumbo, Dalton, 399, 400
Tucson, 416
Tugboat Annie, 287
Tulips Shall Grow, 490, 492
Tunberg, Karl, 426, 427
Tunnel of Love, 15
Turner Classic Movies, iii, 1, 23, 128, 246, 518, 544
Turner, Lana, 146, 412, 456, 500, 505
TV Guide, ii
Twain, Mark, 74, 262, 324, 468
Twentieth Century, 26, 129, 143, 149, 151, 154, 155, 280
Twentieth Century-Fox, 7, 15, 115, 145, 200, 207, 266, 353, 410, 417, 468, 483, 490
Twice Two, 137
Twilight Zone, 46
Two Arabian Knights, 9, 10, 24, 59
Tybalt, 199, 207
Typhoon, 377, 380

U

U.S. Marines, 481, 506, 517
U.S. Senate, 350
UCLA, ii, 1, 31, 42, 79, 147, 220, 249, 261, 313, 380, 549
Ugly Duckling, The, 319, 354
UHF, iii
Ulmer, Edward, 162
Uncle Tom's Cabin, 31
Under Western Stars, 293, 294
Underworld, 9, 26, 27, 33, 36, 45
Uninvited, The, 472
Union Jack, 500
Union Pacific, 249, 309, 352, 353
Unique and Artistic Picture, 6, 7, 9, 12, 14, 16
United Artists, 9, 15, 62, 234, 310
United States, 2, 34, 70, 129, 149, 150, 268, 299, 374, 427, 437, 443, 452, 504, 508

Universal, 50, 105, 137, 159, 162, 163, 191, 208, 229, 246, 264, 310, 379, 386, 473, 490, 519, 522, 524, 552
University of Nevada, 10
Unknown, The, 17, 23, 47, 629
Unsuspected, The, 43
Up the River, 70, 110
USC, 278
Usher, Robert, 416, 468, 469
USS Arizona, 145
USS Enterprise, 430
USSR, 45, 46, 307, 321, 395, 547, 550, 551, 559, 567, 569
Ustinov, Peter, 481

V

Vagabond King, The, 51
Valentine, Joseph, 245, 246, 288, 291, 338, 403, 406
Valentino, Rudolph, 20, 35, 429
Valiant Is the Word for Carrie, 204, 205
Valiant, The, 35, 36, 41, 42
Valium, 507
Vampyr, 41, 86
Van Der Veer, Willard, 50
Van Dyke, W.S., 154, 155, 194, 195
Van Enger, Willard, 570
Van Every, Dale, 244
van Sloan, Edward, 72
Variety, 39, 158
Varsity Show, 226, 227
Veidt, Conrad, 364, 378, 409, 445
Veiller, Anthony, 244
Velez, Lupe, 494
Venice, 126, 178, 191
Venuti, Joe, 51
Verdi, Guiseppe, 238, 247
Verne, Jules, 220
Versailles, 264
Vertov, Dziga, 45
VHS, ii, iii, 86
Victorian, 55, 68, 96, 101, 103, 143, 247, 252, 359, 417, 433, 471, 494, 507, 519, 521, 552
Victory Through Air Power, 343, 554, 559
Vidor, King, 15, 16, 21, 23, 24, 58, 59, 89, 97, 238, 267, 278, 279, 411
Vienna, 47, 134, 203, 219, 289, 375, 376, 415
Villon, Francois, 264, 281
Violent Is the Word for Curly, 205
Virgin Mary, 531, 535, 566
Virginian, The, 61
Vitameatavegamin, 37
Viva Villa!, 142, 143, 147, 155, 156
Vivacious Lady, 288, 291
Volcanoes, 114, 380, 413, 429, 472
Vollbrecht, Karl, 8
von Harbou, Thea, 13, 25, 80
von Sternberg, Josef, 27, 33, 35, 36, 38, 40, 45, 67, 69, 73, 79, 85, 87, 90, 95, 97, 98, 283, 291, 397, 486
von Stroheim, Erich, 33, 39, 41, 45, 47, 134, 162, 268, 464, 549, 550
Vonnegut, Kurt, 116

W

Wagner, Richard, 259, 399, 409, 411, 557
Wagon Master, 309
Waikiki Wedding, 226, 227, 229, 250
Wake Island, 480, 481, 493, 496, 502, 504, 505, 506, 537
Wales, 435, 448, 461, 468
Walk, Don't Run, 530
Walker, Joseph, 160, 288, 292, 338, 340, 454, 457
Walker, Robert, 543
Walker, Vernon L., 135, 377, 474, 523, 568
Wallace, Oliver, 431, 554, 559
Waller, Fats, 189, 221, 563
Wallis, Hal, 255, 527
Walpole, Hugh, 171, 185, 200
Walsh, Raoul, 26, 33, 35, 40, 326, 366, 368
Walter Wanger's Vogues of 1938, 250, 251, 252
Walton, Sir William, 216
Waltons, The, 529
Wanger, Walter, 250, 251, 252, 357, 382
War Against Mrs. Hadley, The, 480, 482
War and Peace, 23
War of 1812, 290
War of the Worlds, The, 403, 476
Ward, Edward, 293, 431, 432, 459, 461, 464, 488, 489, 517, 518, 559, 560
Ware, Darrell, 426, 427
Warner Archives, 37
Warner Brothers, 6, 10, 11, 52, 71, 117, 118, 136, 137, 173, 196, 199, 214, 219, 222, 227, 229, 236, 244, 249, 255, 297, 300, 313, 324, 325, 354, 355, 381, 419, 420, 439, 456, 471, 473, 475, 476, 490, 505, 523, 565, 570, 571
Warner, H.B., 25, 89, 232, 239, 240
Warner, Jack, 6, 142, 152, 173, 527
Warren, Gloria, 488
Warren, Governor Earl, 479
Warren, Harry, 169, 187, 250, 293, 294, 295, 373, 374, 465, 467, 488, 490, 541, 563
Washington, Denzel, 332
Washington, Ned, 366, 367, 373, 465, 563
Watch on the Rhine, 528, 532, 535, 536, 538, 539, 540, 541
Waterloo Bridge (1930), 91
Waterloo Bridge (1940), 367, 372, 403, 406, 562
Waters, Ethel, 221, 562, 564
Watkins, Maurine, 212
Watson, Lucile, 532, 535, 536
Waxman, Franz, 186, 256, 259, 261, 309, 367, 371, 373, 459
Way Down South, 308, 313
Way of All Flesh, The, 9, 16
Way Out West, 124, 234, 235, 243, 247, 249, 257
Wayne, John, 99, 123, 125, 249, 261, 285, 309, 322, 329, 342, 351, 368, 384, 484, 517, 521, 557
Wead, Frank, 284, 285, 286, 287
Weary River, 39
Webb, Ira S., 522, 541, 567
Webb, Kenneth, 160
Webb, Roy, 246, 249, 367, 370, 482, 485, 554, 556

Wedding March, The, 33, 34, 39, 41, 45, 47, 134
Wedekind, Frank, 53
Wee Willie Winkie, 251, 252
Weill, Kurt, 336
Welles, Orson, 18, 98, 224, 323, 374, 397, 404, 409, 424, 426, 435, 440, 445, 446, 448, 458, 494, 504, 513, 530, 561
Wellesley, Gordon, 424, 426
Wellman, William, 9, 22, 23, 33, 40, 51, 73, 95, 224, 225, 228, 233, 242, 262, 304, 531, 535, 558
Wells, H.G., 13, 112, 124, 220
Wenstrom, Harold, 159
Werewolf of London, 183
Werfel, Franz, 539
West of Zanzibar, 17, 36, 42
West Point, 144
West, Adam, 76
West, Claudine, 335, 336, 492, 510
West, Mae, 53, 119, 120, 168, 228, 238, 252, 386, 392
West, Roland, 32
Westerner, The, 361, 394, 395, 408, 416, 417, 419
Westmore, Perc, 85
Westmore, Wally, 136
Weyl, Carl J., 261, 262, 566, 567
Whale, James, 61, 90, 99, 100, 112, 123, 130, 175, 181, 182, 185, 208, 379, 406, 457, 629
What Price Hollywood?, 103, 242
What's Opera, Doc?, 475
What's up, Doc?, 288
Whatever Happened to Baby Jane?, 444
Wheeler, Bert, 467
Wheeler, Lyle, 251, 253, 261, 262, 319, 349, 416
When Ladies Meet (1933), 135
When Ladies Meet (1941), 468, 471
When Worlds Collide, 112, 476
Whipper, Leigh, 531
White Banners, 275, 277, 282
White Christmas, 158, 497, 508
White Heat, 451
White Parade, The, 142, 143, 147, 148
White Shadows in the South Seas, 30, 44
White Zombie, 121, 122, 135
Whiting, Richard A., 216, 217, 251
Whitman, Walt, ii, 301
Whitney, Jack, 377
Whitty, Dame May, 236, 241, 271, 505, 507
Who Killed Cock Robin?, 167, 168
Whoopee!, 79, 80
Wicked Witch, The, 304, 345
Wilcoxson, Henry, 144, 167
Wild Hare, A, 419, 420, 421
Wild, Harry, 288, 290
Wilde, Hagar, 286, 288
Wilde, Ted, 24
Wilder, Billy, 21, 44, 46, 69, 287, 335, 336, 337, 394, 396, 402, 405, 424, 425, 437, 452, 457, 549, 550, 566
Wilder, Thornton, 46, 385, 547, 548
Wiles, Gordon, 87, 105
Wiley, Mason, 7, 37
William Tell Overture, 168
Williams, John, 487

Williams, Ralph Vaughan, 493
Williams, Robert, 93, 95
Williams, Robin, 383
Williams, Warren, 76, 109, 118, 144, 146, 347
Willis, Edwin B., 219, 468, 471, 520, 566, 567
Willkie, Wendell, 423
Willson, Meredith, 366, 369, 459, 463
Willy Wonka and the Chocolate Factory, 557
Wilmarth, William H., 472, 523
Wilson, Carey, 183, 184
Wilson, Dooley, 555
Wilt, David E., 476
Wimperis, Arthur, 492, 510
Wimpy, 222
Wimpy, Rex, 568
Wind, The, 34, 38, 39, 41, 43, 45, 47
Wings, 8, 9, 20, 22, 40, 51, 73, 128, 225, 285, 472, 569
Wings over Honolulu, 245, 246
Winters, Shelley, 237
Winterset, 214, 215, 219, 220
Wisconsin, 471
With Byrd at the South Pole, 50
Wizard of Oz, The, iii, 101, 186, 214, 300, 304, 306, 314, 316, 318, 319, 323, 324, 328, 333, 342, 345, 349, 351, 352, 354, 364, 410
Wodehouse, P.G., 226
Wolcott, Charles, 559, 561, 563
Wolf Man, The, 183, 209, 264, 303, 474, 519
Wolheim, Louis, 10, 24
Woman of Affairs, A, 38, 41, 43
Woman of the Year, 282, 392, 480, 499, 500, 502, 534
Woman's Face, A, 444, 445
Women in War, 377, 380
Women, The, 299, 327, 402
Wonder Man, 243
Wonder of Women, 41, 43
Wong, Anna May, 238
Wood, Sam, 333, 358, 359, 385, 495, 502, 503, 510, 512, 529, 556
Woody Woodpecker, 114, 475, 571
Woolcott, Alexander, 498
Woolley, Monty, 495, 497, 498, 511, 539
World War I, 9, 17, 22, 34, 59, 102, 126, 128, 148, 178, 191, 192, 257, 268, 326, 340, 348, 385, 413, 418, 427, 438, 495, 498, 518
World War II, ii, 11, 16, 44, 104, 119, 139, 151, 268, 285, 327, 340, 355, 372, 379, 383, 390, 412, 427, 430, 441, 458, 464, 466, 477, 482, 490, 495, 496, 506, 518, 528, 530, 531, 536, 546, 548, 549, 553, 559, 561, 565, 573
Wray, Fay, 35, 39, 47, 77, 127, 158
Wrestling Swordfish, 85
Wright, Bob, 293, 373, 374, 488, 489
Wright, Joseph C., 376, 377, 416, 417, 471, 492, 520, 522, 567
Wright, Teresa, 437, 450, 451, 492, 495, 498, 500, 501, 503, 507, 533, 534, 545
Wrigley, Dewey, 517
Wrong Again, 43
Wuthering Heights, 301, 303, 310, 316, 319, 320, 323, 324, 328, 330, 333, 334, 335, 337, 338, 339, 345, 348, 349, 351, 458
Wycherly, Margaret, 450, 451

Wyeth, N.C., 376
Wyler, William, 27, 182, 194, 206, 210, 230, 275, 311, 317, 324, 330, 333, 334, 335, 358, 360, 362, 408, 437, 445, 447, 453, 492, 501, 502
Wylie, Philip, 112
Wynyard, Diana, 108, 109

X

Xanadu, 469

Y

Yank in the R.A.F., A, 472, 474
Yankee Doodle Dandy, 249, 262, 312, 463, 492, 493, 496, 497, 502, 504, 505, 506, 508, 509, 517, 518, 520, 533
Yankee Doodle Mouse, 541, 570
Yearling, The, 416
Yeats-Brown, Francis, 183
Ygor, 306
York, Sergeant Alvin, 438
Yosemite Sam, 475
You Can't Cheat an Honest Man, 299, 327, 386
You Can't Take It with You, 154, 182, 265, 268, 271, 278, 282, 283, 286, 287, 288, 292
You Nazty Spy, 383, 491
You Were Never Lovelier, 488, 490, 517, 519
You'll Find Out, 373, 375
You'll Never Get Rich, 431, 433, 465, 467, 520
You're a Sweetheart, 251, 253
Youmans, Vincent, 161
Young Frankenstein, 181, 352
Young in Heart, The, 256, 259, 261, 288, 292, 309
Young Mr. Lincoln, 162, 258, 299, 303, 306, 308, 310, 328, 331, 343, 389, 419, 542
Young, Brigham, 112
Young, Loretta, 17, 96, 100, 145, 147, 167, 258, 280, 346
Young, Robert, 145, 277, 465
Young, Roland, 239, 240, 259, 292, 473
Young, Victor, 256, 257, 308, 313, 314, 345, 347, 366, 367, 368, 413, 459, 462, 482, 484, 554, 556
Young, Waldemar, 112, 183
Youth on Parade, 488, 490
Youtube, 1
Yurka, Blanche, 200

Z

Zanuck, Darryl F., 118, 145, 165, 172, 184, 196, 202, 224, 231, 266, 284, 359, 383, 400, 410, 453
Zemach, B., 188
Zen, 394
Ziegfeld, Florenz, 80, 197
Zorina, Vera, 565
Zorro, 307
Zorro Rides Again, 249

Endnotes:

[i] *A Short History of the Movies*, 7th edition, Allyn and Bacon, 2000, p. 31.
[ii] Scott Eyman, *Ernst Lubitsch: Laughter in Paradise*, Johns Hopkins UP, 2000, p. 148.
[iii] Qtd. in Scott Eyman, *The Speed of Sound: Hollywood and the Talky Revolution, 1926-1930*, Johns Hopkins UP, 1999, p. 140.
[iv] Anthony Holden, *Behind the Oscar*, Plume, 1995, p. 93.
[v] From DVD special features, "A Thousand Faces," *The Unknown*. TCM Archives, *The Lon Chaney Collection*, Warner Home Video, 2003.
[vi] Also from "A Thousand Faces."
[vii] http://archives.dawn.com/archives/46826
[viii] http://www.silentsaregolden.com/sadiethompsonreview.html
[ix] http://news.google.com/newspapers?nid=1961&dat=19270111&id=fn8hAAAAIBAJ&sjid=aIsFAAAAIBAJ&pg=5020,1224247
[x] Mason Wiley and Damien Bona, *Inside Oscar*, 10th Anniversary Edition, Ballantine Books, 1996, p. 17.
[xi] Scott Eyman, *Mary Pickford: America's Sweetheart*, Plume, 1991, p. 191.
[xii] Karen Swenson, *Greta Garbo: A Life Apart*, Scribner, 1997, p. 193.
[xiii] Charles Affron, *Lillian Gish: Her Legend, Her Life*, University of California Press, 2002, p. 229.
[xiv] http://www.silentsaregolden.com/articles/corinnegriffitharticle.html
[xv] Scott Eyman, *The Speed of Sound: Hollywood and the Talky Revolution, 1926-1930*, Johns Hopkins UP, 1999, p. 244, 329.
[xvi] Mark Vieira, *Irving Thalberg*, University of California Press, 2009, p. 55.
[xvii] http://www.stylist.co.uk/people/joan-crawford-a-life-in-pictures
[xviii] http://www.scribd.com/doc/54173410/The-Greta-Garbo-Handbook-Everything-you-need-to-know-about-Greta-Garbo
[xix] *The Public Enemy* DVD special features, Warner Home Video, 2005.
[xx] "Beer and Blood" documentary on *The Public Enemy* DVD special features, Warner Home Video, 2005.
[xxi] *Little Caesar*, DVD commentary, Warner Home Video, 2005.
[xxii] Andrew Sarris,*"You Ain't Heard Nothin' Yet"* Oxford UP, 2000, p. 149.
[xxiii] Qtd in Donald Spoto, *Possessed*, William Morrow, 2010, p. 93.
[xxiv] Roger Ebert, *Scorsese by Ebert*, University of Chicago Press, 2009, p. 202.
[xxv] Mark Vieira, *Irving Thalberg*, University of California Press, 2009, p. 240.
[xxvi] Karen Swenson, *Greta Garbo: A Life Apart*, Scribner, 1997, p. 258.
[xxvii] Andrew Sarris, *"You Ain't Heard Nothin' Yet"* Oxford UP, 2000, p. 268.
[xxviii] James Curtis, *James Whale: A New World of Gods and Monsters*, University of Minnesota Press, 2003, p. 221.
[xxix] Peter Bogdanovich, *Who the Devil Made It*, Ballantine, 1998, p. 711.
[xxx] Scott Eyman, *Print the Legend*, Johns Hopkins UP, 2001, p. 140.
[xxxi] Alex Ben Block and Lucy Autrey Wilson, *George Lucas's Blockbusting*, It Books, 2010, p. 171.
[xxxii] William K. Everson, *Classics of the Horror Film*, Citadel, 1990, p. 93.
[xxxiii] Peter H. Brown and Jim Pinkston, *Oscar Dearest*, Harper Collins, 1998, p. 26.
[xxxiv] Scott Eyman, *Ernst Lubitsch: Laughter in Paradise*, Johns Hopkins UP, 2000, p. 193.
[xxxv] Qtd. in John Eastman, *Retakes*, Ballantine Books, 1989, p. 93.
[xxxvi] http://www.scifilm.org/musing421.html
[xxxvii] Scott Eyman, *Ernst Lubitsch: Laughter in Paradise*, Johns Hopkins UP, 2000, p. 194.
[xxxviii] Scott Eyman, *Empire of Dreams: The Epic Life of Cecil B. DeMille*, Simon & Schuster, 2010, p. 293.
[xxxix] Pauline Kael, *5001 Nights at the Movies*, Henry Holt and Company, 1991, p. 373.
[xl] Peter H. Brown & Jim Pinkston, Oscar Dearest, Harper & Row, 1987. Davis herself said, "My bosses helped them [her opponents] by sending instructions to all their personnel to vote for somebody else." Qtd. in Anthony Holden, *Behind the Oscar*, Simon & Schuster, 1993, p. 127.
[xli] Donald Spoto, *Possessed*, William Morrow, 2010, pg. 119.
[xlii] http://hollywood-legends.webs.com/ladyofthenight/b.htm
[xliii] http://www.tcm.com/tcmdb/title/79028/Imitation-of-Life/articles.html
[xliv] James Kotsilibas-Davis and Myrna Loy, *Myrna Loy: Being and Becoming*, Donald I. Fine, 1988, p. 88-91.
[xlv] Todd McCarthy, *Howard Hawks: The Grey Fox of Hollywood*, Grove Press, 2000, p. 193.
[xlvi] Scott Eyman, *Ernst Lubitsch: Laughter in Paradise*, Johns Hopkins UP, 2000, p. 223.
[xlvii] Patrick McGilligan, *Alfred Hitchcock: A Life in Darkness and Light*, It Books, 2004, p. 168.
[xlviii] Patrick McGilligan, *Alfred Hitchcock: A Life in Darkness and Light*, It Books, 2004, p. 521.
[xlix] http://rogerebert.suntimes.com/apps/pbcs.dll/article?AID=/20001015/REVIEWS08/10 150301/1023
[l] www.tcm.com/this-month/article/.../It-Happened-One-Night.html
[li] Mason Wiley and Damien Bona, *Inside Oscar*, 10th Anniversary Edition, Ballantine Books, 1996. 54.
[lii] http://www.chicagoreader.com/chicago/the-affairs-of-cellini/Film?oid=1050254
[liii] Alex Ben Block and Lucy Autrey Wilson, *George Lucas's Blockbusting*, It Books, 2010, p. 182.
[liv] http://www.tcm.com/this-month/article/208616|0/Twentieth-Century.html
[lv] Mason Wiley and Damien Bona, *Inside Oscar*, 10th Anniversary Edition, Ballantine Books, 1996, p.56.
[lvi] http://www.nytimes.com/1996/07/31/movies/claudette-colbert-unflappable-heroine-of-screwball-comedies-is-dead-at-92.html
[lvii] Mason Wiley and Damien Bona, *Inside Oscar*, 10th Anniversary Edition, Ballantine Books, 1996, p. 55.
[lviii] Qtd. in David Thomson, *Bette Davis*, Faber and Faber, 2009, p. 17
[lix] Donald Bogle, *Toms, Coons, Mulattoes, Mammies, and Bucks: An Interpretative History of Blacks in American Film*, 4th edition, Continuum, 2001, p. 64.
[lx] http://black-face.com/louise-beavers.htm.
[lxi] http://www.tcm.com/tcmdb/title/1626/Viva-Villa/articles.html
[lxii] http://www.tcm.com/tcmdb/title/2515/Treasure-Island/
[lxiii] http://www.imdb.com/name/nm0750538/
[lxiv] http://www.tcm.com/tcmdb/title/68854/The-Black-Cat/articles.html
[lxv] www.rbmoviereviews.com

[lxvi] Gary Marmorstein, *Hollywood Rhapsody*, Schirmer, 1997, p. 192
[lxvii] Gary Marmorstein, *Hollywood Rhapsody*, Schirmer, 1997, p. 68, 71
[lxviii] Scott Eyman, *Ernst Lubitsch: Laughter in Paradise*, Johns Hopkins UP, 2000, p. 223.
[lxix] Andrew Sarris,*"You Ain't Hear Nothin' Yet"* Oxford UP, 2000, p. 228.
[lxx] rogerebert.suntimes.com/apps/pbcs.dll/article?AID=/20050116/.
[lxxi] Michael Barrier, *Hollywood Cartoons: American Animation in the Golden Age*, Oxford UP, 2003, p. 115.
[lxxii] Mason Wiley and Damien Bona, *Inside Oscar*, 10th Anniversary Edition, Ballantine Books, 1996, p. 63.
[lxxiii] Pauline Kael, *5001 Nights at the Movies*, Henry Holt and Company, 1991, p. 165.
[lxxiv] Mason Wiley and Damien Bona, *Inside Oscar*, 10th Anniversary Edition, Ballantine Books, 1996, p. 61.
[lxxv] David Thomson, *Showman*, Abacus, 1993, p. 183.
[lxxvi] Scott Eyman, *Print the Legend*, Johns Hopkins UP, 2001, p. 159-160.
[lxxvii] www.searchquotes.com/.../...the_behind_of_an_elephant./128677/
[lxxviii] Gary Marmorstein, *Hollywood Rhapsody*, Schirmer, 1997, p. 193.
[lxxix] goatdog.com/moviePage.php?movieID=748
[lxxx] http://www.tcm.com/this-month/article/220861|0/Ruggles-of-Red-Gap.html
[lxxxi] *Top Hat* DVD commentary, Turner Home Entertainment, 2005.
[lxxxii] Charlotte Chandler, *The Girl Who Walked Home Alone*, Applause Books, 2007, p. 108.
[lxxxiii] http://movies.nytimes.com/movie/review?res=9502EEDB1239E632A25757C2A9639C946494D6CF
[lxxxiv] Scott Eyman, *Print the Legend*, Johns Hopkins UP, 2001.
[lxxxv] *Steamboat Round the Bend* DVD commentary, *Ford at Fox Collection*, 20th Century Fox, 2007.
[lxxxvi] http://www.jayrosenblattfilms.com/press-nytr082000.php
[lxxxvii] Gary Marmorstein, *Hollywood Rhapsody*, Schirmer, 1997, p. 85.
[lxxxviii] James Curtis, *James Whale: A New World of Gods and Monsters*, University of Minnesota Press, 2003, p. 246.
[lxxxix] Gary Marmorstein, *Hollywood Rhapsody*, Schirmer, 1997, p. 78.
[xc] Brendan G. Carroll, *The Last Prodigy*, Amadeus Press, 1997, p.250, 254.
[xci] Brendan G. Carroll, *The Last Prodigy*, Amadeus Press, 1997, p. 243.
[xcii] Pauline Kael, *5001 Nights at the Movies*, Henry Holt and Company, 1991, p. 672.
[xciii] http://movies.nytimes.com/movie/review?res=9807E5DD173CE53ABC4E52DFB467838E629EDE
[xciv] http://www.tcm.com/tcmdb/title/69748/Broadway-Melody-of-1936/articles.html
[xcv] *Gold Diggers of 1935* DVD commentary, Warner Home Video, 2006.
[xcvi] *Top Hat* DVD commentary, Turner Home Entertainment, 2005.
[xcvii] Daniel Eagan, *America's Film Legacy*, Continuum Publishing Group, 2009, p. 253.
[xcviii] Qtd. in http://filmfoodie.blogspot.com/2010/05/great-ziegfeld.html
[xcix] http://movies.nytimes.com/movie/review?res=9906EFDF1F3FEE3BBC4F51DFBE66838D629EDE
[c] Mason Wiley and Damien Bona, *Inside Oscar*, 10th Anniversary Edition, Ballantine Books, 1996, p. 74.
[ci] The full story of the trade-off is in Anthony Holden, Behind the Oscar, p. 134.
[cii] Emmanuel Levy, *George Cukor*, William Morrow and Company, 1994, p. 91
[ciii] *Pigskin Parade* DVD special features, 20th Century Fox, 2007.
[civ] David Thomson, *Showman*, Abacus, 1993, p. 251.
[cv] *Swing Time* DVD special features, Turner Home Entertainment, 2005.
[cvi] Emmanuel Levy, *George Cukor*, William Morrow and Company, 1994, p. 91.
[cvii] Mason Wiley and Damien Bona, *Inside Oscar*, 10th Anniversary Edition, Ballantine Books, 1996, p. 82.
[cviii] *Make Way for Tomorrow*, DVD special features, Criterion, 2010.
[cix] Qtd. in Andrew Sarris, *"You Ain't Heard Nothin' Yet"* Oxford UP, 2000, p. 334.
[cx] http://quotes.lucywho.com/browse/keywords/pinch-quotes.html
[cxi] Peter H. Brown and Jim Pinkson, *Oscar Dearest*, Harper Collins, 1988, p. 12.
[cxii] www.imdb.com/name/nm0856921/bio
[cxiii] upcomingdiscs.com/2005/04/26/stella-dallas/
[cxiv] Mason Wiley and Damien Bona, *Inside Oscar*, 10th Anniversary Edition, Ballantine Books, 1996, p. 81.
[cxv] http://www.tcm.com/tcmdb/title/27419/The-Awful-Truth/articles.html
[cxvi] http://www.tcm.com/tcmdb/title/309/Maytime/articles.html
[cxvii] Qtd. in Rudy Behlmer, *America's Favorite Movies*, F. Ungar Pub, 1982, p. 55.
[cxviii] Rudy Behlmer, *America's Favorite Movies*, F. Ungar Pub, 1982, p. 85.
[cxix] http://www.allmovie.com/movie/v112188
[cxx] http://www.tcm.com/tcmdb/title/1577/Marie-Antoinette/articles.html
[cxxi] Gary Marmorstein, *Hollywood Rhapsody*, Schirmer, 1997, p. 213.
[cxxii] http://www.cinescene.com/flicks/flicks122005.htm#citadel
[cxxiii] Jan Herman, *A Talent for Trouble*, Da Capo Press, 1997, p. 178.
[cxxiv] http://anecdotage.com/index.php?aid=20266
[cxxv] *Angels with Dirty Faces* DVD commentary track, Warner Home Video, 2005.
[cxxvi] Pauline Kael, *5001 Nights at the Movies*, Henry Holt and Company, 1991, p. 104.
[cxxvii] Roger Ebert, *The Great Movies II*, Broadway, 2006, p. 8-9.
[cxxviii] Jan Herman, *A Talent for Trouble*, Da Capo Press, 1997, p. 177, 182.
[cxxix] Pauline Kael, *5001 Nights at the Movies*, Henry Holt and Company, 1991, p. 465.
[cxxx] http://movies.nytimes.com/movie/review?res=EE05E7DF173DE577BC4B53DFB0668383629EDE
[cxxxi] http://www.tcm.com/tcmdb/title/453/Three-Comrades/articles.html
[cxxxii] Roger Ebert, *The Great Movies II*, Broadway, 2006, p. 8-9.
[cxxxiii] *Angels with Dirty Faces* DVD commentary track, Warner Home Video, 2005.
[cxxxiv] http://www.tcm.com/tcmdb/title/15778/The-Great-Waltz/articles.html
[cxxxv] Roger Ebert, *The Great Movies II*, Broadway, 2006, p. 8.
[cxxxvi] http://www.youtube.com/watch?v=2jbZrocd6vs&feature=related
[cxxxvii] Qtd. in Tino Balio, *Grand Design: Hollywood as a Modern Business Enterprise, 1930-1939*, Vol. 5 of the *History of the American Cinema*, University of California Press, 1996, pg. 1.
[cxxxviii] Molly Haskell, *Frankly, My Dear*, Yale UP, 2010, p. xiii.
[cxxxix] Molly Haskell, *Frankly, My Dear*, Yale UP, 2010, p. 207.
[cxl] Molly Haskell, *Frankly, My Dear*, Yale UP, 2010, p. 214.
[cxli] Molly Haskell, *Frankly, My Dear*, Yale UP, 2010, p. 209-210.
[cxlii] Letter from Melchor Lengyel, *The New York Times*, June 19, 1940; qtd. in Svetlana Boym, *Ninotchka*, p. 155.

cxliii Email to author from the Academy's Margaret Herrick Library; 7/16/2011.
cxliv I am indebted to Gaylyn Studlar and Matthew Bernstein's brilliant study *John Ford Made Westerns* for this information; p. 191.
cxlv Rudy Behlmer, *America's Favorite Movies*, F. Ungar Pub, 1982, p. 117.
cxlvi Brendan G. Carroll, *The Last Prodigy*, Amadeus Press, 1997, p. 286.
cxlvii Molly Haskell, *Frankly, My Dear*, Yale UP, 2010, p. 74.
cxlviii *Dark Victory* DVD special features, Warner Home Video, 2005.
cxlix Mason Wiley and Damien Bona, *Inside Oscar*, 10th Anniversary Edition, Ballantine Books, 1996, p. 94, quoting *The New York Daily News*.
cl Andrew Sarris, *"You Ain't Heard Nothin' Yet"* Oxford UP, 2000, p. 390.
cli Mason Wiley and Damien Bona, *Inside Oscar*, 10th Anniversary Edition, Ballantine Books, 1996, p. 99.
clii Scott Eyman, *Print the Legend*, Johns Hopkins UP, 2001, p. 206.
cliii Qtd, in http://www.eyeforfilm.co.uk/reviews.php?id=3385.
cliv Qtd. in Scott Eyman, *Print the Legend*, Johns Hopkins UP, 2001, p. 204.
clv *Hollywood Reporter*, qtd in Mason Wiley and Damien Bona, *Inside Oscar*, 10th Anniversary Edition, Ballantine Books, 1996, p. 95.
clvi http://www.imdb.com/title/tt0031679/trivia
clviiQtd. in Jan Herman, *A Talent for Trouble*, Da Capo Press, 1997, p. 196.
clviii http://www.tcm.com/tcmdb/title/96324/Wuthering-Heights/articles.html
clix www.tcm.com/this-month/article/.../The-Rains-Came.html
clx http://www.imdb.com/title/tt0032138/soundtrack
clxi Molly Haskell, *Frankly, My Dear*, Yale UP, 2010, p. 157-58.
clxii http://www.tcm.com/tcmdb/title/586/Dark-Victory/articles.html
clxiii http://brandeisspecialcollections.blogspot.com/2008/04/victor-young-collection-39-linear-feet.html
clxivhttp://www.tcm.com/tcmdb/title/87215/The-Private-Lives-of-Elizabeth-and-Essex/articles.html
clxvhttp://news.google.com/newspapers?nid=1964&dat=19390119&id=rklRAAAAIBAJ&sjid=   tjMNAAAAIB AJ&pg=3076,1707383
clxvi Patrick McGilligan, *Alfred Hitchcock: A Life in Darkness and Light*, It Books, 2004, p. 283.
clxvii Qtd. in Joseph McBride, *Searching for John Ford*, St. Martins Press, 2001, p. 309.
clxviii Rudy Behlmer, *America's Favorite Movies*, F. Ungar Pub, 1982, p. 129.
clxix *Rebecca* DVD special features, MGM 2008.
clxx Qtd. in Patrick McGilligan, *Alfred Hitchcock: A Life in Darkness and Light*, It Books, 2004, p. 260.
clxxi http://www.amazines.com/Cooking/article_detail.cfm/3441492?articleid=3441492
clxxiihttp://movies.nytimes.com/movie/review?res=9C05E7DF1630E43ABC4F53DFB566838B659EDE
clxxiii http://en.wikipedia.org/wiki/The_Great_Dictator#Score
clxxiv *Paul Bowles on Music*, ed. byTimothy Mangan and Irene Hermann, University of California Press, 2003, p. 31.
clxxv http://www.tcm.com/tcmdb/title/87781/Rebecca/articles.html
clxxvi Qtd. in Joseph Epstein, *Fred Astaire*, Yale UP, 2009, p. 104.
clxxvii *Alfred Hitchcock*, by Alfred Hitchcock, Francois Truffaut, and Helen G. Scott, Revised Edition, Simon & Schuster, 2005, p. 135.
clxxviii *Rebecca* DVD special features, MGM 2008.
clxxix http://www.tcm.com/tcmdb/title/76858/The-Great-Dictator/articles.html
clxxx Joseph McBride, *Searching for John Ford*, St. Martins Press, 2001, p. 314.
clxxxi Scott Eyman, *Print the Legend*, Johns Hopkins UP, 2001, p. 222.
clxxxii http://www.imdb.com/title/tt0032551/trivia
clxxxiii Pauline Kael, *5001 Nights at the Movies*, Henry Holt and Company, 1991, p. 419.
clxxxiv Mason Wiley and Damien Bona, *Inside Oscar*, 10th Anniversary Edition, Ballantine Books, 1996, p. 104.
clxxxv Glenn Hopp, *Billy Wilder: The Cinema of Wit*, Taschen, 2003, p. 26.
clxxxvi http://www.tcm.com/tcmdb/title/600/Dr-Ehrlich-s-Magic-Bullet/articles.html
clxxxvii Mason Wiley and Damien Bona, *Inside Oscar*, 10th Anniversary Edition, Ballantine Books, 1996. p. 109.
clxxxviii http://www.tcm.com/tcmdb/title/76817/The-Grapes-of-Wrath/articles.html
clxxxix http://www.tcm.com/tcmdb/title/81770/The-Long-Voyage-Home/articles.html
cxc *Rebecca* DVD special features, MGM 2008.
cxci Lawrence J. Quirk, *The Films of Robert Taylor*, Lyle Stuart, 1979, p. 12.
cxcii http://www.tcm.com/tcmdb/title/27848/The-Westerner/articles.html
cxciii http://www.tcm.com/tcmdb/title/67587/Arise-My-Love/articles.html
cxciv http://www.nytimes.com/learning/general/onthisday/bday/0506.html
cxcv www.tyrone-power.com/bloodandsand_notes.html
cxcvihttp://movies.nytimes.com/movie/review?res=9504EED81F3DE33BBC4B51DFB366838A659EDE
cxcvii *Citizen Kane* DVD special features, Turner Home Entertainment, 2001.
cxcviii Pauline Kael, *5001 Nights at the Movies*, Henry Holt and Company, 1991, p. 85.
cxcix *Citizen Kane*, DVD commentary, from both Roger Ebert and Peter Bogdanovich, Turner Home Entertainment, 2001.
cc www.hollywoodsgoldenage.com/moguls/orson_welles.html
cci Mason Wiley and Damien Bona, *Inside Oscar*, 10th Anniversary Edition, Ballantine Books, 1996, p. 114.
ccii blogs.indiewire.com/peterbogdanovich/the_southerner
cciii http://www.imdb.com/title/tt0033729/soundtrack
cciv *Suspicion*, DVD commentary, Turner Home Entertainment, 2004.
ccv Brendan G. Carroll, *The Last Prodigy*, Amadeus Press, 1997, p. 300-301.
ccvi http://www.nysun.com/arts/warner-bros-celebrates-hollywoods-jazz-age/82767/
ccvii Brendan G. Carroll, *The Last Prodigy*, Amadeus Press, 1997, p. 159.
ccviii http://www.tcm.com/tcmdb/title/89/Citizen-Kane/articles.html
ccix http://www.tcm.com/tcmdb/title/81524/The-Little-Foxes/
ccx http://www.tcm.com/tcmdb/title/55/Blossoms-in-the-Dust/articles.html
ccxi *Blood and Sand*, DVD commentary, 20th Century Fox 2007.
ccxii *Citizen Kane*, DVD commentary, Roger Ebert, Turner Home Entertainment, 2001.
ccxiii Michael S. Shull and David E Wilt, *Doing Their Bit*, 2nd edition, McFarland, 2004, p. 38.
ccxiv Maltin, Leonard, *Of Mice and Magic*, Plume, 1987, pg. 120-122.

ccxv Jeanine Basinger, *The World War II Combat Film: Anatomy of a Genre*, Columbia University Press: New York, 1986, p. 28-34.
ccxvi Pauline Kael, *5001 Nights at the Movies*, Henry Holt and Company, 1991, p. 671-672.
ccxvii http://www.independent.co.uk/news/world/americas/the-castropedia-fidels-cuba-in-facts-and-figures-432478.html
ccxviii Pauline Kael, *5001 Nights at the Movies*, Henry Holt and Company, 1991, p. 486.
ccxix http://www.vanityfair.com/hollywood/classic/features/magnificent-obsession-200201
ccxx http://movies.nytimes.com/movie/review?res=9804E5DC1039E33BBC4052DFB4678389659EDE
ccxxi http://goatdog.com/moviePage.php?movieID=780
ccxxii Lubitsch, qtd. in Annette Insdorf, *Indelible Shadows: Film and the Holocaust*, Cambridge UP, 2002, p. 67.
ccxxiii http://www.tcm.com/tcmdb/title/683/The-Magnificent-Ambersons/articles.html
ccxxiv *Moontide* DVD commentary, 20th Century Fox, 2008.
ccxxv http://www.threemoviebuffs.com/review/formeandmygal
ccxxvi http://www.tcm.com/tcmdb/title/168/George-Washington-Slept-Here/articles.html
ccxxvii http://www.tcm.com/tcmdb/title/36536/Rudyard-Kipling-s-Jungle-Book/articles.html
ccxxviii Andrew Sarris, *"You Ain't Heard Nothin' Yet"* Oxford UP, 2000, p. 129.
ccxxix Mason Wiley and Damien Bona, *Inside Oscar*, 10th Anniversary Edition, Ballantine Books, 1996, p. 124.
ccxxx http://movies.nytimes.com/movie/review?res=9D05E7DC153DE13BBC4F51DFB766838F659EDE
ccxxxi http://www.tcm.com/tcmdb/title/575/Air-Force/articles.html
ccxxxii http://www.tcm.com/tcmdb/title/85227/The-North-Star/articles.html
ccxxxiii http://www.imdb.com/title/tt0035884/reviews
ccxxxiv Jann Pasler, *Confronting Stravinsky*, University of California Press, 1988, p. 337.
ccxxxv http://eislermusic.com/life.htm
ccxxxvi http://wordsofnote.wordpress.com/articles/propaganda-and-peasants/
ccxxxvii *Victory Through Air Power*, DVD introduction by Leonard Maltin, *Walt Disney Treasures: On the Front Line*, Walt Disney Video 2004.
ccxxxviii http://movies.nytimes.com/movie/review?res=940DE0D71E39E33BBC4A52DFB5668388659EDE

www.ingramcontent.com/pod-product-compliance
Lightning Source LLC
Chambersburg PA
CBHW020726160426
43192CB00006B/128